I0803402

Amazing Gardens

Amazing Gardens

VIVIENNE HAMBLY

amber
BOOKS

This new edition first published in 2025

First edition published in 2022

Copyright © 2022 Amber Books Ltd

Published by Amber Books Ltd
United House
North Road
London N7 9DP
United Kingdom
www.amberbooks.co.uk
Instagram: amberbooksltd
Facebook: amberbooks
Twitter: @amberbooks
Pinterest: amberbooksltd

All rights reserved. With the exception of quoting brief passages for the purpose of review no part of this publication may be reproduced without prior written permission from the publisher. The information in this book is true and complete to the best of our knowledge. All recommendations are made without any guarantee on the part of the author or publisher, who also disclaim any liability incurred in connection with the use of this data or specific details.

ISBN: 978-1-83886-525-2

Project Editor: Michael Spilling
Designer: Mark Batley
Picture Research: Terry Forshaw

Printed in China

FSC
www.fsc.org
MIX
Paper | Supporting
responsible forestry
FSC® C109093

Contents

Introduction

Gardening today rests on traditions built up over millennia. Our first attempts at ornamental horticulture began in the Fertile Crescent, the productive lands stretching from the Tigris and Euphrates in modern-day Iraq and Syria, to the Nile in Egypt. Here, nutrient-rich soils and reliable water supply meant populations could not only settle but establish the social hierarchies that permitted decorative cultivation. Since then, gardens and gardening have come to represent as many interests as there are places in the world. Religious symbolism is innate to many gardens in the Far East. Medicinal plants inspired the first European botanic gardens. Monarchs built gardens to display wealth or to trump rivals. Invading forces, whether Roman, Norman, Mughal or British, established gardens in statements of strength and acquisition. Still other gardens are outlets for creative energy, offer respite from personal difficulty or provide escape from the humdrum of life. Meanwhile, the most forward-looking gardens have sustainability and biodiversity at their heart.

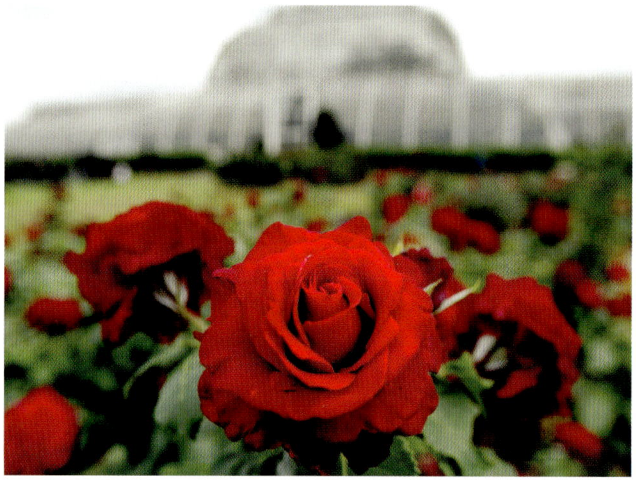

ABOVE:
Royal Botanic Gardens, Kew, England
These gardens in London date from 1759, today, RBG Kew is at the forefront of botanical research.

OPPOSITE:
Tirta Gangga, Bali, Indonesia
In east Bali, this water garden was built by the Karangasem royal family in 1948.

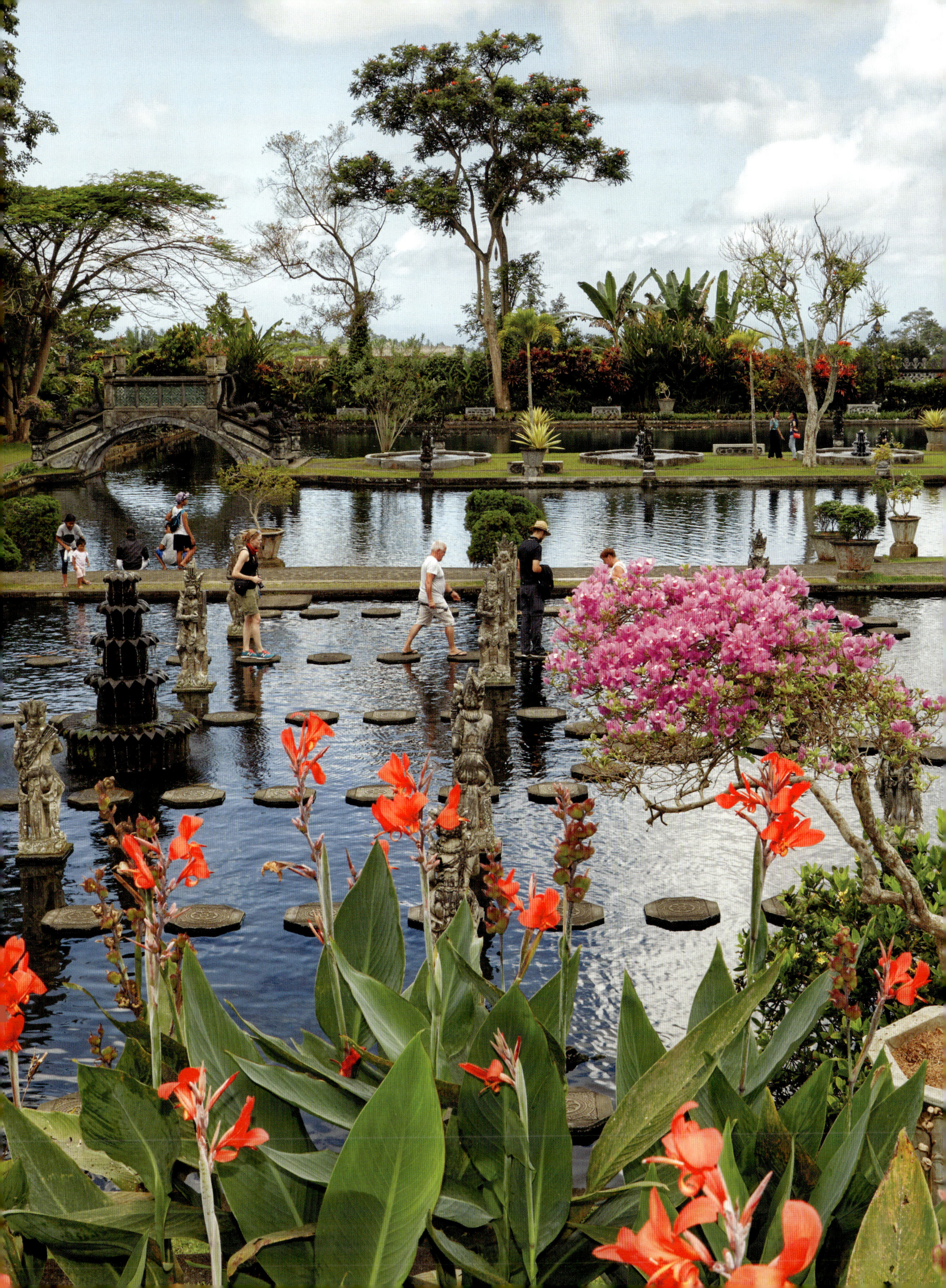

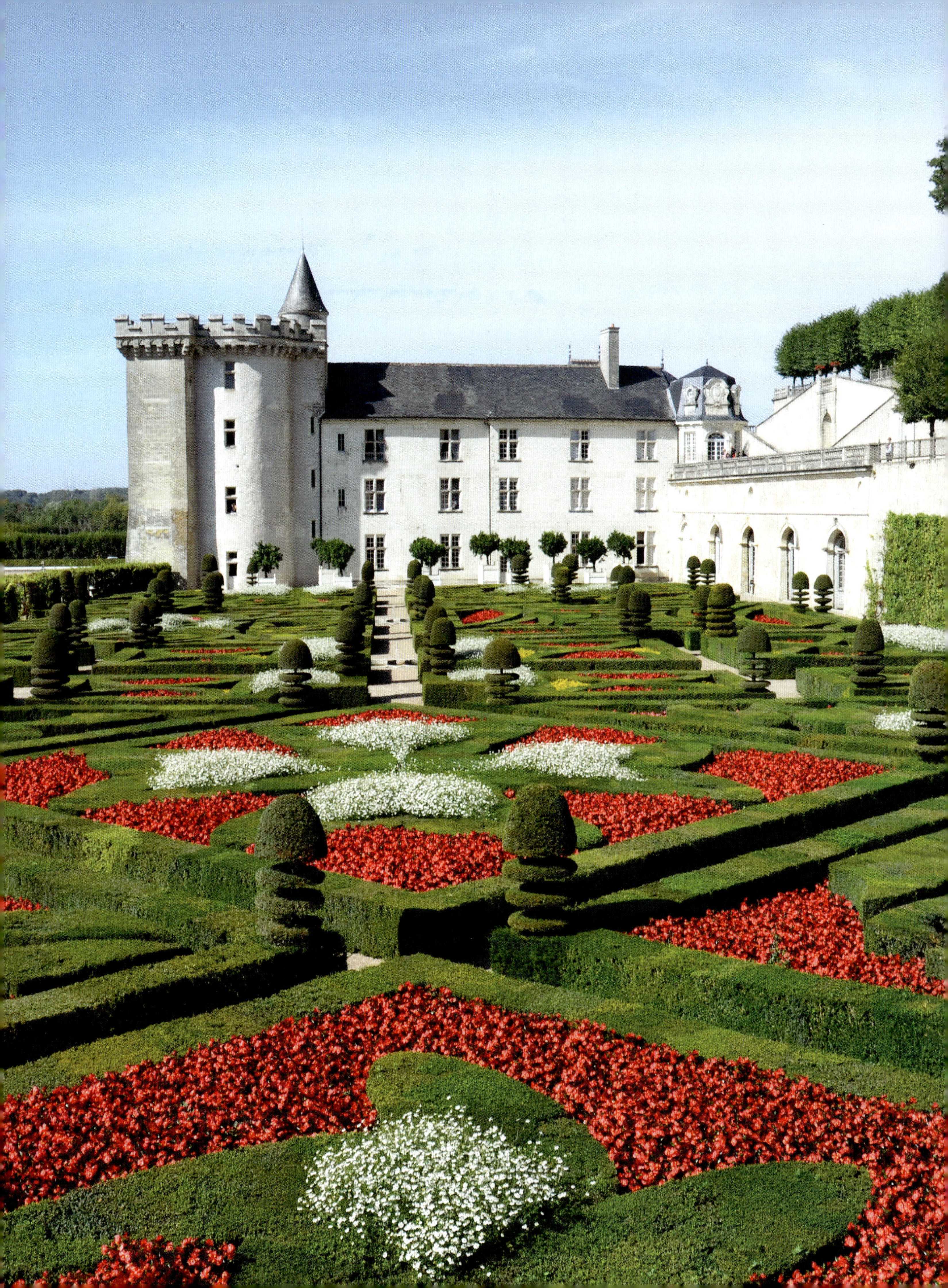

Europe

It is difficult to overstate the influence of this diverse, densely populated continent on botanical tradition around the world. In 1758 in Sweden, Carl Linnaeus developed binomial nomenclature, a system of categorising plants that has come to be used in all spheres of formal horticulture and botany, often at the cost of indigenous knowledge. From Europe's courts and palaces were planned invasions on opposite sides of the globe. Colonial settlers introduced European patterns of gardening to their host countries. If commercial crops such as cocoa, tea and coffee were not being moved from colony to colony, specimen plants were returned by plant hunter-explorers to private nurseries and botanic gardens for collection. It is also impossible to ignore the fact that many great gardens were built with the spoils of the slave trade. For all this, Europe's gardens are by and large the finest in the world. They reflect the continent's creative life, the entangled, often brutal nature of its politics, and have led to extraordinary scientific innovation. Botanical gardens once established to further medicinal knowledge are now at the forefront of global conservation efforts, and they continue to aid the search for cures to our deadliest diseases. The artificial lakes of the English landscape movement, emulated across Europe, were the forerunners of canal transport systems. Expansive glasshouses which were often built to accommodate the influx of exotic plants from around the world, whether palms or pineapples, laid the foundations of modern skyscrapers. Artists like Derek Jarman fashioned intensely personal gardens from unlikely circumstances, while Louis XIV's Palace of Versailles was so extravagant, so ornate, it was envied from St Petersburg to Rome.

OPPOSITE:
Château de Villandry, Indre-et-Loire, France
Archaeologists have dated some work at Château de Villandry to 1532. Its current incarnation is the much more recent vision of Joachim Carvallo, who, having restored the building in the 1900s, implemented the opulent Renaissance-style planting we see today.

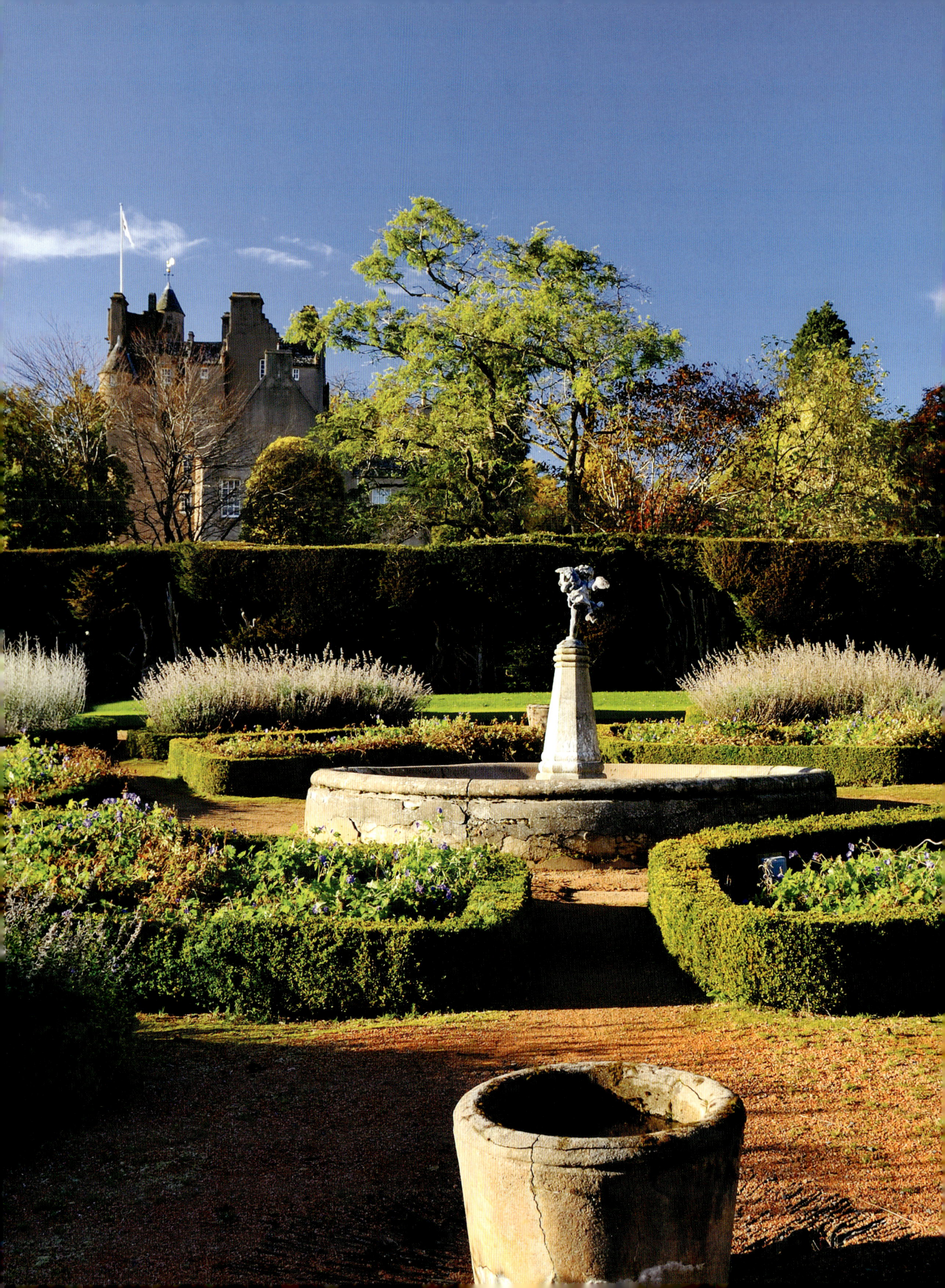

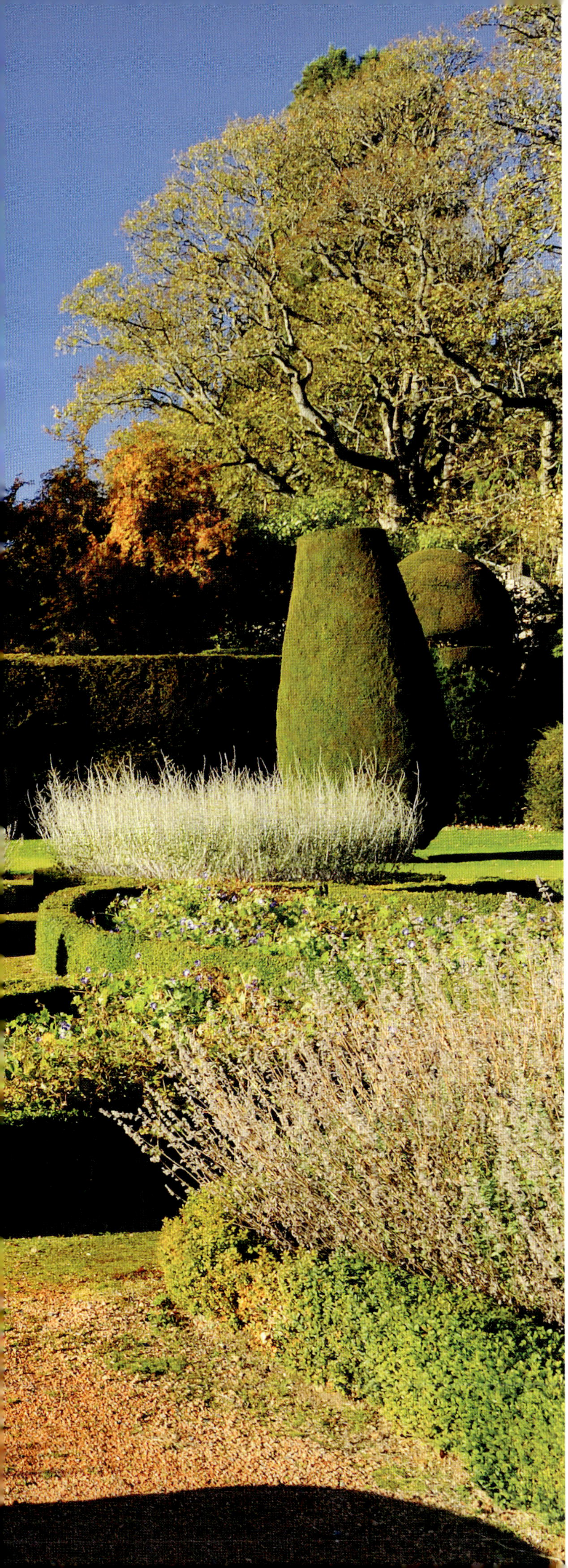

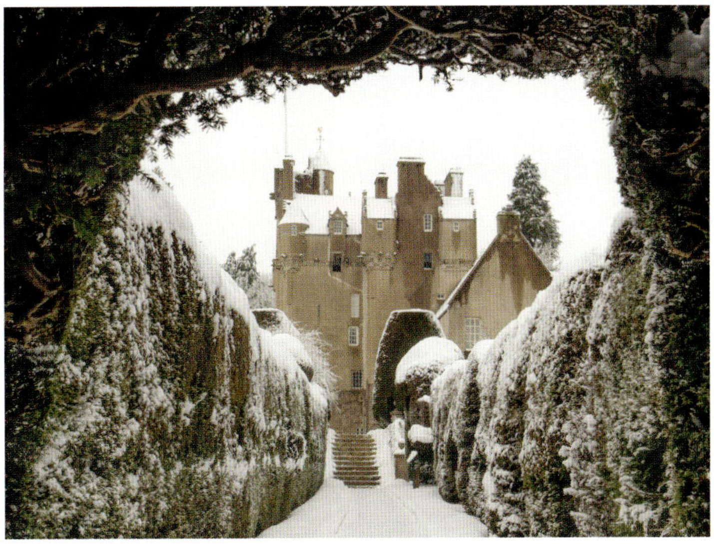

LEFT & ABOVE:

Crathes Castle, Aberdeenshire, Scotland

Now in the care of the National Trust for Scotland, 16th-century Crathes Castle was for 350 years the home of the Burnett family. In the early 20th-century walled garden built by Sir James Burnett and his wife Sybill, roses and herbaceous borders abound. Some yew planting here, in topiary and hedging, is believed to date from 1702.

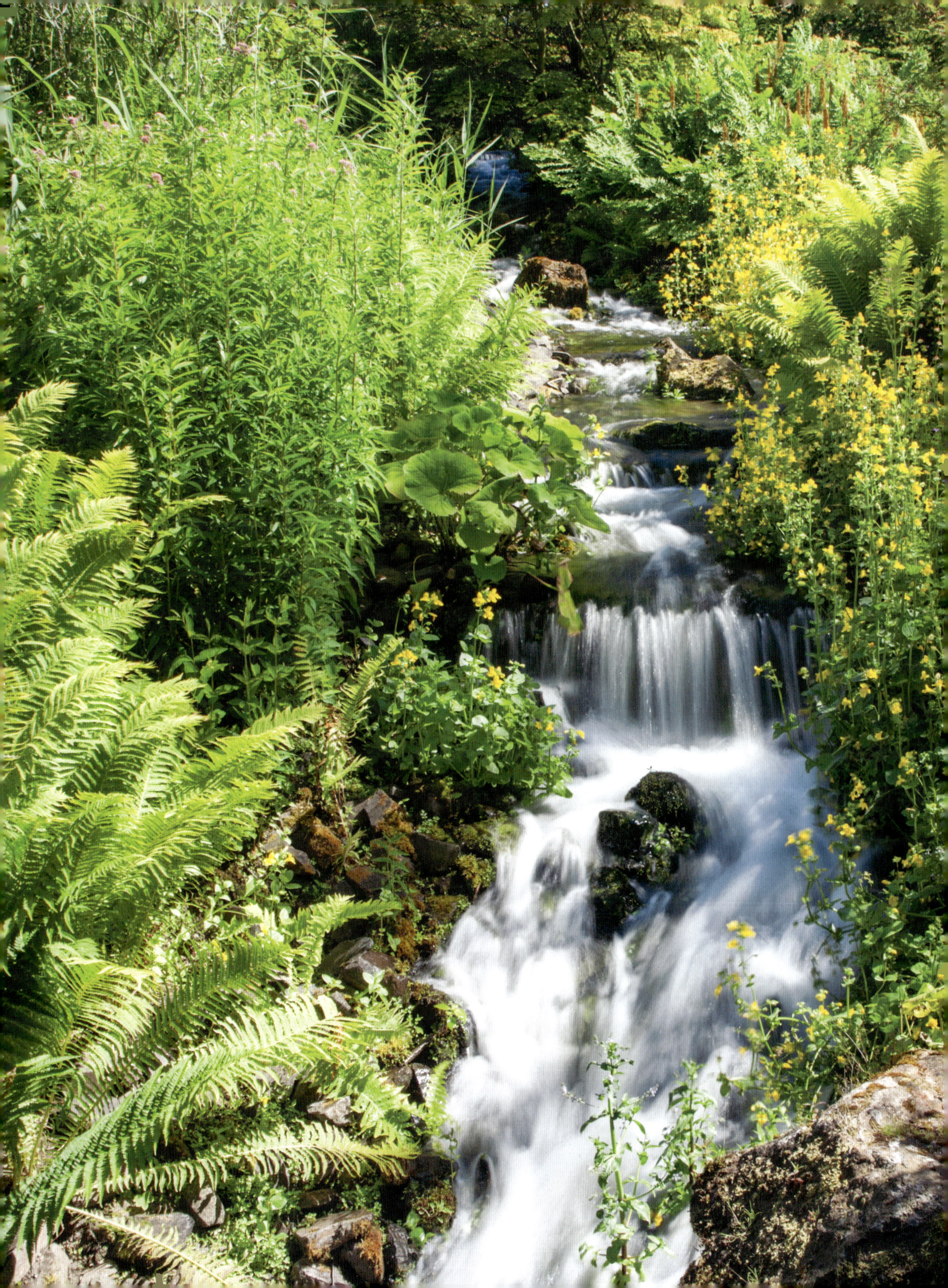

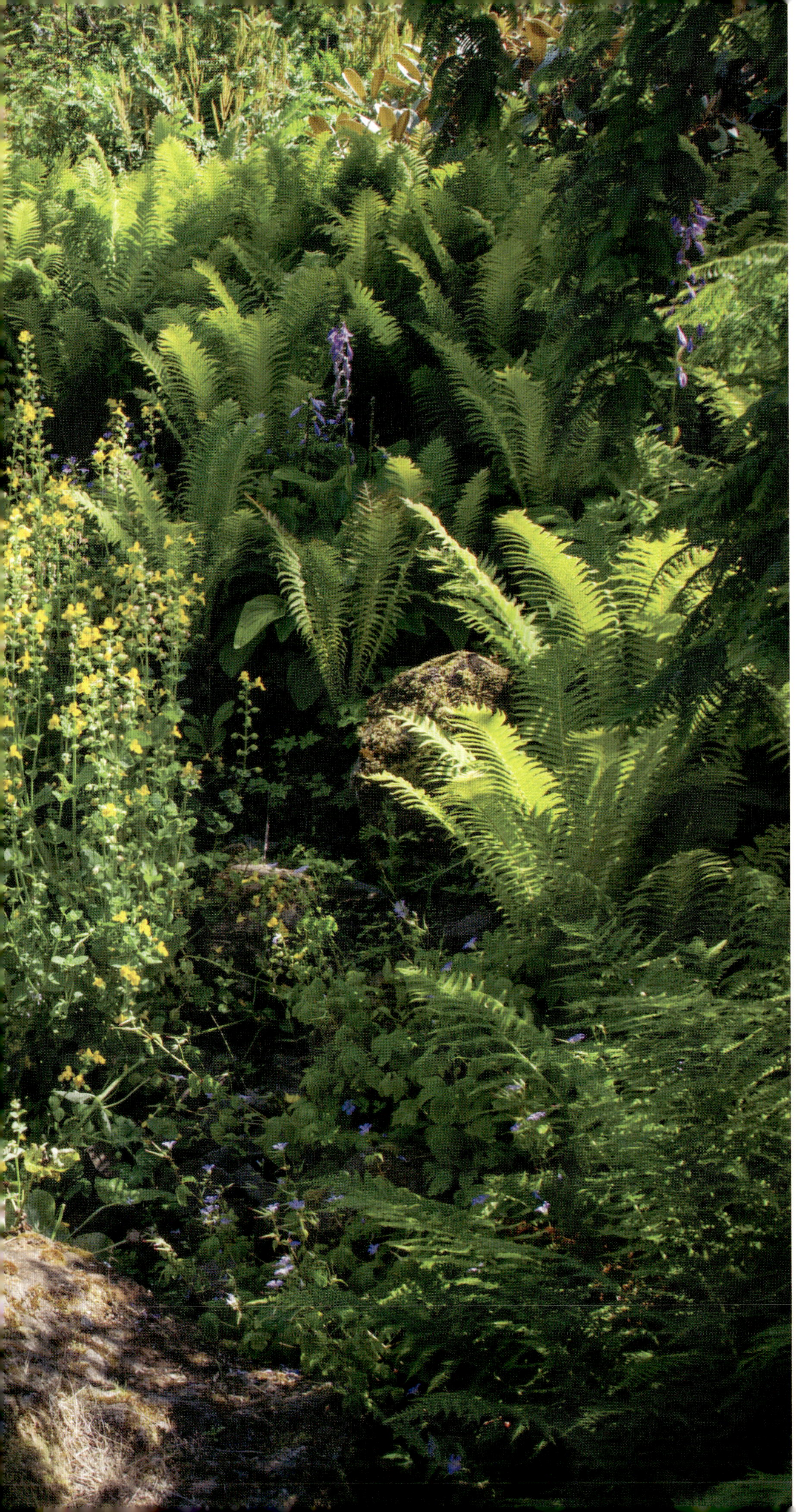

Royal Botanic Garden Edinburgh, Scotland
Like many early gardens, the function of the RBGE was practical: it was founded in 1670 with the express purpose of supplying plants for study and medical treatment. Now 300 years old, its scope is wide-ranging and global, with energies directed towards education, conservation and science programmes.

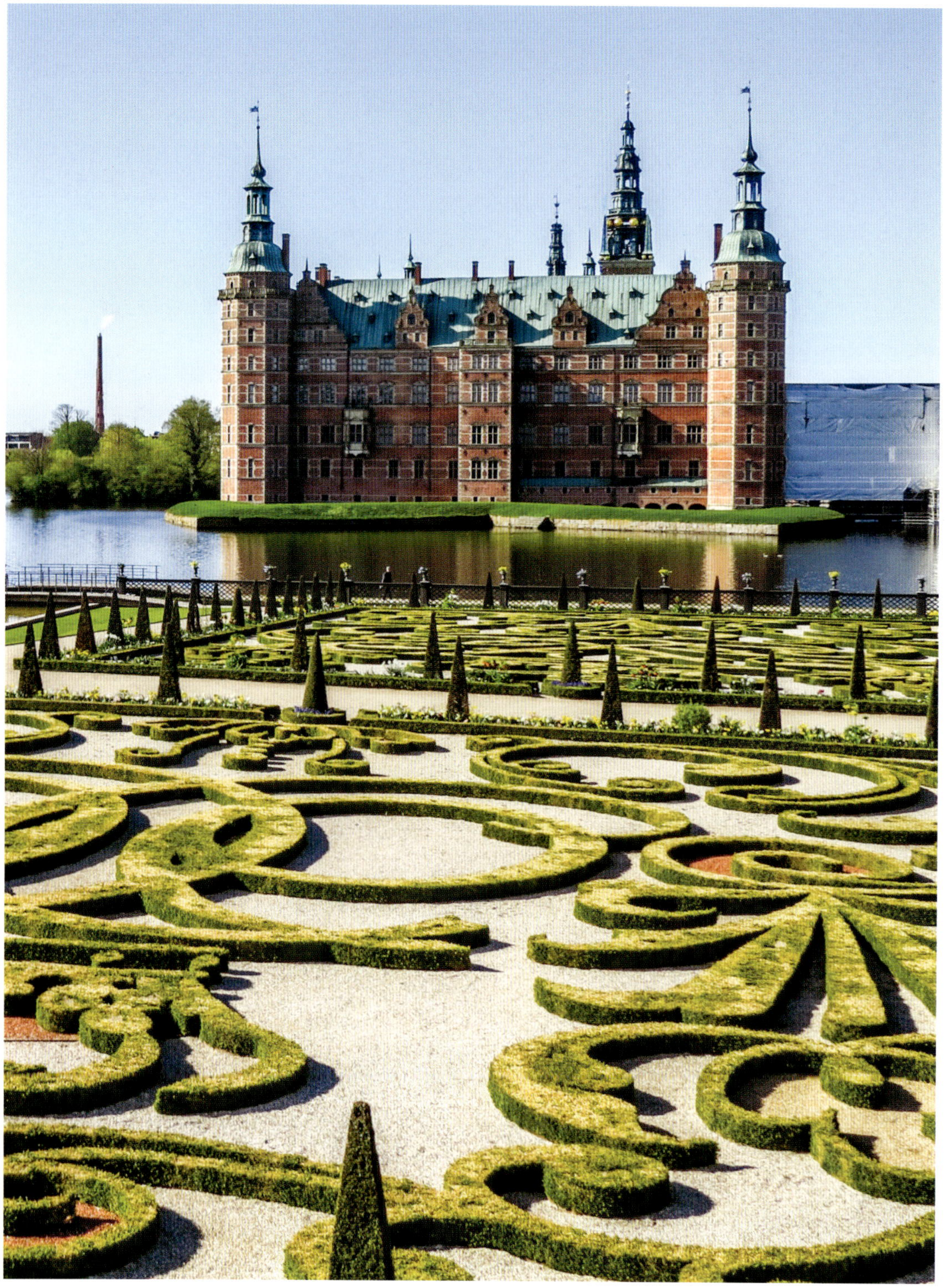

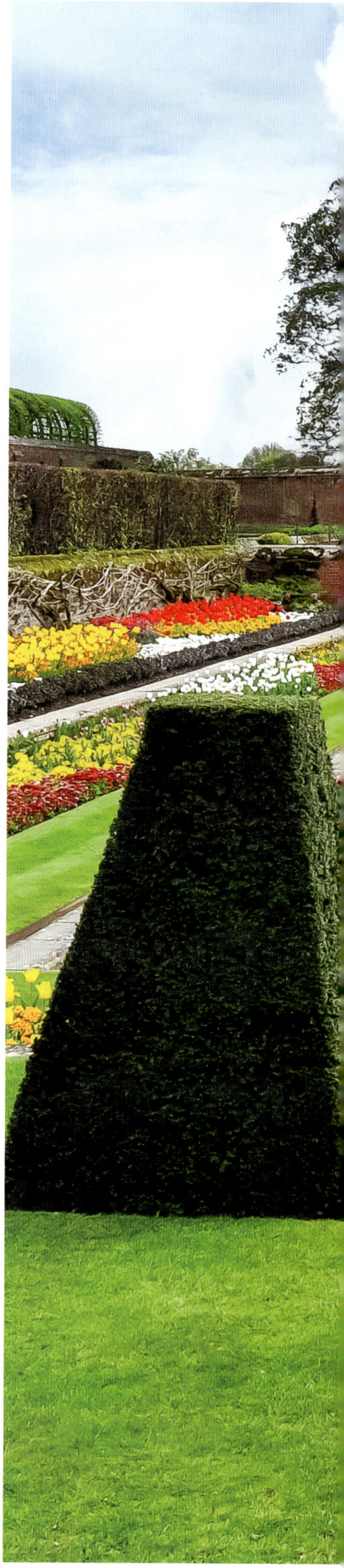

ABOVE:
Frederiksborg Castle, Hovedstaden, Denmark
An example of early 17th-century architecture, Frederiksborg Castle was built by King Christian IV between 1600 and 1621 and named for his father, Frederick. In the Baroque garden, around 65,000 box trees shape the monograms of certain royals. By contrast, the informal Landscape garden is typical of this 19th-century style, with paths, canals and shrubberies contriving to make a 'natural' landscape.

RIGHT & OVERLEAF:
Hampton Court Palace, Surrey, England
The home of England's most notorious king, Henry VIII, this magnificent palace on the banks of the river Thames is surrounded by 24ha (60 acres) of formal garden and a further 303ha (750 acres) of parkland. Garden highlights include the restored Baroque-style Privy Garden, Kitchen Garden and the world's oldest puzzle maze, dating from around 1700.

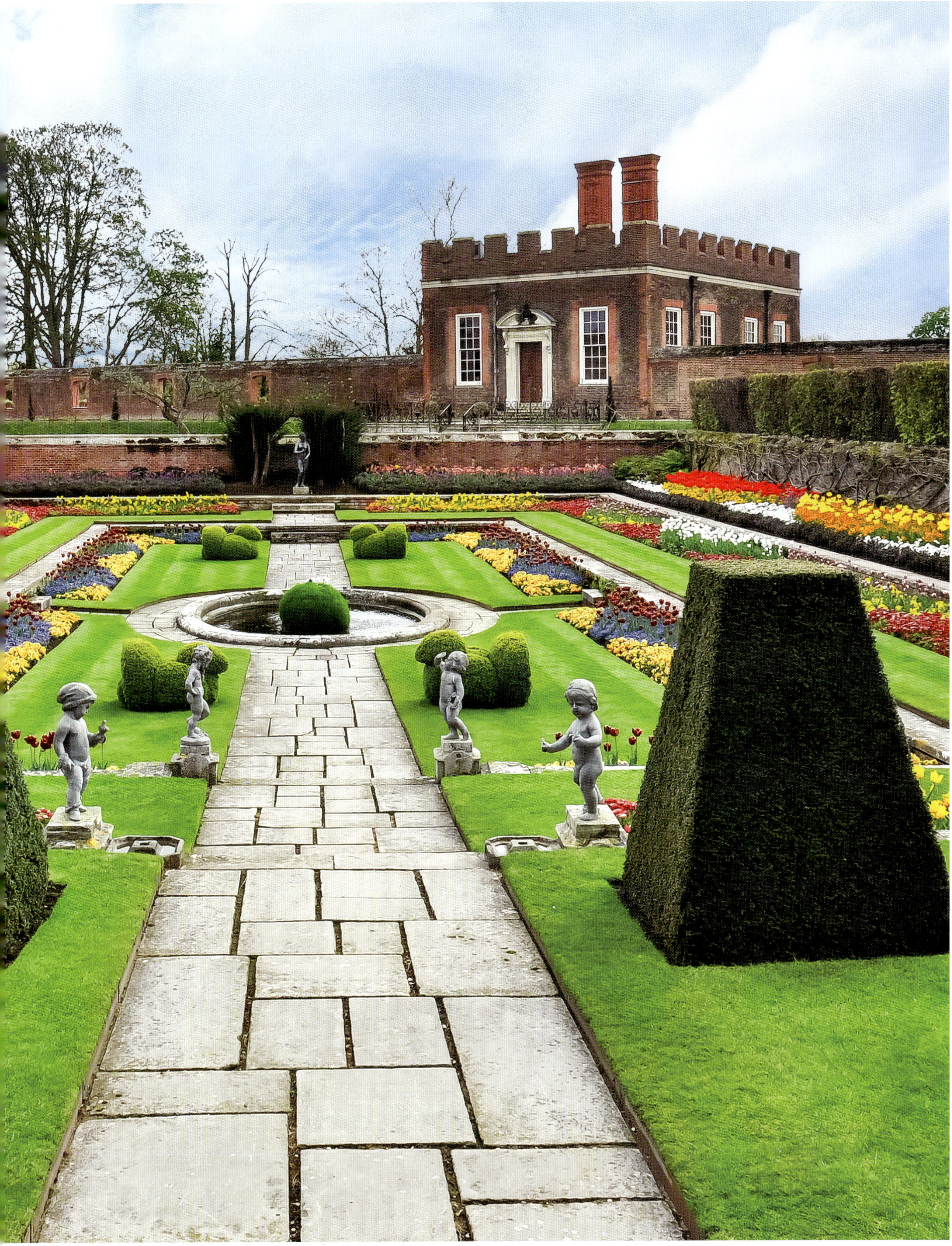

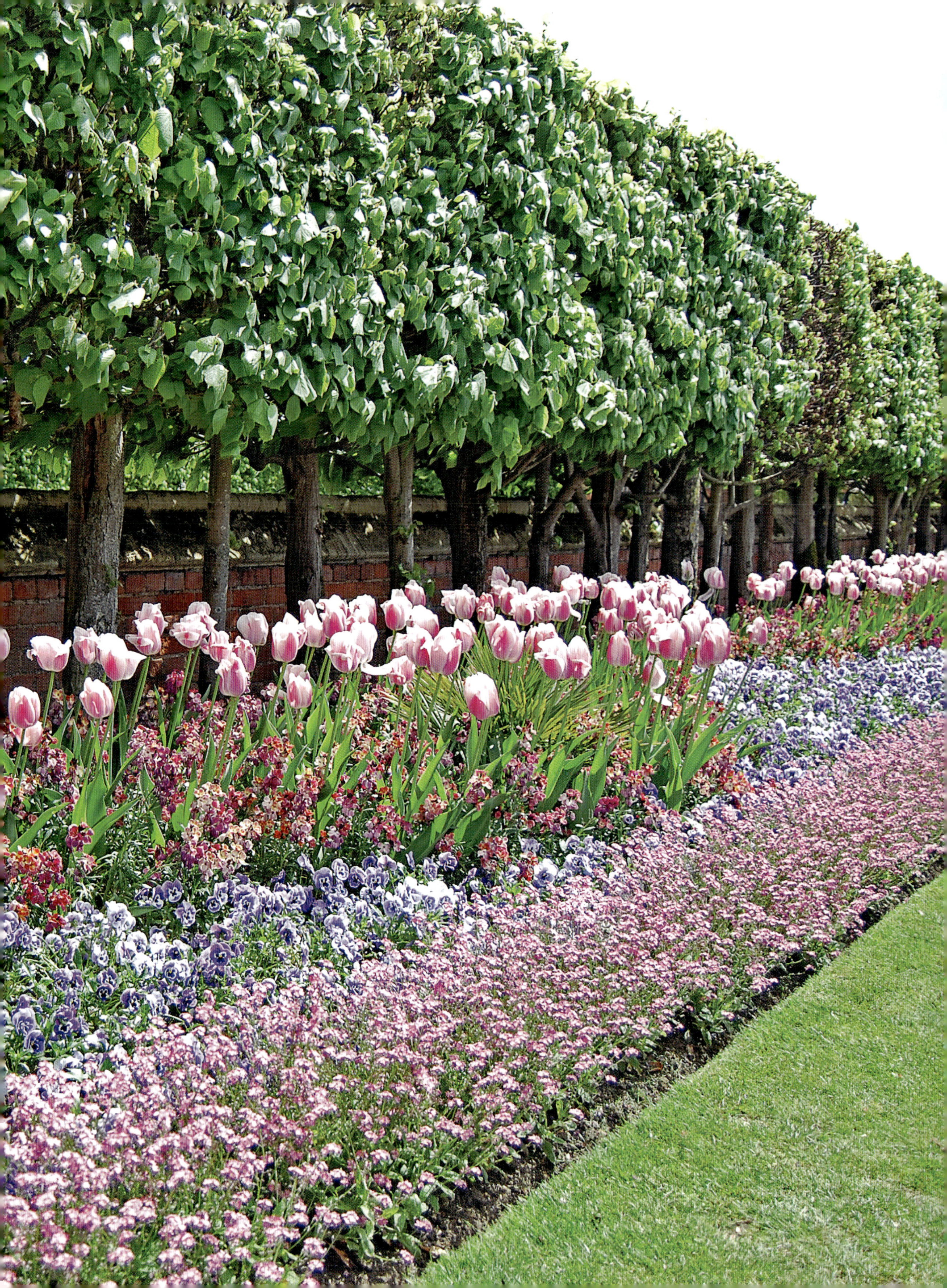

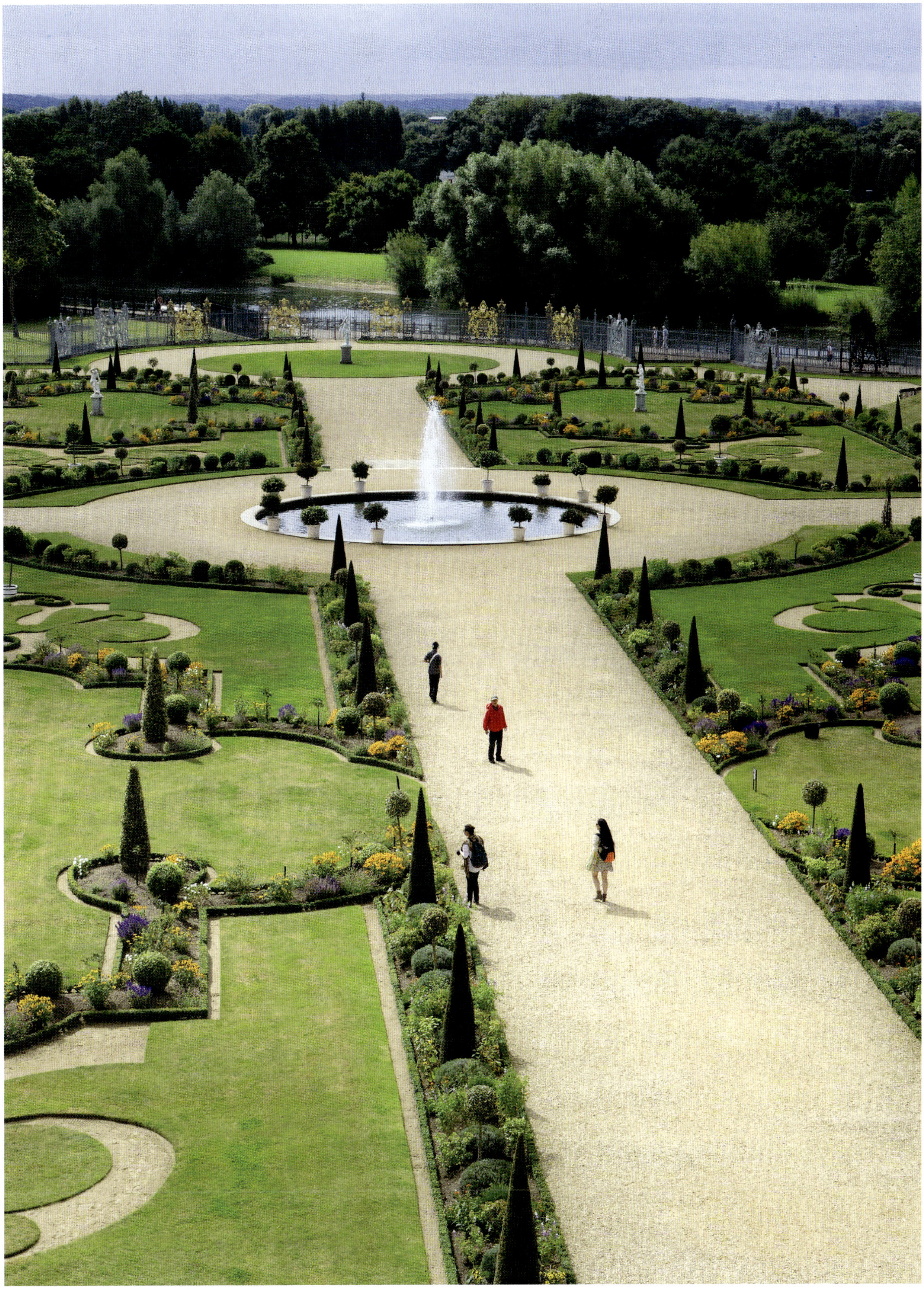

RIGHT AND BOTTOM RIGHT:

Forde Abbey, Dorset, England

In the gentle hills of southern England, Forde Abbey is a former Cistercian retreat with a garden 900 years in the making. While the Great Pond is the only remaining monastic element, successive generations have shaped the garden here. New features include a floral labyrinth and meadow planting.

TOP RIGHT:

The Newt, Somerset, England

The Newt is a restored historic estate near Bruton. In May 2019, it opened its newly cultivated gardens, designed by renowned landscape artist Patrice Taravella. The Parabola garden shown is based on French techniques of fruit growing. Every inch of its inner walls is now covered in apple trees, tightly pruned and meticulously trained. Most are planted against the walls, county by county, arranged in a Baroque-style maze. This geographical way of displaying them is the basis for the recent National Collection status awarded to The Newt by Plant Heritage.

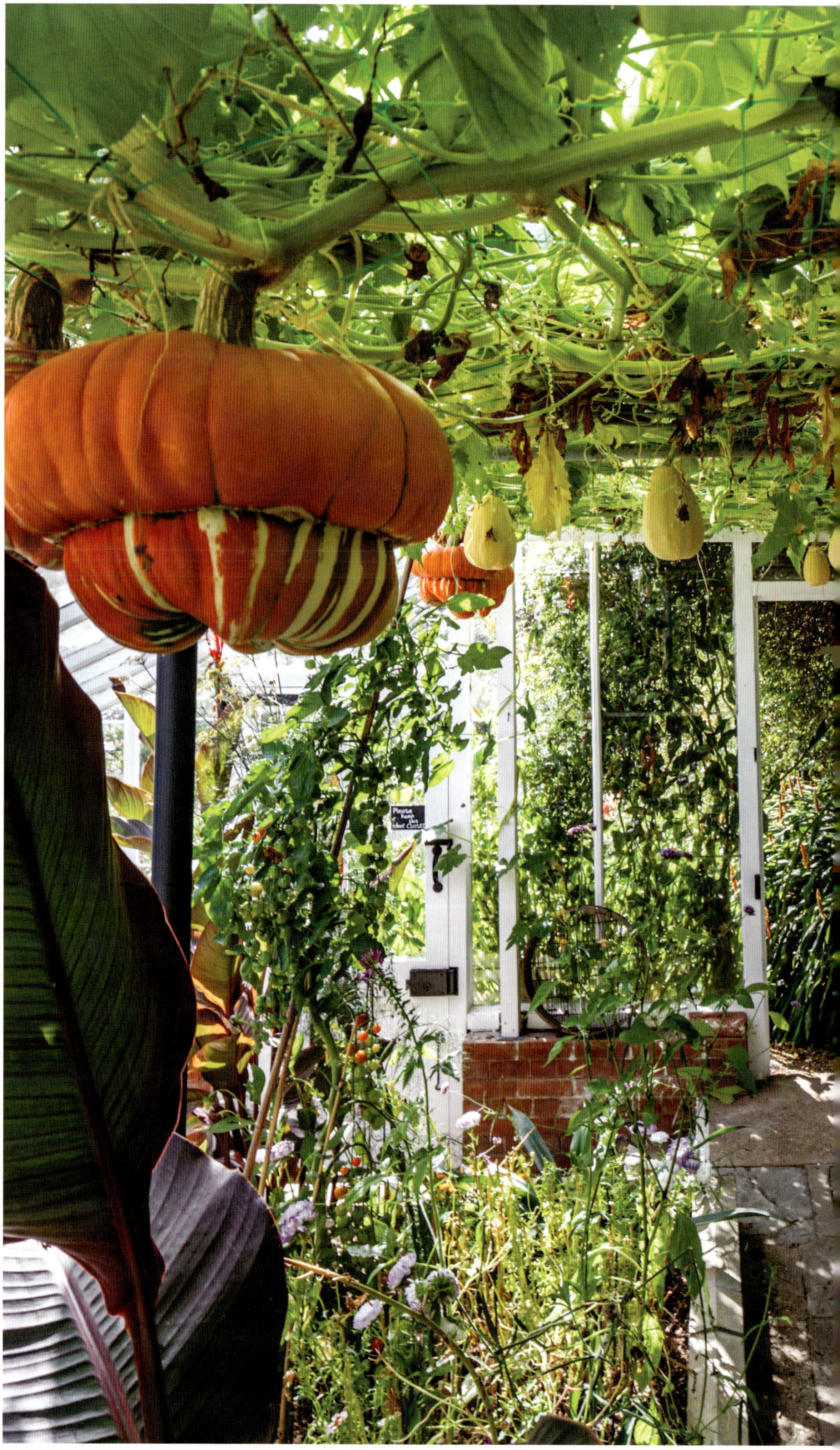

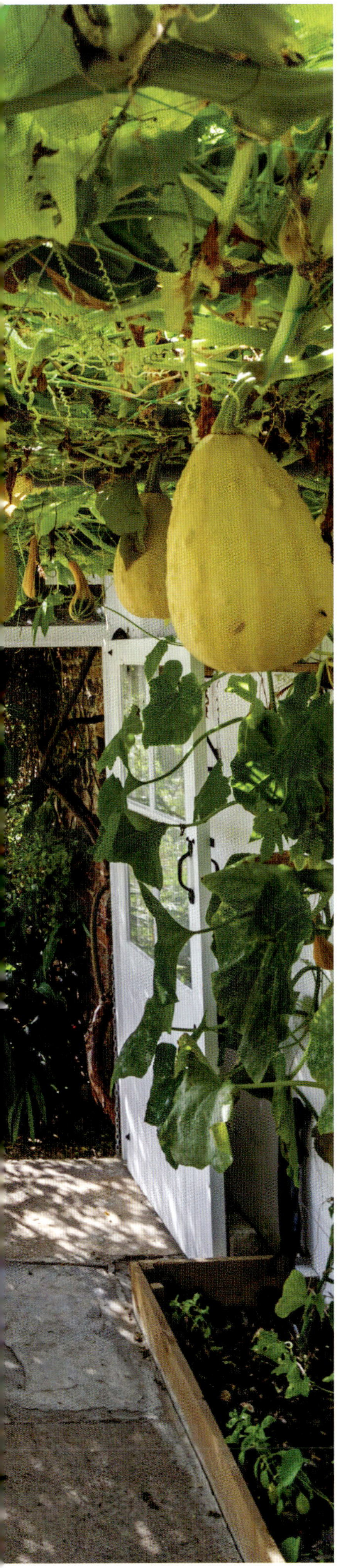

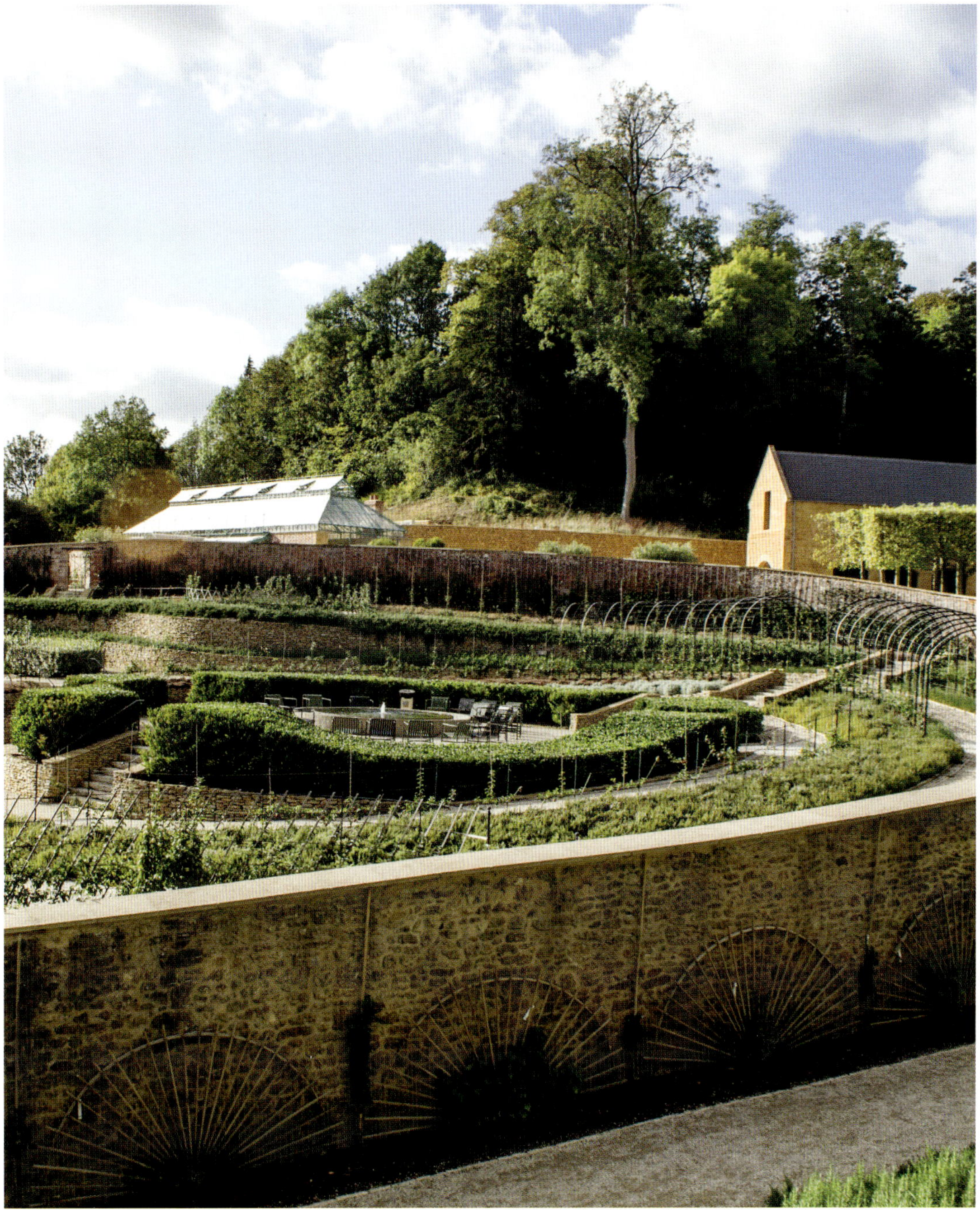

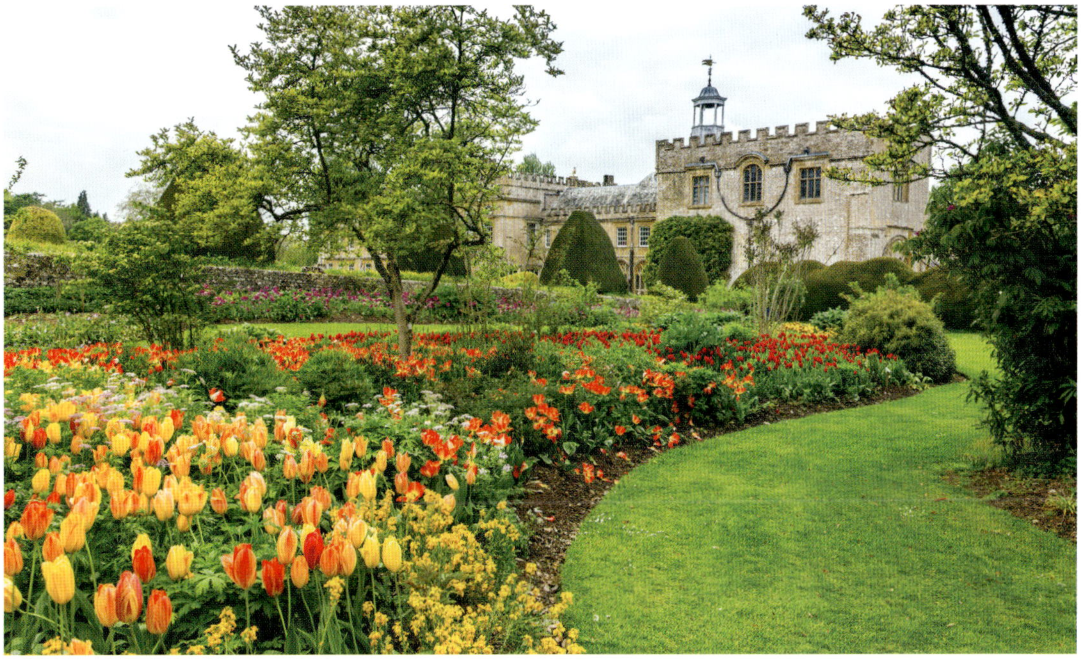

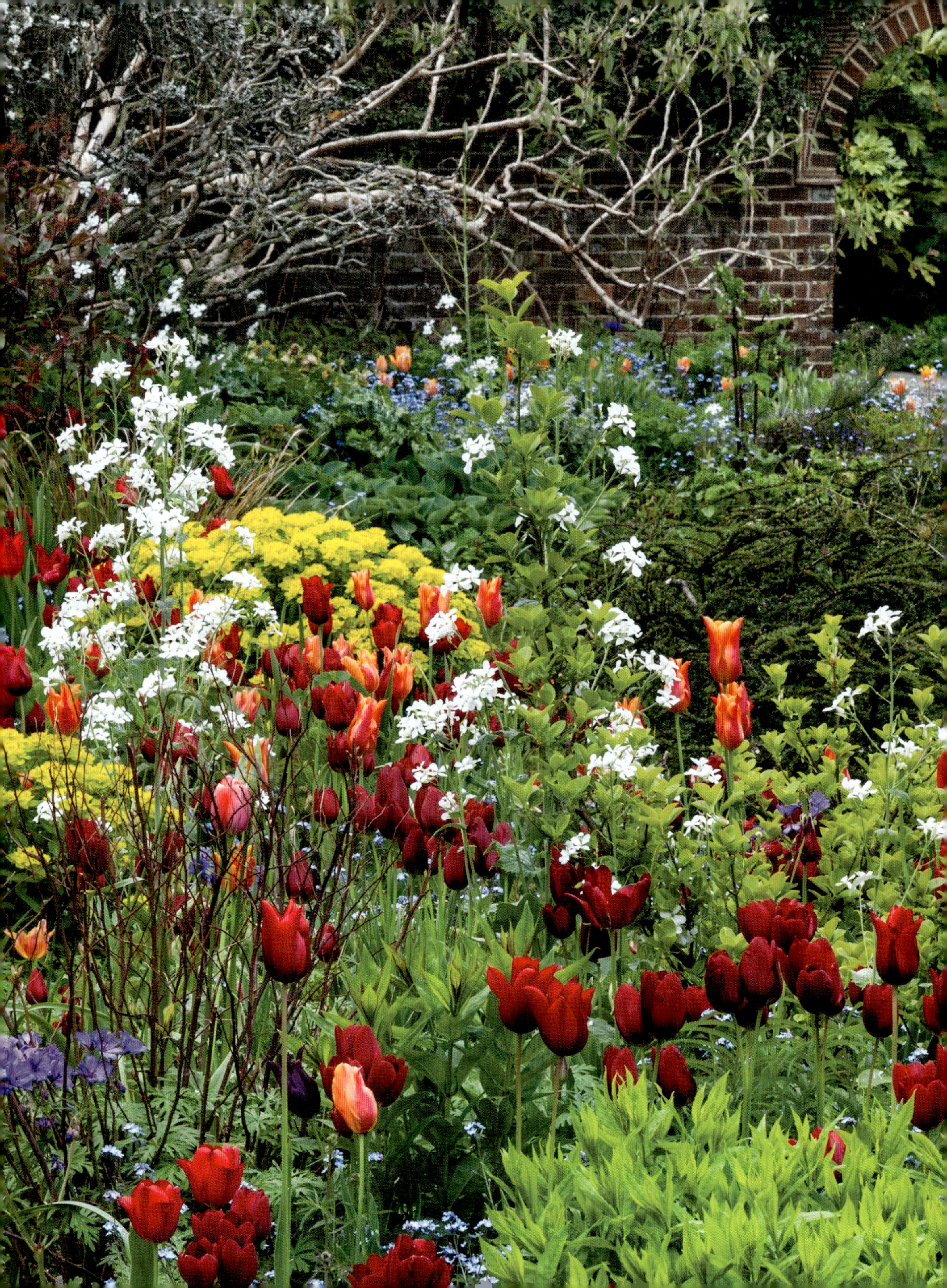

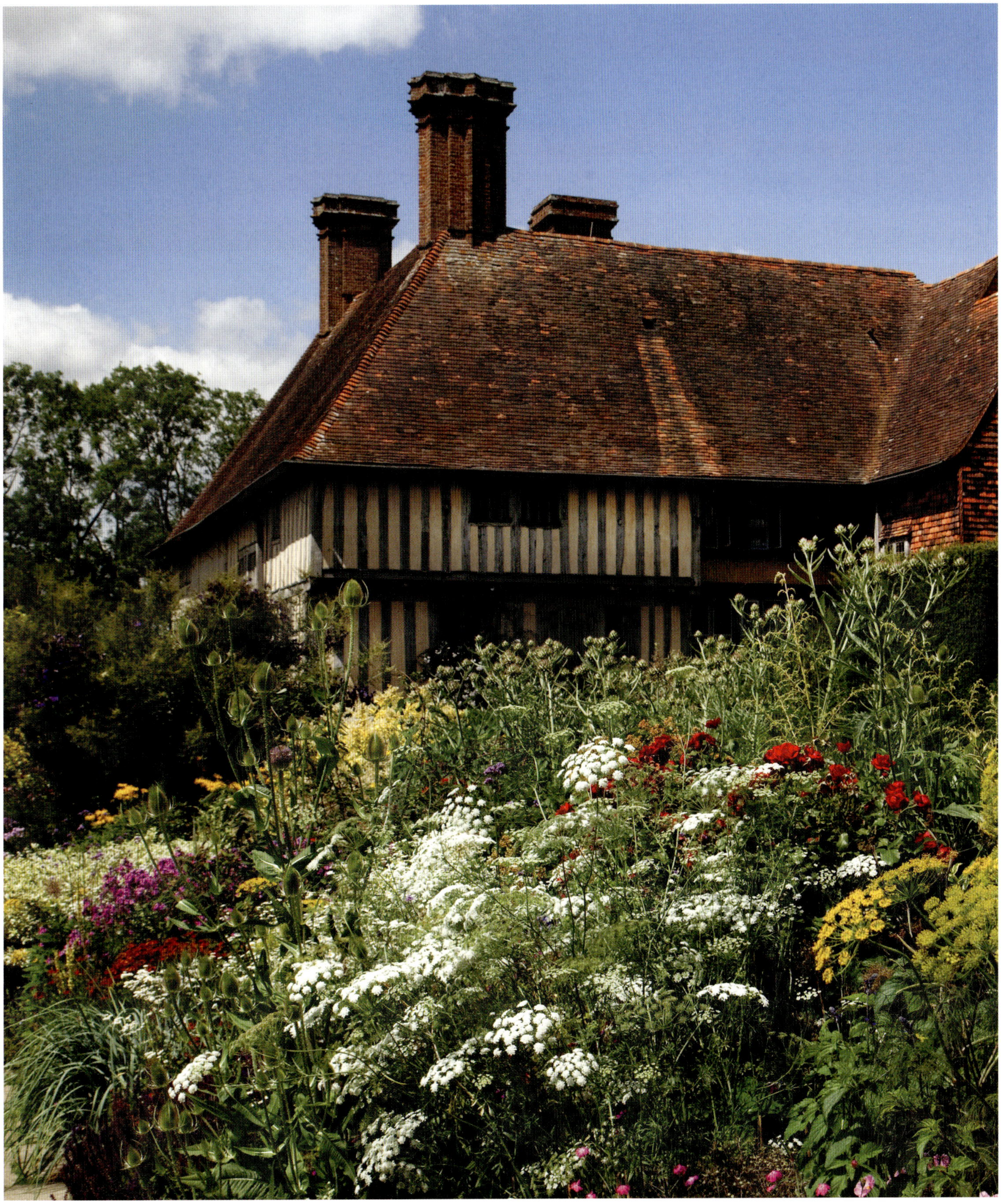

ALL PHOTOGRAPHS:

Great Dixter, East Sussex, England

Sir Edwin Lutyens made additions to this 15th century building and garden in the early 20th century, but it is the gardener and gardening writer Christopher Lloyd (1921–2006) who put his family home on the map. The spirit of Lloyd's colourful, inventive planting combined with quirky topiary is now maintained by Fergus Garrett and the Great Dixter Charitable Trust. Influential through its learning programmes, the garden has gathered legions of fans around the world.

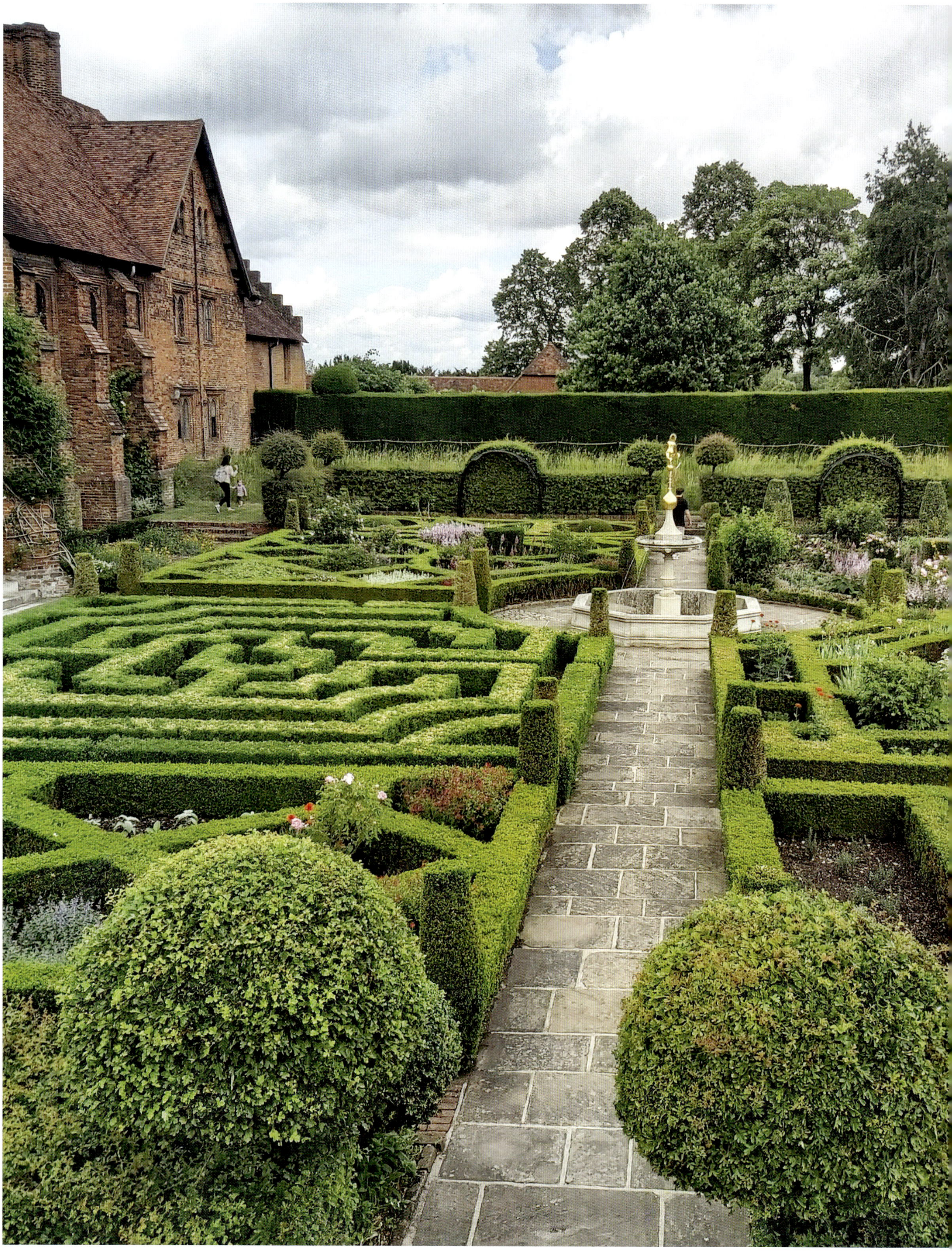

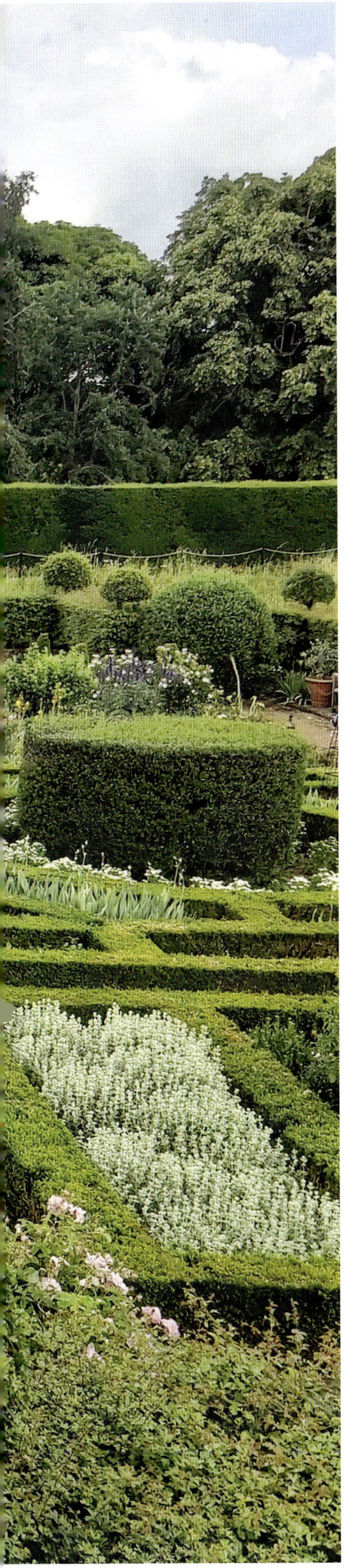

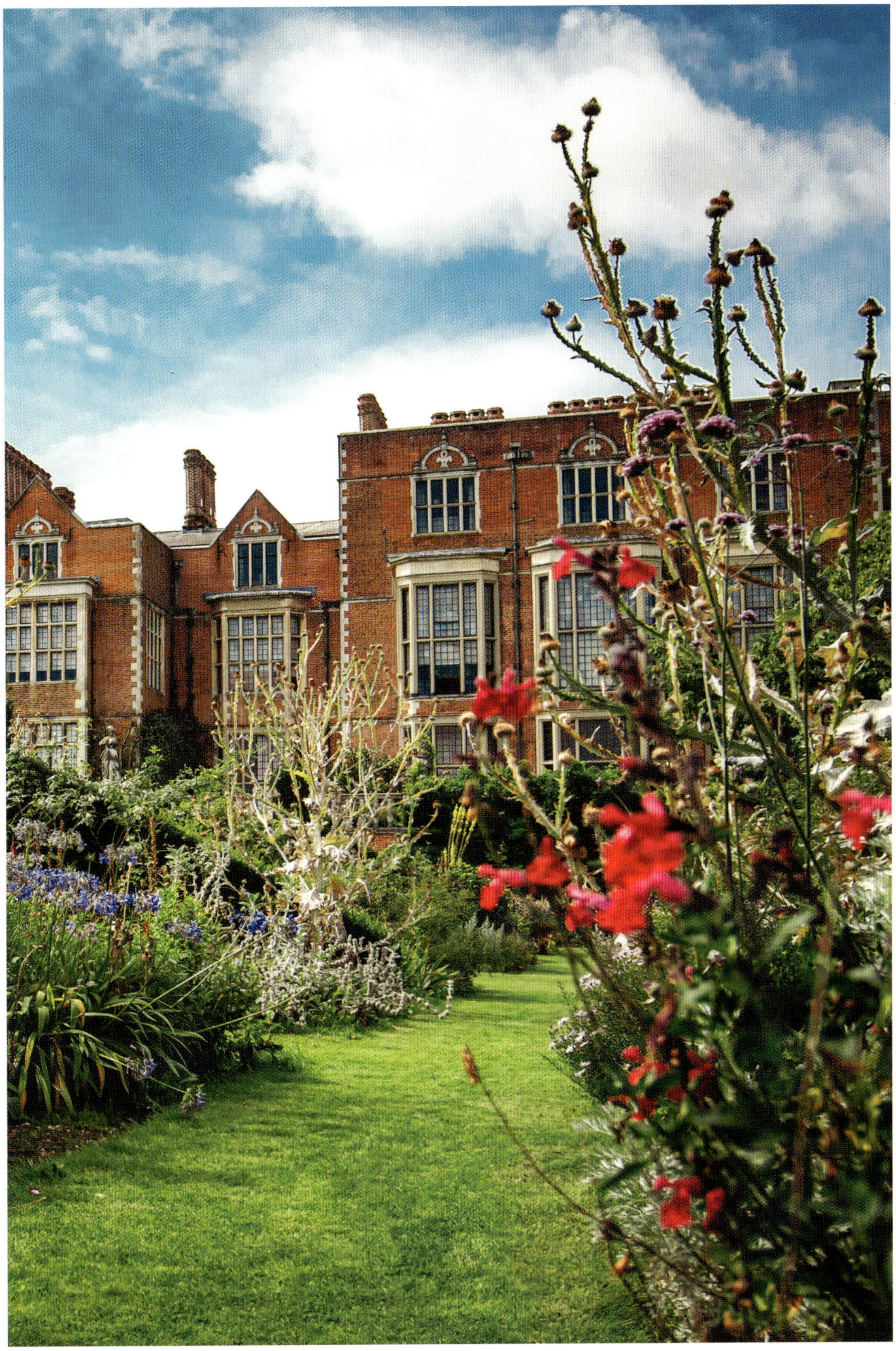

ALL PHOTOGRAPHS:

Hatfield House, Hertfordshire, England

This Jacobean house 21 miles north of London, was built in 1611 by first Earl of Salisbury Robert Cecil, although it is based on an older palace, in which Elizabeth I learned she would be Queen. The house has remained the property of the Cecil family ever since. Highlights include parterres in the East Garden, a maze, yew hedges and topiary, and a walk of pleached lime trees.

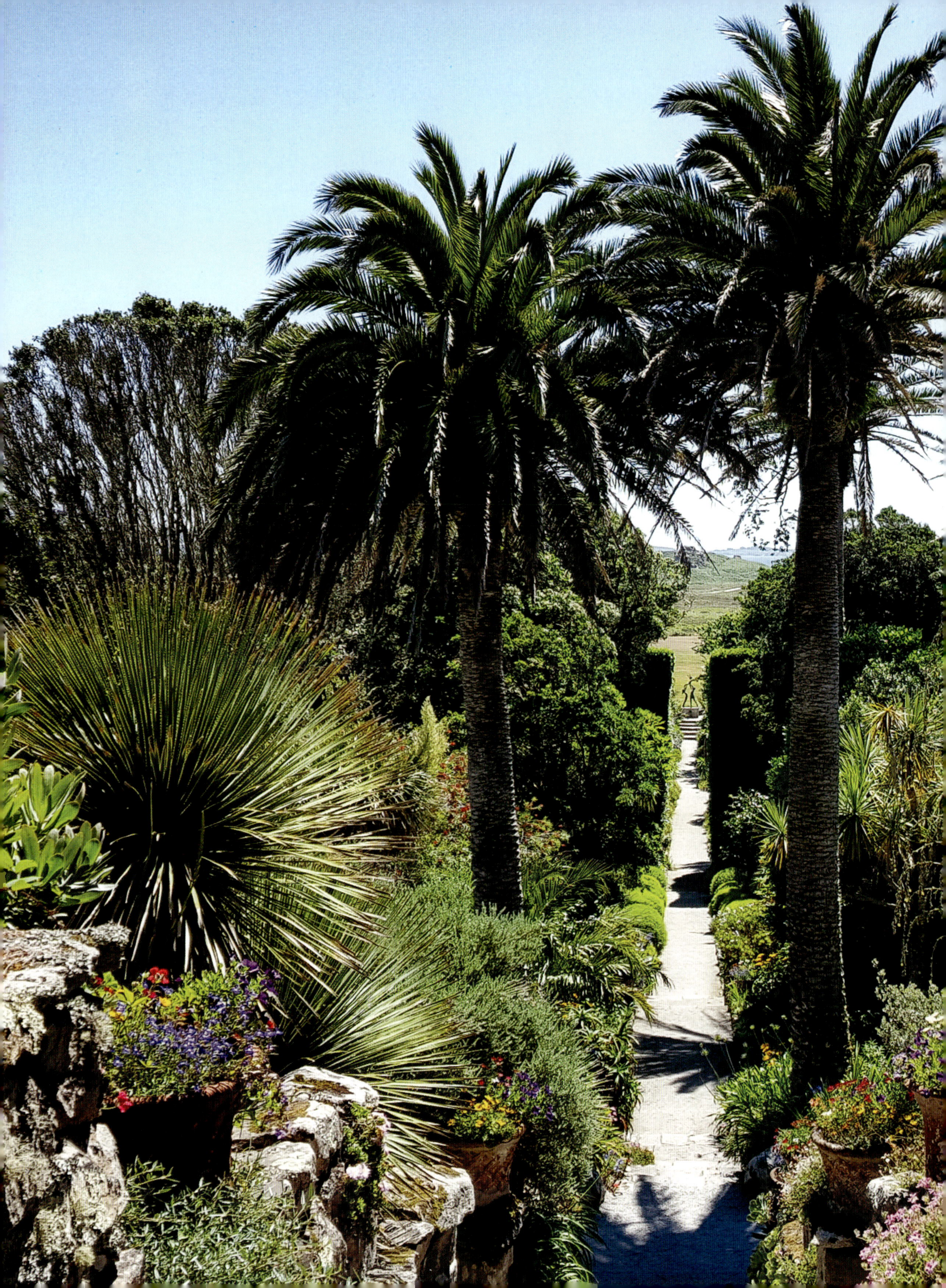

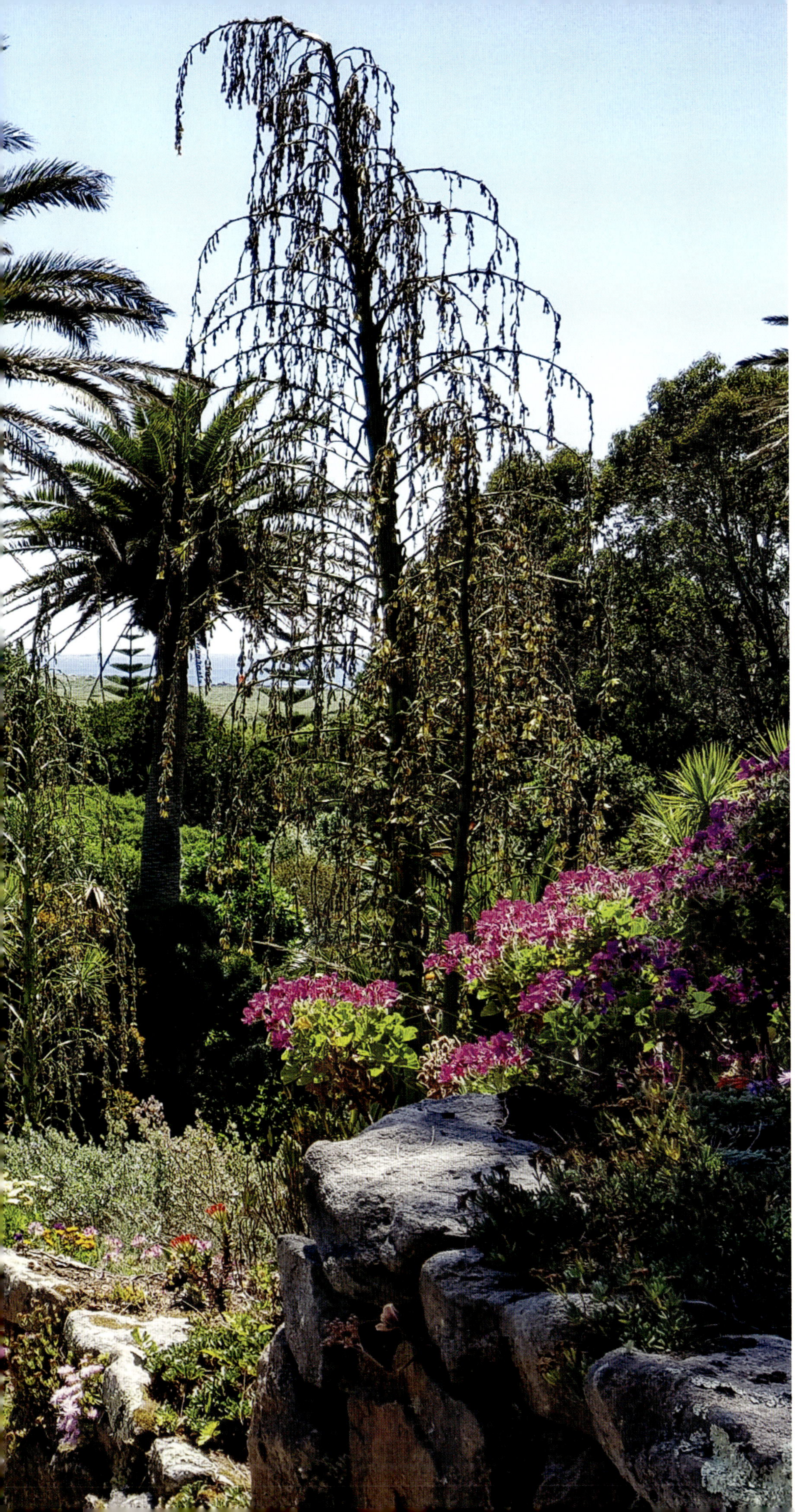

Tresco Abbey Gardens, Isles of Scilly, England
Tresco is one of five inhabited islands in the Isles of Scilly archipelago, 28 miles southwest of Cornwall. Here the subtropical Tresco Abbey Gardens, warmed by the effects of the Gulf Stream, were established around the ruins of a Benedictine abbey in the 18th century. Around 20,000 subtropical plants thrive in what must be one of the most picturesque gardens in the world.

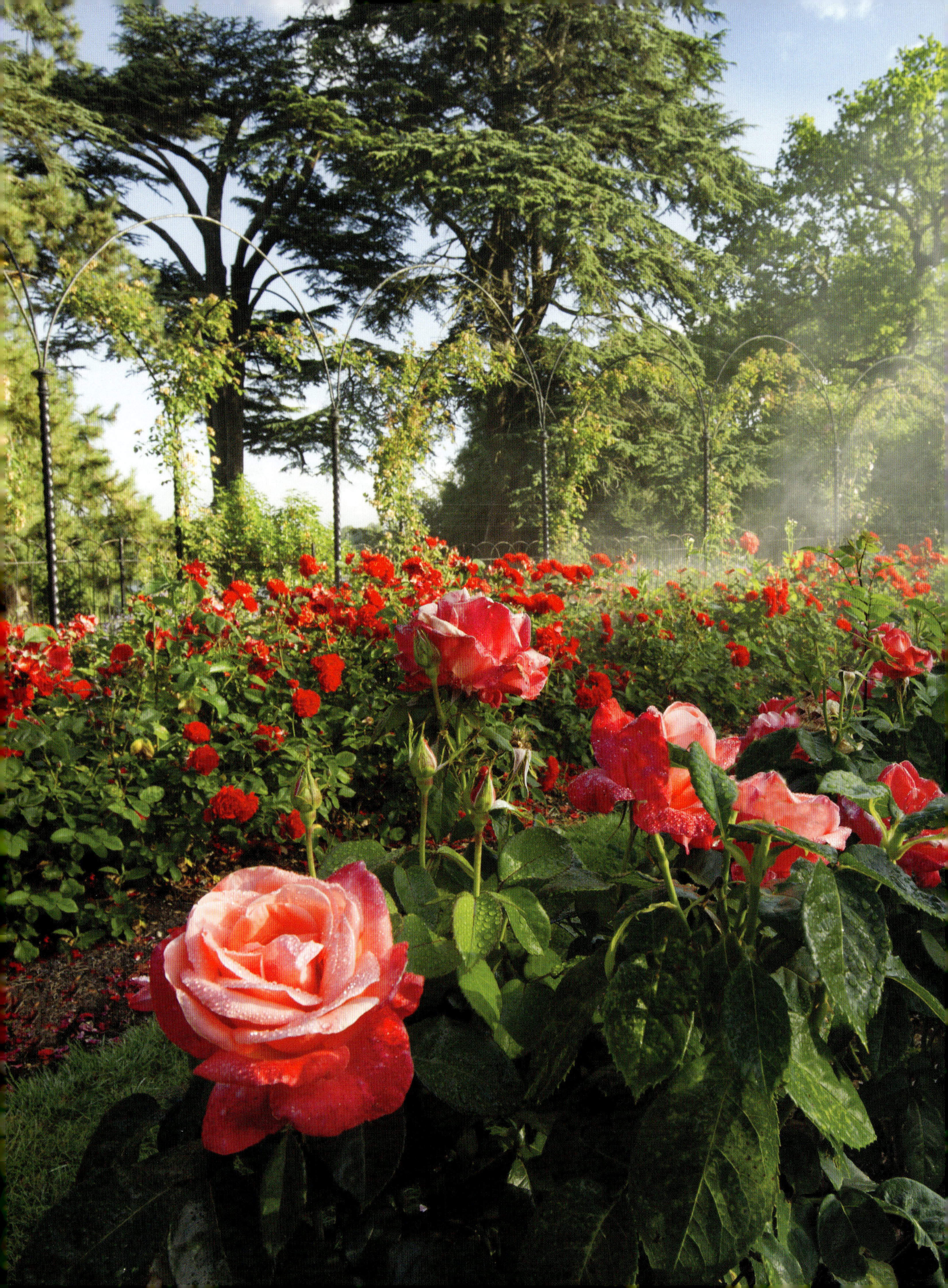

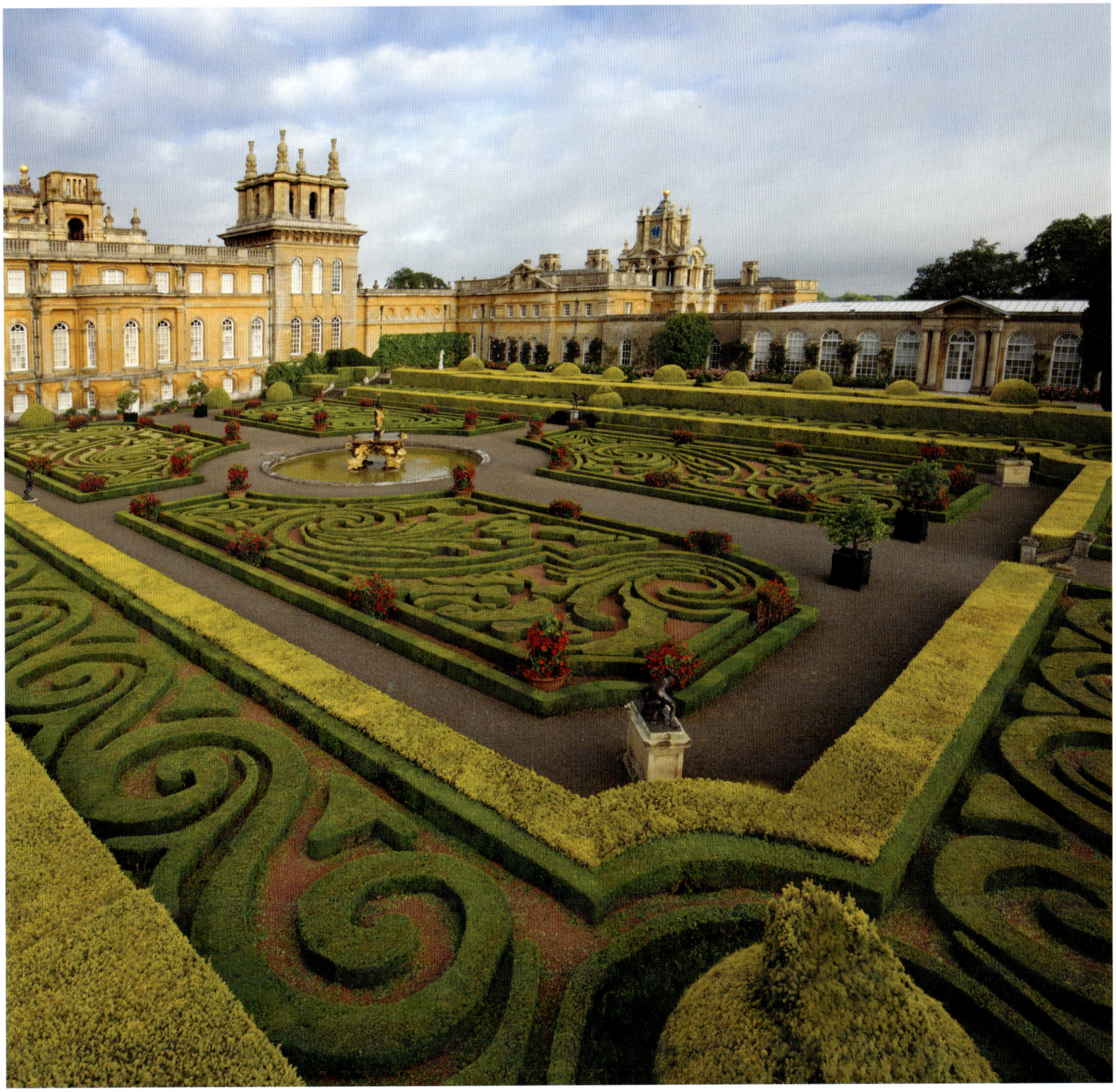

ALL PHOTOGRAPHS:

Blenheim Palace, Oxfordshire, England

The seat of the Dukes of Marlborough since 1704, this UNESCO World Heritage Site is the only non-royal, non-episcopal palace in the country. The land for the palace was given to the first Duke of Marlborough following his success at the Battle of Blenheim (1704). In recent decades, it has become known for being the birthplace of Sir Winston Churchill.

Sir Lancelot 'Capability' Brown designed a substantial landscape park in 1764. Formal gardens surrounding the palace feature water terraces, a rose garden and an Italian garden. Beyond, the Walled Garden houses a three-kilometre (two-mile) long yew maze.

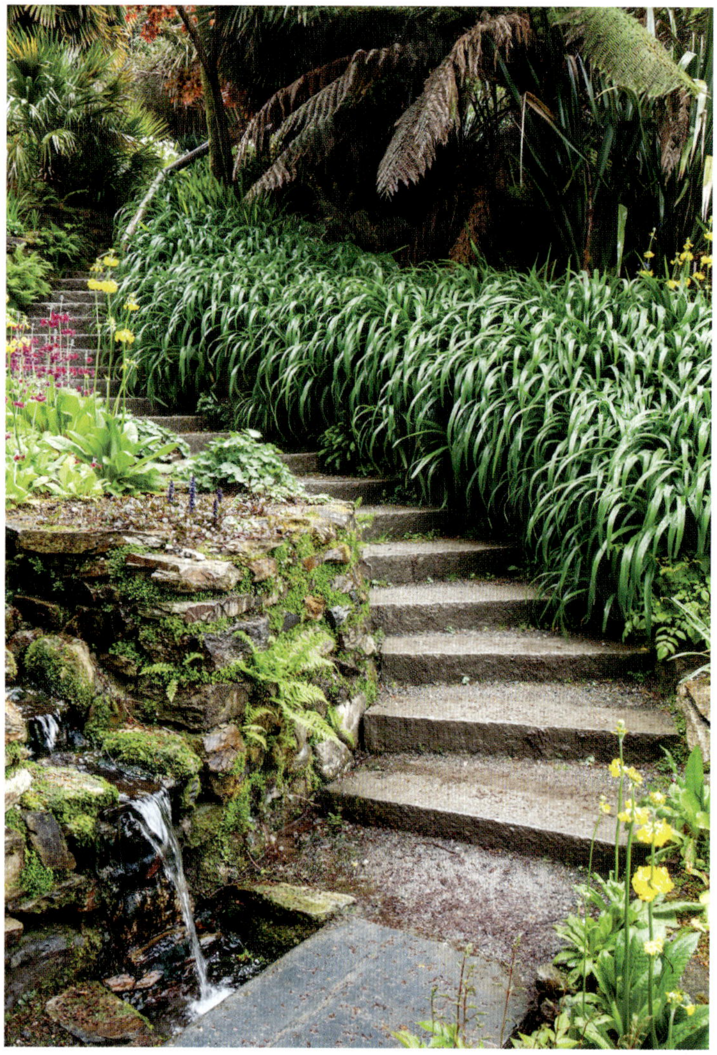

ALL PHOTOGRAPHS:

Trebah, Cornwall, England

Some 10.5ha (26 acres) make up the subtropical gardens of this Cornish property on the river Helford, near Falmouth. It was established in 1831 by Charles Fox and latterly restored by Tony Hibbert. The mild climate and acidic soil provide ideal conditions for 140-year-old rhododendrons, magnolias, camellias and hydrangeas, which thrive here.

Polgwidden beach, at the foot of the gardens, was used to launch the World War II offensive on Omaha Beach in Normandy, France.

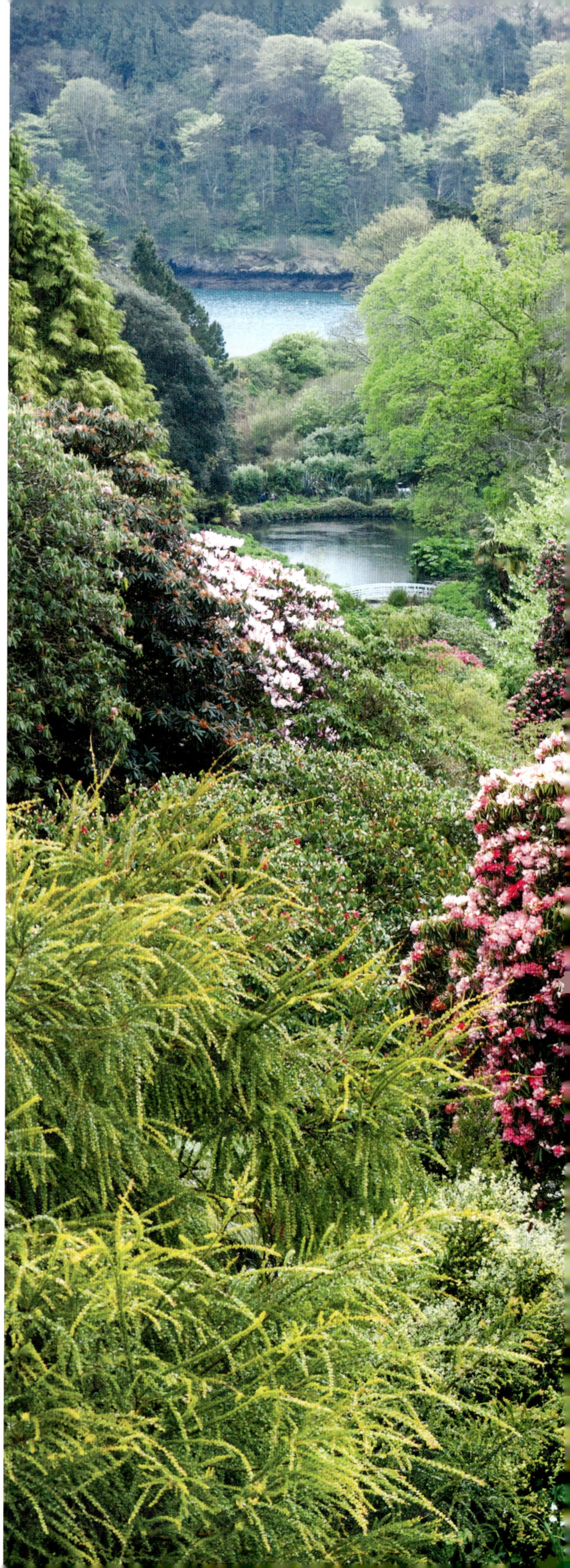

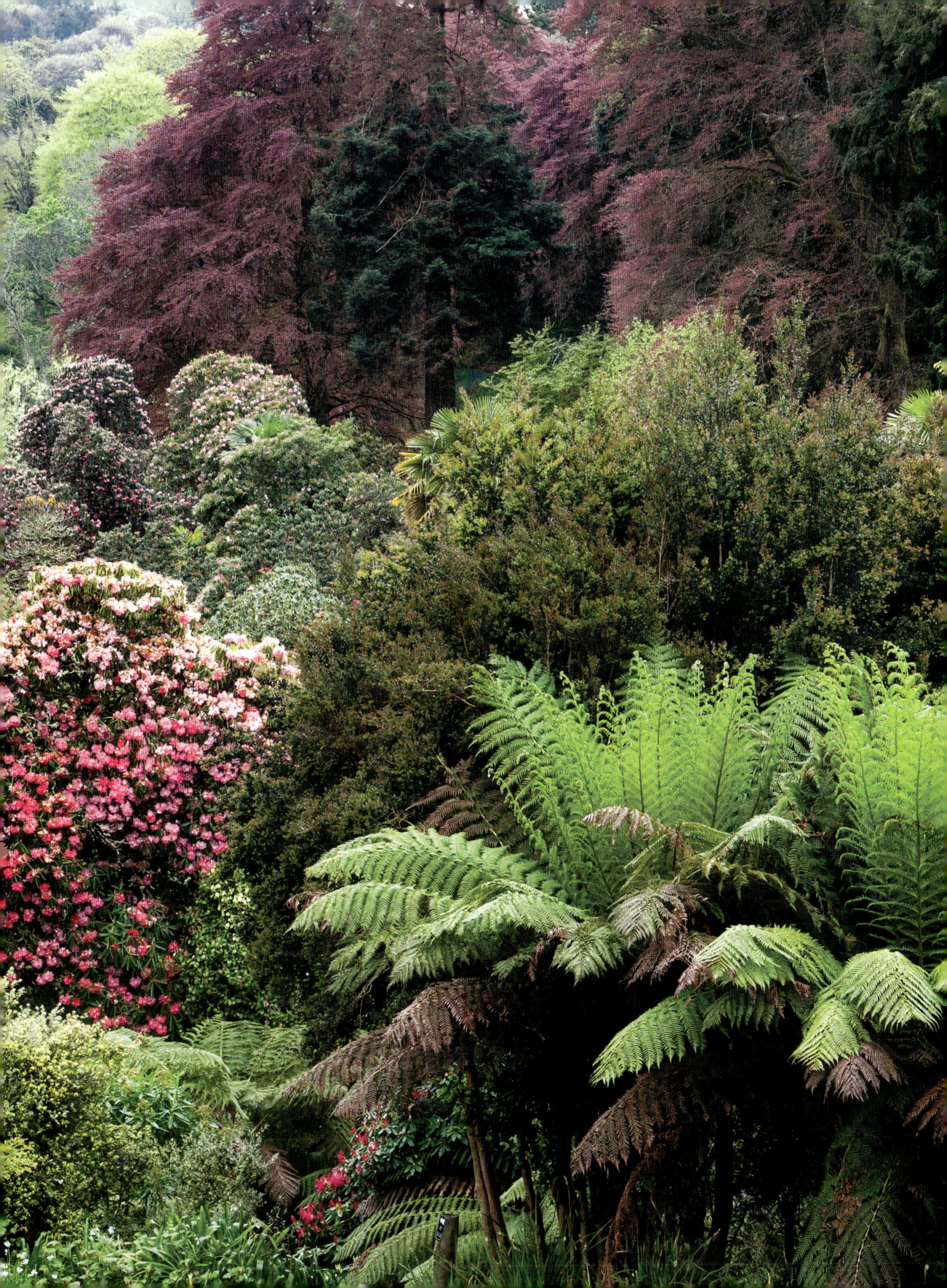

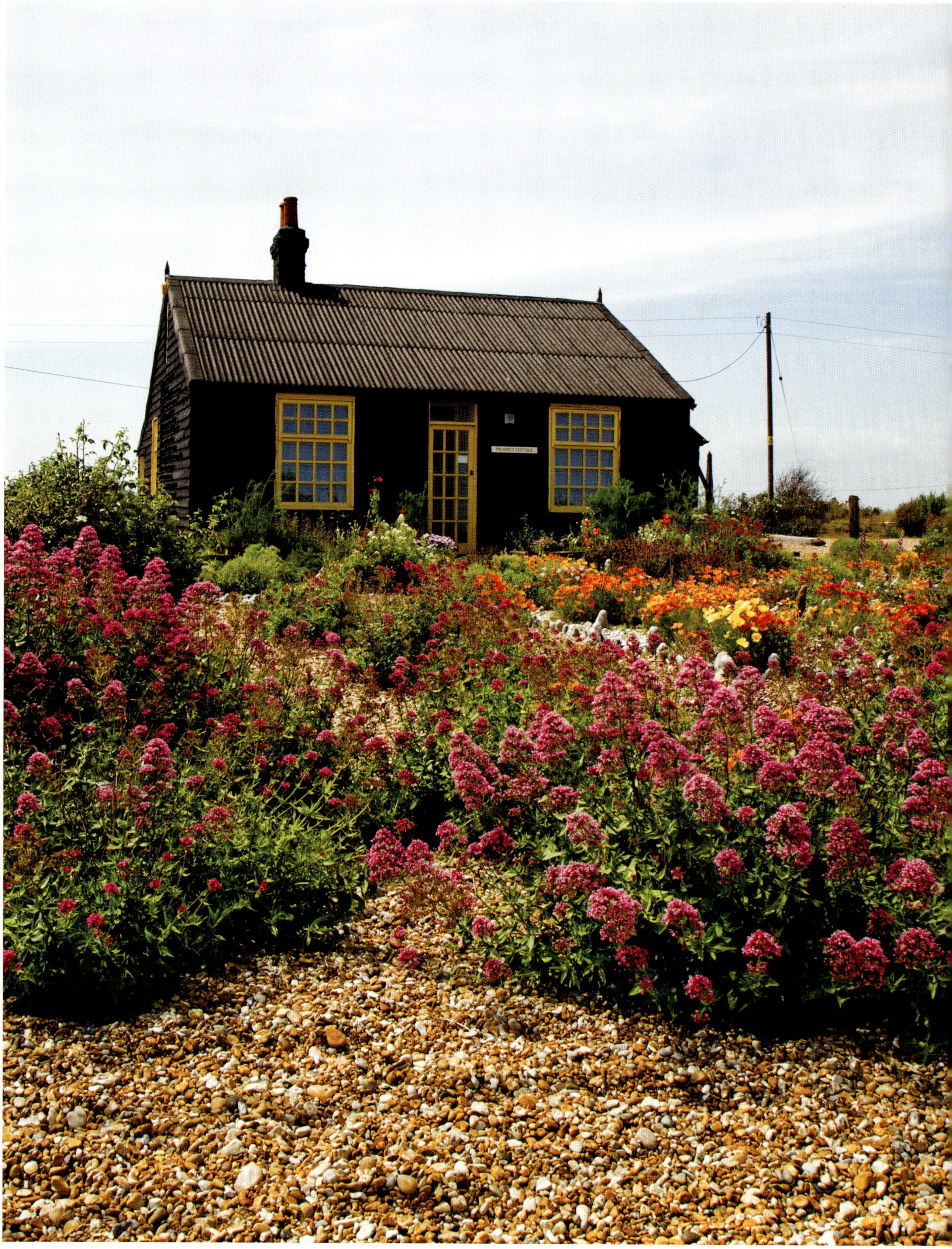

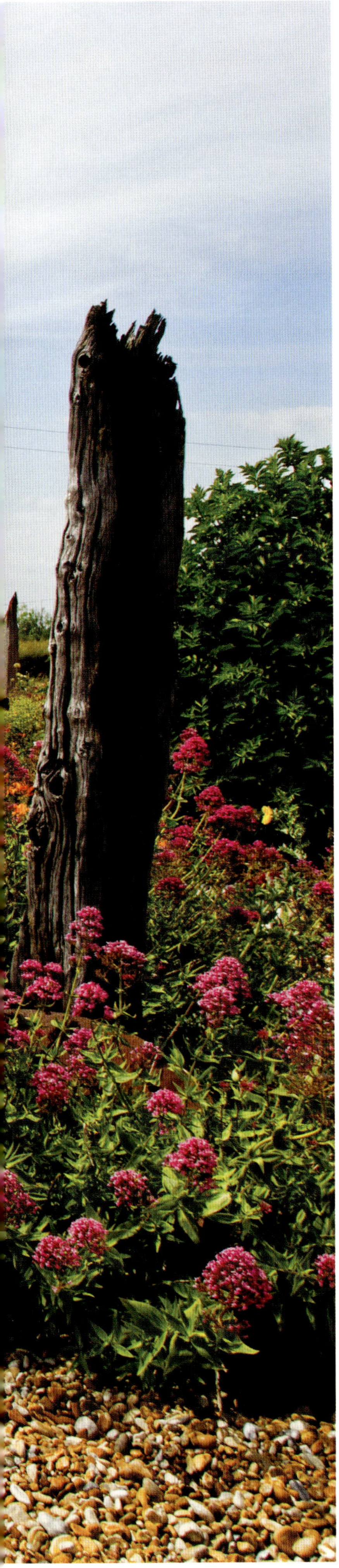

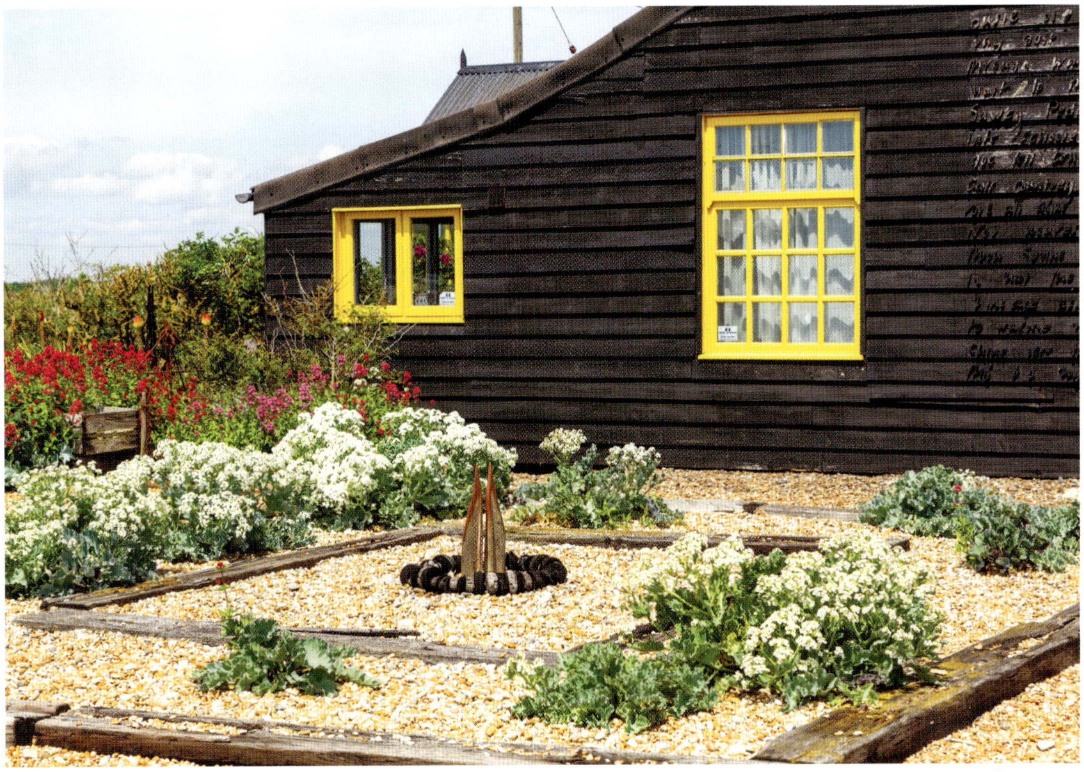

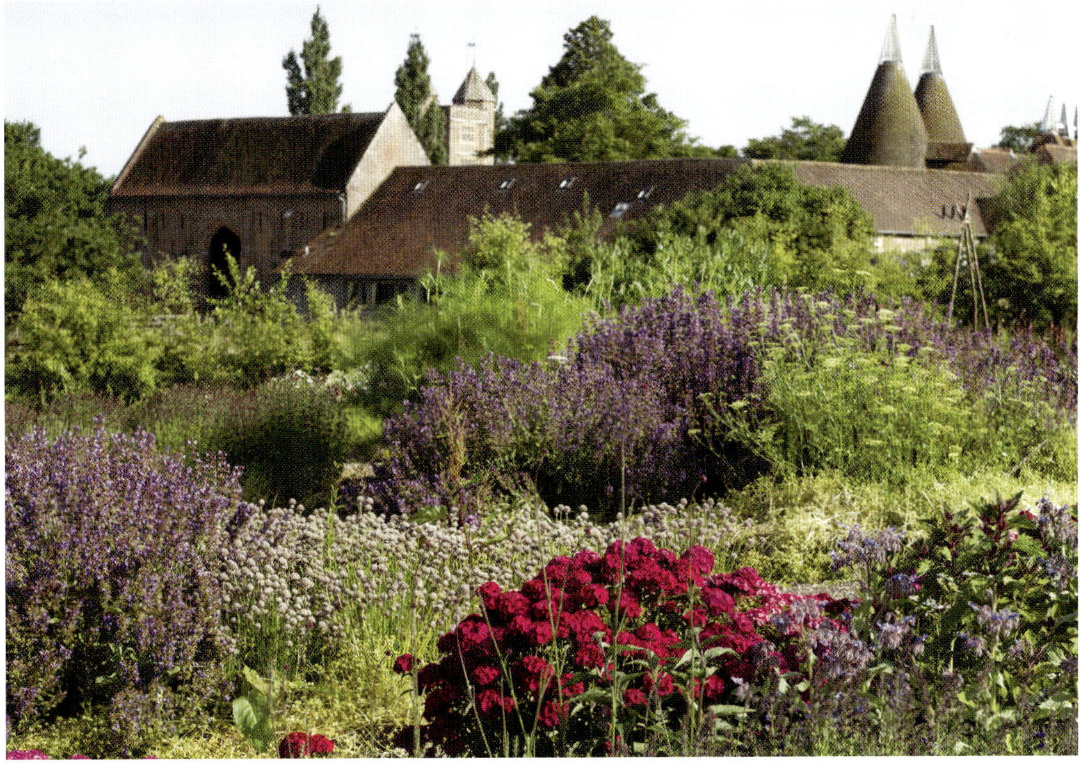

LEFT AND ABOVE TOP:
Prospect Cottage, Kent, England
Some say that the greatest work of Derek Jarman (1942–1994) was not film-making for which he was known, but the garden he created beside Dungeness nuclear power station. Buying a former fisherman's cottage in 1984, Jarman fashioned the garden from flotsam, shingle and hardy plants. In 2020, the cottage, at risk of falling into private ownership, was bought for the nation thanks to a £3.5 million fund-raising campaign.

ABOVE BOTTOM AND OVERLEAF:
Sissinghurst Castle Garden, Kent, England
Few gardens in the world enjoy the popularity of Sissinghurst, the life's work of Vita Sackville-West and Harold Nicolson, who bought the Tudor property in 1930. The White Garden, in particular, has inspired amateur gardeners for decades. The property is now in care of the National Trust and in 2021, a dry-climate garden based on Harold and Vita's travels to the Greek island of Delos was opened.

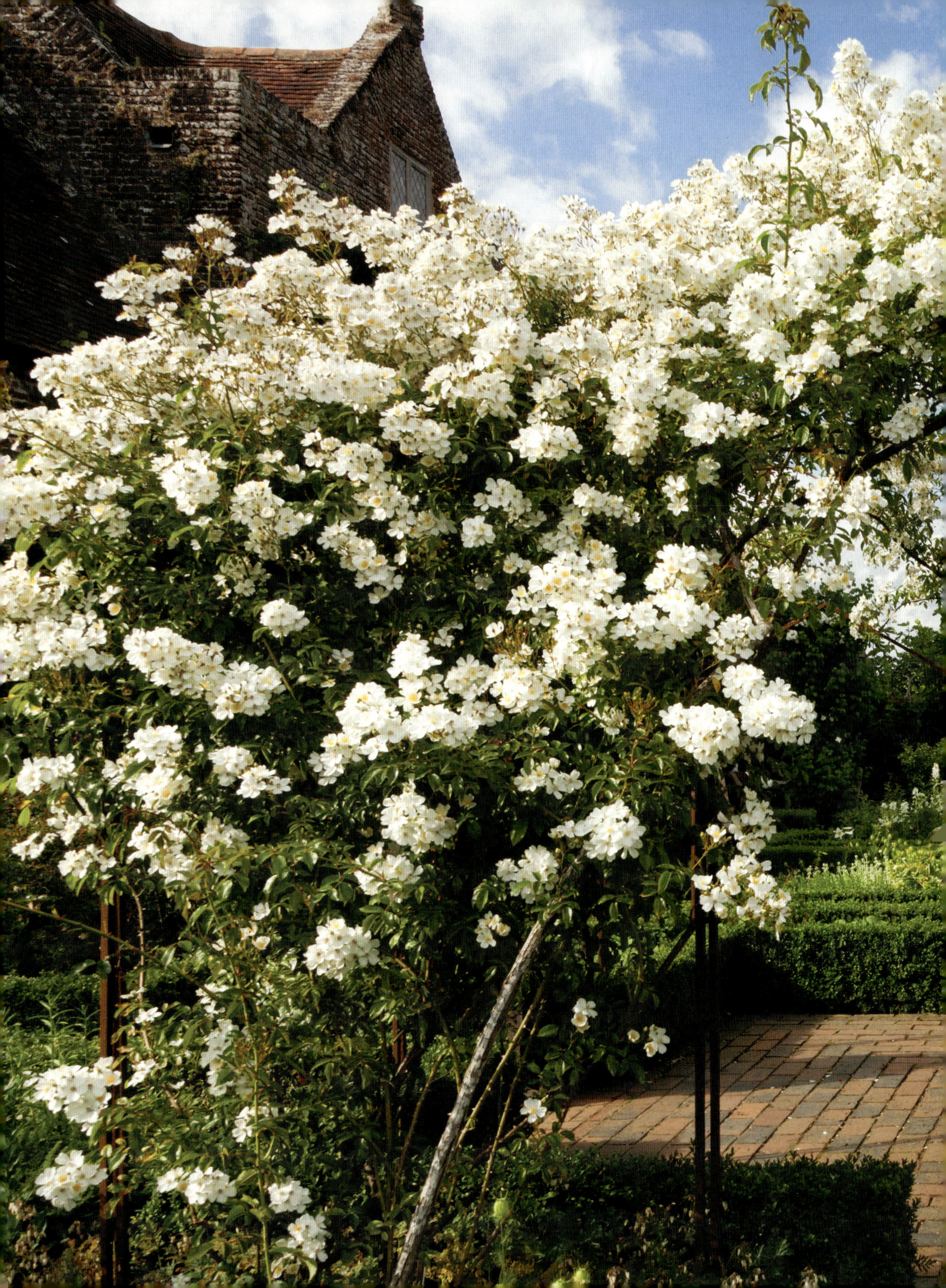

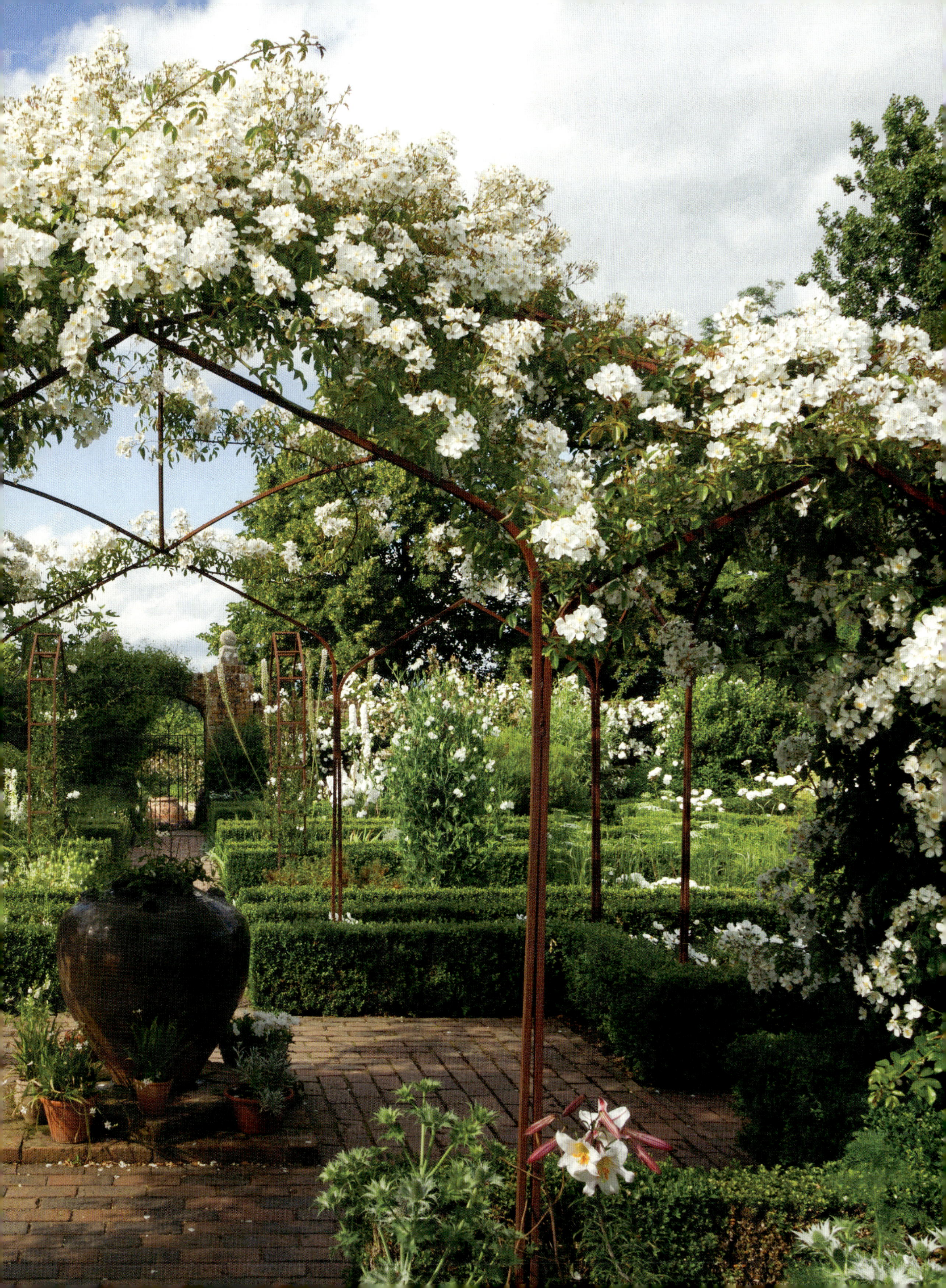

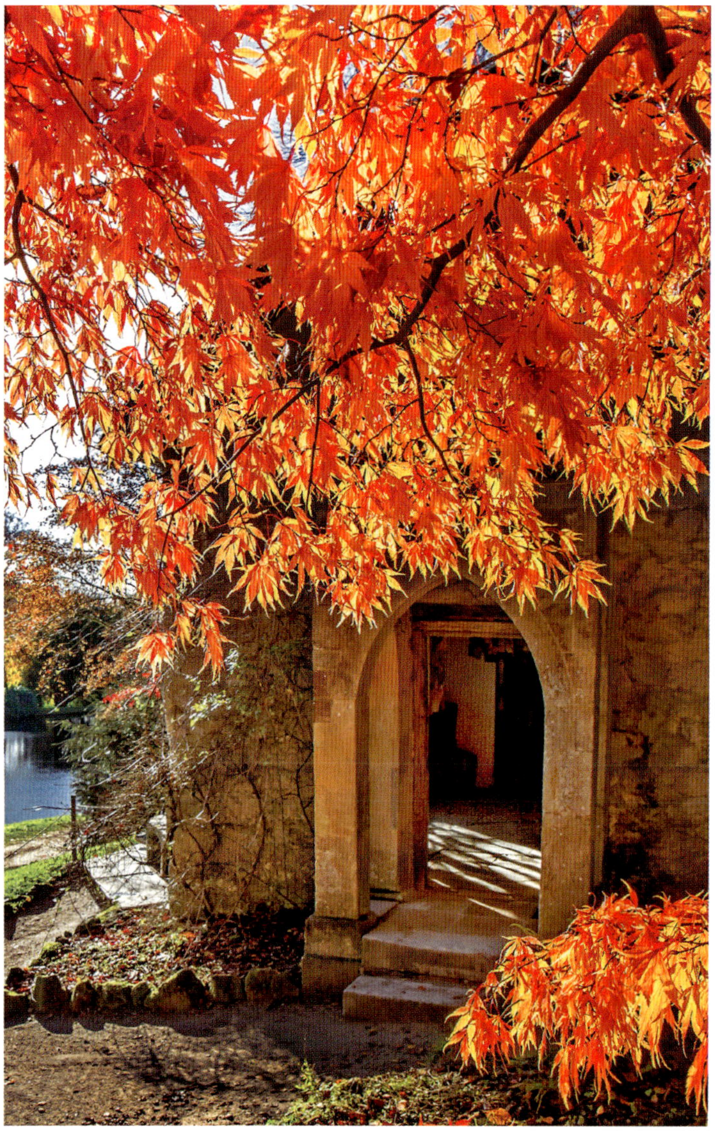

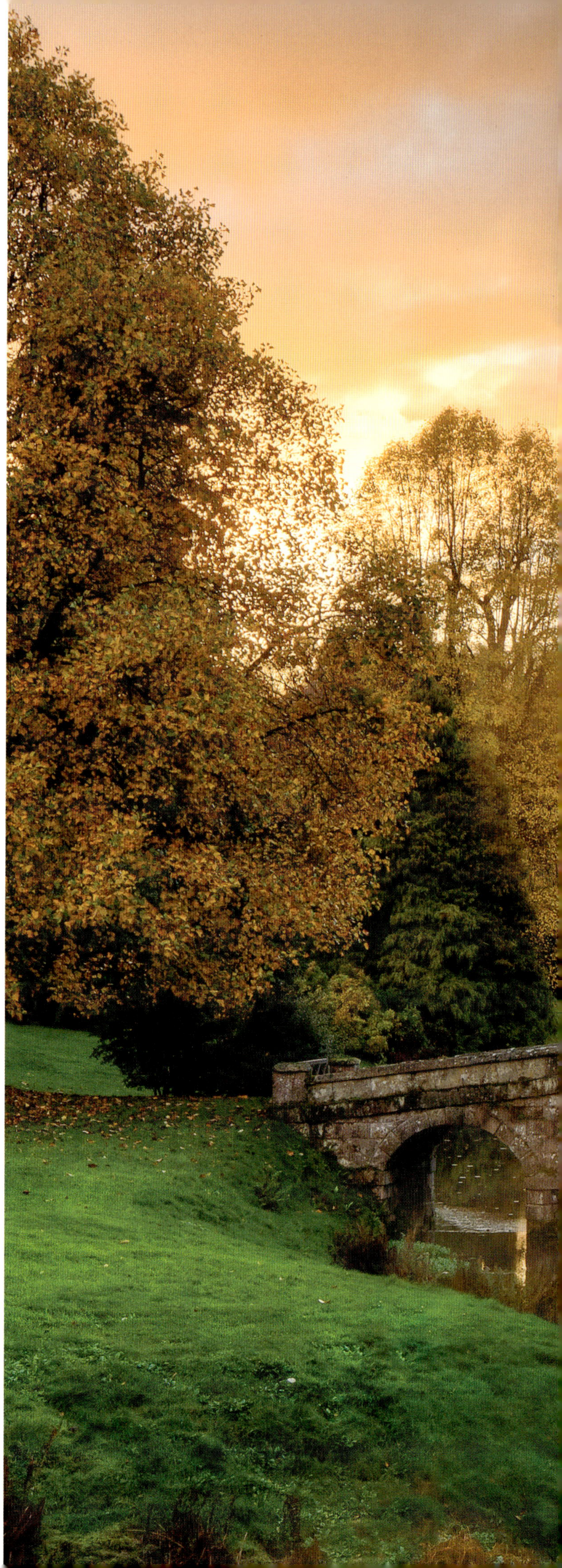

ALL PHOTOGRAPHS:

Stourhead, Wiltshire, England

The property of the Stourton family for half a century, Stourhead came into the possession of the Hoares, the banking family, in 1717. The house, one of England's greatest Palladian mansions, remained in the family until 1949, when it was given to the National Trust. The surrounding mid-18th century gardens are in the English landscape style with an artificial lake and views framed by classical follies and monuments.

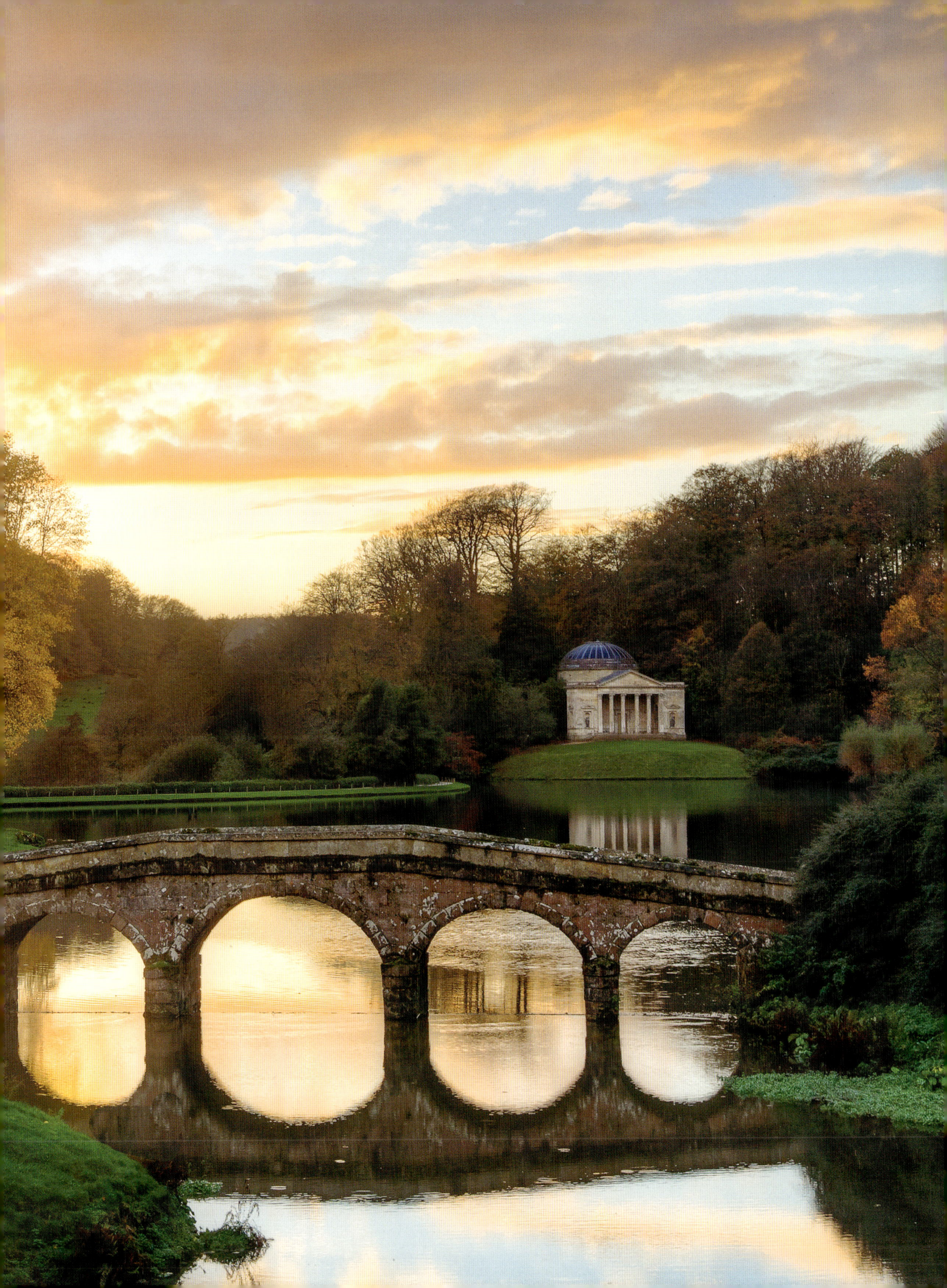

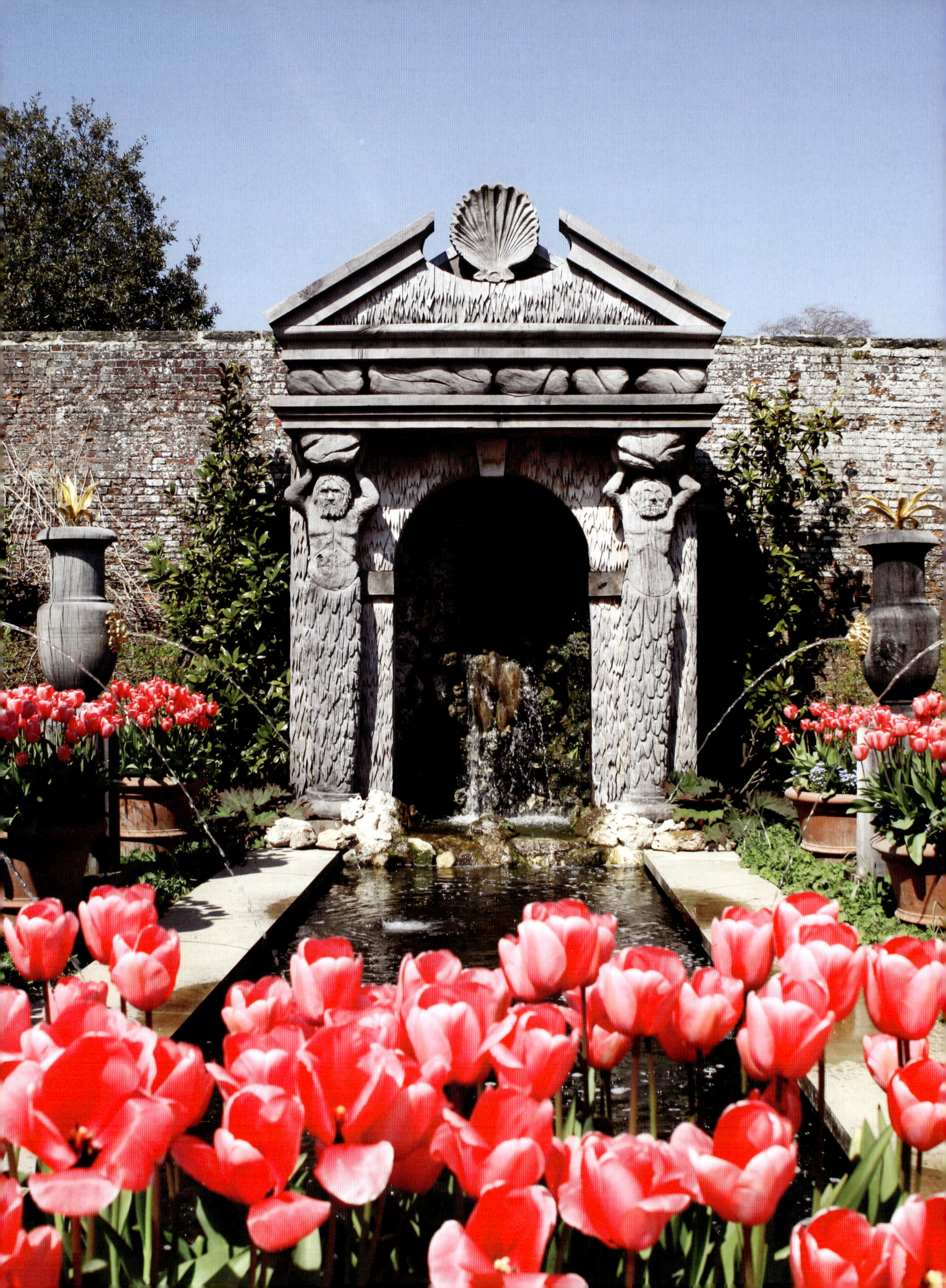

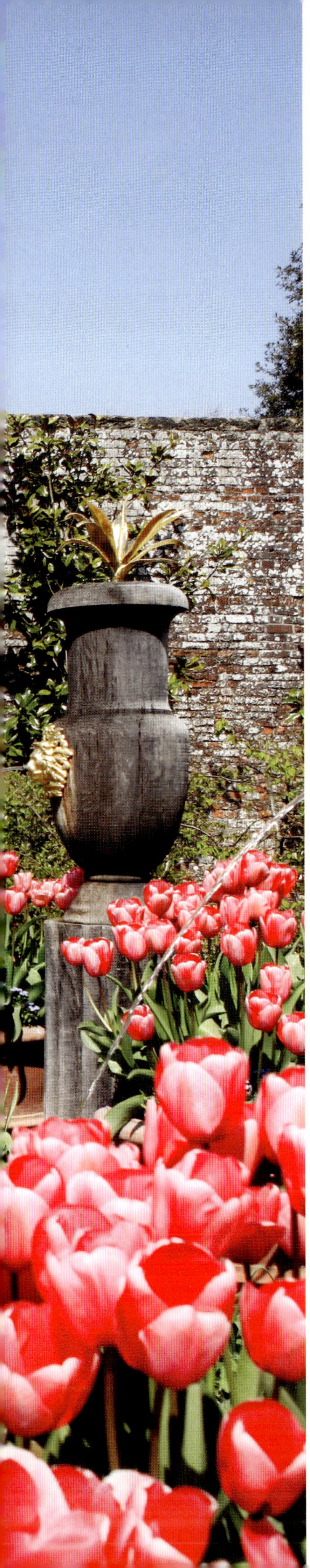

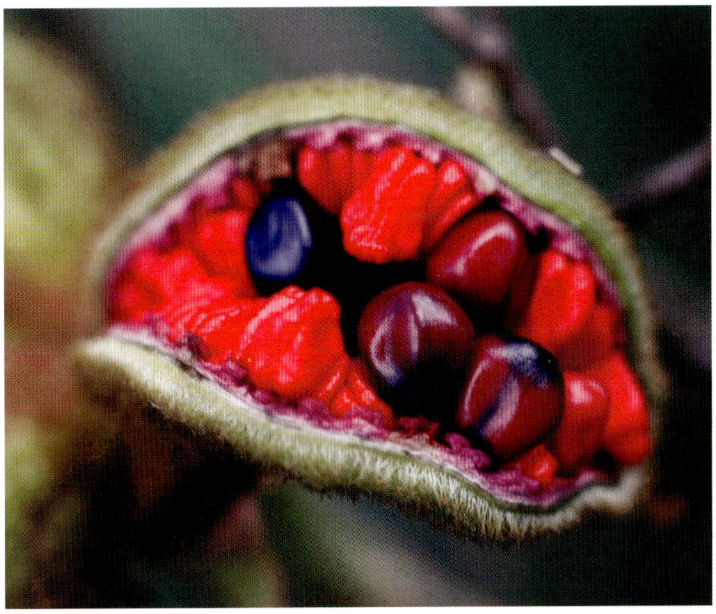

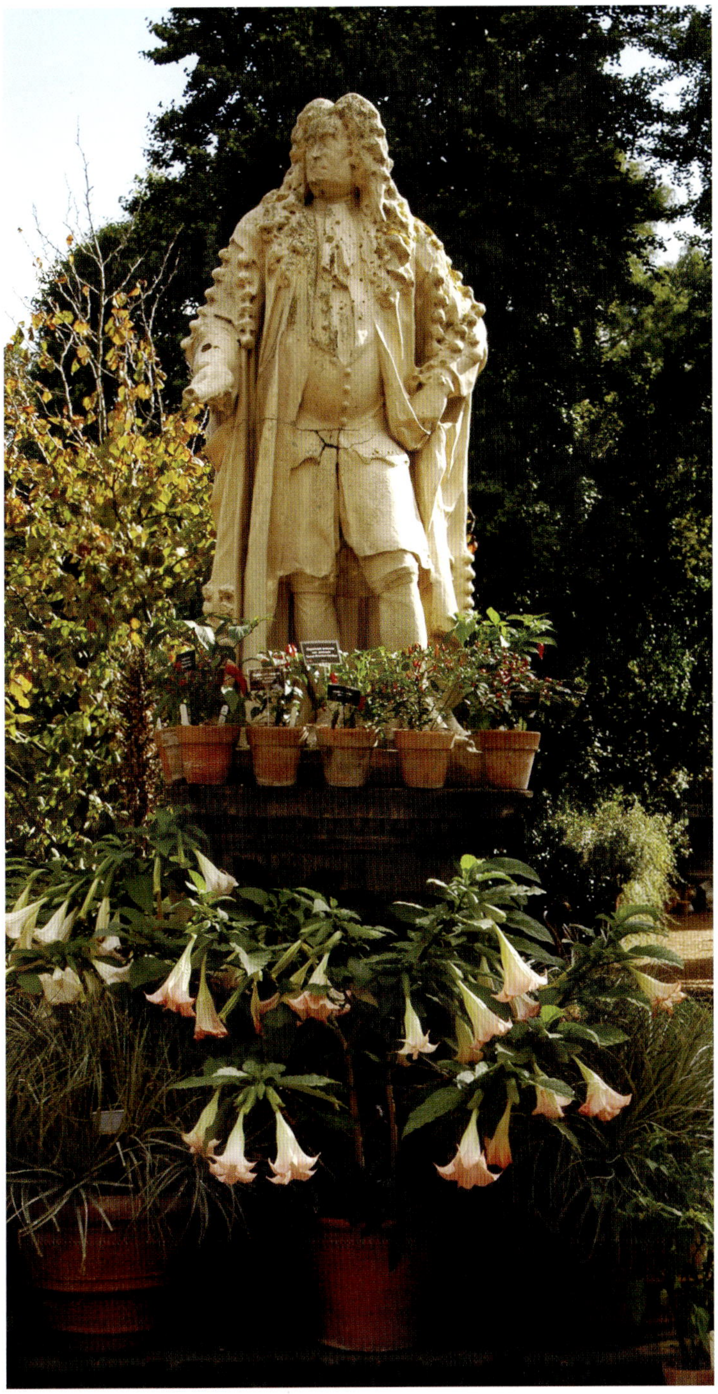

FAR LEFT:

Arundel Castle, West Sussex, England

Positioned on a hill in the pretty village of Arundel, this castle dates to 1067 and Charles de Montgomery, first holder of the earldom of Arundel which was given to him by William the Conqueror. The densely arranged gardens, which include substantial glasshouses, are packed with spring bulbs, while the Rose Garden comes to the fore in summer. Opened in 2008, the Collector Earl's garden, containing a pergola and central canal, is a memorial to the 14th Earl of Arundel.

LEFT TOP AND BOTTOM:

Chelsea Physic Garden, London, England

Beside the banks of the river Thames, central London, the four-acre Chelsea Physic Garden has been the site of medicinal plant growing since 1673. Use of property was secured in 1712 by Sir Hans Sloane and the garden continues to pay an annual rent of £5 to his descendants.

On his travels to the West Indies, Sloane had noticed Jamaicans drinking cocoa with water to settle the stomach. A renowned physician, Sloane adapted their recipe, which led the Cadbury brothers to sell drinking chocolate under his name. Today around 5,000 edible and medicinal plants feature in this green space.

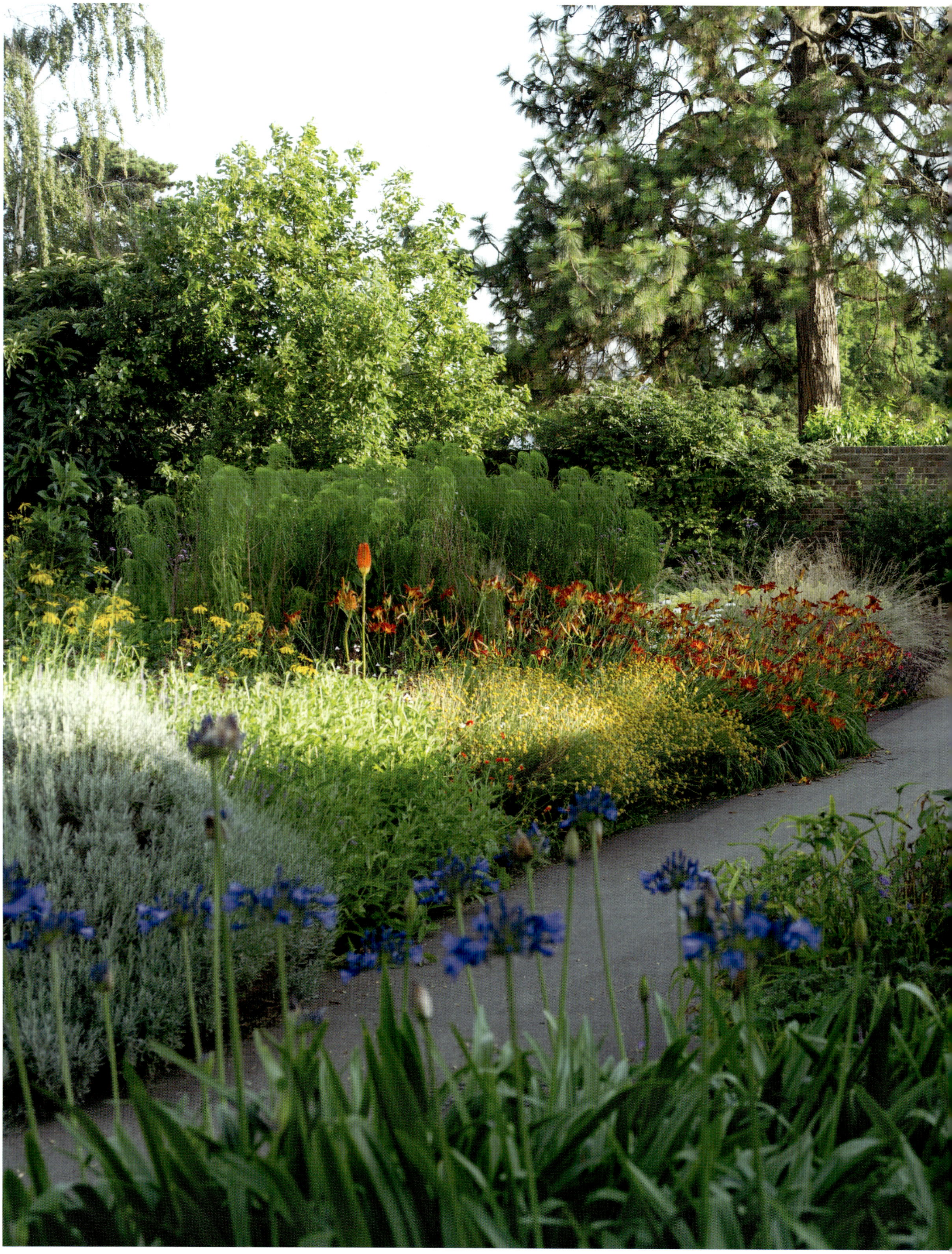

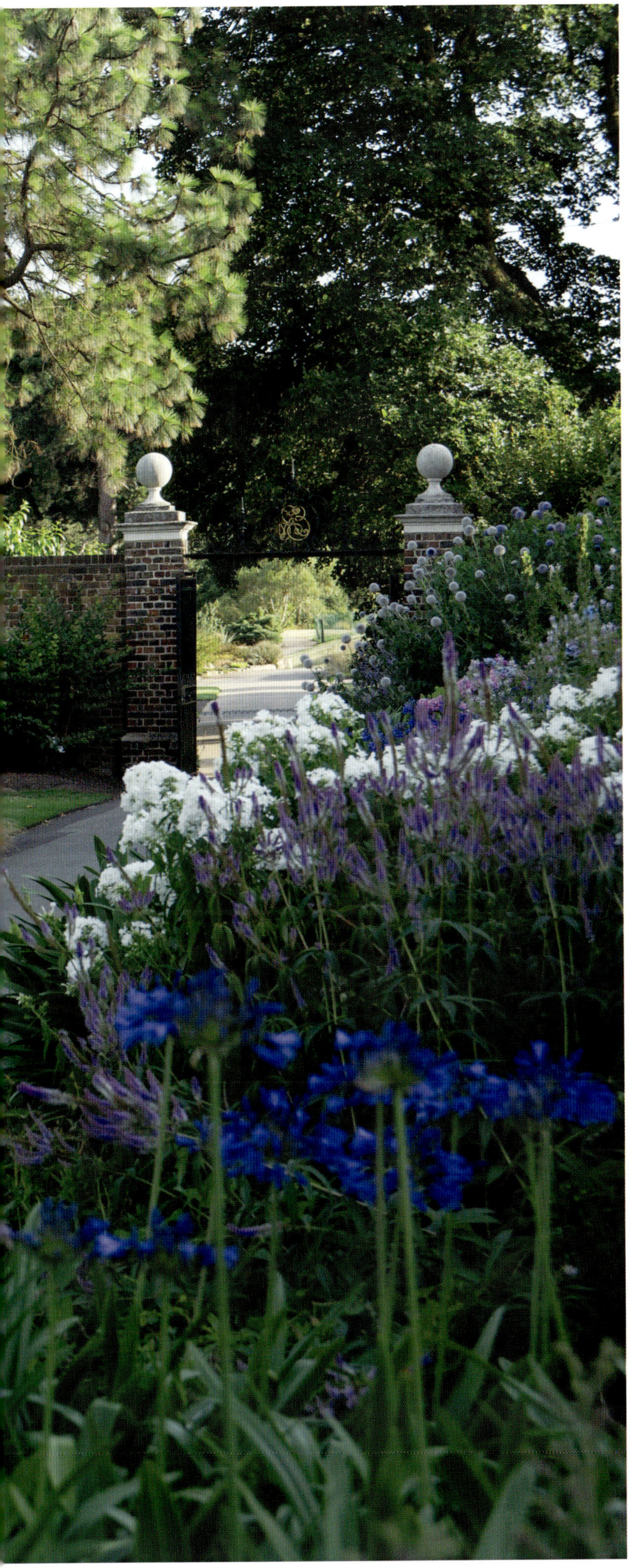

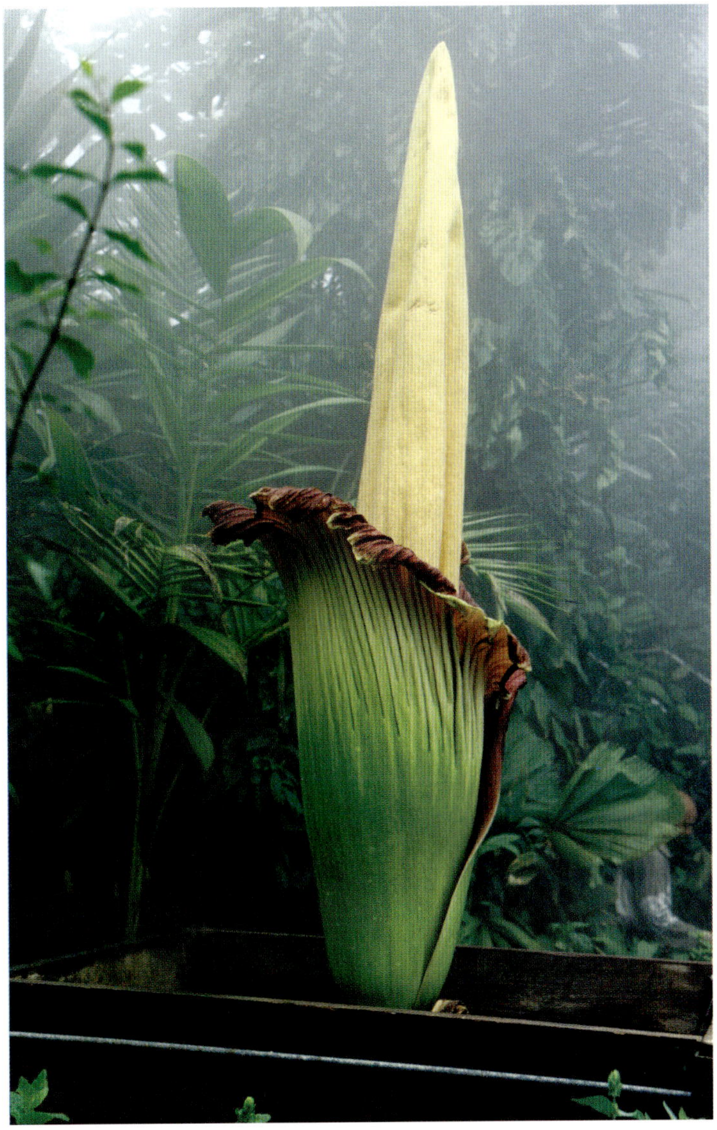

ALL PHOTOGRAPHS:

Royal Botanic Gardens, Kew, Surrey, England

Possibly the greatest garden in the world, RBG Kew was formally opened in 1840, although it had been operating from its site in southwest London from at least 1759. Much of the garden's original work was to source plants with commercial potential from new territories, relying on the endeavours of robust plant-hunter explorers. Such activities gathered pace under the first director, William Hooker.

The plant titan arum (*Amorphophallus titanum*) is famed for smelling of rotting flesh when it flowers (above). It is housed in the Princess of Wales Conservatory.

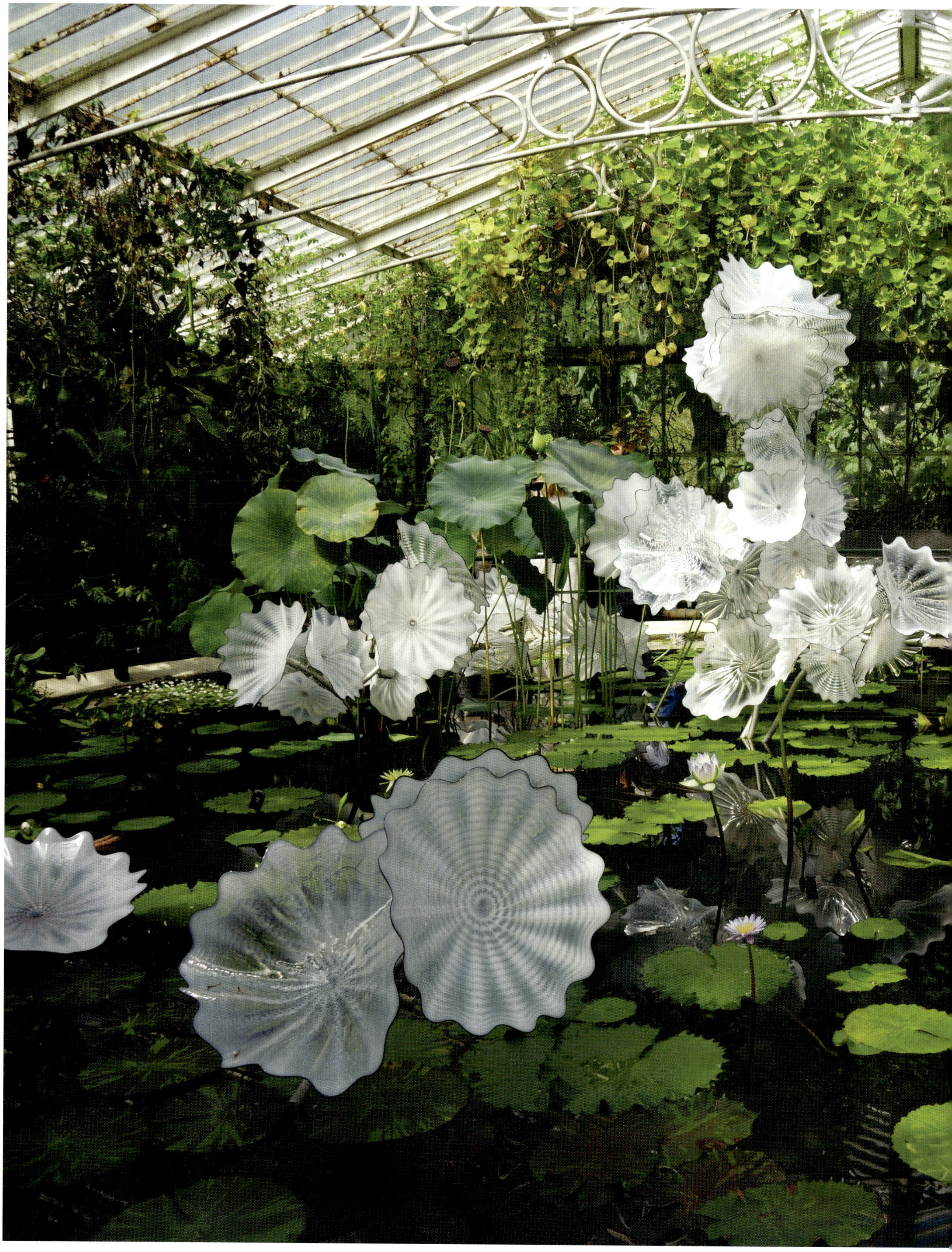

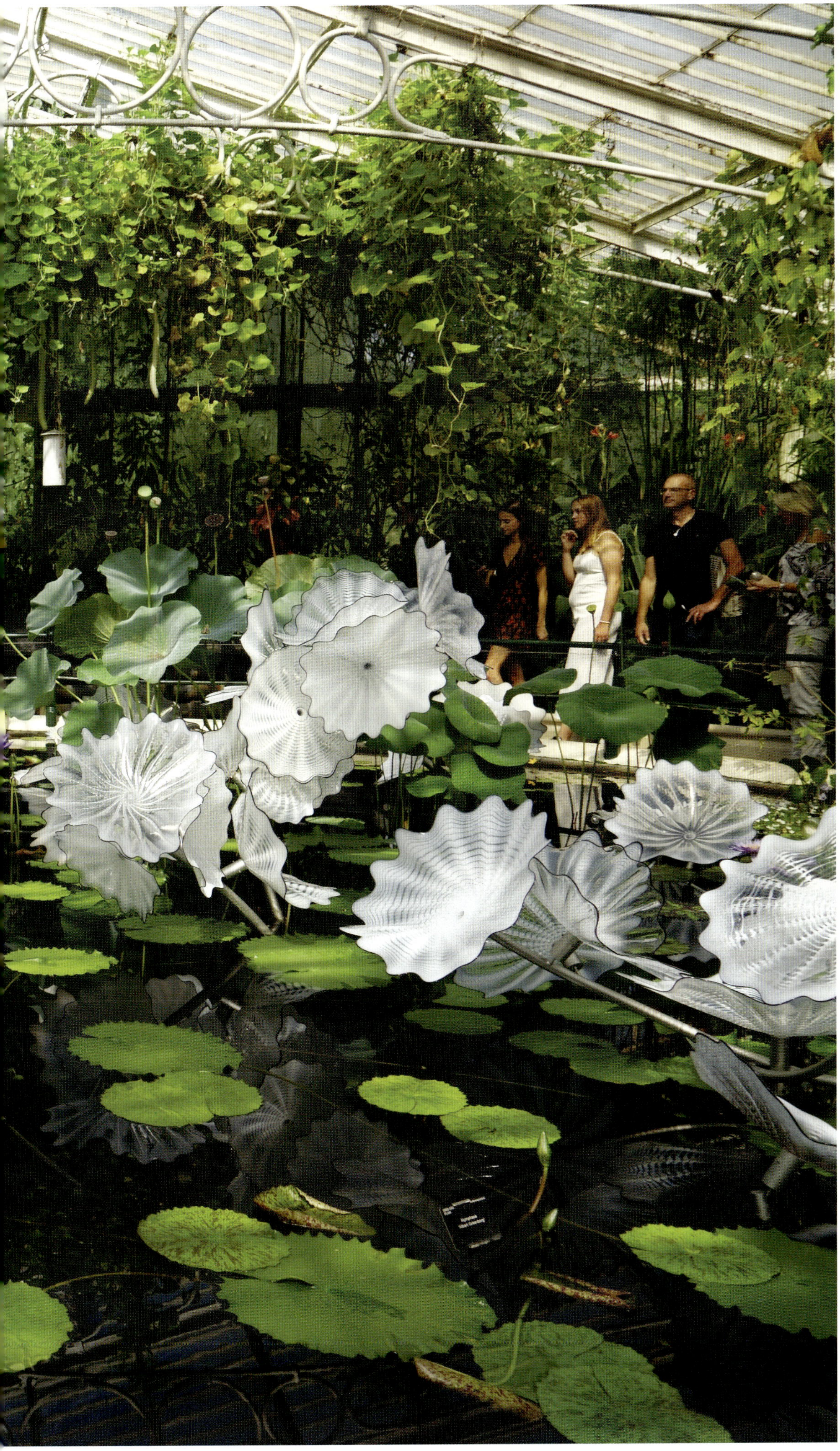

LEFT:

Royal Botanic Gardens, Kew, Surrey, England

While reckoning with its imperial past, the current focus of RBG Kew is broadly on conservation and maintaining biodiversity. The Millennium Seed Bank at the gardens' second site, Wakehurst, holds in secure conditions seeds of roughly 39,000 species from around world.

OVERLEAF (BOTH PHOTOGRAPHS):

Eden Project, Cornwall, England

Two unmistakable geodesic domes filled with plant specimens from around the world form the backbone of the Eden Project in Cornwall. The brainchild of Sir Tim Smit, the garden grew out of an old quarry site, took two-and-a-half years to build, and opened formally in 2001. While there is plenty of outdoor planting, tropical and Mediterranean biomes are housed beneath the domes. Rainwater harvesting and green energy strategies put sustainability at the heart of the garden.

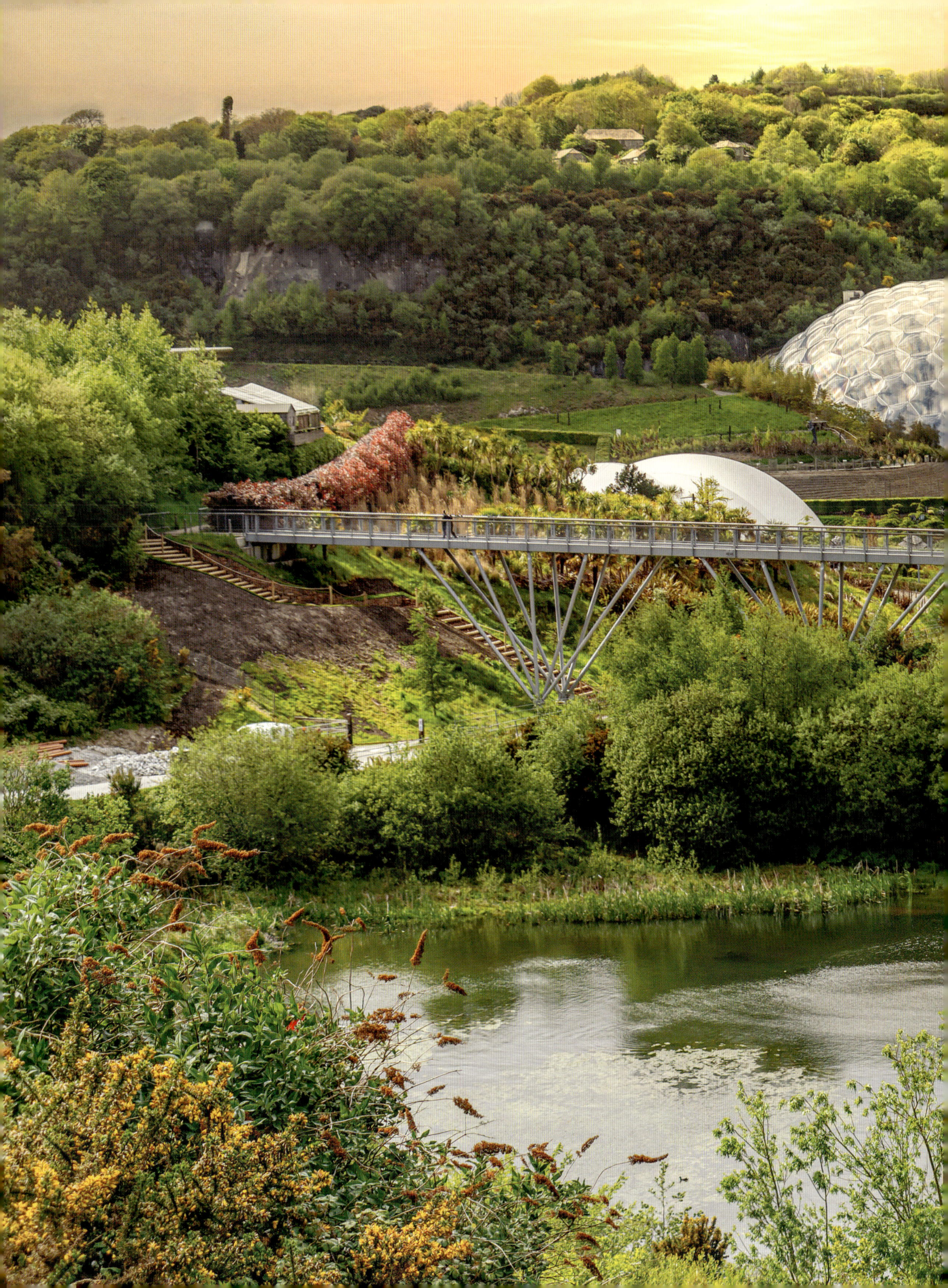

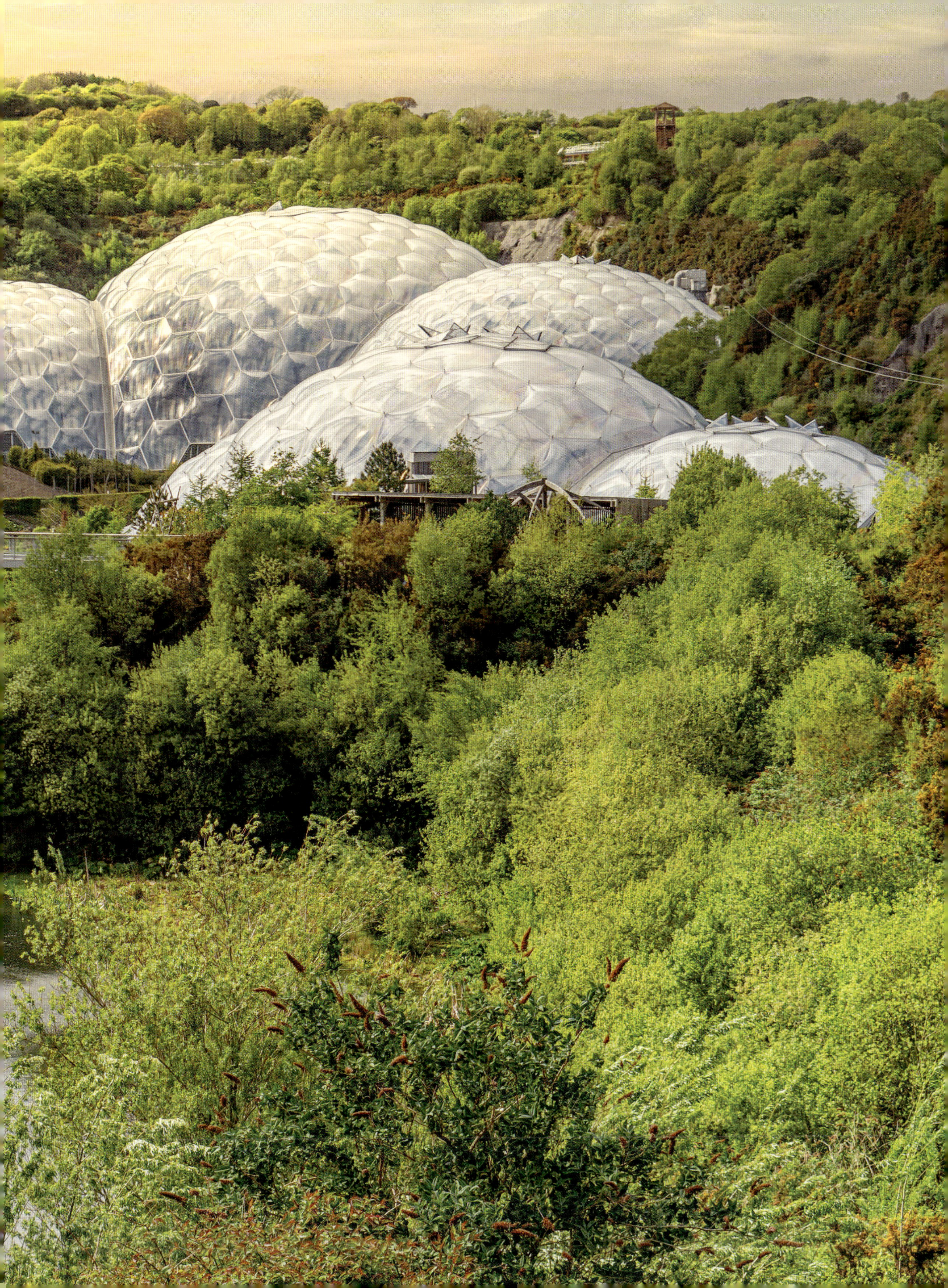

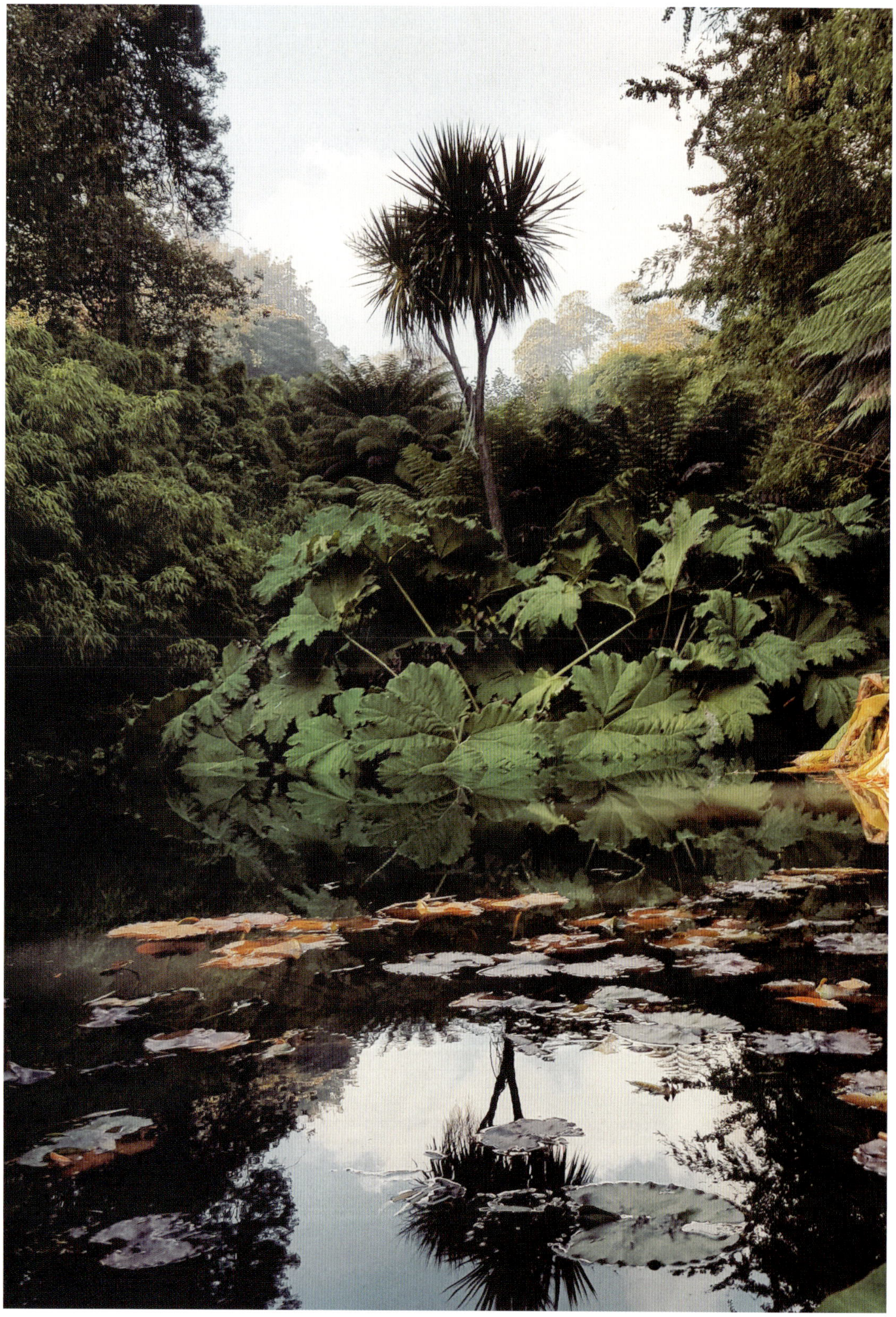

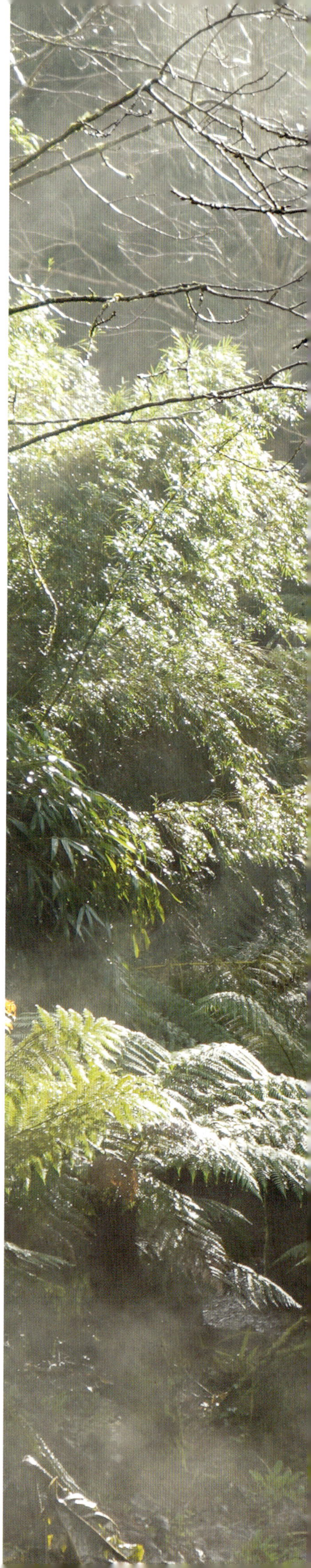

ALL PHOTOGRAPHS:

Lost Gardens of Heligan, Cornwall, England

After World War I took the lives of many gardeners who went to fight in the trenches, the gardens at Heligan were left to ruin, to be reclaimed only in the 1990s by Sir Tim Smit. By that time, they were so overgrown, metal detectors were used to locate old tools and greenhouse parts. While the Walled Garden here is an exercise in immaculate productive gardening, steeply sloping wilder sections include the Jungle and the Lost Valley which are planted with gunnera and tree ferns.

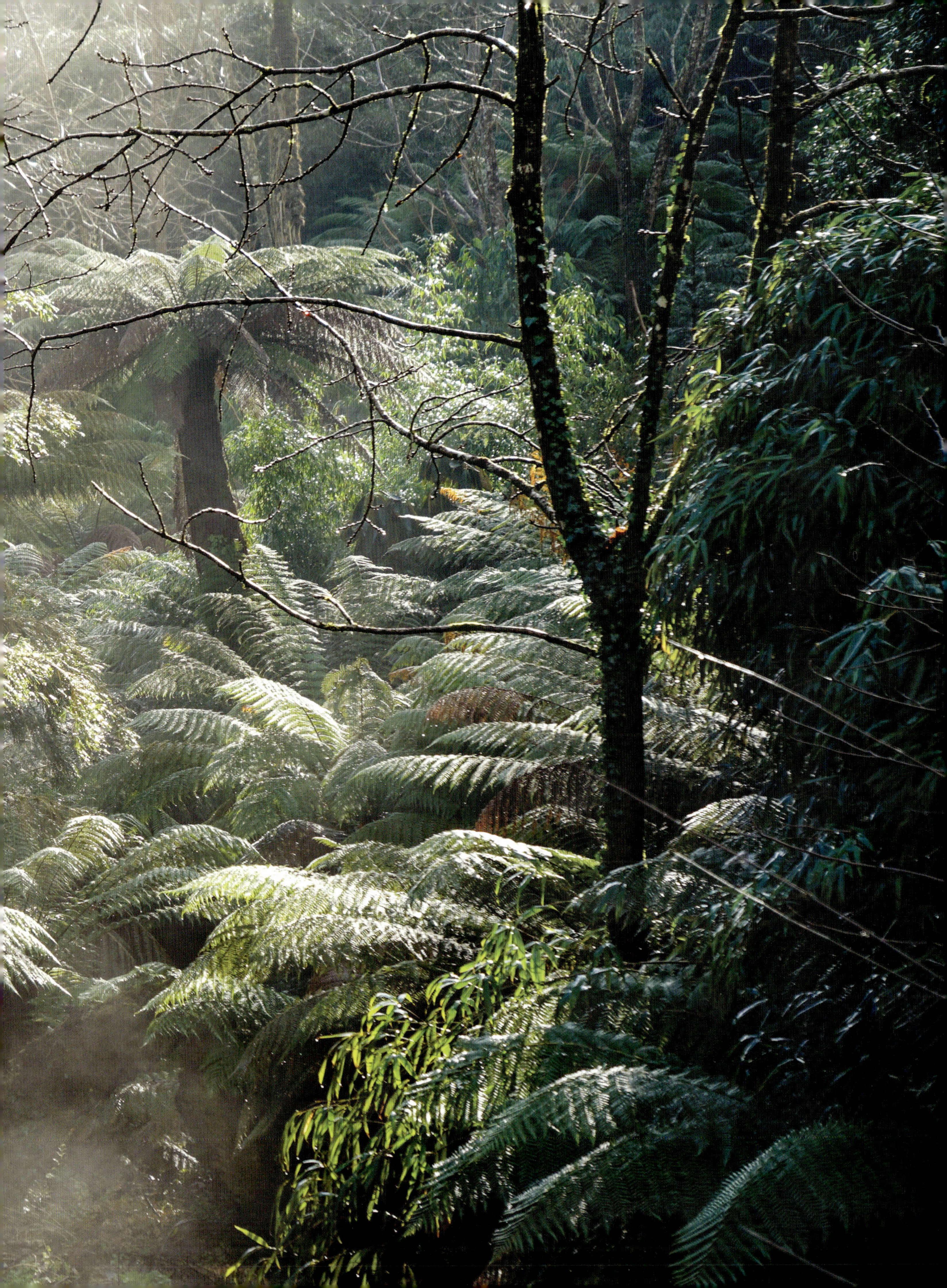

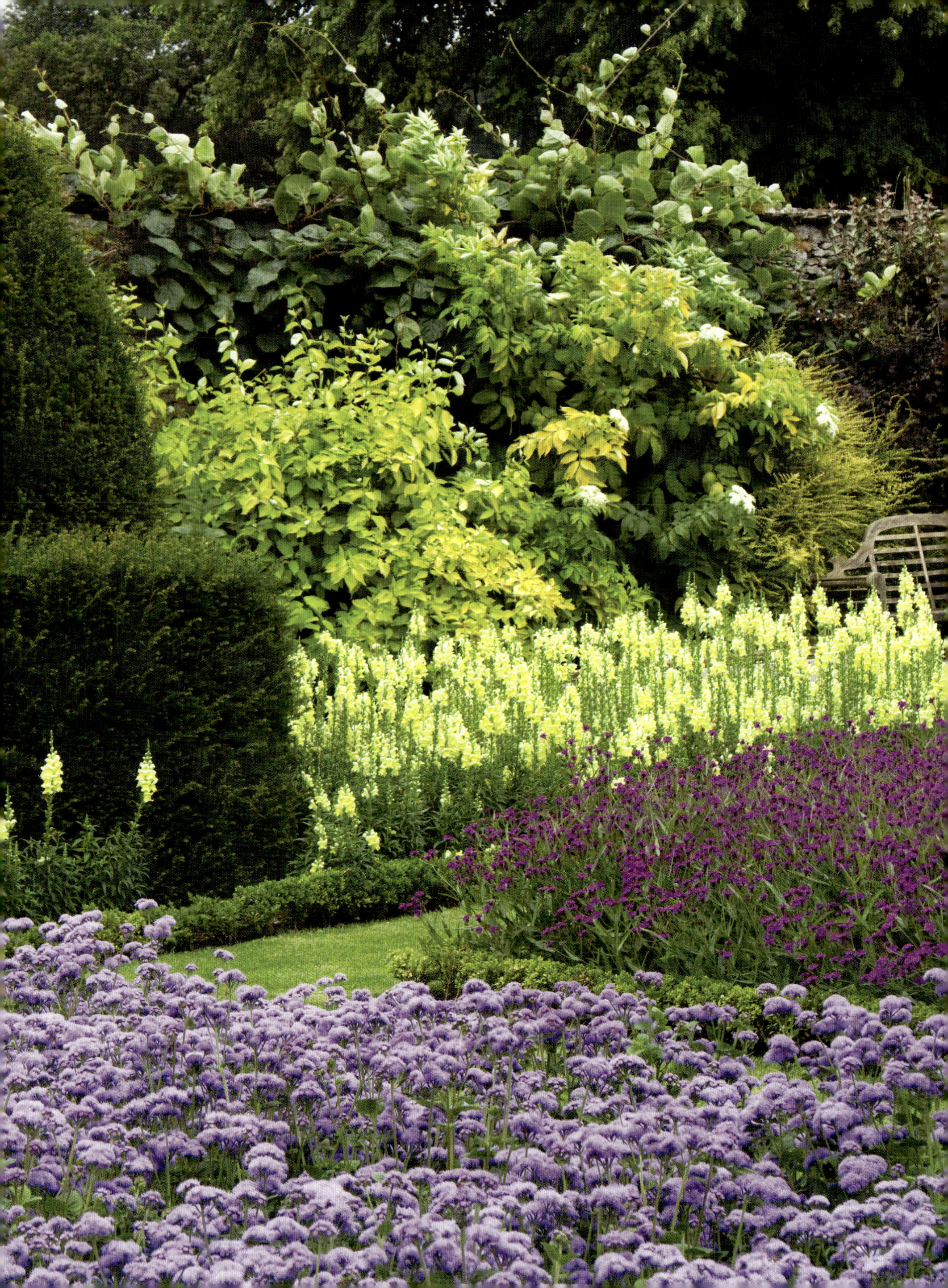

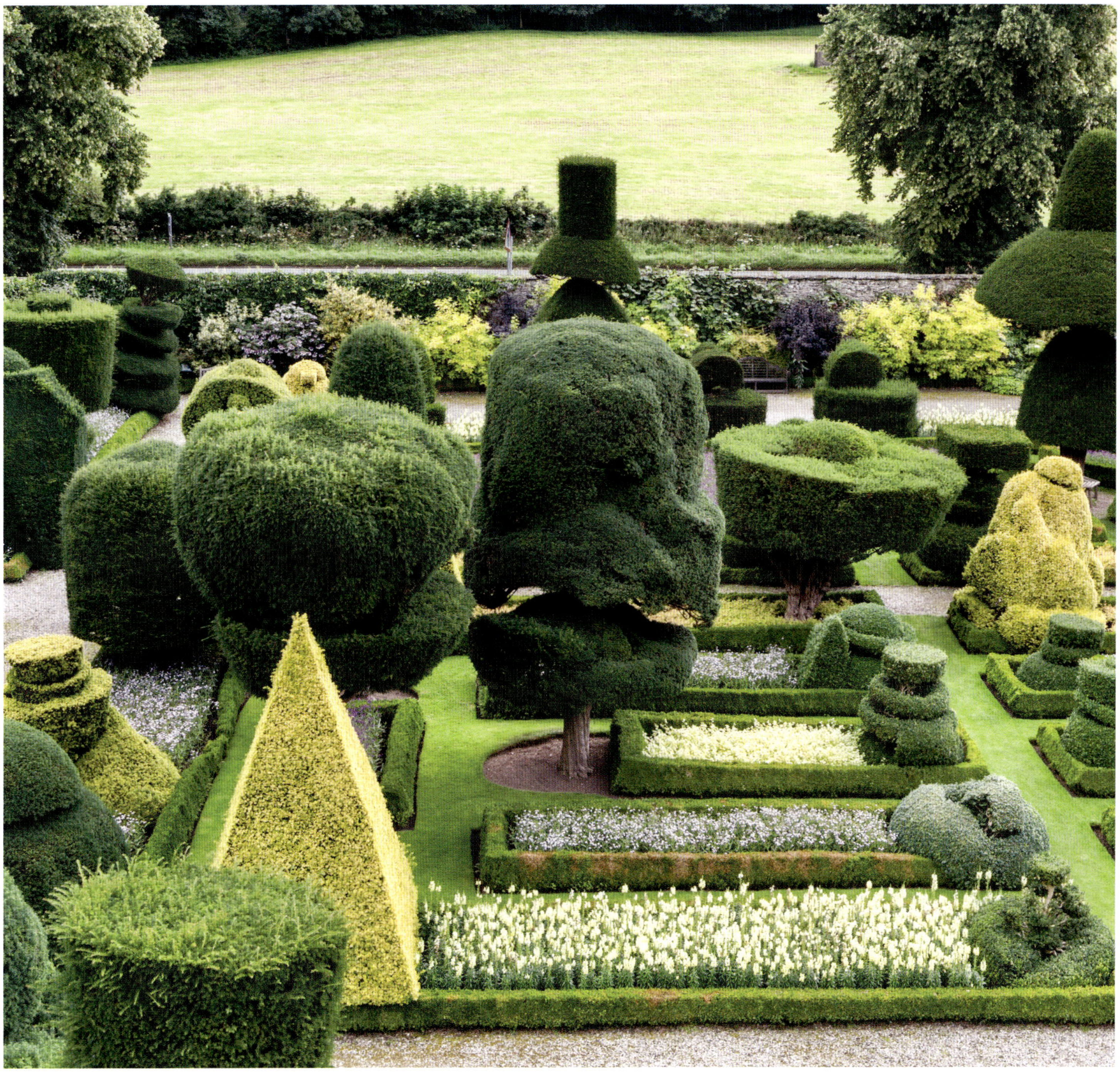

ALL PHOTOGRAPHS:

Levens Hall, North Yorkshire, England

Quirky topiary forms, both abstract and geometric, are a hallmark of this garden dating from the 1690s. The clipped yew and box shapes constitute what is believed to be the world's oldest topiary garden. Herbaceous borders, lawns, roses and a productive garden complete the scene.

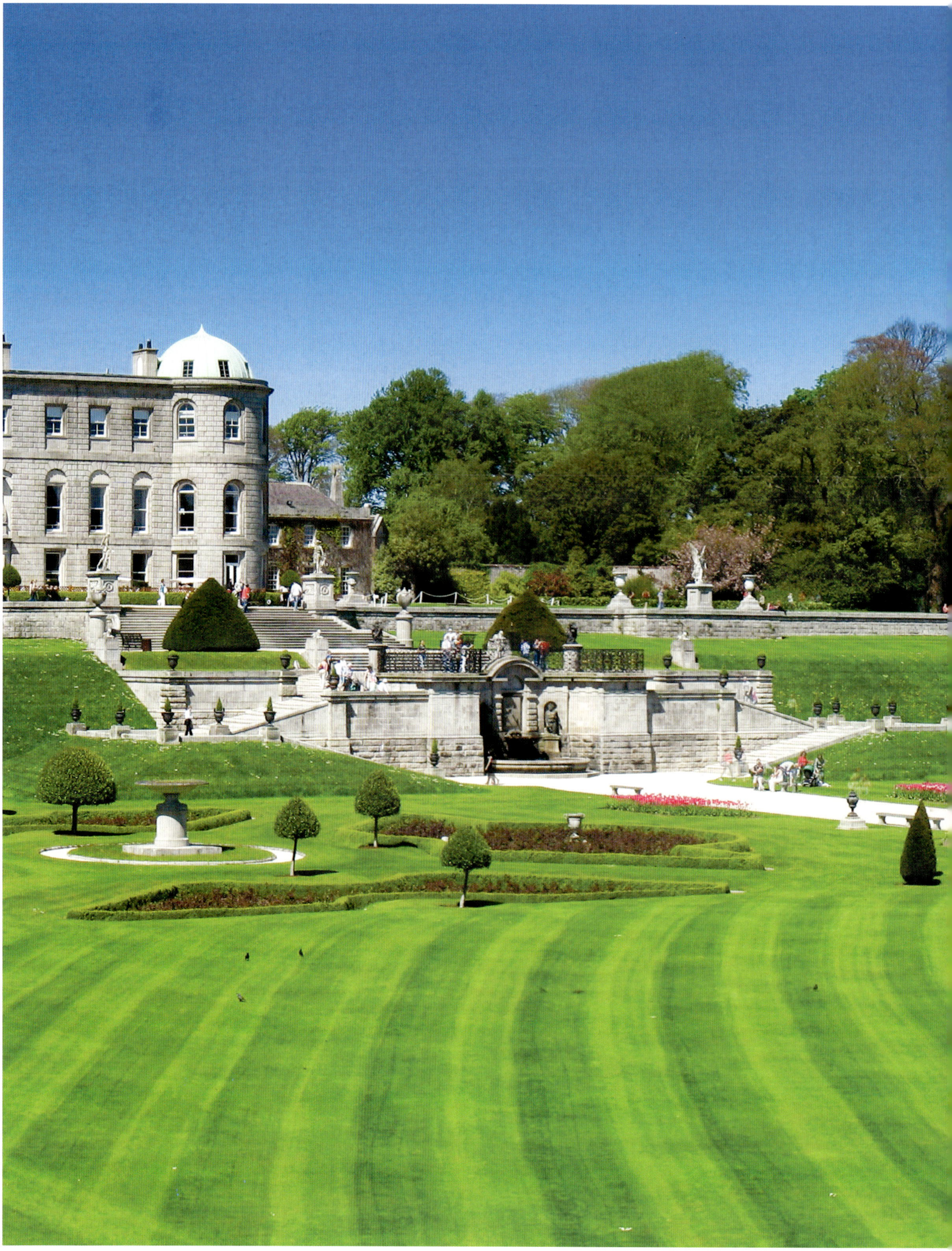

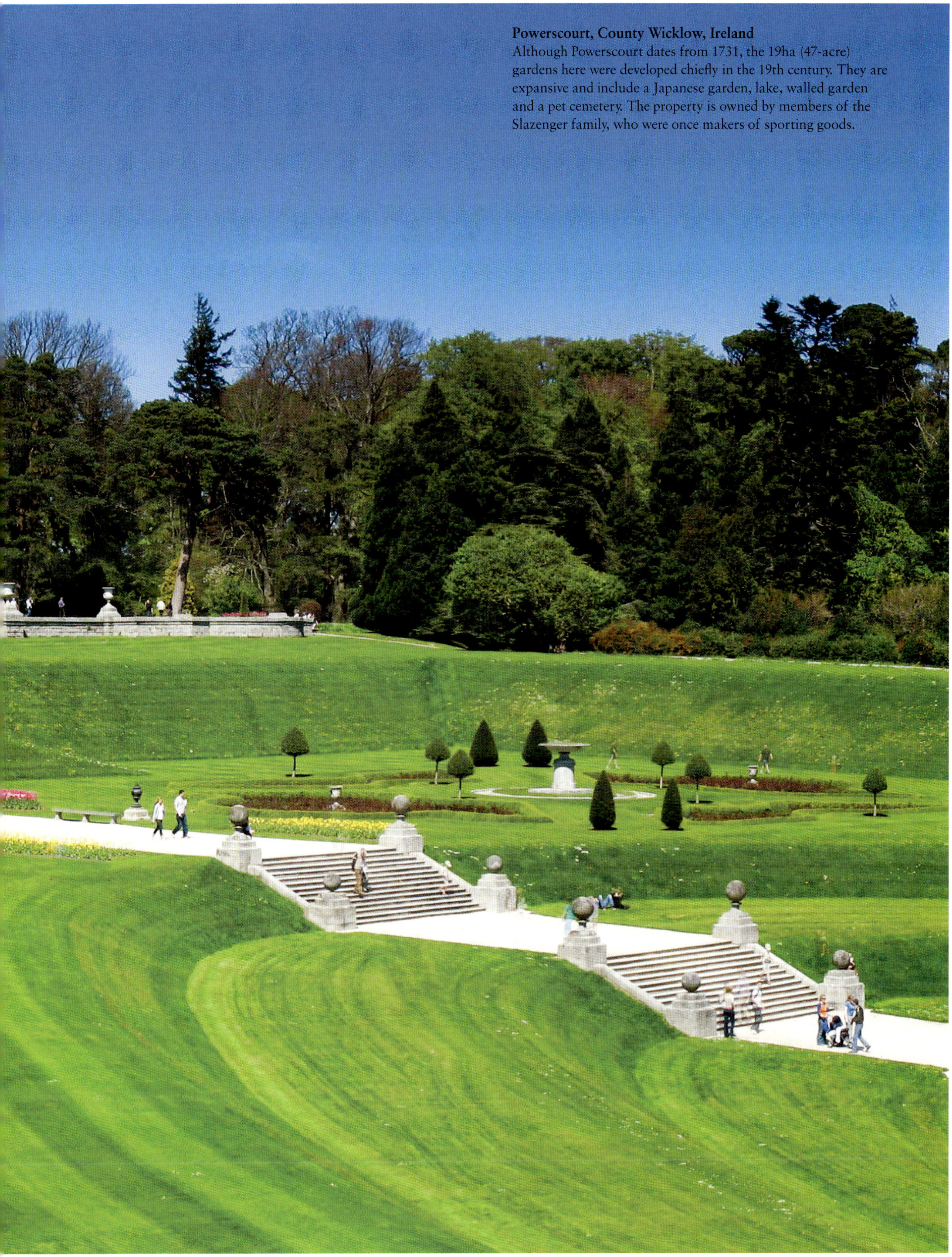

Powerscourt, County Wicklow, Ireland
Although Powerscourt dates from 1731, the 19ha (47-acre) gardens here were developed chiefly in the 19th century. They are expansive and include a Japanese garden, lake, walled garden and a pet cemetery. The property is owned by members of the Slazenger family, who were once makers of sporting goods.

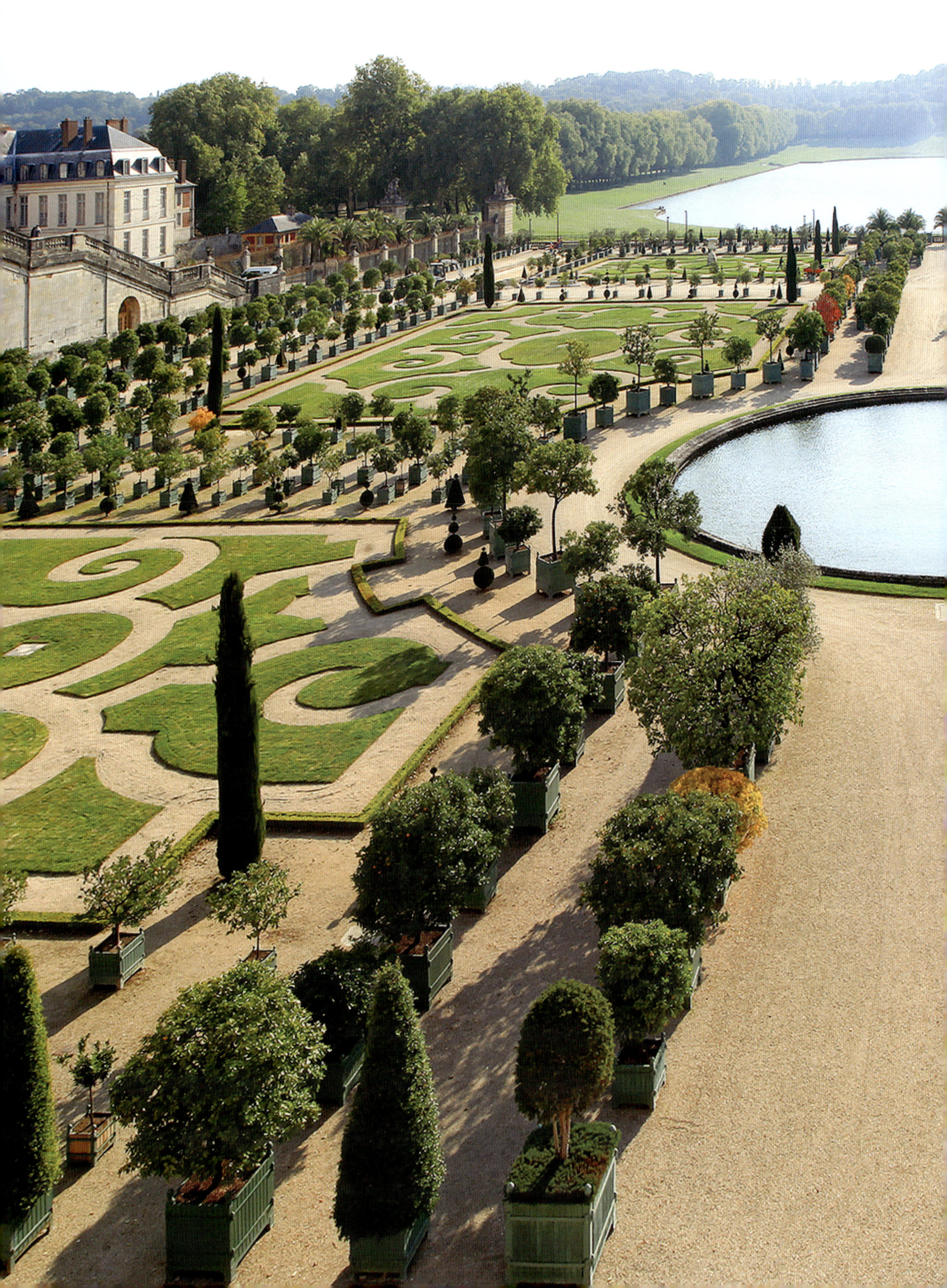

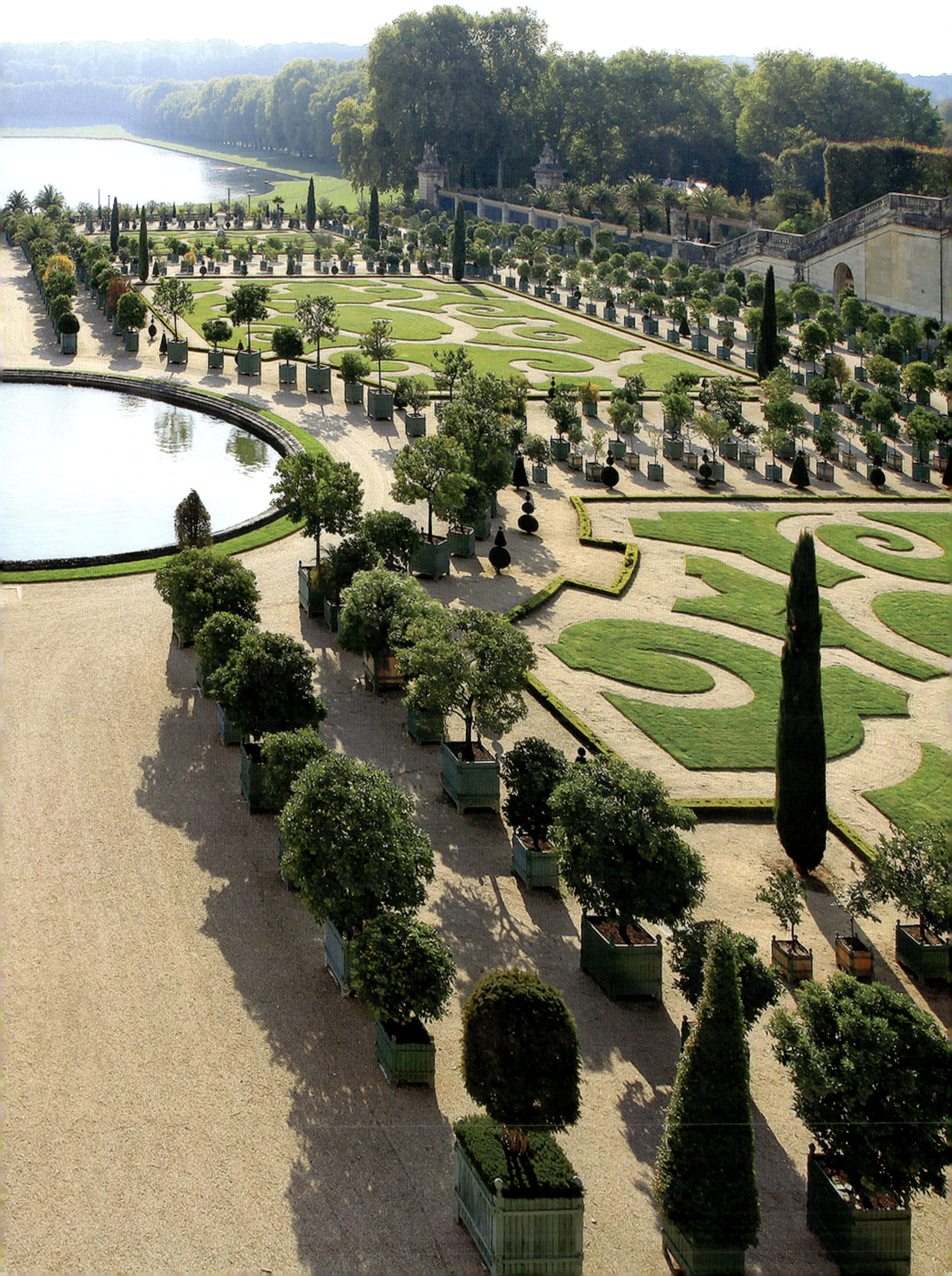

PREVIOUS PAGES & RIGHT:
Palace de Versailles, Île-de-France, France
Louis XIV placed as much emphasis on the gardens at the Palace of Versailles as he did the building. In 1661, he instructed André Le Nôtre to create, over four decades, what would become one of the world's most admired gardens. The intensely formal designs include parterres, clipped hedging, fountains and canals. Aspects of this UNESCO World Heritage Site were replanted in the early part of this century.

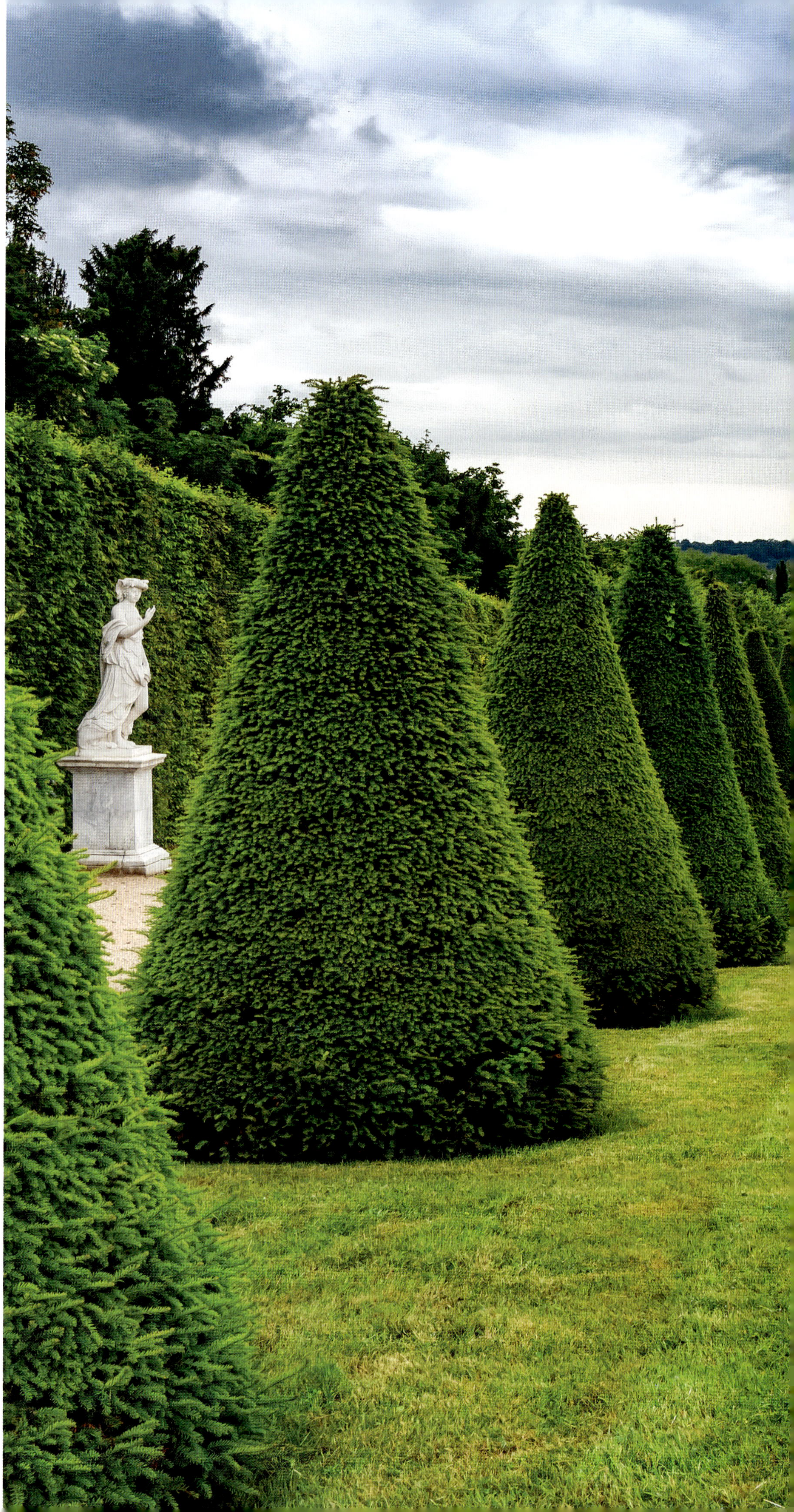

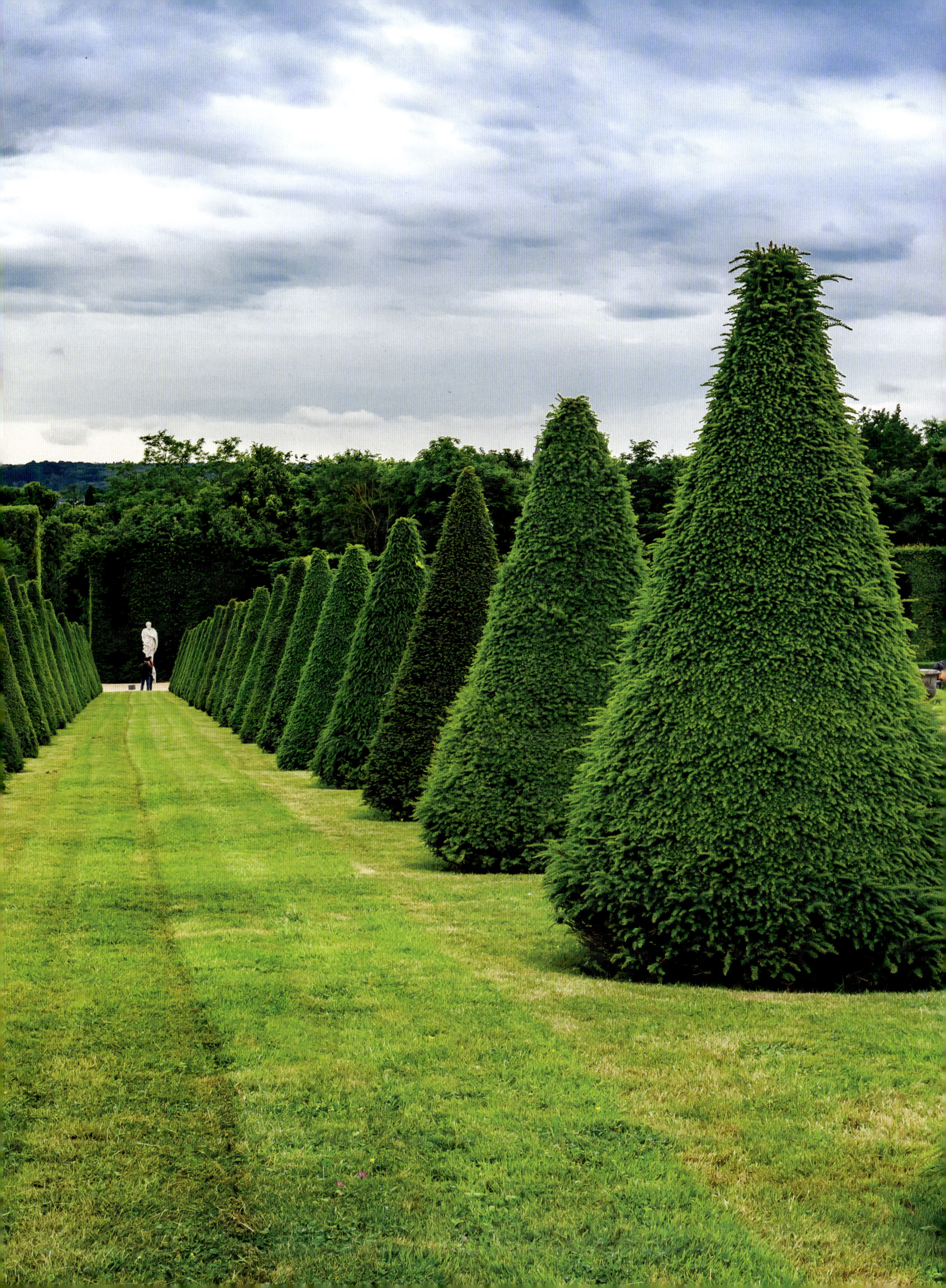

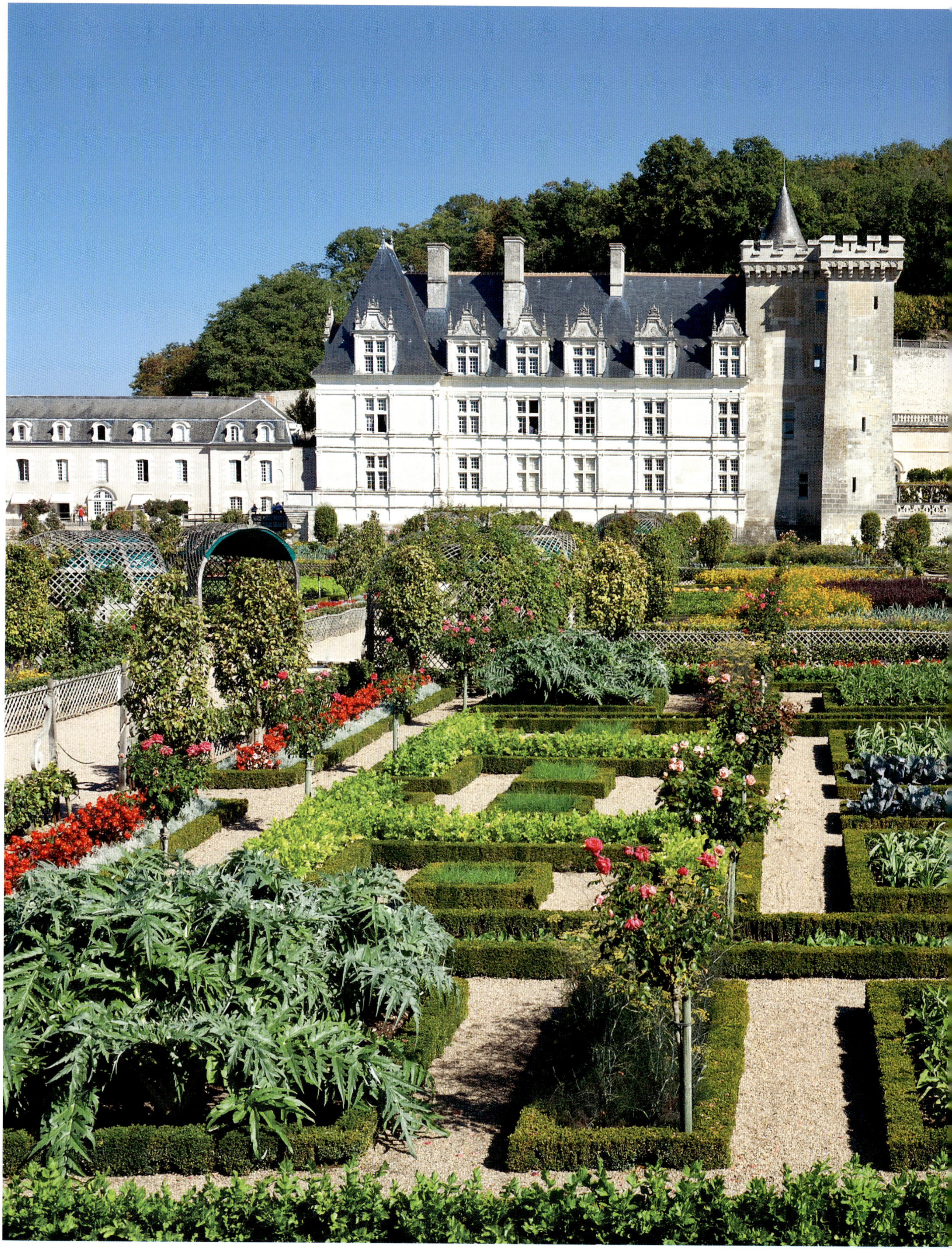

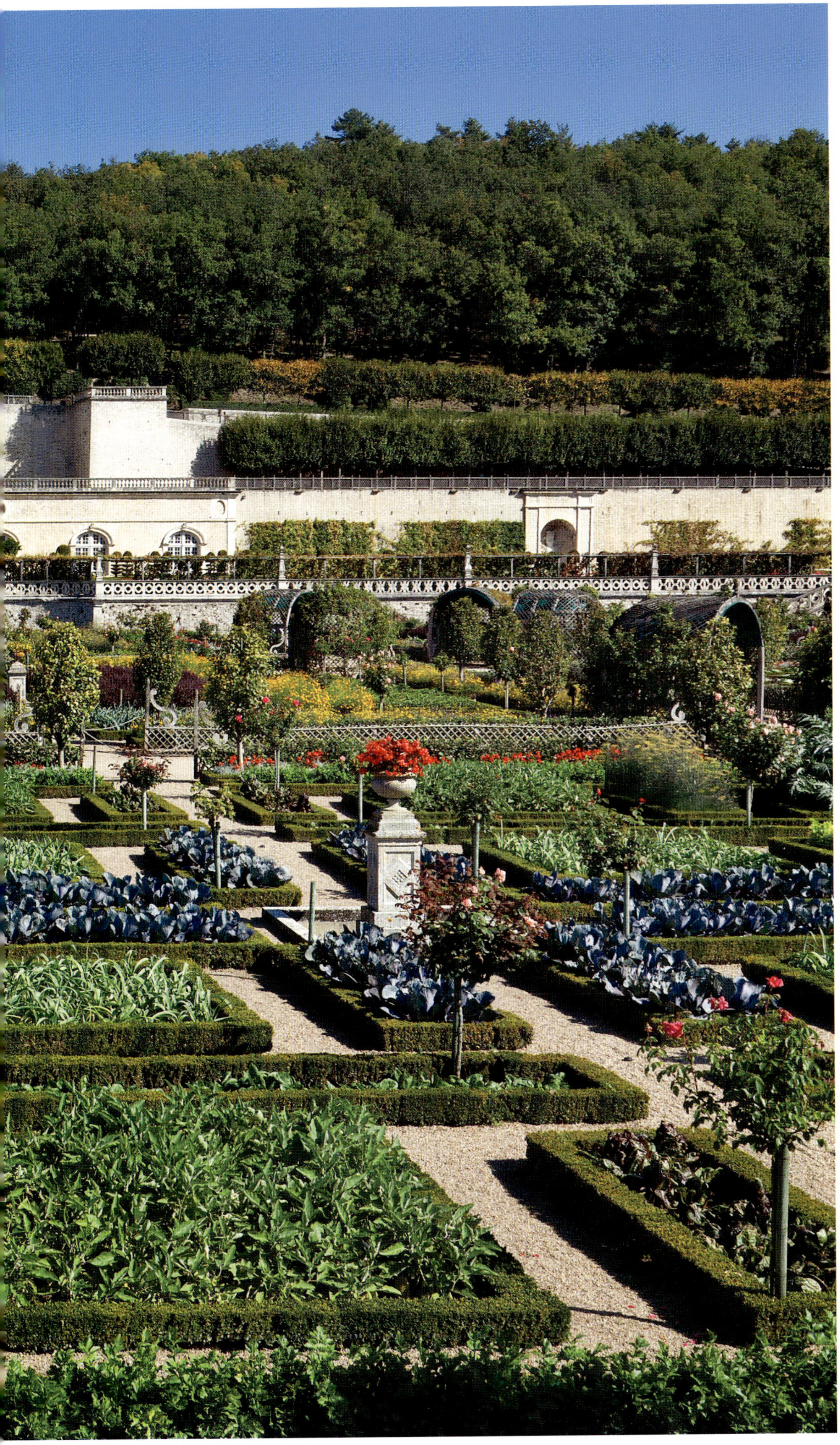

Château de Villandry, Indre-et-Loire, France
In the gardens of the Renaissance-era Château de Villandry, organic productive spaces are among the most exceptional. In autumn, decorative cabbages jostle with leeks, late tomatoes, kale and squash. These particular spaces are the vision of Joachim Carvallo and his American wife Anne Coleman, great-grandparents of the current owner, Henri Carvallo.

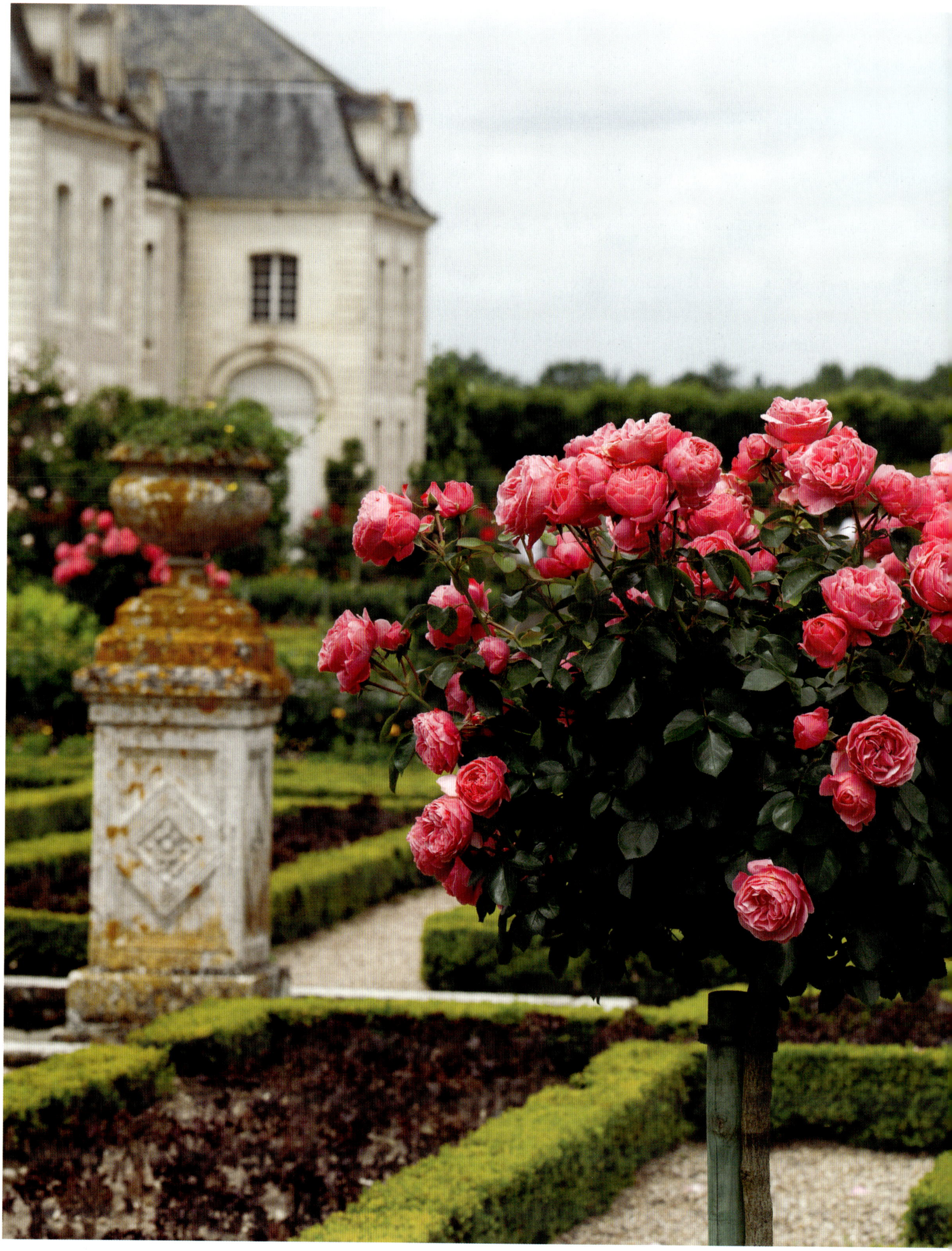

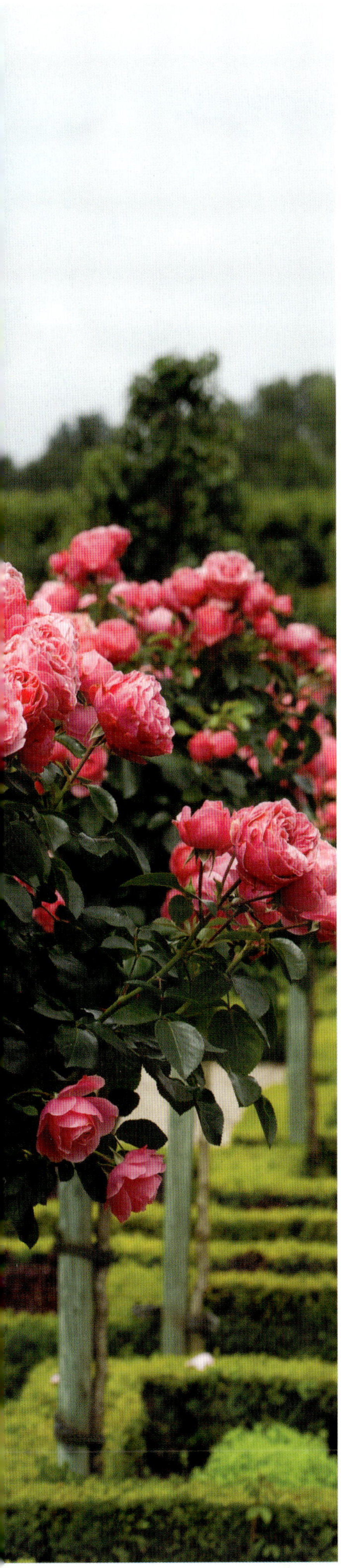

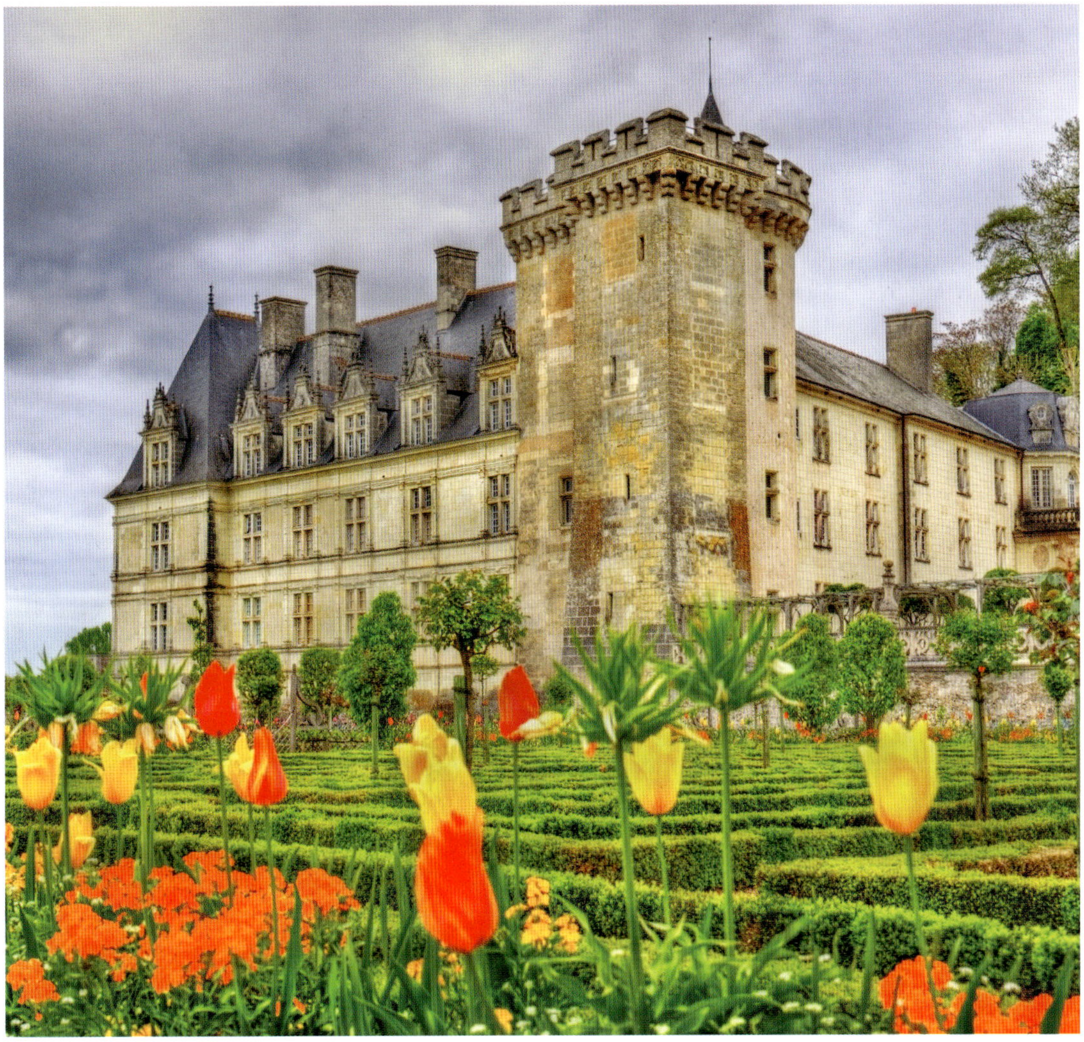

ALL PHOTOGRAPHS:

Château de Villandry, Indre-et-Loire, France

The gardens here date to the construction of the château in 1532, with archaeologists revealing the presence of a decorative kitchen garden near the house. Around the 18th century, the grounds were designed in the style of an English park, in the style promulgated by 'Capability' Brown, Humphry Repton and William Kent, particularly. In the early 1900s, having restored the château to its Renaissance splendour, Carallo ordered the Renaissance arrangements we see today.

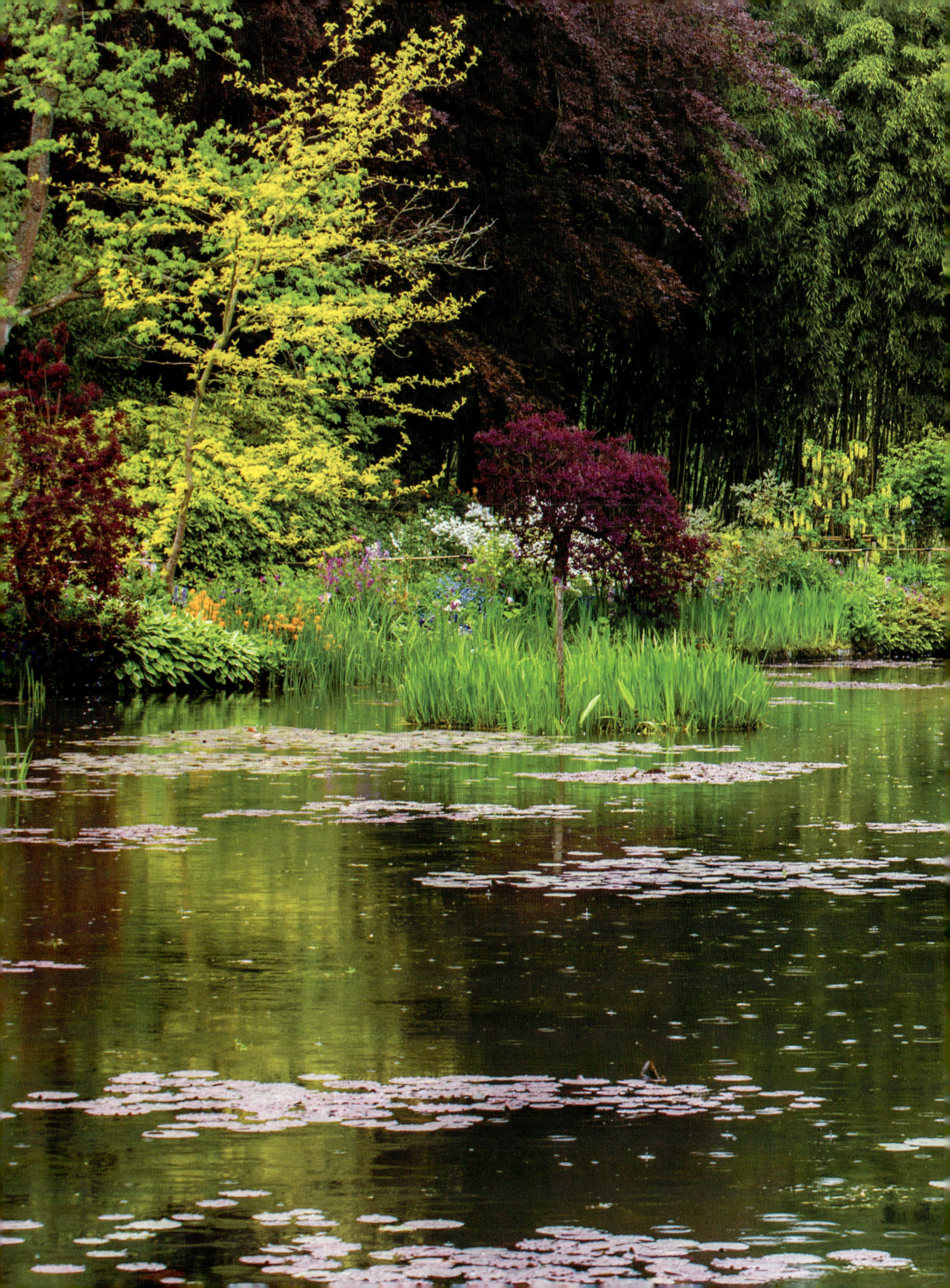

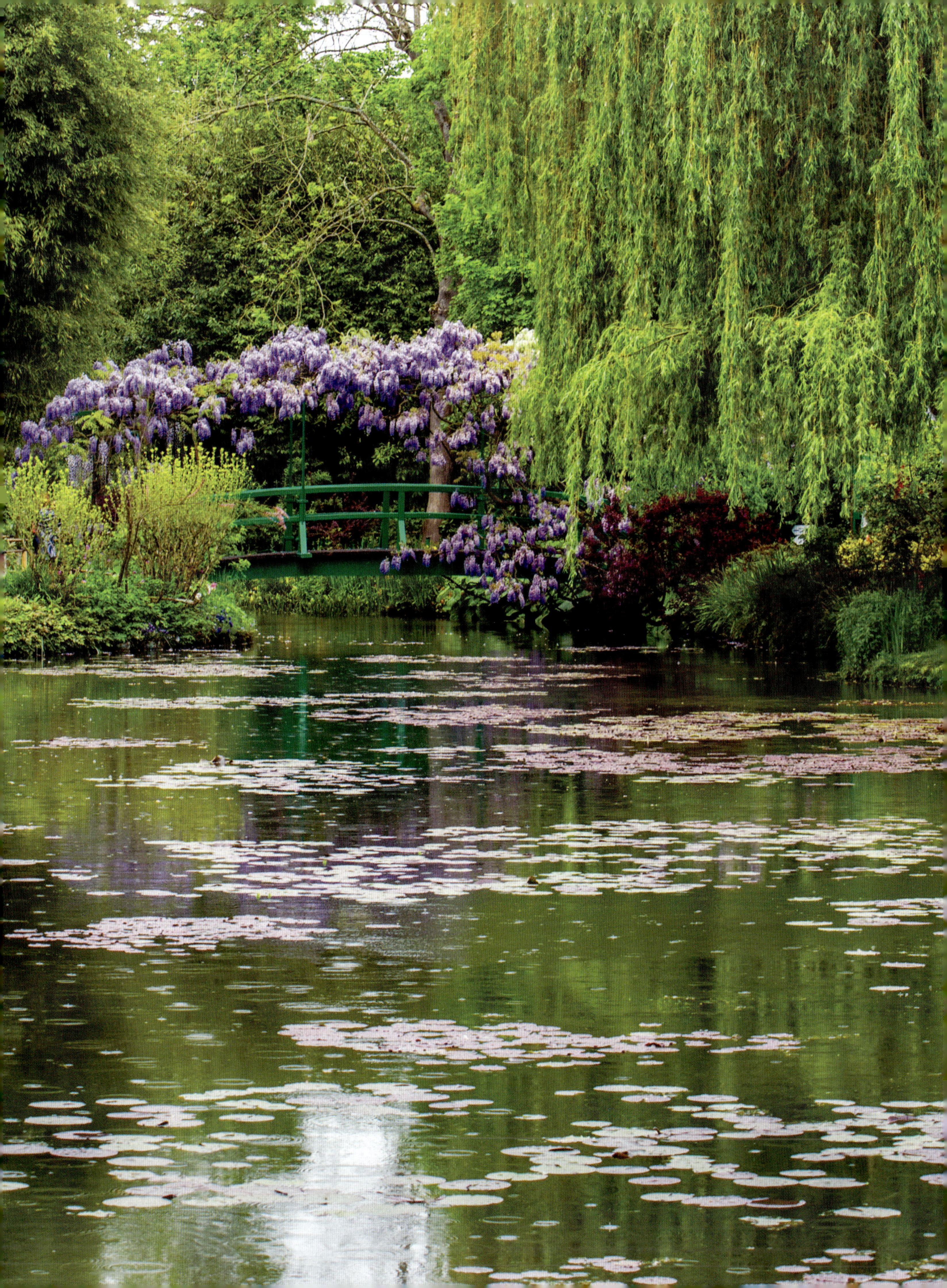

PREVIOUS PAGES AND RIGHT:
Monet's Garden at Giverny, Eure, France
This most famous painter's garden, begun in the 1880s, is a garden of two parts. Its Japanese water garden, some distance from the house, was inspired by prints the painter collected and it was later immortalised in his paintings. The second garden, close to the house, focuses on symmetry and perspective achieved through flower beds, fruit trees and climbing roses.

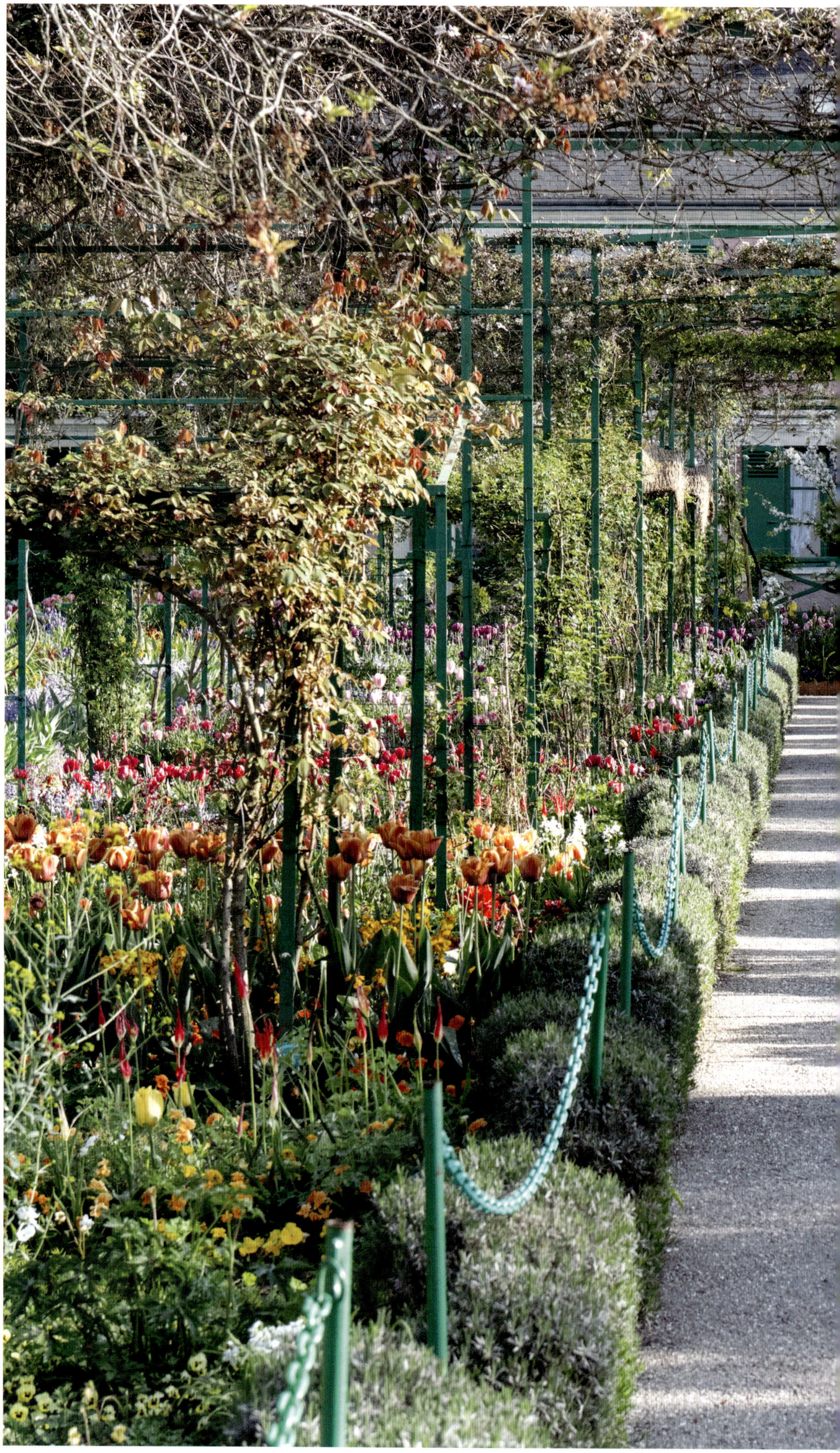

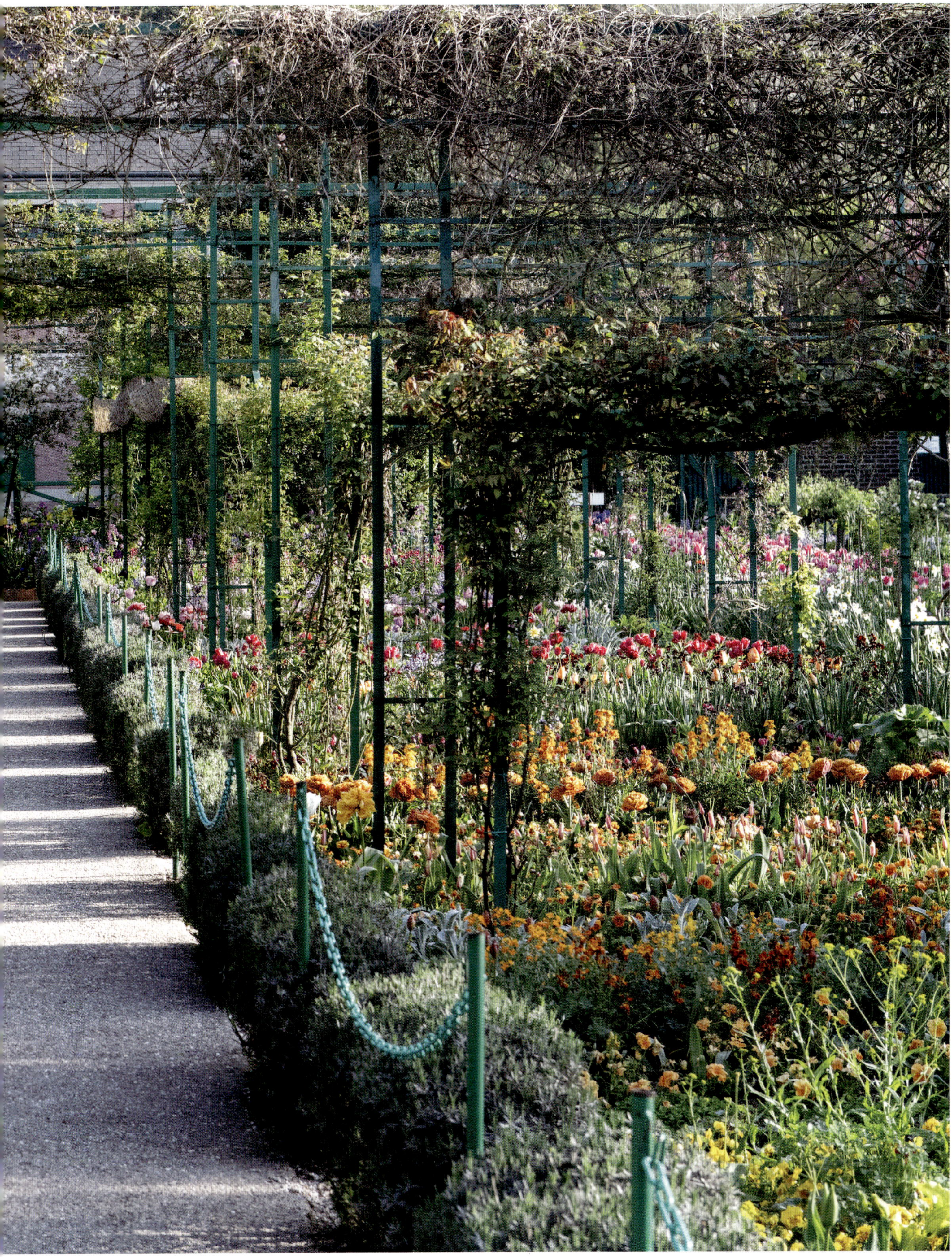

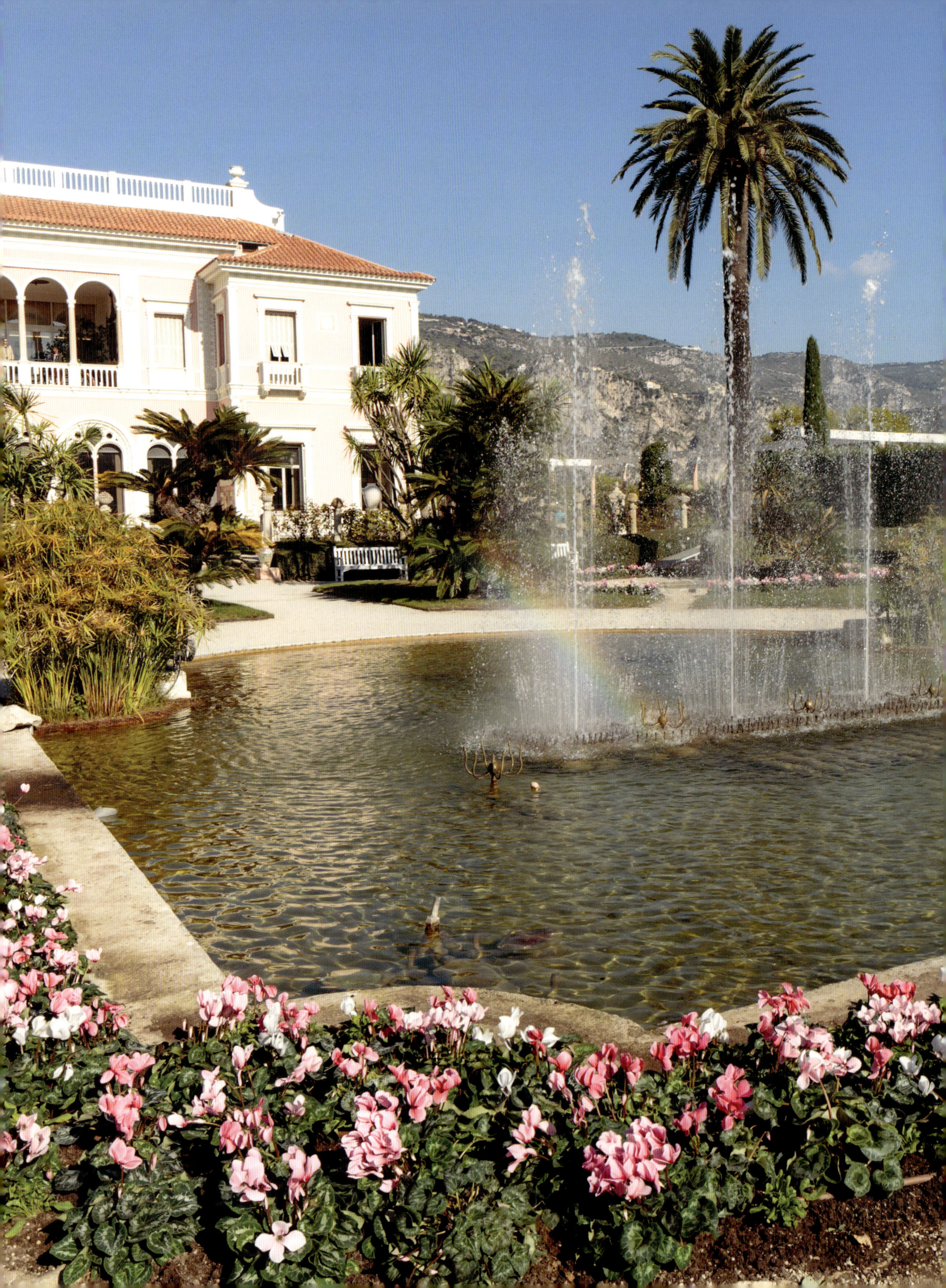

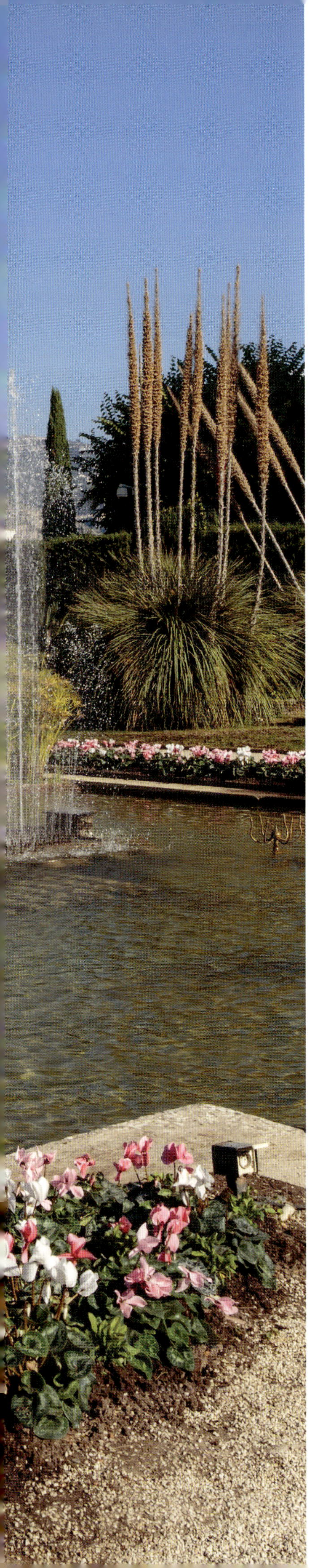

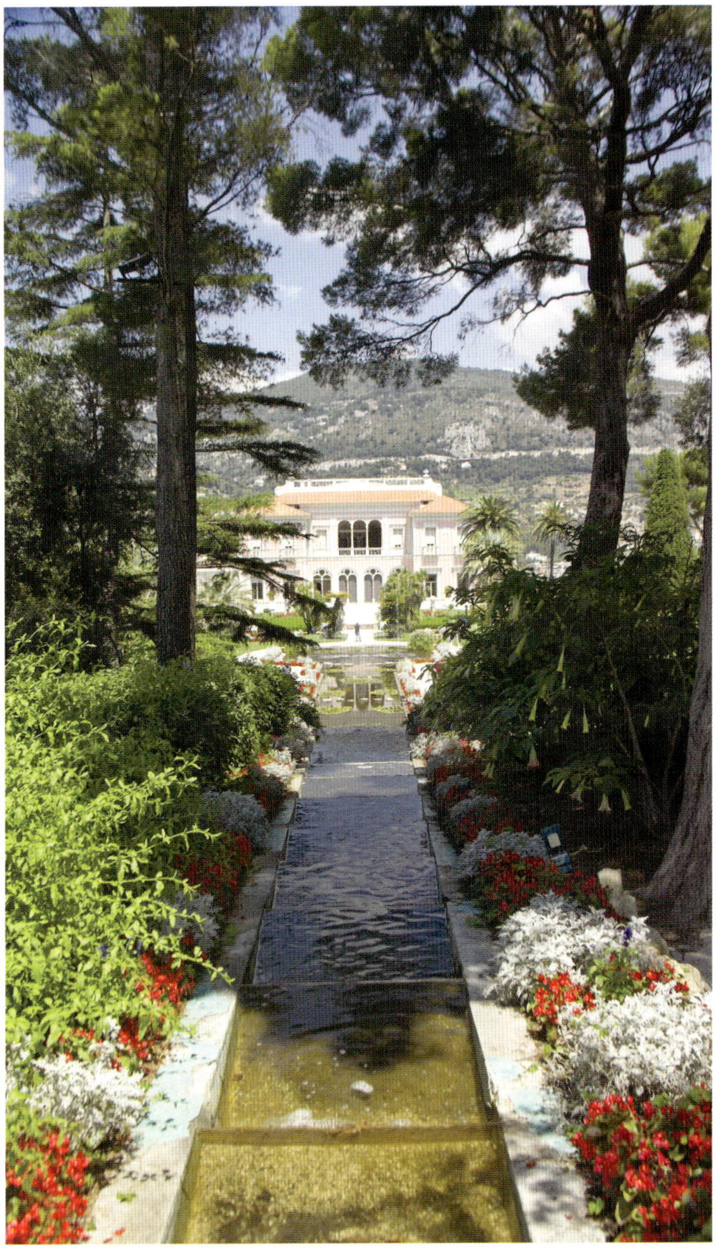

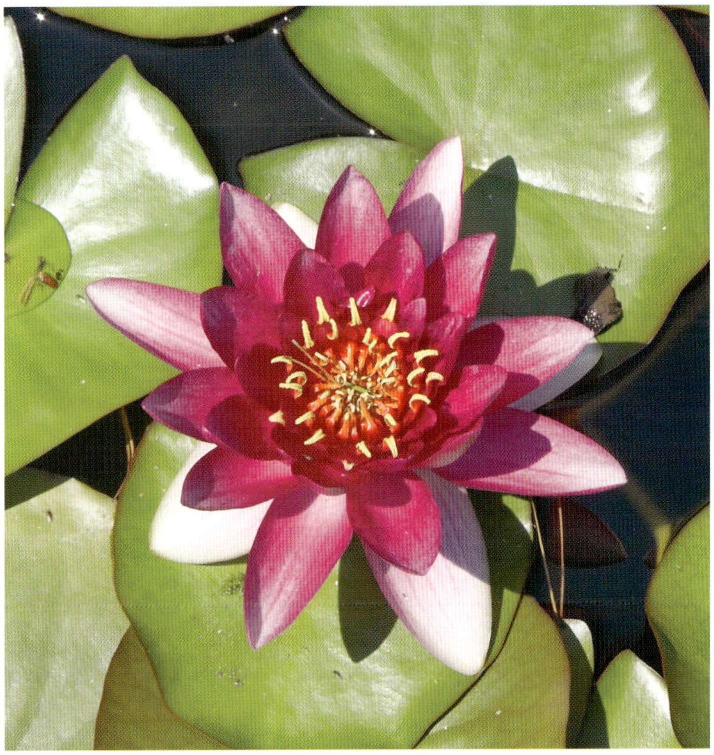

ALL PHOTOGRAPHS:

Villa Ephrussi de Rothschild, Alpes-Maritimes, France

Between glamorous Nice and Monaco, on the promontory of Saint-Jean-Cap-Ferrat, Villa Ephrussi de Rothschild is the vision of Baroness Beatrice de Rothschild (1864–1934), who imagined the main garden in the shape of a ship's deck. Built from 1907–12, the organic garden comprises eight themed rooms, including French, Spanish, Japanese, Provençal and Florentine. The captivating garden has been classified as one of the Remarkable Gardens of France.

ALL PHOTOGRAPHS:

Jardin Exotique, Monaco

In 1933, the Exotic Garden of Monaco was built into a cliffside overlooking the Mediterranean. A botanical garden, its striking setting is the ideal location for collections of succulents and cacti gathered from around the world. These collections were started as early as 1865.

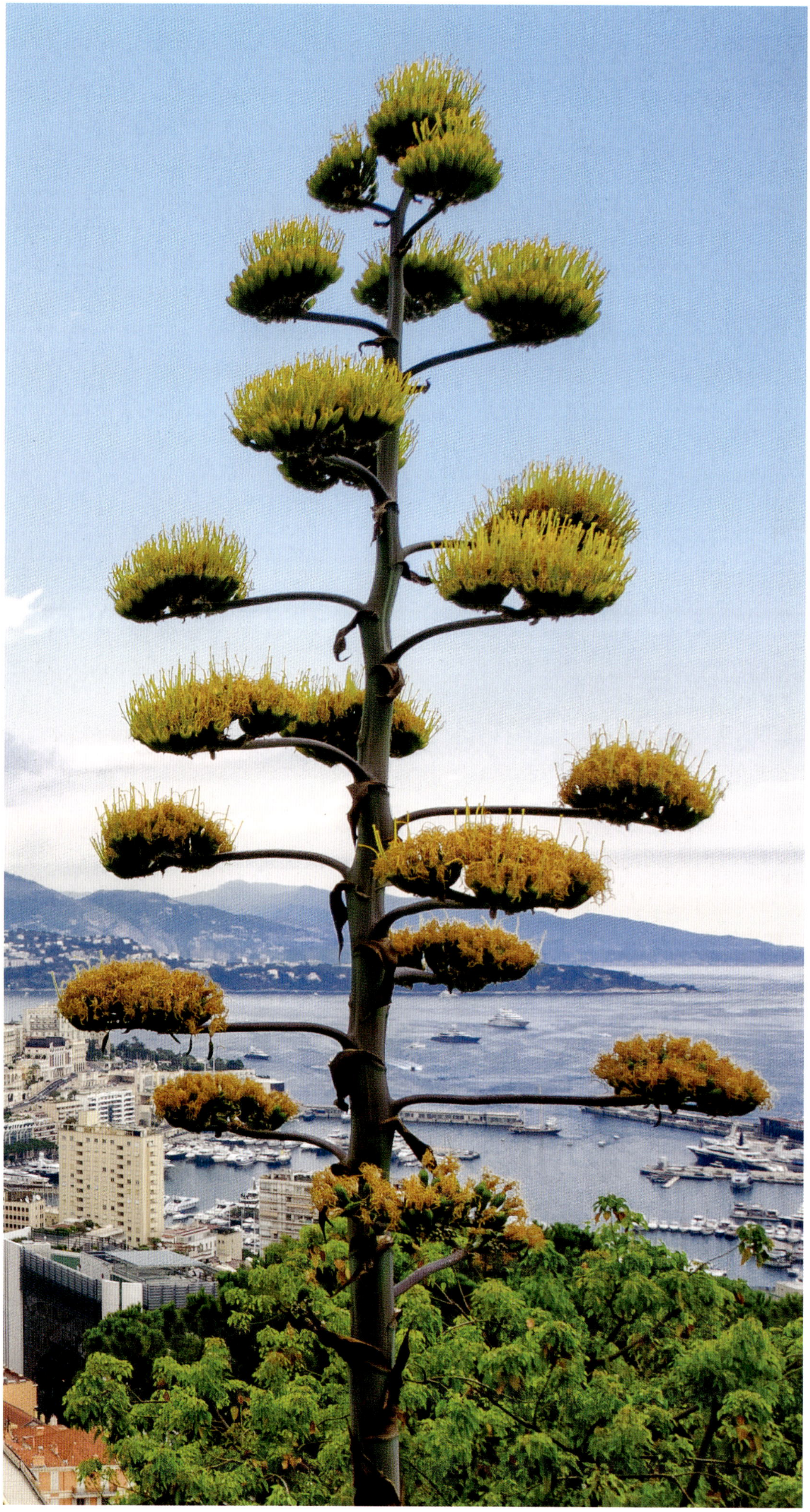

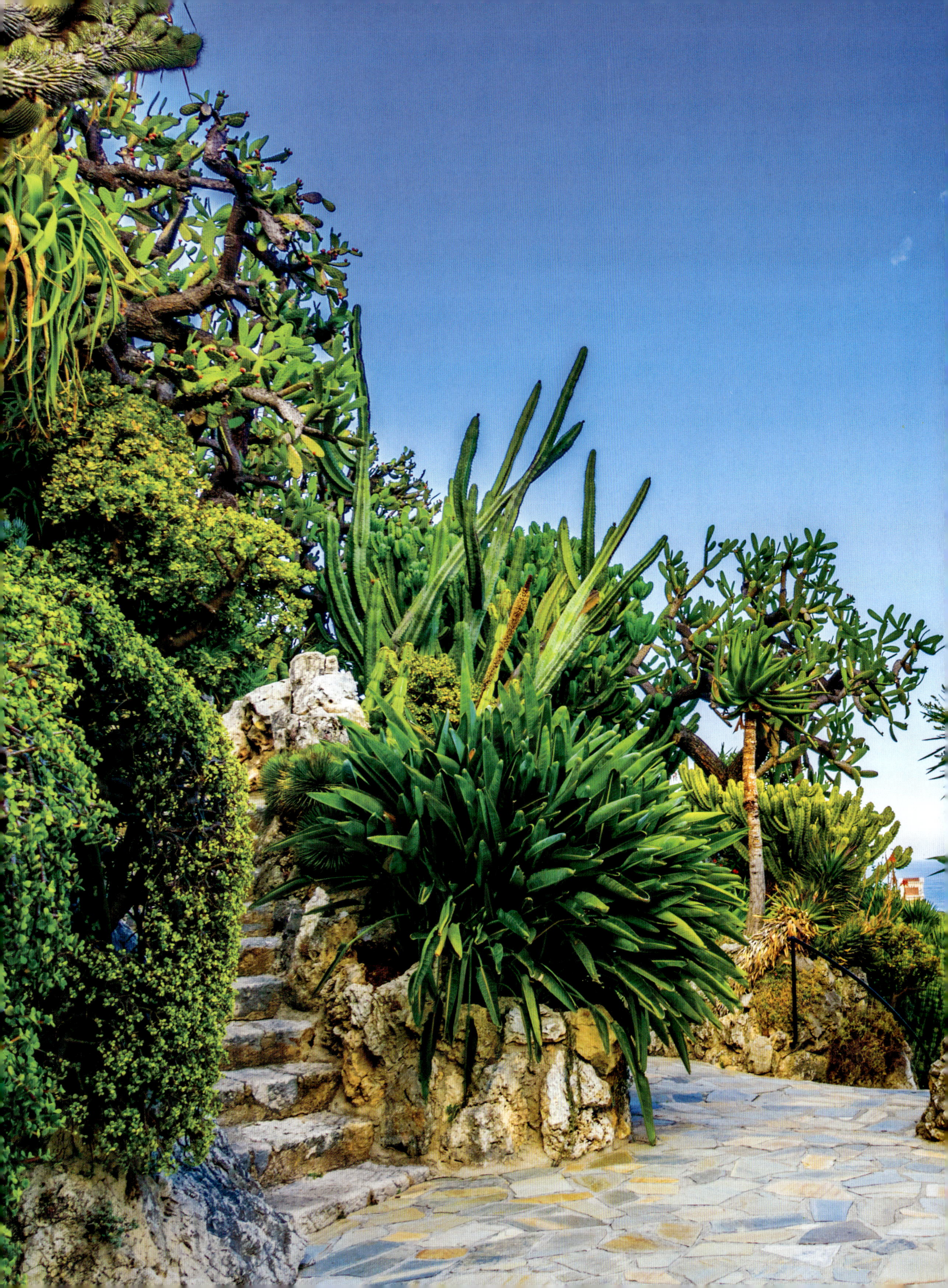

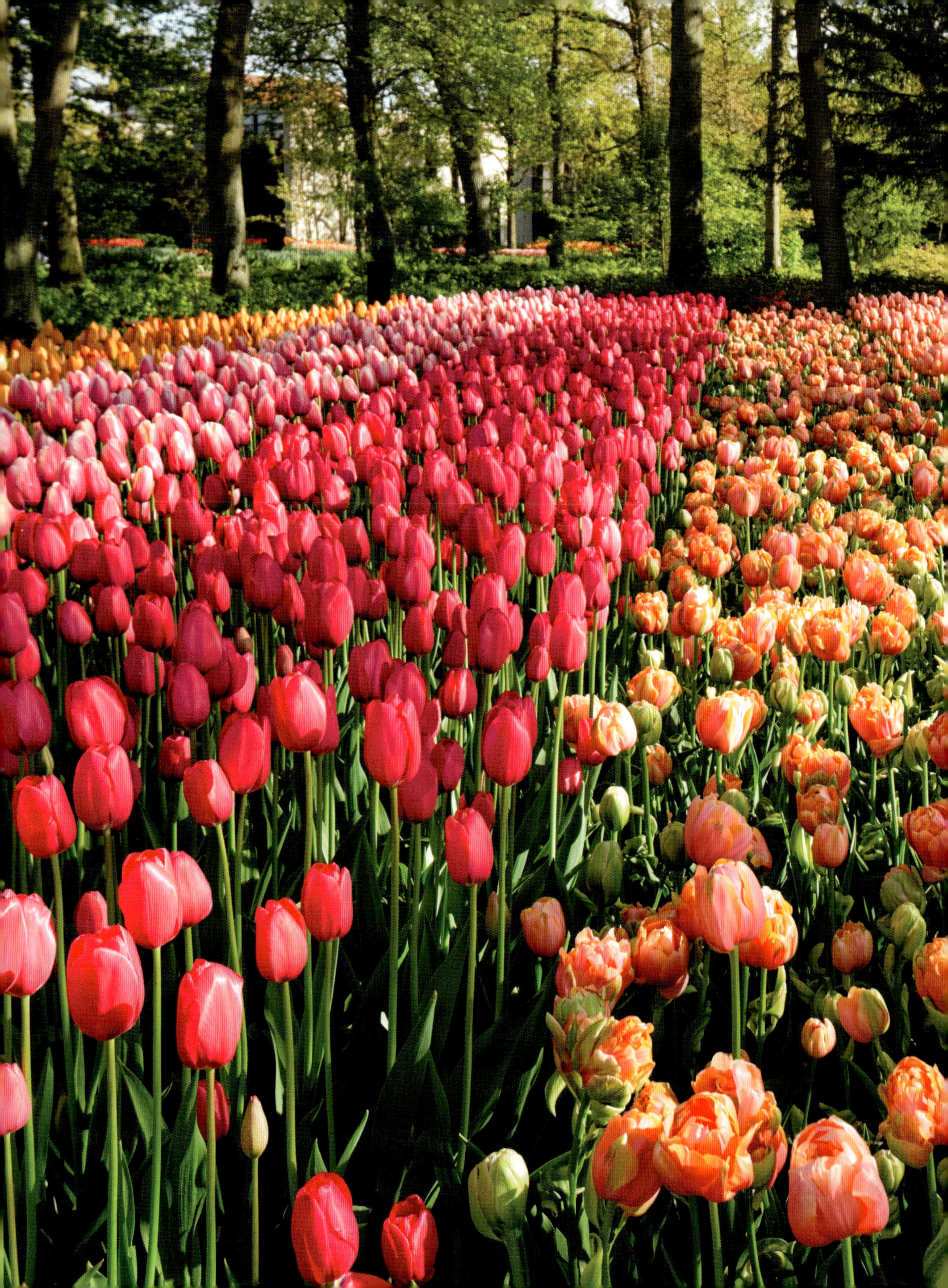

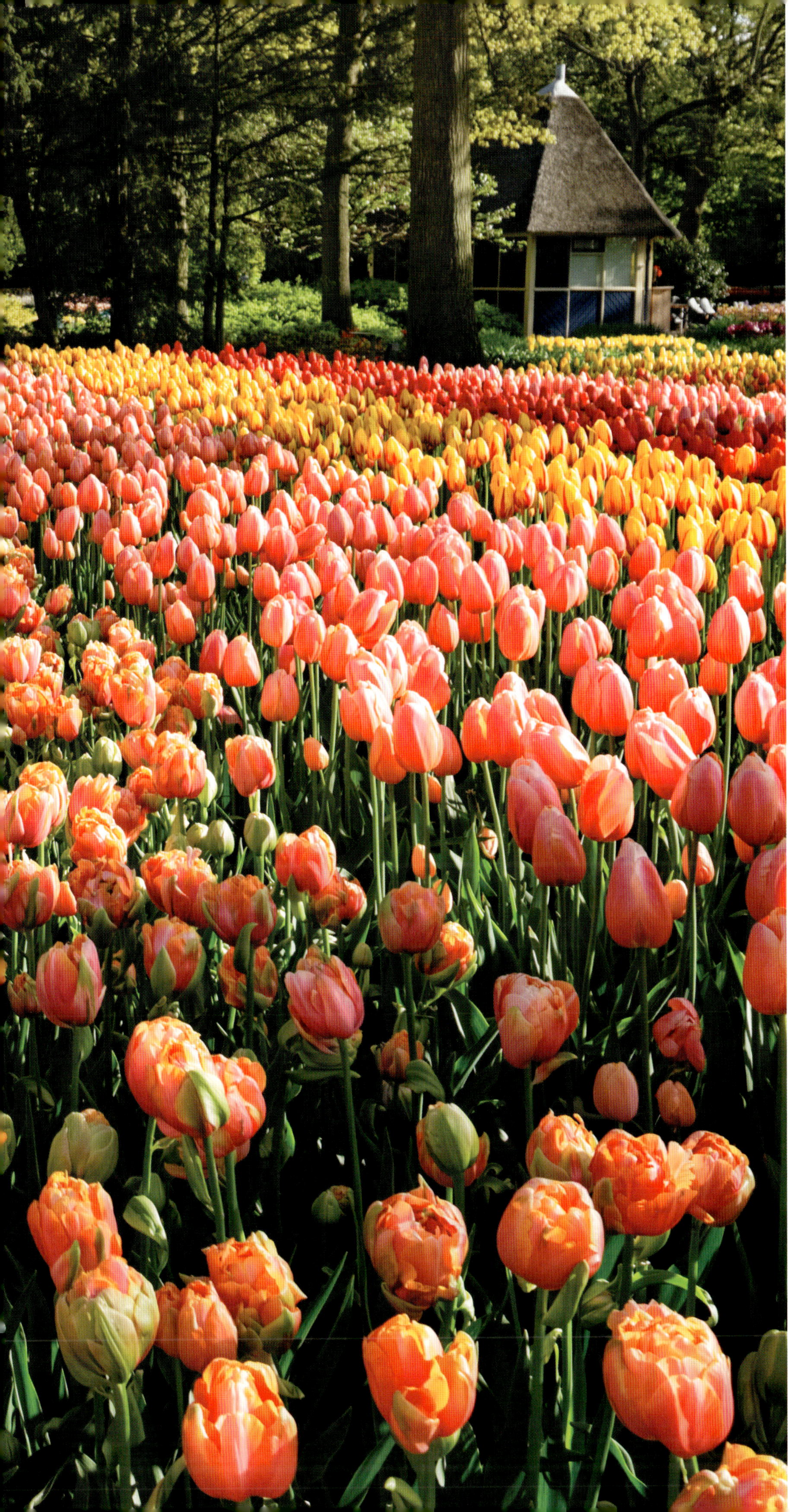

Keukenhof, Lisse, Netherlands
Without doubt, Keukenhof offers the most admired display of spring bulbs in the world. Each year, from March to May, around seven million bulbs come into flower in the 200ha (494-acre) park, in what is now one of Europe's key tourist attractions. Although the garden dates to the 15th century and Countess Jacoba van Beieren, the displays we see today began as recently as 1949, when a group of 20 bulb specialists thought to put on a spring display.

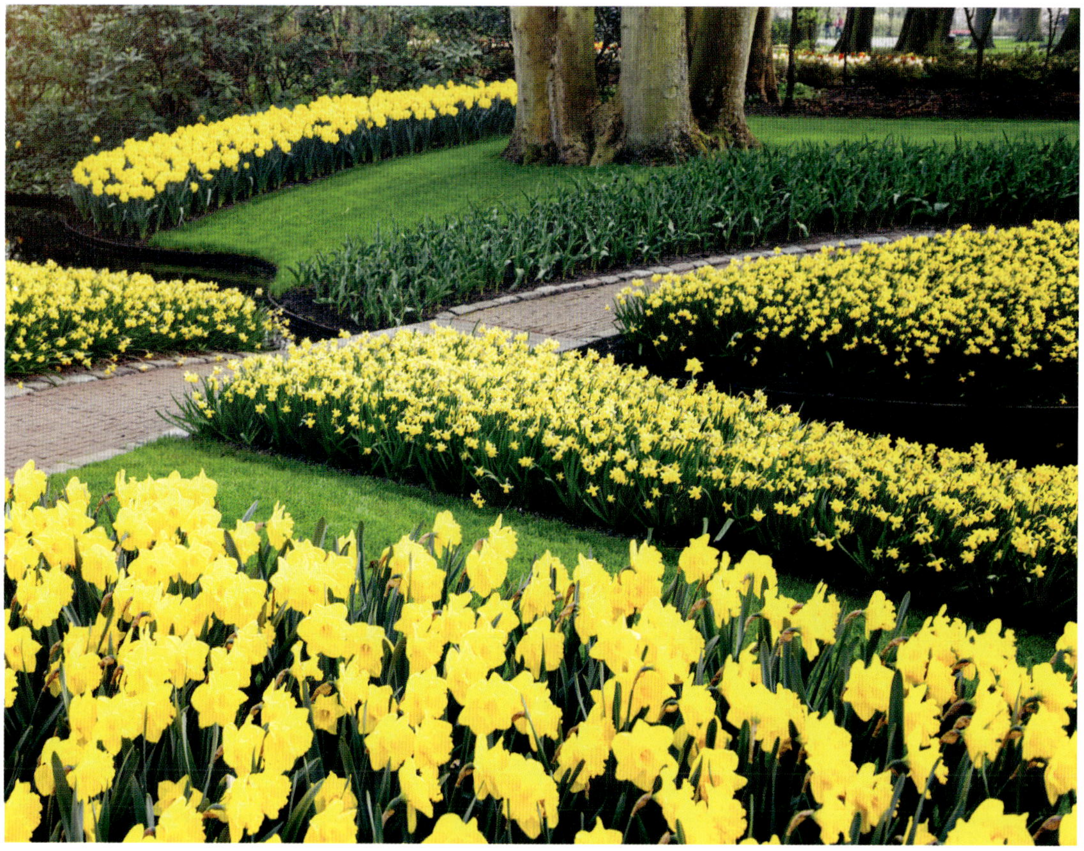

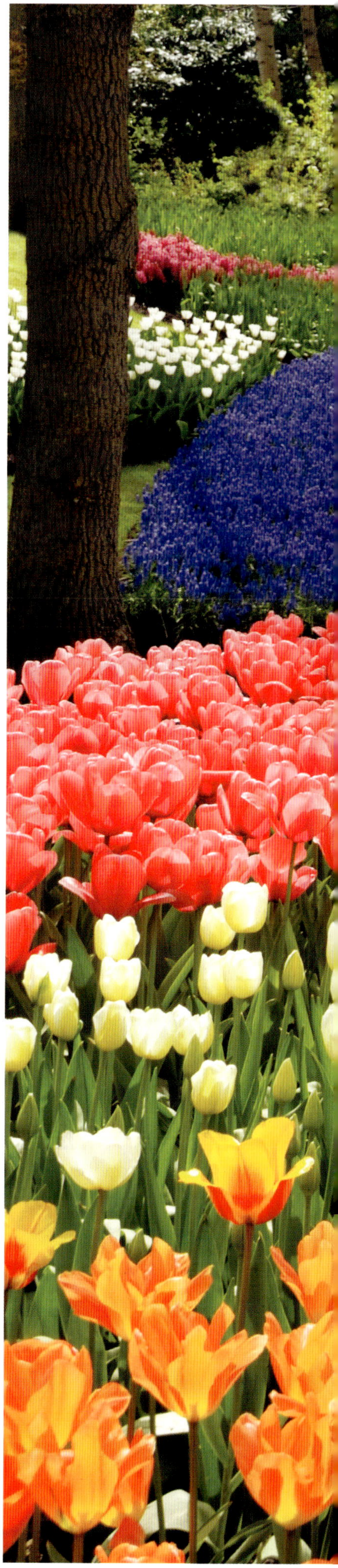

ALL PHOTOGRAPHS:
Keukenhof, Lisse, Netherlands
Now described as a living catalogue of the work of 100 bulb breeders, Keukenhof reflects the bulb and cut-flower growing heritage of this country, which reached its infamous peak in the tulipmania of the 17th century. Around 500 growers of cut-flowers also take part in nearly two dozen flower shows here.

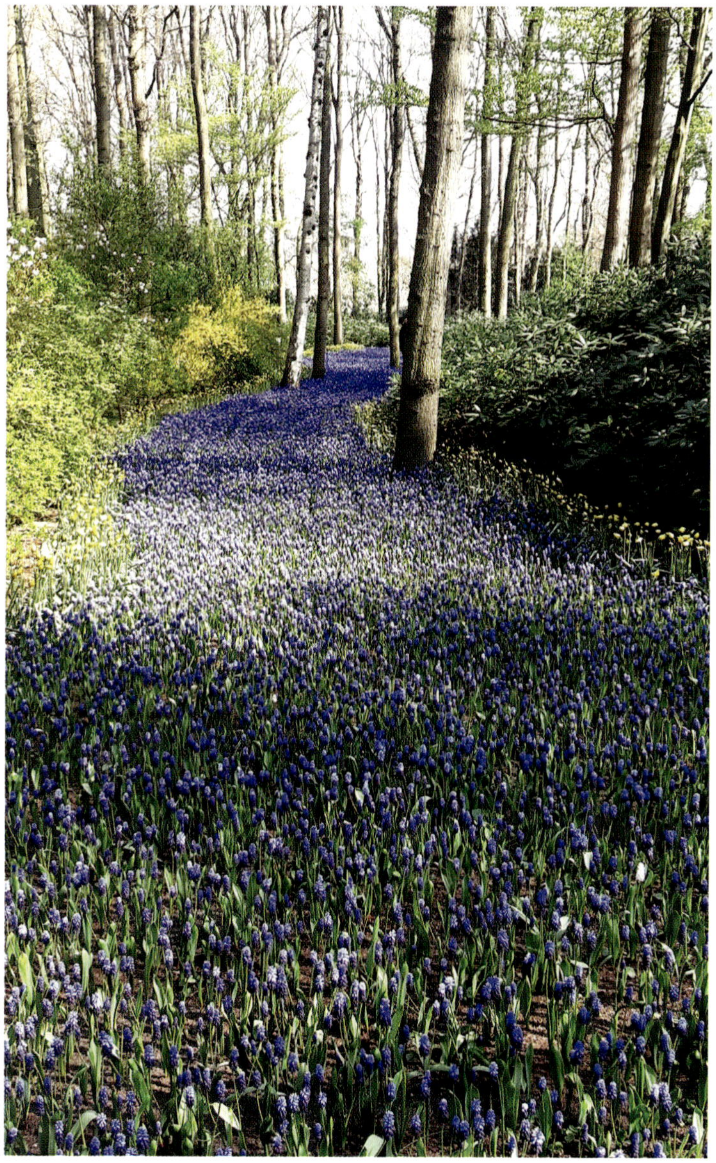

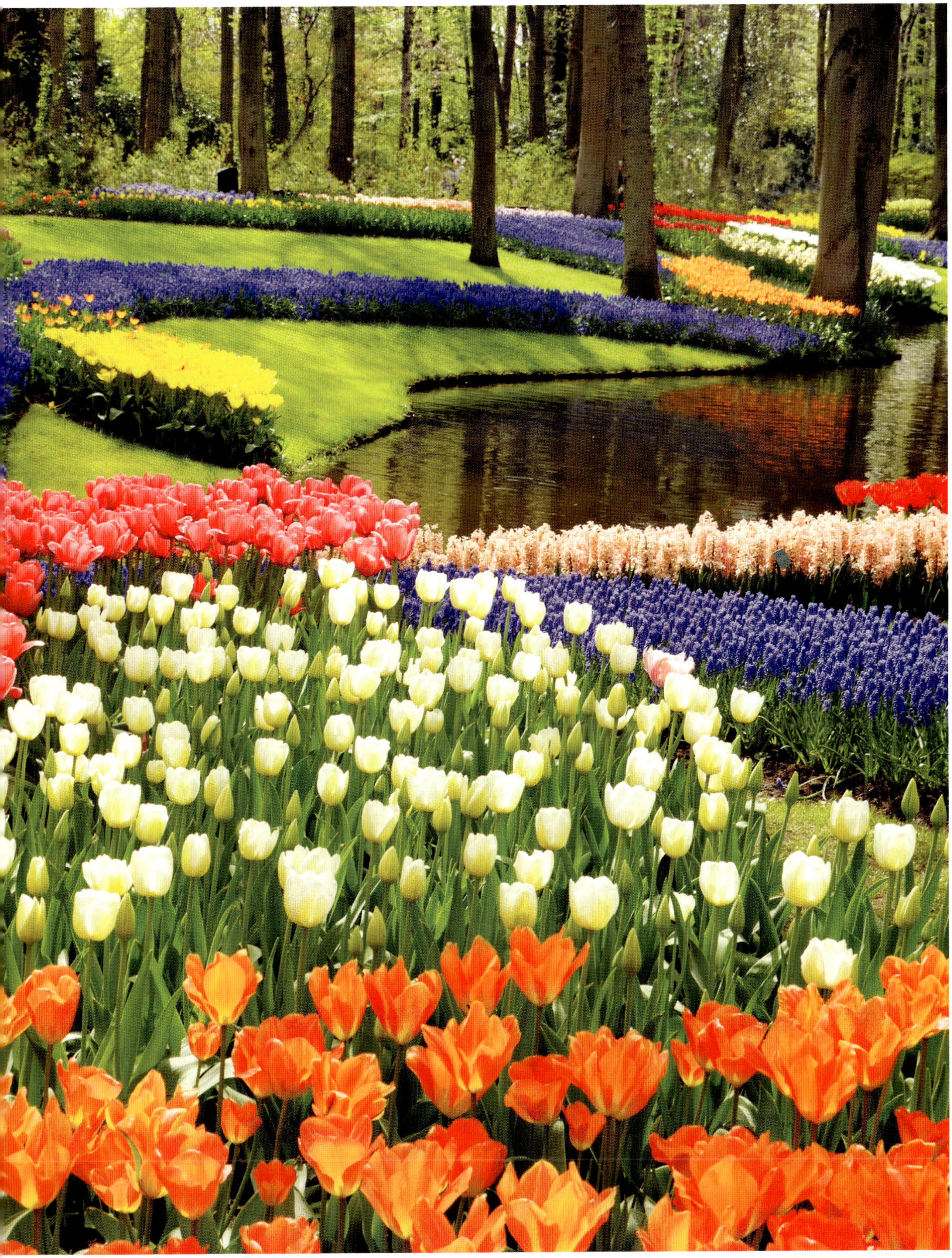

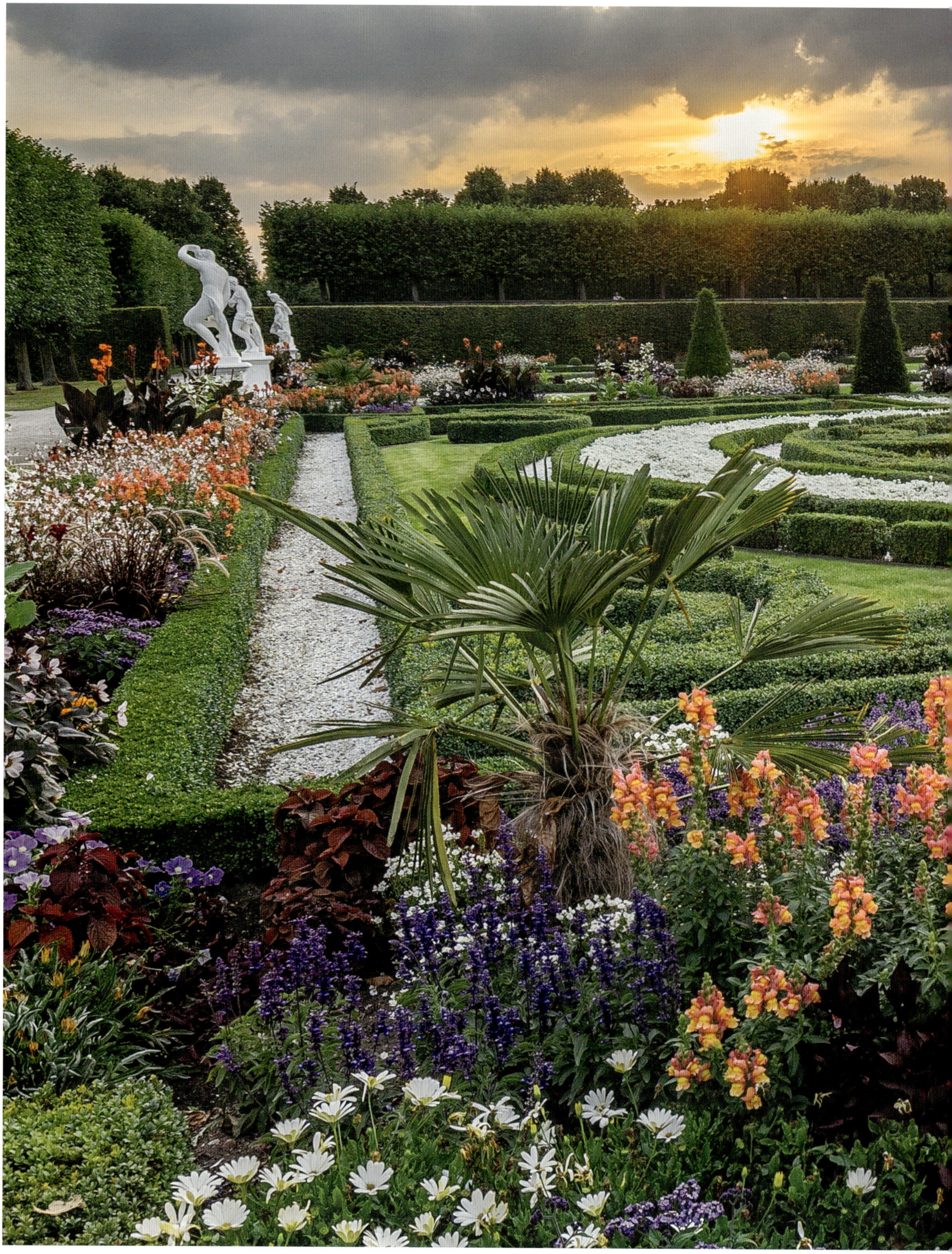

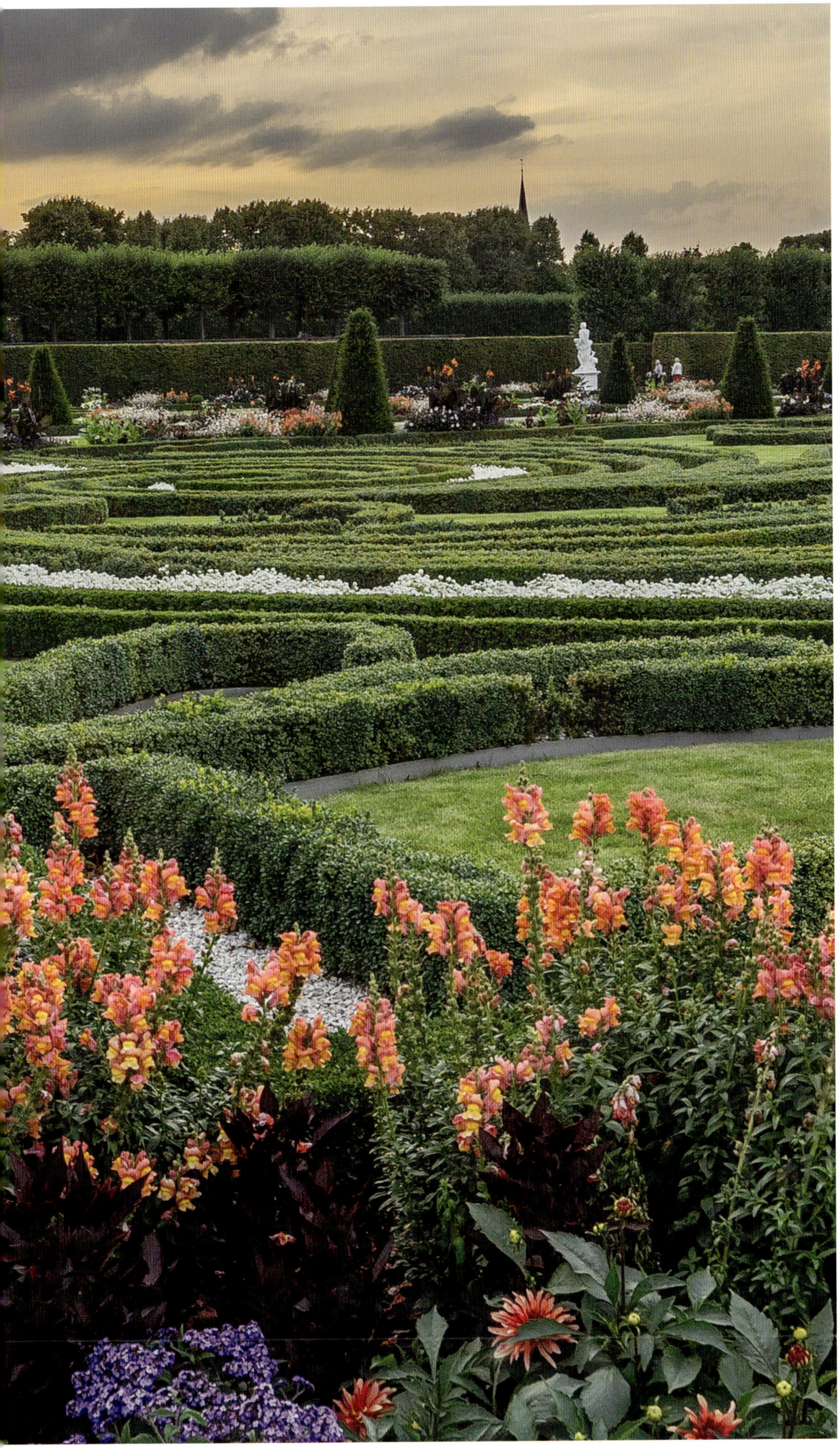

Herrenhausen Palace, Lower Saxony, Germany
Britain's centuries-old links with Europe become apparent at Schloss Herrenhausen, Hanover, erstwhile palace of King George II and King George III, who also held the Duchy of Brunswick-Lüneburg. It was in fact an heir to the British throne, Sophia of Hanover, who initiated the construction of these grand palace gardens in 1683. The Great Garden here epitomises Baroque style and is unchanged from its 300-year-old plan. Other gardens are designed in the English landscape style.

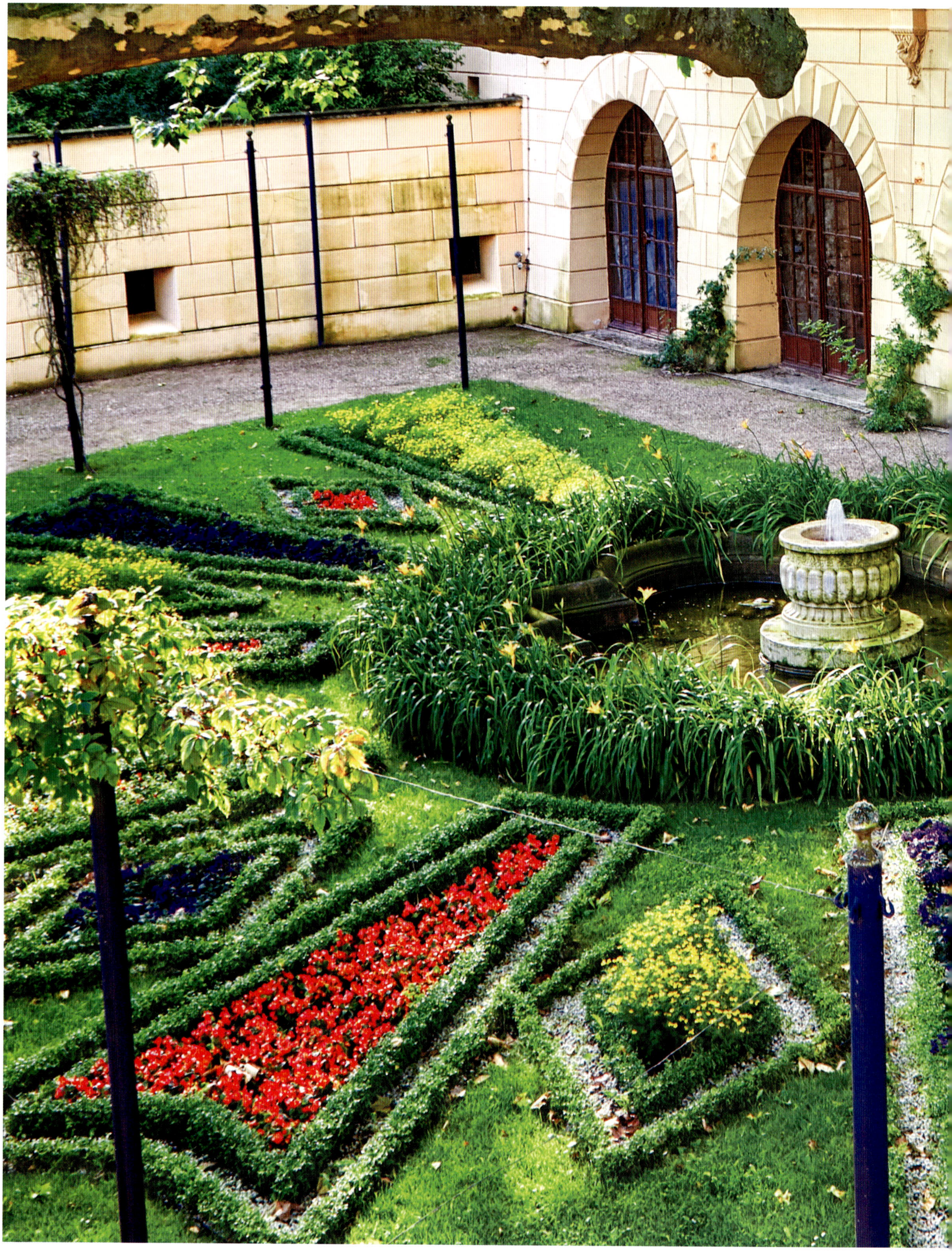

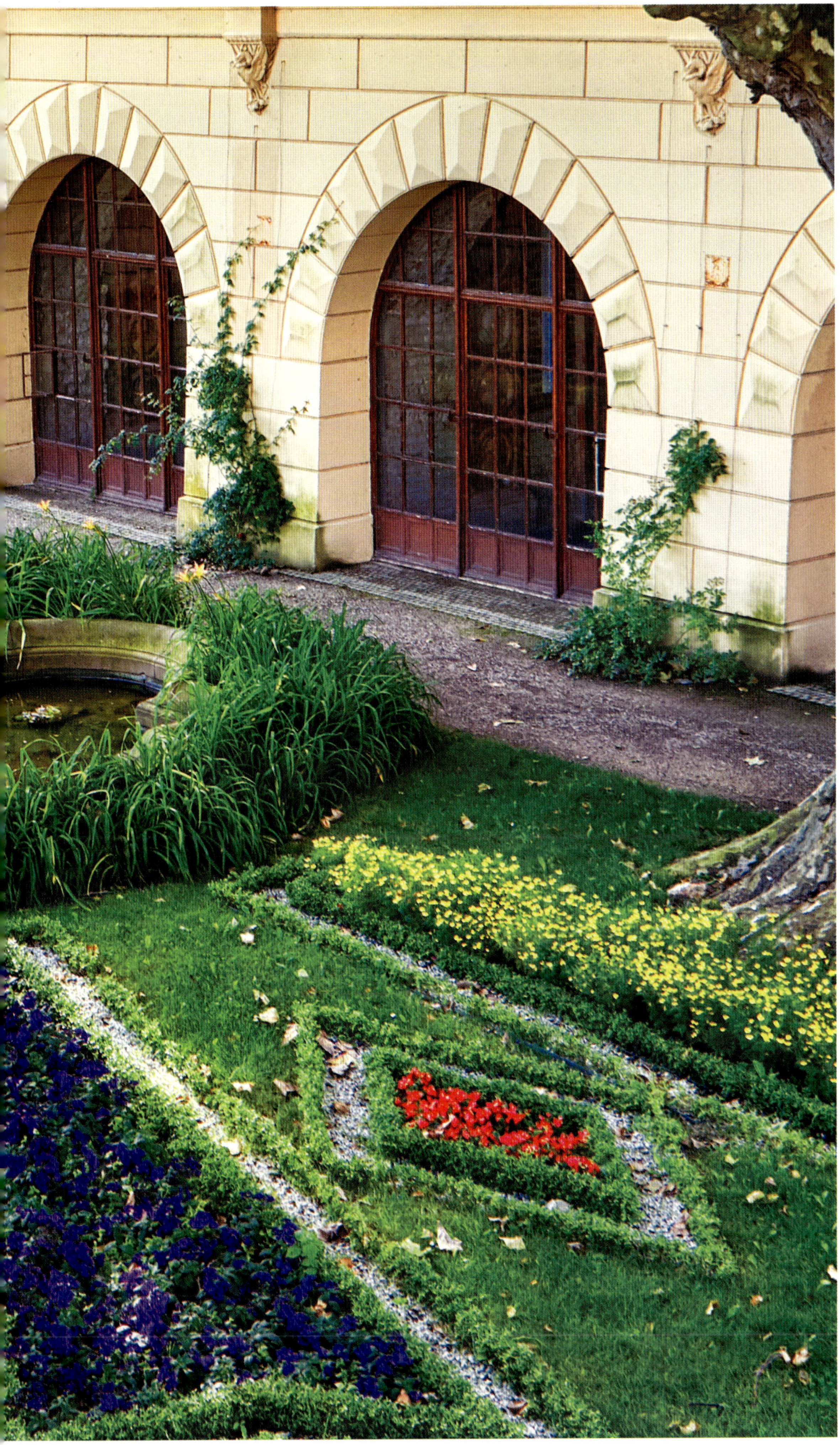

LEFT:

Schwerin Castle, Mecklenburg-Vorpommern, Germany

Some kind of fortification has existed on the site of Schwerin castle for at least the past millennium. The current building was constructed around an older structure in the mid-1800s, for Friedrich Franz II, Grand Duke of Mecklenburg-Schwerin, although the castle is now a public building. The island location in the city of Schwerin must be one of the most romantic imaginable. Baroque features date from 1748, with newer elements introduced in the 1800s.

OVERLEAF:

Sanssouci Palace and Park, Brandenburg, Germany

This UNESCO World Heritage Site was built between 1745 and 1747. Sanssouci translates literally as 'without a care', and it was the name Friedrich the Great, King of Prussia, gave to this summer palace in the city of Potsdam.

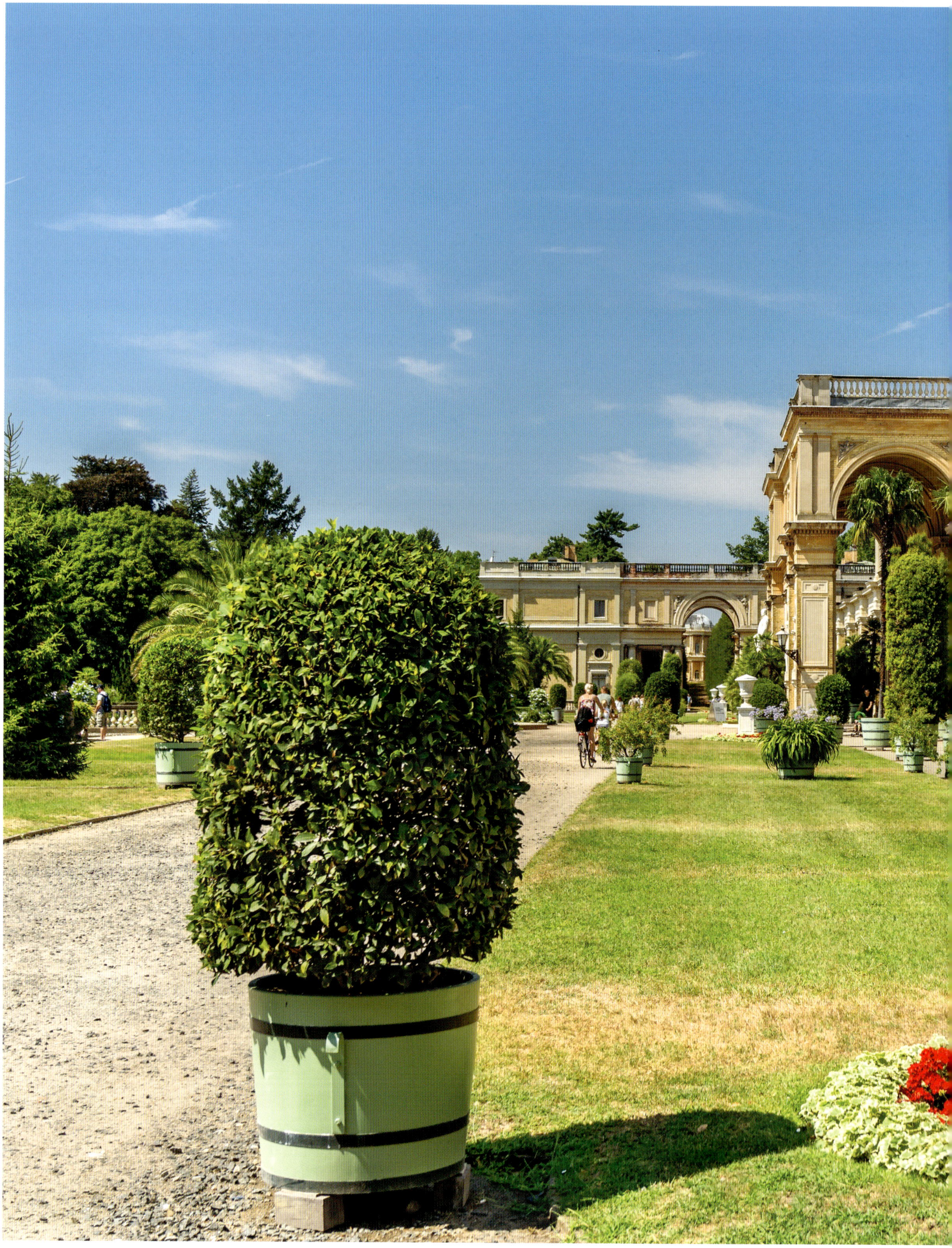

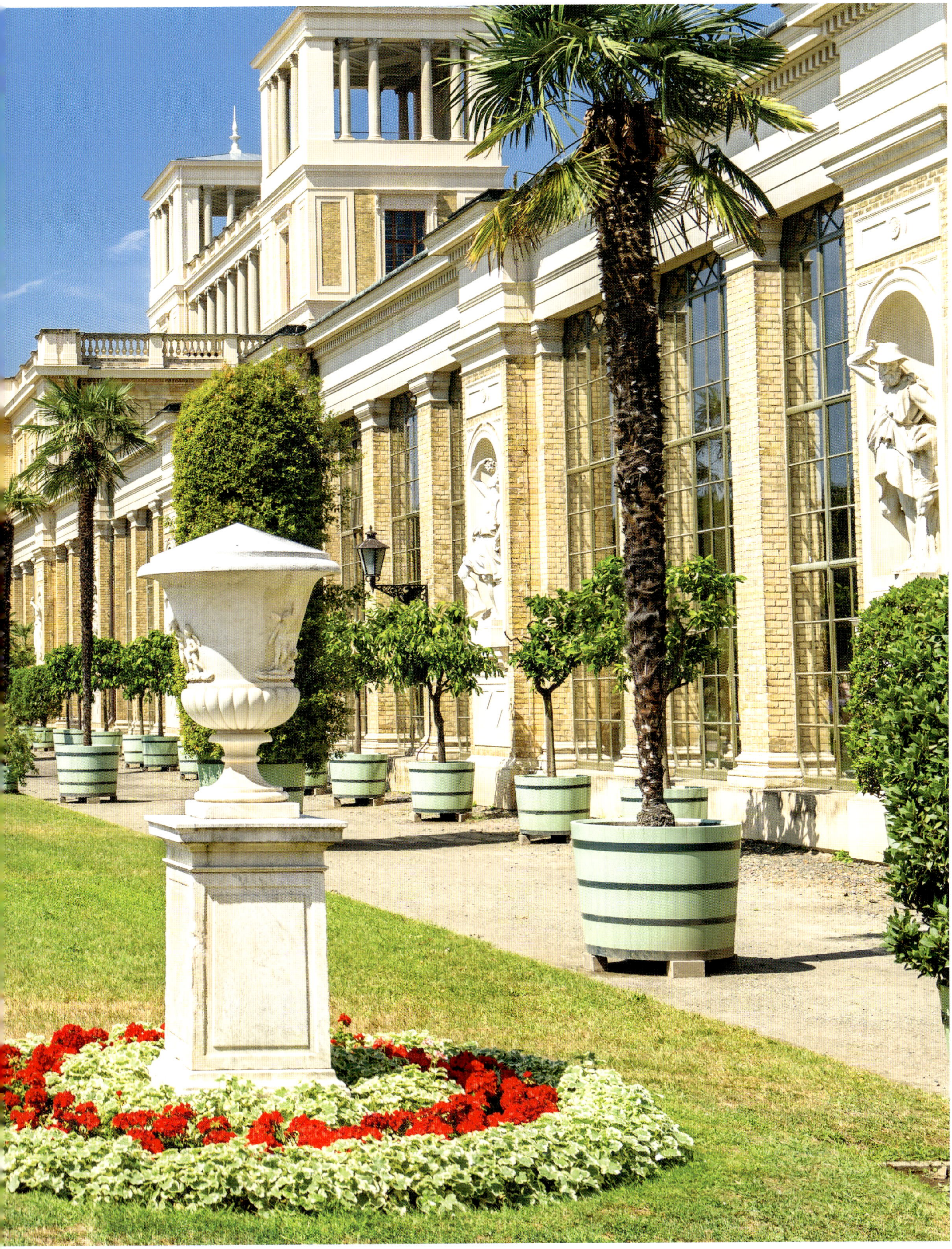

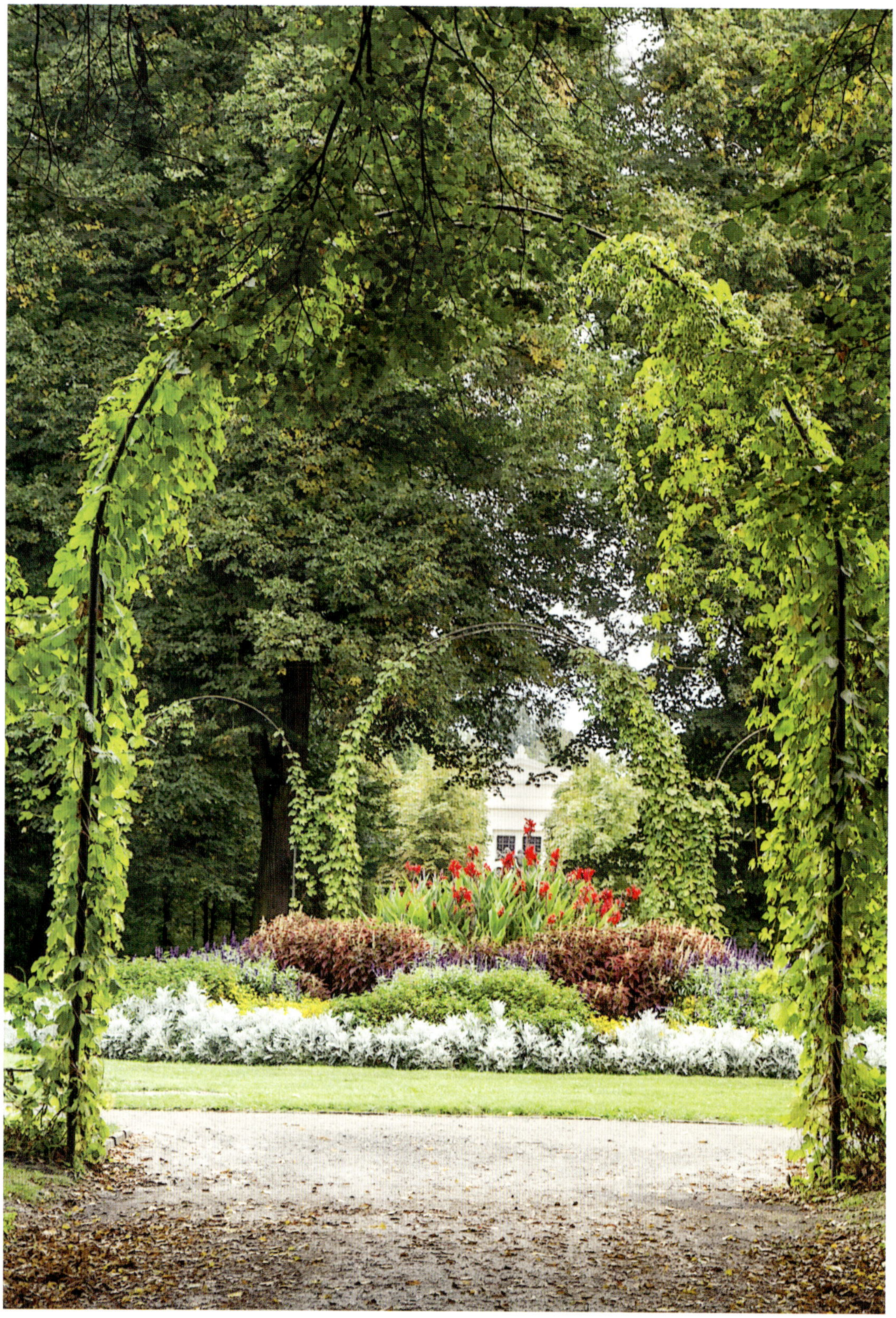

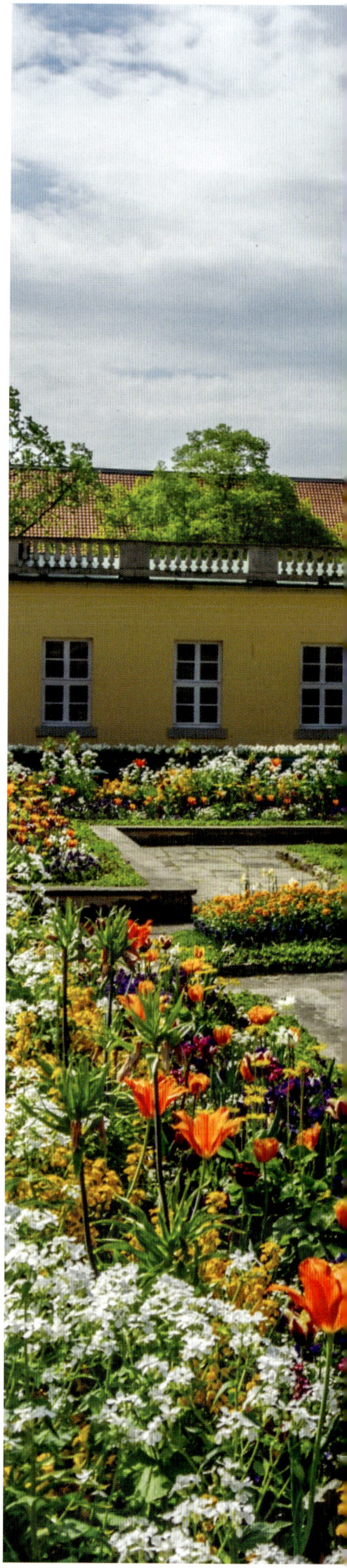

ALL PHOTOGRAPHS:

Sanssouci Palace and Park, Brandenburg, Germany

Formal terraces lead down from the palace to the Baroque-style garden designed in the 19th century by Peter Joseph Lenné. The expansive grounds include such features as a grotto, neoclassical temples, a large fountain and a Chinese house, incorporating rococo and chinoiserie elements. The last attraction to be built here was the Orangery Palace, ordered by Wilhelm IV. This handsome building is an ideal place for overwintering tender plants.

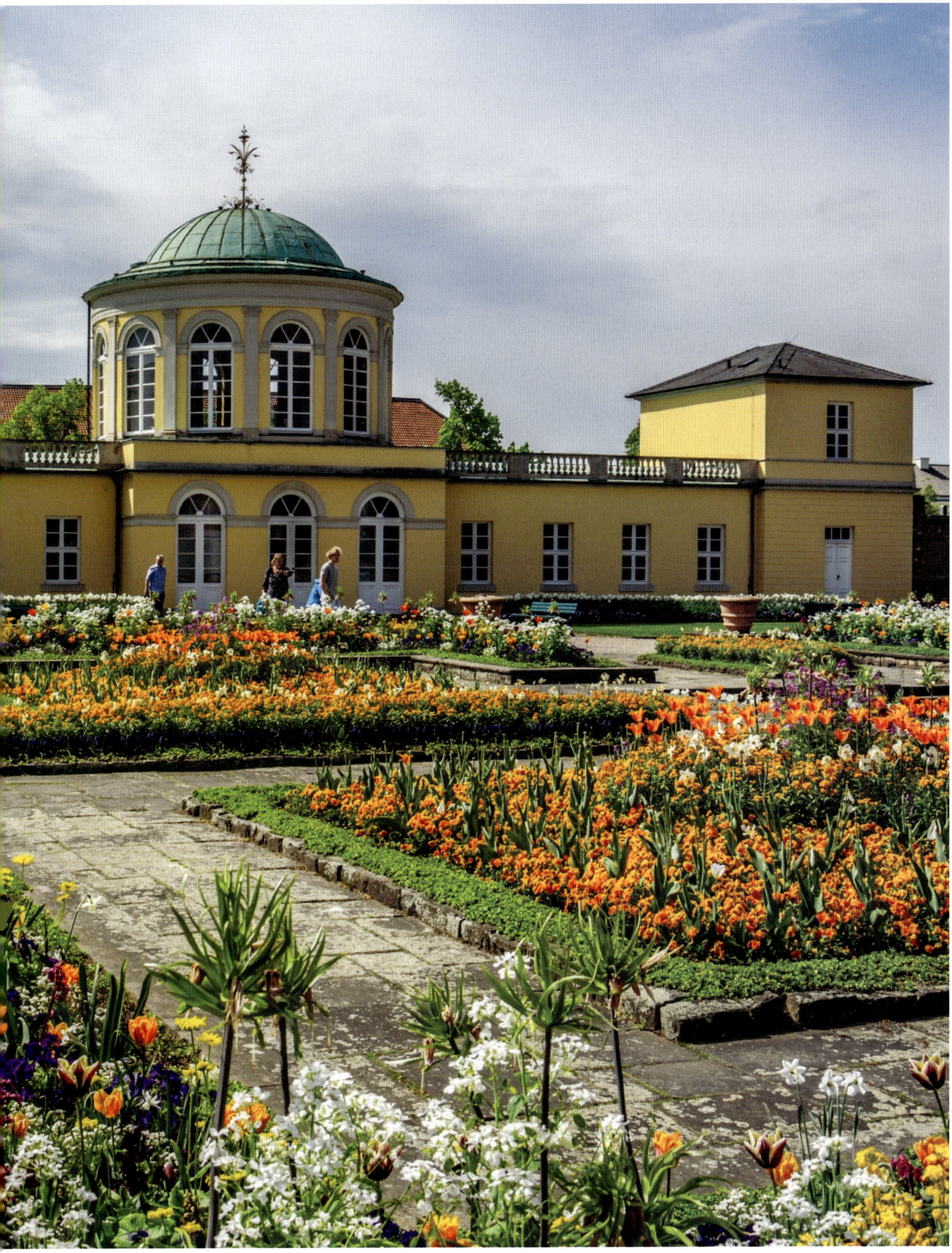

Mirabell Palace and Gardens, Salzburg, Austria
Sharp-eyed fans of *The Sound of Music* will recognize the Pegasus Fountain in Salzburg's Mirabell Palace gardens: it is where Julie Andrews, as Maria, and the children danced and sang 'Do Re Mi' in the 1965 film. This Salzburg landmark was built in 1606 but the gardens that we see were laid out in 1690. Classically Baroque in style, they include a rose garden fountain, orangery and hedge theatre.

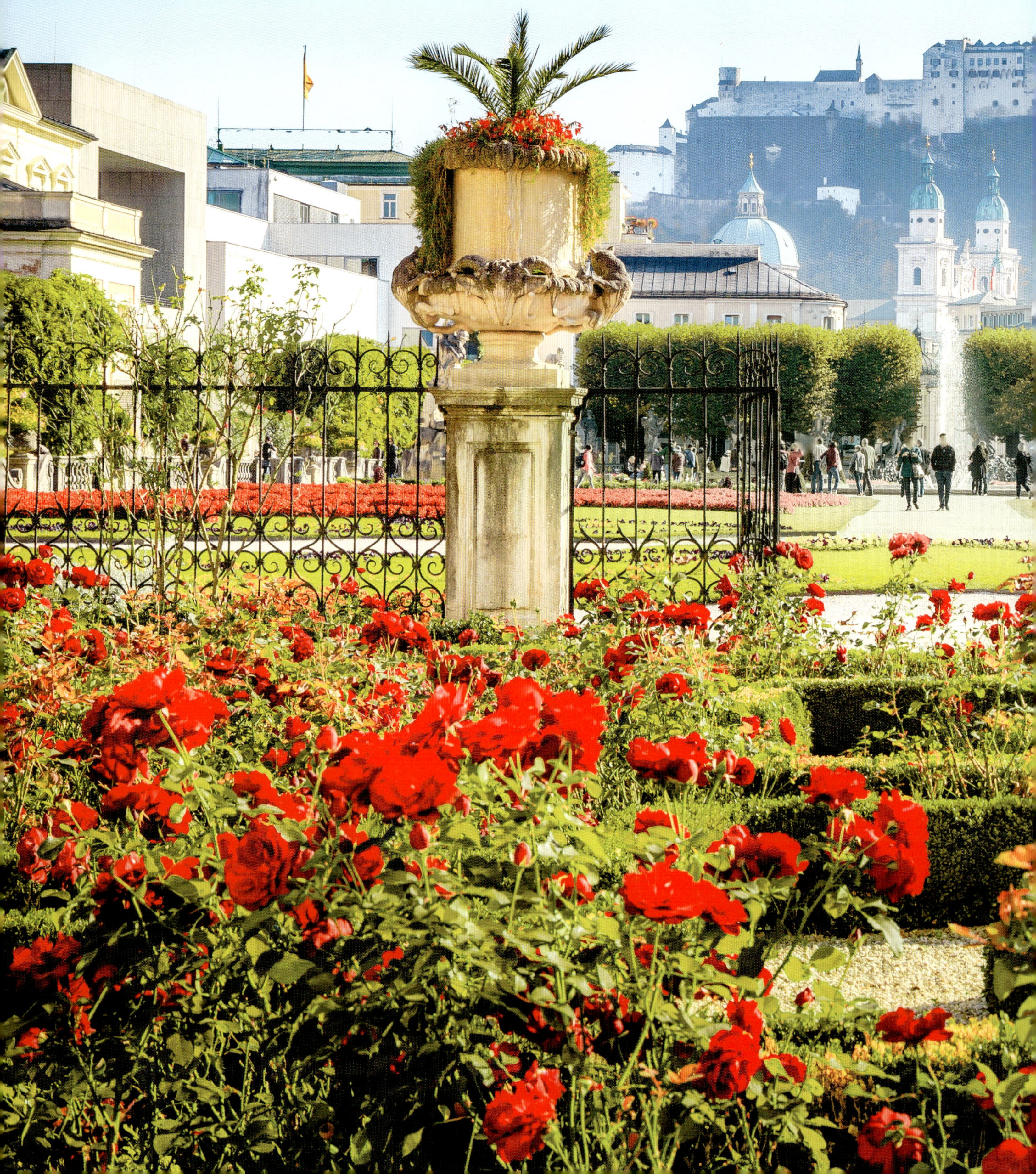

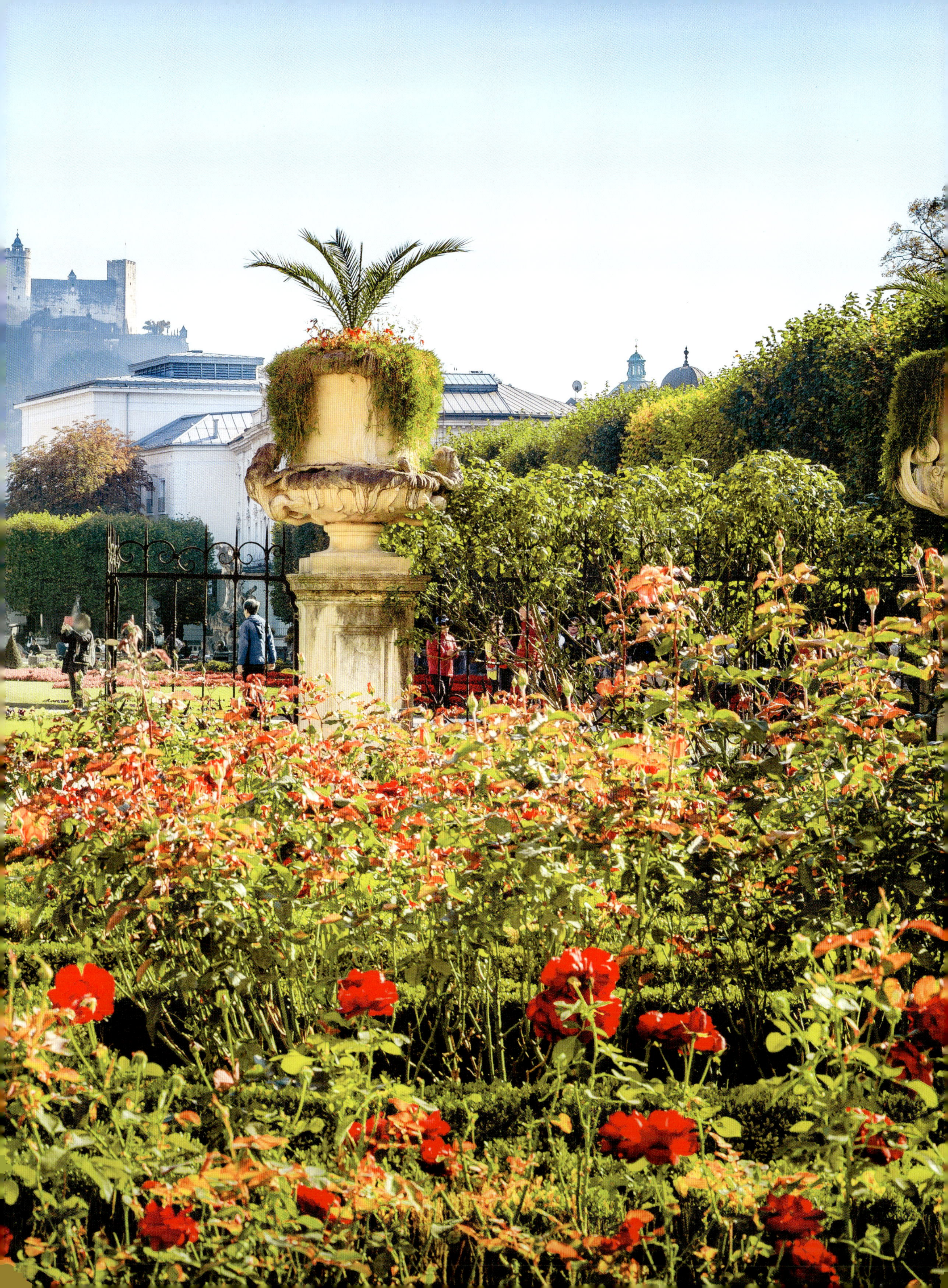

Volksgarten, Vienna, Austria
This public park in Austria's only metropolitan city was laid out in 1821 by Ludwig Remy and opened to the public in 1823. Volksgarten translates as 'people's garden', reflecting the fact that it was built over city fortifications destroyed by Napoleon in 1809. In time, other fortifications which were no longer needed were removed and the park was expanded. The public space became so popular that Johann Strauss I even wrote a piece entitled Volksgarten Quadrille.

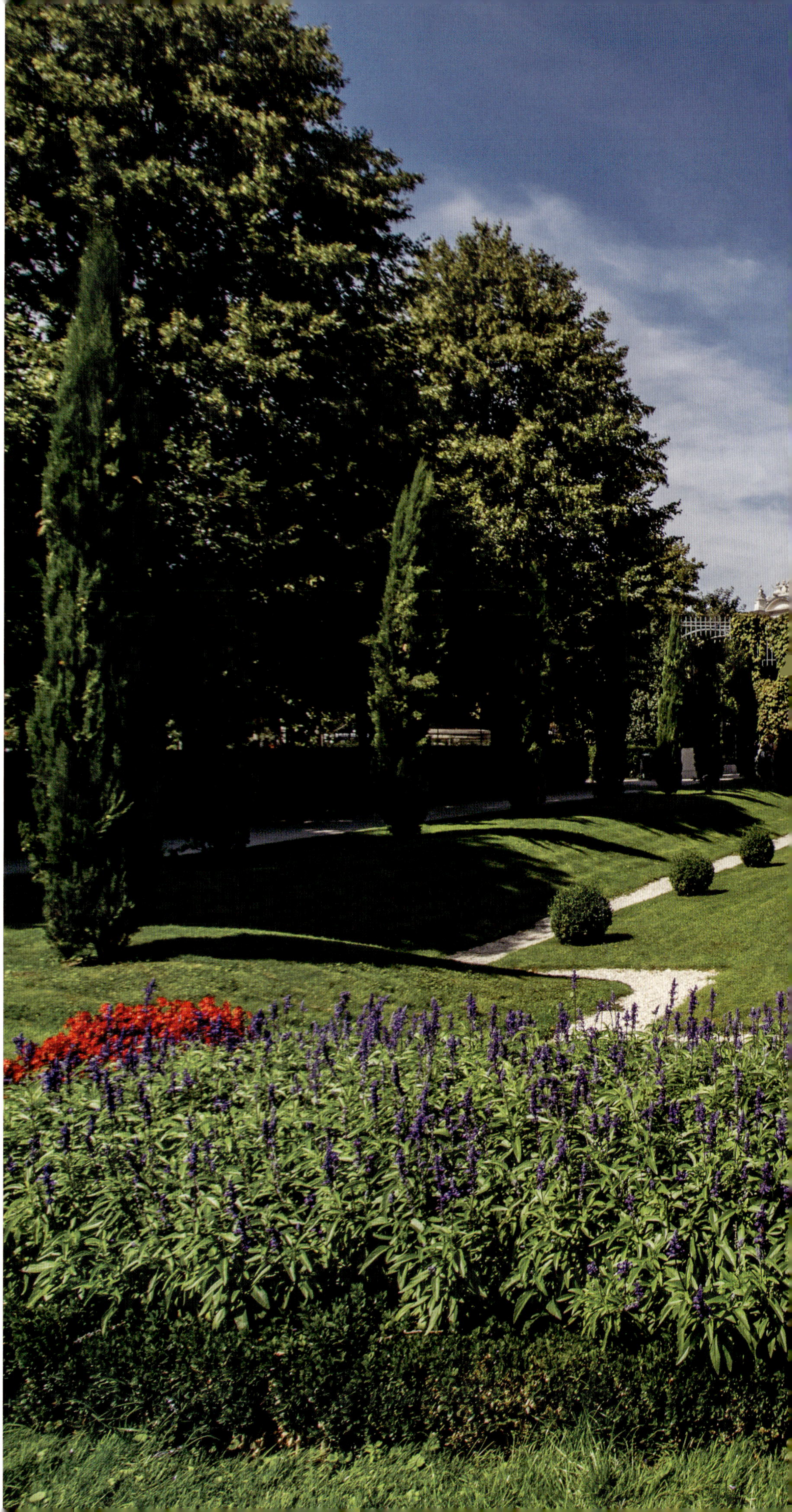

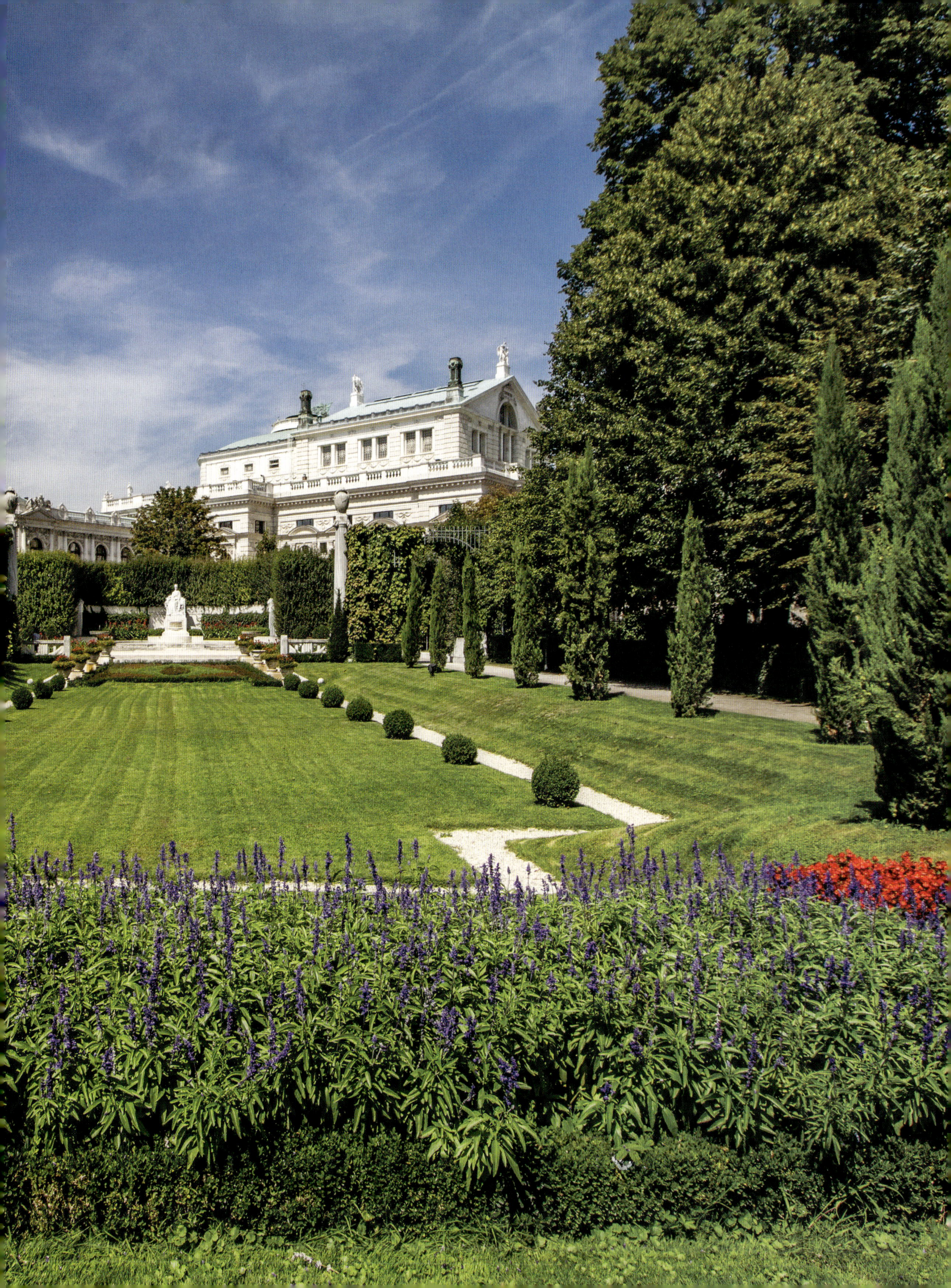

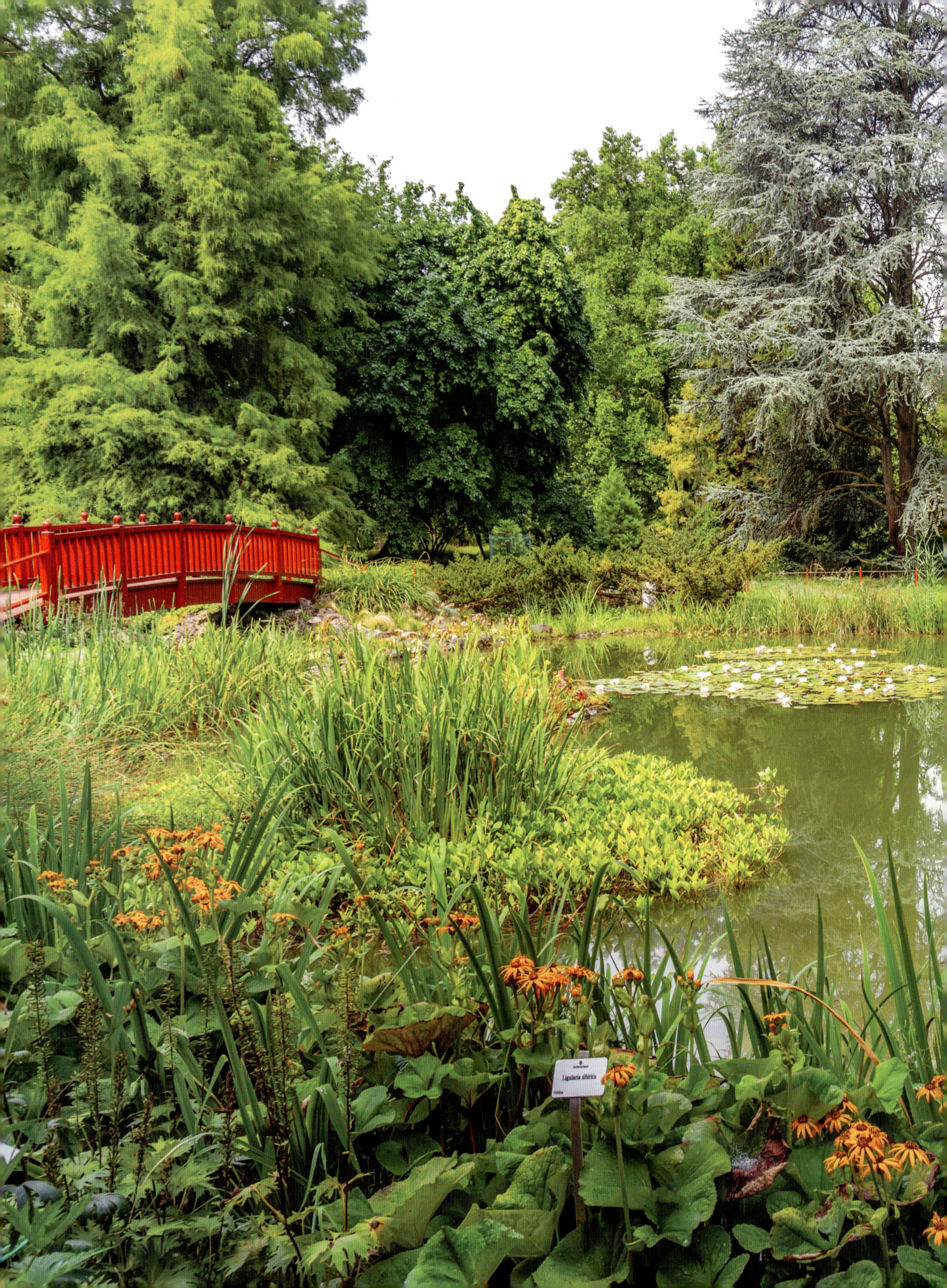
Ligularia sibirica

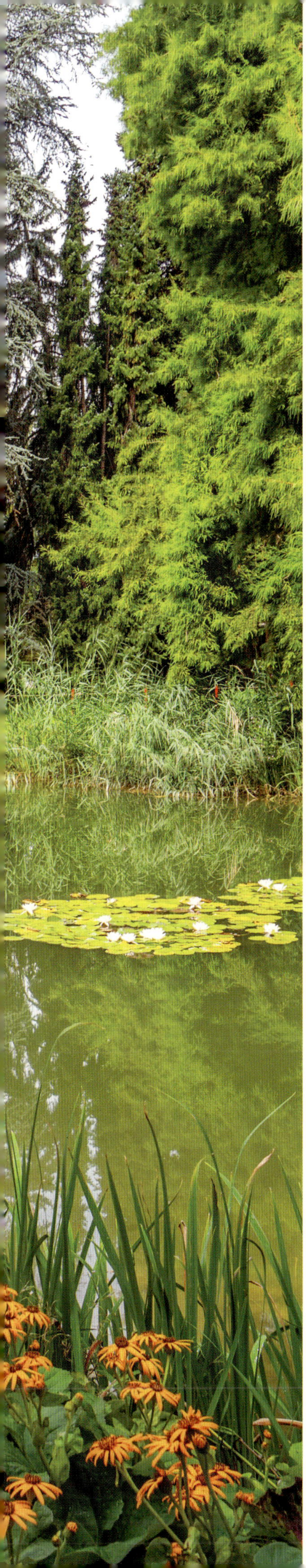

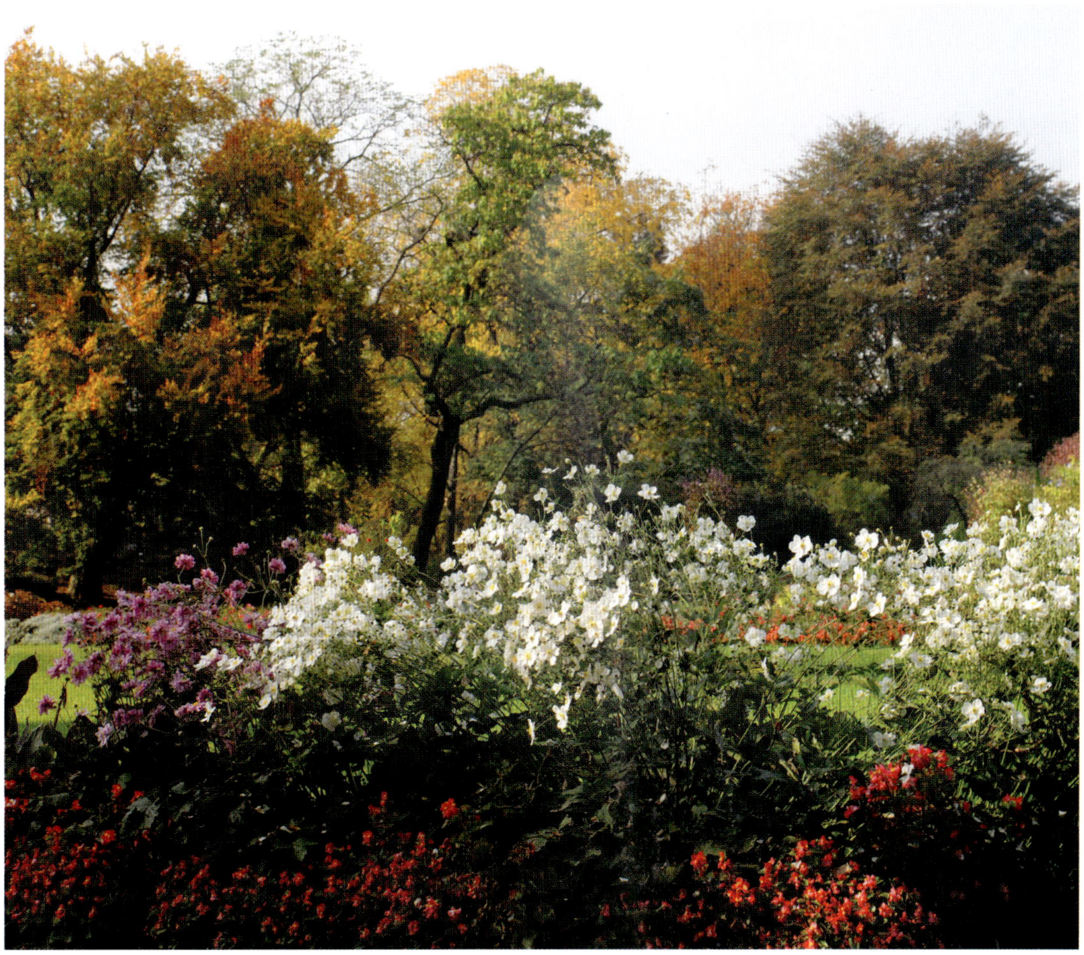

LEFT AND ABOVE:

Zagreb Botanical Garden, Croatia

Laid out in 1890, this botanical garden is attached to the Faculty of Science at Zagreb University. It contains around 5,000 different specimens, and has a particular focus on preserving native flora. Within the 2ha (5-acre) garden in the heart of the city, find flower parterres, glasshouses, a rock garden and an arboretum in the English landscape style.

RIGHT:

Caserta Royal Palace and Park, Campania, Italy

Drawing heavily from Versailles and covering 4ha (9.8 acres), the UNESCO World Heritage Site outside Naples comprises fountains, pools and cascades, in what UNESCO describes as 'a triumph of Italian Baroque'. It was built for Charles III, King of Naples and Italy and later King of Spain, by Luigi Vanvitelli. A later English landscape garden was designed for Queen Maria Carolina, sister of Marie Antoinette, by John Andreas Graefer.

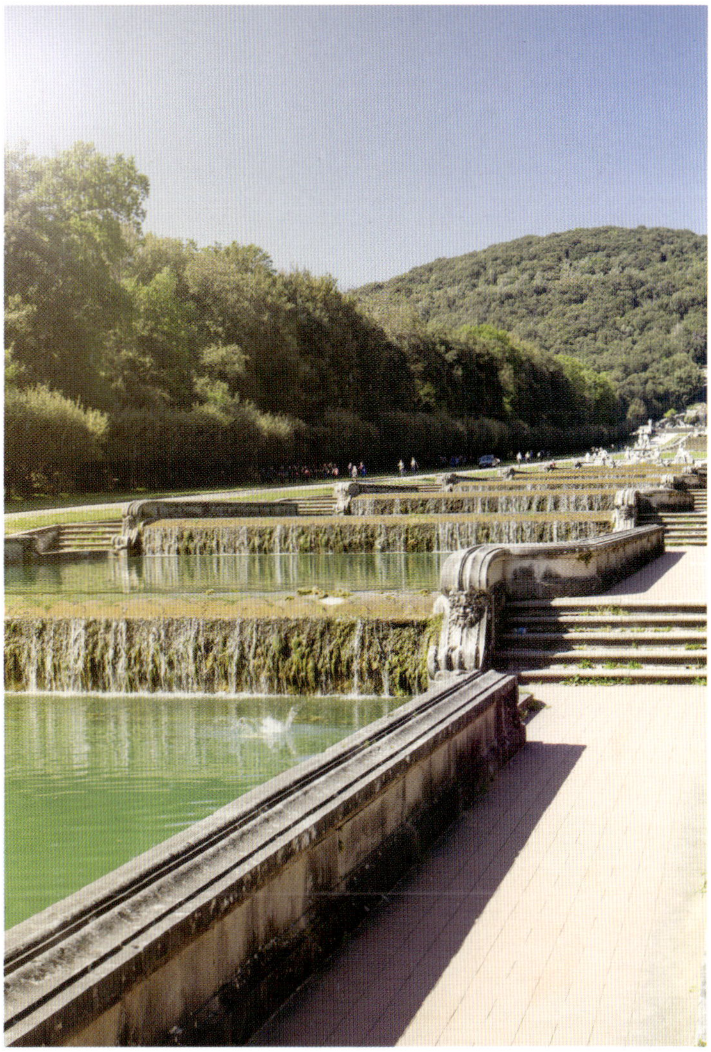

La Venaria Reale, Piedmont, Italy
This Baroque palace near Turin was built for the Royal House of Savoy in the 17th and 18th centuries, but by the 20th it had fallen to ruin. An extensive restoration programme now puts this UNESCO World Heritage Site on the map. The gardens offer 80ha (200 acres) of Baroque splendour, including terraces, sculptures, canals and the largest potager in Italy.

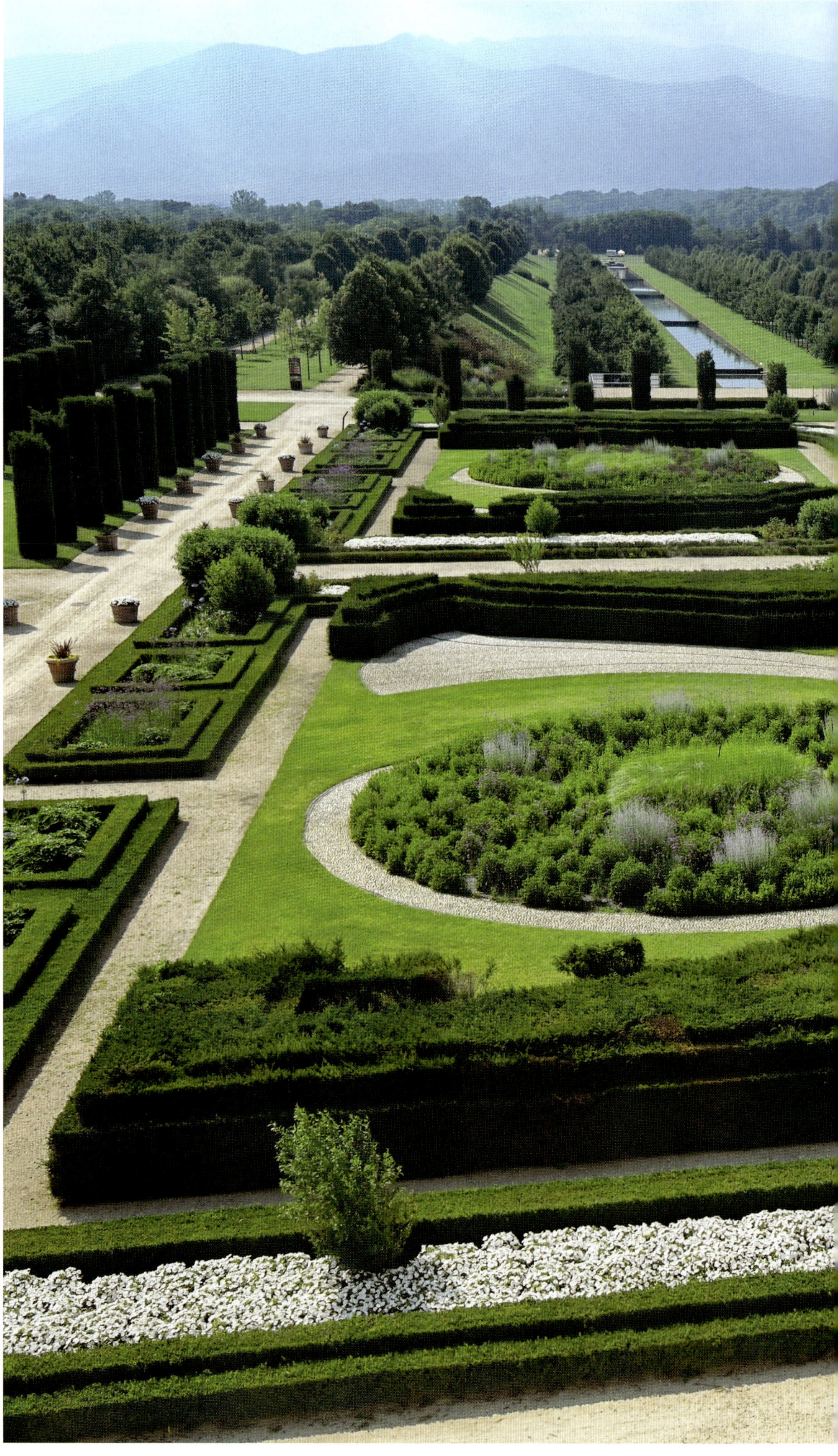

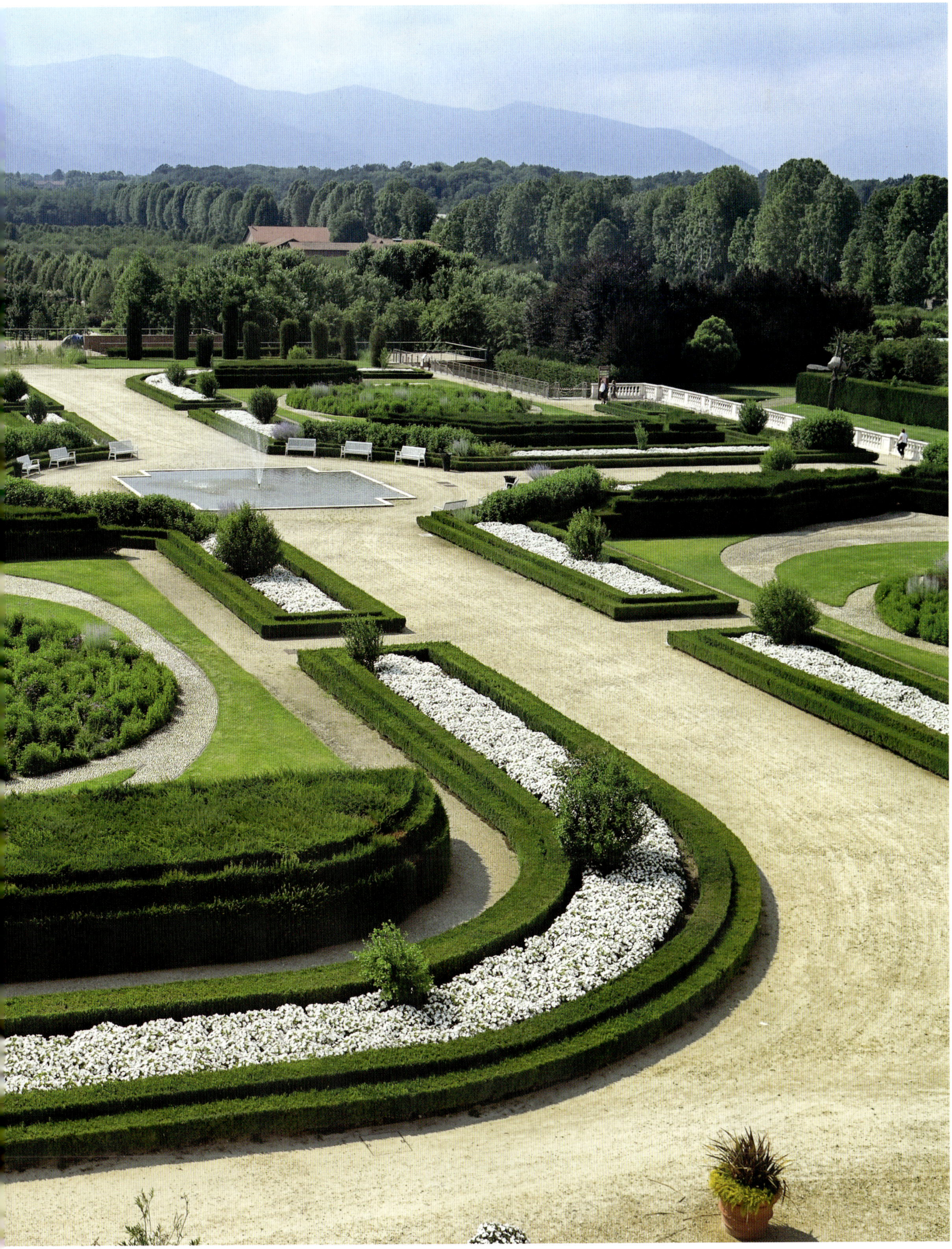

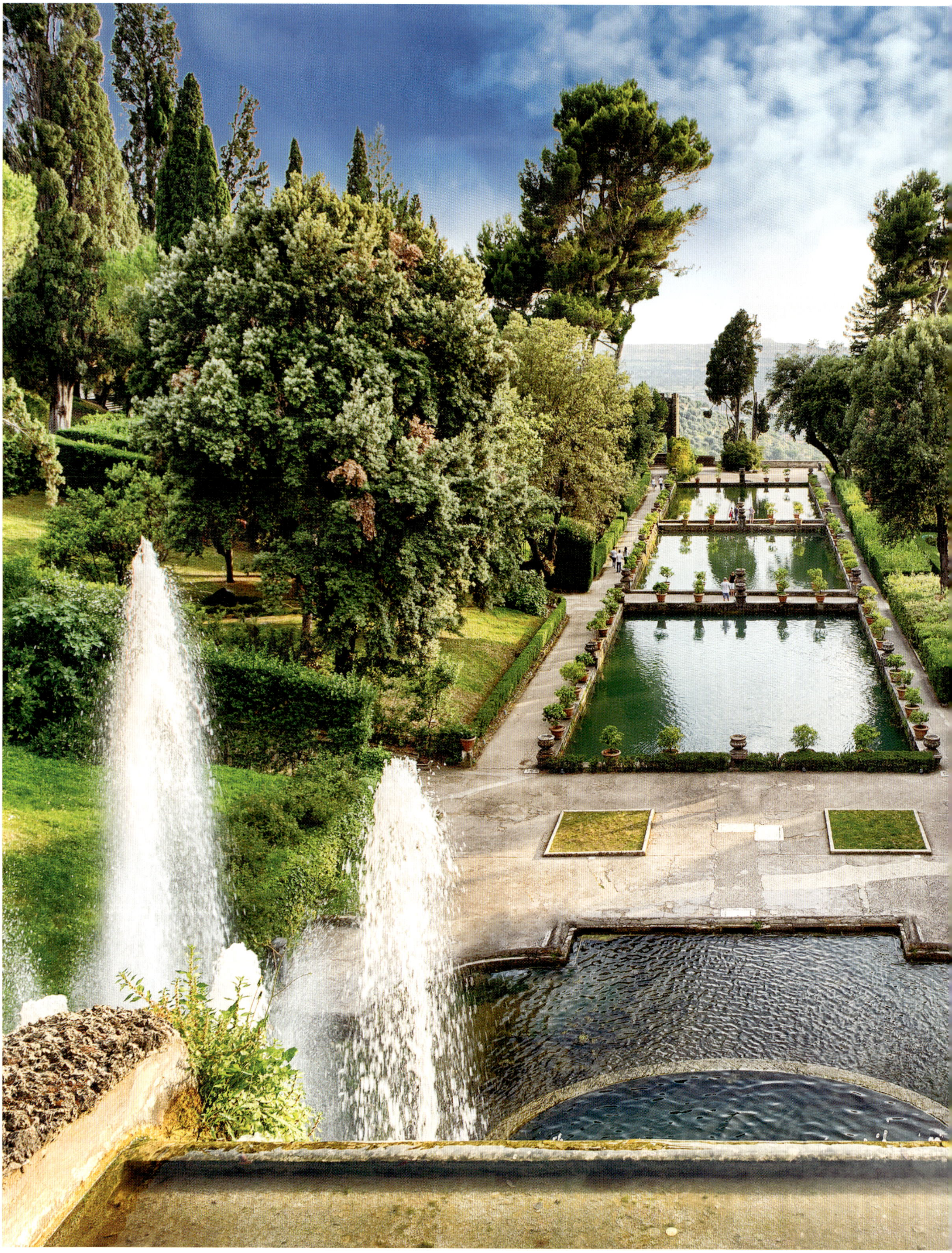

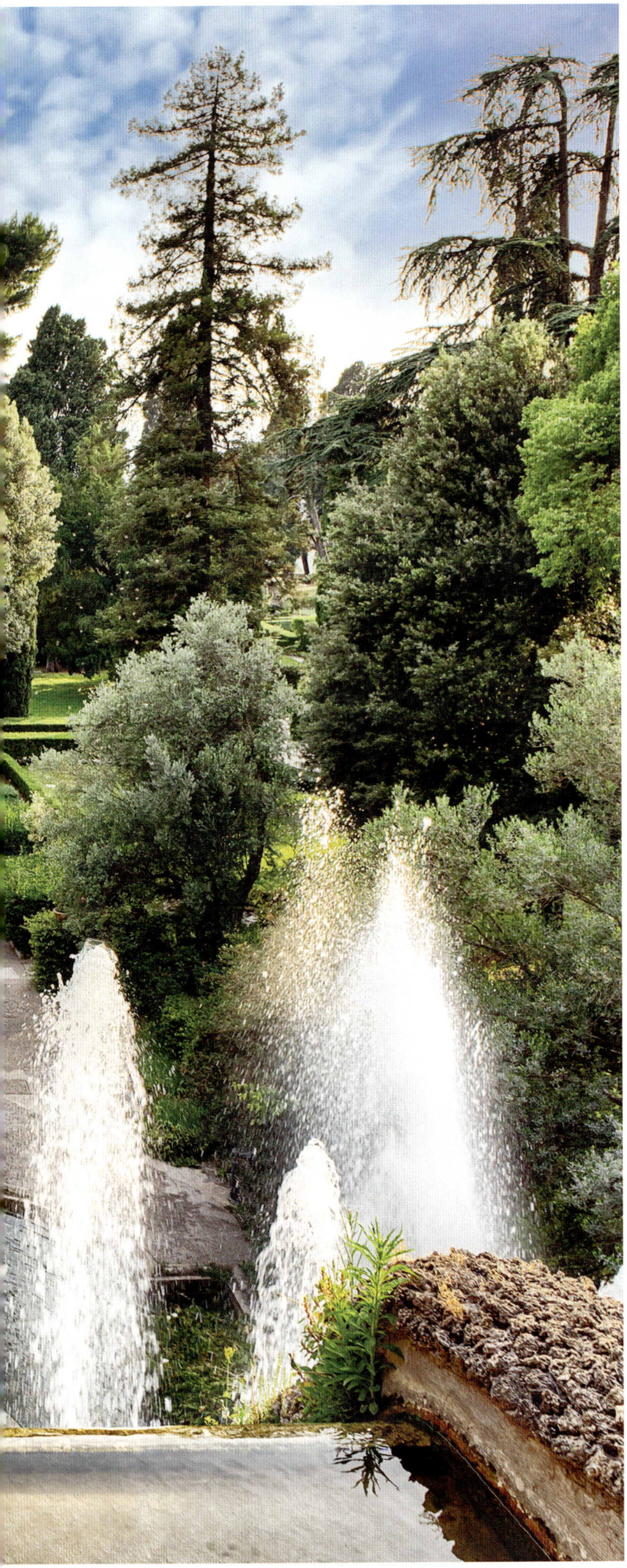

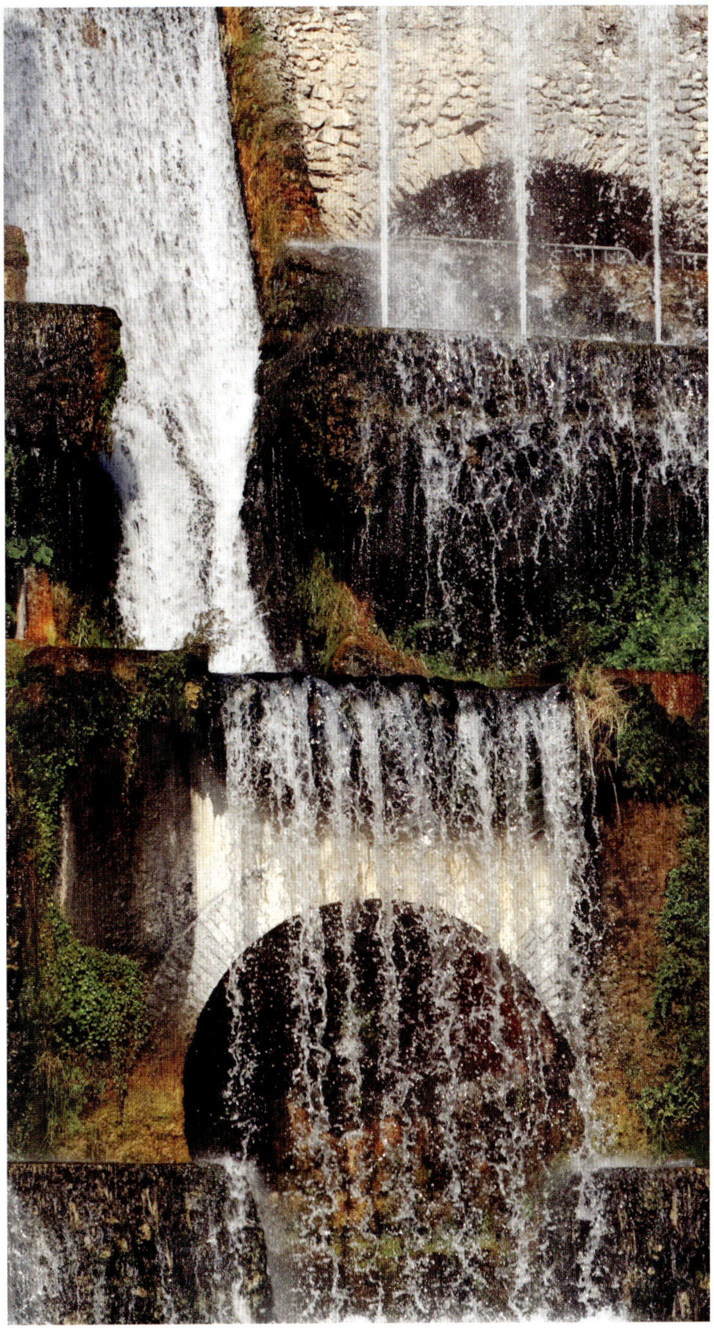

BOTH PHOTOGRAPHS:

Villa d'Este, Lazio, Italy

One of the most famous gardens of all, Villa d'Este in Tivoli is a superb example of Renaissance design and has provided the pattern for many subsequent garden designs. The UNESCO World Heritage Site was laid out by Pirro Ligorio, for Cardinal Ippolito II d'Este of Ferrara in the mid-16th century. Two slopes descend to a terrace in which water features heavily. The Fountain of Organ is an early feat of engineering.

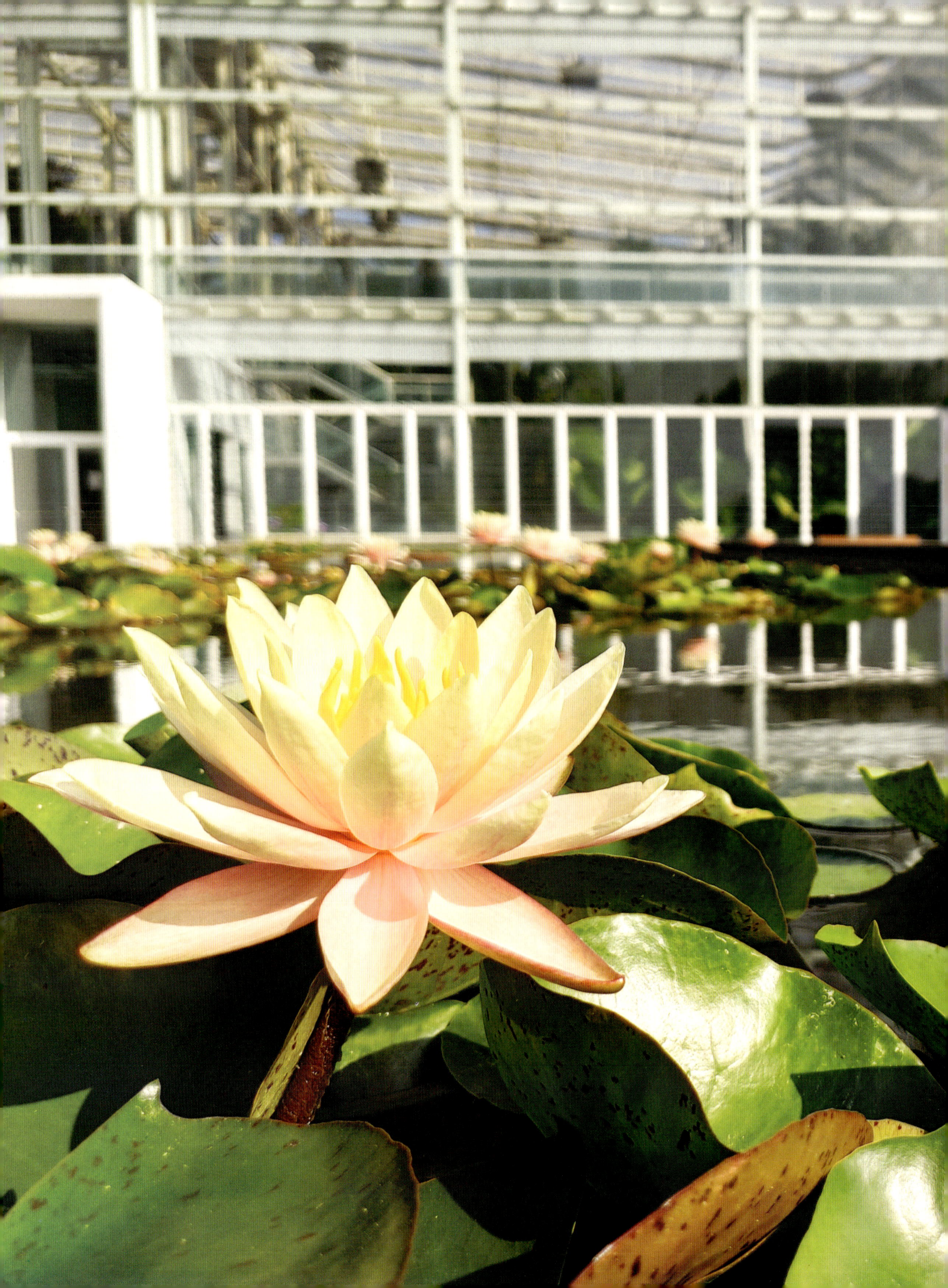

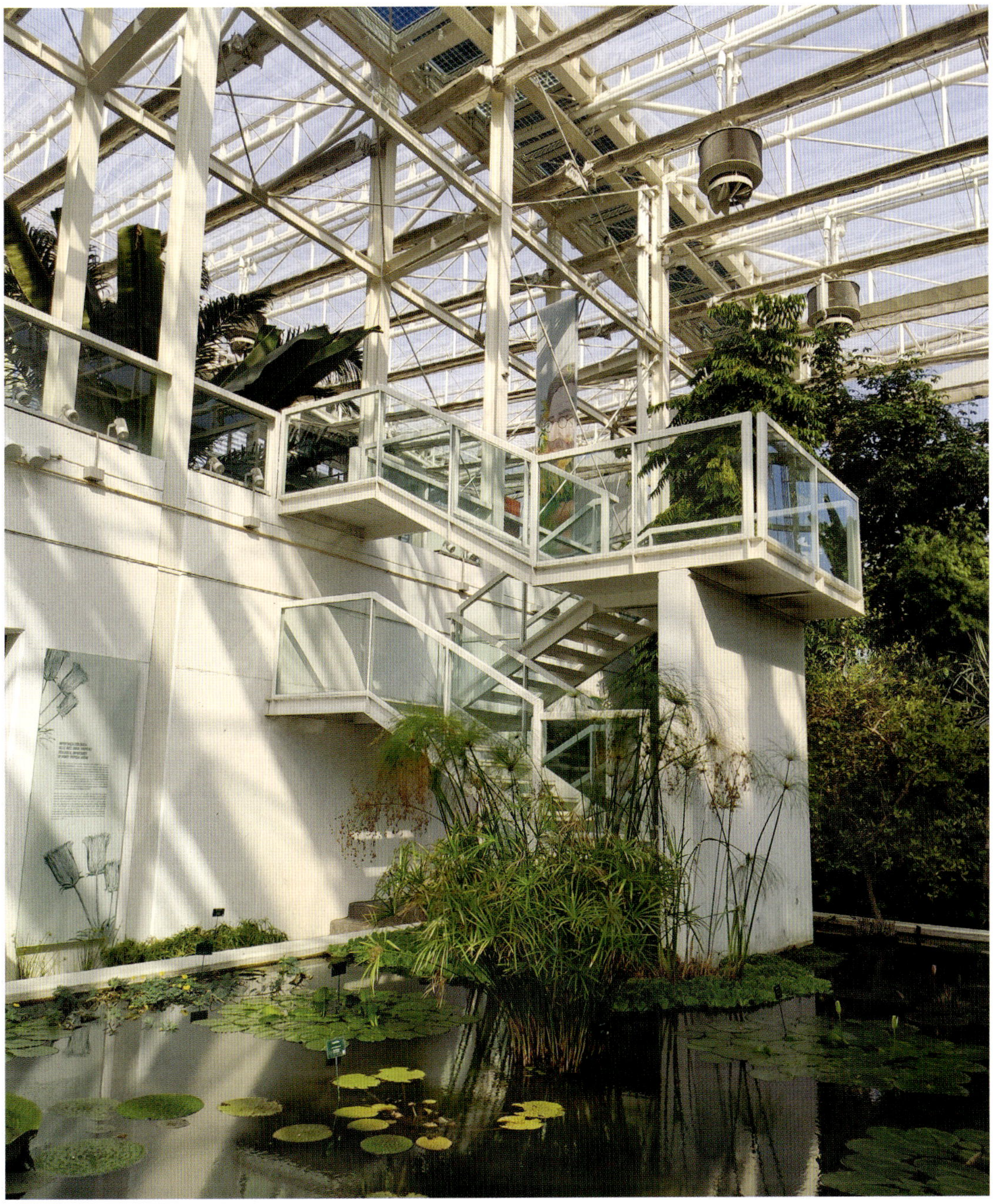

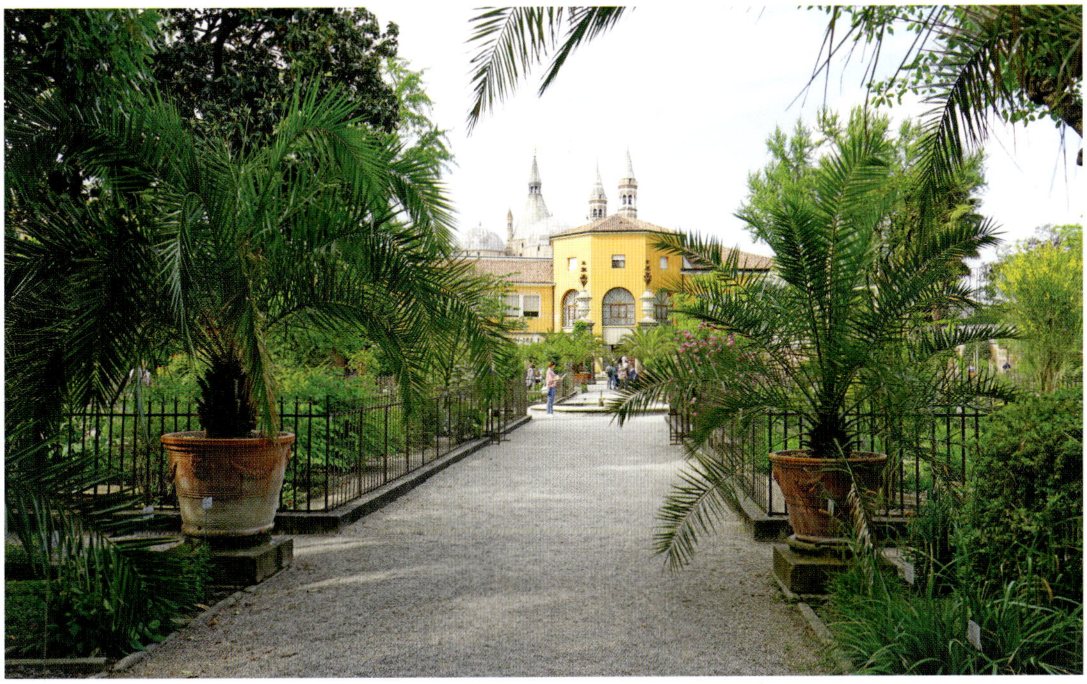

ALL PHOTOGRAPHS:
Orto Botanico di Padova, Veneto, Italy
Although the botanic garden in Pisa pips this garden by a year, the botanic garden of Padua, founded in 1545, has never moved from its site, putting it in the running for oldest botanic garden in the world. It was initiated by the Senate of the Venetian Republic as a place where medicinal plants could be studied. Today it is a UNESCO World Heritage Site.

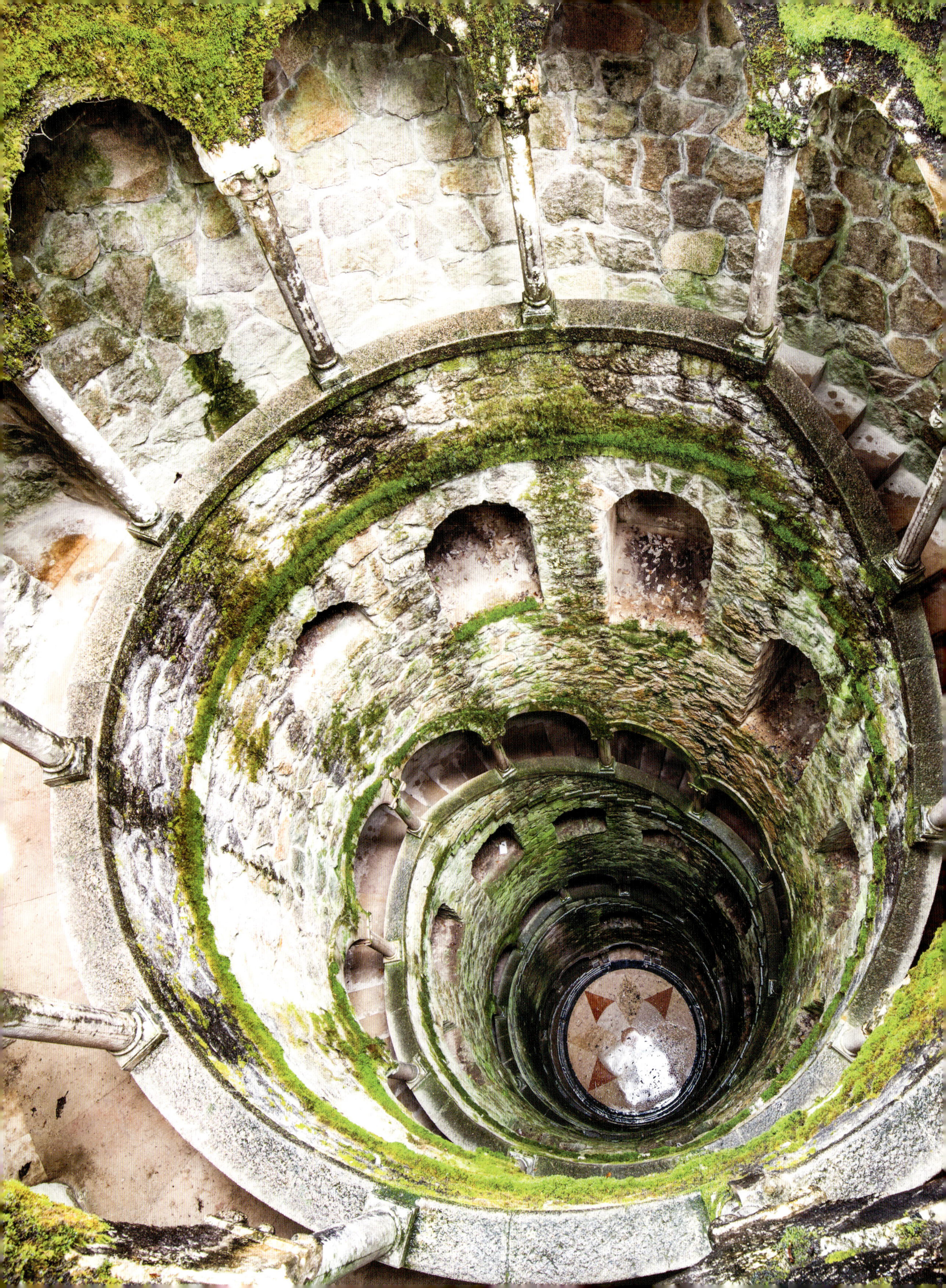

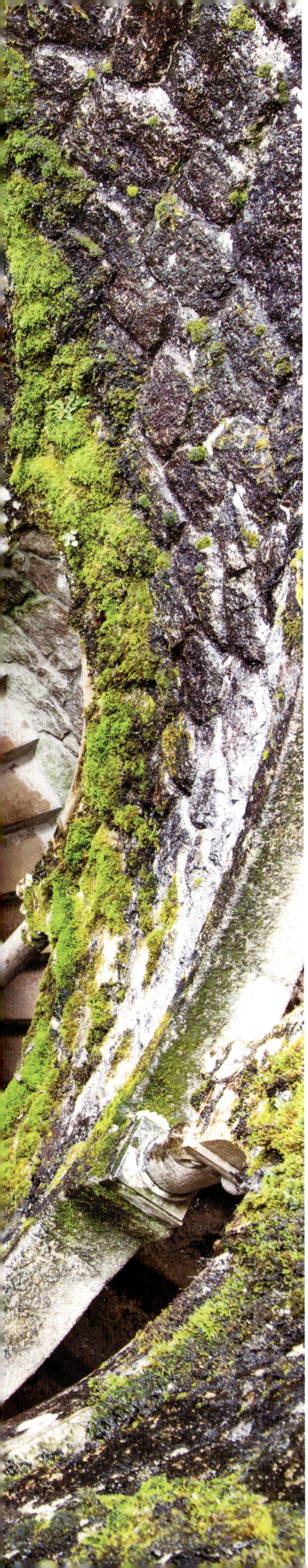

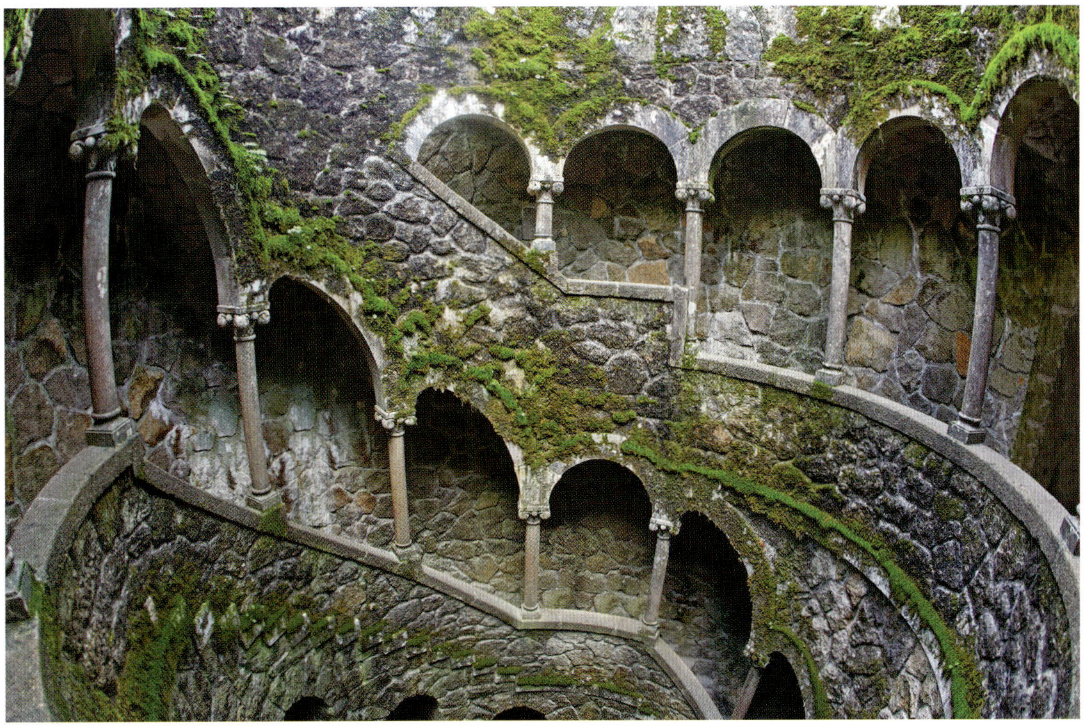

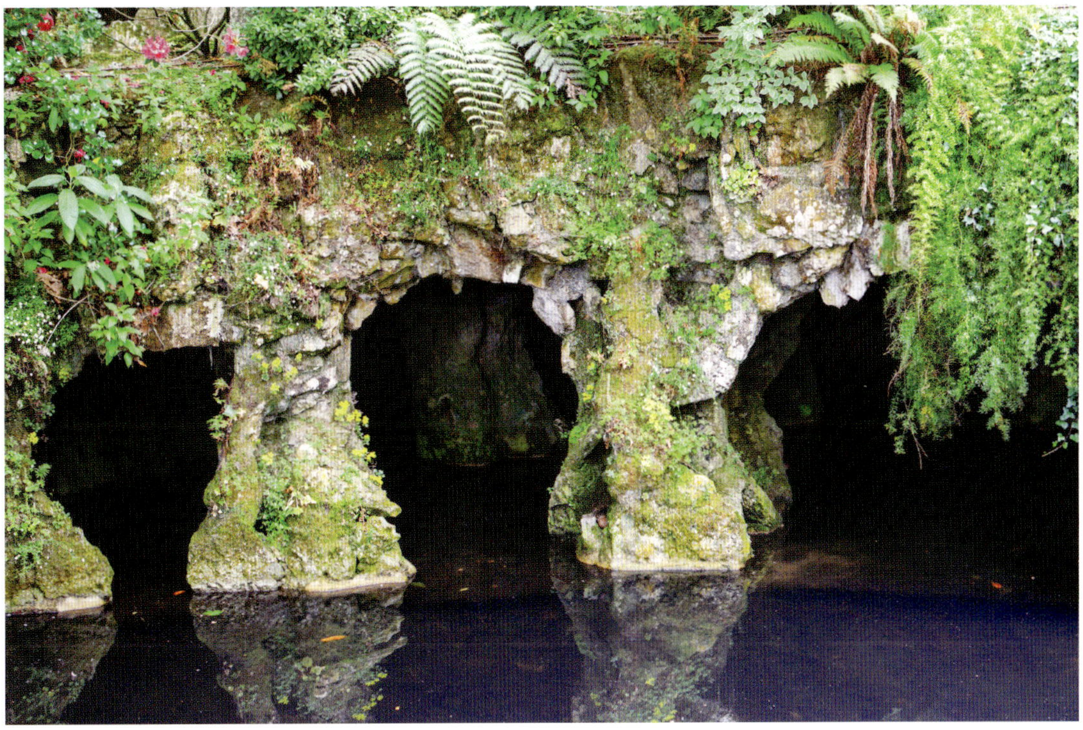

ALL PHOTOGRAPHS:
Quinta da Regaleira, Lisbon, Portugal
In the wooded hills above Lisbon, the village of Sintra is the site of a number of remarkable gardens. Key among them is this palace, the 4ha (9.8-acre) grounds of which are a confection of grottoes, wells, fountains and lakes built for Carvalho Monteiro in the late 19th century by Luigi Manini, an Italian architect. The complex is a UNESCO World Heritage Site.

Alhambra, Granada, Spain
The influence of Islamic garden spans north India to Spain, where in Granada the Alhambra is one of the most exalted gardens in the world. Positioned on a rocky hill, the palace was built in the 13th century by Muhammad I of Granada, also known as Ibn al-Ahmar. By the 14th century, various rooms had been built for successive rulers, but as with so many Islamic gardens, water as well as containment and exposure are key features here.

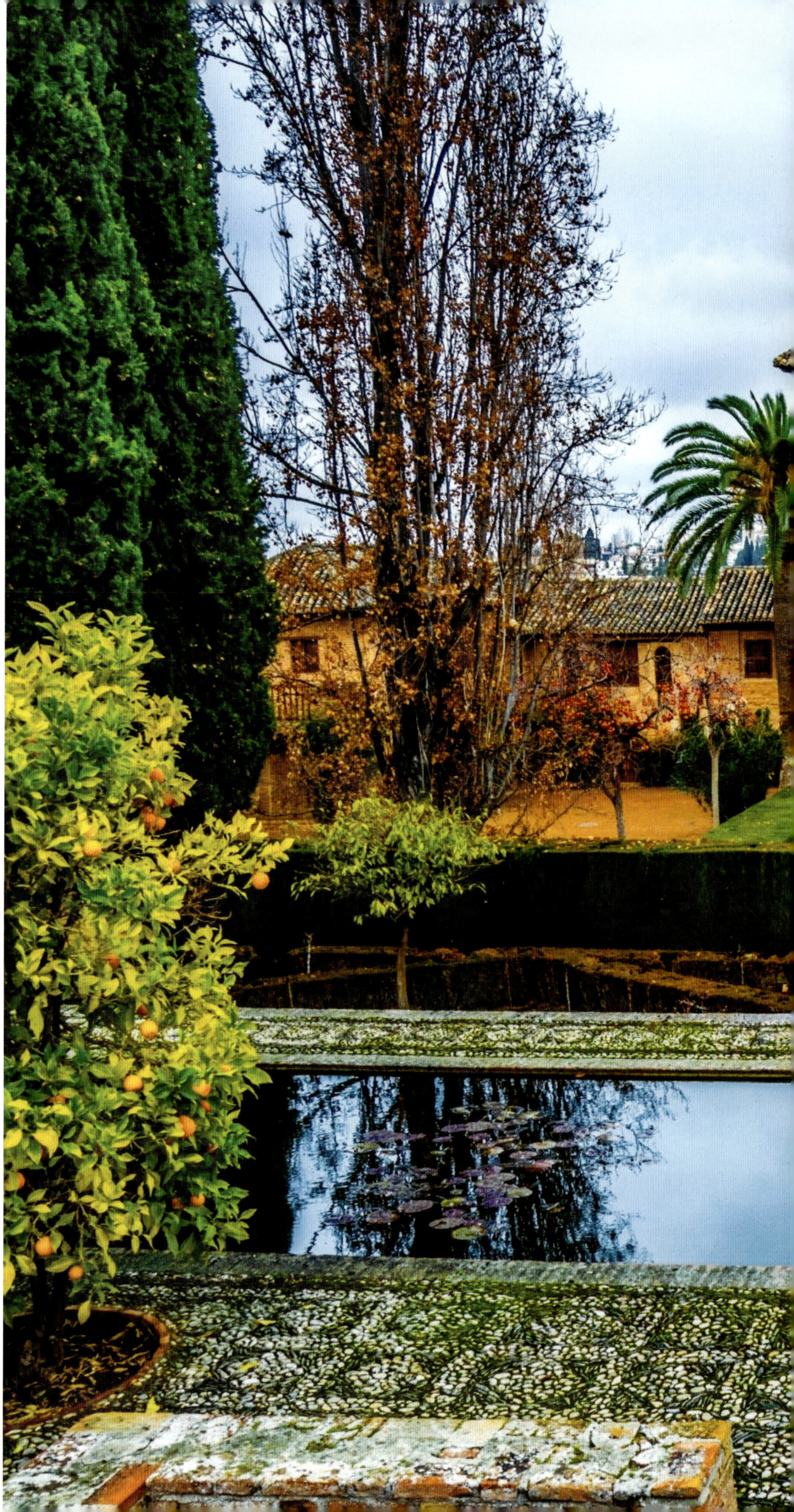

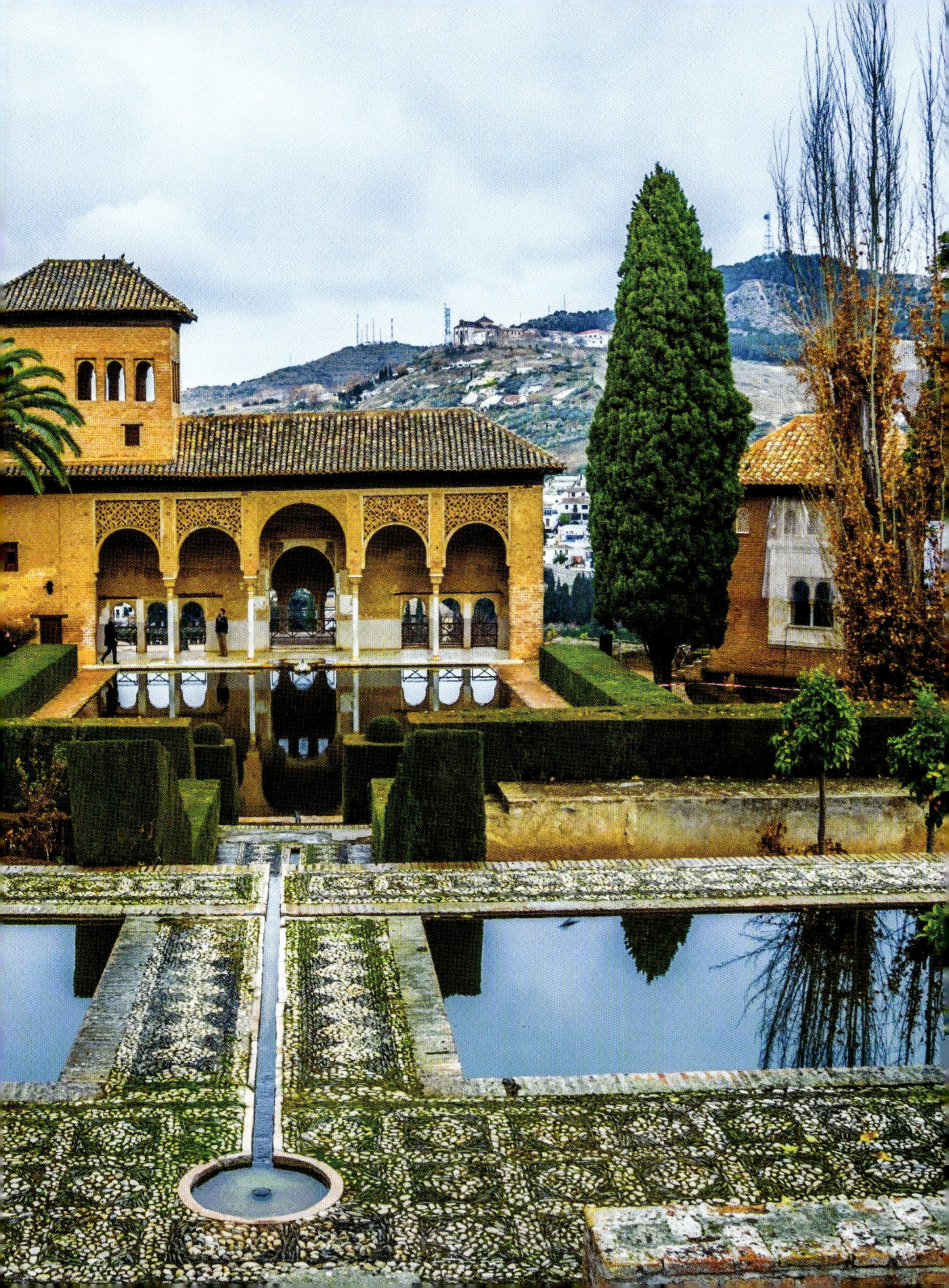

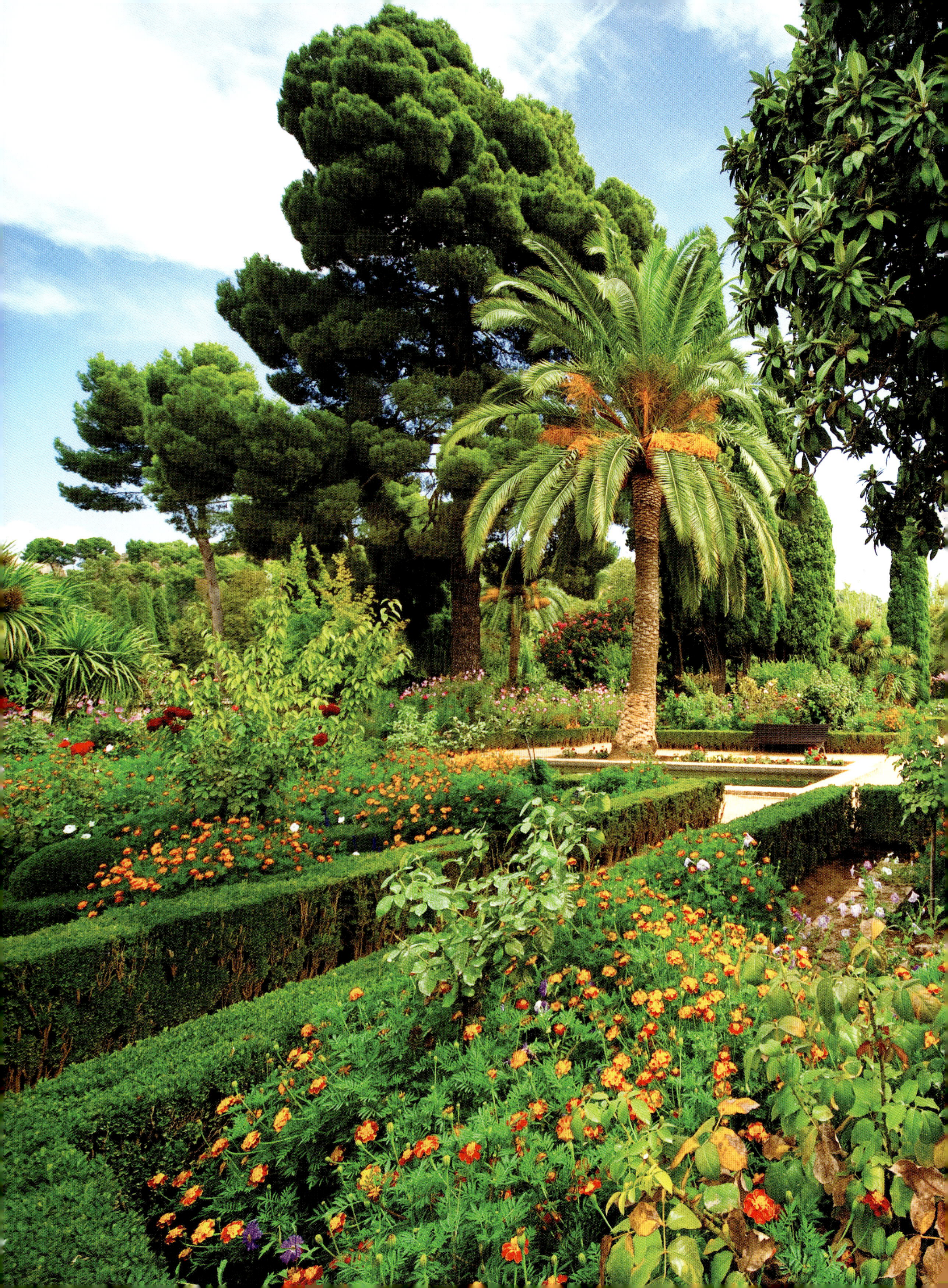

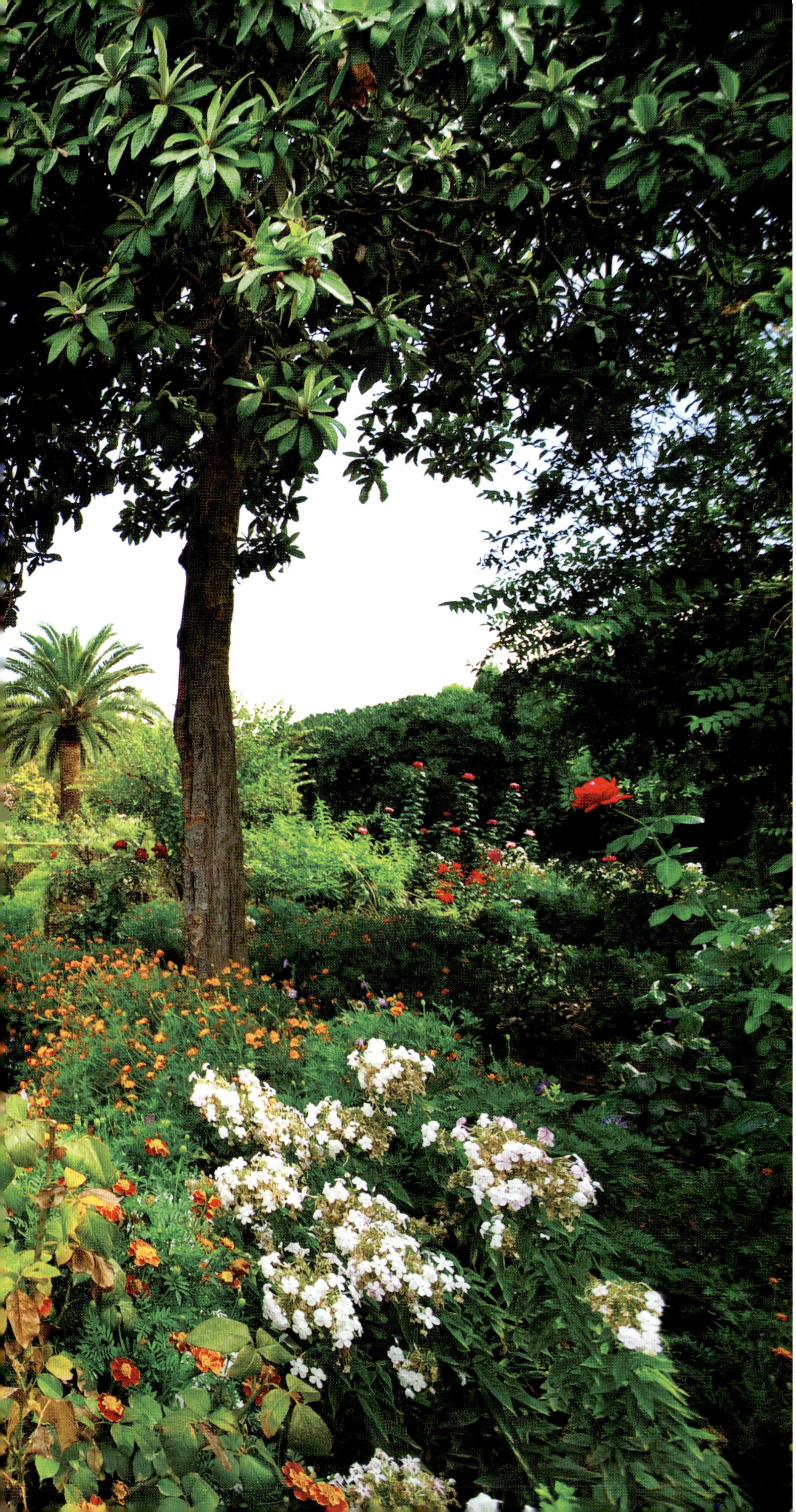

LEFT AND OVERLEAF LEFT TOP:

Alhambra, Granada, Spain

Columns, passages and courtyards offer a sublime visitor experience. Sections of the gardens include the Court of the Myrtiles and the Court of the Lions, which was built for Muhammad V and takes the form of the iconic Islamic chahar bagh, a square divided into four, with a central water feature. It is a UNESCO World Heritage Site.

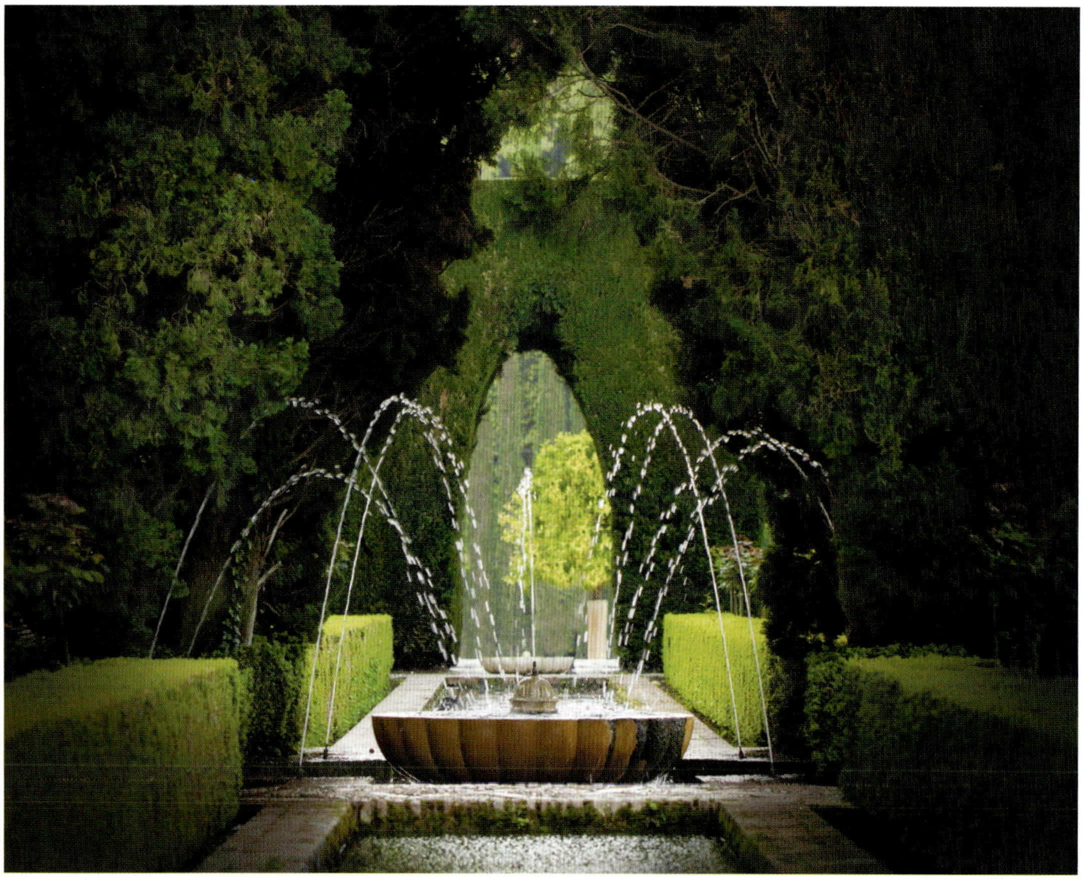

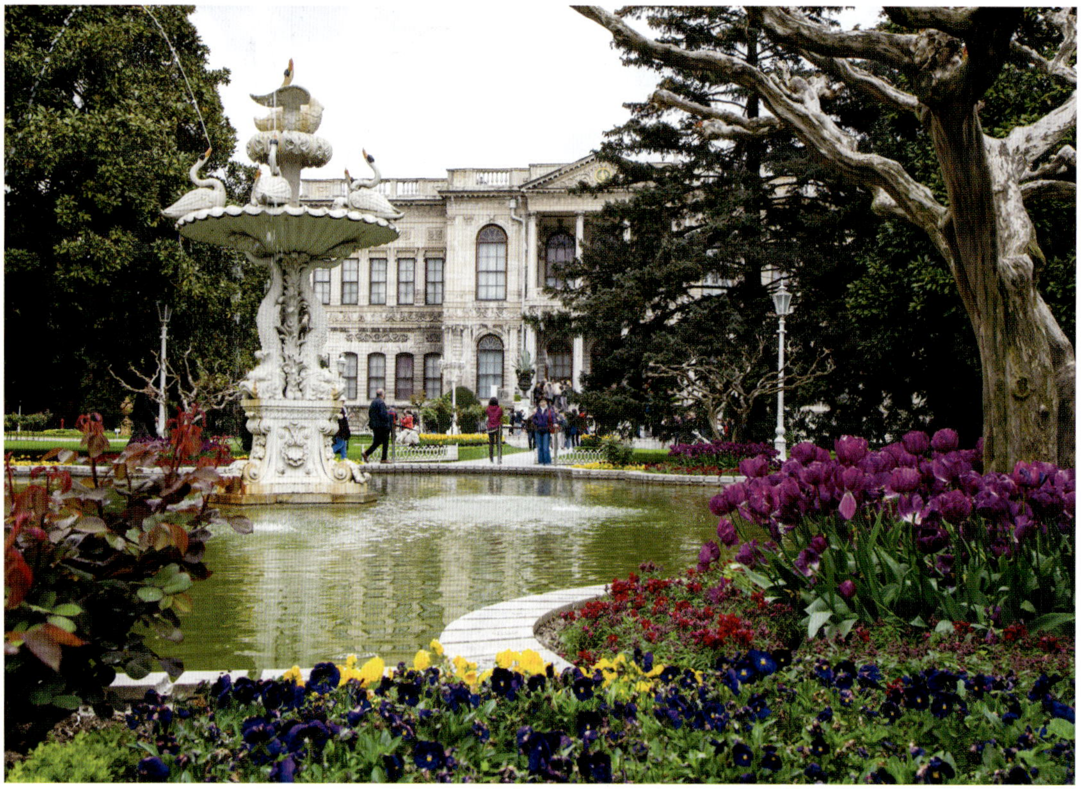

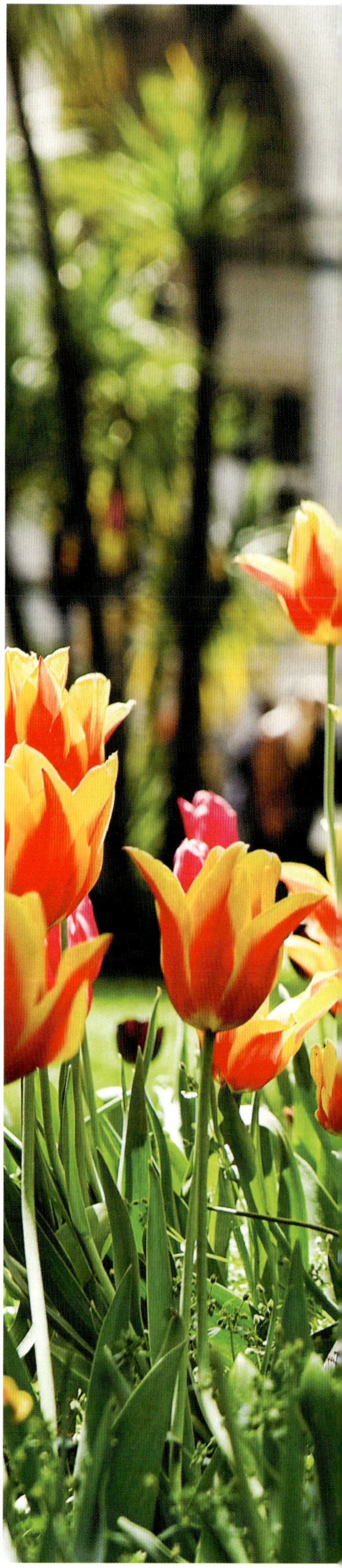

ABOVE BOTTOM AND RIGHT:

Topkapi Palace, Istanbul, Turkey

In Istanbul, overlooking the Bosphorus and the Sea of Marmara, the Ottoman sultan Mehmed the Conqueror built a large garden to cement his presence in the region. The gardens here are a sequence of interlinking rooms, housed within a much larger garden periphery. As in all Islamic gardens, water features prominently.

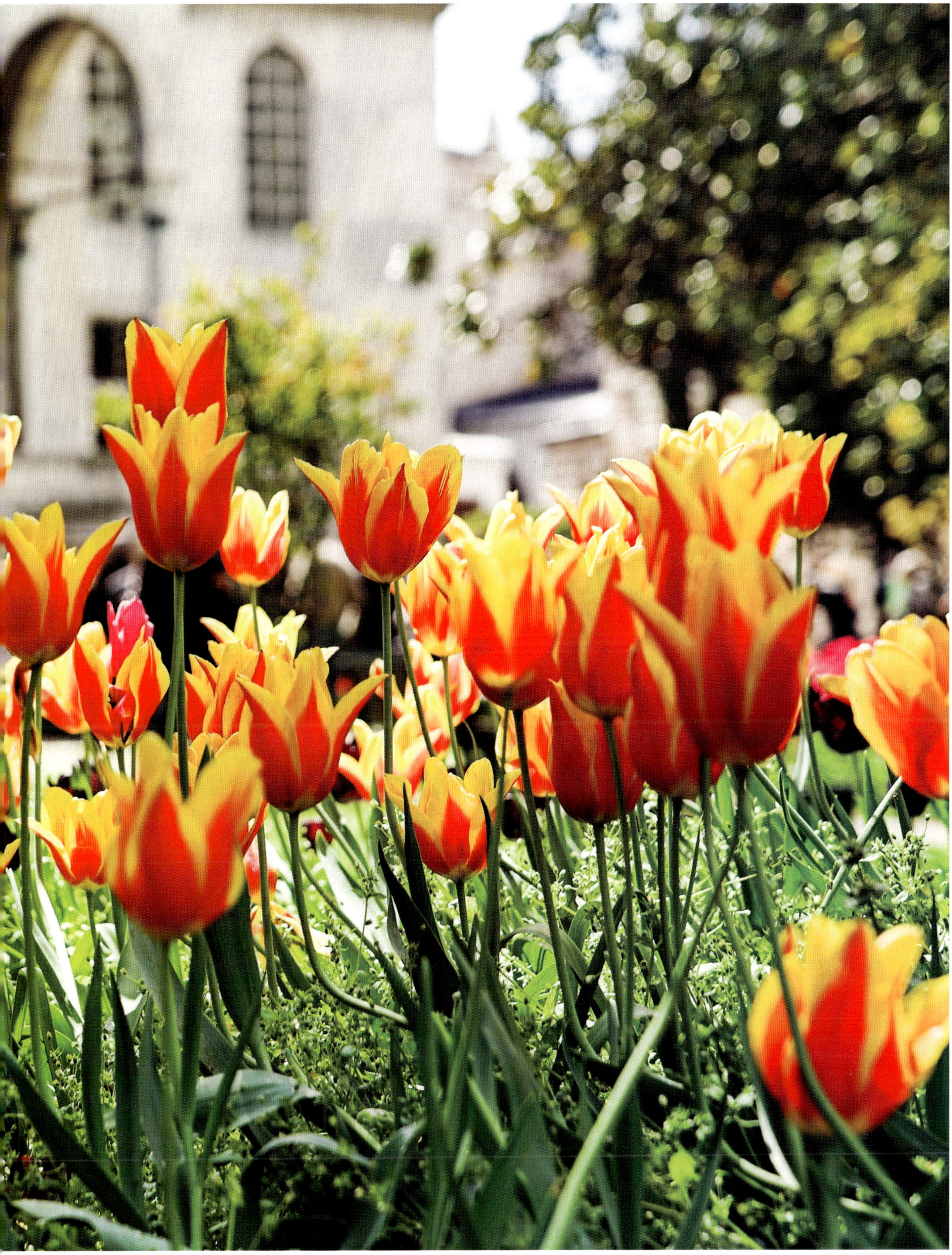

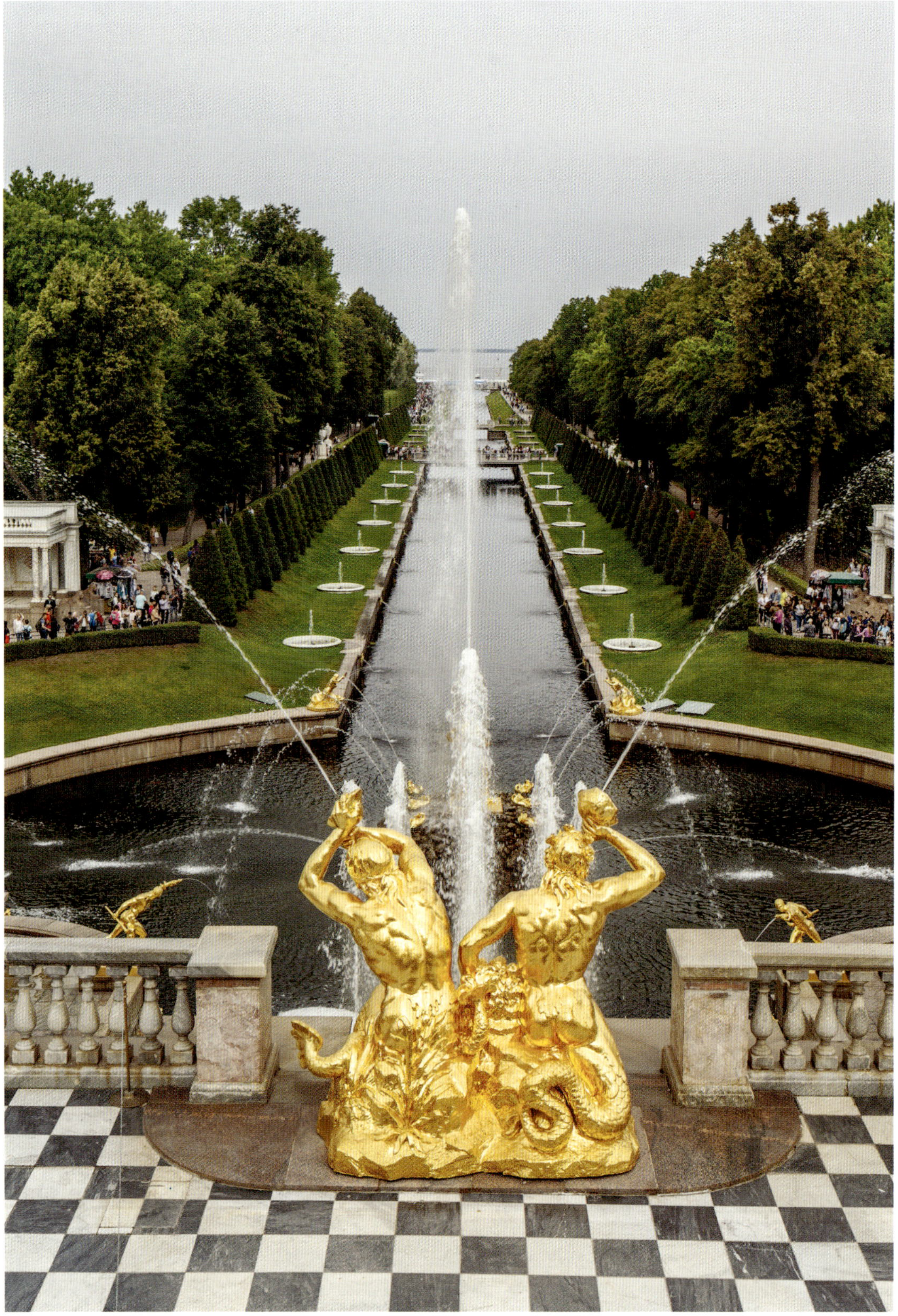

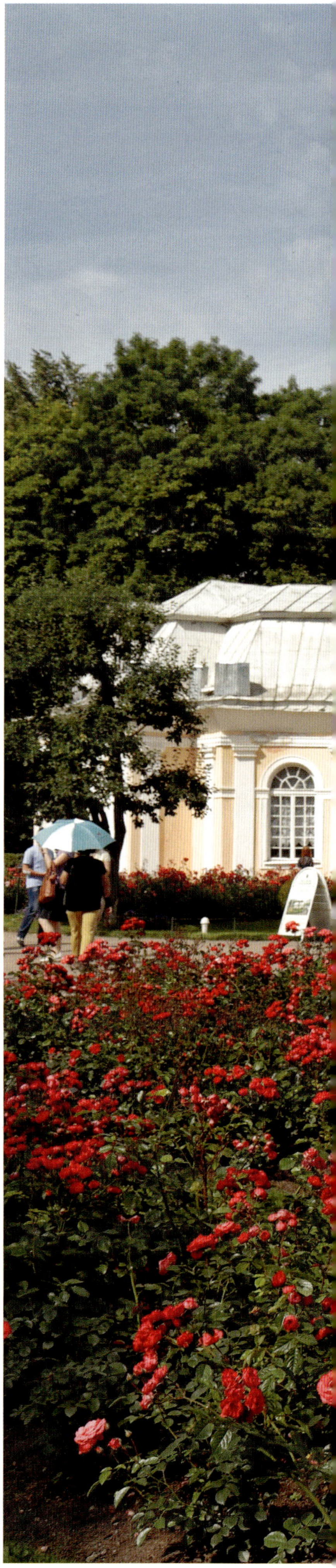

ABOVE & RIGHT:

Peterhof Palace, St Petersburg, Russia

A range of gardens styles prevails at this notable palace, which has won acclaim for its 64 fountains, terraces and cascades richly symbolic of Russian might. It was ordered by Peter the Great in the 18th century, who wished for his palace to rival Versailles – he went as far as appointing Jean-Baptiste Alexandre Le Blond, a contemporary of Versailles designer André Le Nôtre.

Inevitably for such a great garden, Peterhof has seen its fortunes fluctuate over centuries. It was raided by German forces in World War II, when the palace was captured and left to burn. The fountains were ruined and fighting took place in the Lower Gardens. Extensive restoration projects have brought this property back to life and the site marked its 300th anniversary in 2003.

OVERLEAF:

Kadriorg Palace, Tallinn, Estonia

After capturing Tallinn in 1710, Peter the Great ordered Kadriorg Palace for his wife, Catherine, and work began on it in 1718. It was little used, however, and much of what we see today is the 19th century vision of Nicholas I of Russia. Baroque planting was restored in the late 1990s.

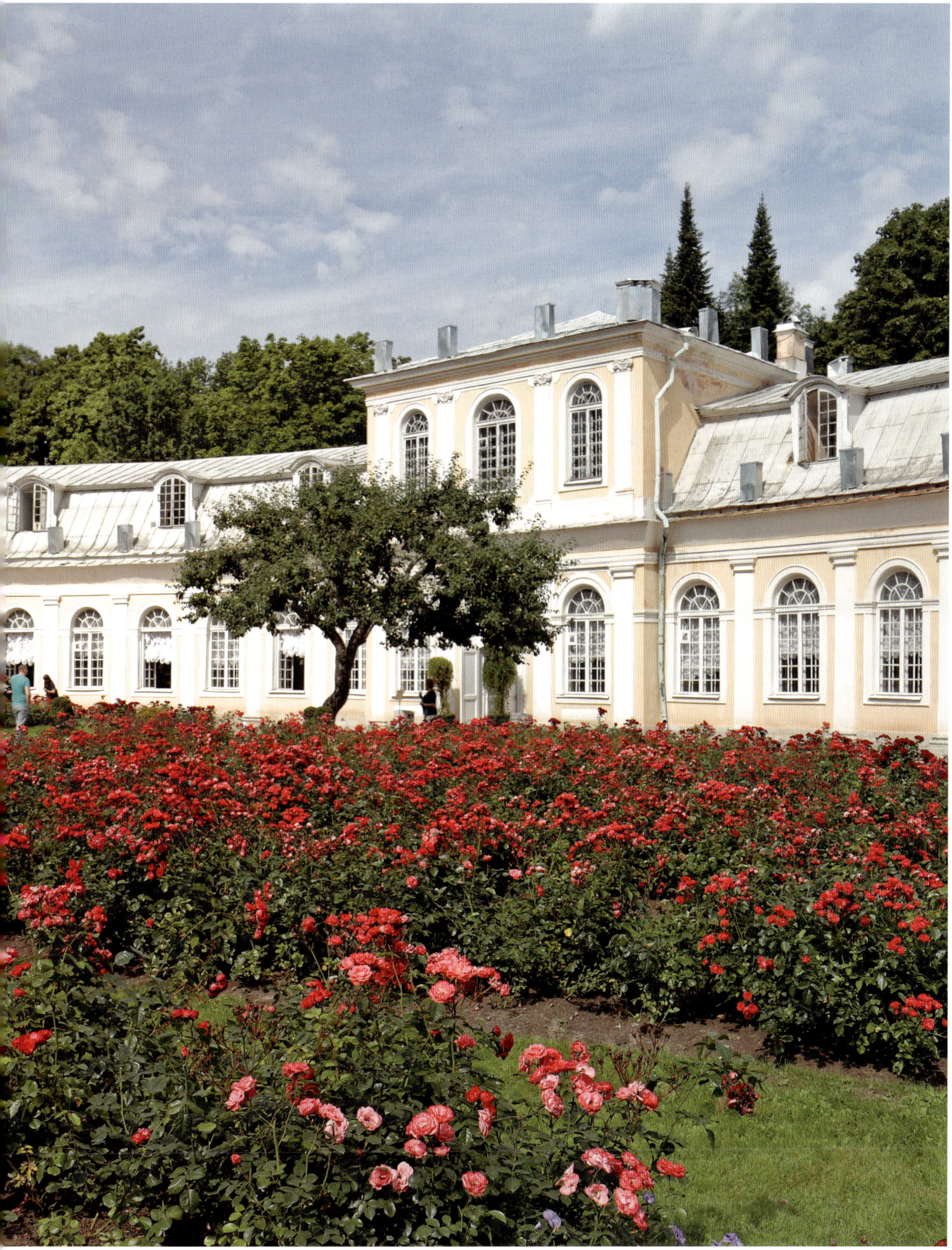

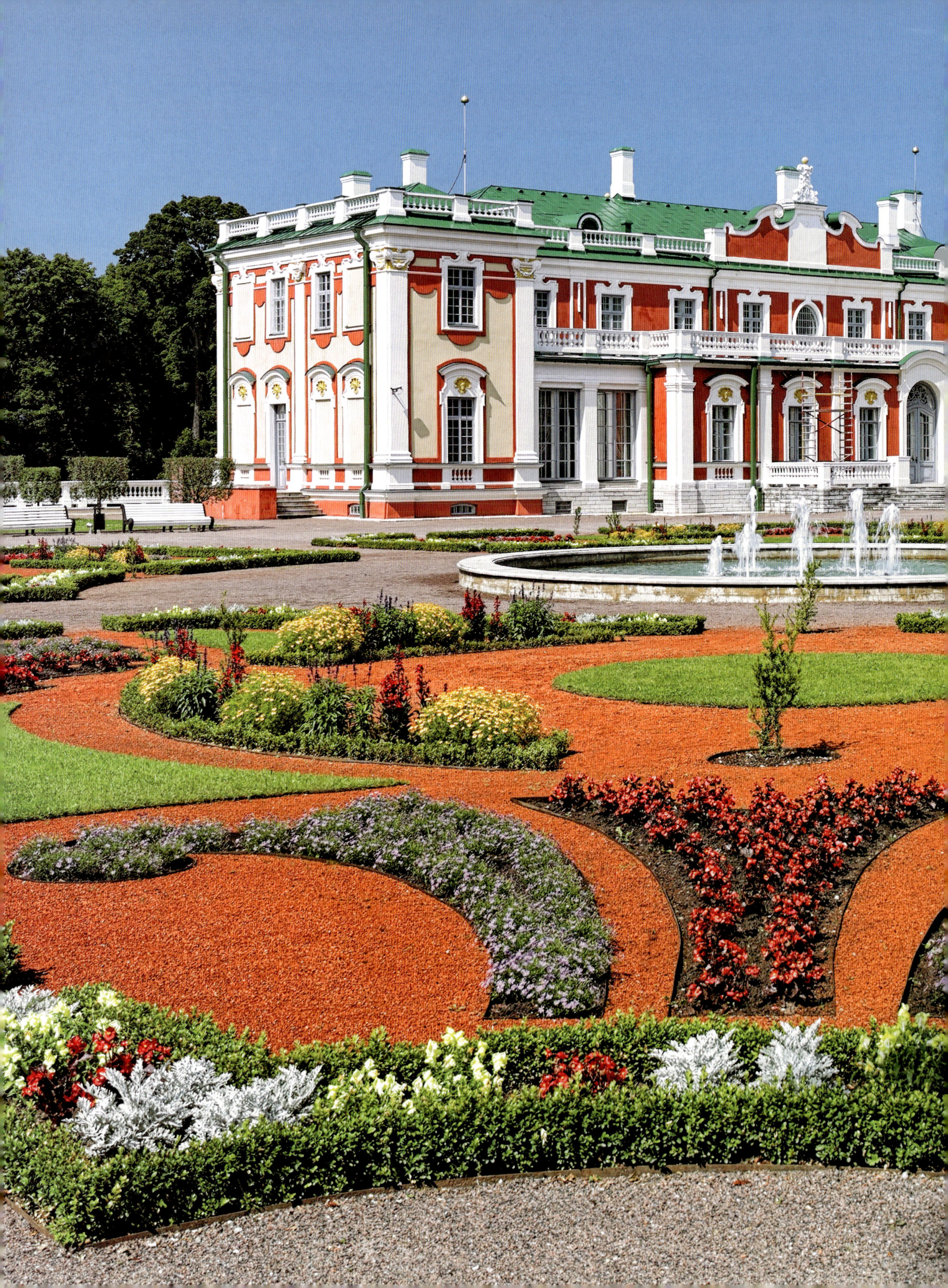

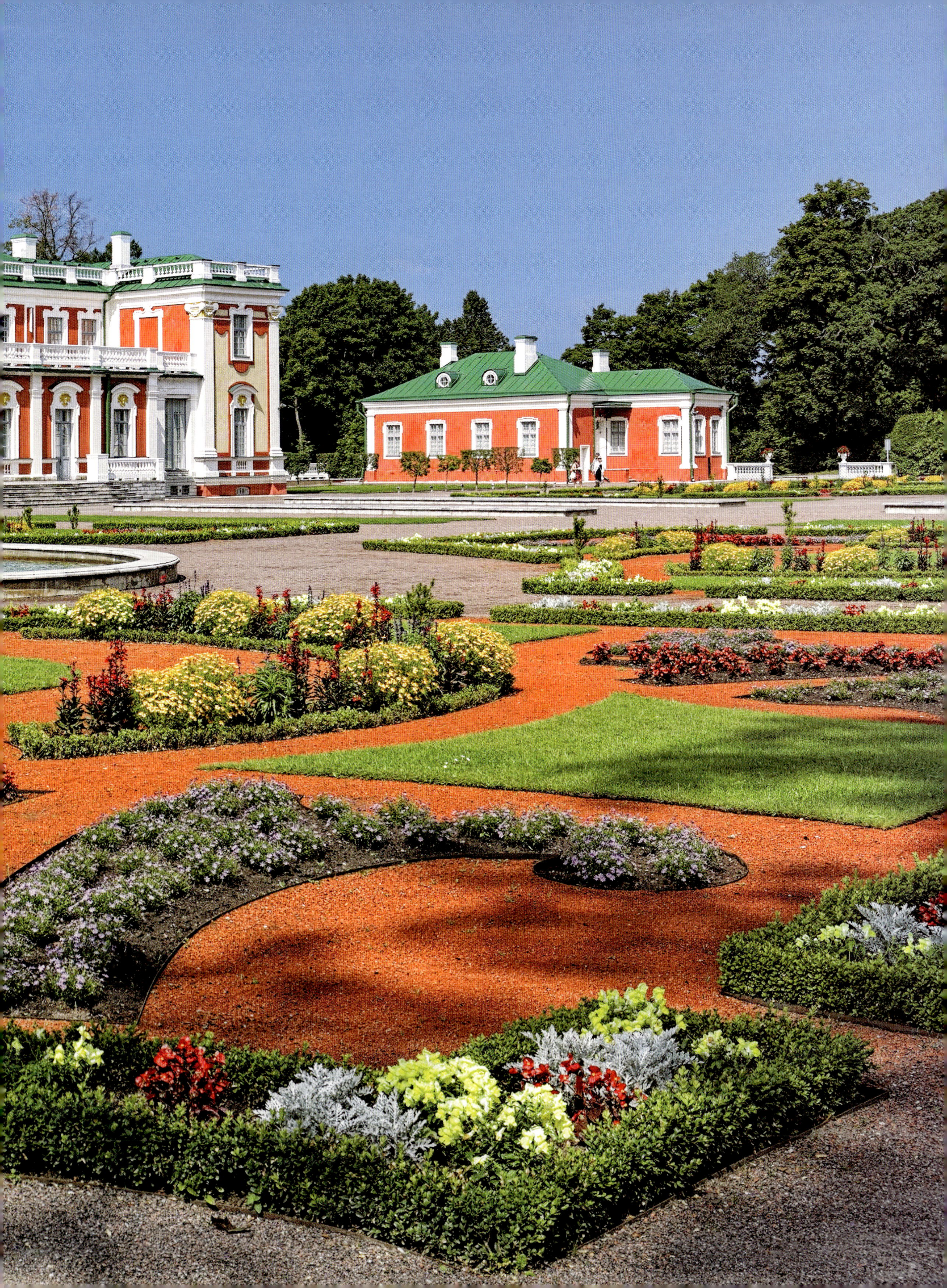

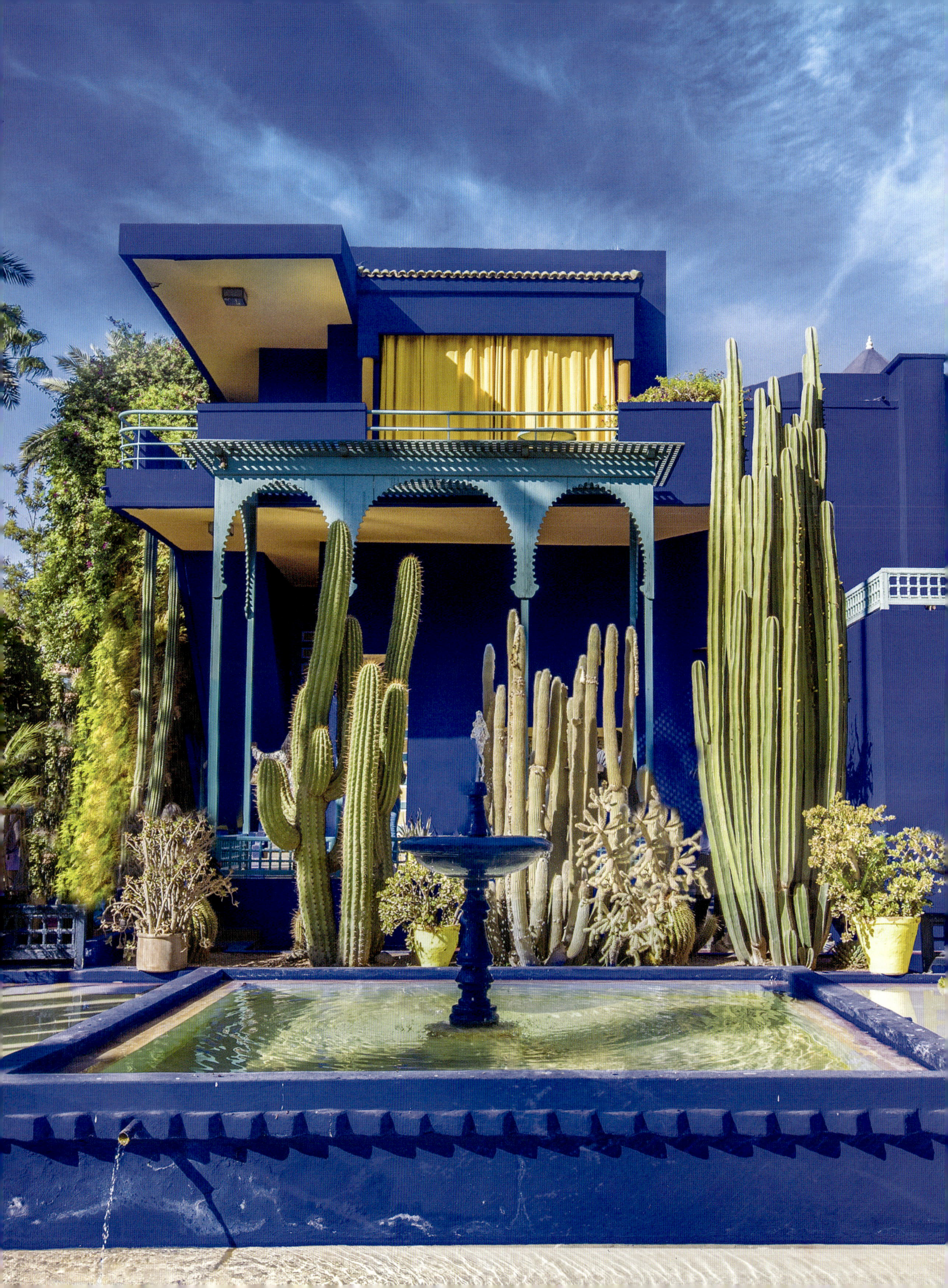

Africa and the Middle East

For much of Africa, the act of survival defines what may be grown. In the north, where resources are scant, the Berbers or Amazighs must be nomadic to live. South of the Sahara, all the way down to the Nguni tribes of southern Africa, subsistence farmers hold up the continent, with rare capacity for ornamental gardening. Yet, where ornamental gardens do exist, they are magnificent, often reflecting the colonial powers that scrambled for this resource-rich continent. In Morocco, the French painter Jacques Majorelle was so taken with the colours used by the Amazigh around him, that he splashed cobalt blue across walls and fountains to create a compelling spectacle of a garden in this arid country. The tropical islands of Mauritius and the Seychelles saw both French and British rule which is echoed in their long-established botanic gardens. On the very tip of the continent, the first white settler at the Cape of Good Hope, now Cape Town, Jan van Riebeeck, planted a defensive hedge on a farm in 1660. In what is now Kirstenbosch National Botanical Garden a remnant remains, but far more striking today is a Camphor Avenue planted by the British in 1898.

Arab influences have trickled into East Africa for centuries but it is in the Middle East itself that the classic Islamic garden, the chahar bagh, is most pronounced. In Iran, on the banks of the River Koshk, the Bagh-e Eram takes its name from what we can only dream of: paradise.

OPPOSITE:

Jardin Majorelle, Marrakesh-Safi, Morocco

In Marrakesh, this extraordinary garden, one of the most striking and best-known in Africa, was originally the work of French painter Jacques Majorelle. The artist began work here in 1924 and painted walls, fountains and rills in a distinctive cobalt blue he had seen used in Amazigh or Berber communities.

Jardin Majorelle, Marrakesh-Safi, Morocco
The garden was bought in 1980 by fashion designer Yves Saint Laurent and Pierre Bergé, his partner. Their intention was to restore the property, which had fallen into neglect after Majorelle's divorce in the 1950s and death in 1963. The Musée Berbère is at the heart of the garden and contains Amazigh artefacts initially collected by Majorelle. In 2017, a further museum housing the items from the collection of Yves Saint Laurent and Pierre Bergé was opened. The ashes of Laurent, who died in 2008, are scattered in the garden.

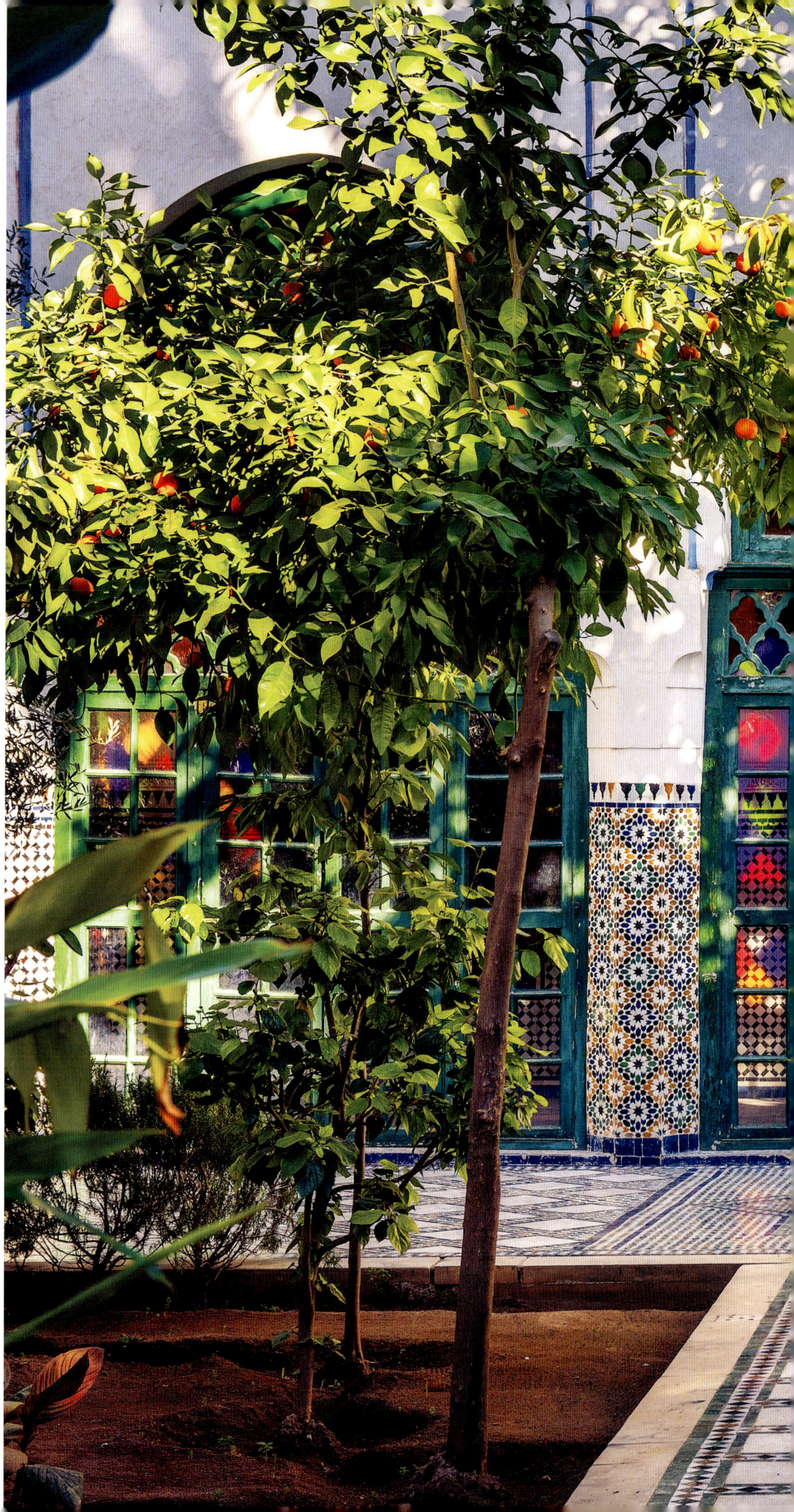

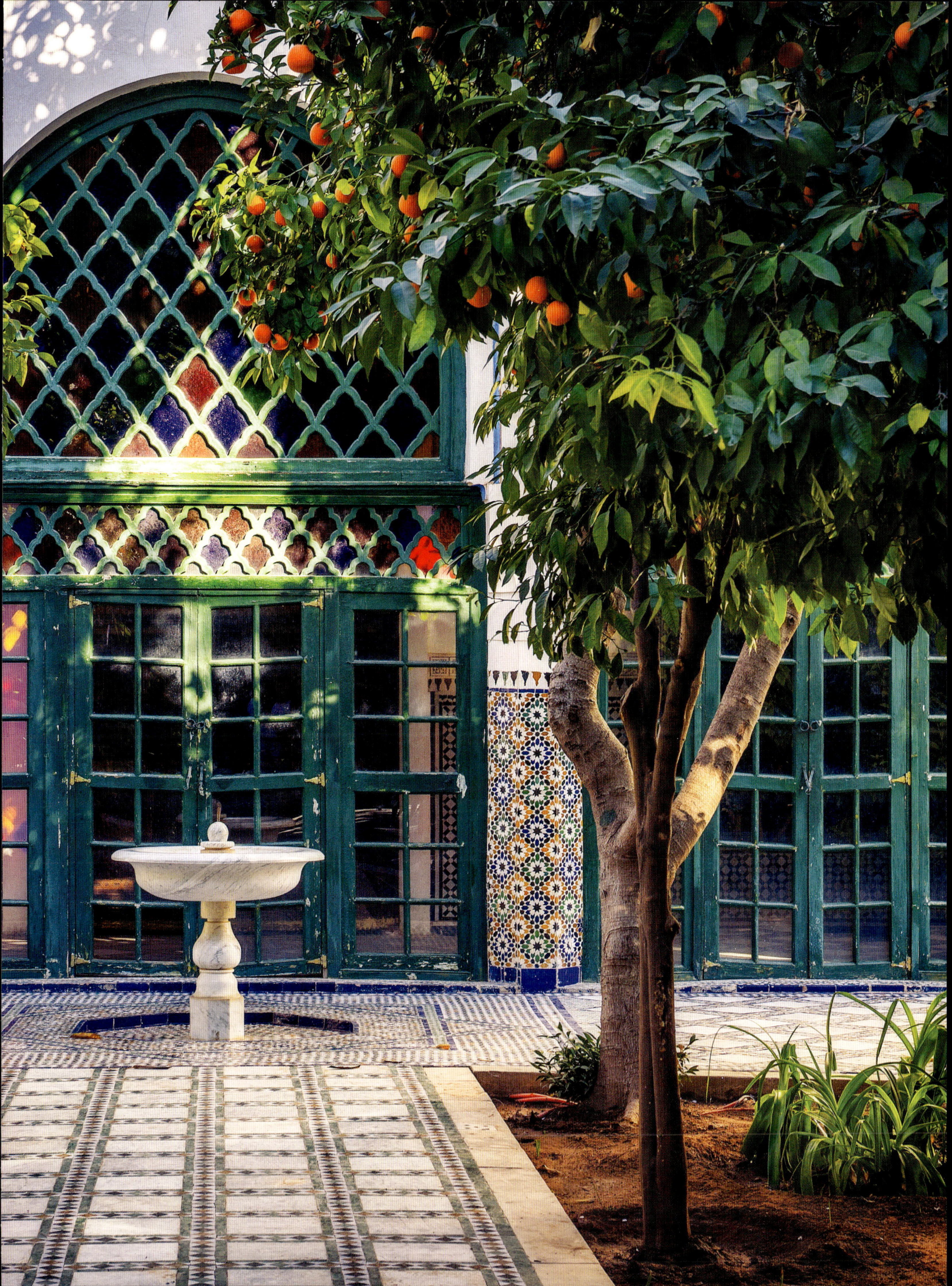

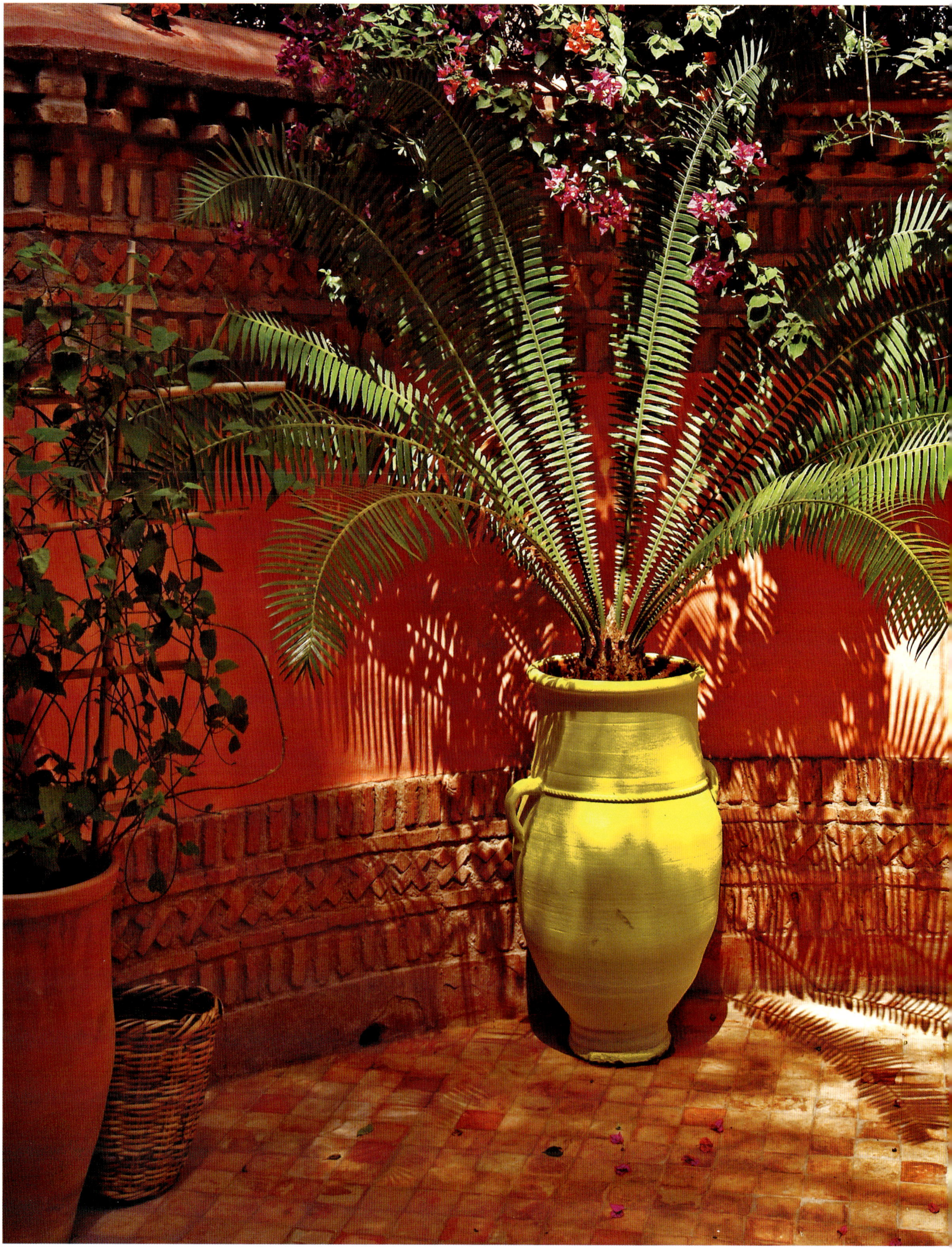

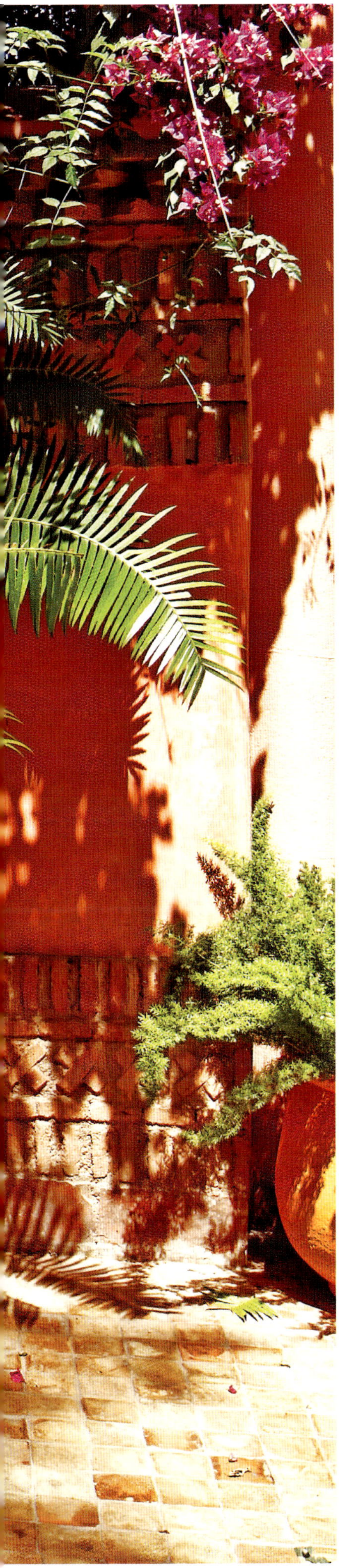

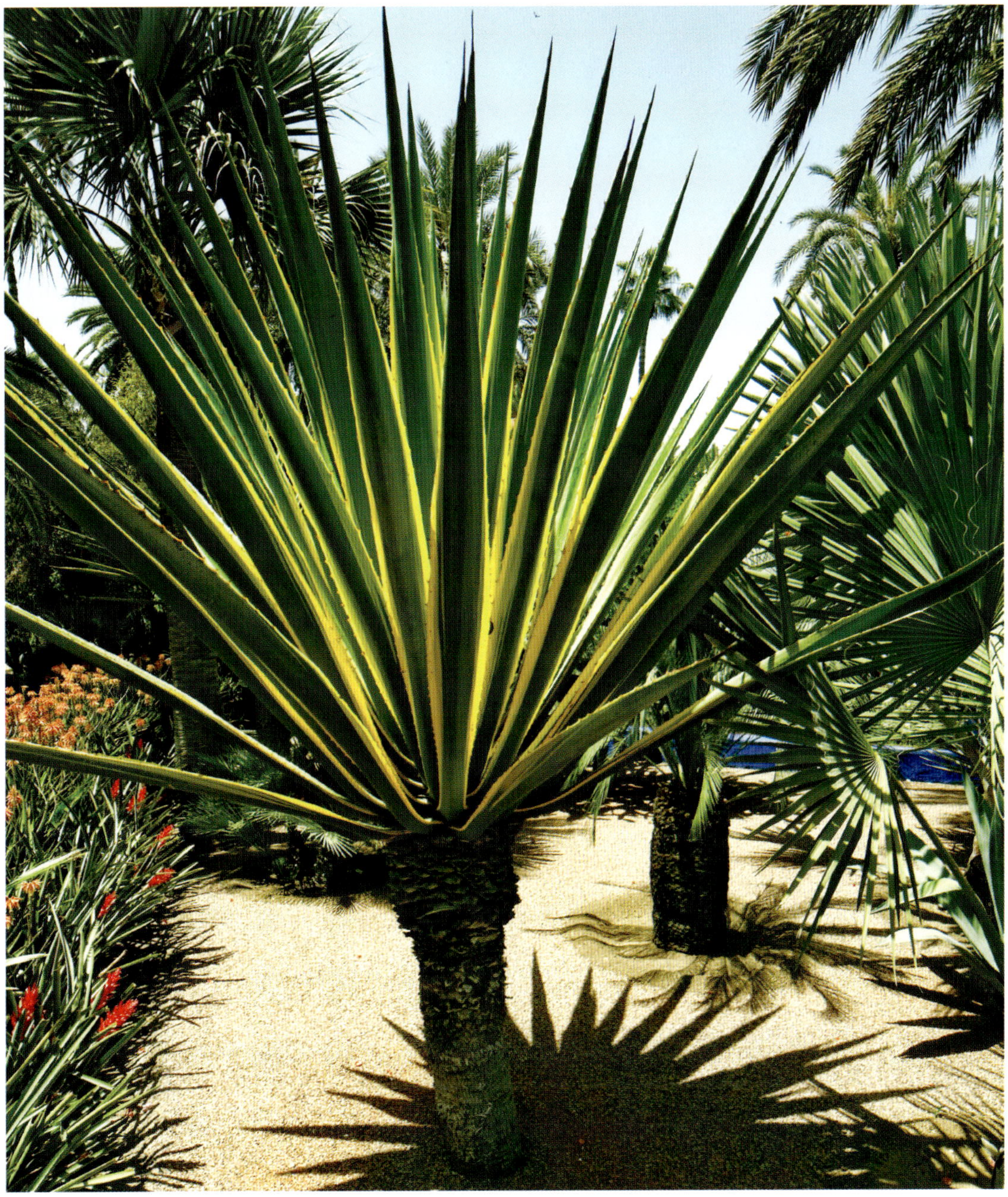

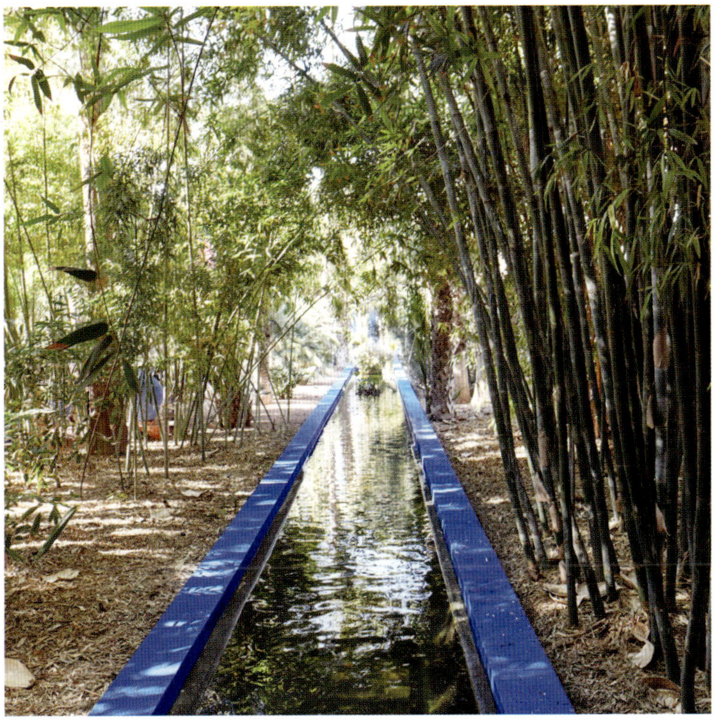

ALL PHOTOGRAPHS:
Jardin Majorelle, Marrakesh-Safi, Morocco
In addition to painting, Majorelle was also a keen plant collector and spent decades working on the garden. Water, whether in fountains, furrows or rills, is dominant here, in echoes of traditional Islamic gardens. There is a fine collection of cacti, while bamboos, succulents and palms add to the mood of the property.

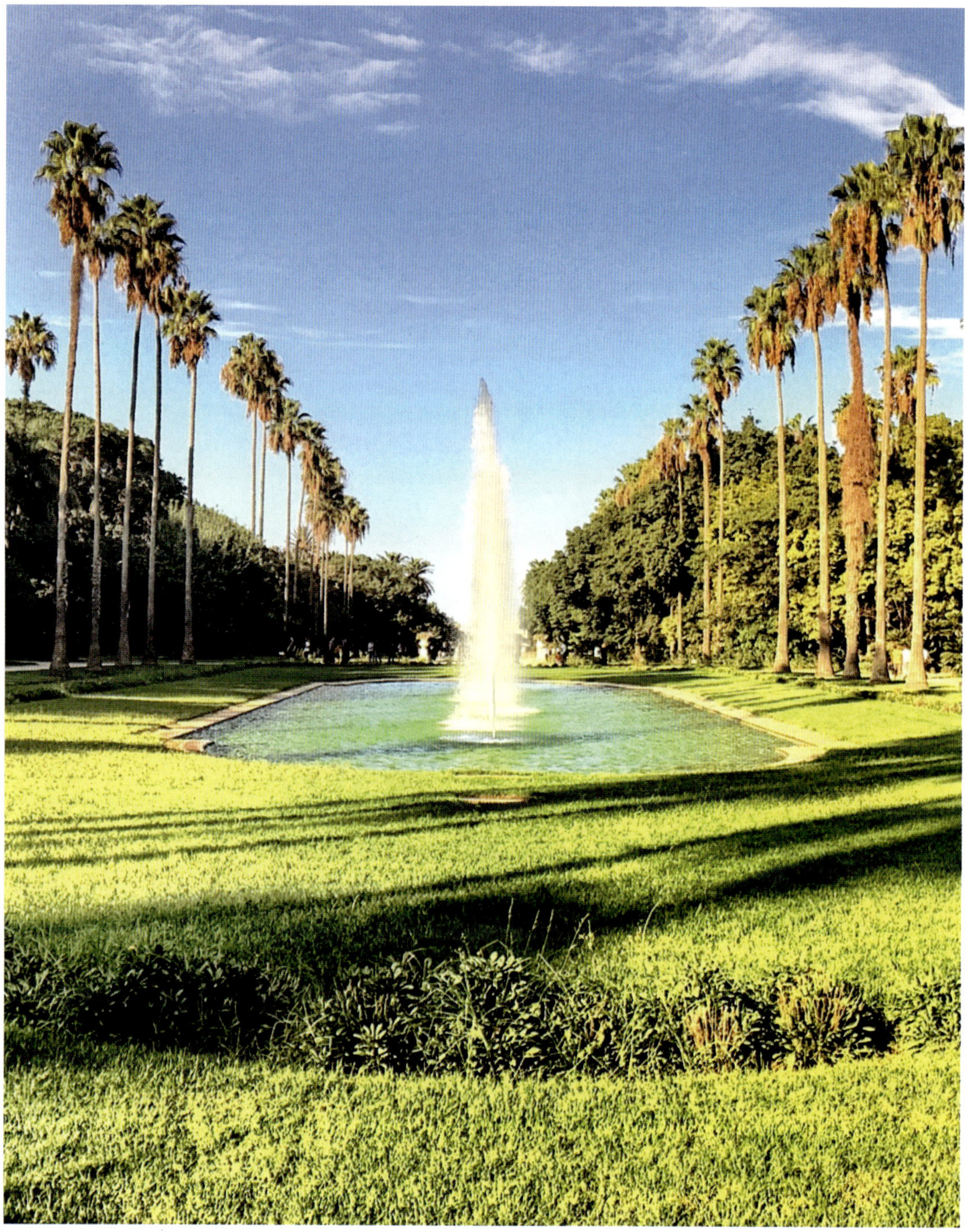

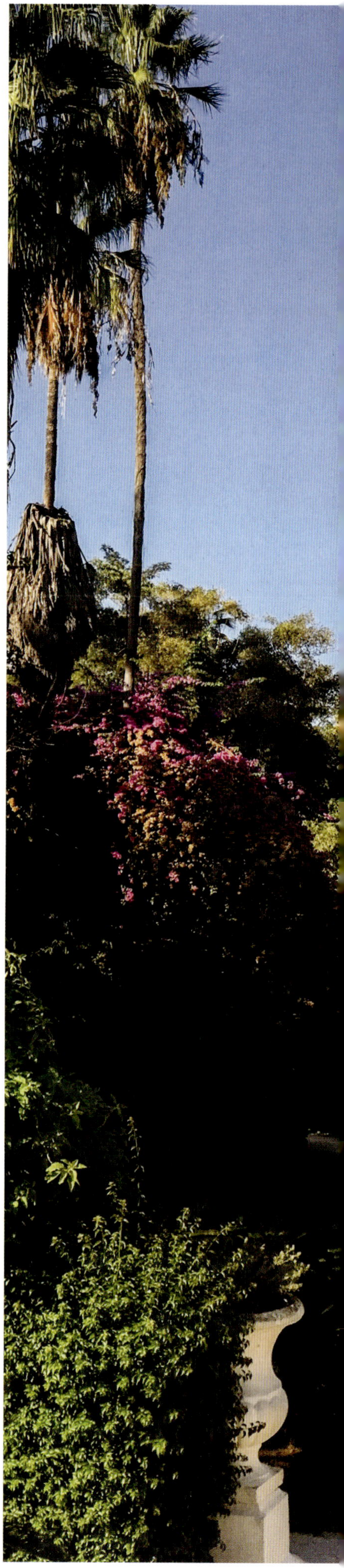

BOTH PHOTOGRAPHS:

El-Hamma Botanical Garden, Algiers, Algeria

Fashioned from drained ground in the Bay of Algiers in 1832, this 32ha (79-acre) botanical garden carries the influences of its French and English colonial powers. Bougainvilleas and palm trees create lush vistas here, and a broad walk affords views down to the sea. Initially used as a trial garden, it is today a popular public park.

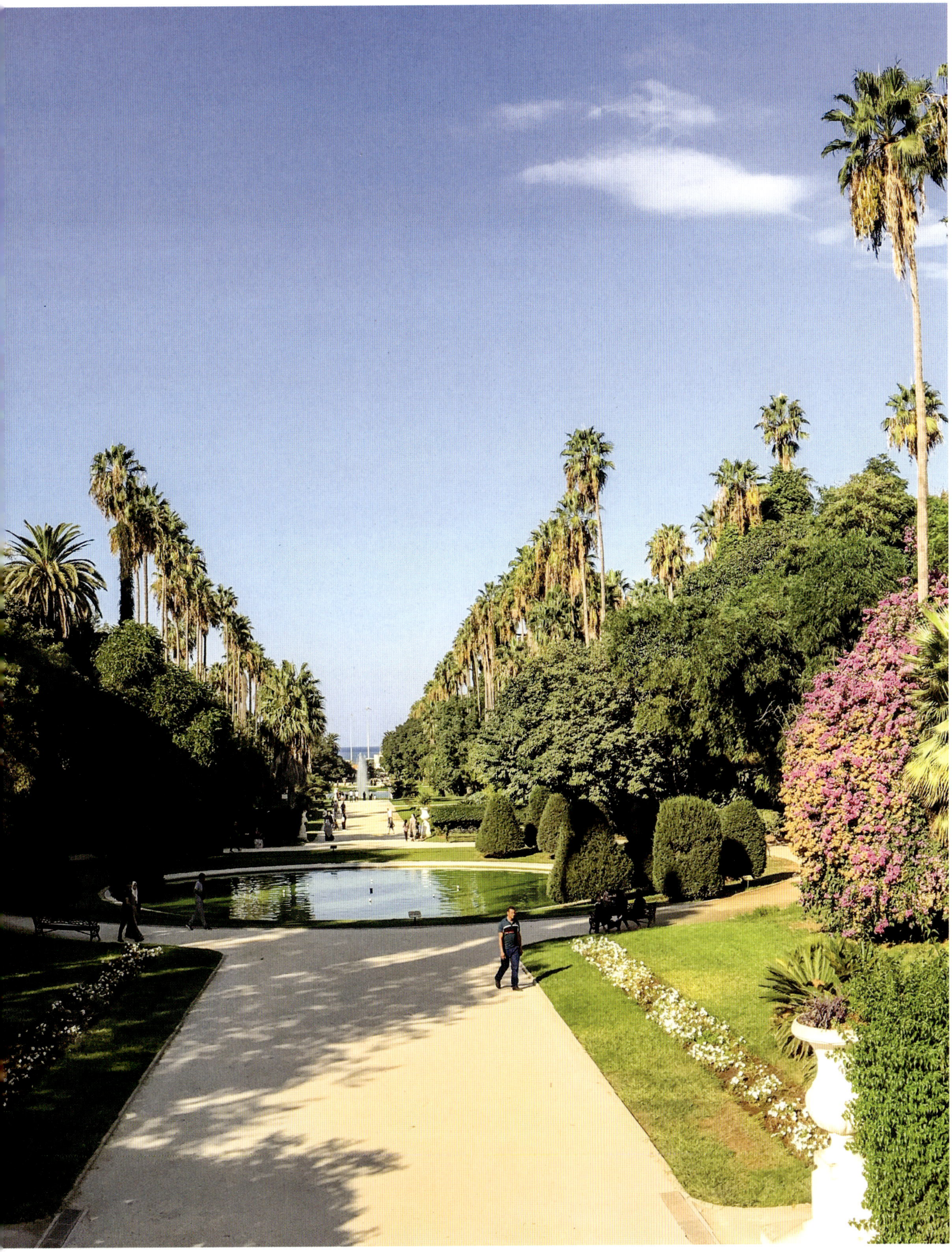

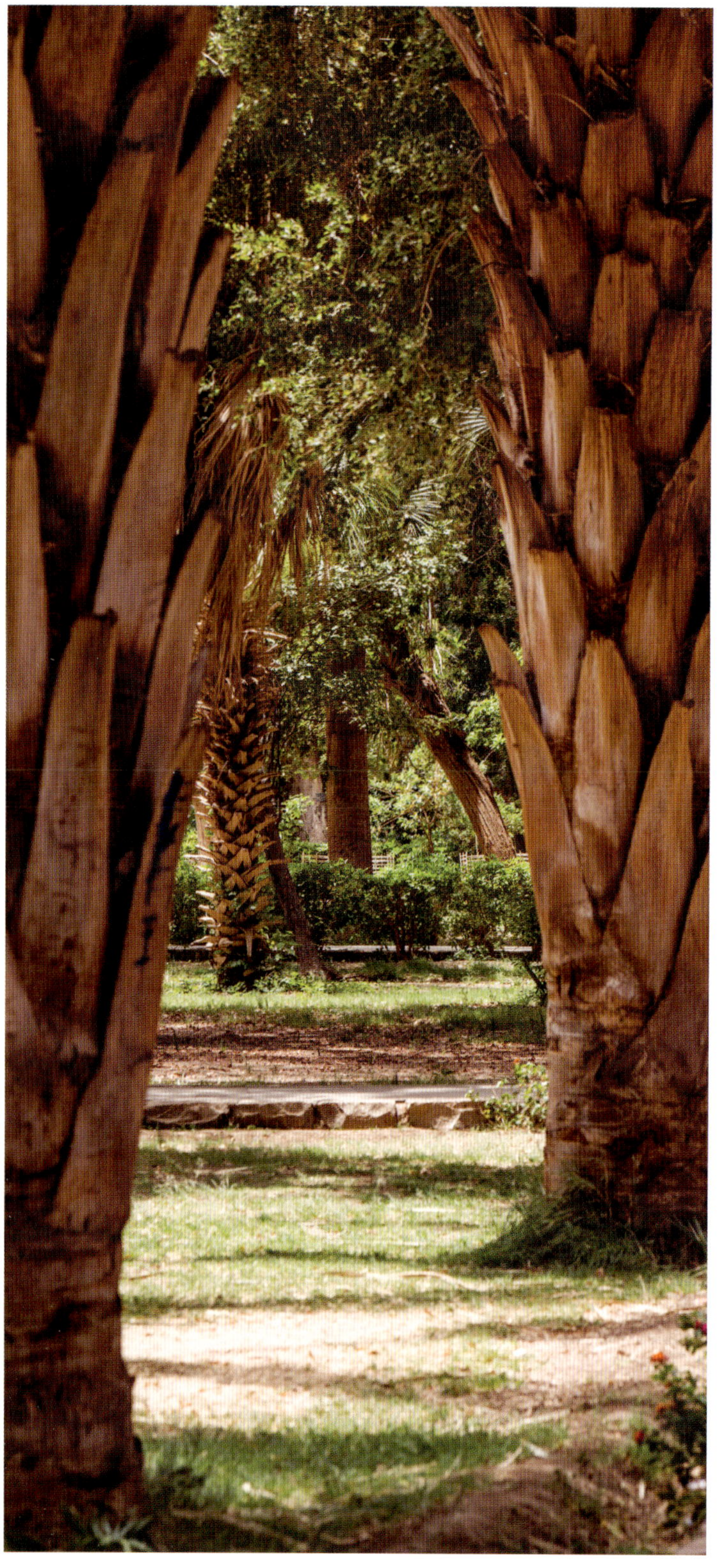

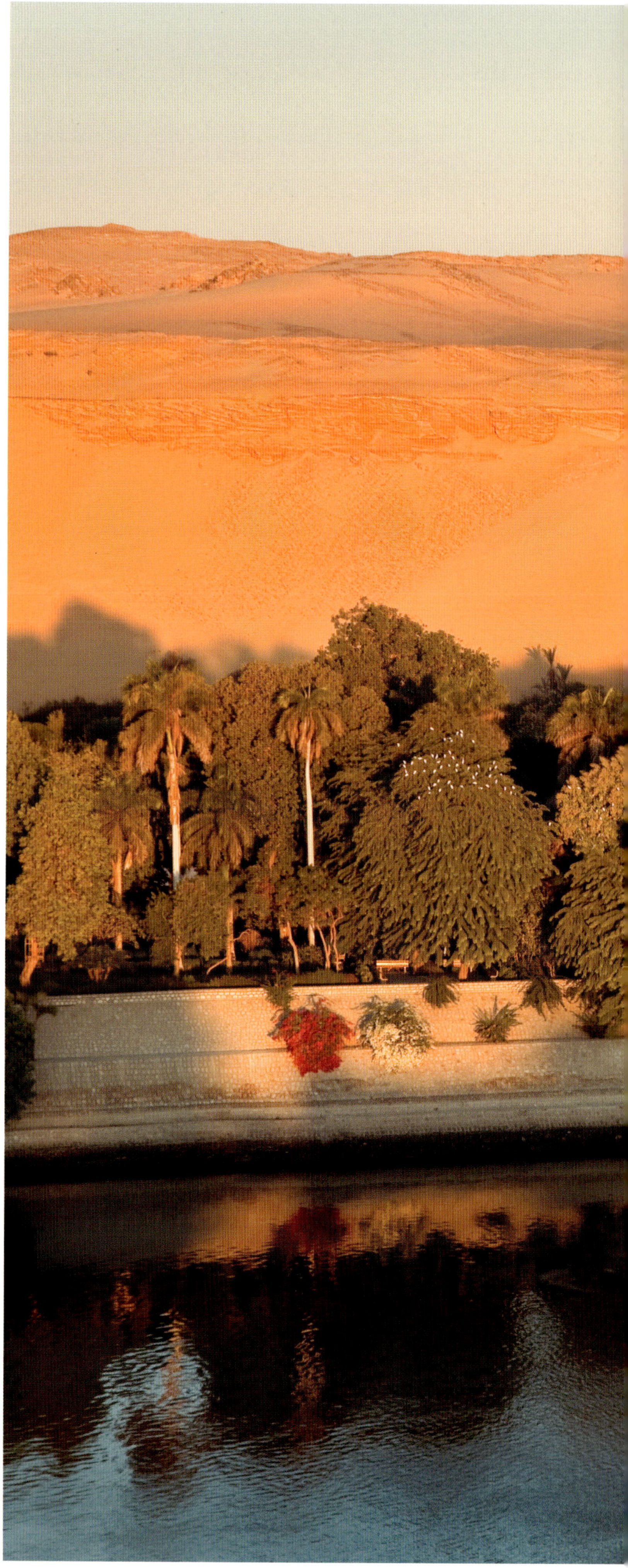

BOTH PHOTOGRAPHS:

Aswan Botanical Garden, Aswan, Egypt

A striking backdrop of sand dunes defines the Aswan Botanical Garden, which occupies the entire El Nabatat Island, on the river Nile. The island was once in the possession of Lord Kitchener and has also been known as Kitchener's Island. Kitchener planned paths and irrigation patterns that made cultivation here possible. He also began a collection of tropical plants from around the world, which is now maintained by the Botanical Research Institute on the island.

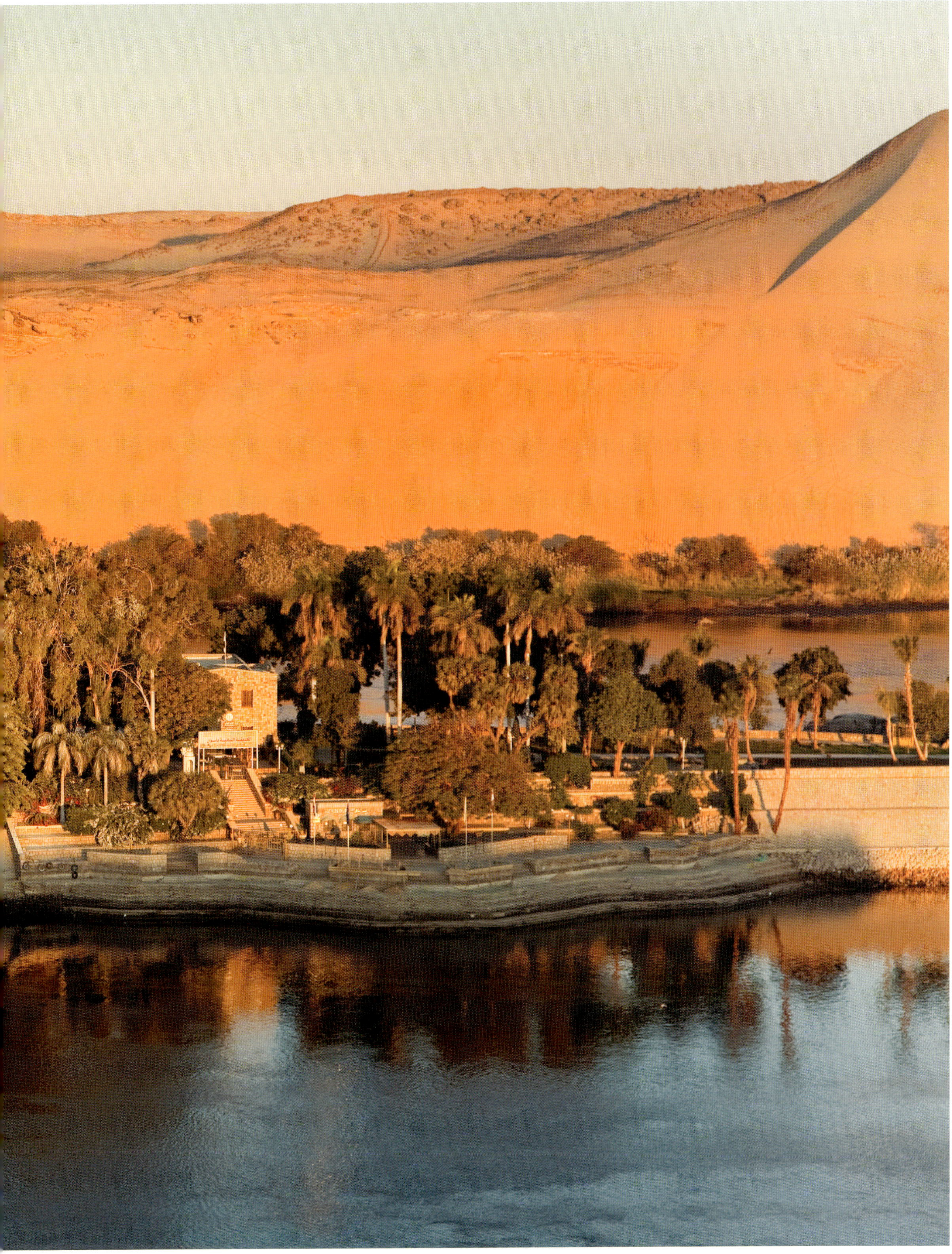

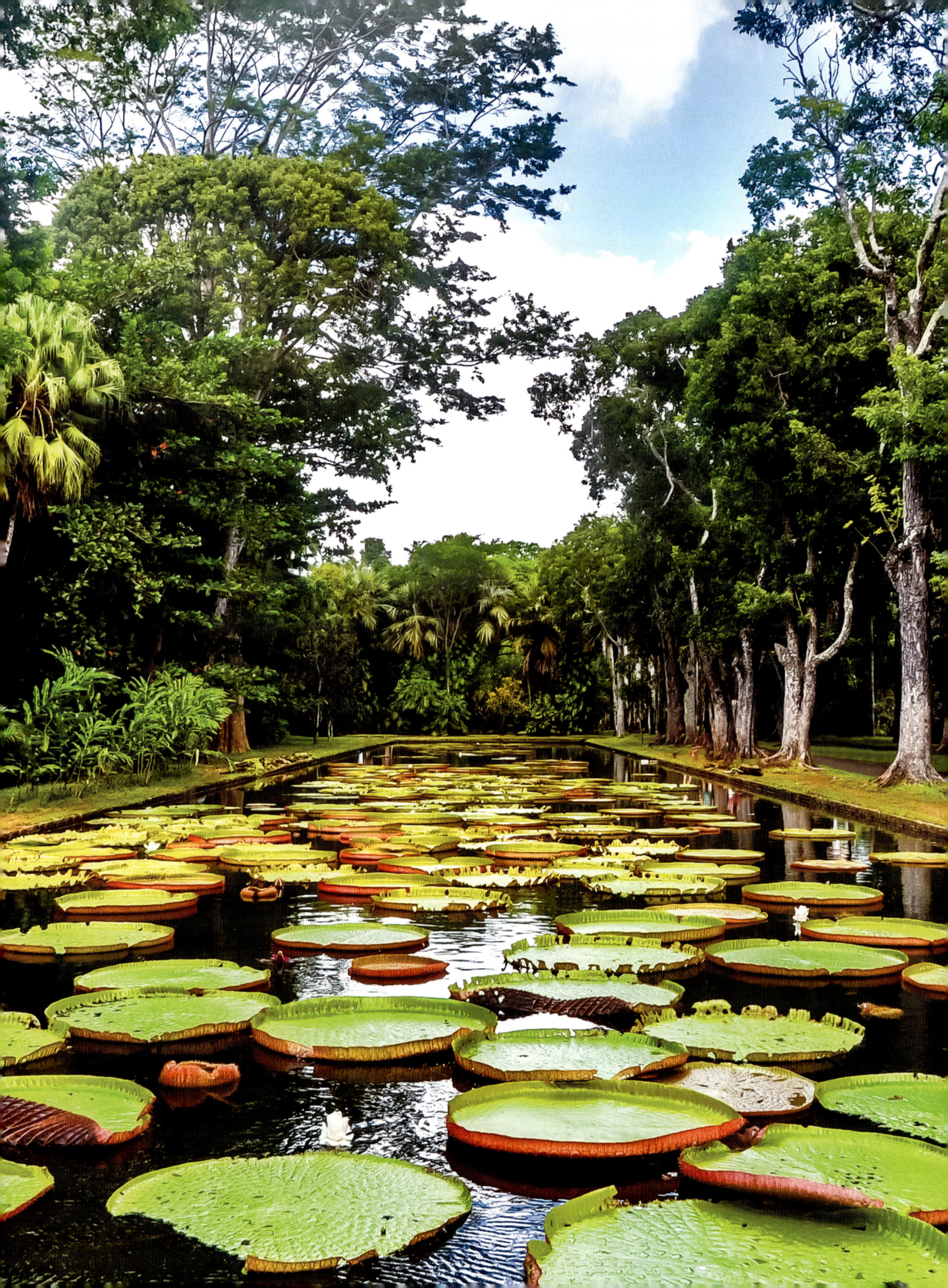

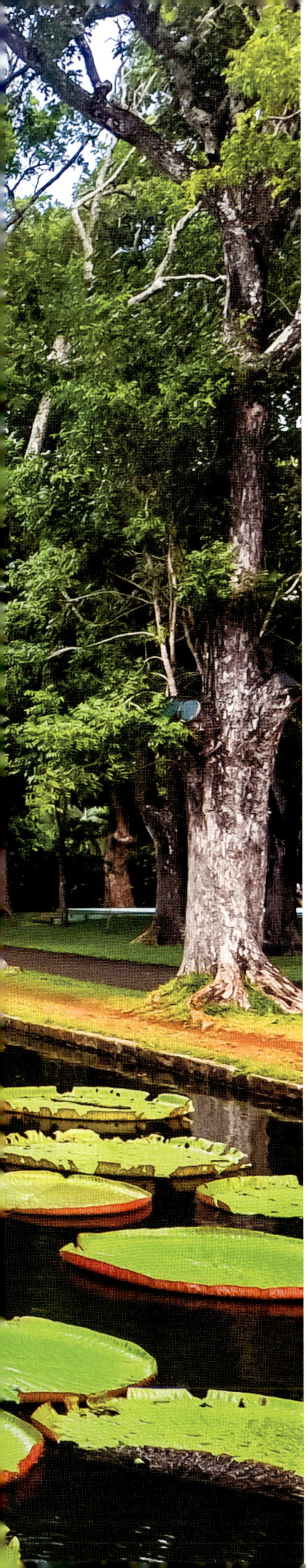

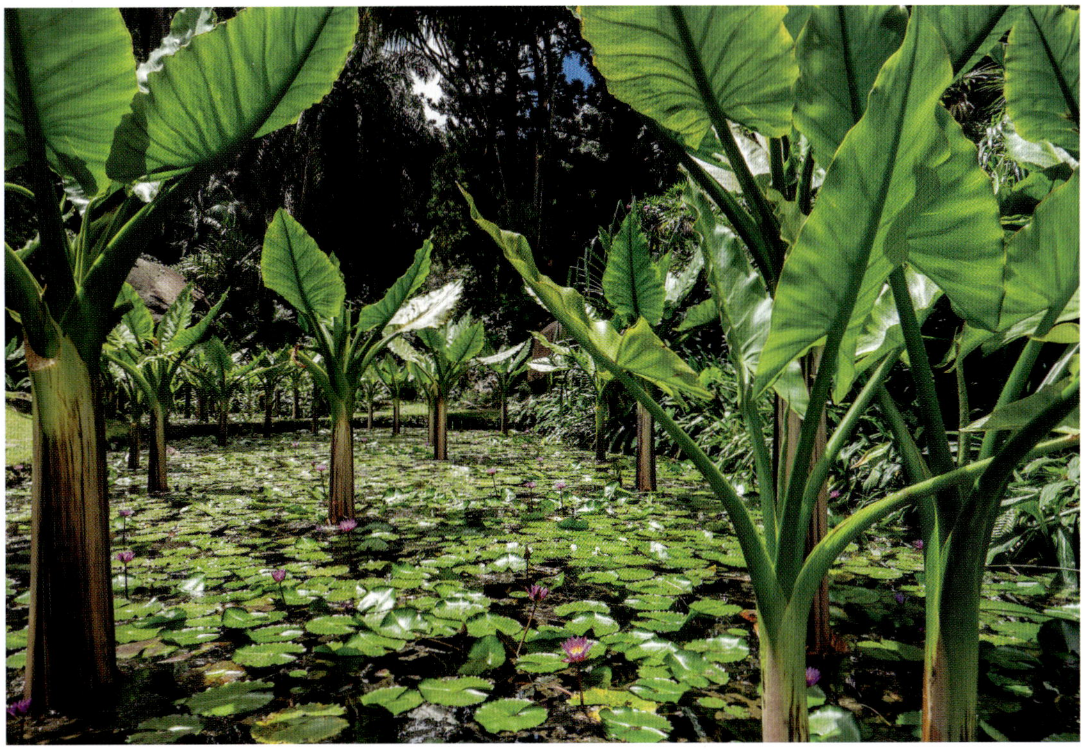

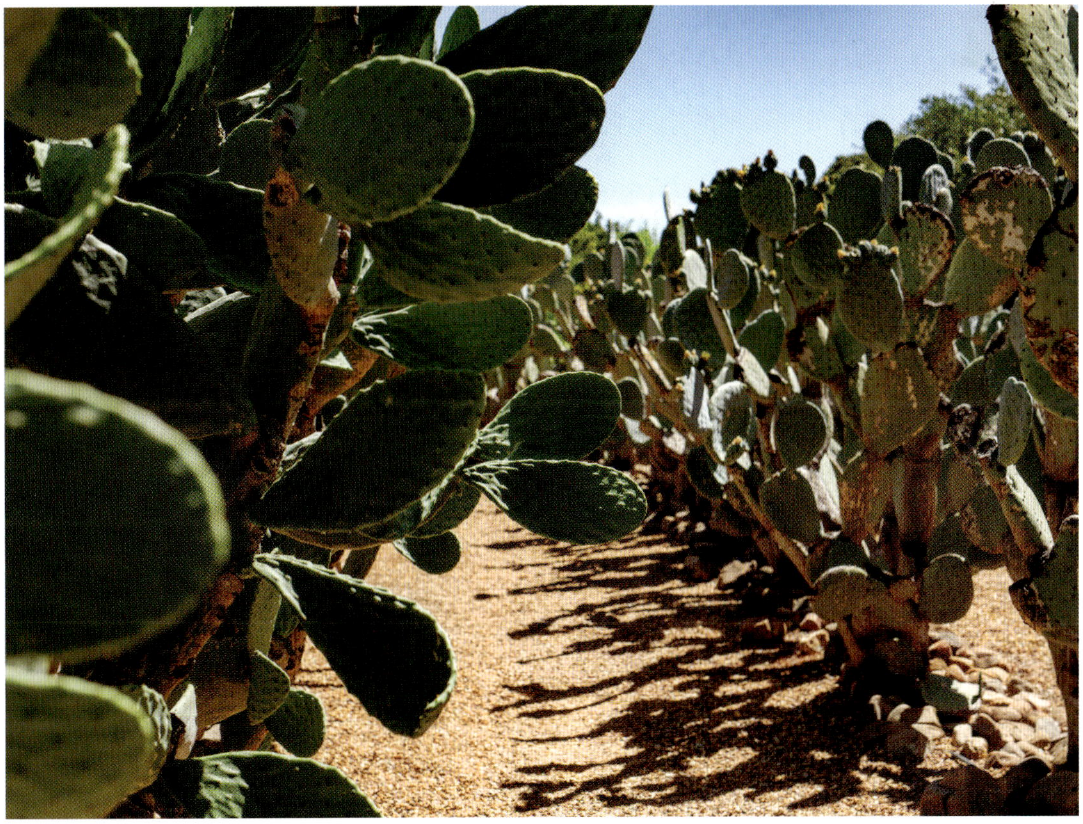

LEFT:
Sir Seewoosagur Ramgoolam Botanical Garden, Port Louis, Mauritius
The oldest botanical garden in the Southern Hemisphere was established in 1770, when the island was a French colony and dominated by the French East India Company. The garden is named after the first prime minister of Mauritius and contains 80 tropical palm species.

ABOVE TOP:
Seychelles Botanical Gardens, Mahé
Like Mauritius, the Seychelles were colonized by both the French and the British, and during this time the botanical gardens in Victoria, on the island of Mahé, were set up to trial crops with commercial potential. Today environmental education and sustainable tourism efforts are key activities of this lush space.

ABOVE BOTTOM AND OVERLEAF:
Babylonstoren, Western Cape, South Africa
On one of the oldest Cape-Dutch farms in the country, now a hotel, French designer Patrice Taravella has created a decorative productive garden of 15 rooms. These are set against the imposing Simonsberg mountain and include a prickly-pear maze, ponds planted with edible water lilies, and thousands of clivias which bloom in spring.

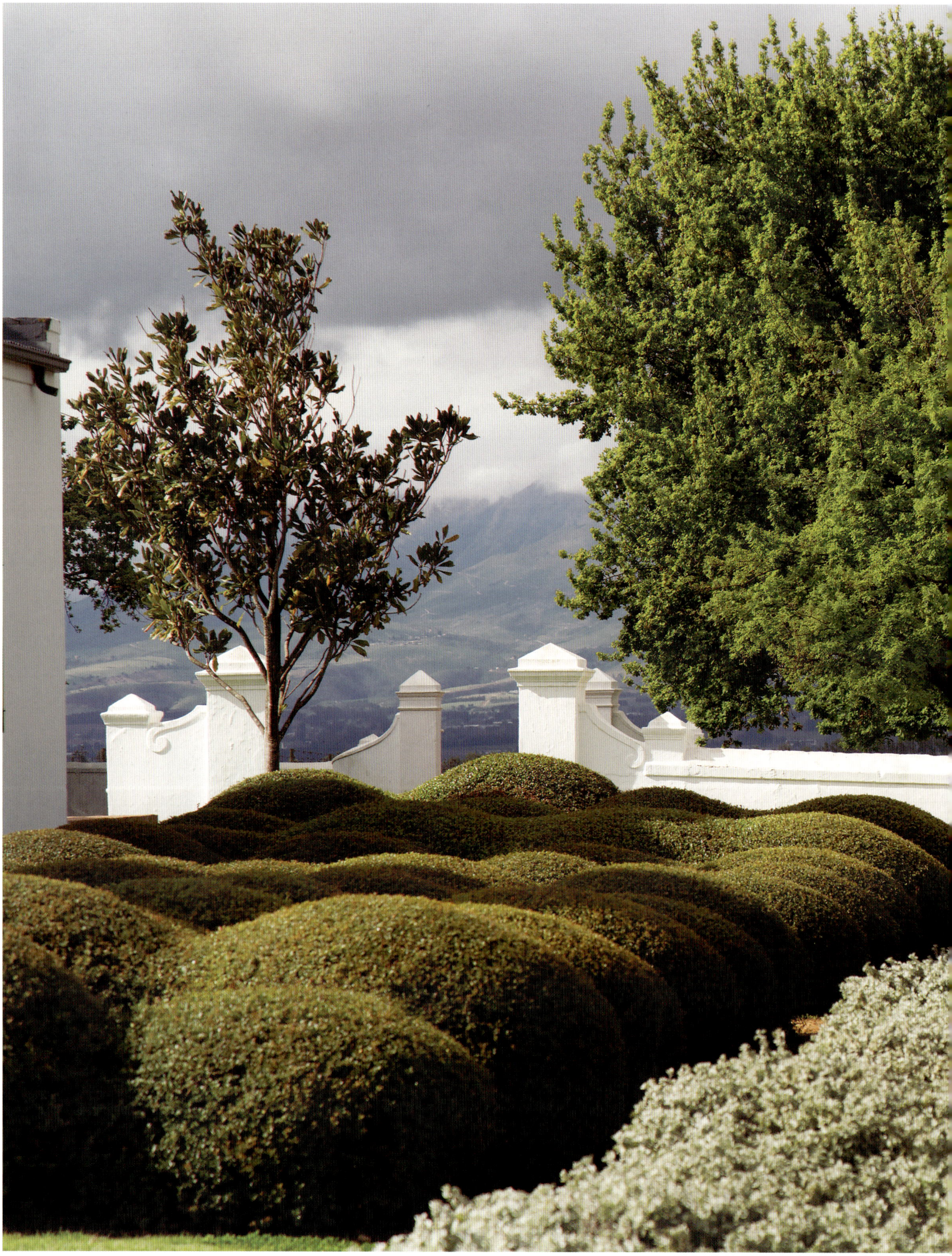

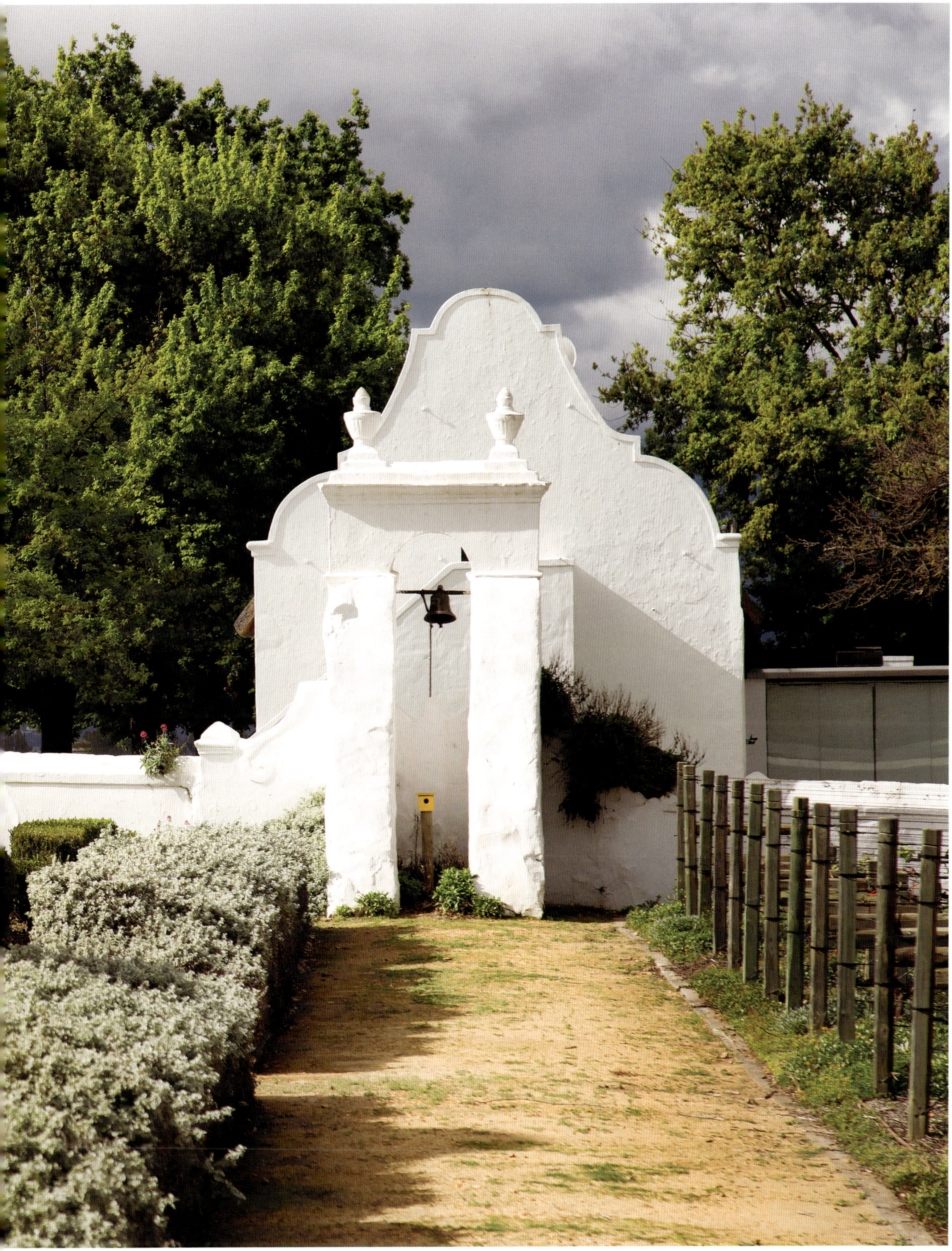

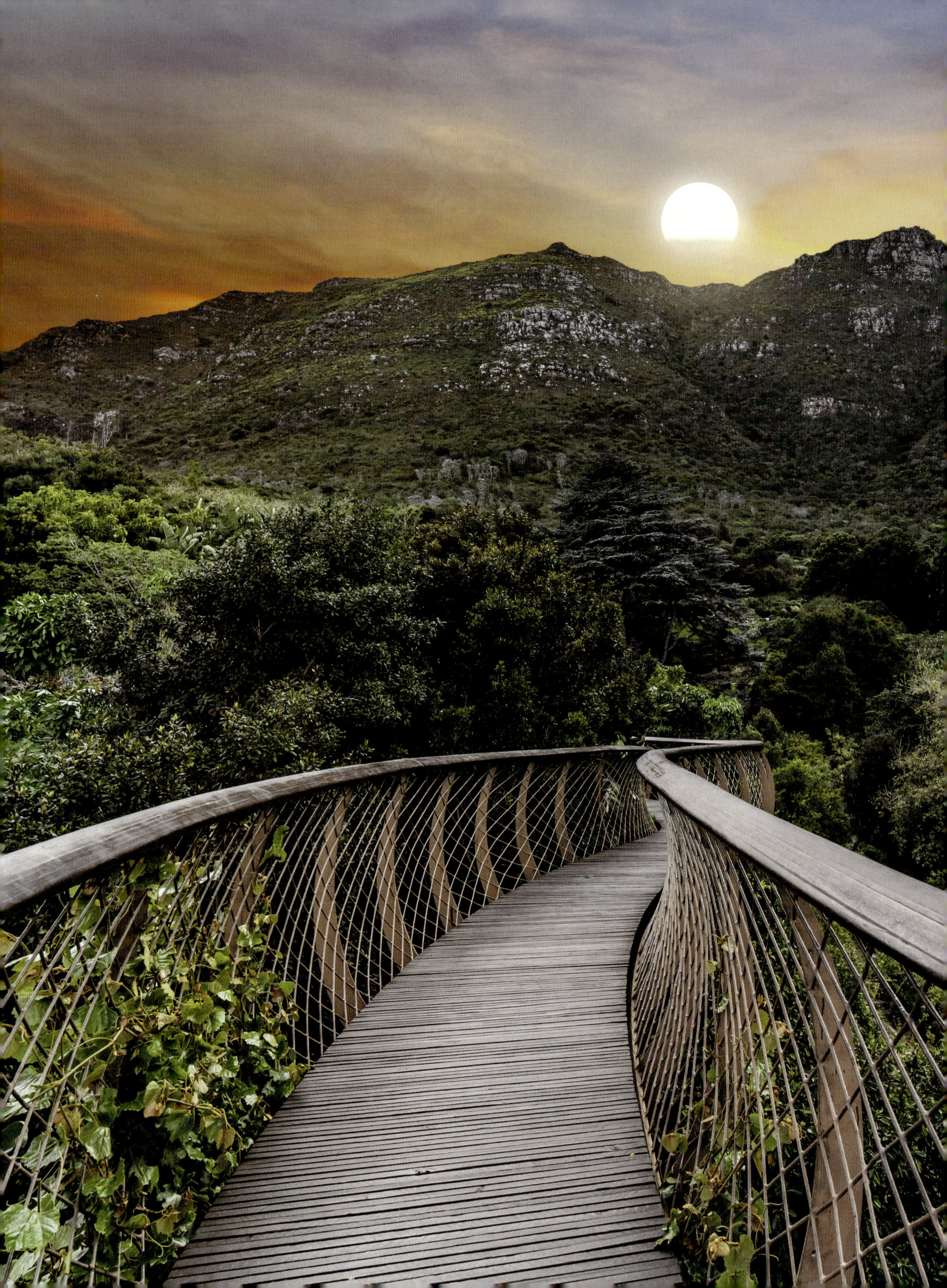

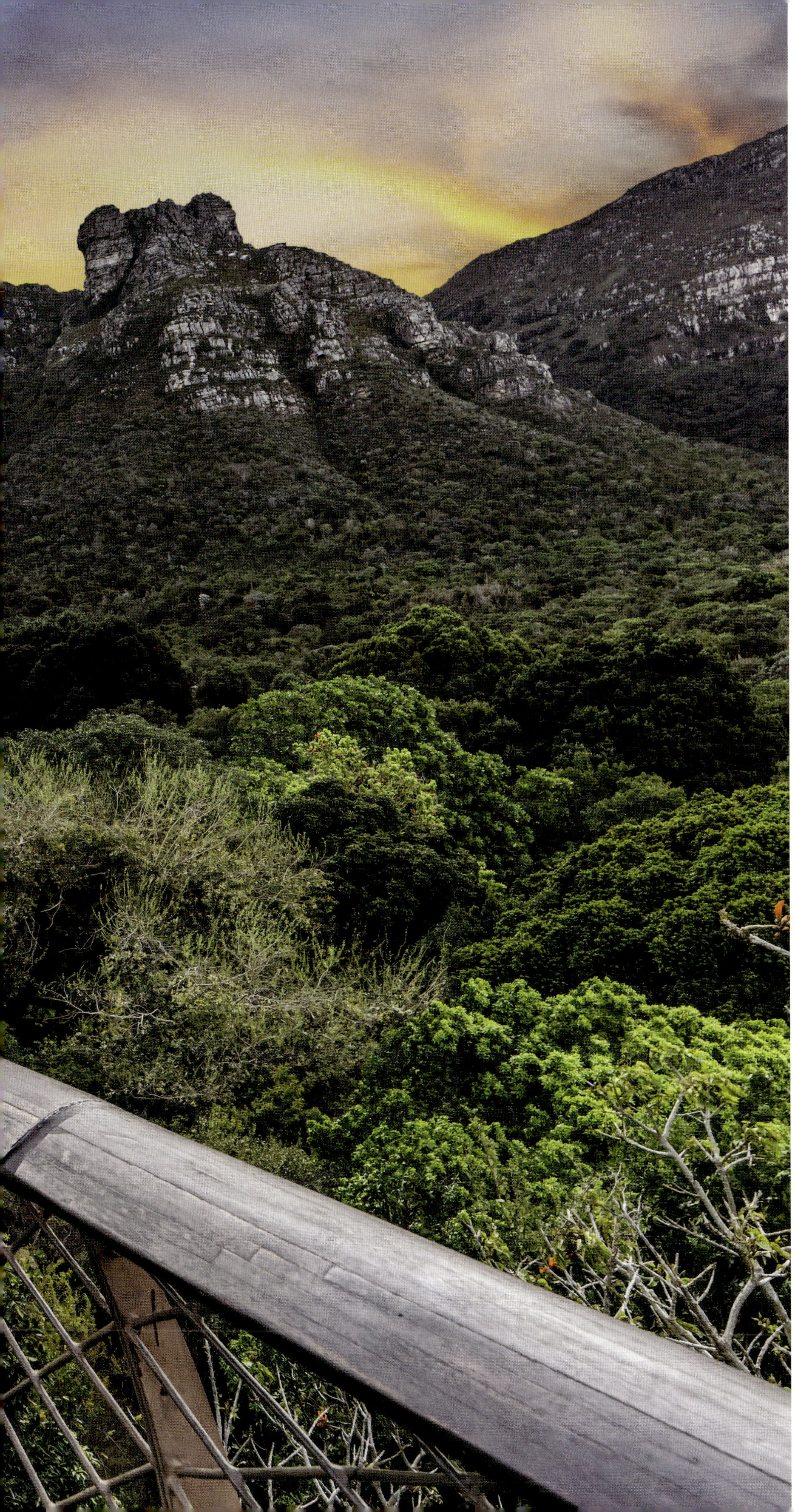

Kirstenbosch National Botanical Garden, Western Cape, South Africa
This truly unique garden spanning 528ha (1300 acres) on the slopes of Table Mountain, Cape Town, is one of the most important botanical gardens in the world for its role in supporting the species-dense Fynbos biome. First inhabited by indigenous Khoikhoi people, and then by European settler-farmers, it was founded in 1913 and became part of a UNESCO World Heritage Site in 2004. The Camphor Avenue was planted in 1898. A new, 130m (425ft) long skywalk marks the garden's centenary.

Meidan Emam, Isfahan, Iran
Open squares are fundamental to contemporary urban planning but one of the largest in the world dates from the early 17th century. Built by Abbas I the Great, this square is also known as Naqsh-e Jahan, translating as 'Image of the World'.

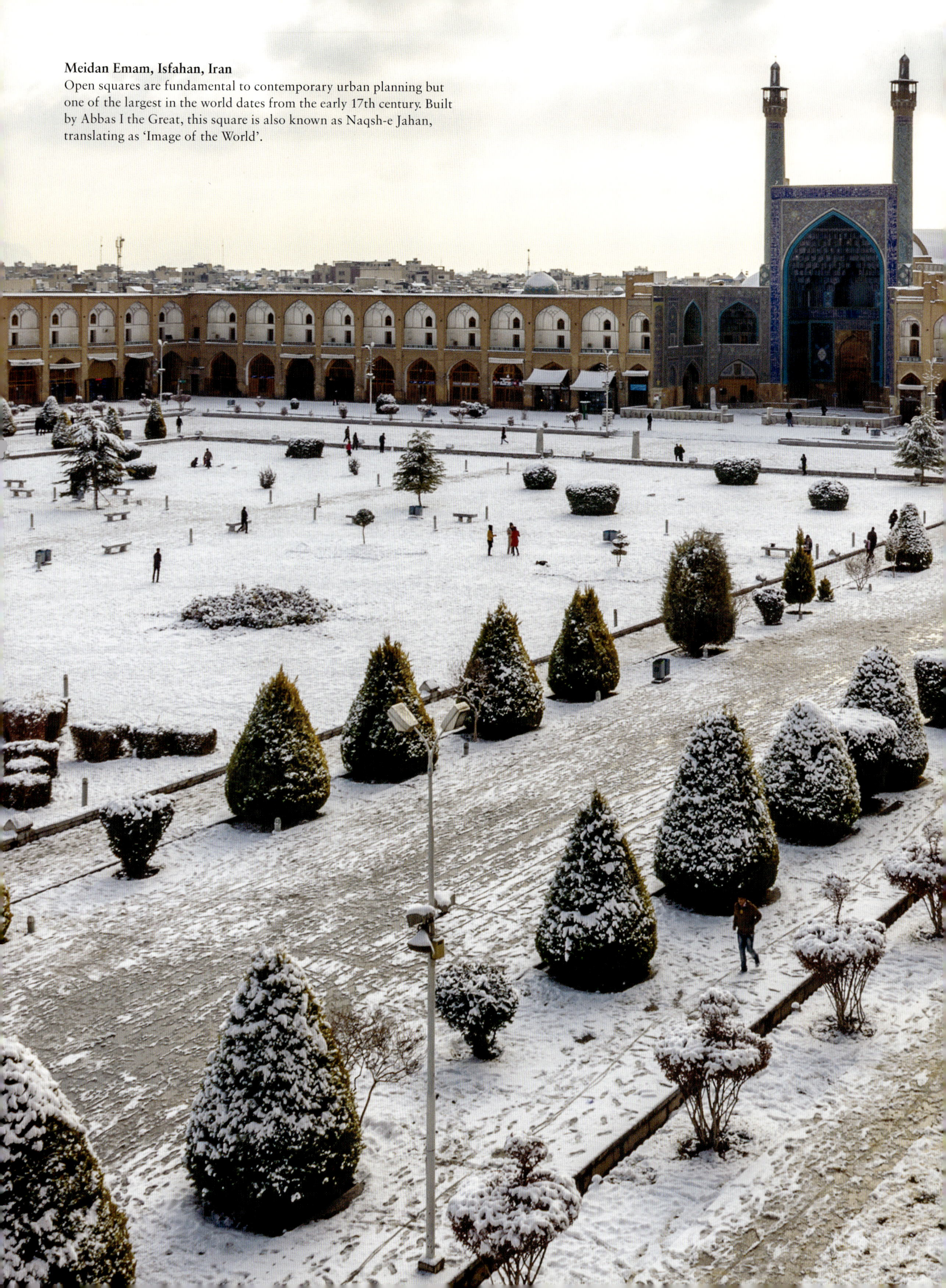

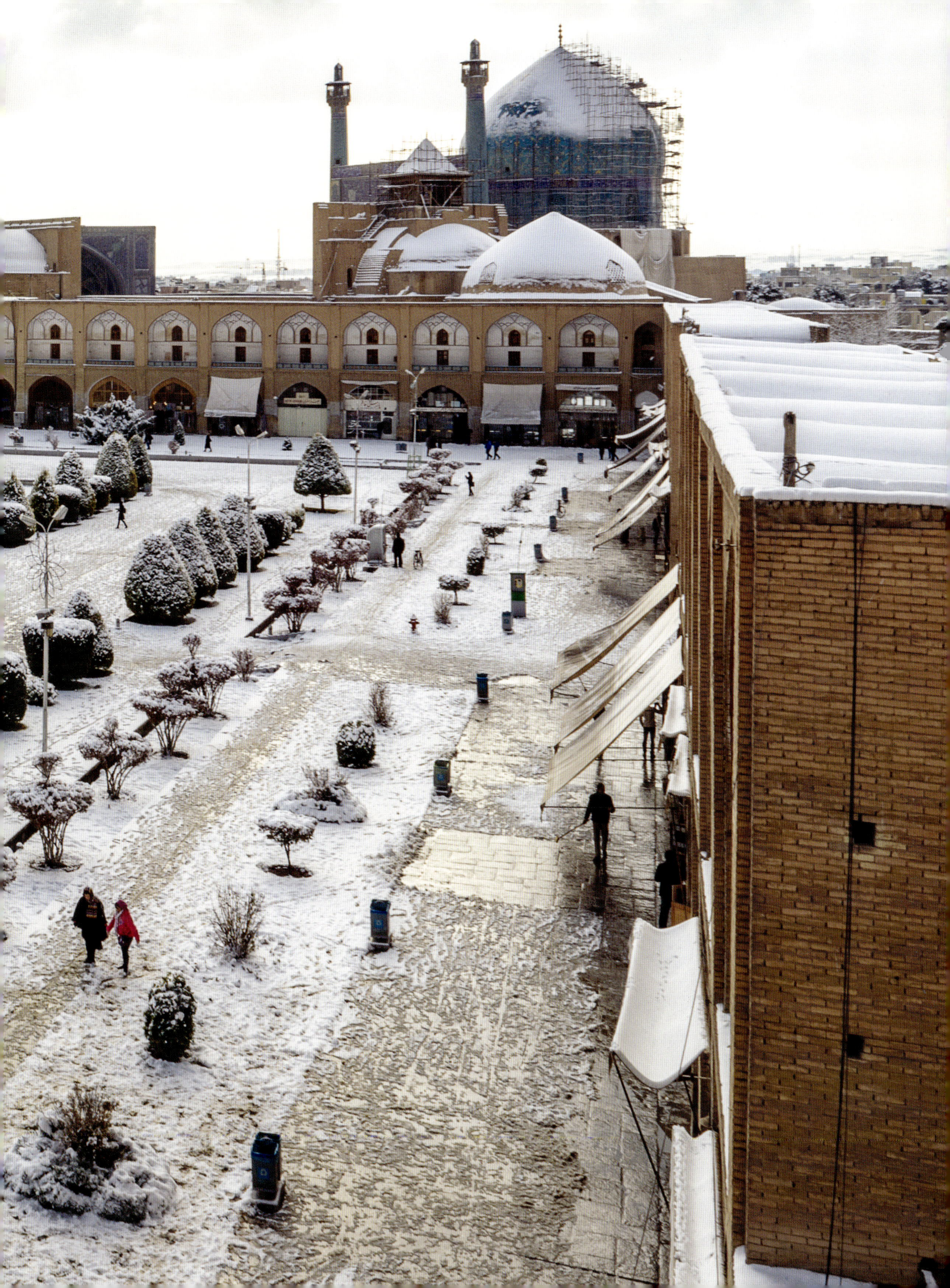

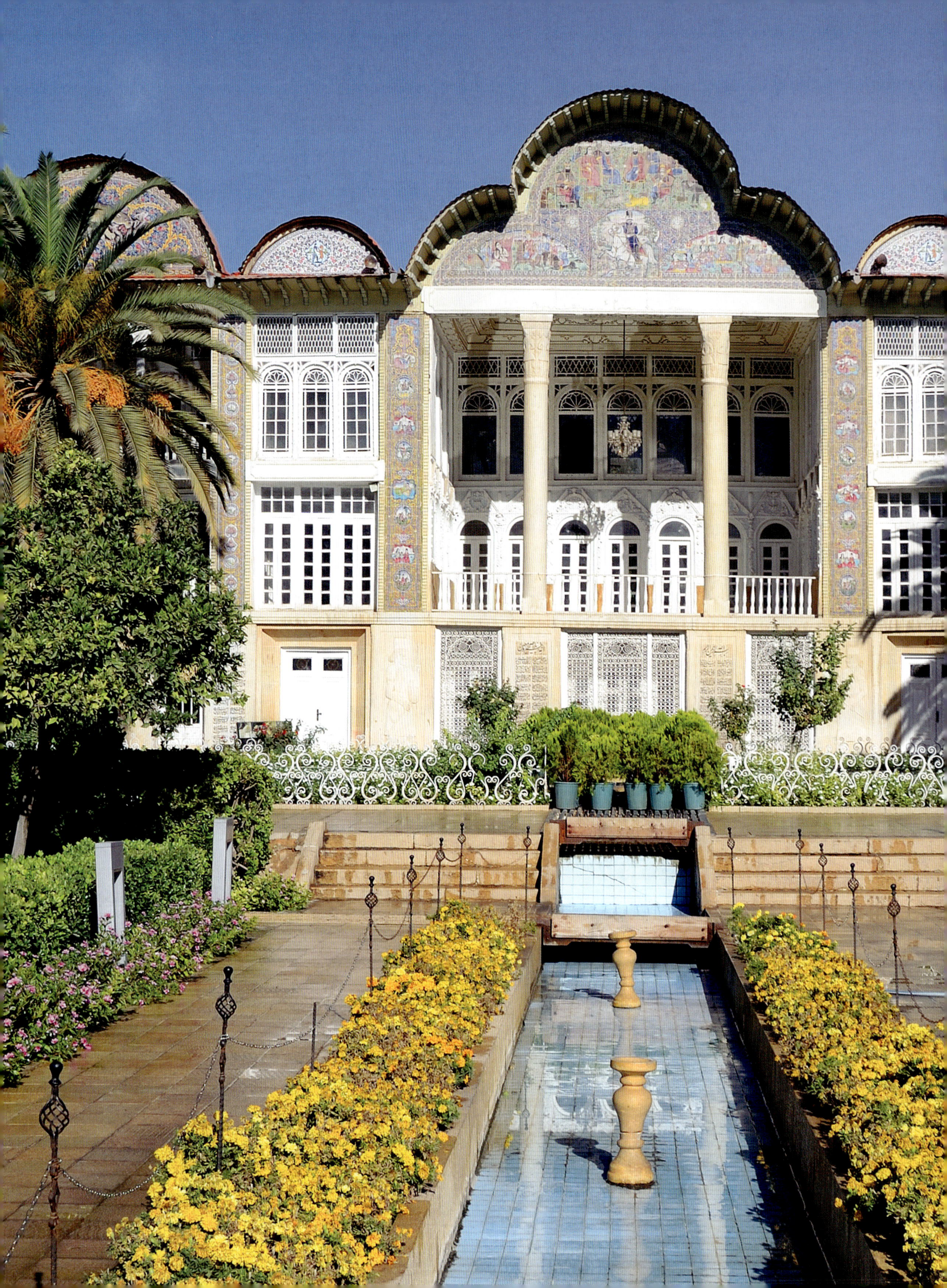

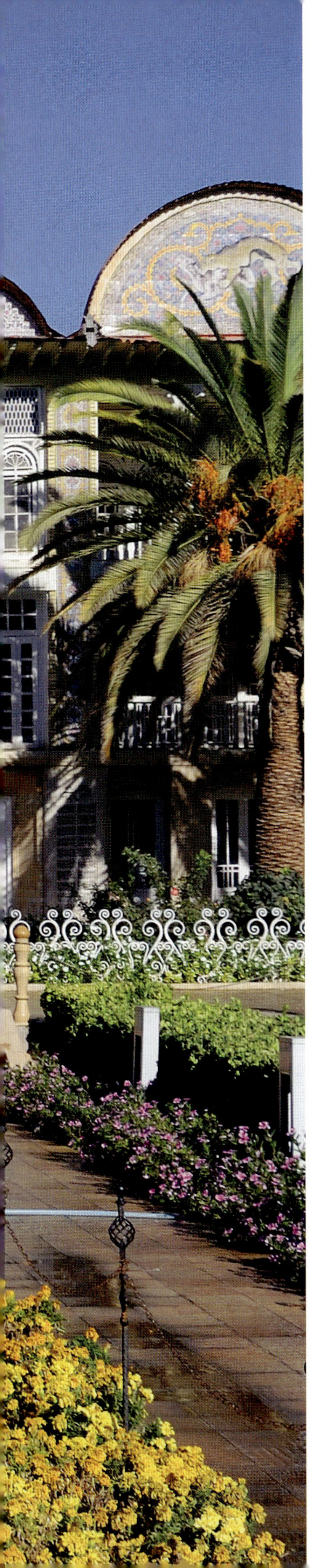

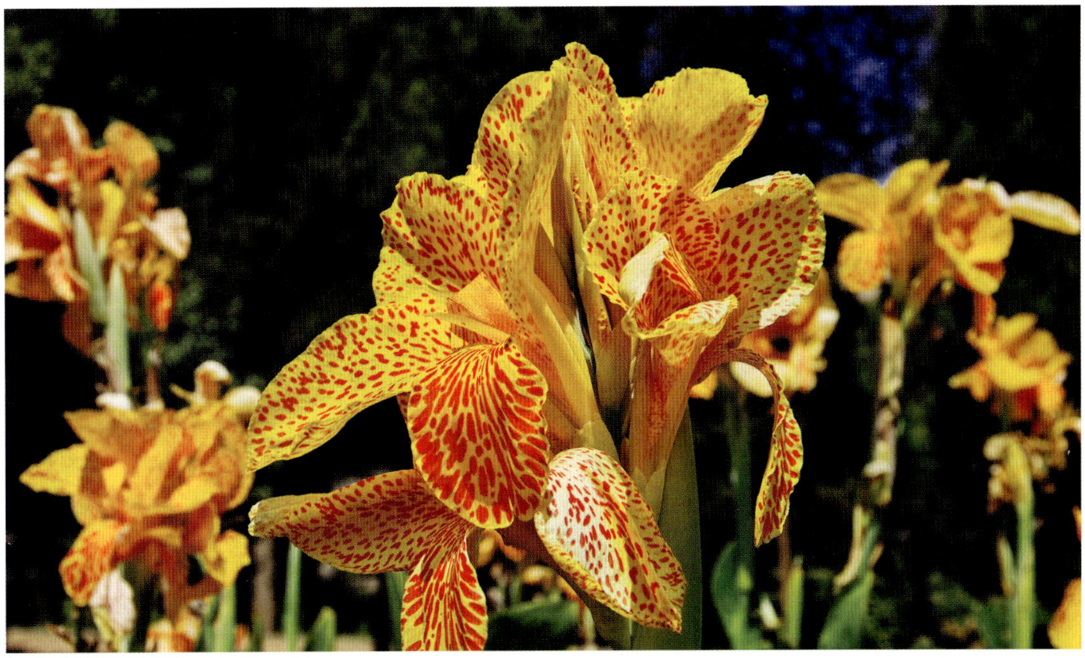

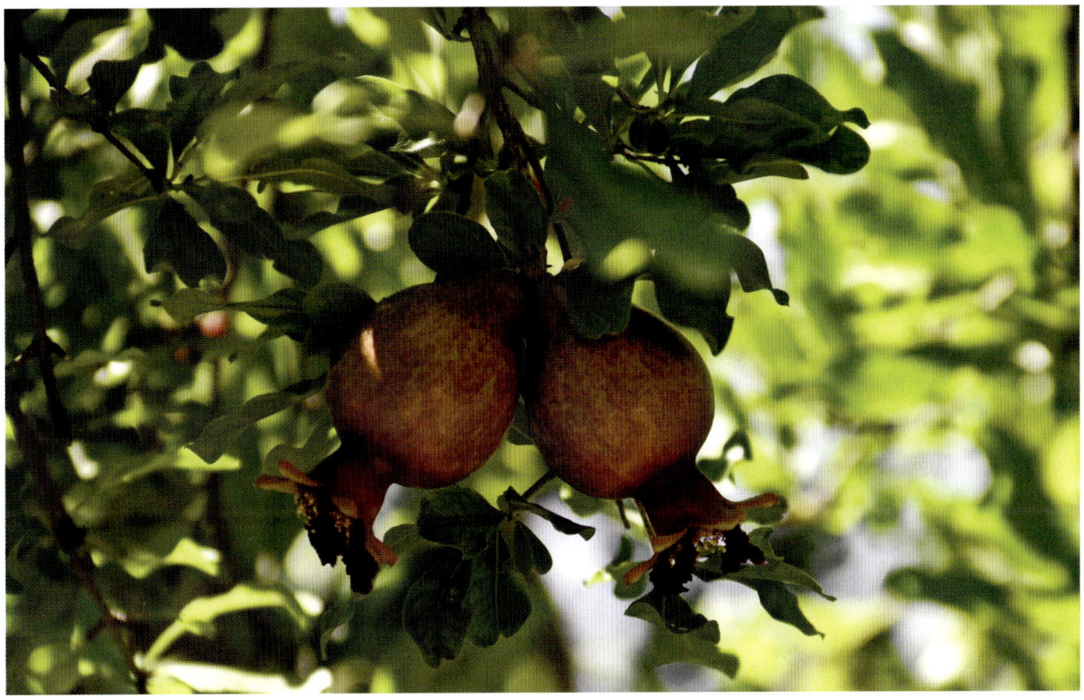

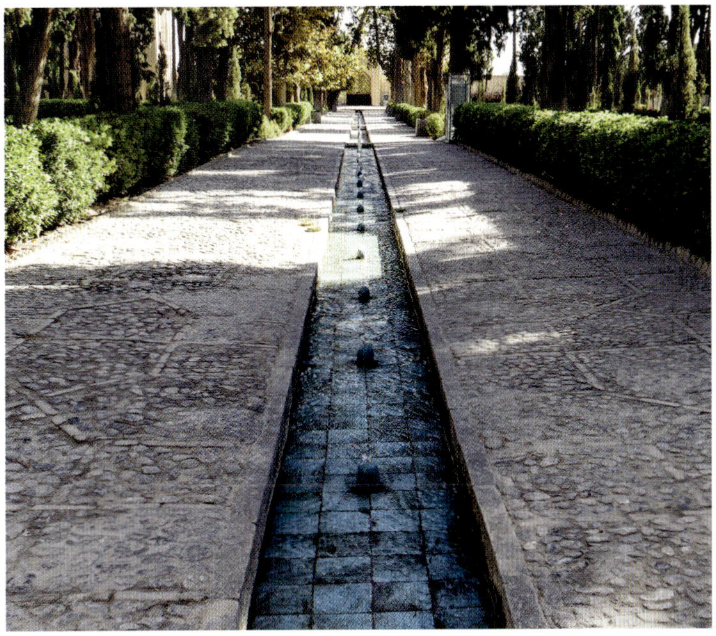

ALL PHOTOGRAPHS:
Bagh-e Eram, Shiraz, Iran
On the banks of the river Koshk lies a defining Islamic paradise garden, the name of which is the Persian word for heaven. The garden is thought to have been founded around the 12th century, and is one of nine Persian gardens in Iran awarded UNESCO World Heritage Site status for exemplifying the diversity of Islamic garden design. Water, in rills and fountains, is a central theme, as is abundant floristic planting.

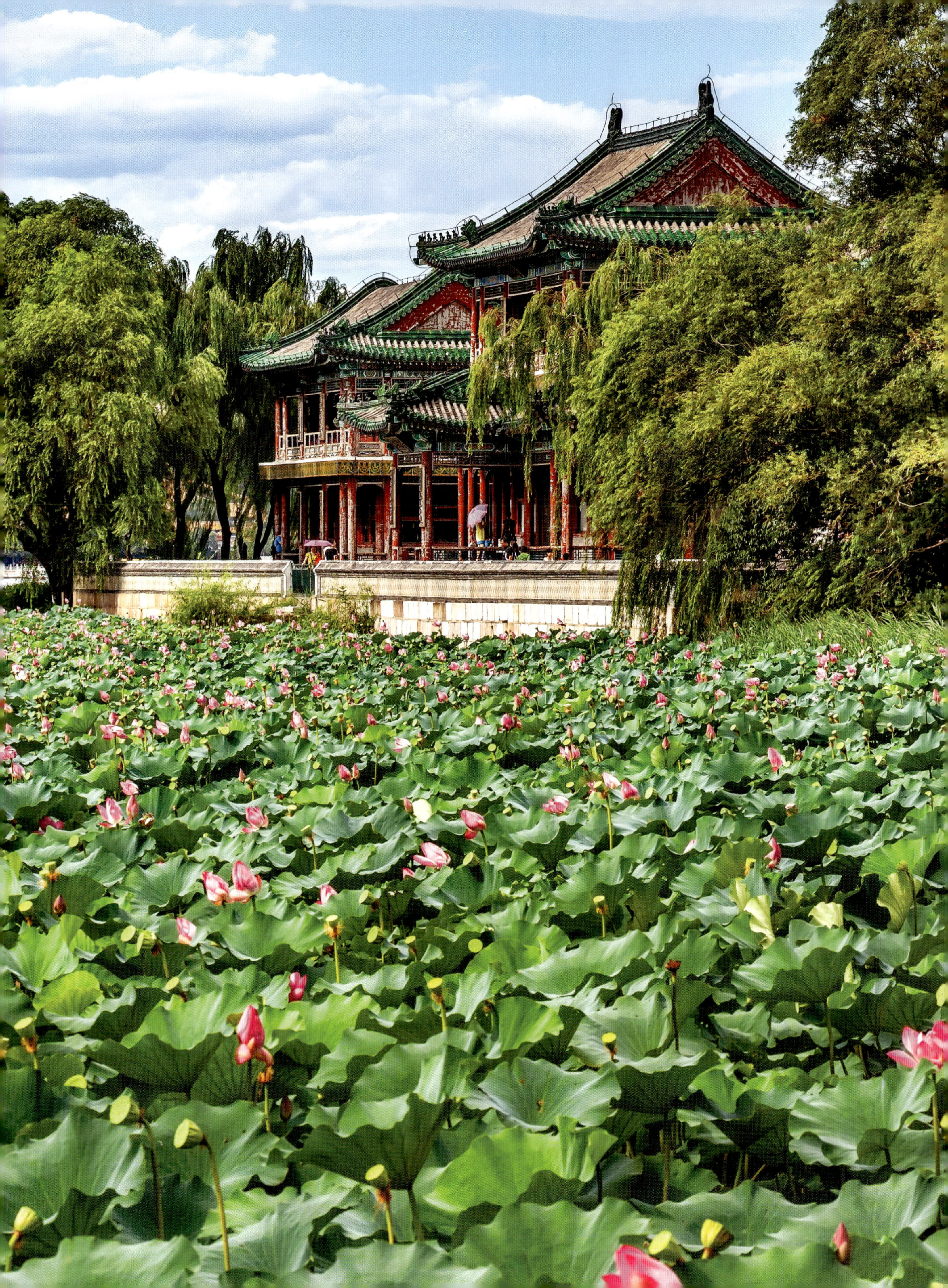

Asia

From Japanese gardens tended in minute detail for centuries, to the most modern, subtropical conceptions in Singapore, Asia holds an extraordinary collection of gardens.

Much of the region's horticultural tradition emerged from China, where farming along the Yellow River and Yangtze River floodplains inevitably led to ornamental practices. Documents from as early as the 4th century BCE describe gardening for pleasure exclusively. Of the many horticultural landscapes in this vast and diverse country, the classical gardens in the city of Suzhou, all UNESCO World Heritage Sites, are among the best known.

Across the Yellow Sea and the Sea of Japan, the relative seclusion of the Japanese islands brought about a unique gardening tradition, although gardening practice has been influenced by neighbouring China and Korea. Gardens here are laden with symbolism, integral to Shinto beliefs and are at once about control and respect for landscape. Kenroku-en is one of the most compelling.

The Indian subcontinent has seen waves of rulers come and go, yet it was the Mughals who left an indelible horticultural mark here, beginning with Babur, who introduced the classic, quadrilateral Islamic garden or chahar bagh from Persia. Later, British colonialists sought to make their own impression on the jewel in the crown of the British Empire. At first this was through the commercially minded East India Company, but later Sir Edwin Lutyens, who earlier designed Surrey gardens, was commissioned to lay out New Delhi, and Lord Curzon, Viceroy of India, refashioned the Taj Mahal to his taste. Our seemingly inexorably changing climate and the pressure on cities comes to the fore in densely populated Singapore where the Gardens by the Bay have been constructed with sustainability high on the agenda.

OPPOSITE:
Summer Palace, Beijing, China
With its layout based on Chinese mythology, the Summer Palace in Beijing comprises a sequence of connecting lakes, islands, hills, gardens and palaces. The largest feature is manmade Kunmig Lake, which covers 2.2 square km (0.85 square miles).

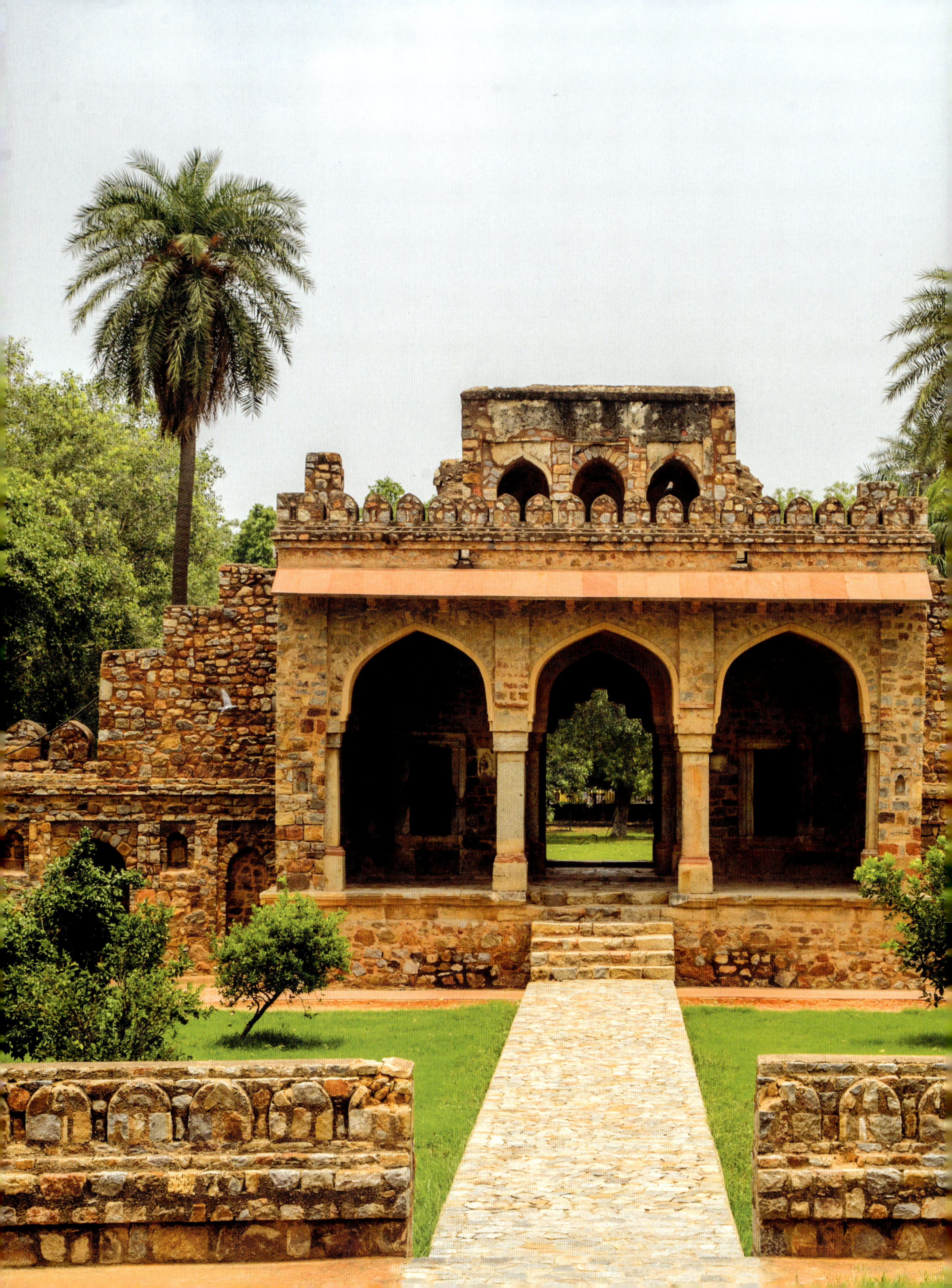

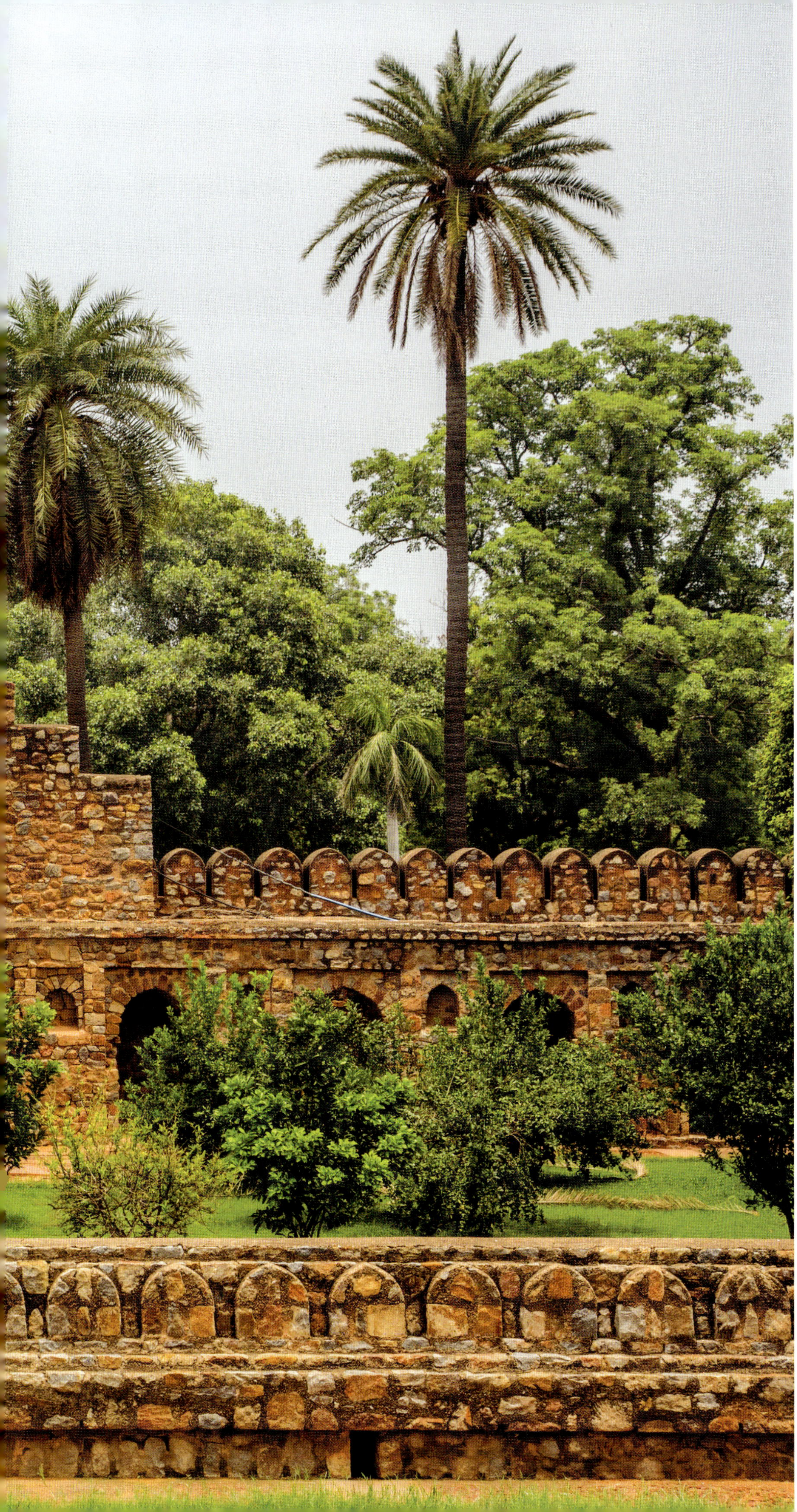

Humayun's Tomb, Delhi, India
Built for the second Mughal emperor Humayun in Delhi, this is the oldest of the Mughal garden-tombs on the Indian subcontinent. It was commissioned by the emperor's widow, Empress Bega Begum, in the mid-1500s, and designed by influential Mirak Mirza Ghiyas and Sayyid Muhammad, father and son. Inspired by the tastes of the first Mughal emperor, Babur, who had himself been moved by the gardens of Samarkand, the complex is a classic chahar bagh. Representing the afterlife in Islamic tradition, it a walled space divided into four by intersecting rills, with a central water source.

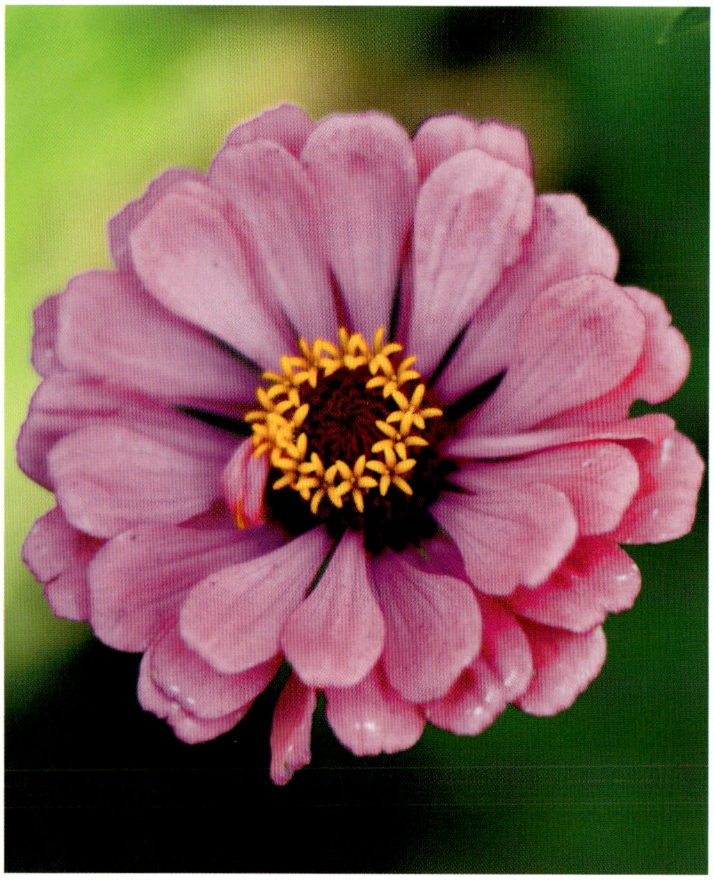

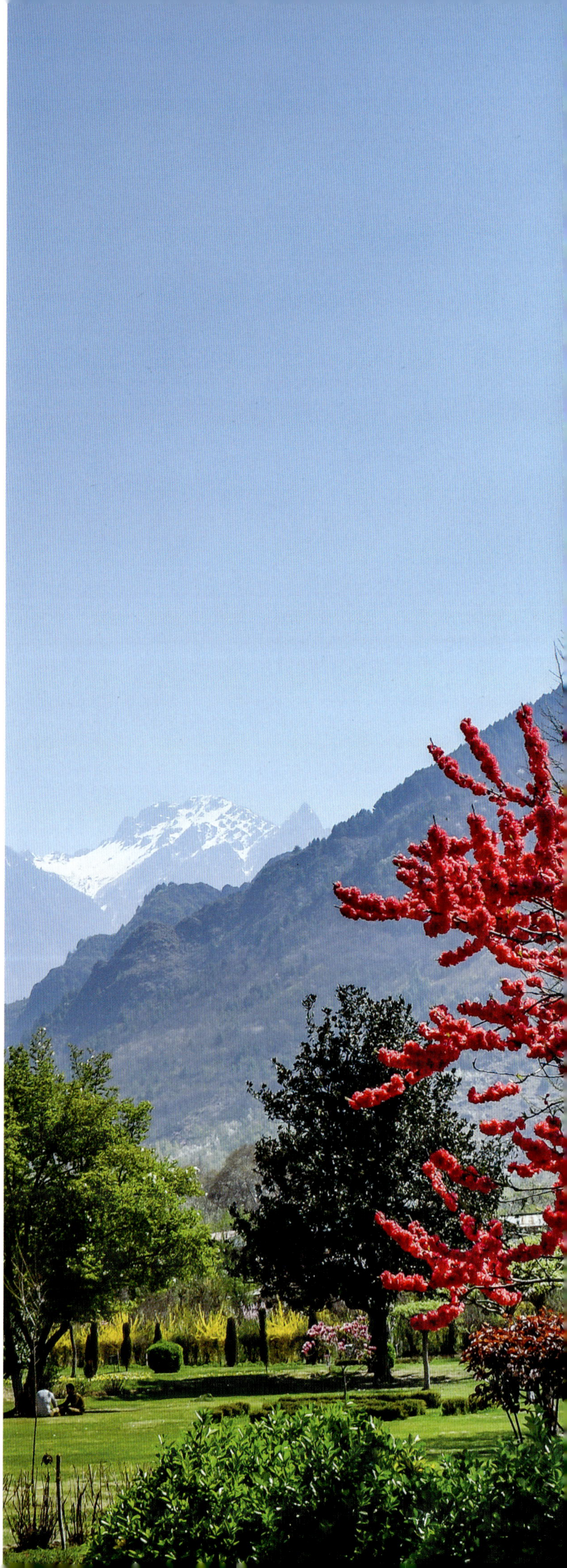

BOTH PHOTOGRAPHS:
Shalimar Gardens, Jammu and Kashmir, India
Emperor Akbar, the son of Humayun, fell in love with Kashmir when he visited in the late 1500s. Around Lake Dal in Srinagar, some 700 gardens were built, but Shalimar Bagh is one of the most enduring. Built in 1619 as an expression of love for his wife Noor Jahan, it is now a public park.

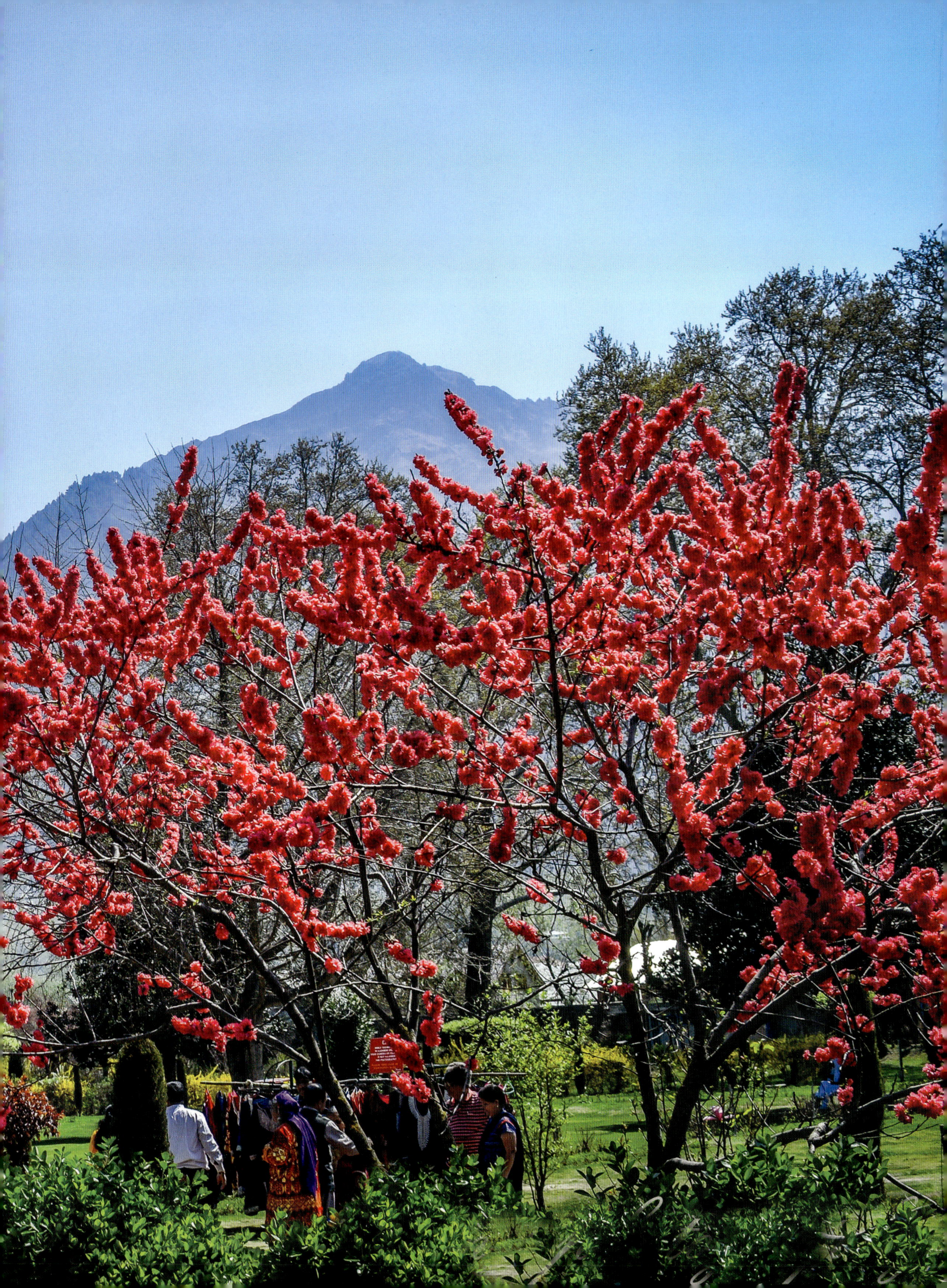

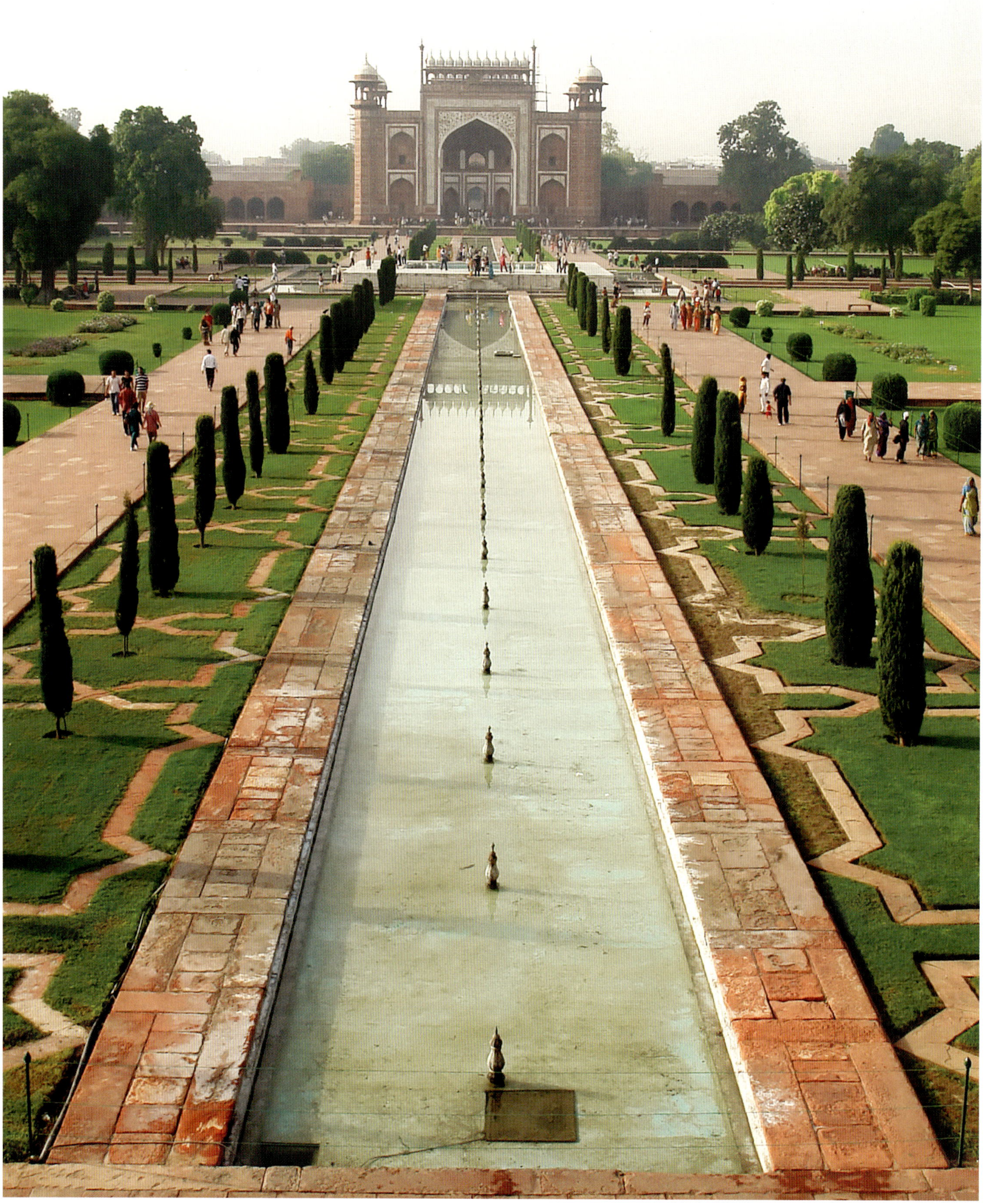

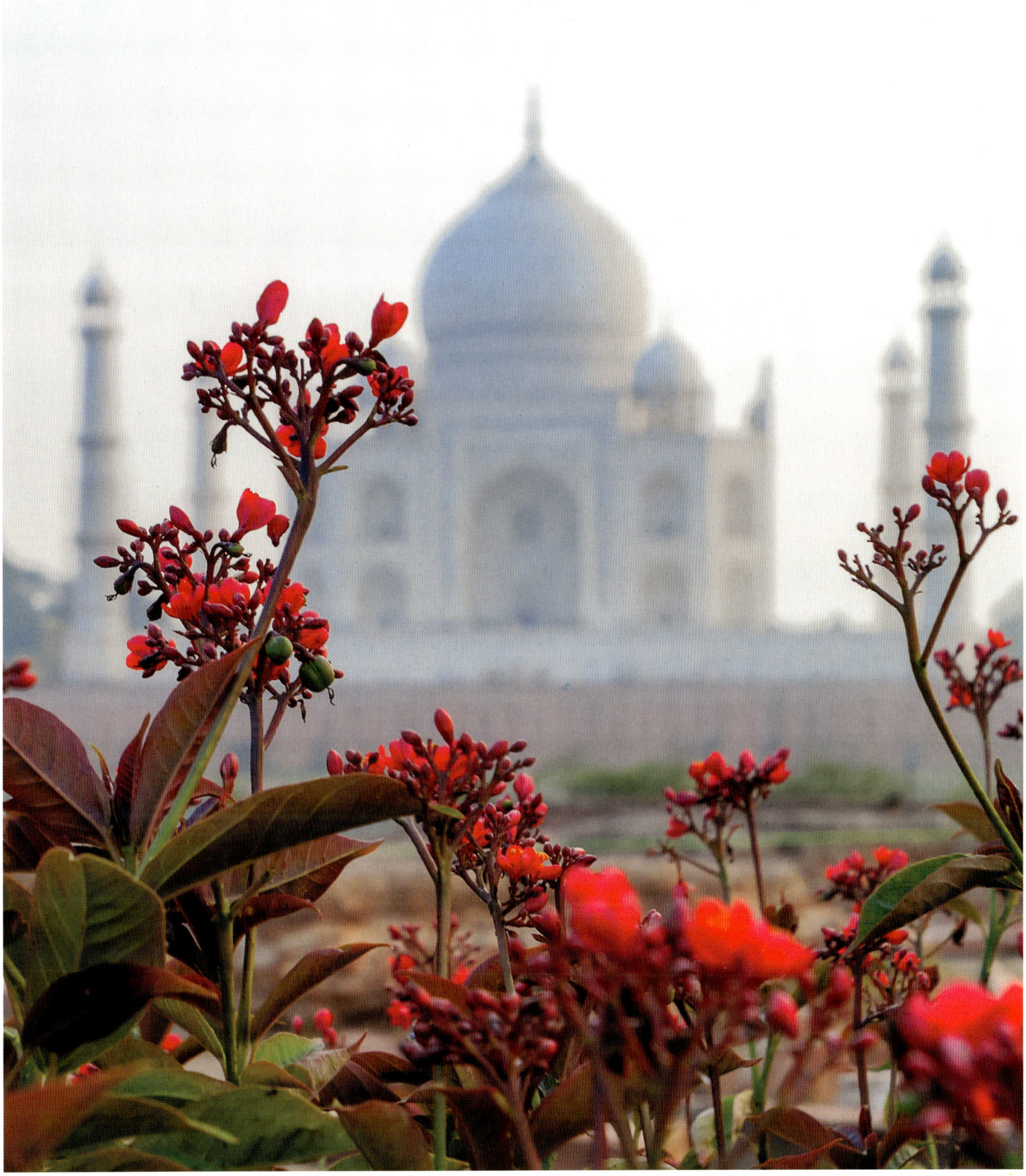

BOTH PHOTOGRAPHS:

Taj Mahal, Uttar Pradesh, India

This incomparable complex in Agra was built between 1632 and 1653 by Emperor Shah Jahan, grandson of Akbar, for his wife, Mumtaz Mahal, who died in childbirth. The Taj Mahal was arranged in the Mughal style, and was intended as an intimate paradise garden planted with roses, narcissus, marigolds and jasmine. Shah Jahan's creation was remodelled in the early 20th century by Lord Curzon, Viceroy of India from 1898 to 1905, who was influenced by English parks. Under his direction, cypress trees were planted between the mausoleum and the gateway to the gardens.

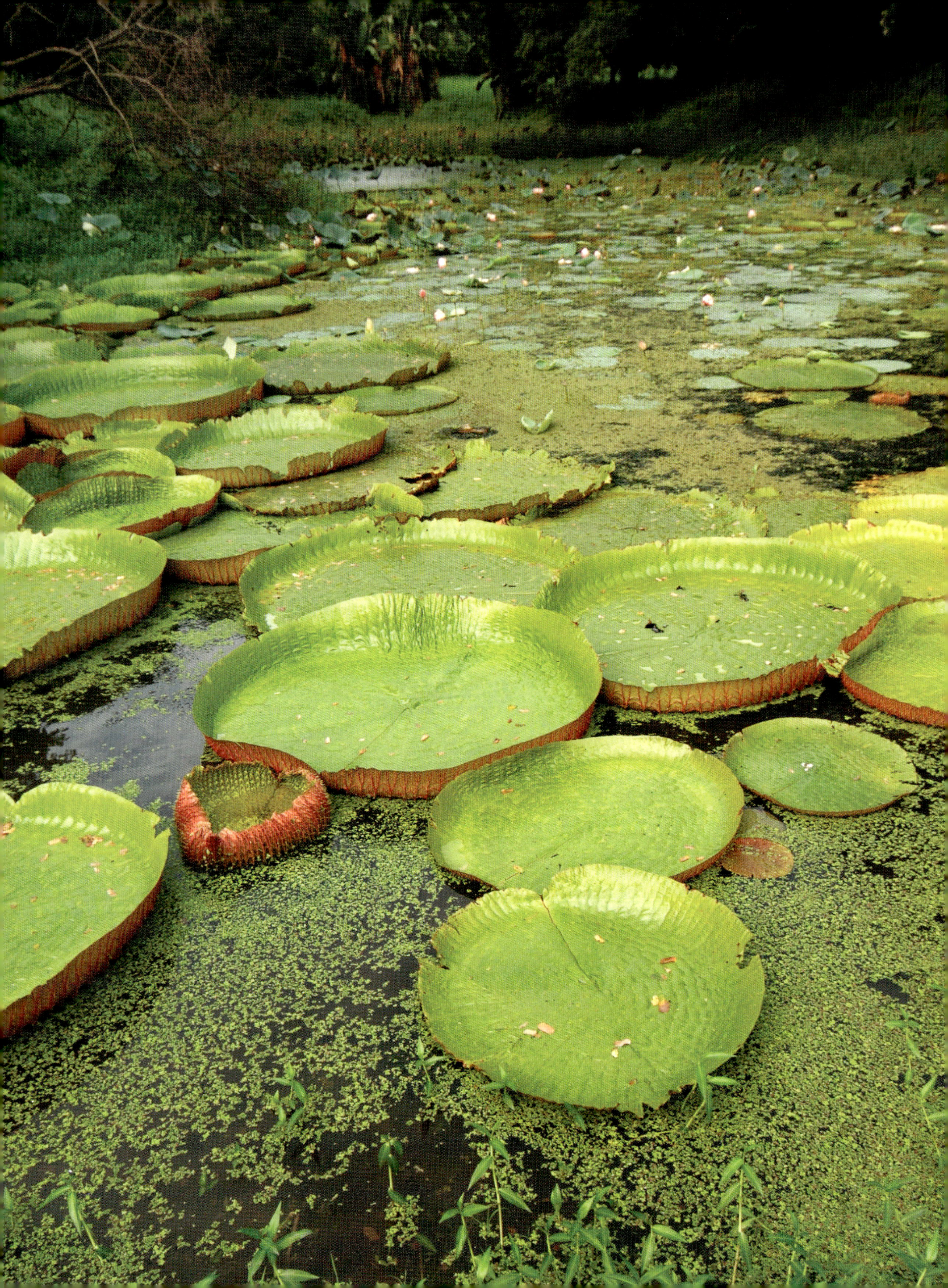

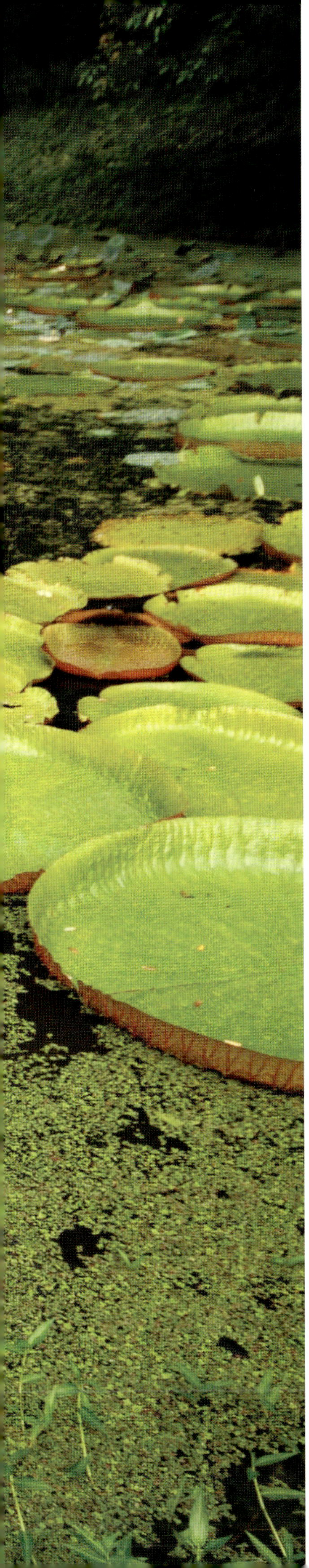

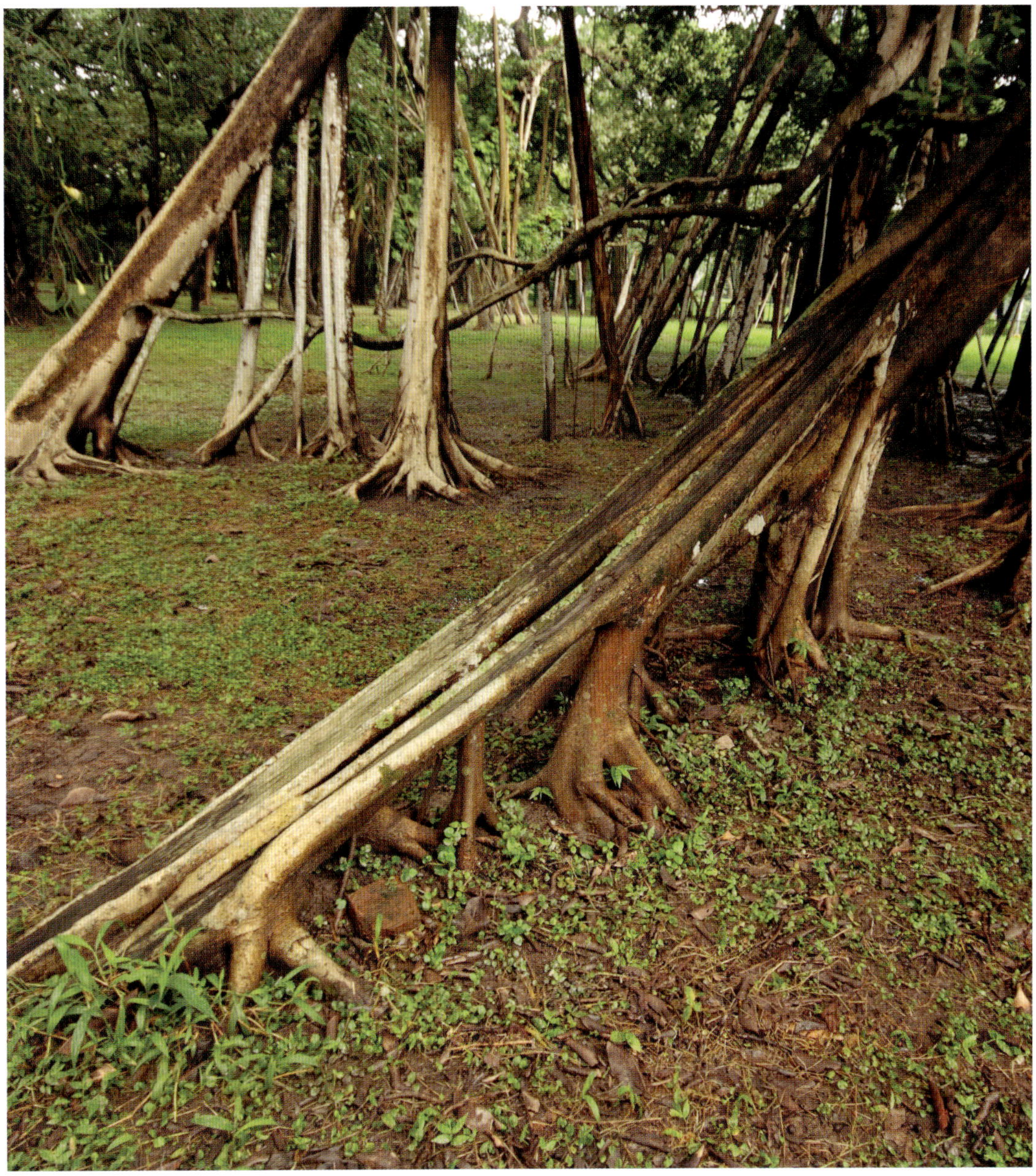

BOTH PHOTOGRAPHS:

Acharya Jagadish Chandra Bose Indian Botanic Garden, West Bengal, India

For centuries Kolkata was the apex of colonial trade with the East. The botanical garden here, on the banks of the great Hooghly river, was established in 1787 by an official in the East India Company. Like most botanical gardens of the British Empire, it was used for trialling plants with a commercial value. Key among these was tea – *Camellia sinensis* and *Camellia assamica* – the success of which precipitated India's substantial tea industry. Today the 109ha (269-acre)garden of lakes, long walks and vistas has a collection of some 12,000 plants, of which The Great Banyan, at 330m in circumference, is believed to be the largest tree in the world. The tree is supported with stilts.

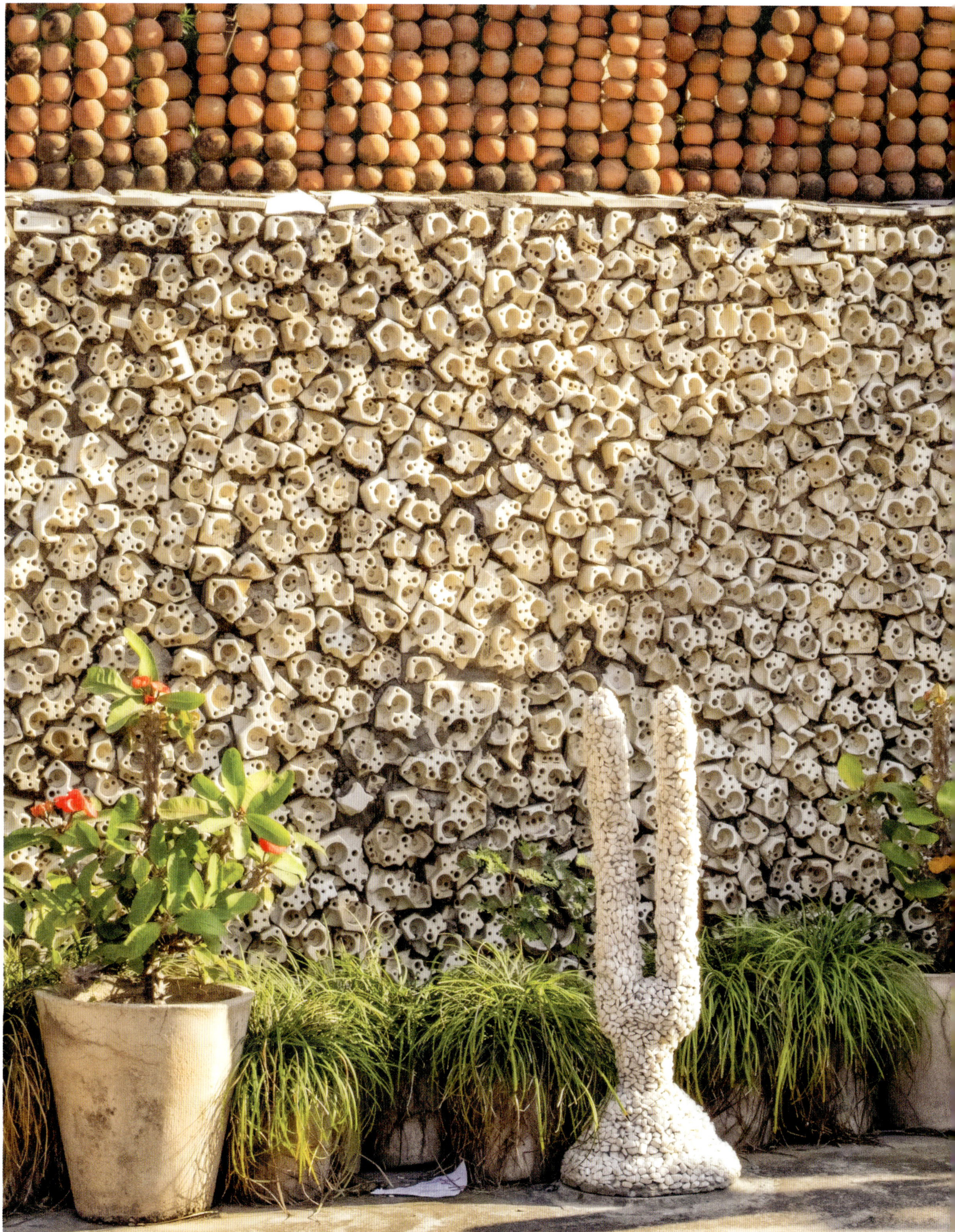

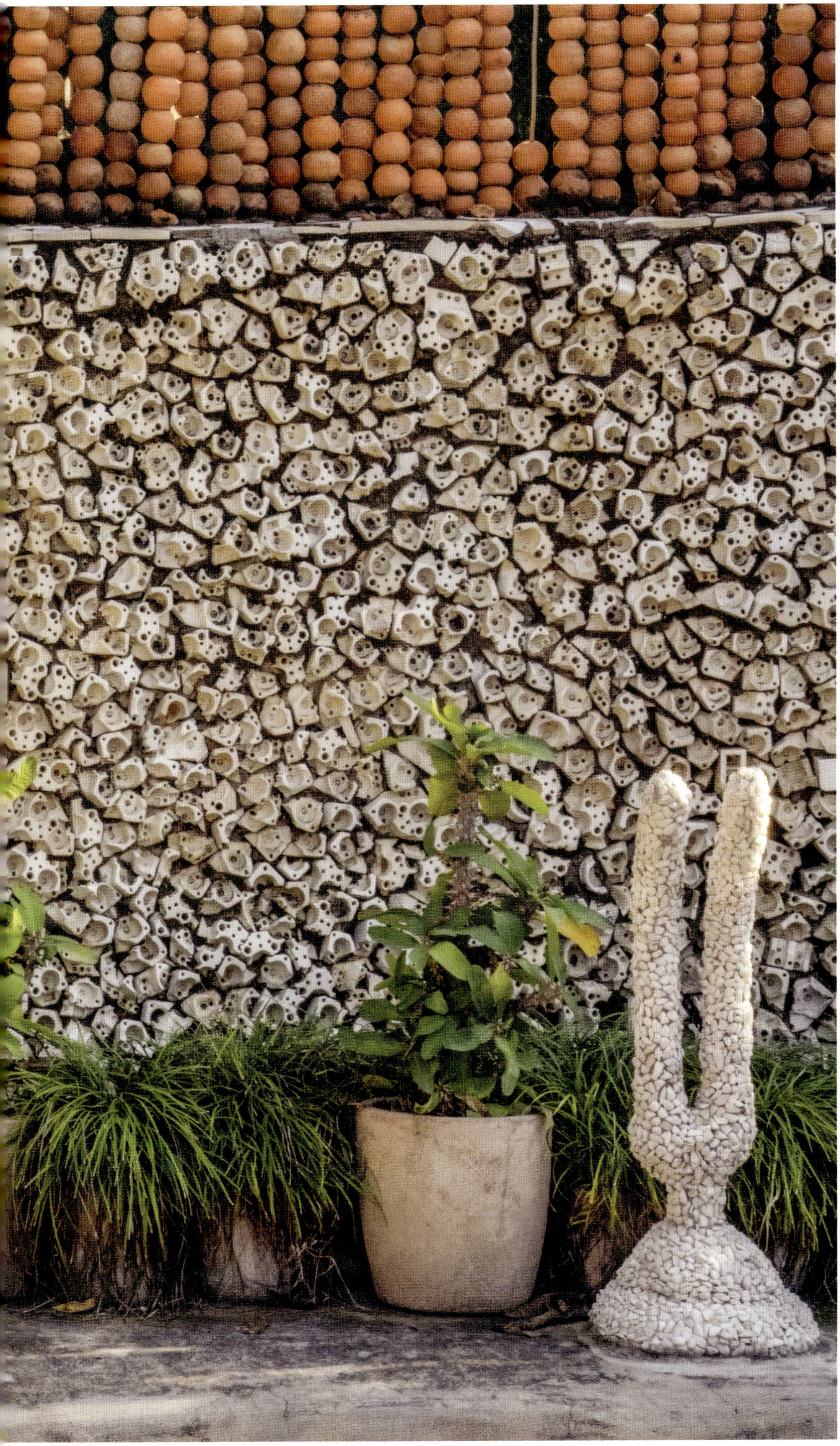

Rock Garden of Chandigarh, Punjab and Haryana, India

It was a transport official of modest means, Nek Chand, who one day in the mid-1960s cleared a circle of jungle in his home city of Chandigargh, north India, to make a garden. Working by night to avoid detection, Chand gradually constructed a series of interlinking courtyards spanning several acres to house the sculpture he fashioned from discarded materials. It was a decade before he was discovered by city authorities and controversially given a salary and a small staff to continue his work. Today there are several thousand sculptures in the grounds, which are supported by the Nek Chand Foundation.

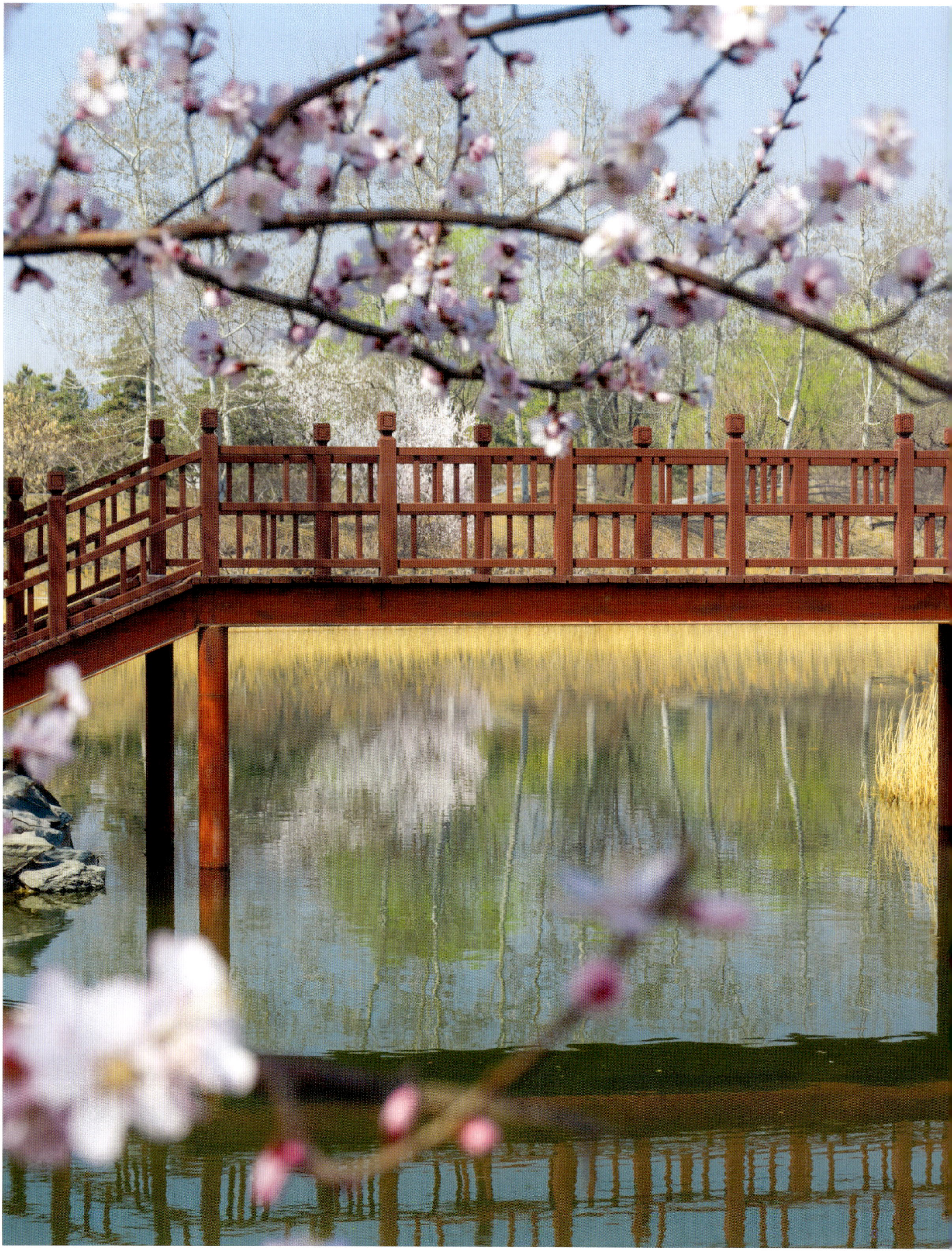

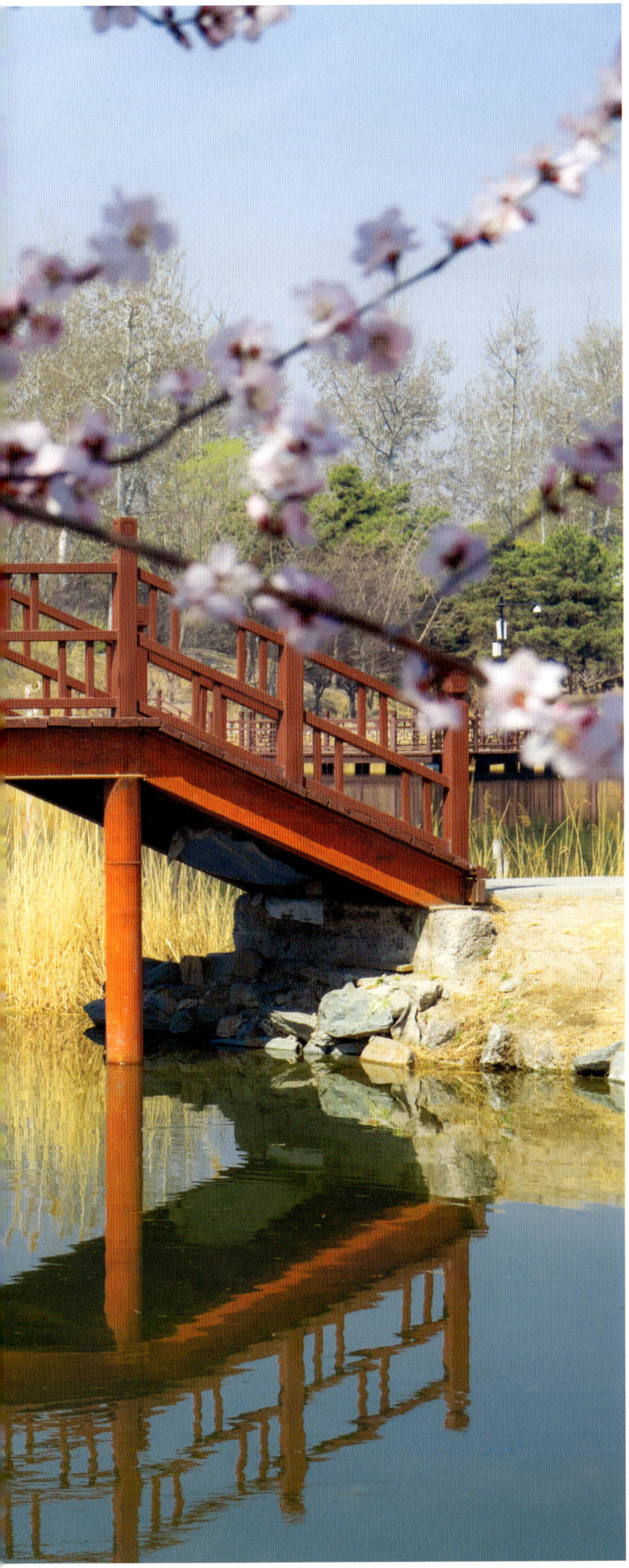

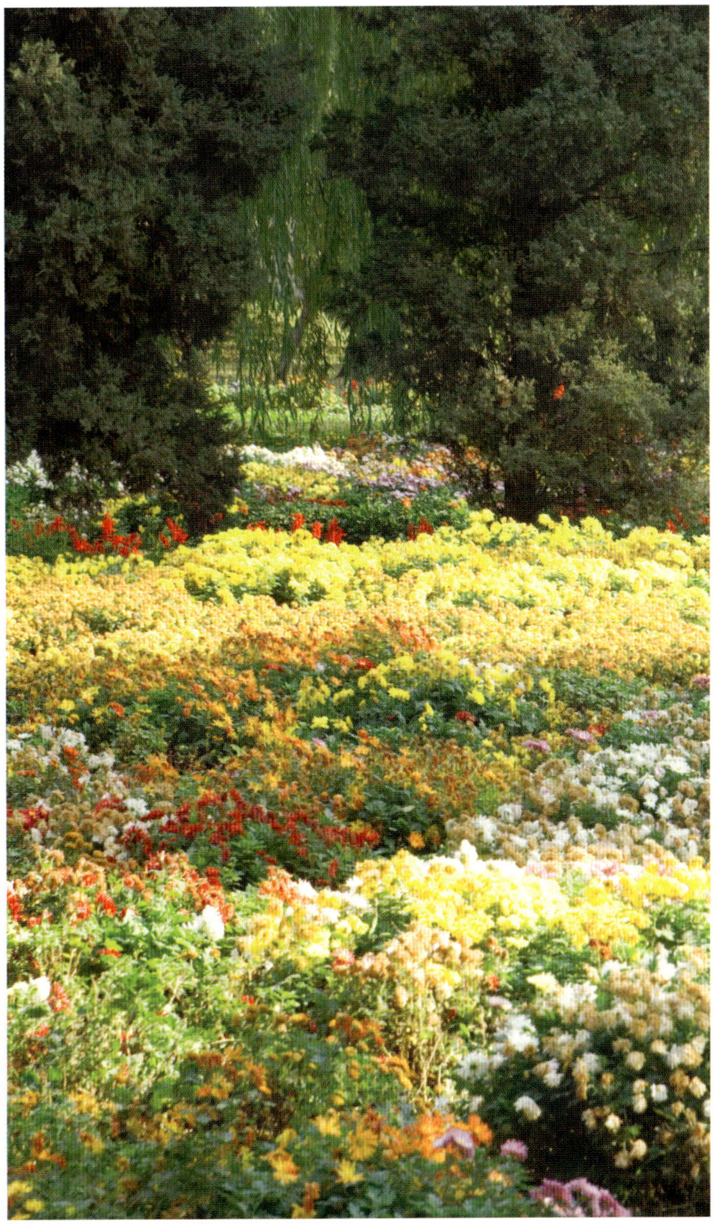

BOTH PHOTOGRAPHS:

Summer Palace, Beijing, China

This perfectly preserved UNESCO World Heritage Site dates from the 12th century but took much of its current form under Qing Emperor Qianlong (1735–1796). Spread over almost 3km (2 miles), it epitomises the Chinese landscape aesthetic in its intention to balance human life with nature: 90 percent of the garden is designed for spiritual well-being. The Summer Palace has been damaged and restored under various regimes since it was first constructed, and is now a major tourist attraction.

Humble Administrator's Garden, Suzhou, China
The Hall of Distant Fragrances and the Pavilion in the Lotus Breeze are just two compelling features in the Humble Administrator's Garden, in Suzhou, west of Shanghai. Built in the classical and defining Suzhou style, the property dates from the 12th century but was developed in the 16th century by a retired government officer, the humble administrator. The historic garden is a UNESCO World Heritage Site.

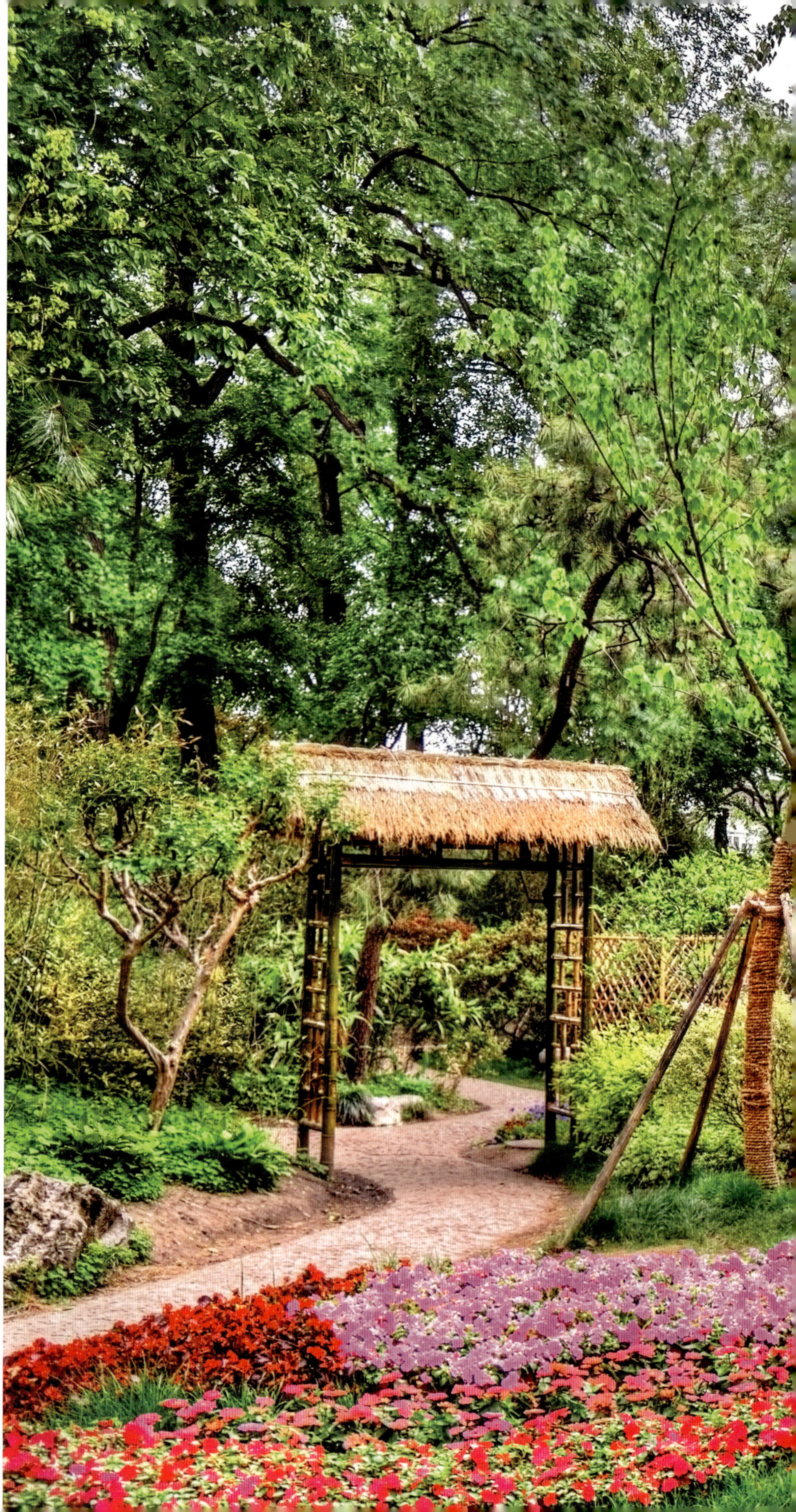

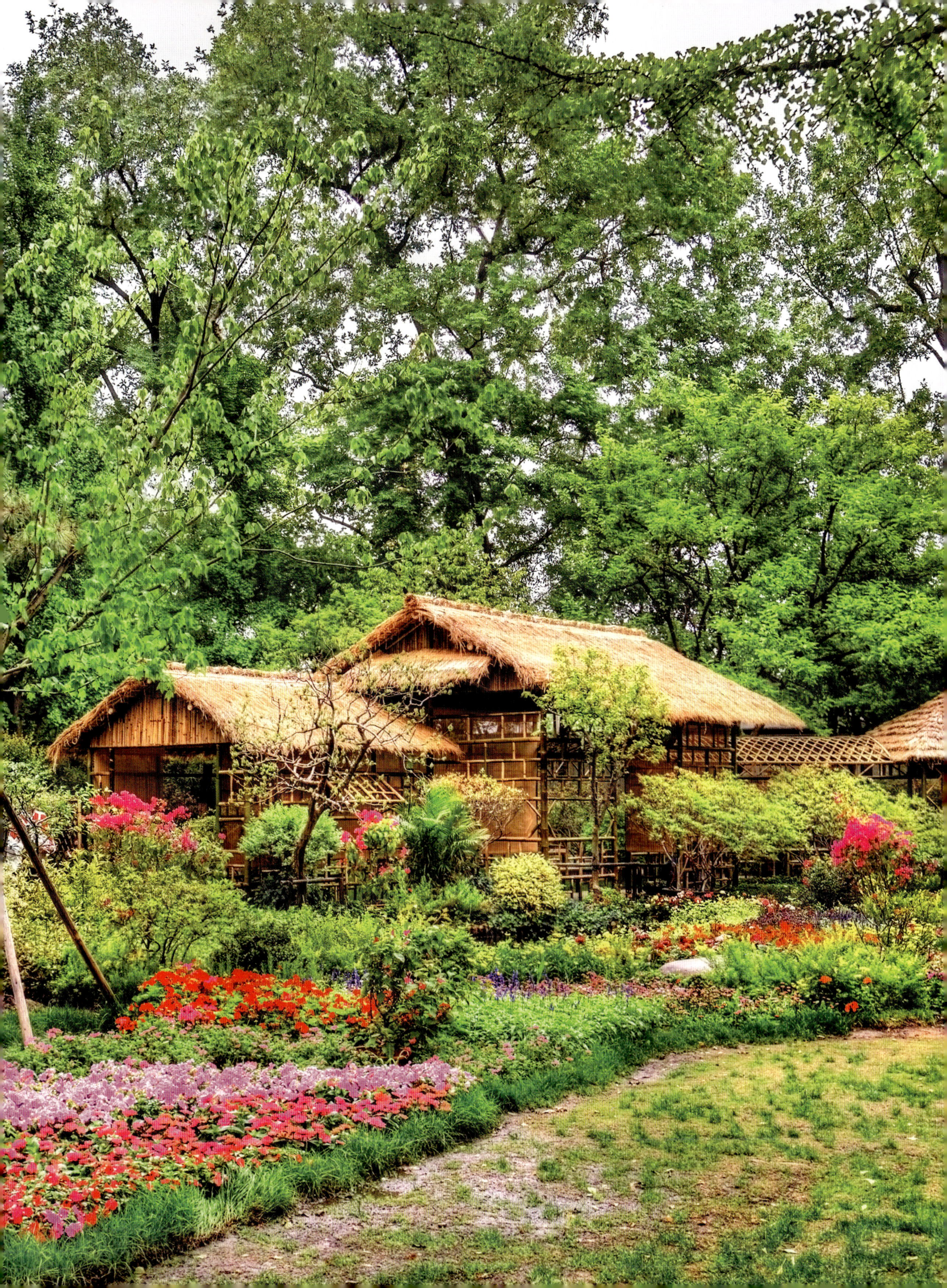

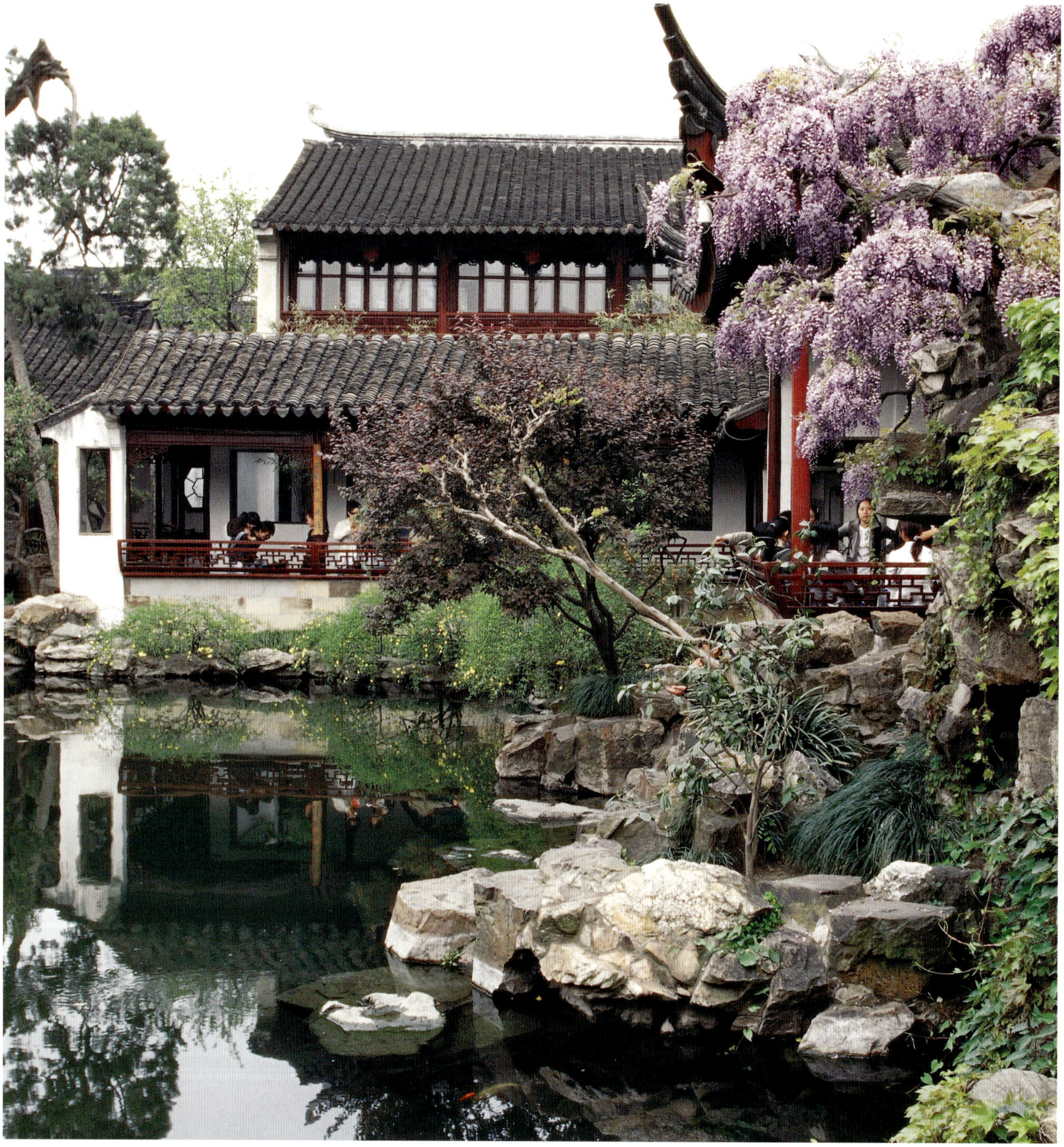

BOTH PHOTOGRAPHS:

Master-of-Nets Garden, Suzhou, Jiangsu, China

In Suzhou, this small but perfectly formed garden, a UNESCO World Heritage Site, is only an acre in size, but as in other classical gardens in this region, each element is exquisitely considered. It is a scholar's garden, with such elements as the Chapel of Accumulated Emptiness and the Pavilion Where the Moon Meets the Wind. Although it was first laid out in the 12th century by Shi Zhengzhi, the garden was redesigned by Song Zongyuan in 1785, with many features dating from this time. The garden is intended to express the simple life of a fisherman.

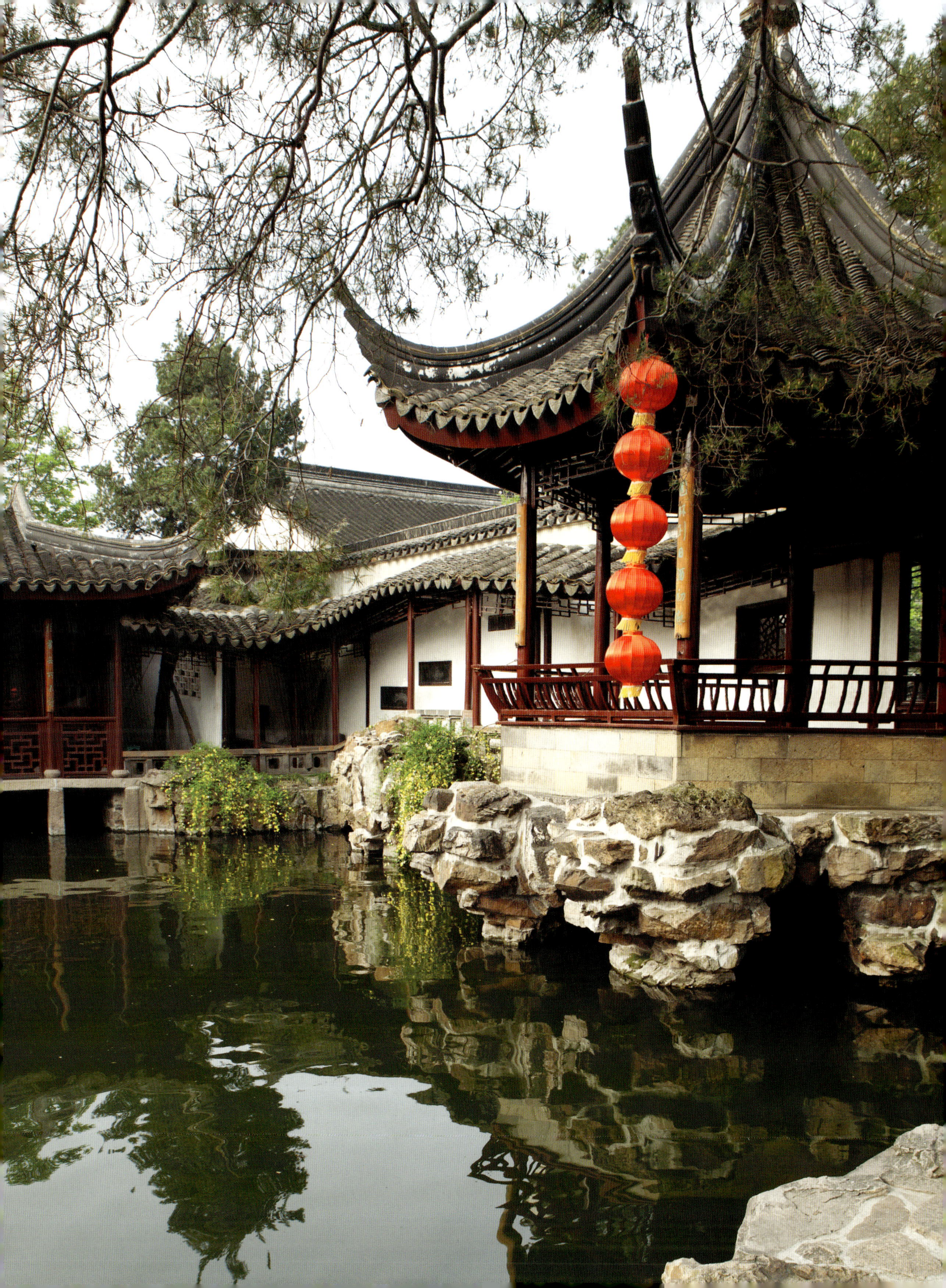

Kenroku-en, Ishikawa, Japan

With Koraku-en and Kairaku-en, Kenroku-en in Kanazawa is known as one of the Three Great Gardens of Japan. It was developed over 200 years from the 17th to the 19th centuries. The oldest building in the garden is a teahouse, built in 1774. The legs of a stone lantern resemble the shape of a *koto*, the Japanese national instrument. The lantern has become heraldic of the garden. In winter, ropes support tree branches to protect them from heavy snows in a technique known as *yukitsuri*.

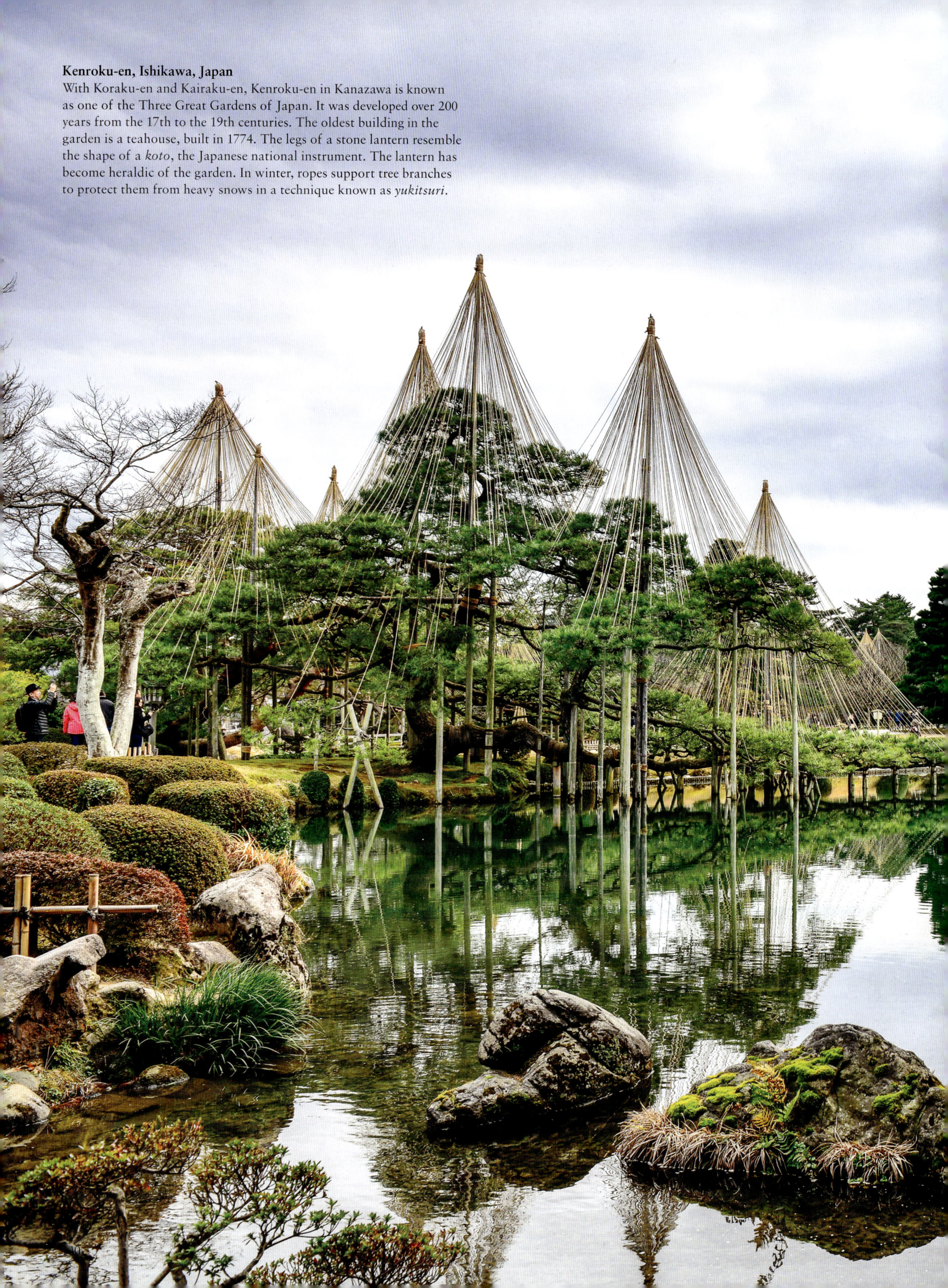

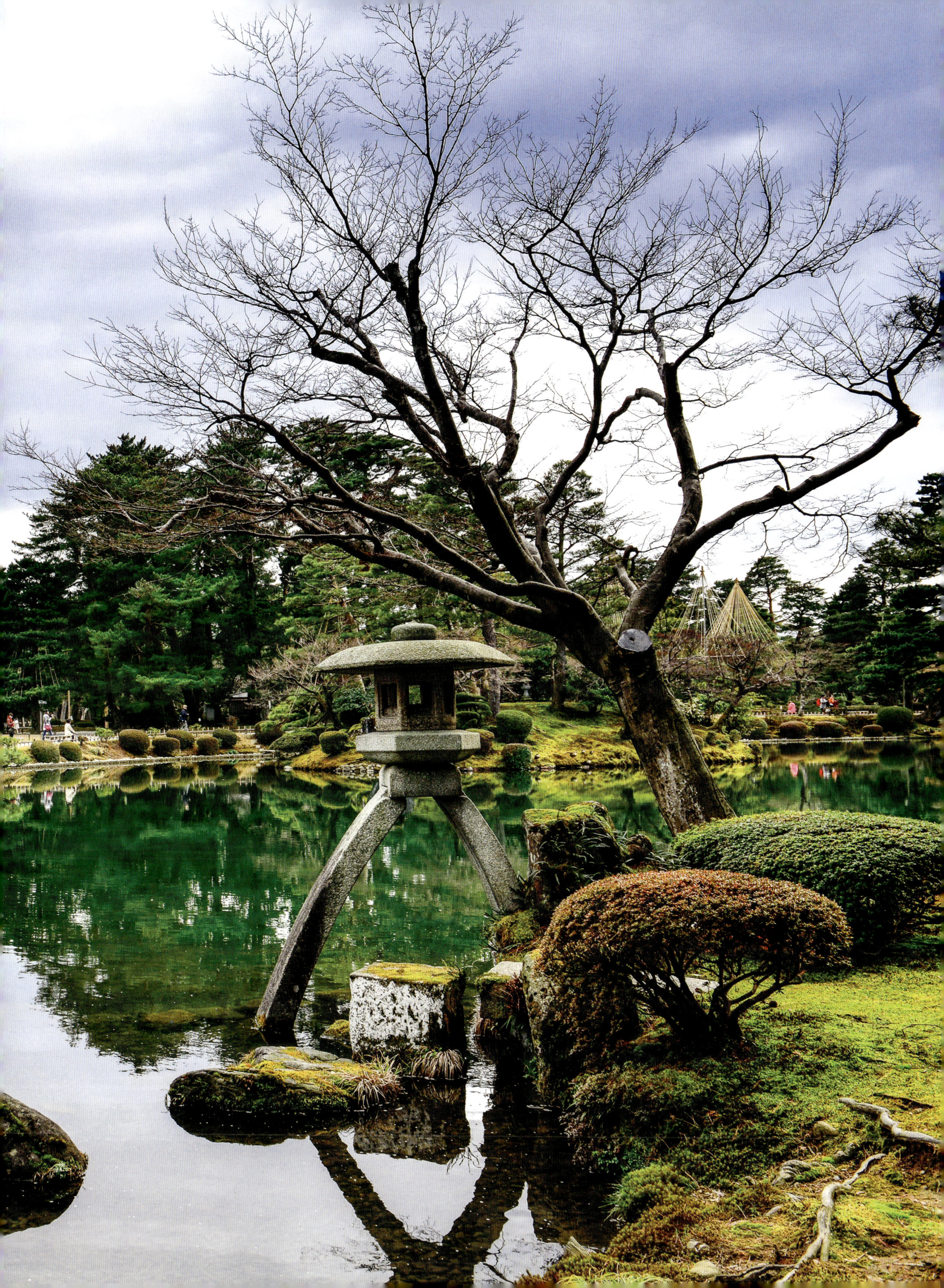

RIGHT AND OVERLEAF TOP LEFT:

Koishikawa Koraku-en Garden, Tokyo, Japan

Few could have imagined how important a green lung for the city of Tokyo this park would become back when it was built in 1629 in the Edo period. One of the oldest parks in the city, it was instigated by Tokugawa Yorifusa and remained in this ruling family until 1869, when it was ceded to the Meiji government. It is at its best in spring and autumn, when it is coloured with blossom and turning leaves respectively.

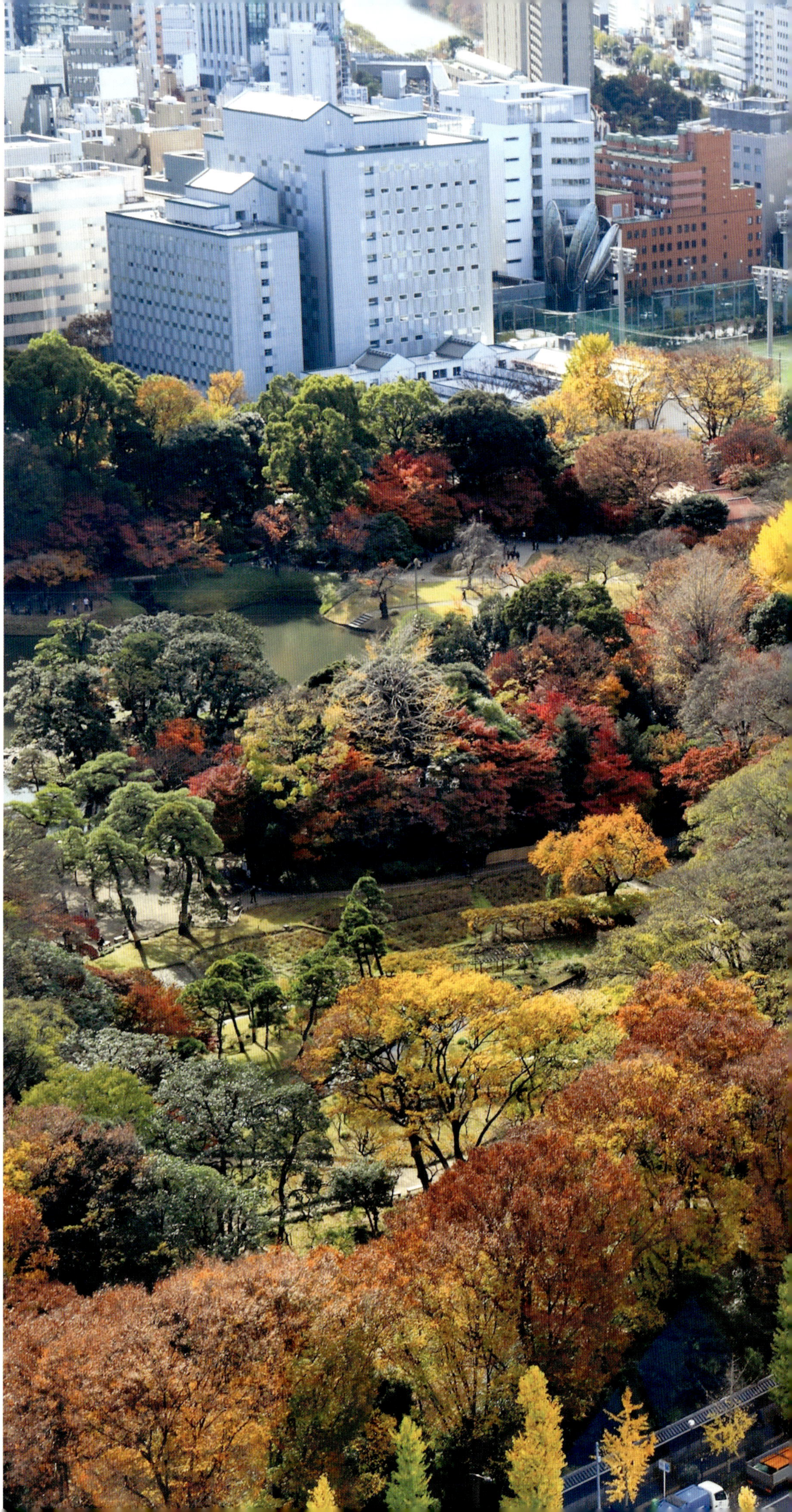

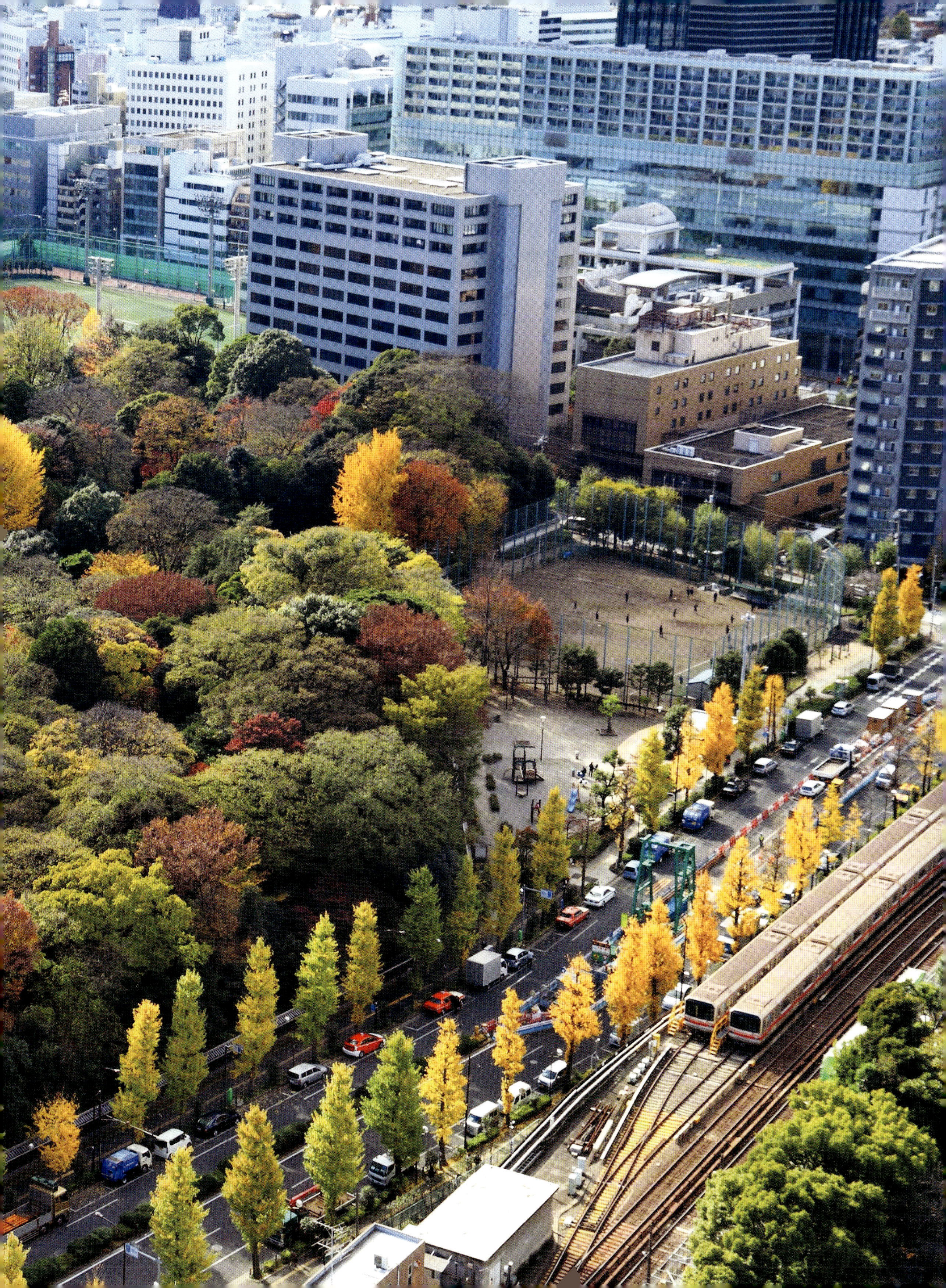

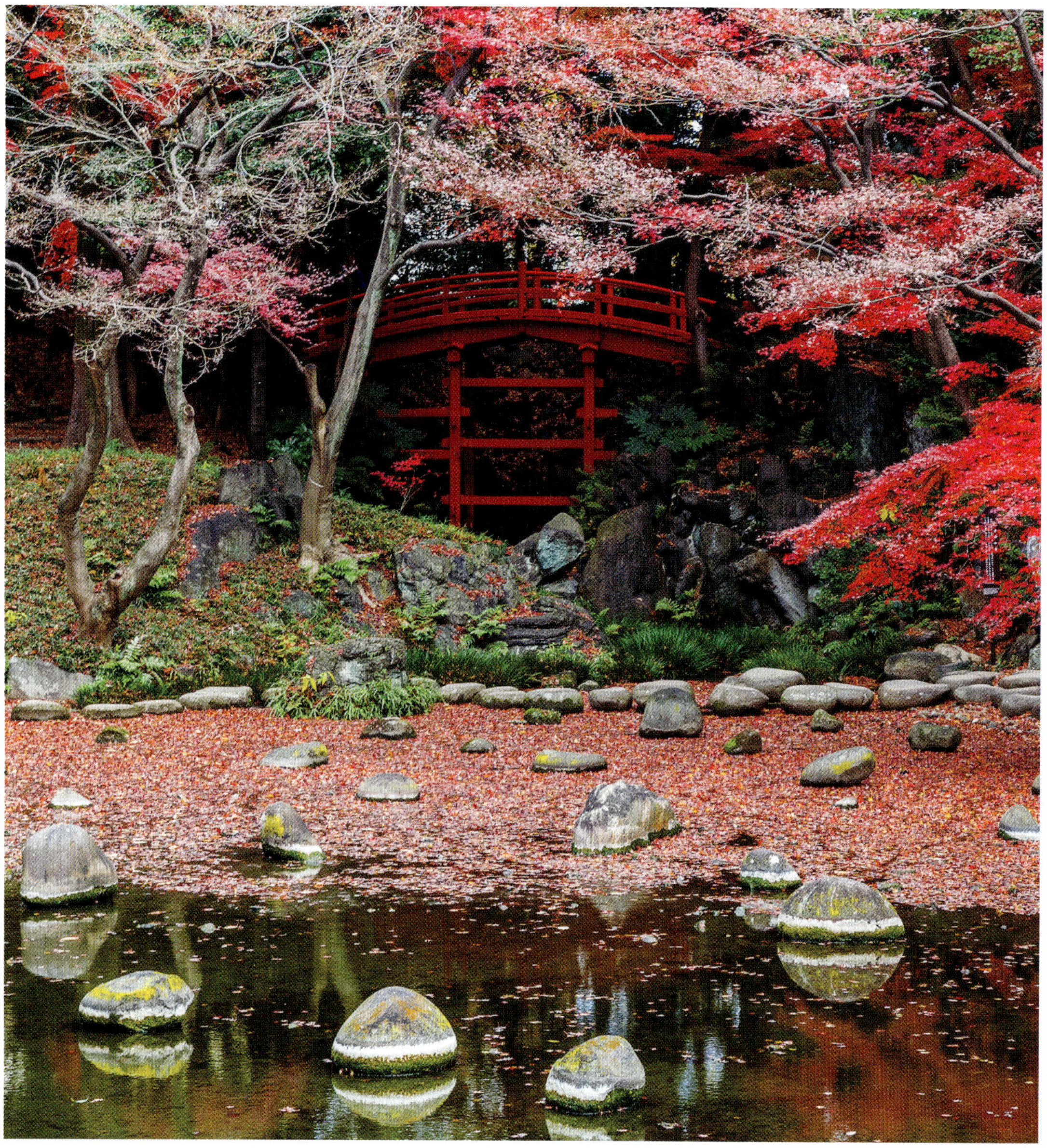

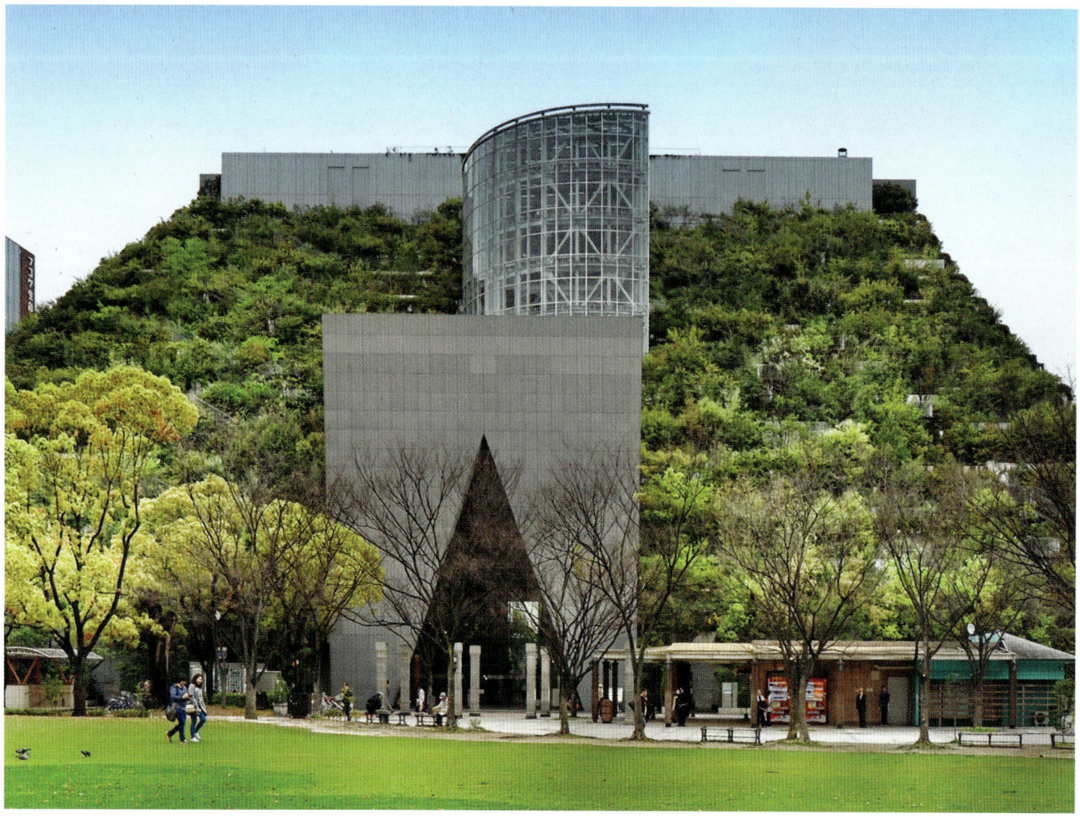

RIGHT AND LEFT BOTTOM:

ACROS building, Fukuoka City, Japan

Roof gardens and living walls are meaningful responses to climate change and habitat loss in dense cities, where they can also offer a pleasing design aesthetic. The ACROS Fukuoka Prefectural International Hall in Fukuoka City was at the forefront of green architecture when it was completed in 1994. Designed by Argentinian green architect Emilio Ambasz, it features an inclining wall of 15 planted terraces which are open to the public. Zig-zagging walkways lead to a roof garden.

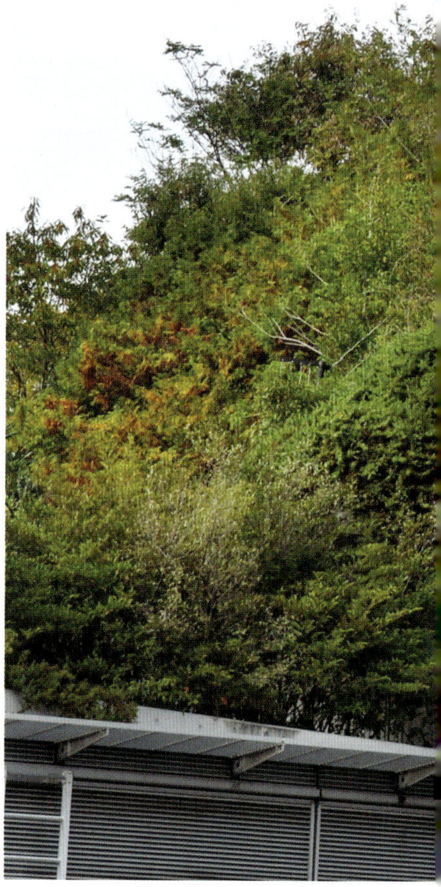

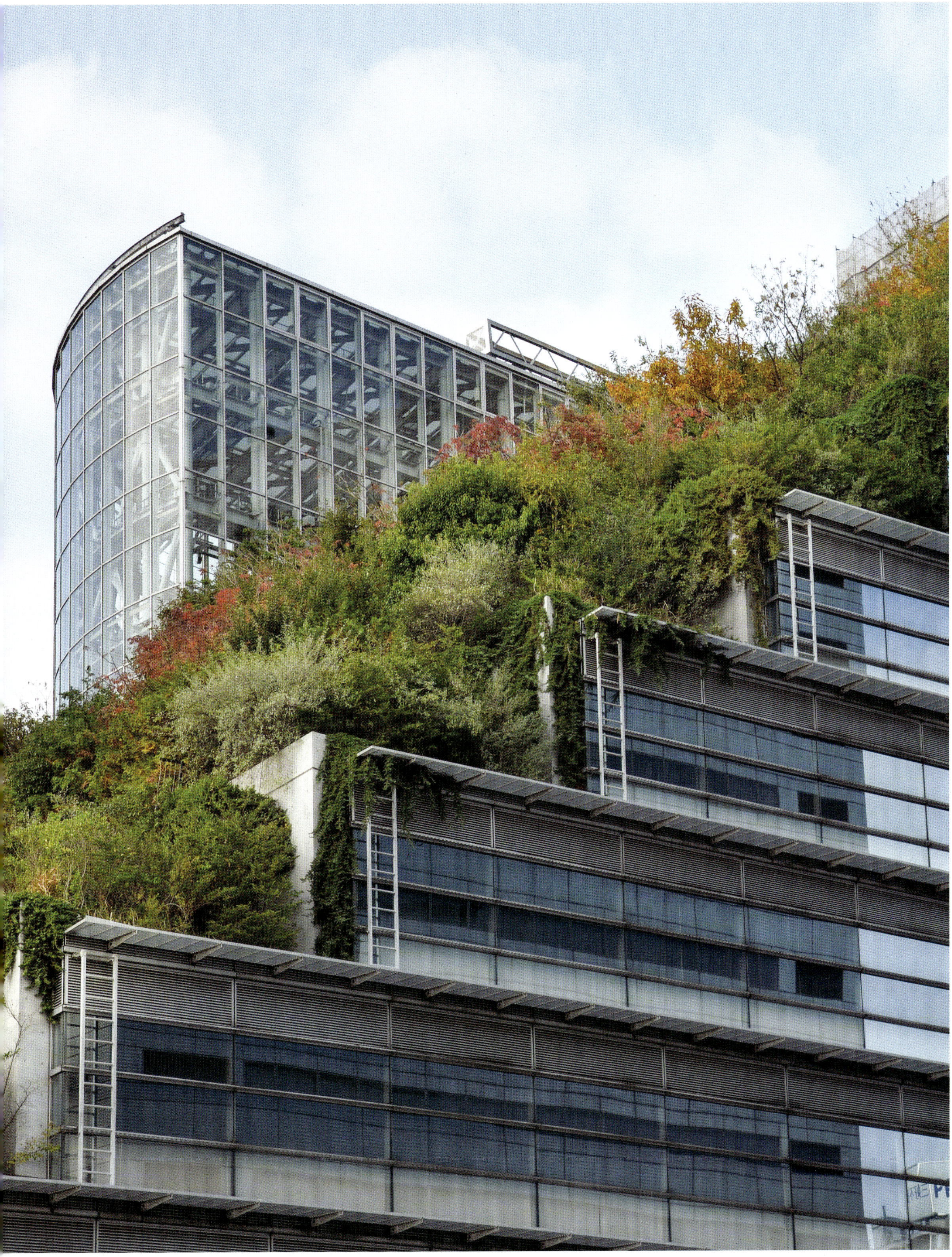

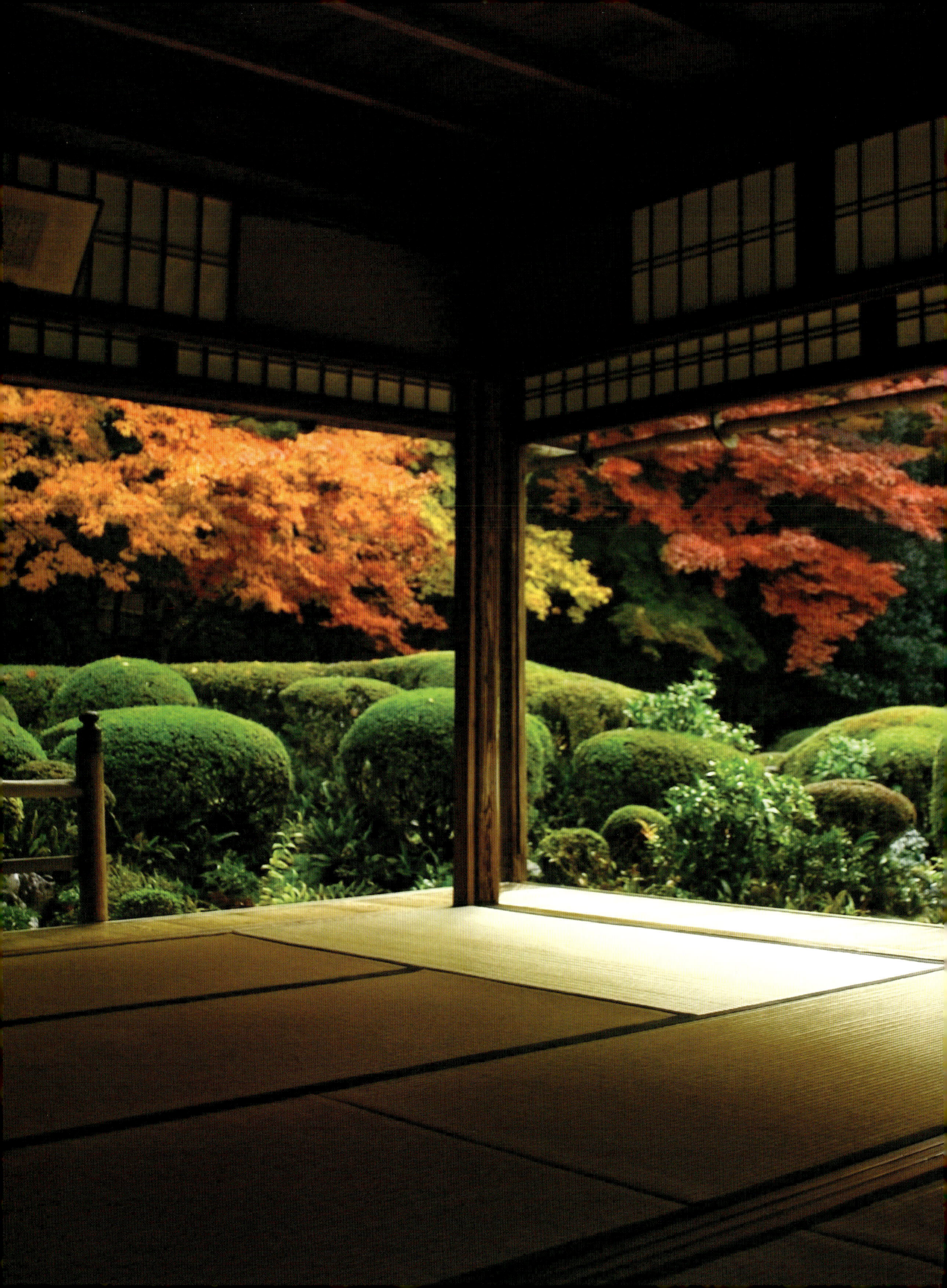

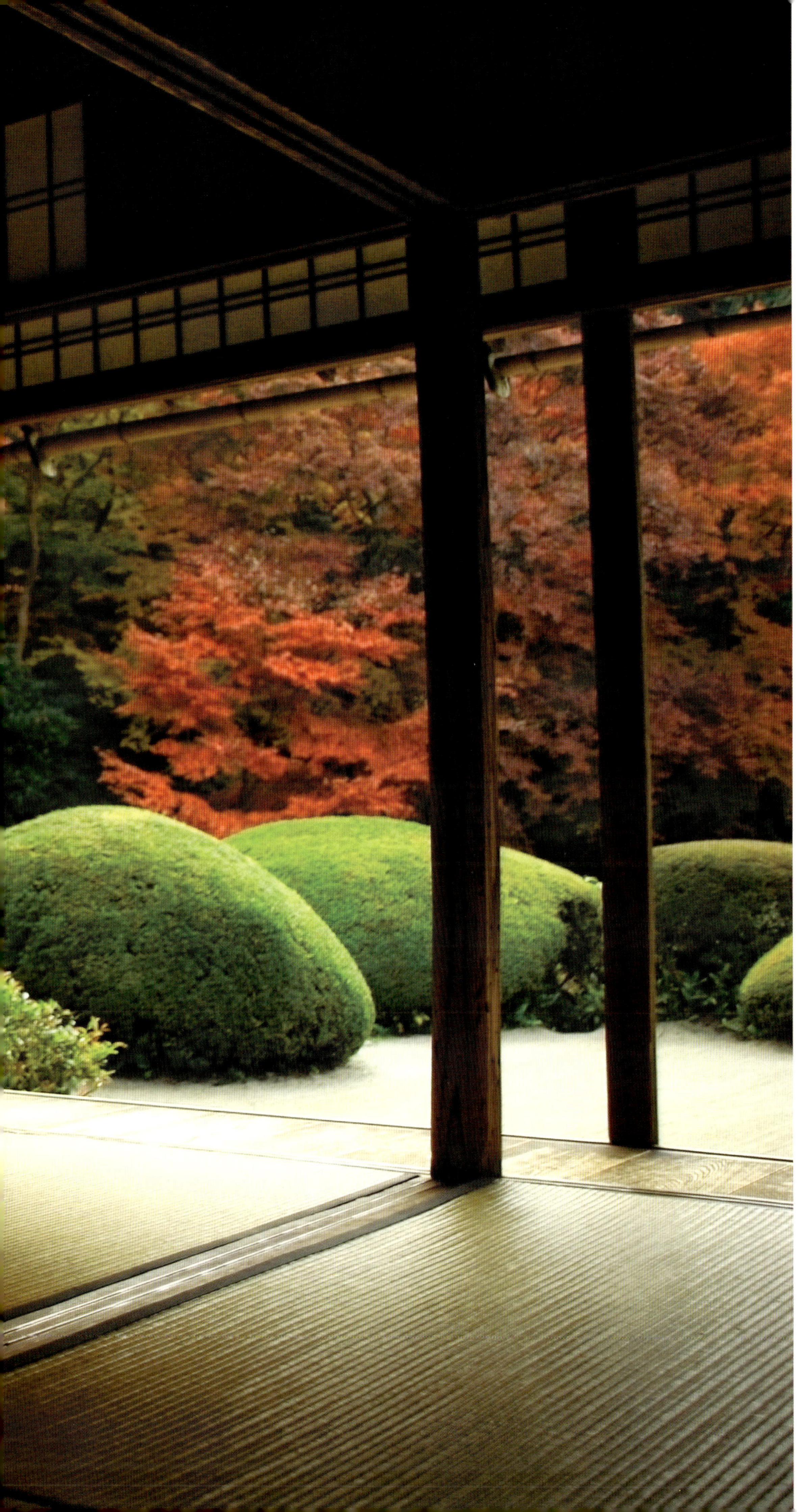

Shisen-do temple, Kyoto, Japan
Ishikawa Jozan built Shisen-do as a mountain retreat or hermitage in 1641. The samurai-turned-poet sought retreat from the pressures of life and that same tranquil air remains in the garden today. It is from the hermitage that Jozan wrote the poetry in the Chinese style for which he became known. Azaleas and maples bring colour to the garden in spring and autumn; their forms contrast with the controlled aesthetic of clipped shrubs and a gravel garden.

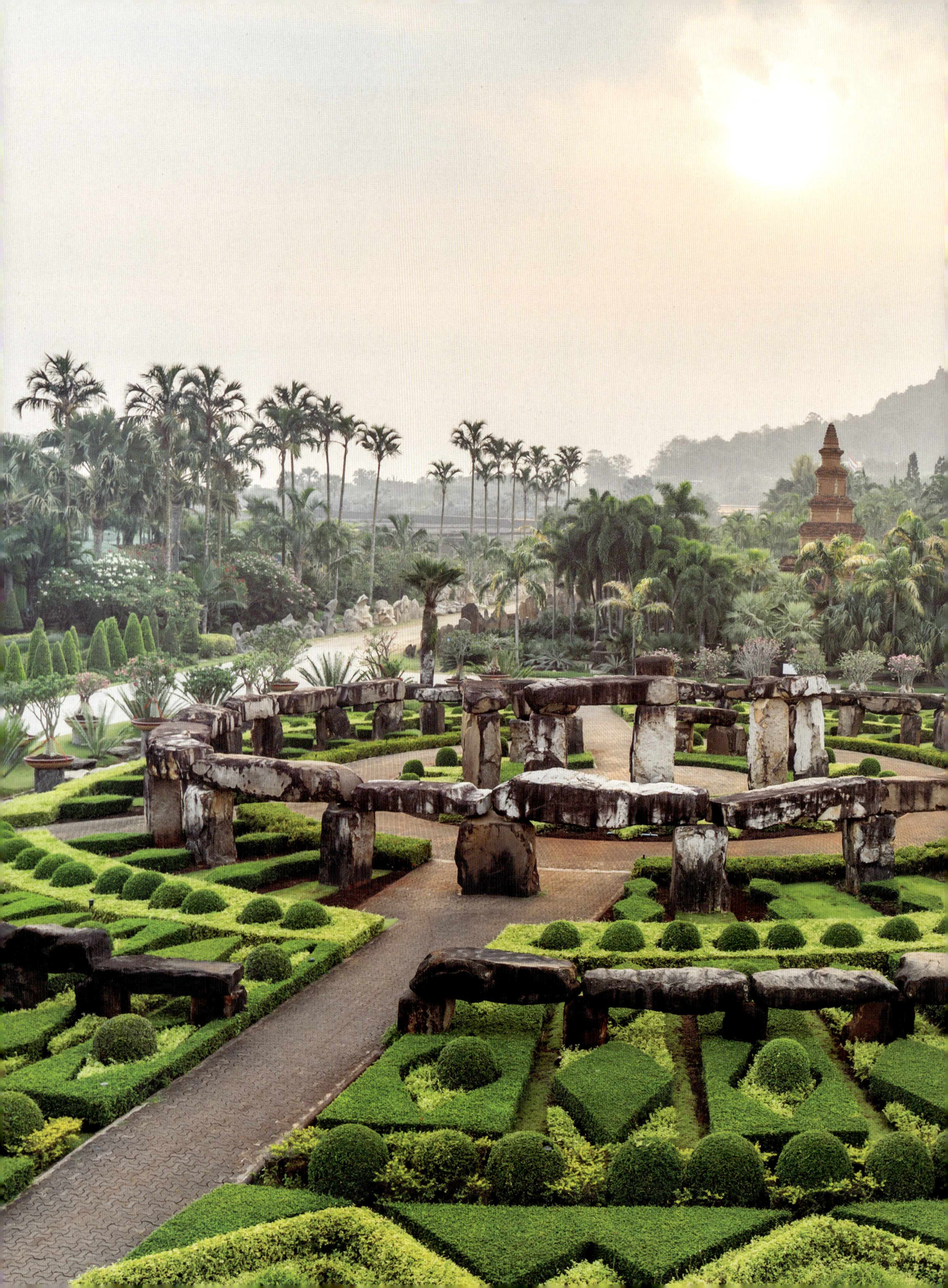

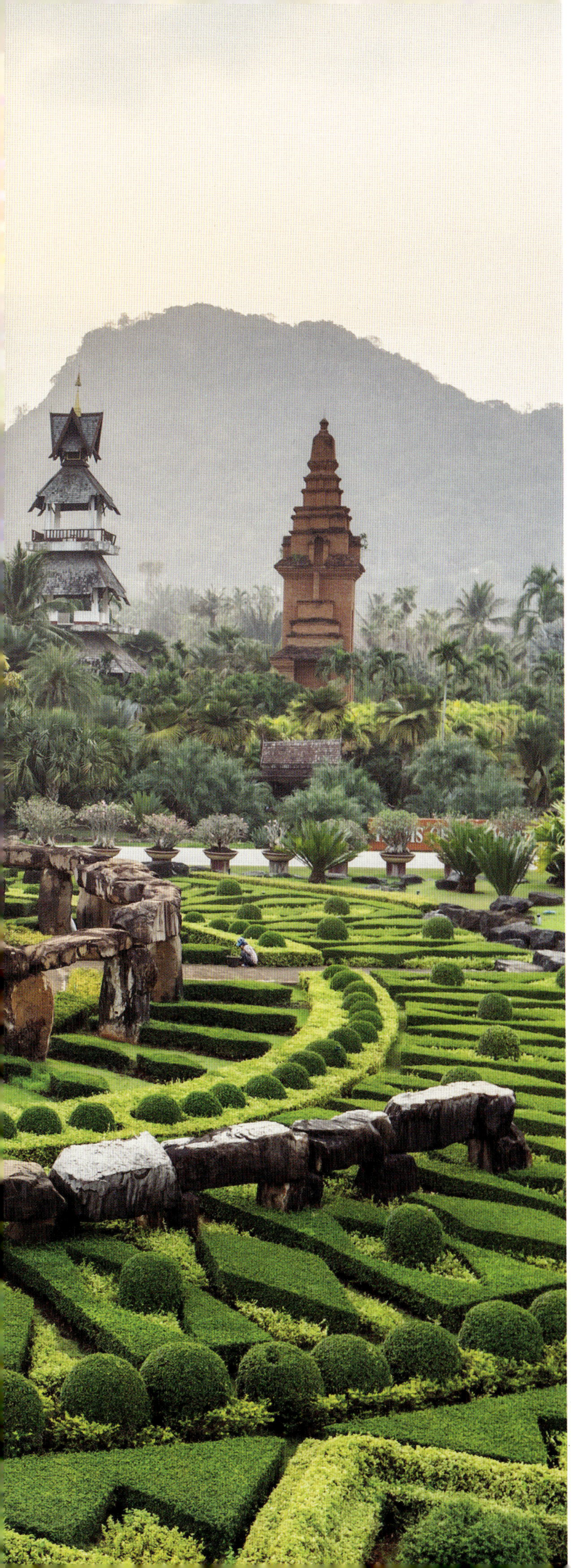

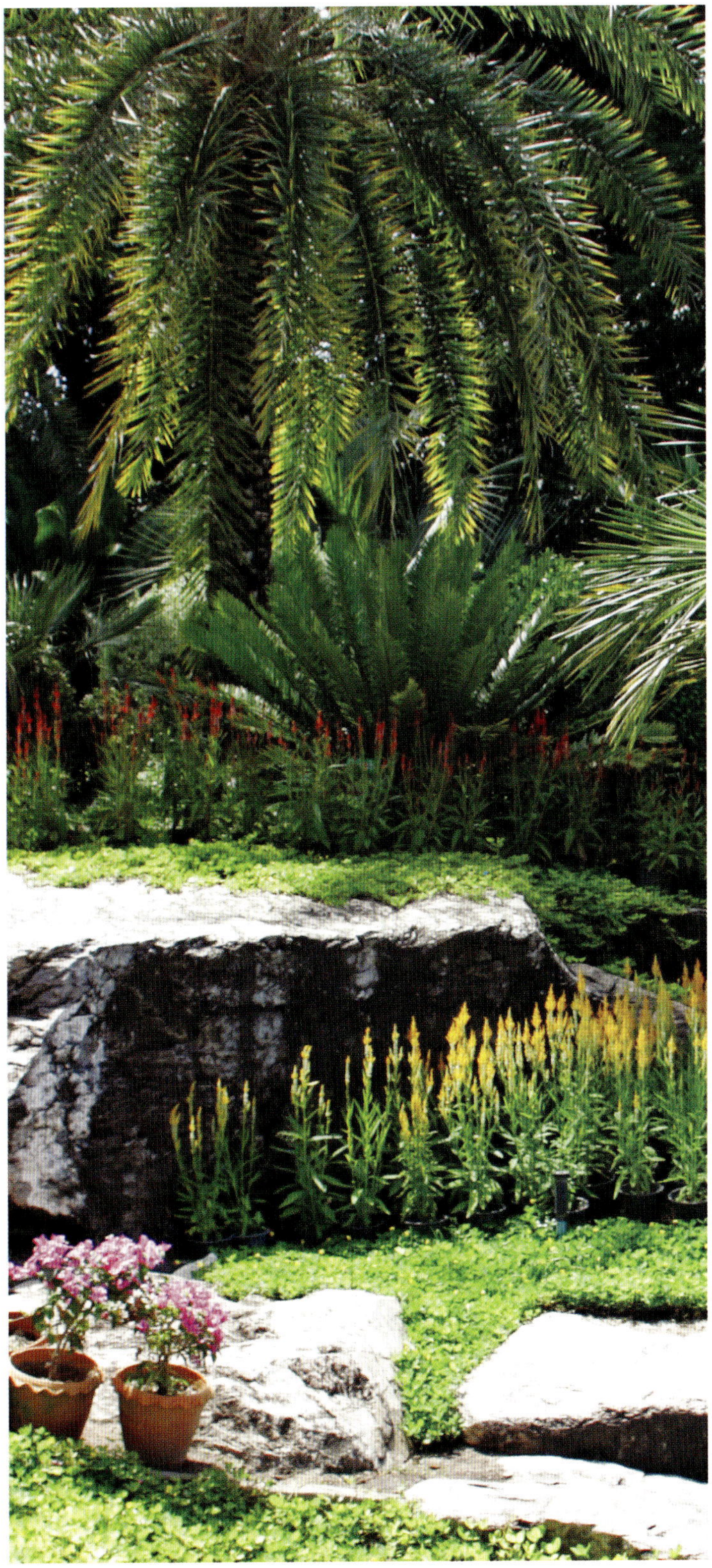

BOTH PHOTOGRAPHS:

Nong Nooch Tropical Garden, Pattaya City, Thailand

Spread over 200ha (500 acres), this tropical garden is one of the largest in Southeast Asia. At first it was intended the land would be given to a commercial plantation but upon seeing ornamental gardens abroad, the owners changed tack. Opened to the public as a tourist destination in 1980, today its extraordinary attractions include palm, orchid and cycad collections, a Thai topiary garden, French- and Italian-style gardens, and Stone Henge garden.

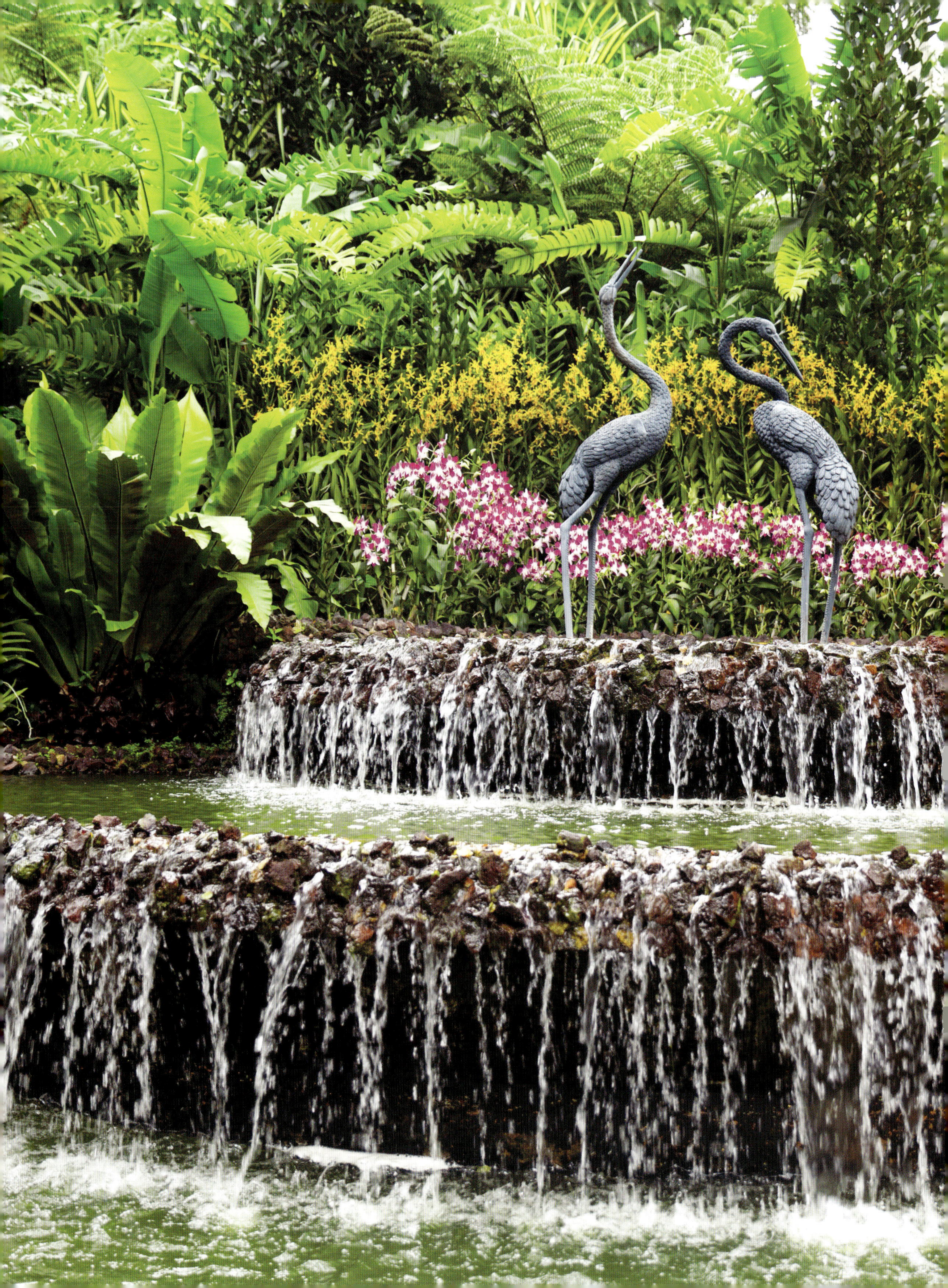

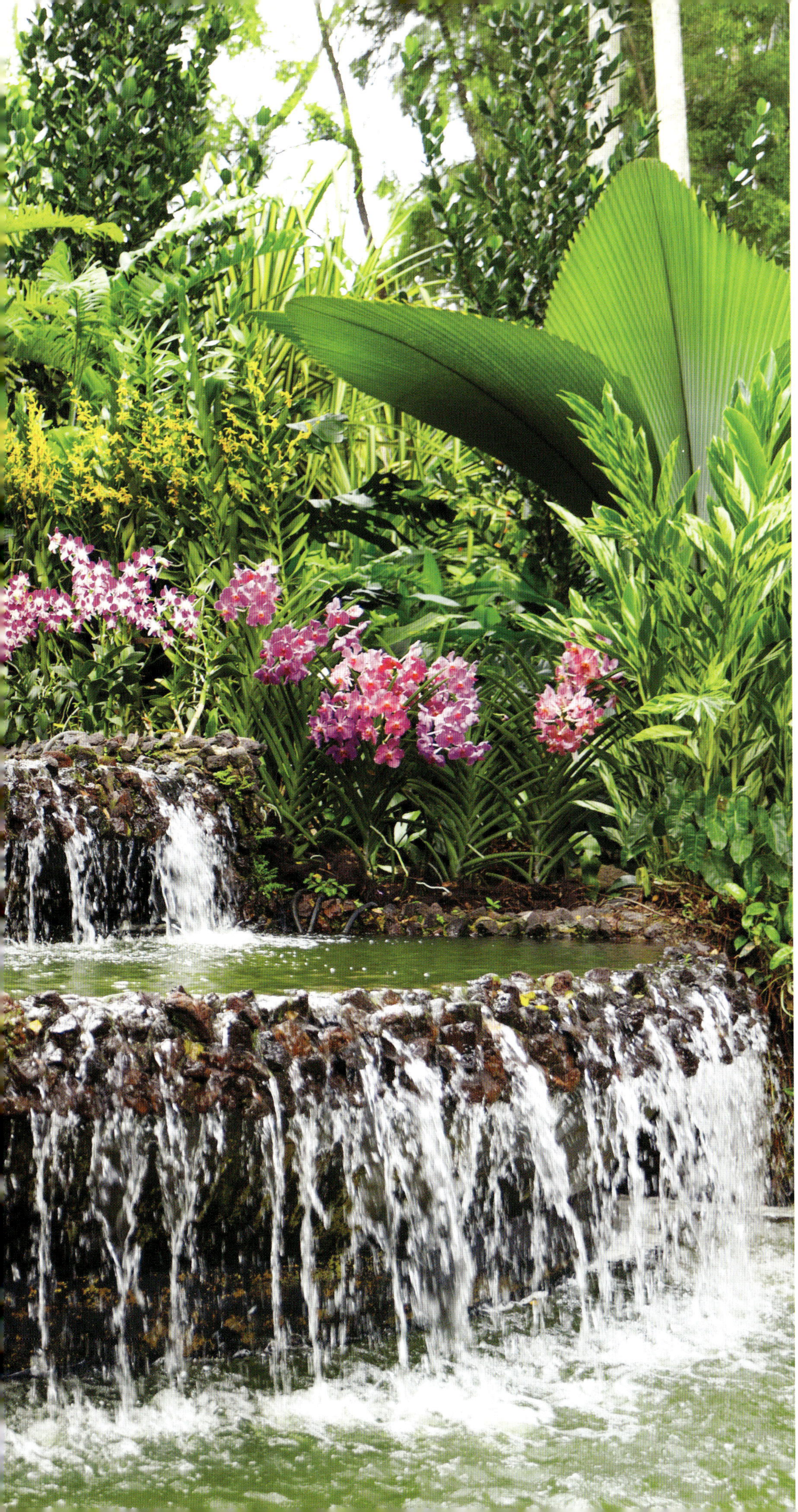

Singapore Botanic Gardens, Singapore
One of the world's most important botanical gardens, this UNESCO World Heritage Site was founded in 1882. Among the first plants trialled here was the Pará rubber tree (*Hevea brasiliensis*) and success spawned commercial plantations across the region. Described as the 'Kew of the East', the institution has maintained a notable orchid breeding programme since 1928, while the Herbarium houses around 750,000 specimens from the Malesian region. The gardens are an important green lung in the city.

Gardens by the Bay, Singapore

If the Singapore Botanic Gardens focus is on regional plants, the Gardens by the Bay take quite the opposite approach. Hundreds of thousands of plant species from around the world are assembled in this vast public garden covering over 100ha (247 acres). Domes, skywalks and cloud forests and the world's largest glass greenhouse may be found here. Opened in 2011, the gardens have a strong sustainability focus, with features such as photovoltaic cells contained within the garden's iconic Supertree Observatory.

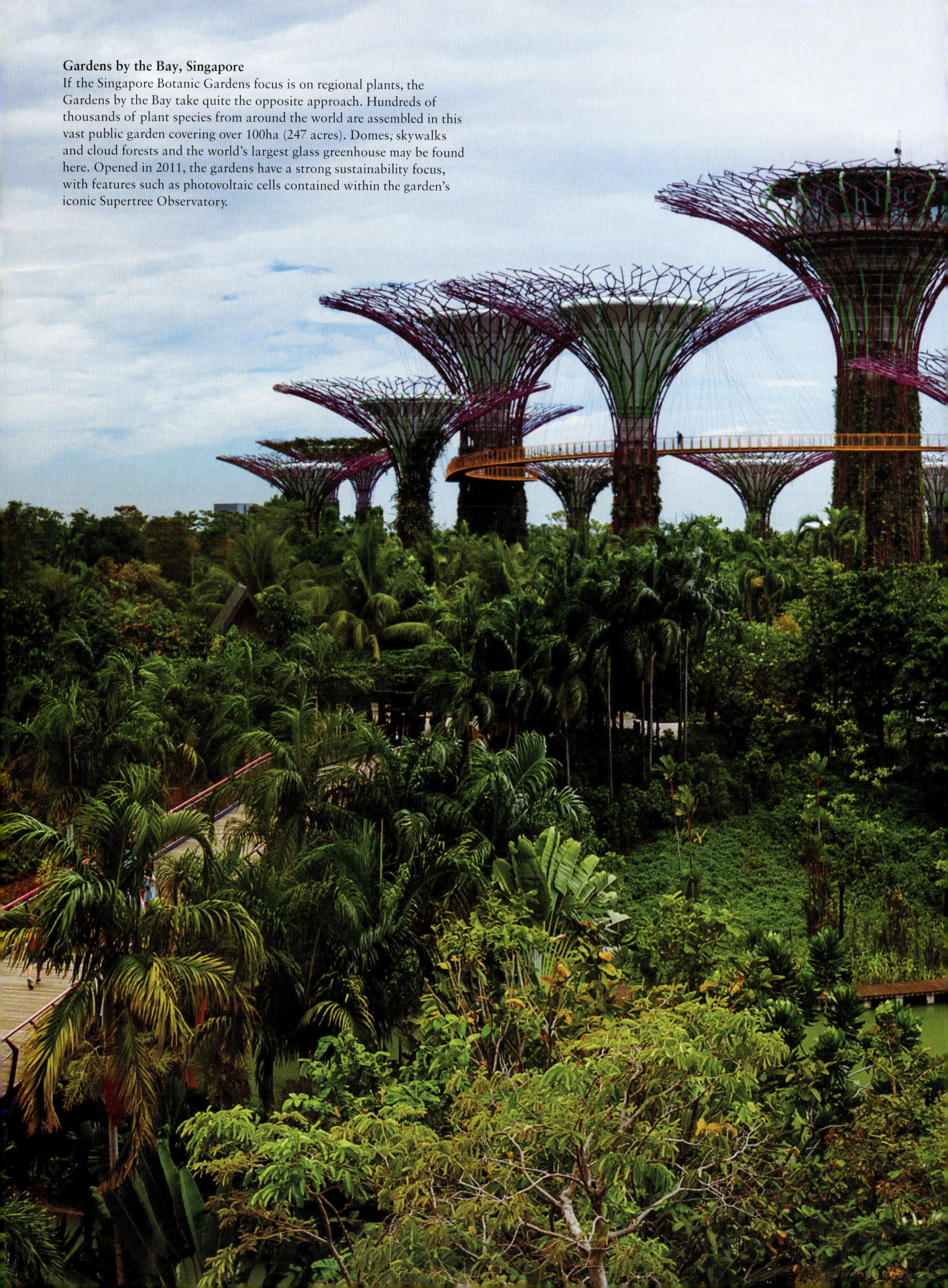

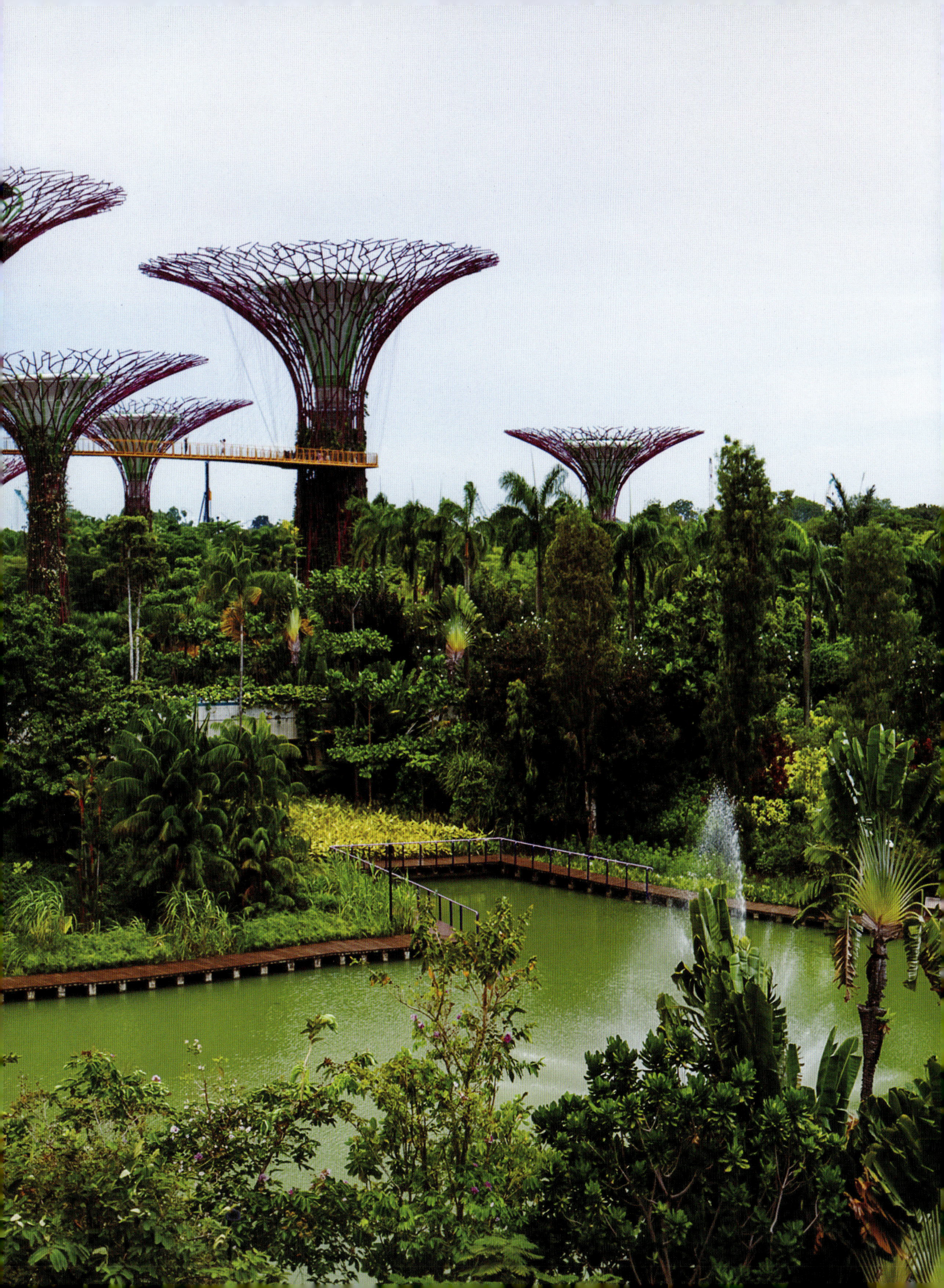

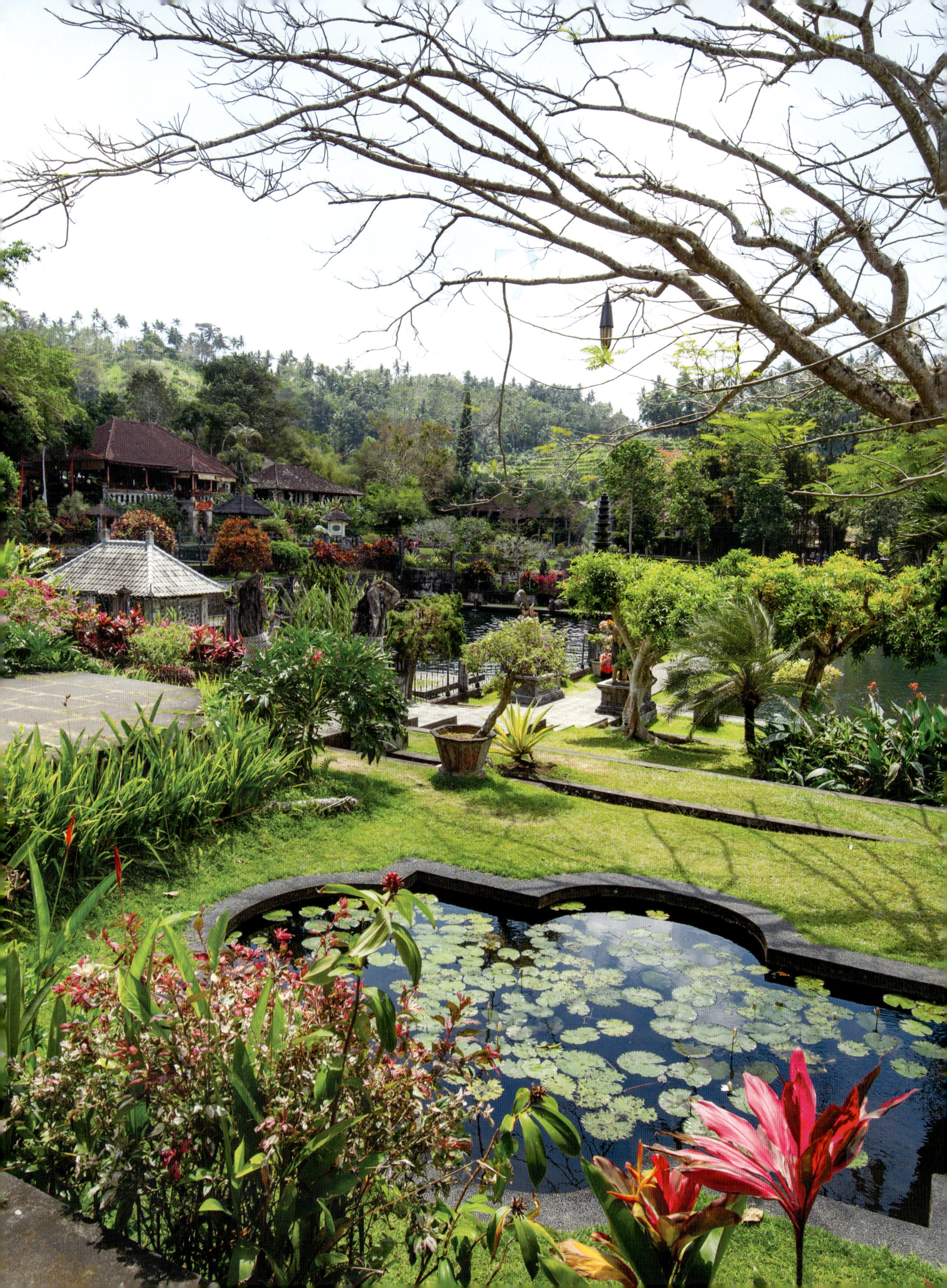

Australasia and the Pacific

A panoply of influences, styles and intentions shape the gardens of this great region, which ranges from the rainforests of equatorial Indonesia to the icy glaciers of South Island, New Zealand.

In Bali, religious persuasions have led to water gardens offering peace and solitude, in spite of being within range of an active volcano.

Across Australia, city founders established parks and gardens to cement an identity on a region, but now find that identity shifting as Australia becomes more international and the role of Aborigine people is acknowledged. Today botanic gardens strive to collect, protect and promote the extraordinary indigenous flora of this vast continent.

Research increasingly confirms what many have long known – which is that gardening can have a profound positive influence on mental health. In New South Wales, Wendy Whitely created a relative Eden from wasteland, and in doing so has overcome her own demons.

Other, intensely personal gardens are the result of creative vision and a direct response to landscape, whether that is farmland or snow-capped mountains.

OPPOSITE:

Tirta Gangga, Bali, Indonesia

This 1.2ha (3-acre) water garden in east Bali was built to create a place of relaxation and holiness for residents and visitors. The name derives from the holy river Ganges, in India. Tirta Gangga has a look of great age but in fact dates only from 1948. With the active volcano of Mount Agung in the background, its three levels feature fountains and decorative ponds.

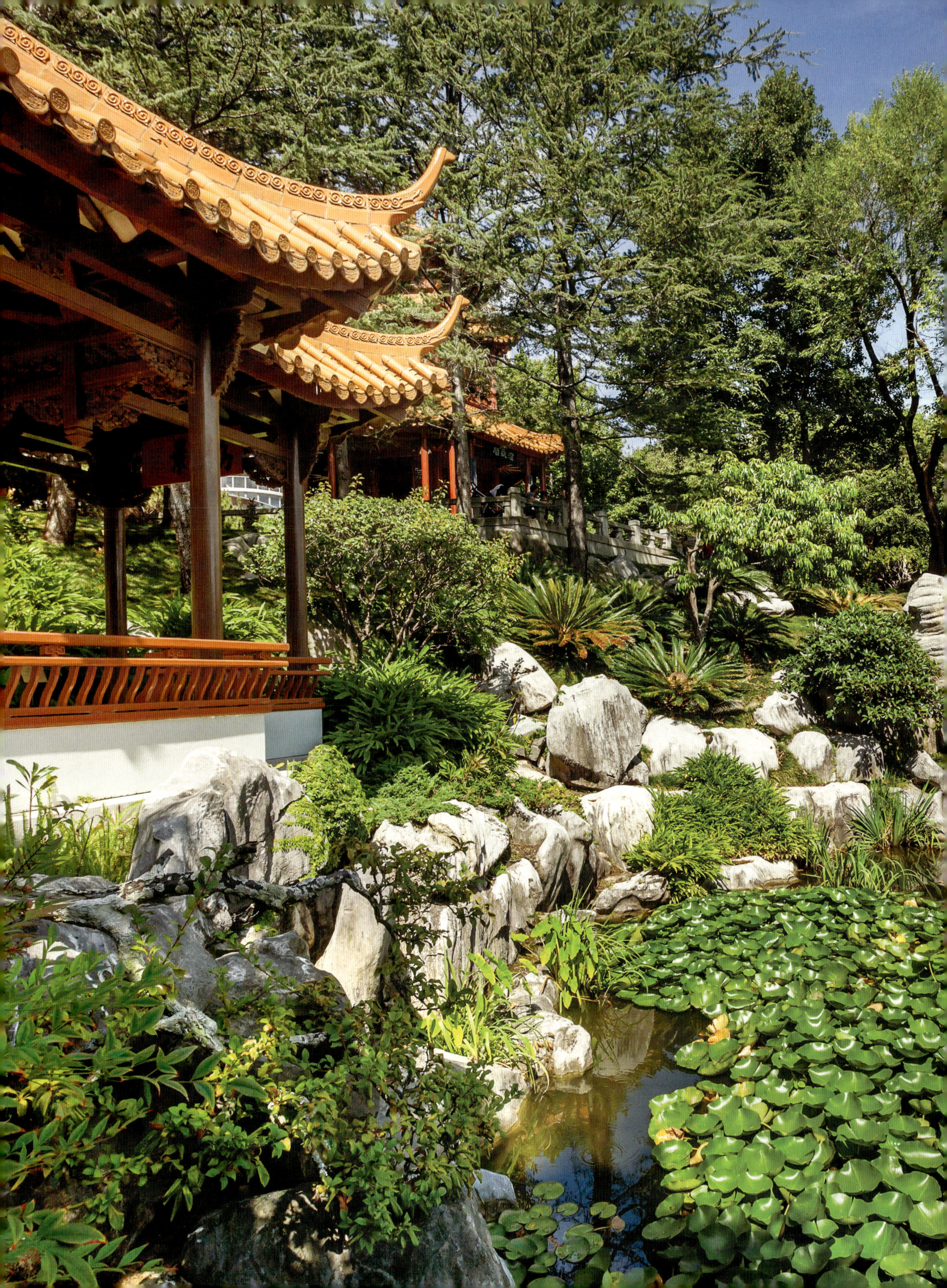

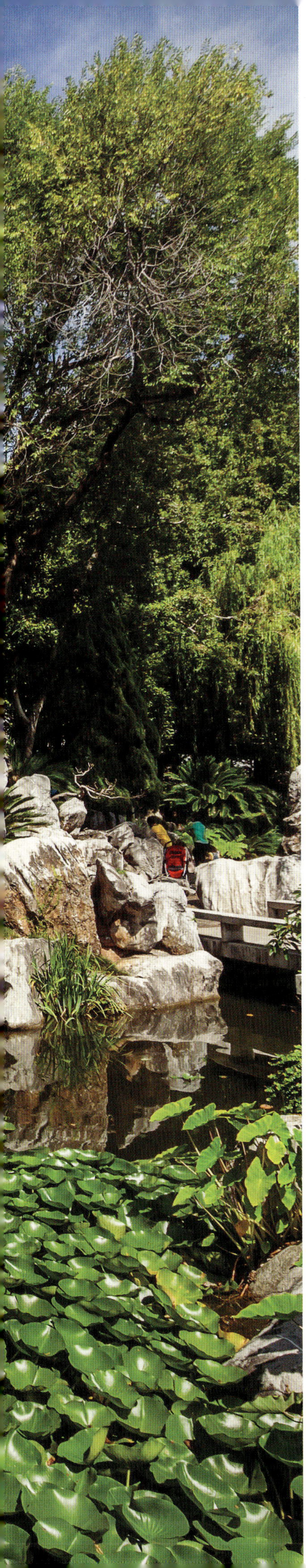

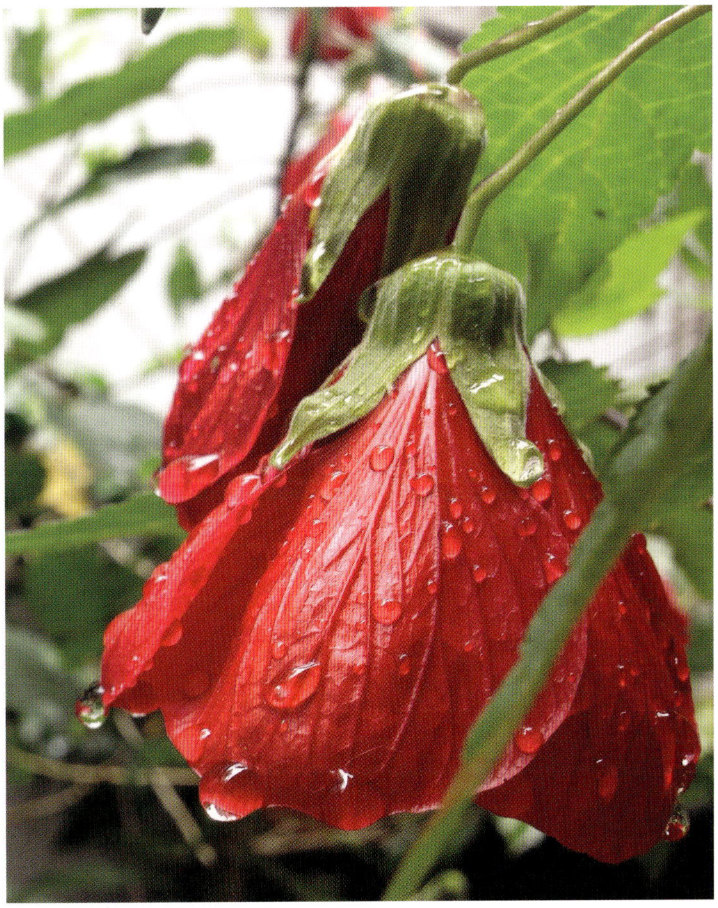

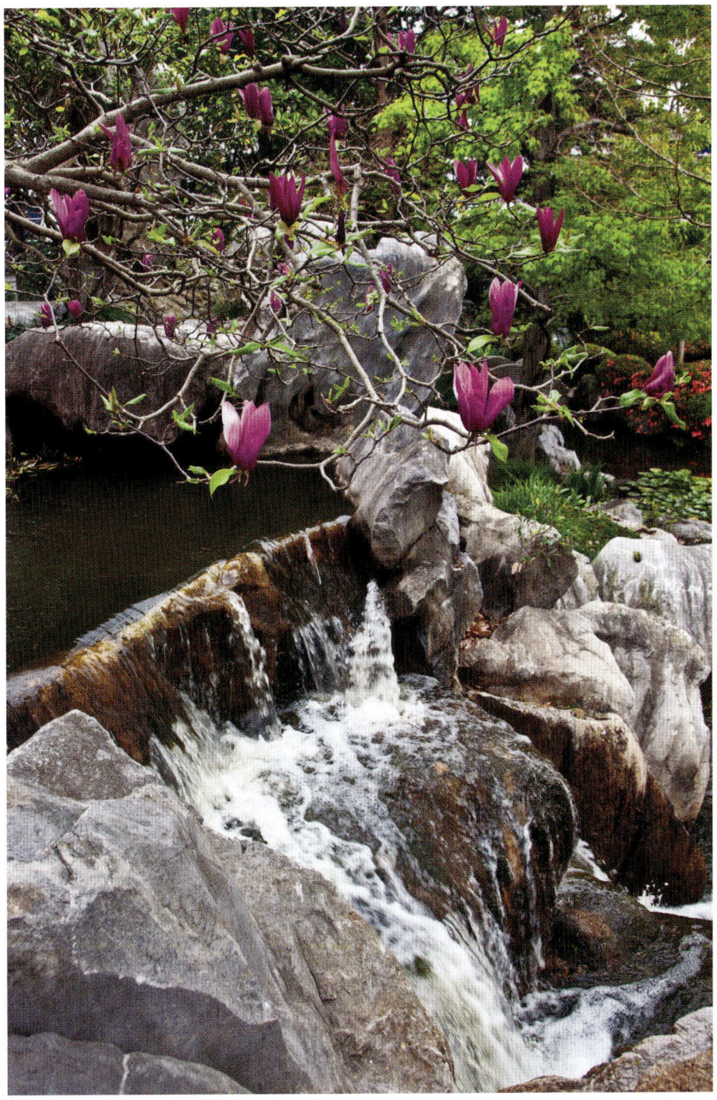

ALL PHOTOGRAPHS:

Chinese Garden of Friendship, New South Wales, Australia

To mark Australia's bicentennial celebrations, these gardens in a goods yard in Darling Harbour, Sydney, were opened in 1988. In a gesture of goodwill, the 1ha (2.47-acre) gardens were initiated by the city's Chinese community, and are designed in the *lingnan* style typical of the city of Guangzhou. Plants include magnolias and abutilon, also known as Chinese lantern.

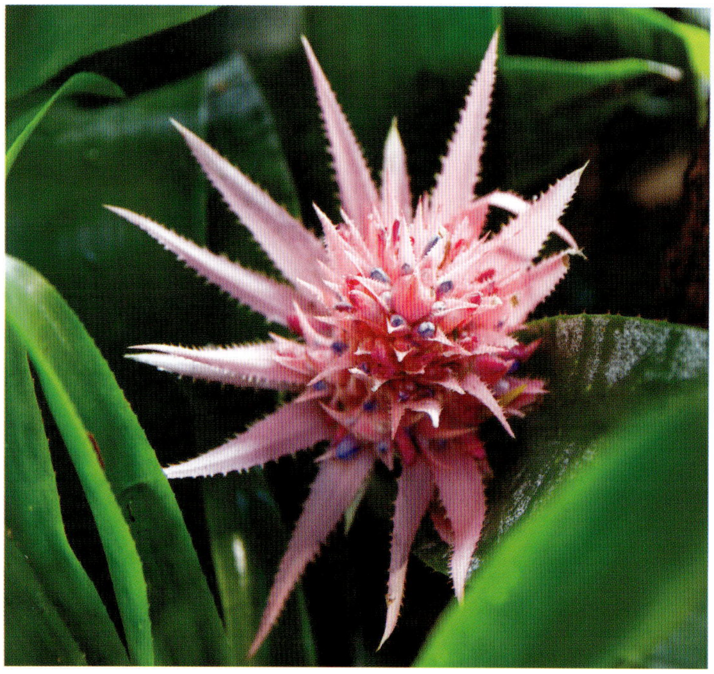

BOTH PHOTOGRAPHS:
Wendy's Secret Garden, New South Wales, Australia
On the north shore of Sydney Harbour, Wendy Whiteley began to garden a tract of abandoned public land after overcoming heroin addiction and the death of her husband and daughter. The sloping site has views of the city skyline and planting is lush with palms and native flora.

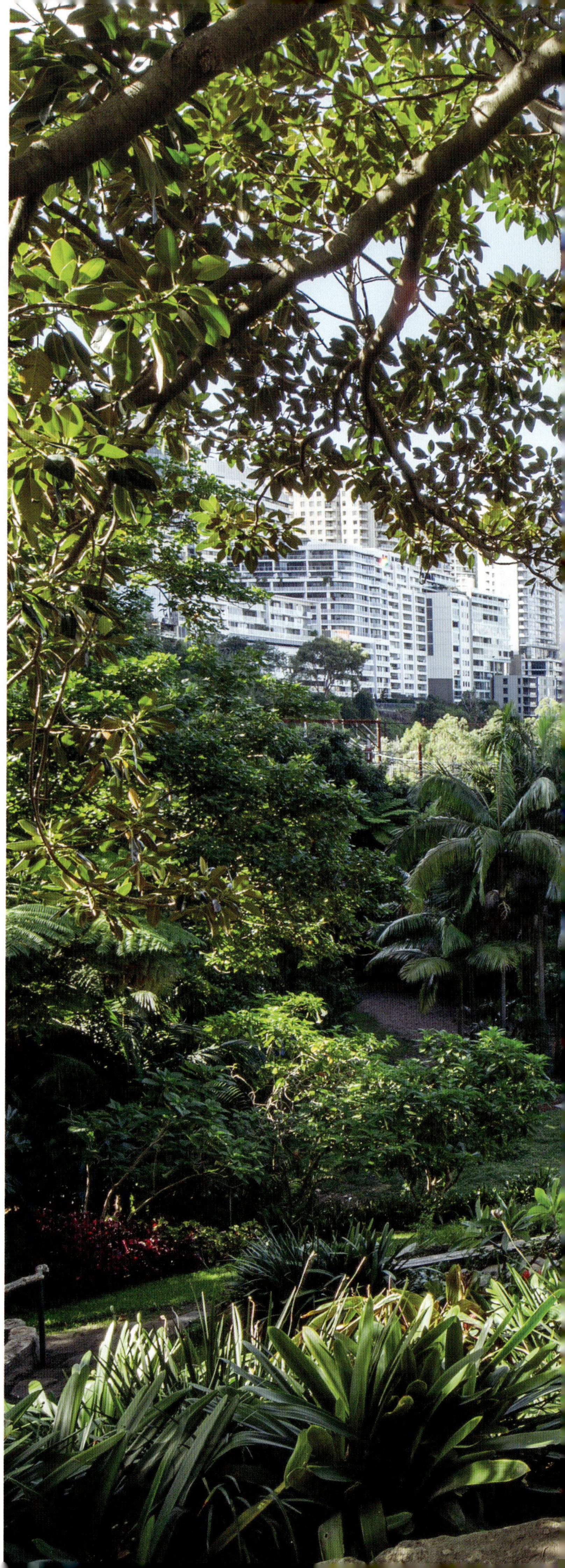

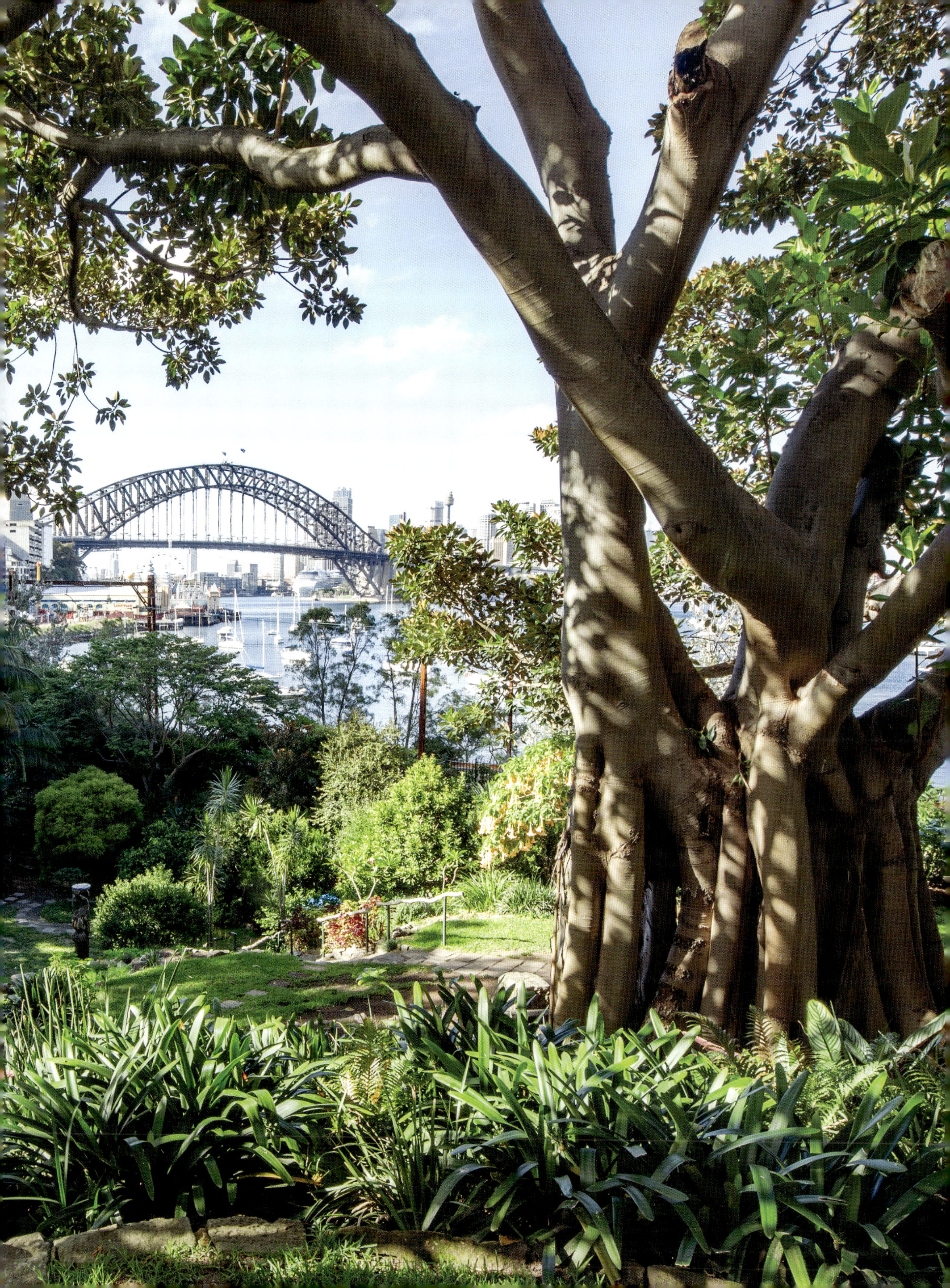

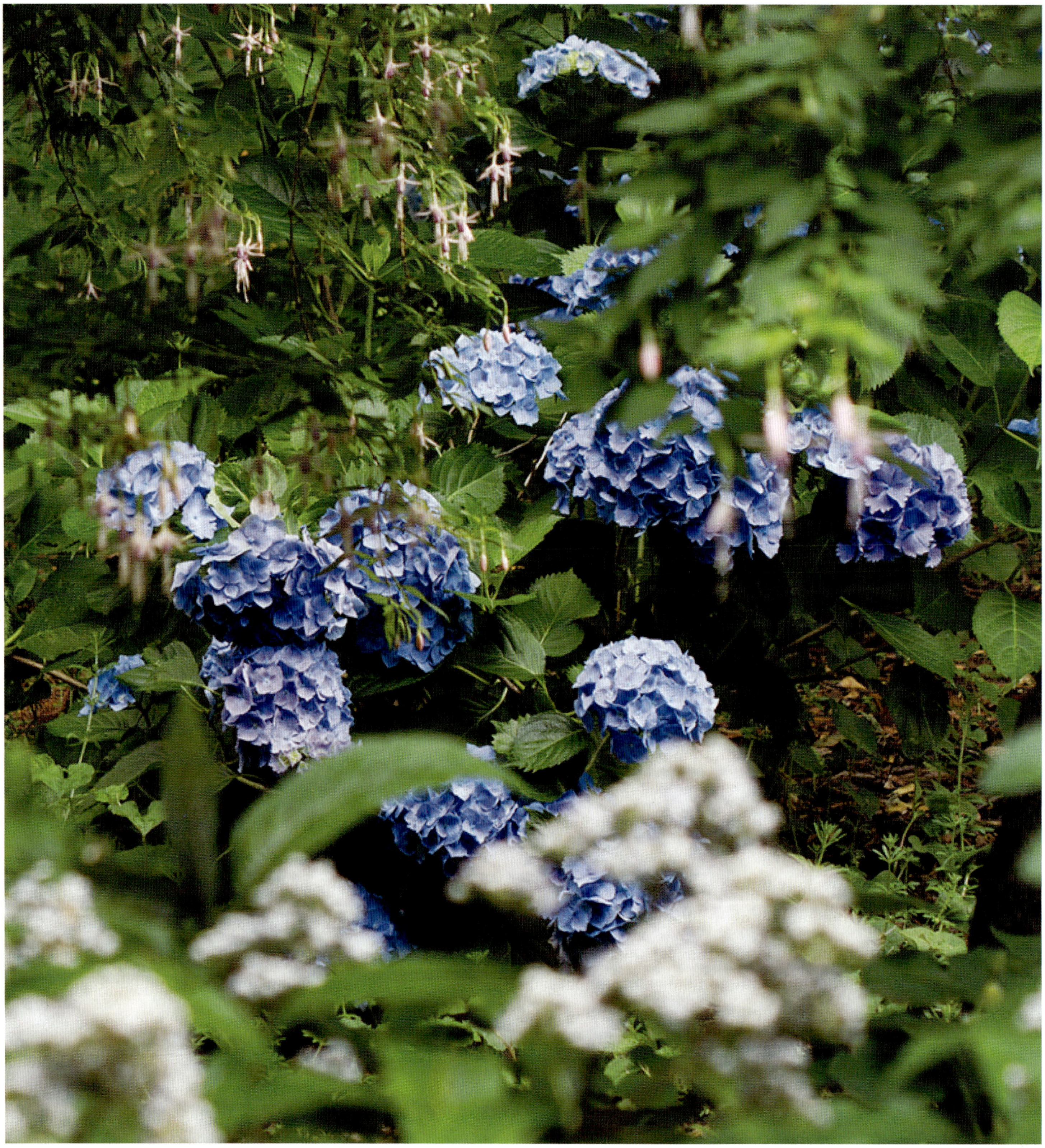

BOTH PHOTOGRAPHS:

Adelaide Botanical Gardens, South Australia, Australia

In this state capital, the botanic gardens and the associated state herbarium work to contribute to sustainability and biodiversity with living, cultural and preserved collections. The 51ha (126-acre) garden was opened in 1857 in response to pressure to establish a public garden in the city. The Bicentennial Conservatory is one of the largest in the Southern Hemisphere.

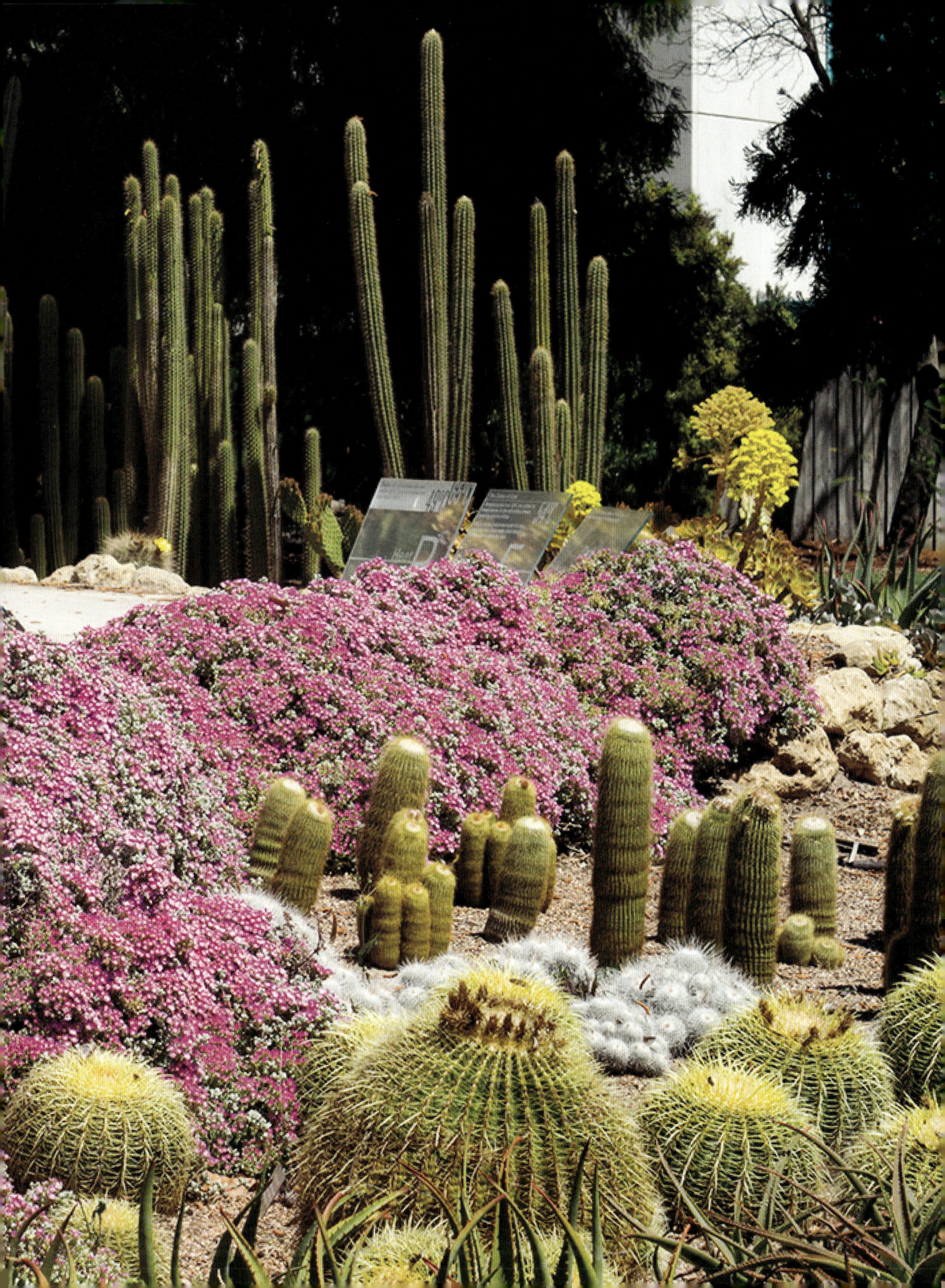

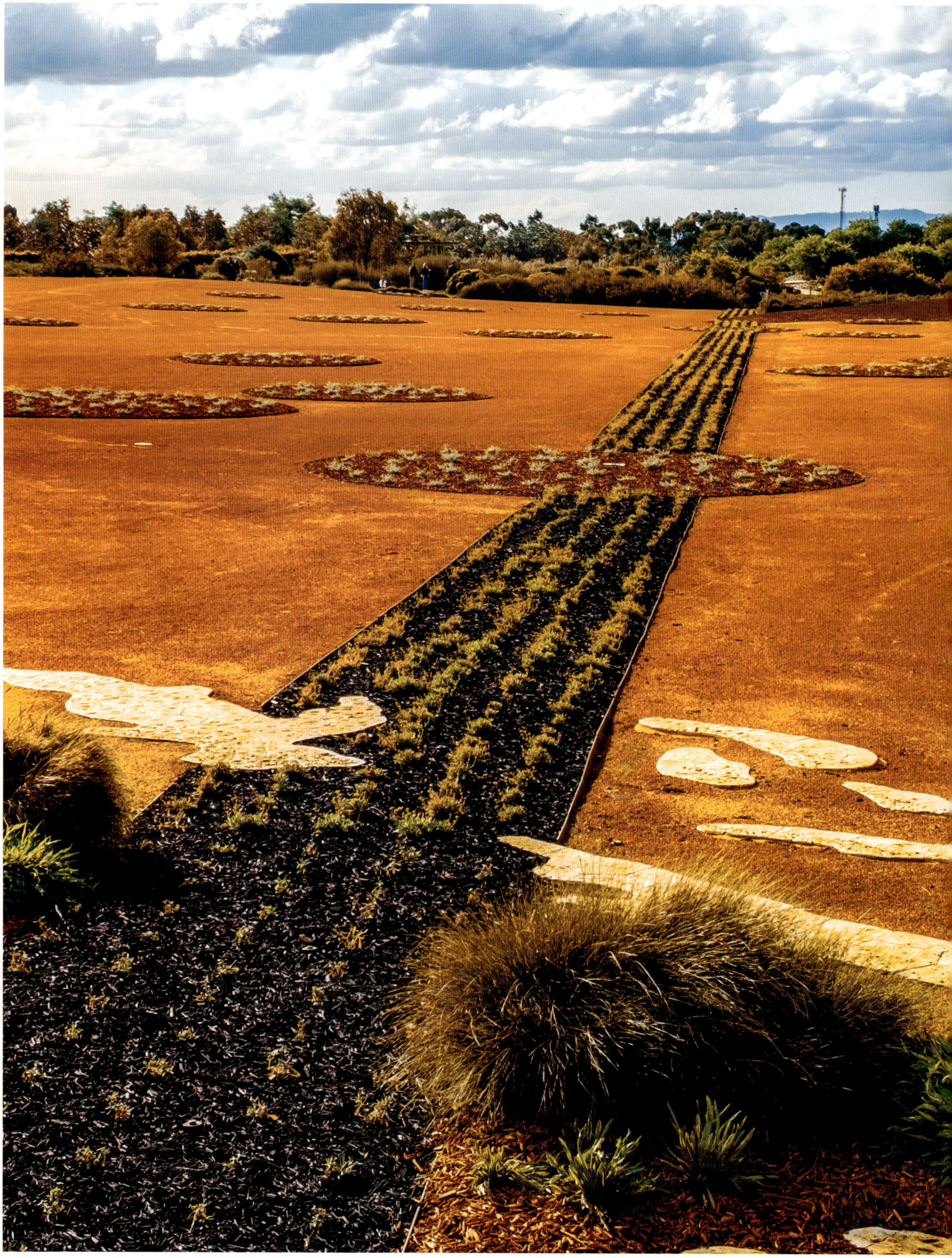

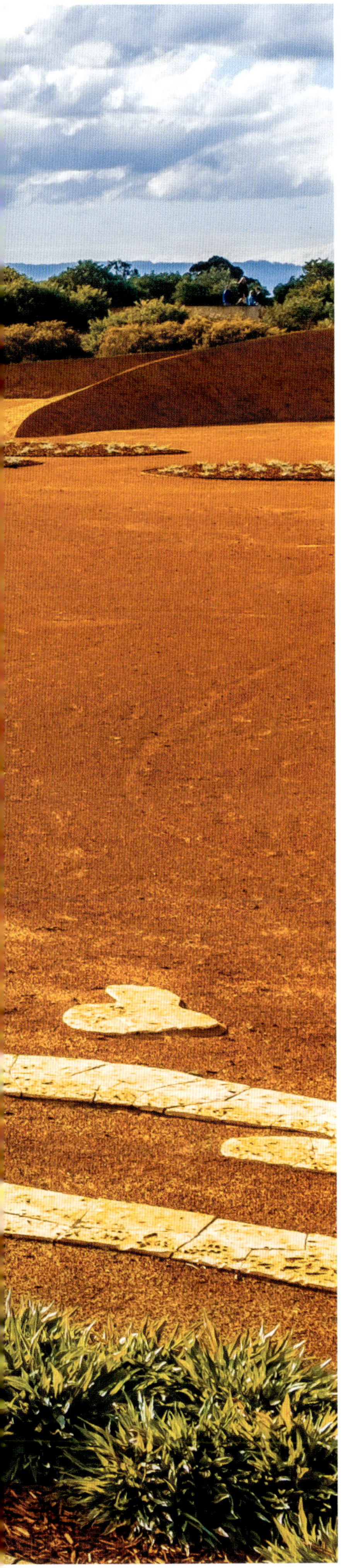

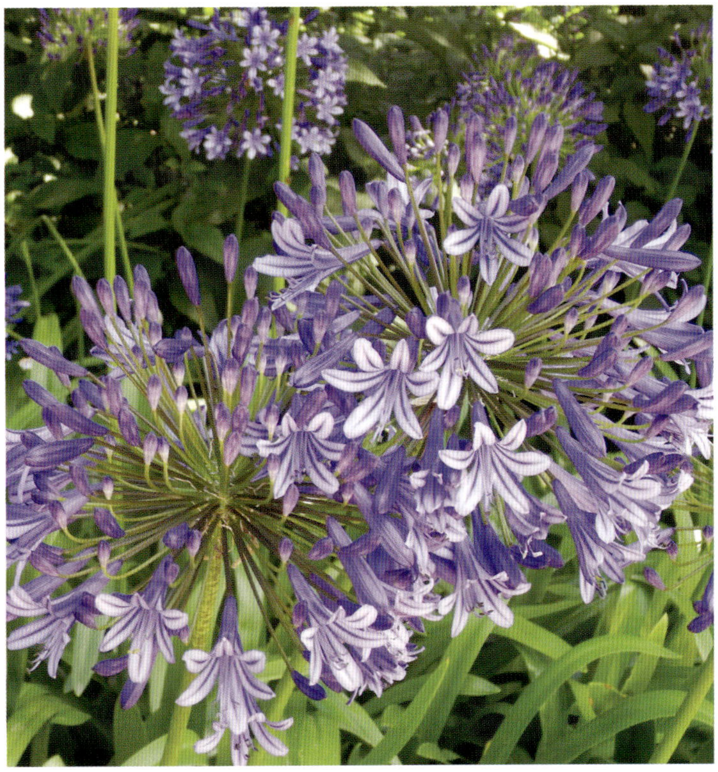

ALL PHOTOGRAPHS:

Royal Botanic Gardens, Victoria, Australia

On the banks of the Yarra river, Melbourne, with lawns, lakes and garden beds, this public garden houses over two dozen living plant collections. The visitor can find collections of eucalypts, cycads, ferns and plants from New Zealand, New Caledonia, Southern Africa and South China. A second site in Cranbourne features a striking, contemporary dry garden planted with around 1,700 plant types from southeast Australia.

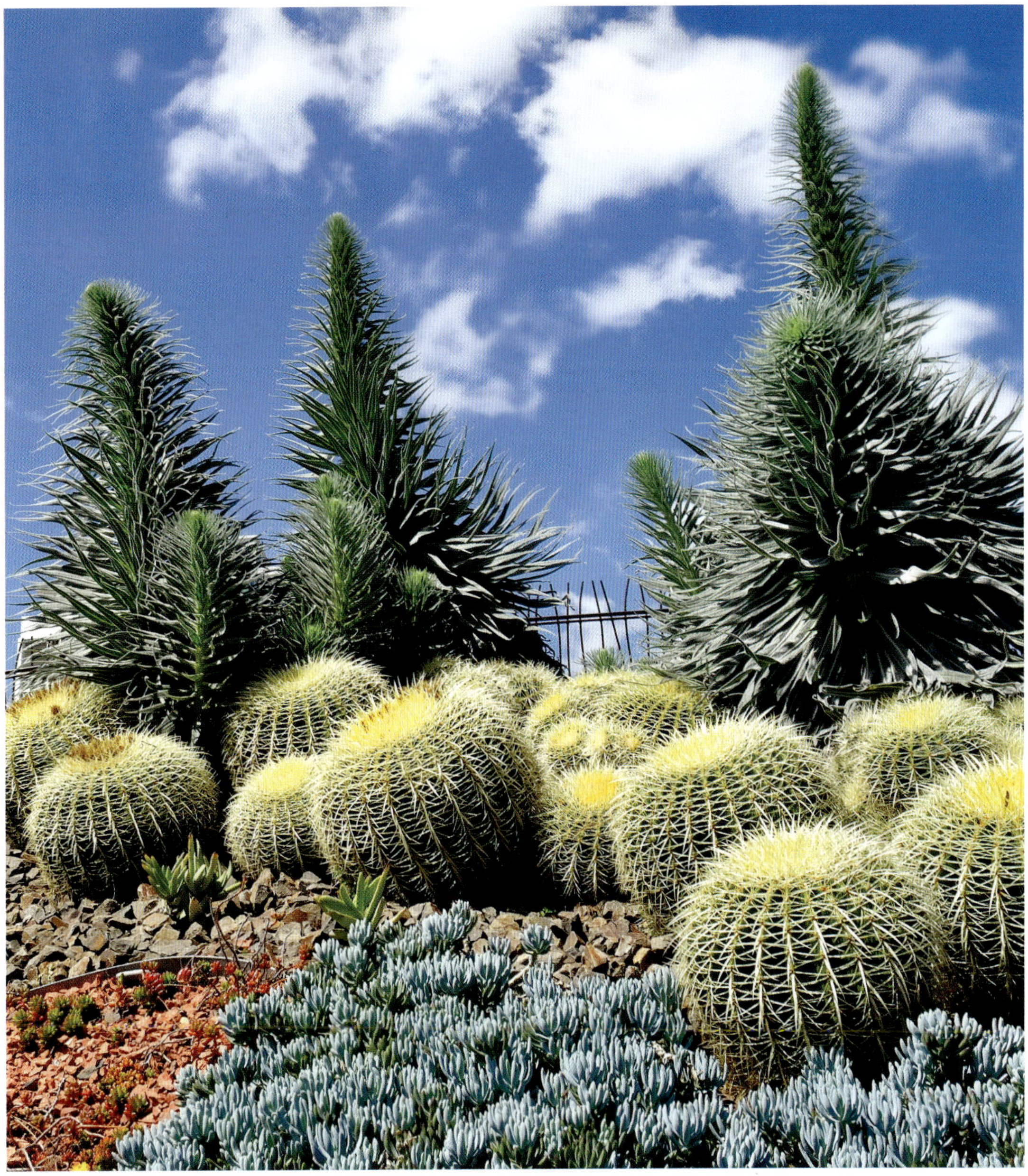

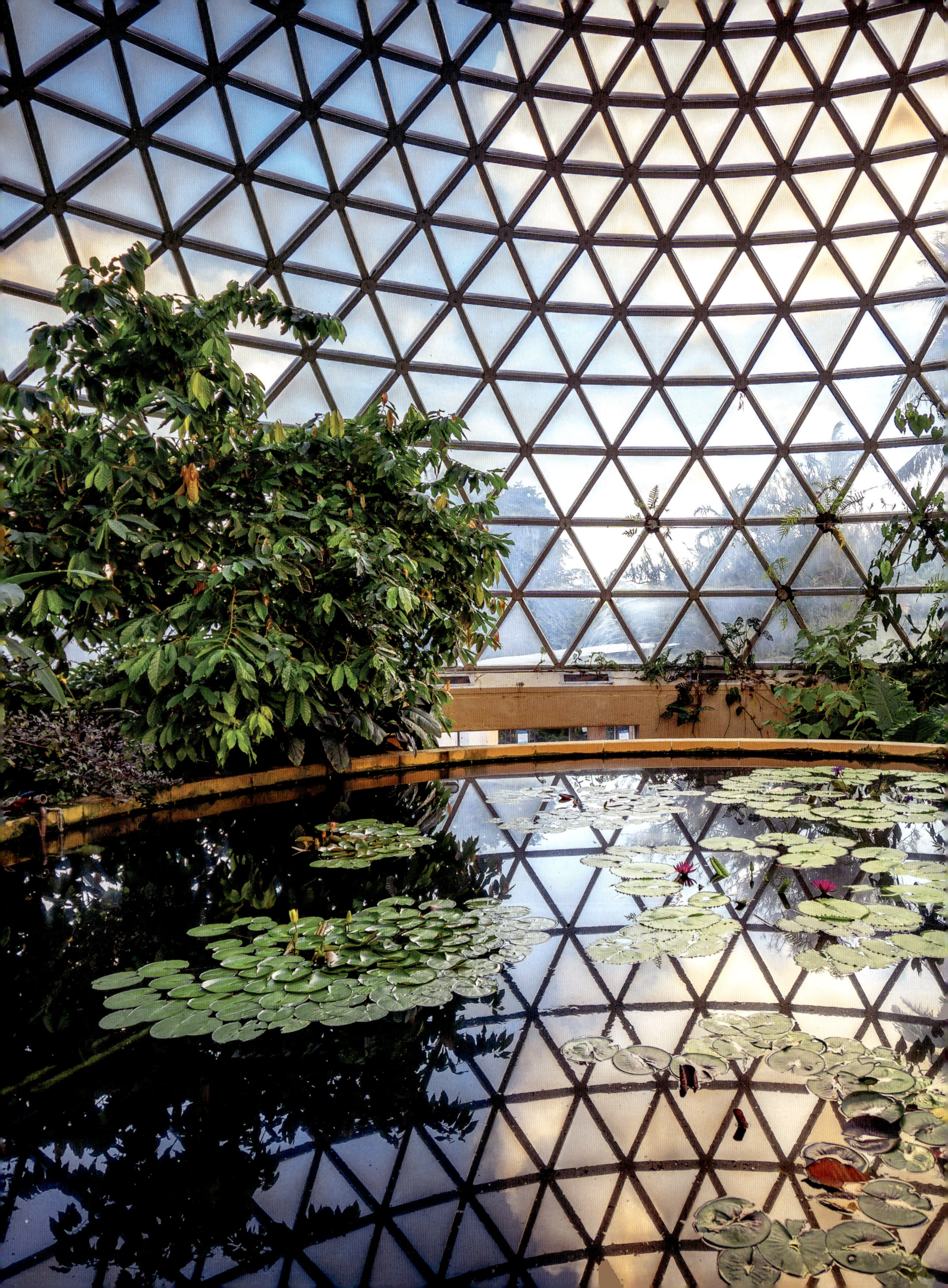

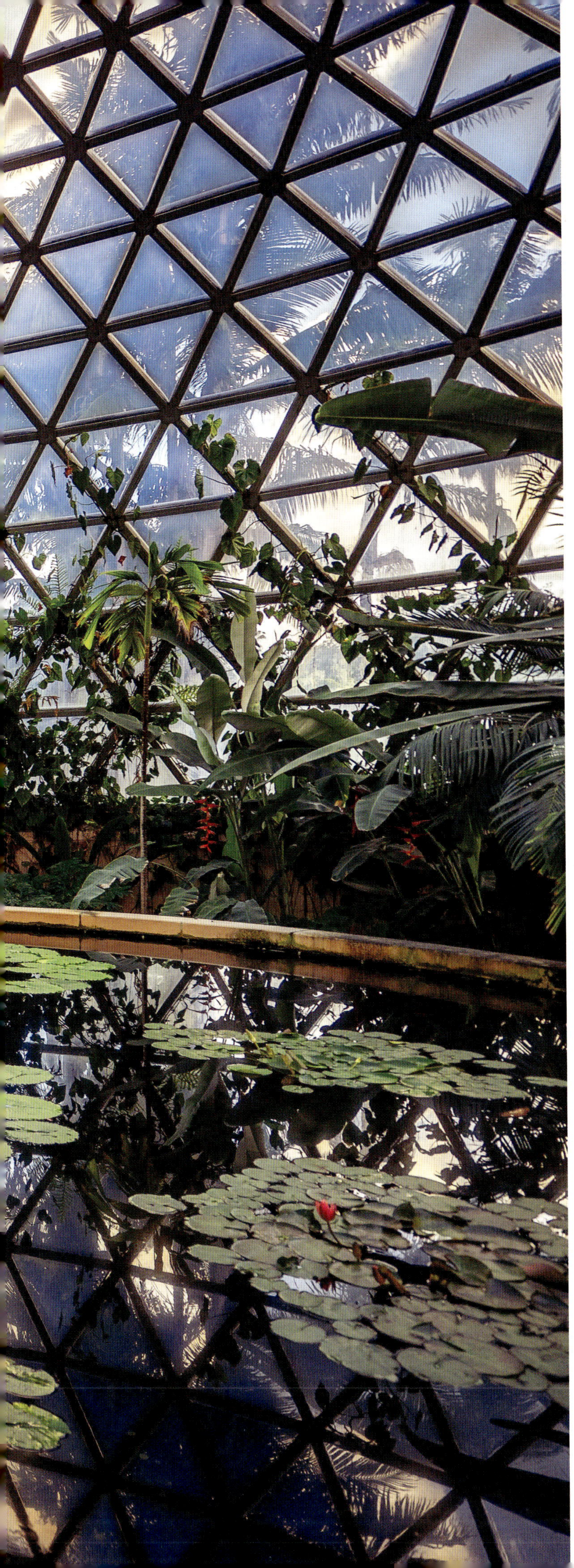

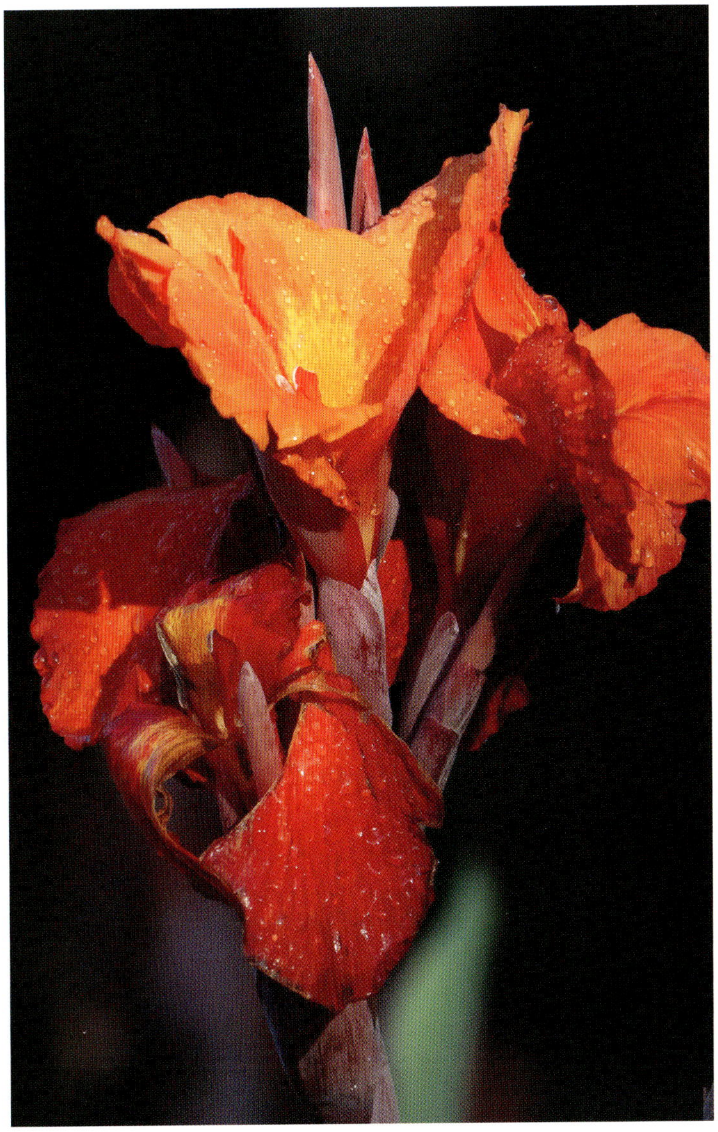

BOTH PHOTOGRAPHS::

Brisbane Botanic Gardens, Queensland, Australia

At the foot of Mount Coot-tha, these gardens in subtropical Brisbane hold significant collections of rainforest plants. The 56ha (138-acre) garden was opened in 1976, and attractions include fern and bonsai houses and a Japanese garden. There are also plant collections from the Pacific Islands around Australia and a geodesic dome housing tropical specimens.

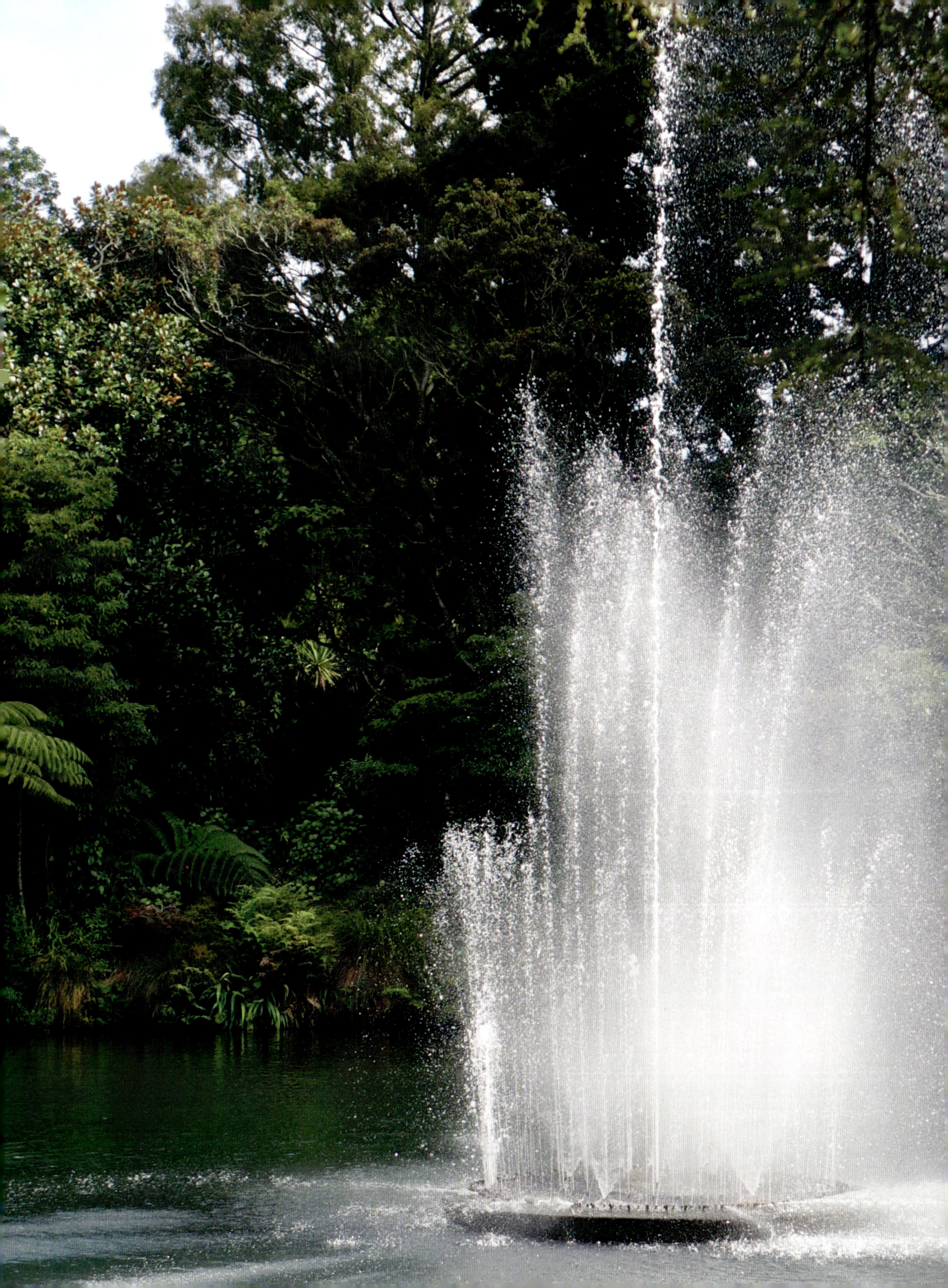

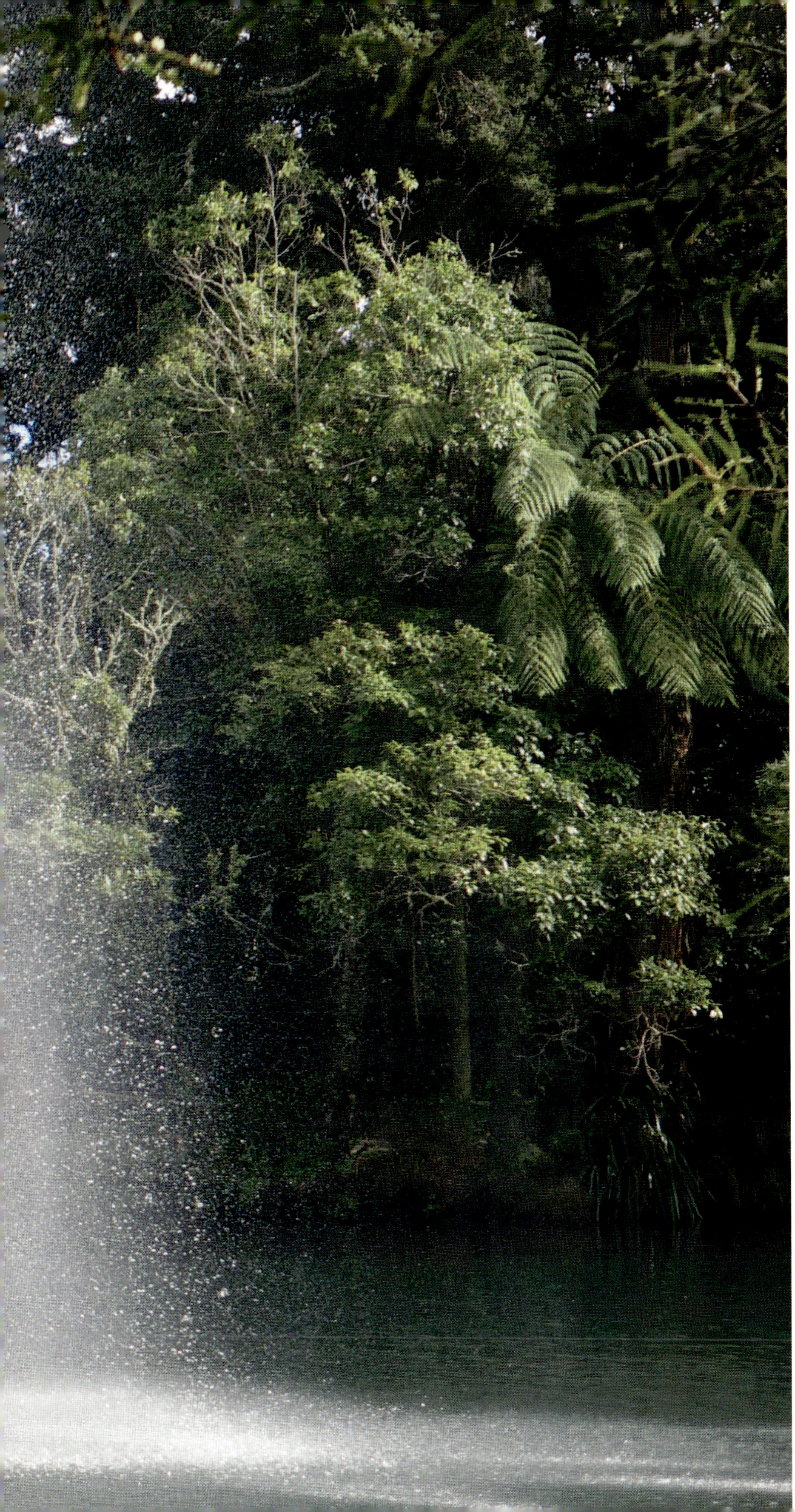

Pukekura Park, Taranaki, New Zealand
Originally swamp or wetland, this popular public space in New Plymouth was opened in 1876. It covers 52ha (128 acres), and includes gardens and recreational areas. The Queen Elizabeth II Fountain was built in 1955 to mark a Royal visit to this key member of the British Commonwealth. Other features are Japanese and Chinese Gardens and a water lily lake.

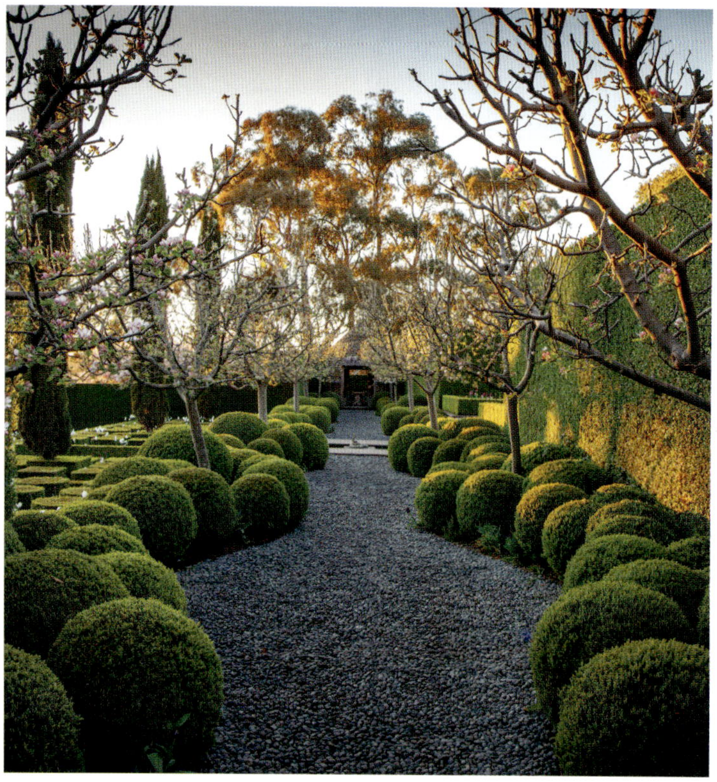

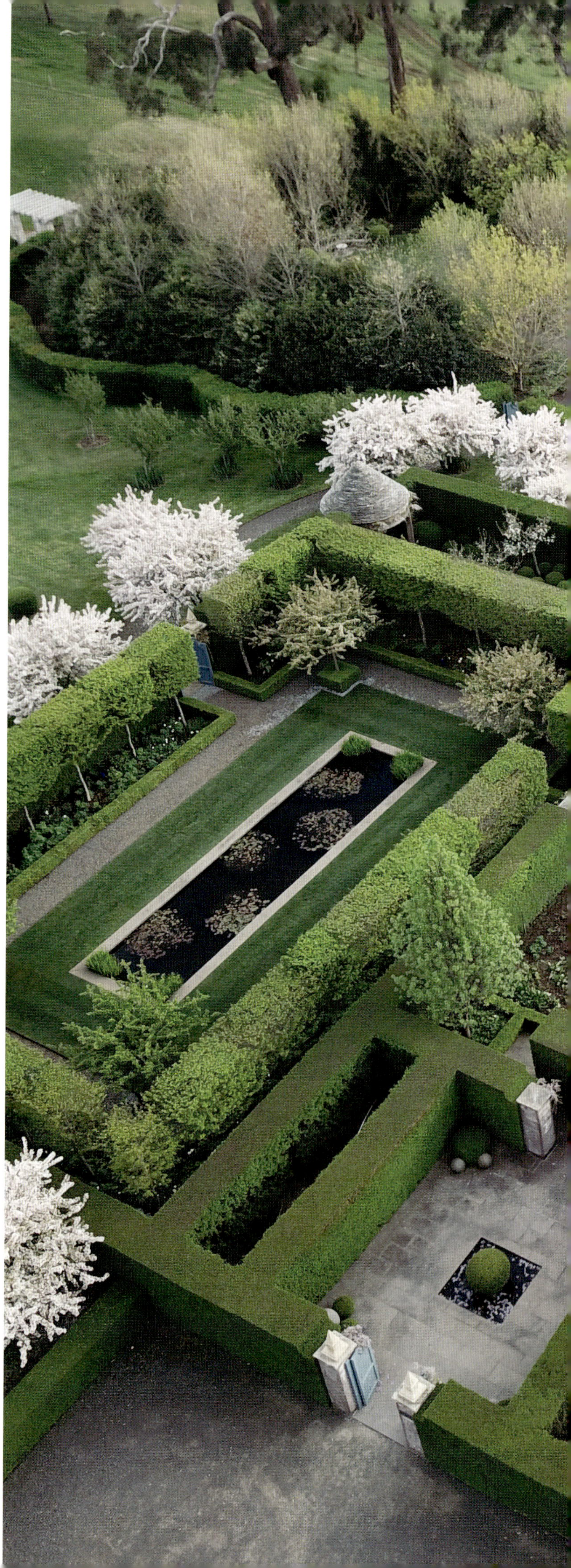

BOTH PHOTOGRAPHS & OVERLEAF:
Stonefields, Victoria, Australia
Paul Bangay is one of Australia's best-known garden designers and his property Stonefields, near Daylesford, reflects a lifetime of gardening. Tucked between some of Victoria's premier wine estates, this large farm bears Italian influences with formal hedges and topiary providing a sense of enclosure. The garden contains such classic elements as a rose parterre, reflective pond and a rill, which runs the length of the space.

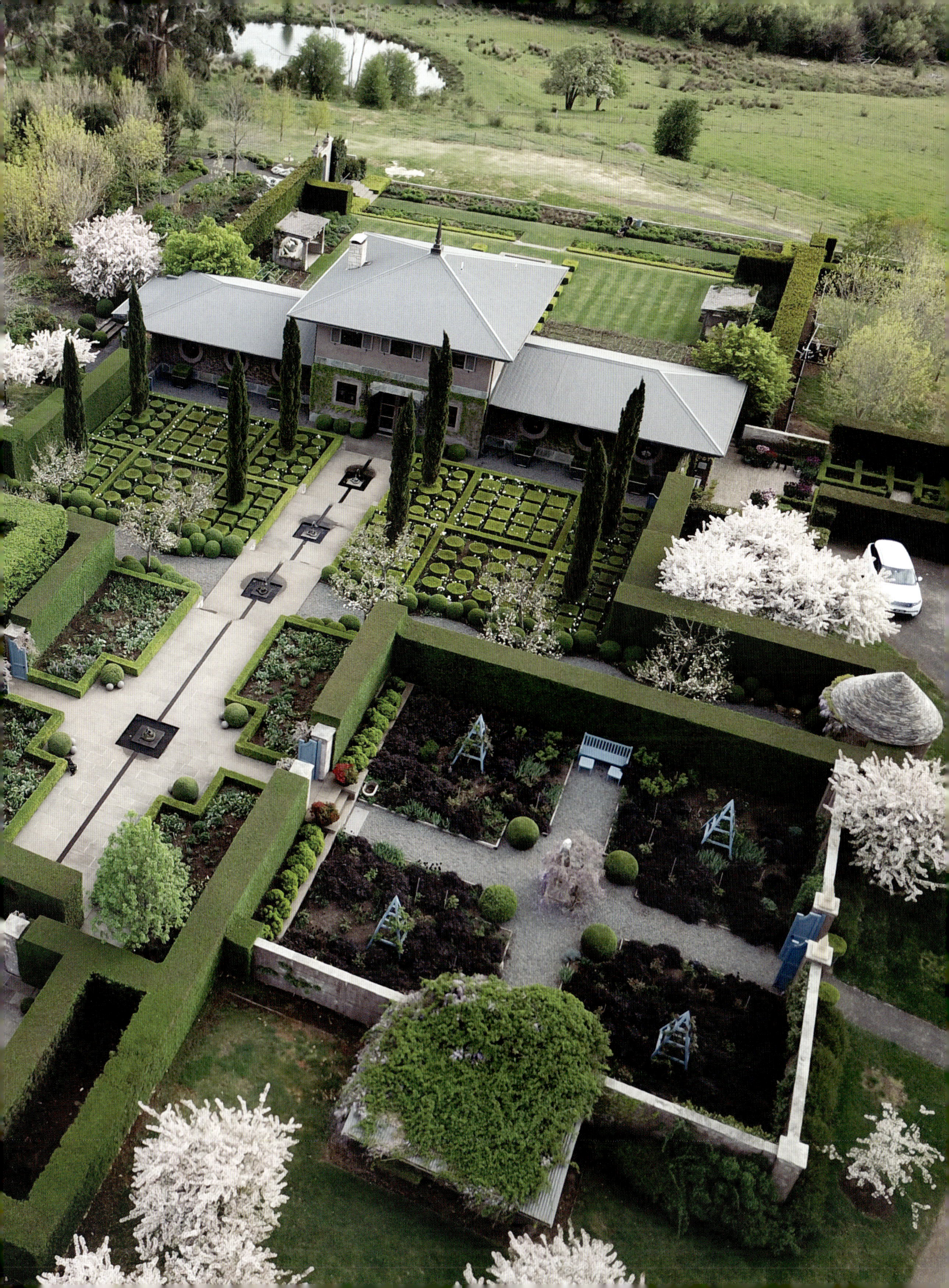

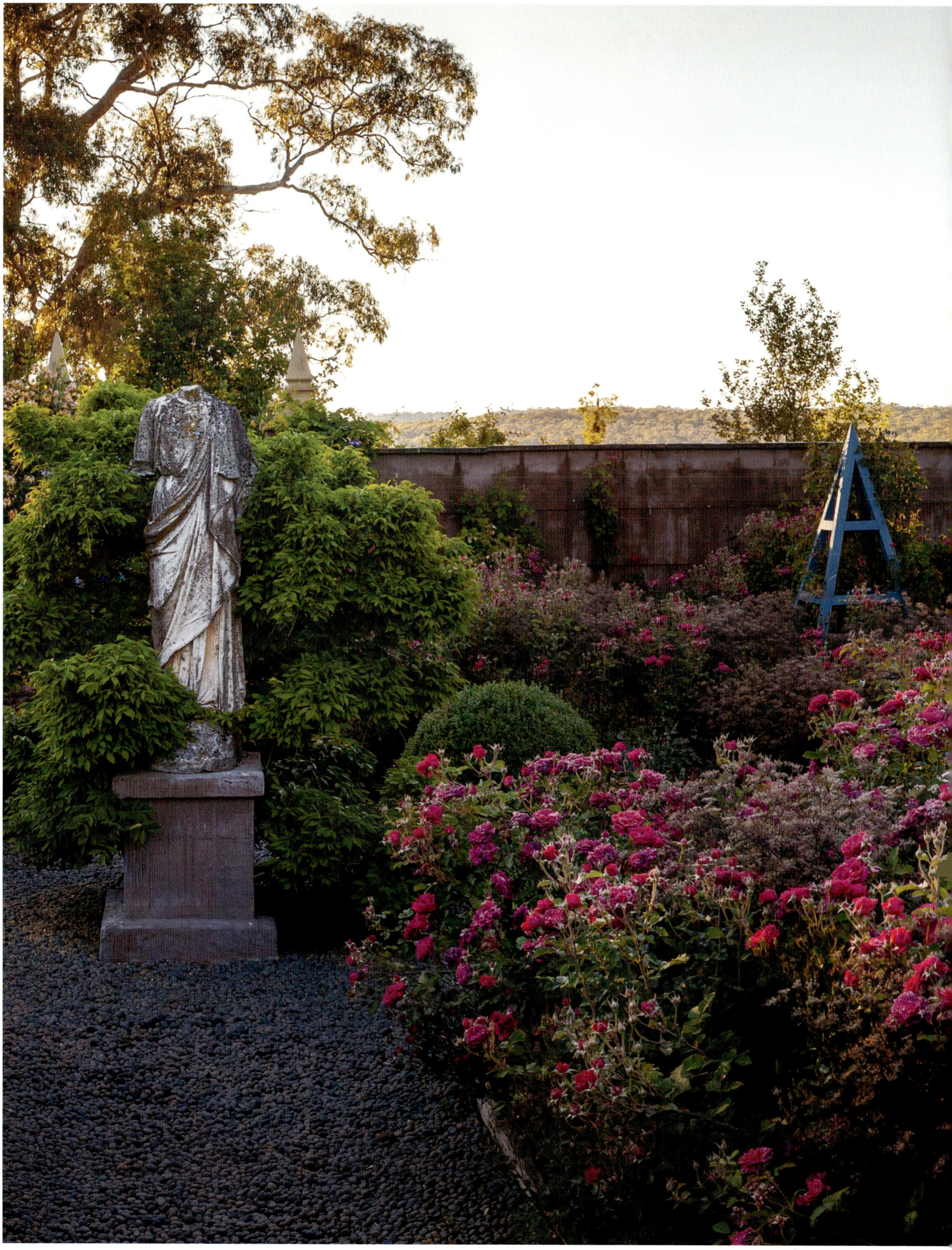

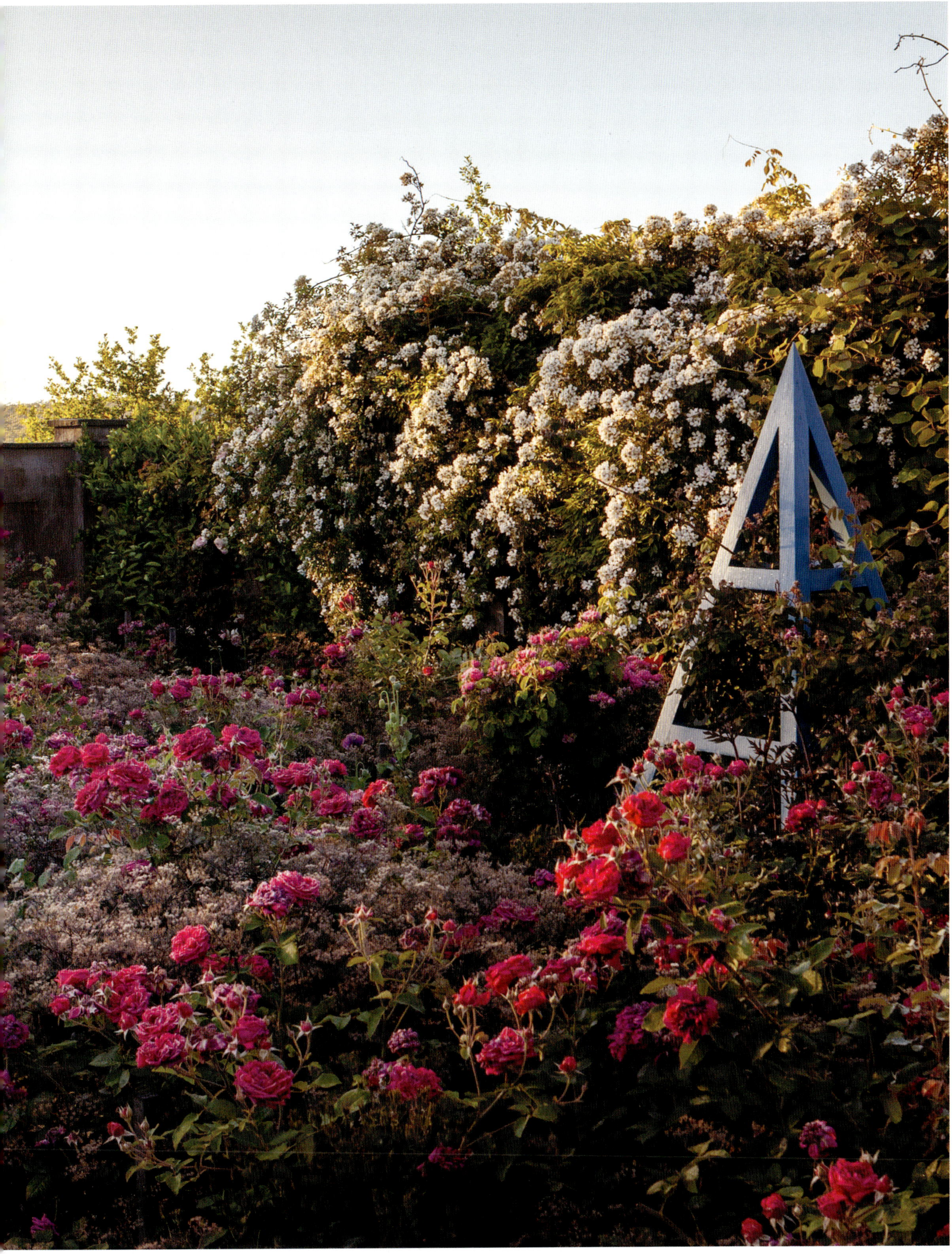

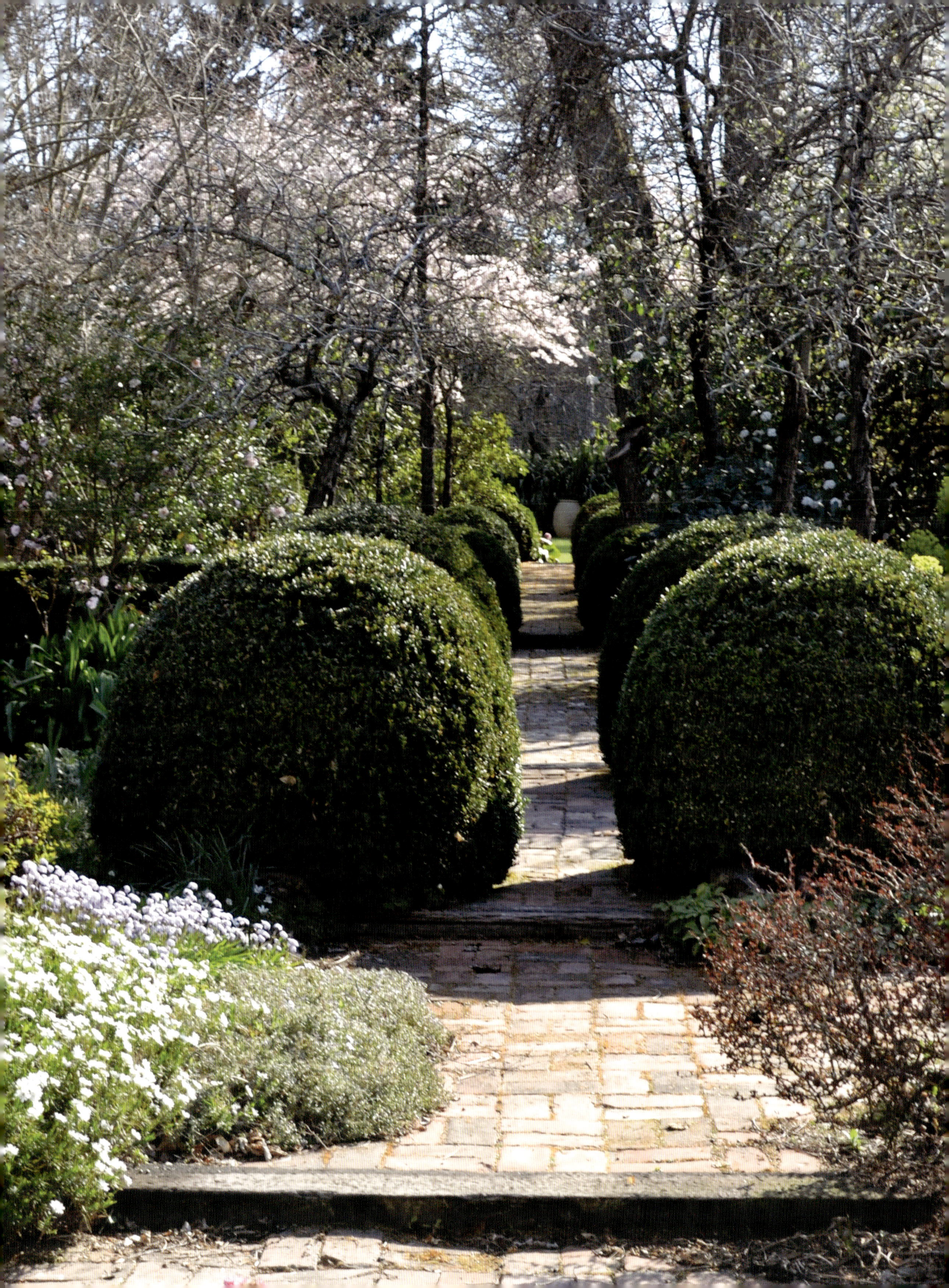

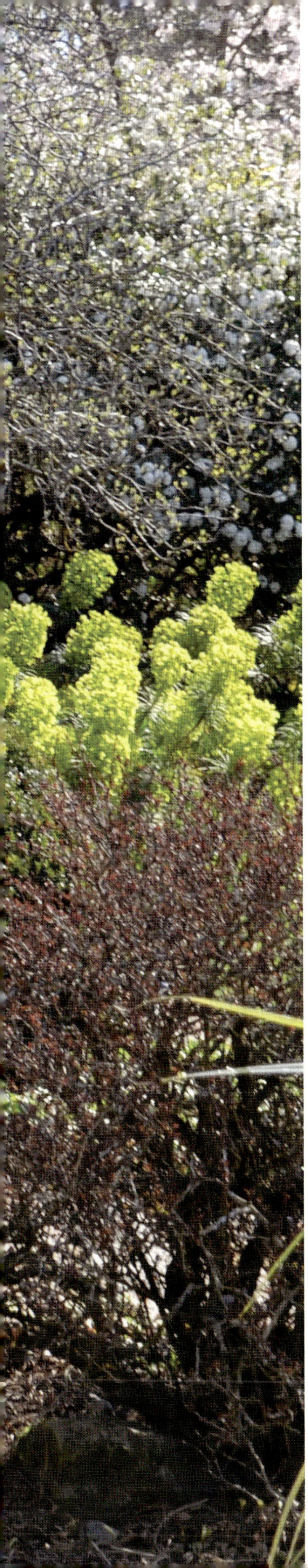

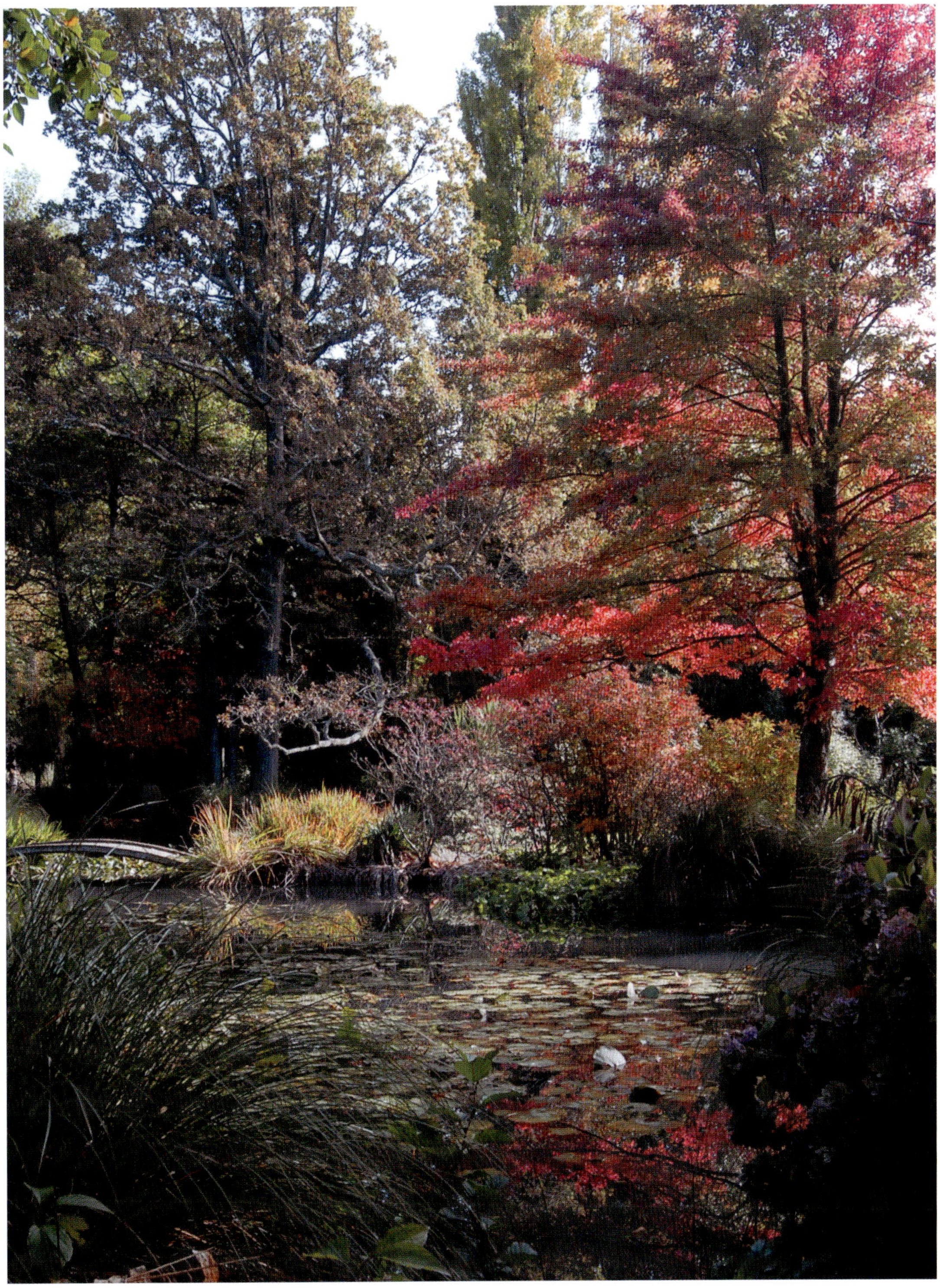

BOTH PHOTOGRAPHS:

Flaxmere Garden, Canterbury, New Zealand

This garden on a sheep farm in North Canterbury has been developed over 50 years by Penny and John Zino. With Mount Tekoa in the distance, vistas are key here – as is water, which is contained in five ponds across the property. Planting includes many native New Zealand species which are combined with rhododendrons and roses. A woodland area comes to the fore in autumn.

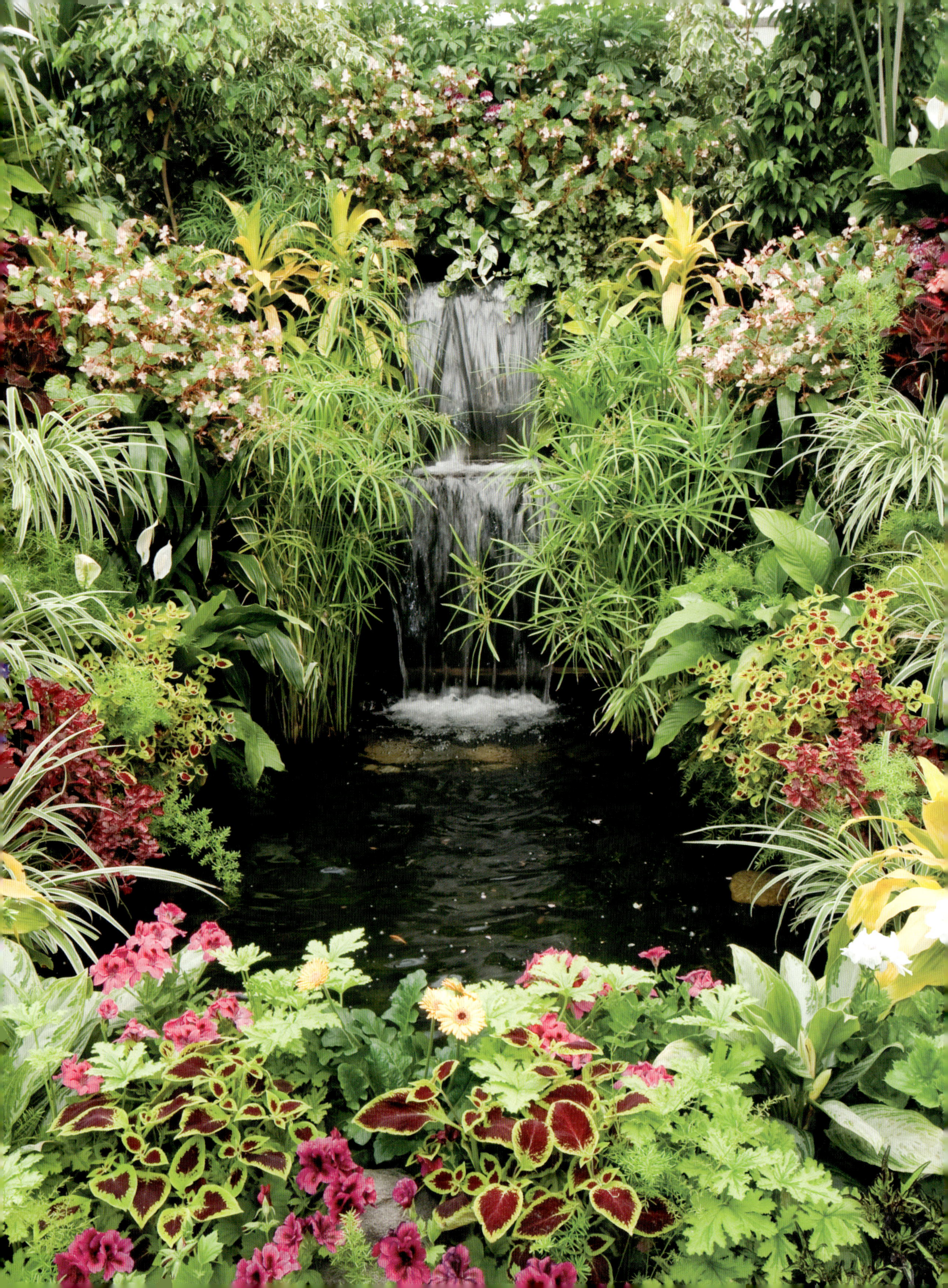

North and South America

From the great, sweeping, temperate landscapes of North America to the richly biodiverse latitudes of Central America and down to the subtropical and tropical regions of South America, these two continents hold an awe-inspiring range of horticultural feats.

Some, like the many post-war Japanese gardens in the United States, have been built to encourage good relations between communities. Others are expressions of the new-found wealth of their owners, who might have grown rich from pharmaceuticals or mining at the turn of the last century. In these gardens nothing but the finest would do. Gardens have also always been an outlet for creativity, providing a splendid canvas on which to effect one's imaginings. Edward James and Edith Wharton knew this well.

As we progress into the 21st century, thoughts turn to the First Nations, resilience, sustainability and biodiversity. Gardens with these themes in mind acknowledge the richness of our natural heritage and the profound influence it has on our quality of life.

The futuristic Seattle Spheres present a biophilic working space that may well become common place in the near future. Meanwhile abandoned railway lines and empty city spaces are planted for humans and urban wildlife alike.

OPPOSITE:
Butchart Gardens, British Columbia, Canada
When Jennie Butchart wondered what to do with a disused limestone quarry on the property she and her husband, Robert, owned outside Victoria in 1904, she turned it into a densely planted sunken garden.

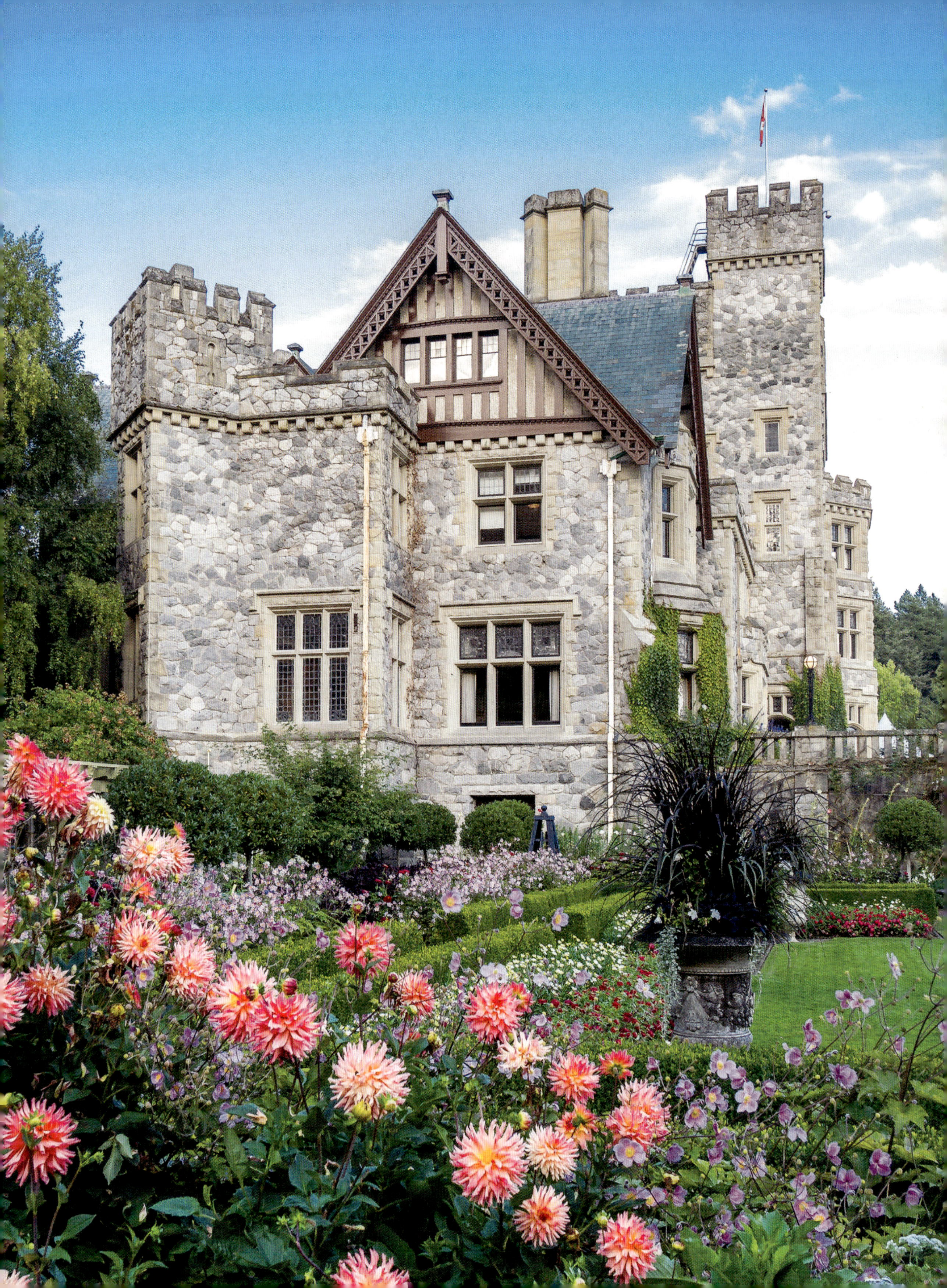

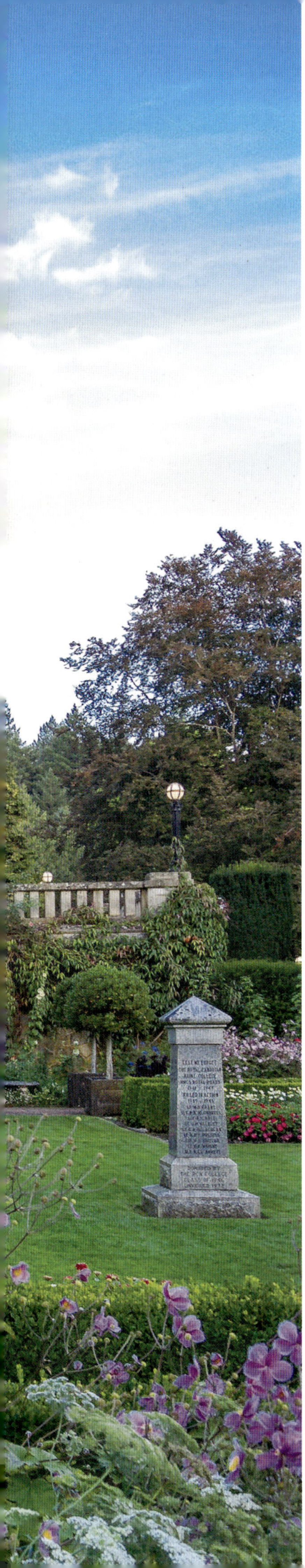

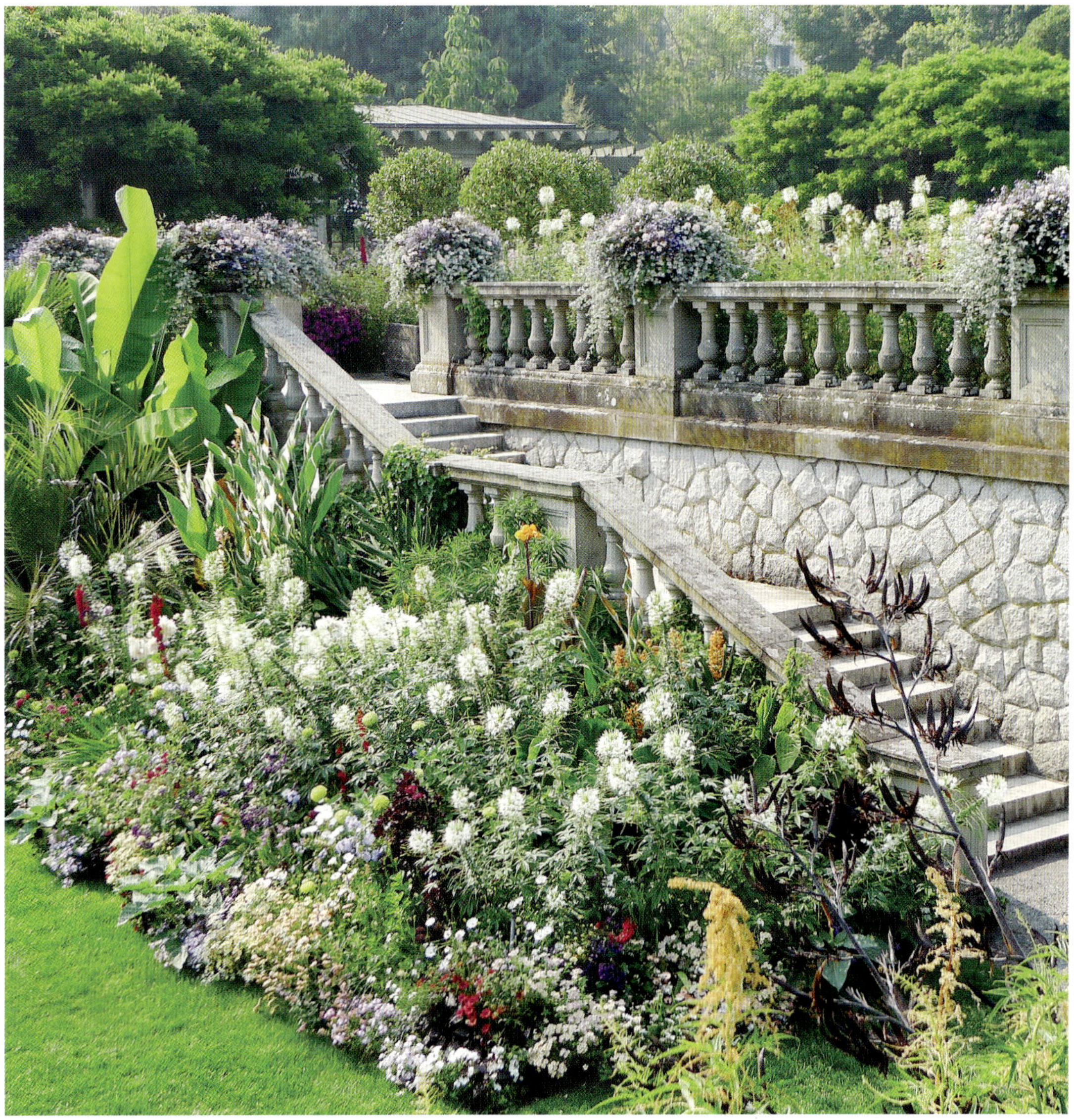

BOTH PHOTOGRAPHS:

Hatley Castle, British Columbia, Canada

The Edwardian mansion of one of British Columbia's most prominent businessmen, James Dunmuir, was built in 1908 on Vancouver Island. Garden designers Franklin Brett and George D. Hall laid out the property in English country house style, and included Victorian design elements to make the garden appear older – and more prestigious – than it was. Today herbaceous borders, a rose garden, Italian garden and a Japanese garden are key attractions.

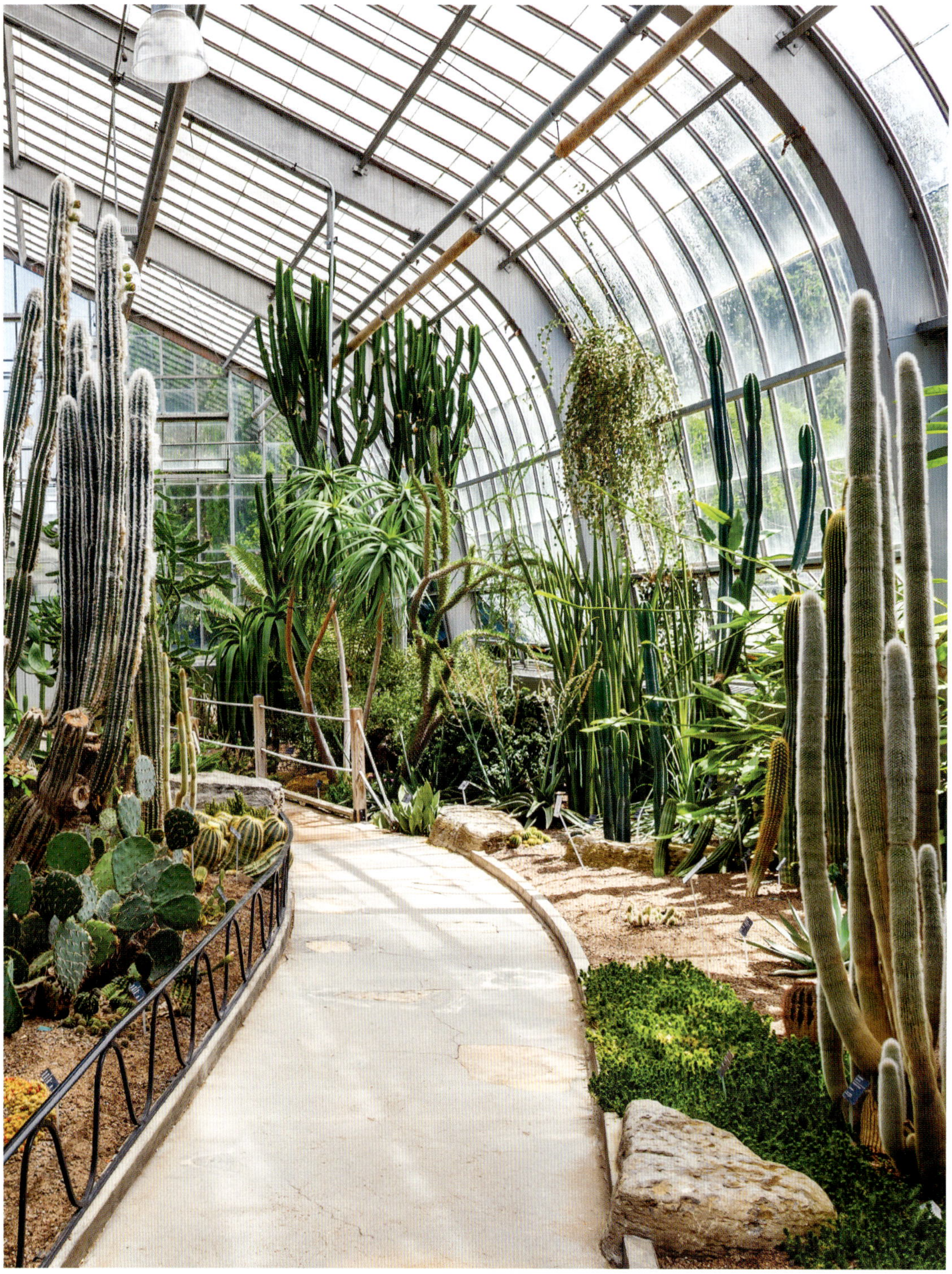

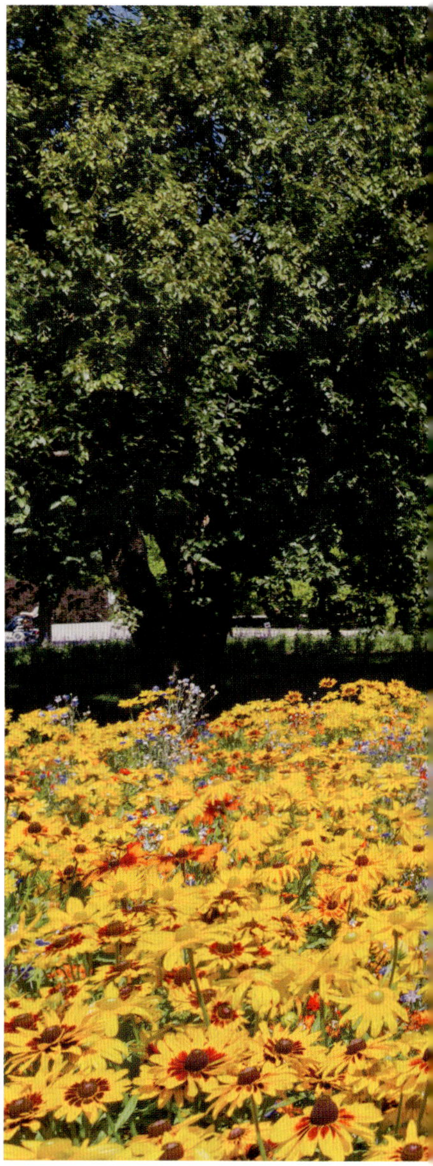

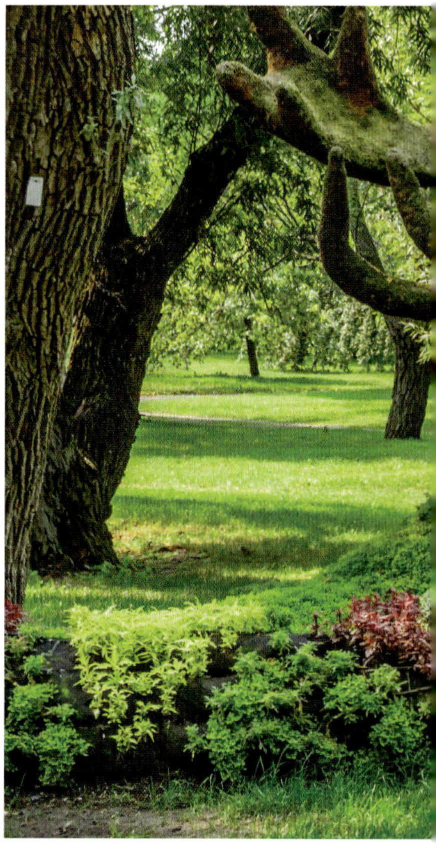

ALL PHOTOGRAPHS:
Montreal Botanical Garden, Quebec, Canada
Some 21,000 different plants are contained in the Montreal Botanical Garden founded in 1931. The orchid genus *Teuscheria*, native to Central America, was named after the first curator of the garden, Henry Teuscher. First Nations, Chinese and Japanese gardens run alongside 10 greenhouses, a large lake and traditional rose, perennial and shrub gardens. In 2013 the garden hosted the international living sculpture exhibition *Mosaïcultures Internationales*

OVERLEAF:
Butchart Gardens, British Columbia, Canada
Jennie Butchart's vision for a disused lime quarry was developed over several generations, beginning in 1904. Butchart's rose garden, Italian garden and Japanese garden remain. In 2004, two Totem Poles were dedicated in the garden to mark the centenary of the garden and the cultural heritage of First Nations in the area.

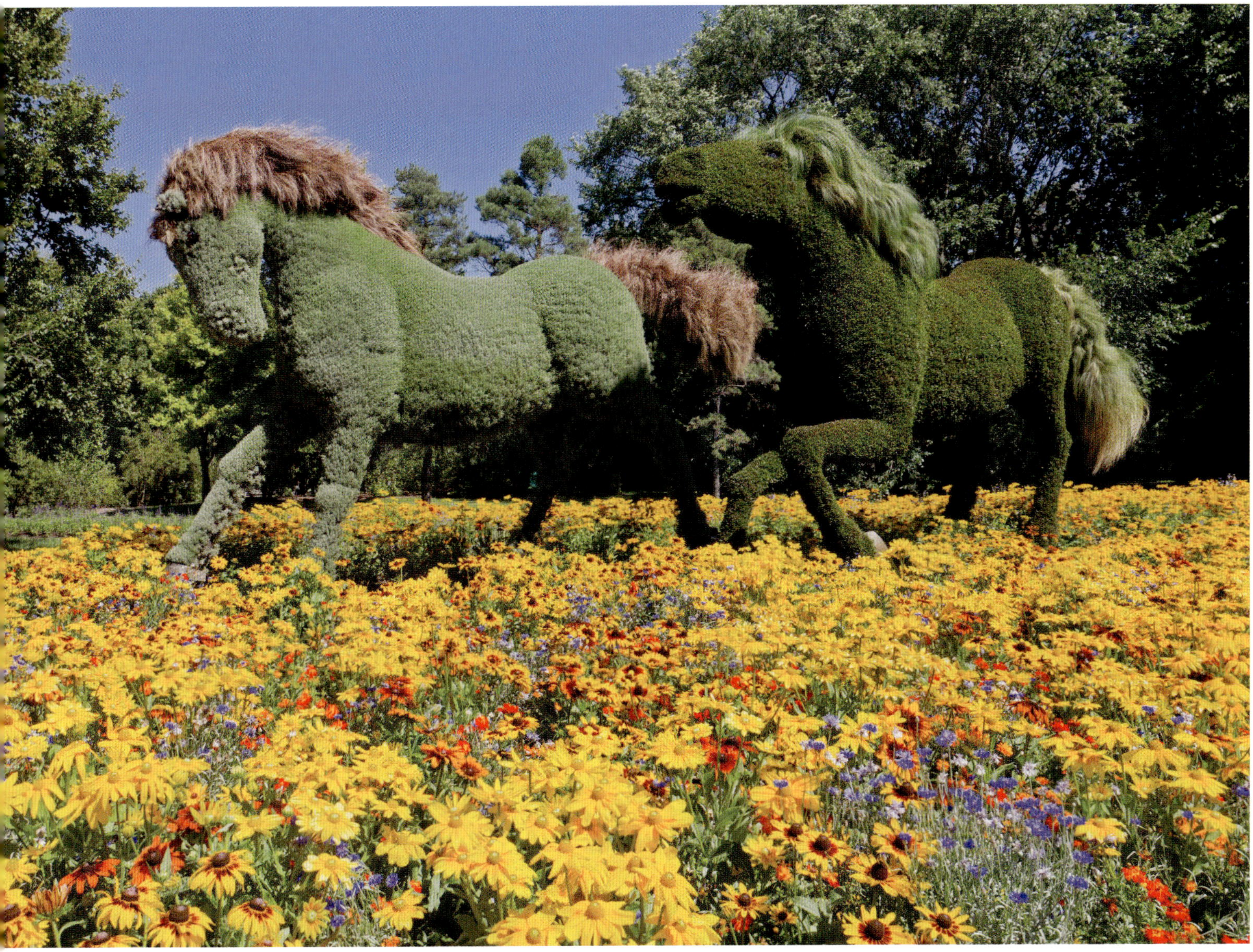

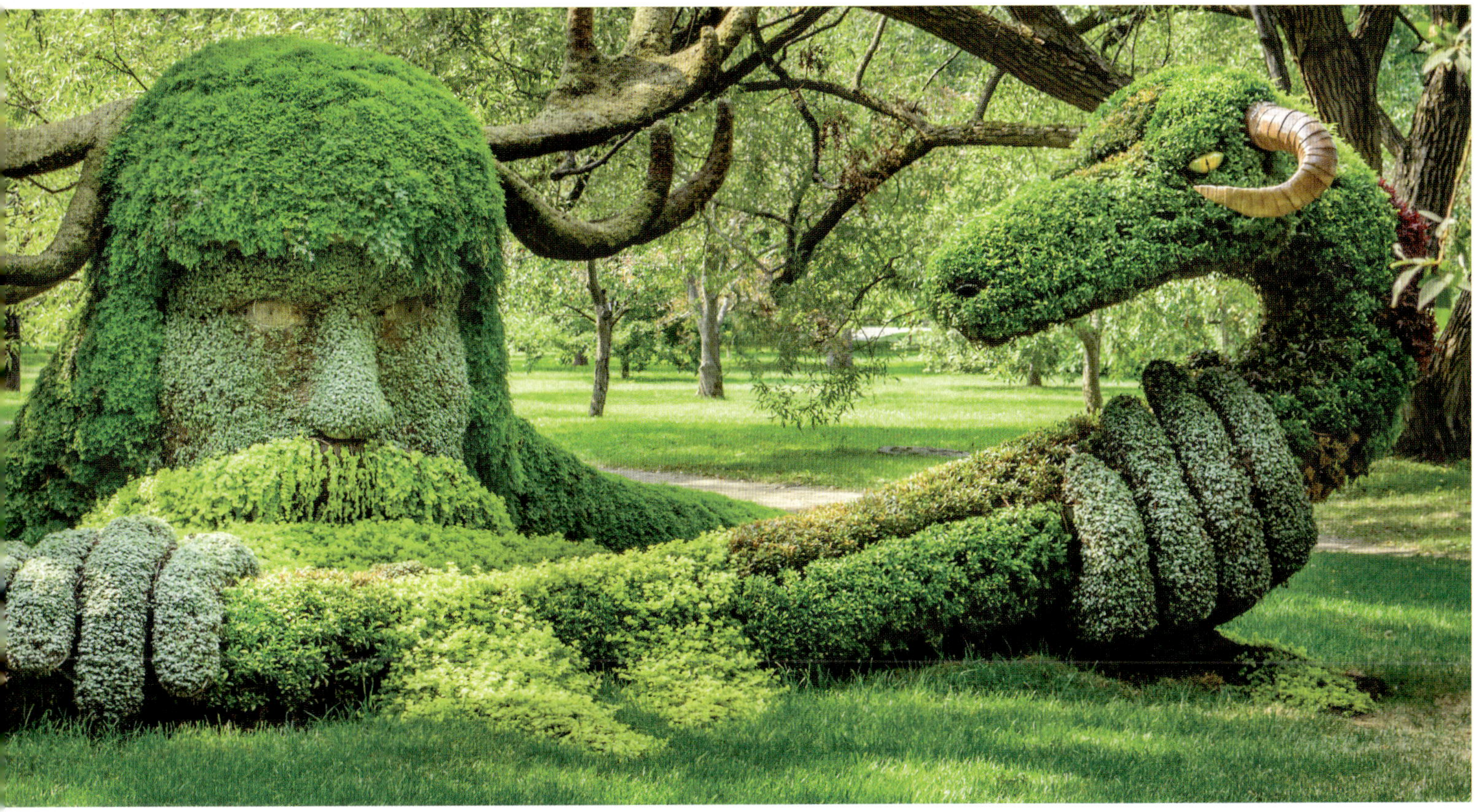

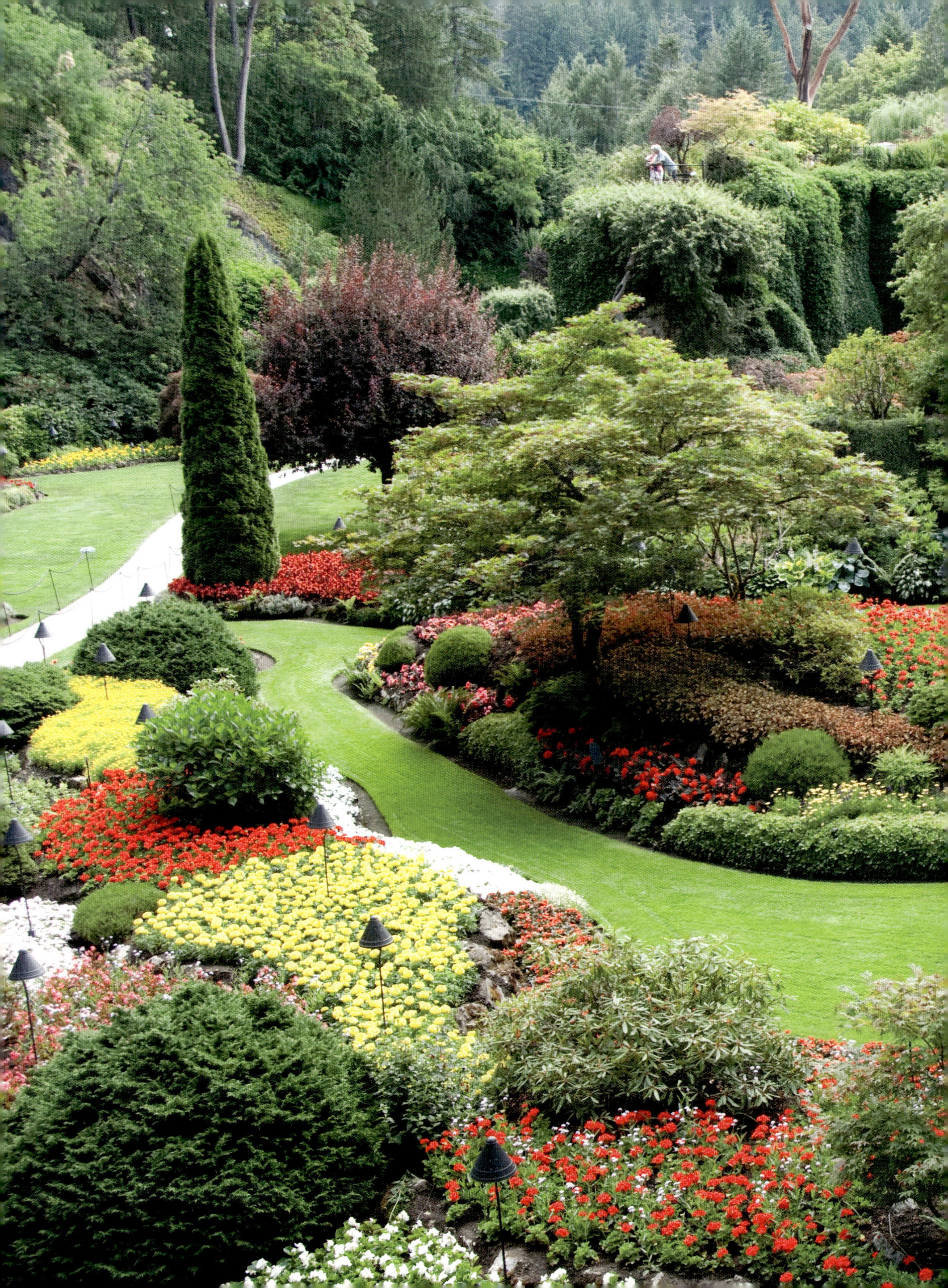

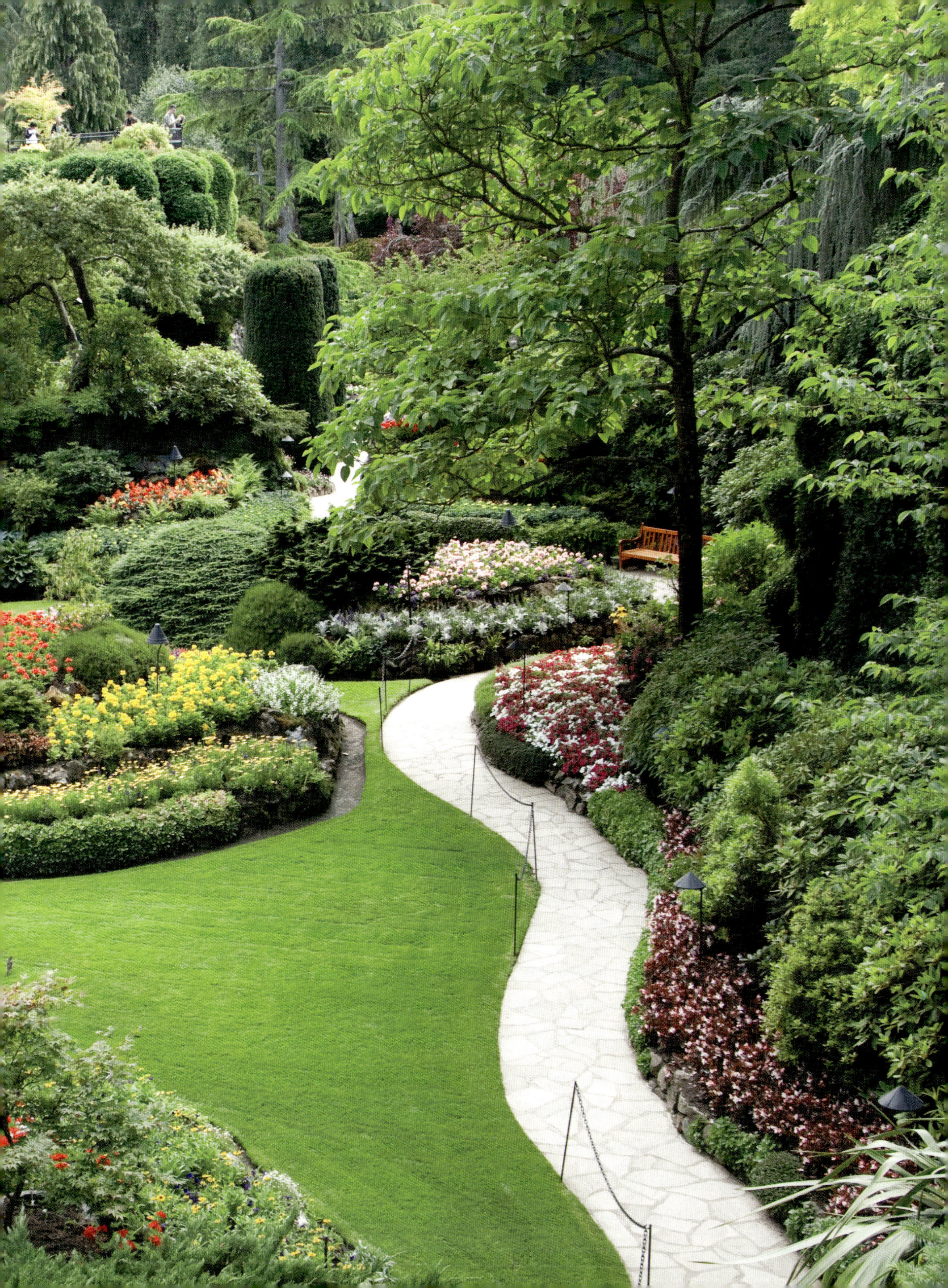

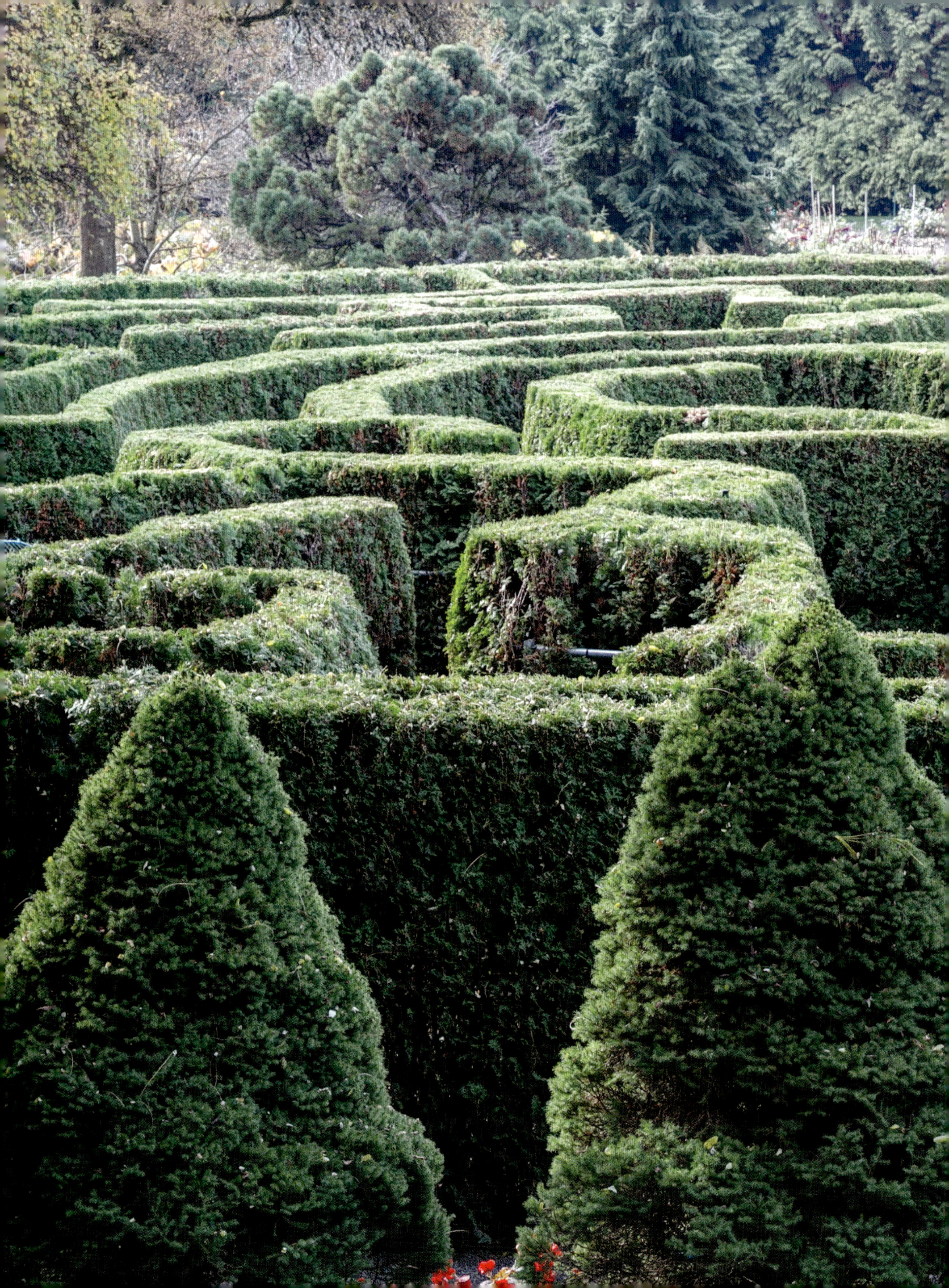

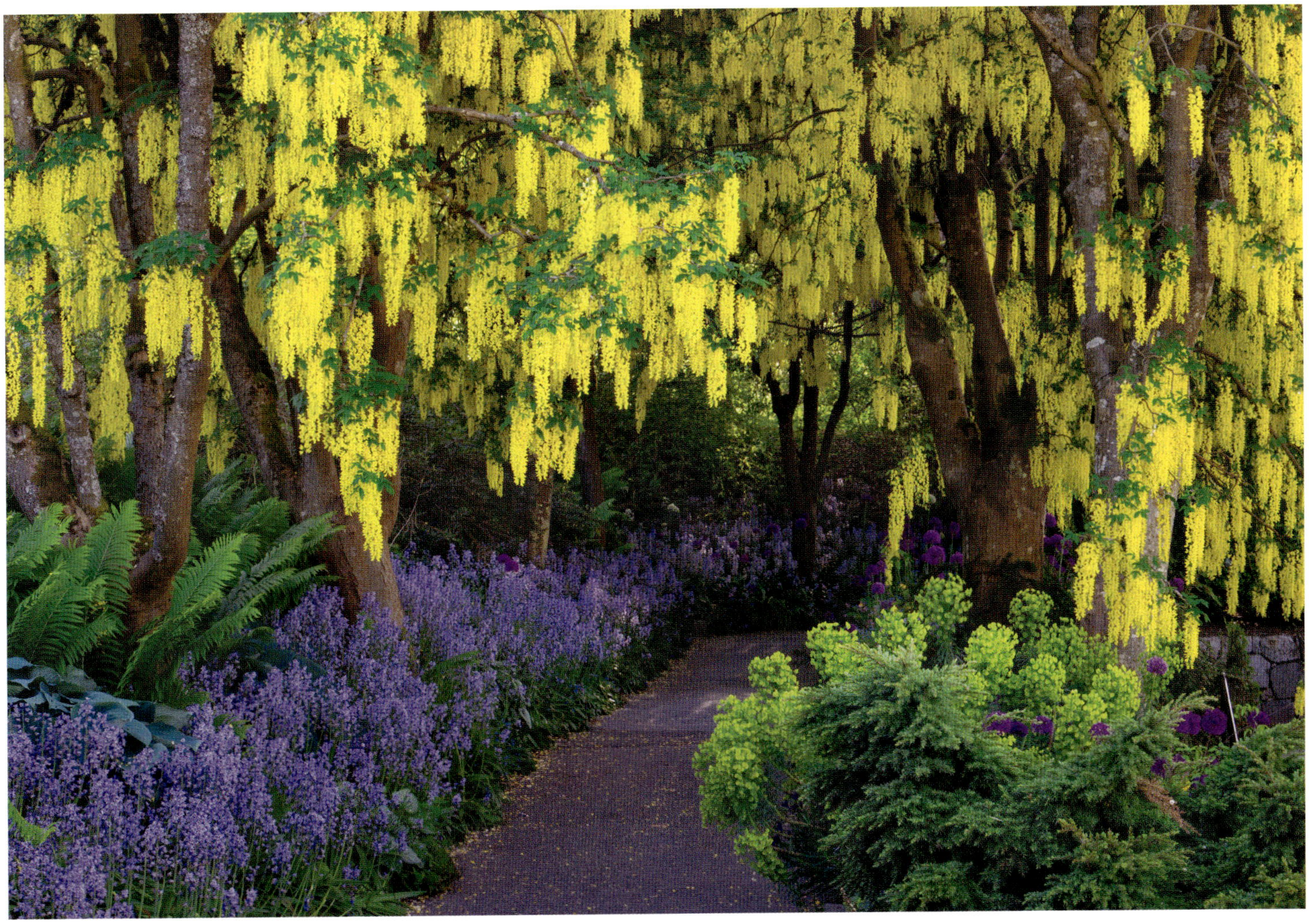

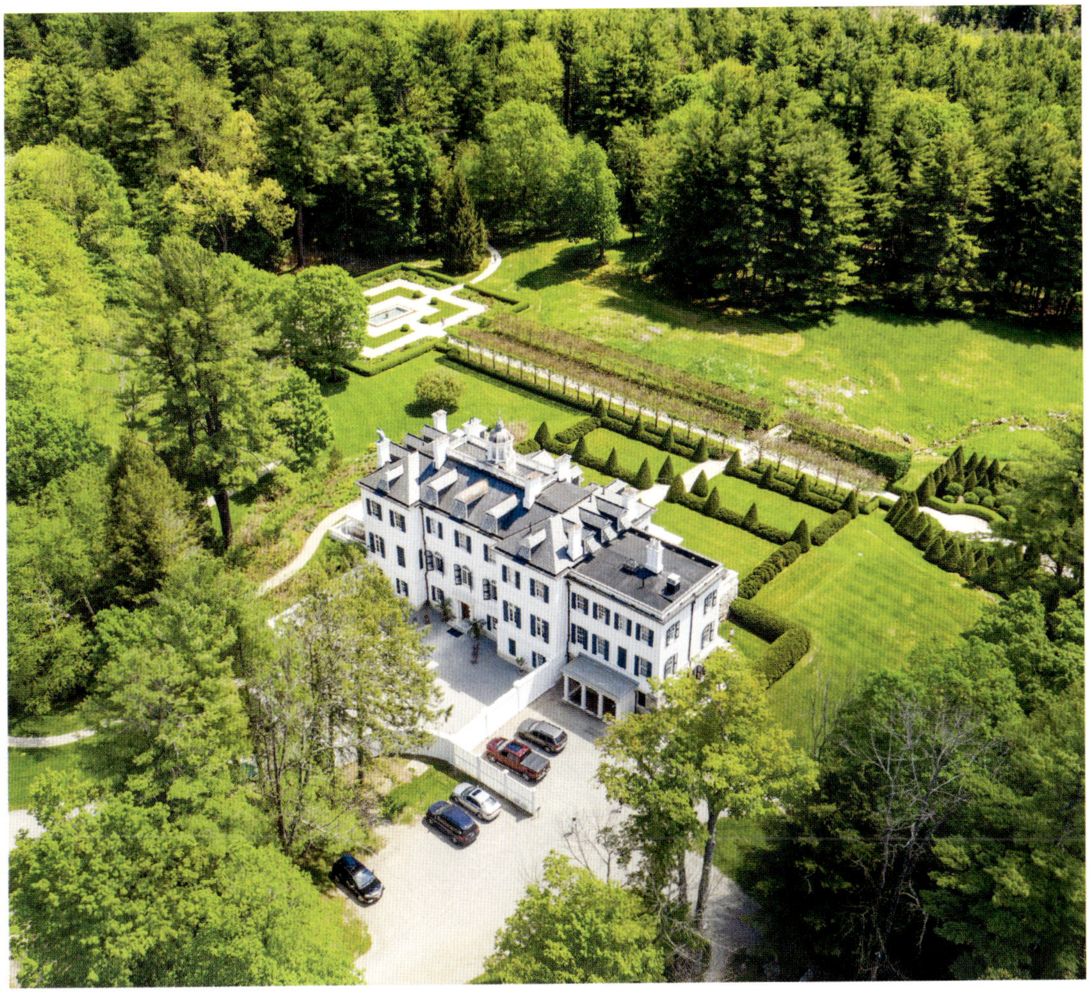

ABOVE AND OPPOSITE:

VanDusen Botanical Garden, British Columbia, Canada

It is difficult to miss the maze of 3,000 planted cedars (*Thuja occidentalis* 'Fastigiata') in the VanDusen Botanical Garden towards the south of Vancouver. A hexagonal Korean pavilion was donated to the garden from the Korean people – it is surrounded by the Cypress Pond. Attached to the garden is the Bloedel Conservatory, which has a special focus on palms and tropical plants.

LEFT:

The Mount, Massachusetts, USA

Novelist Edith Wharton designed and built The Mount in 1902. The first woman to win a Pulitzer prize for her novel *The Age of Innocence* (1920), she documented the wealthy New York life of which she was a part. Yet The Mount was where, with her niece Beatrix Farrand, she turned her hand to gardening.

LEFT AND OVERLEAF:

The Mount, Massachusetts, USA

The elegant New England garden is a series of outdoor rooms that includes a sunken Italian garden, gravel promenades and a rock garden.

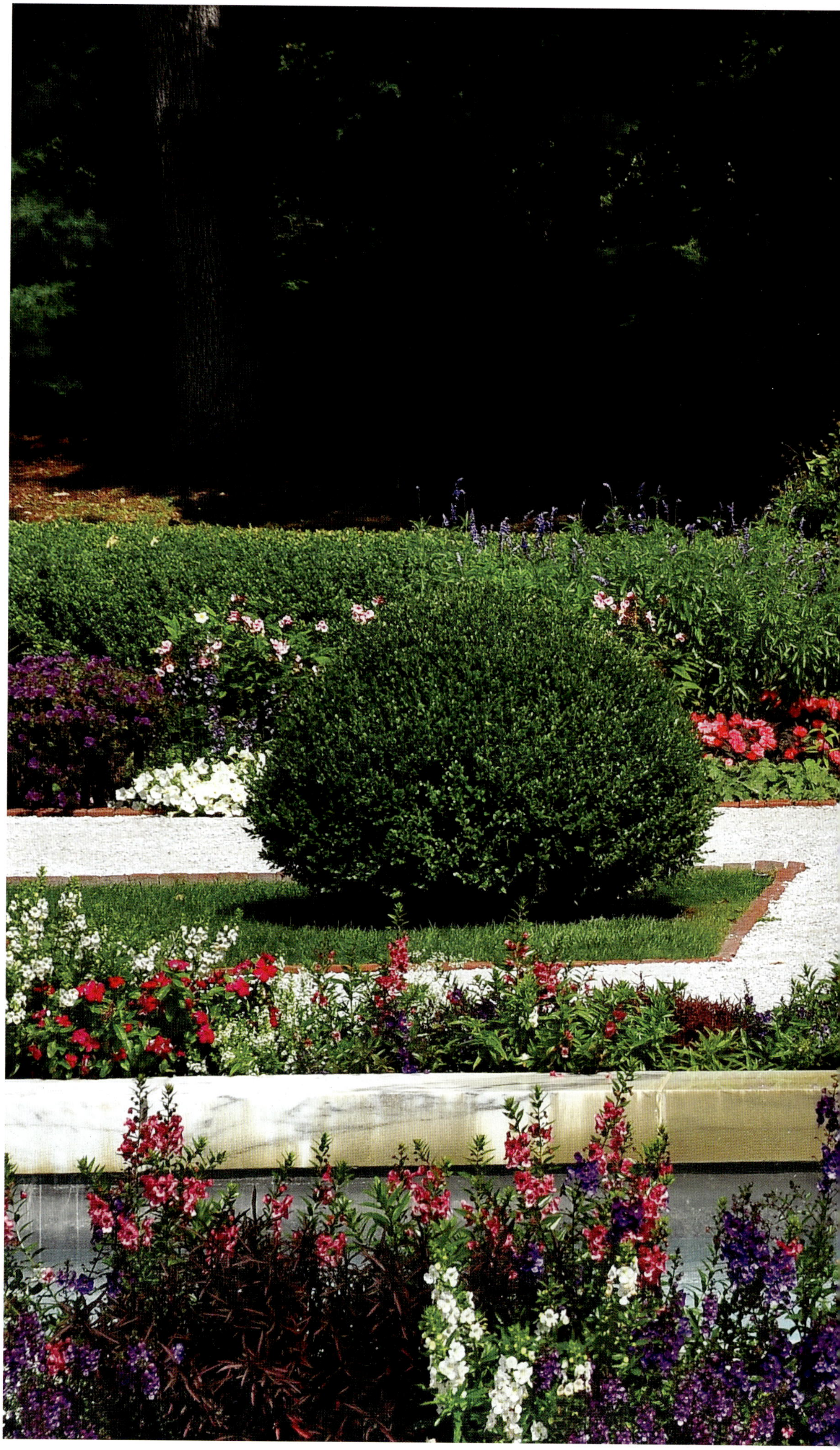

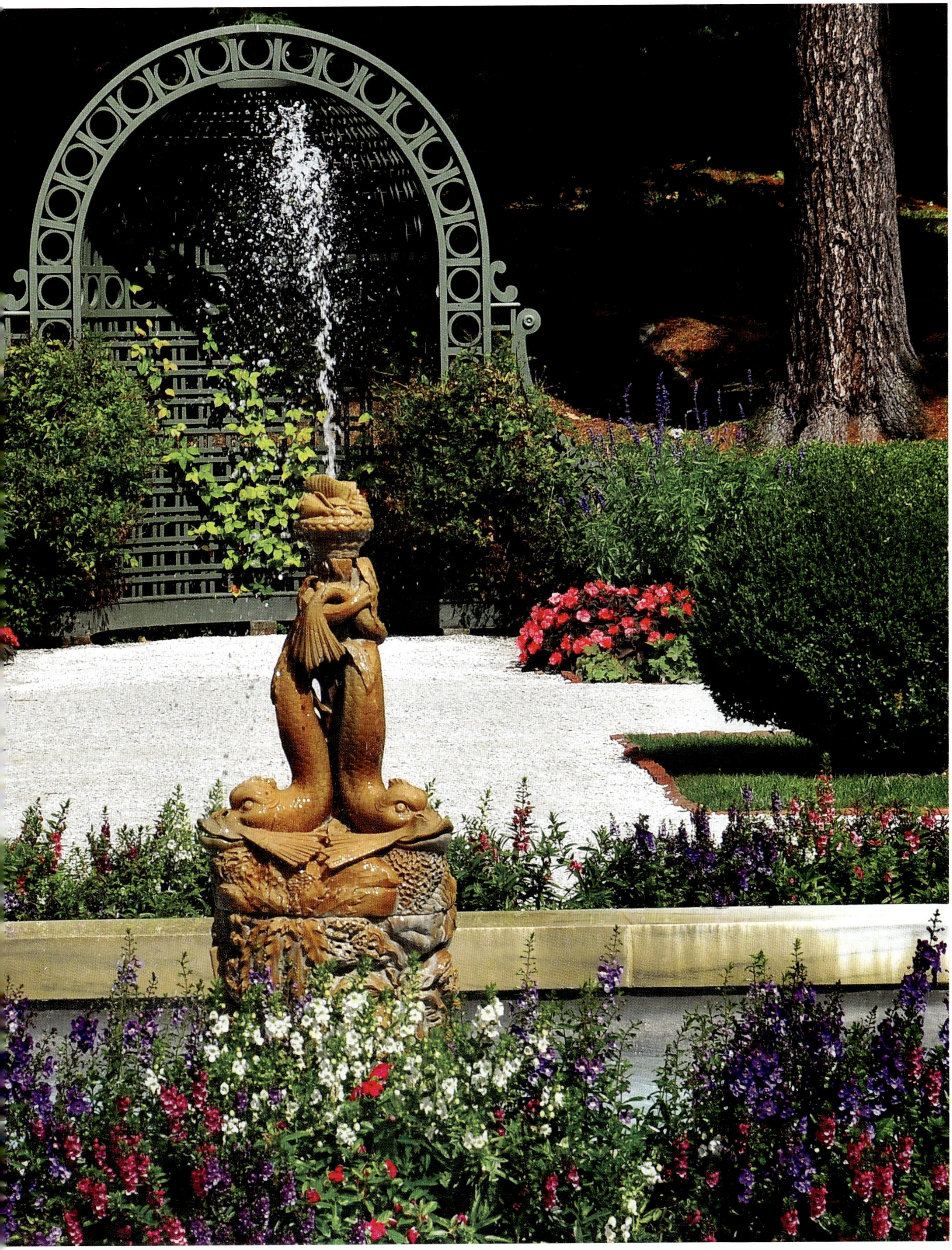

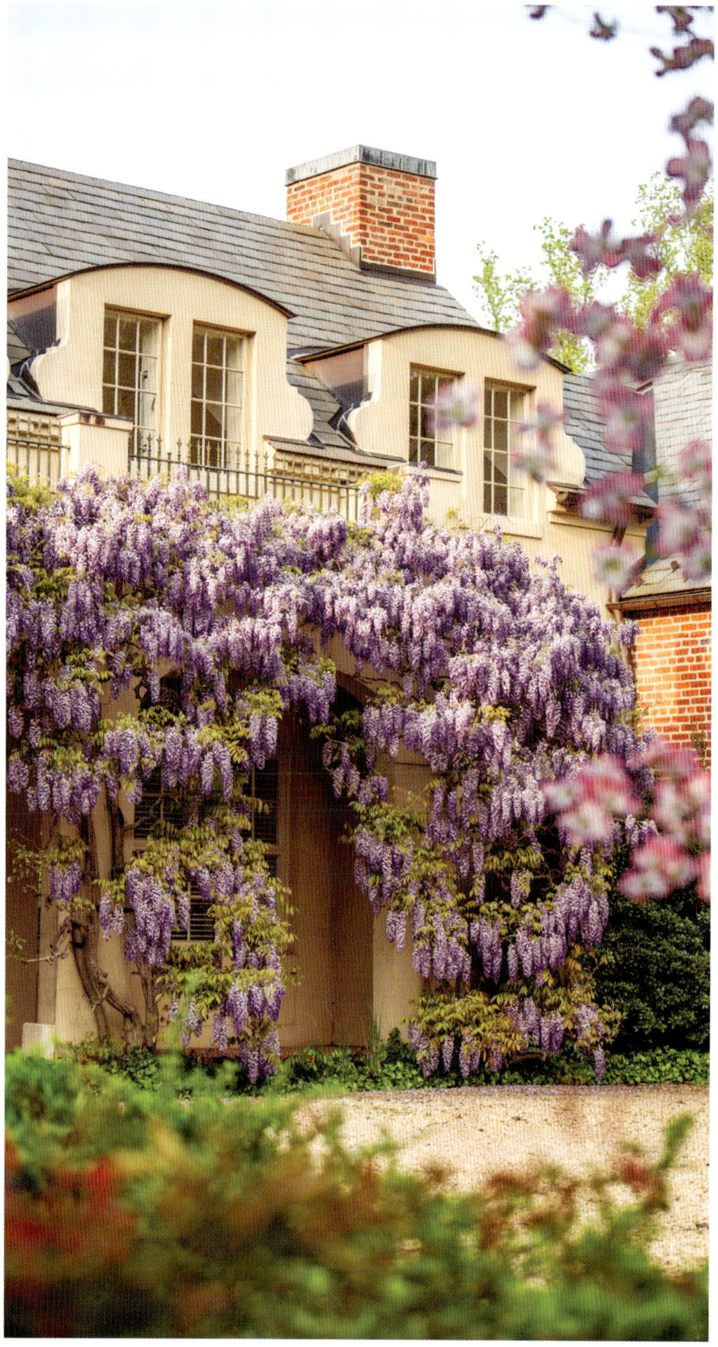

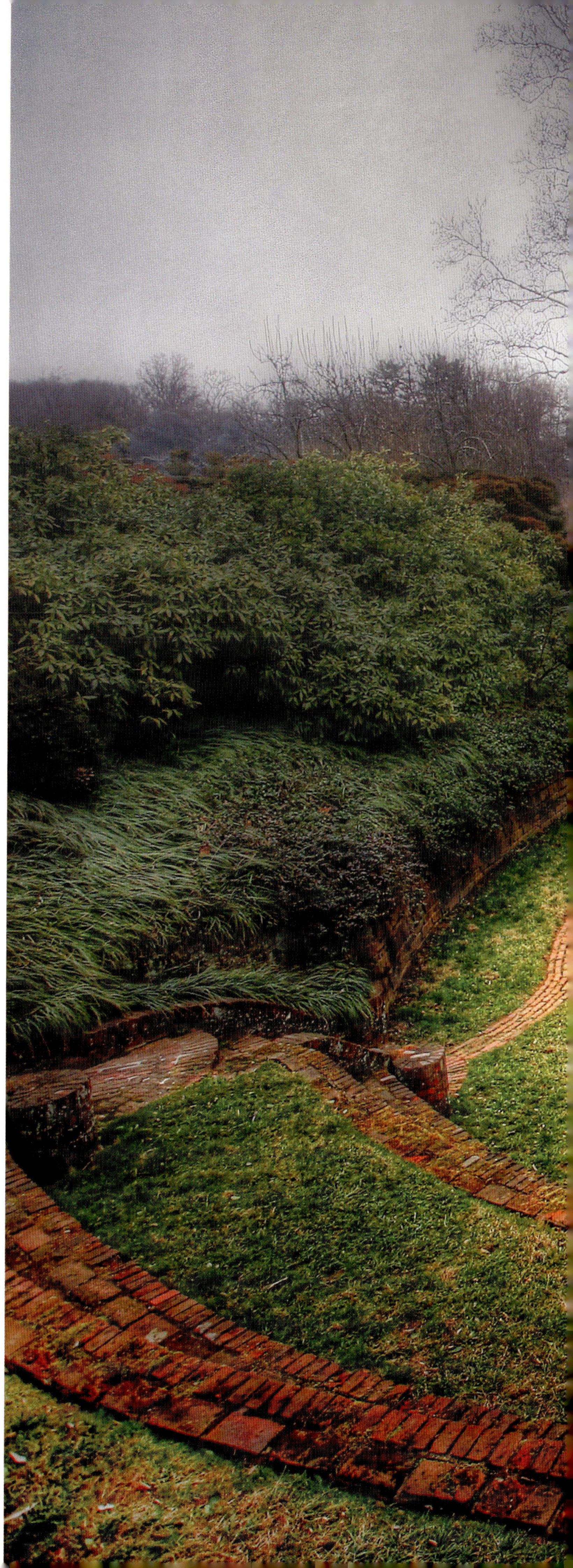

BOTH PHOTOGRAPHS:

Dumbarton Oaks, Washington, D.C., USA

Born in 1872, Beatrix Farrand designed hundreds of upper-class gardens on the US coasts, including spaces at the New York Botanical Garden and The White House, but at Dumbarton Oaks she excelled. One of her few surviving works, it was owned by Robert and Mildred Bliss, who commissioned her to create a mix of formal and informal bedding arrangements drawing from Arts and Crafts, and classic English and Italian elements. The collaboration began in 1921 and ended nearly 30 years later. Farrand died in seclusion in Maine in 1959. Dumbarton Oaks is now a Harvard University humanities research institute, and the gardens remain open to view.

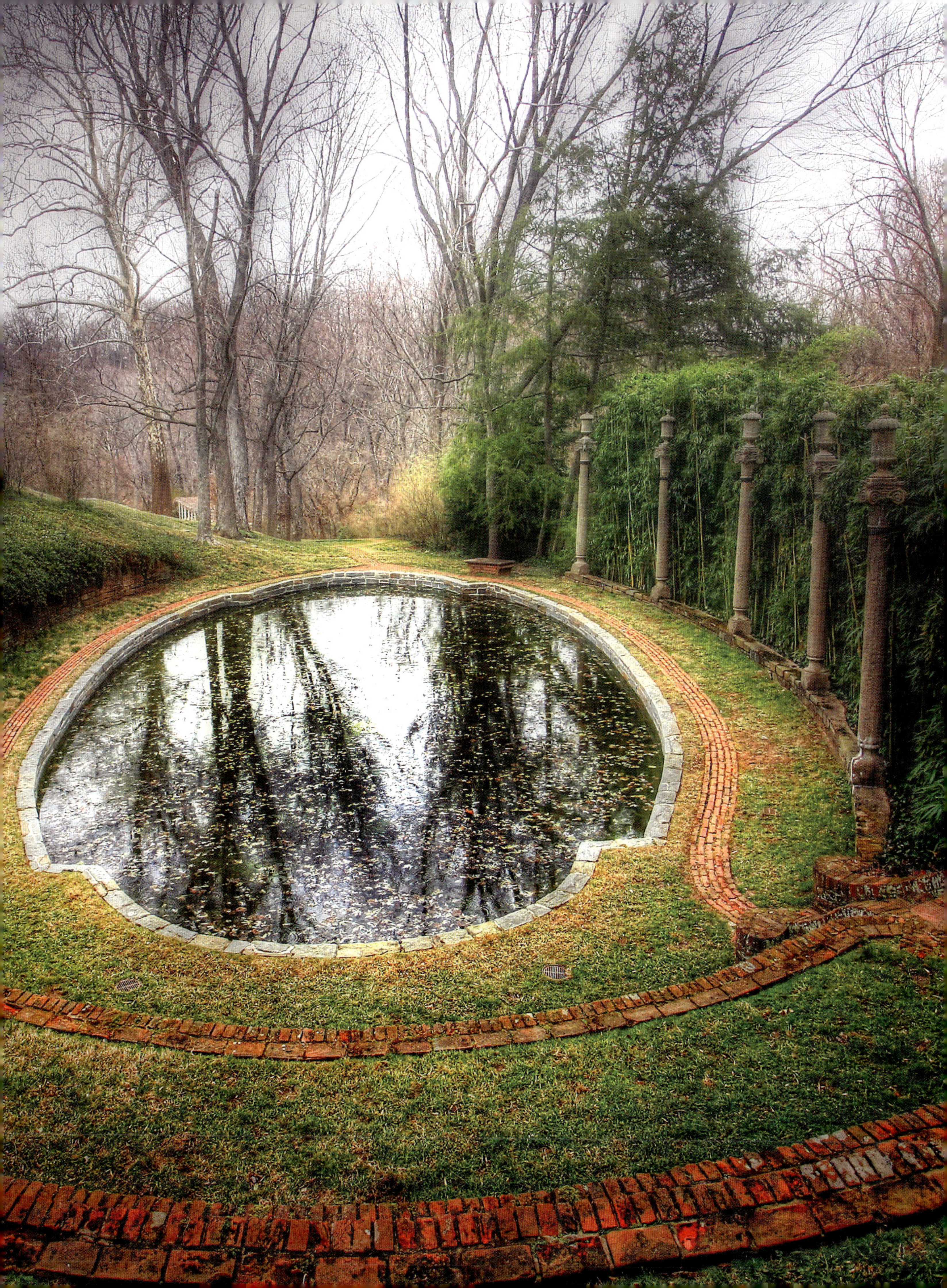

RIGHT AND OVERLEAF

ALL PHOTOGRAPHS:

Atlanta Botanical Garden, Georgia, USA

Comparatively new in botanical garden terms, the Atlanta Botanical Garden opened in 1976 upon the petition of local residents. The garden's mission is to aid botanical education, conservation, research and enjoyment. It regularly hosts popular exhibitions from the likes of glass sculptor Dale Chihuly, whose fantastical creations have been shown around the world. In 2010 the garden was expanded and modernised.

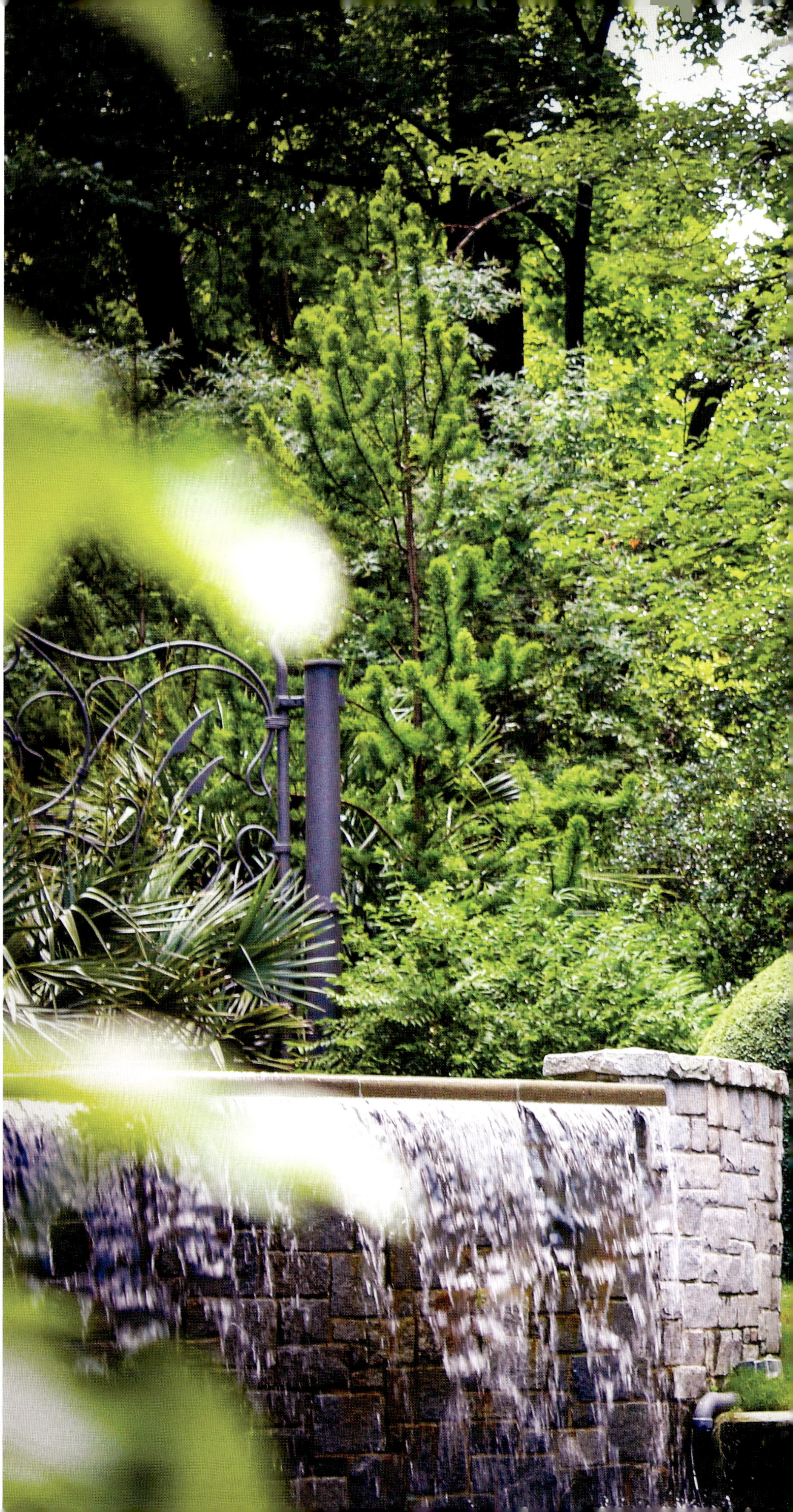

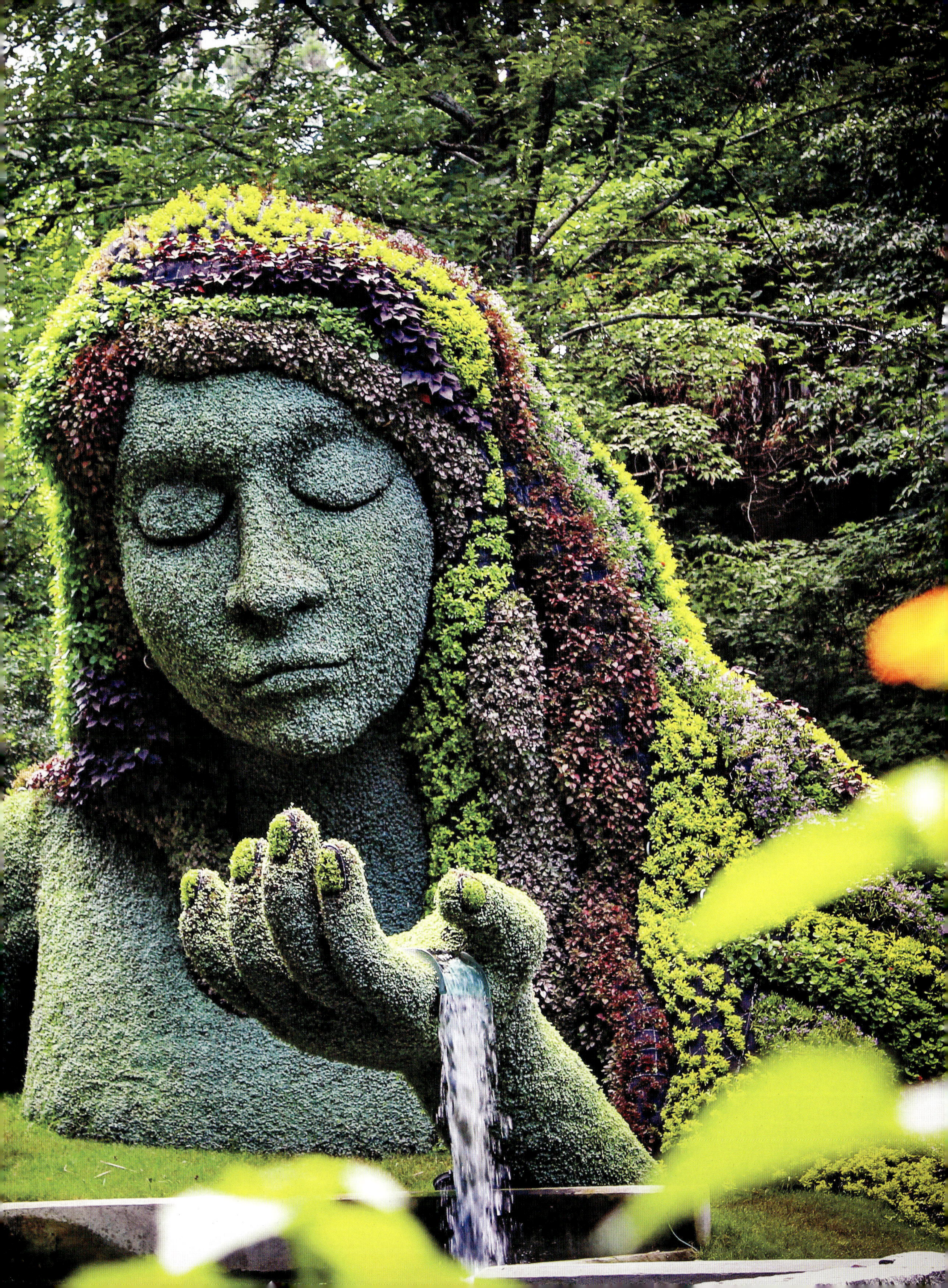

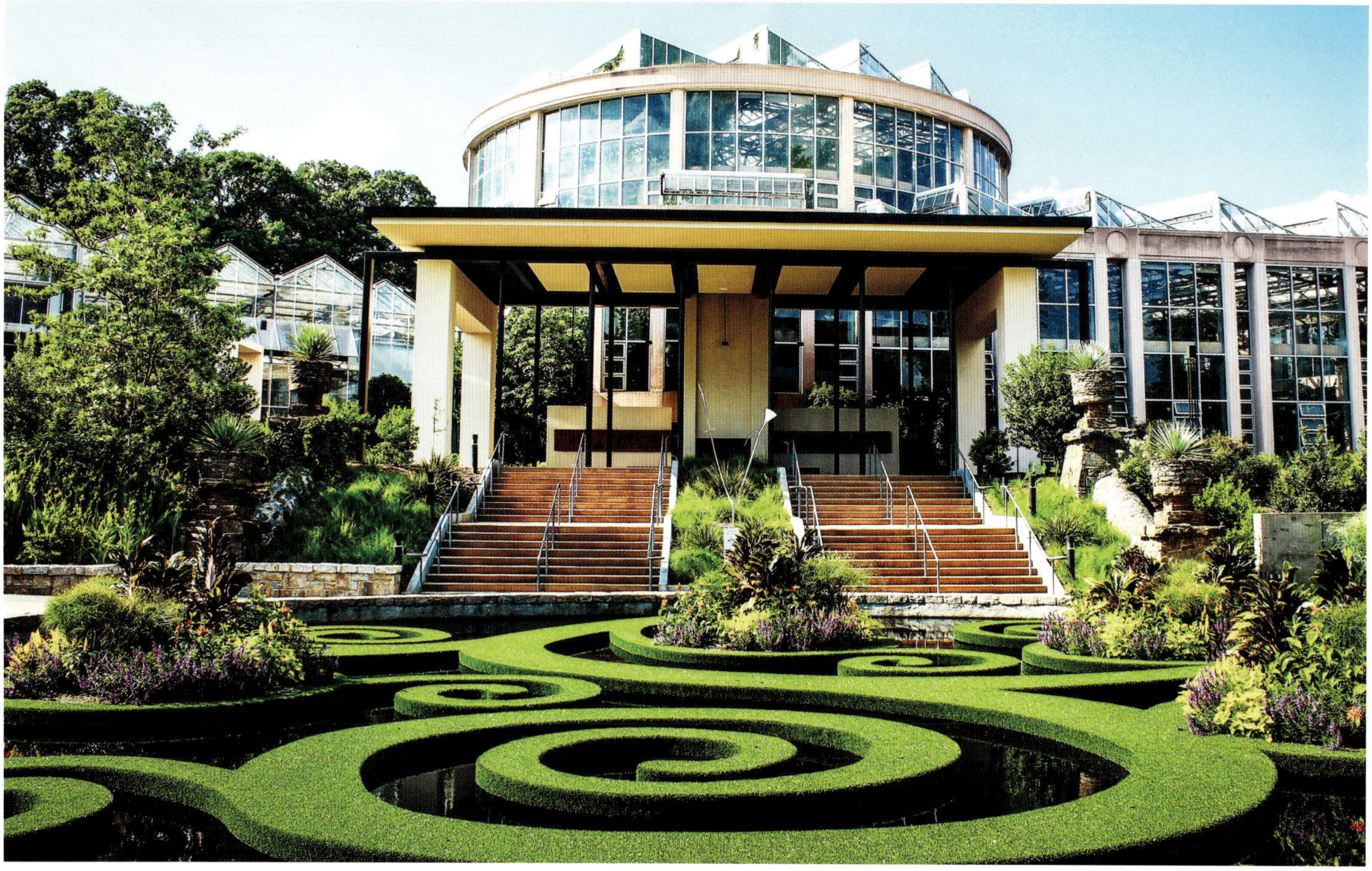

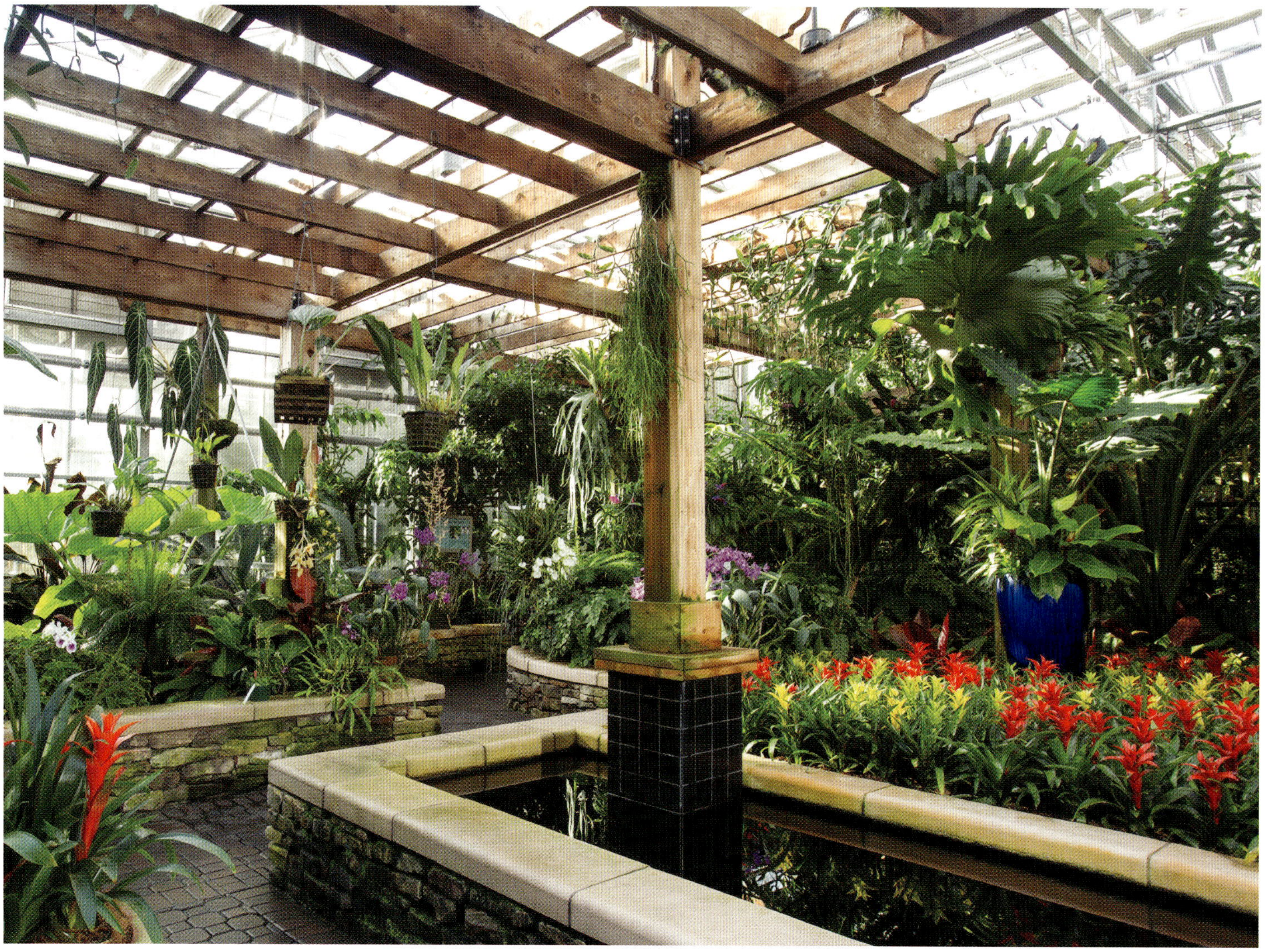

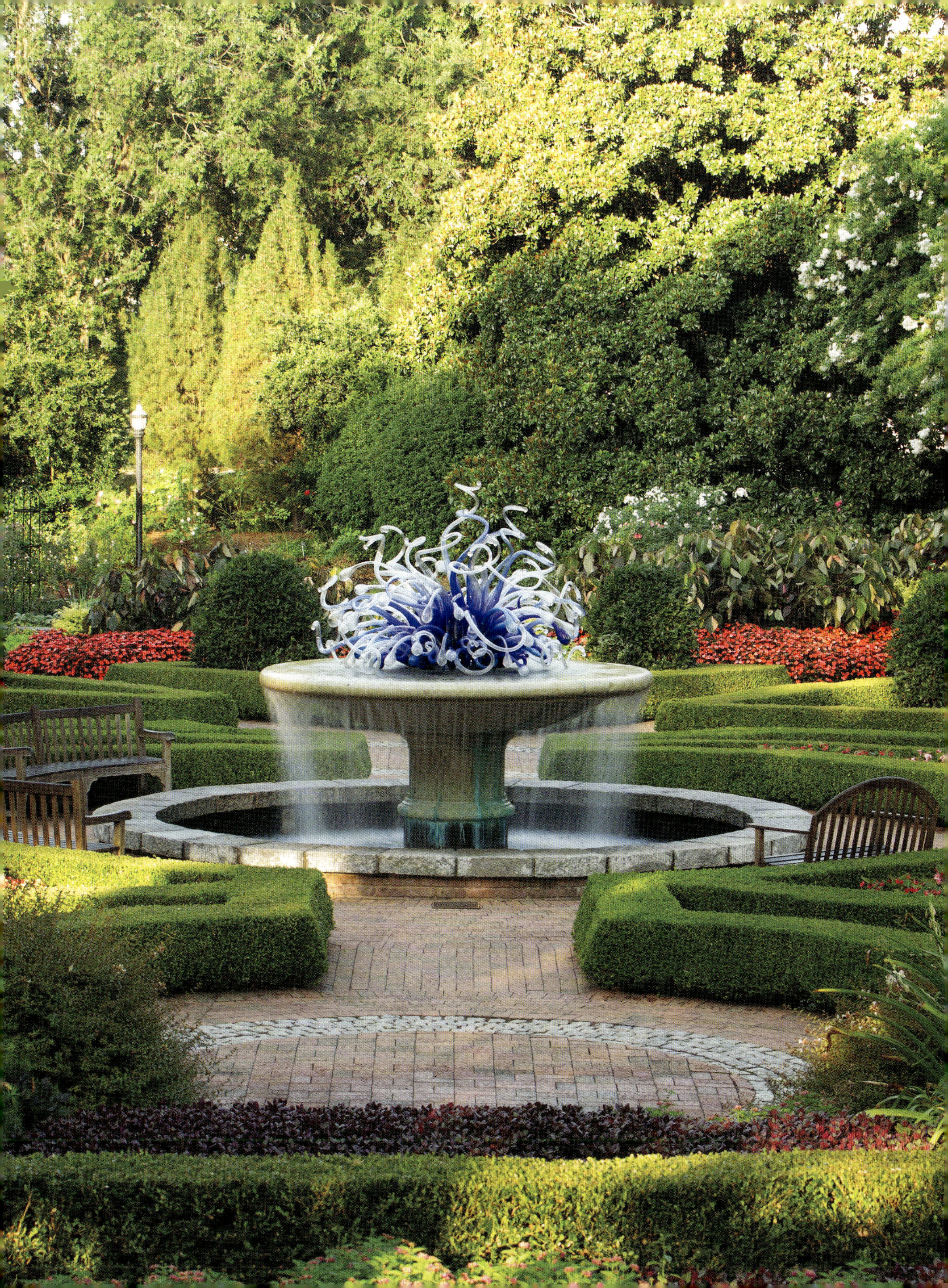

Garfield Park Conservatory, Illinois, USA
One of the largest conservatories in the United States, with nearly a hectare under glass, this notable Chicago conservatory dates to the 19th century. The largest room in the conservatory is the Palm House, which at 65ft high and 90ft wide accommodates 70 palms from around the world. The glasshouses and the surrounding park are listed on the National Register of Historic Places.

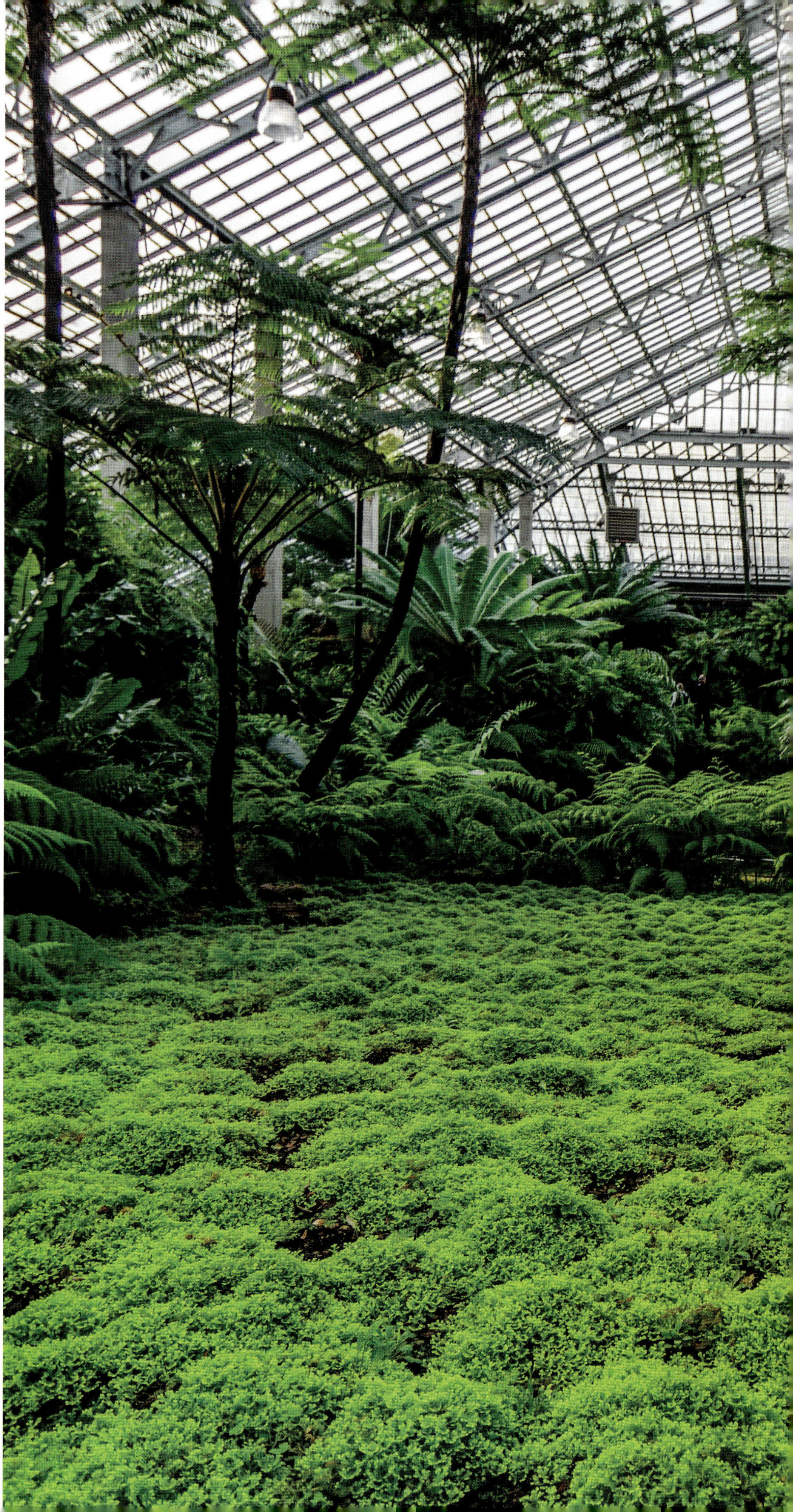

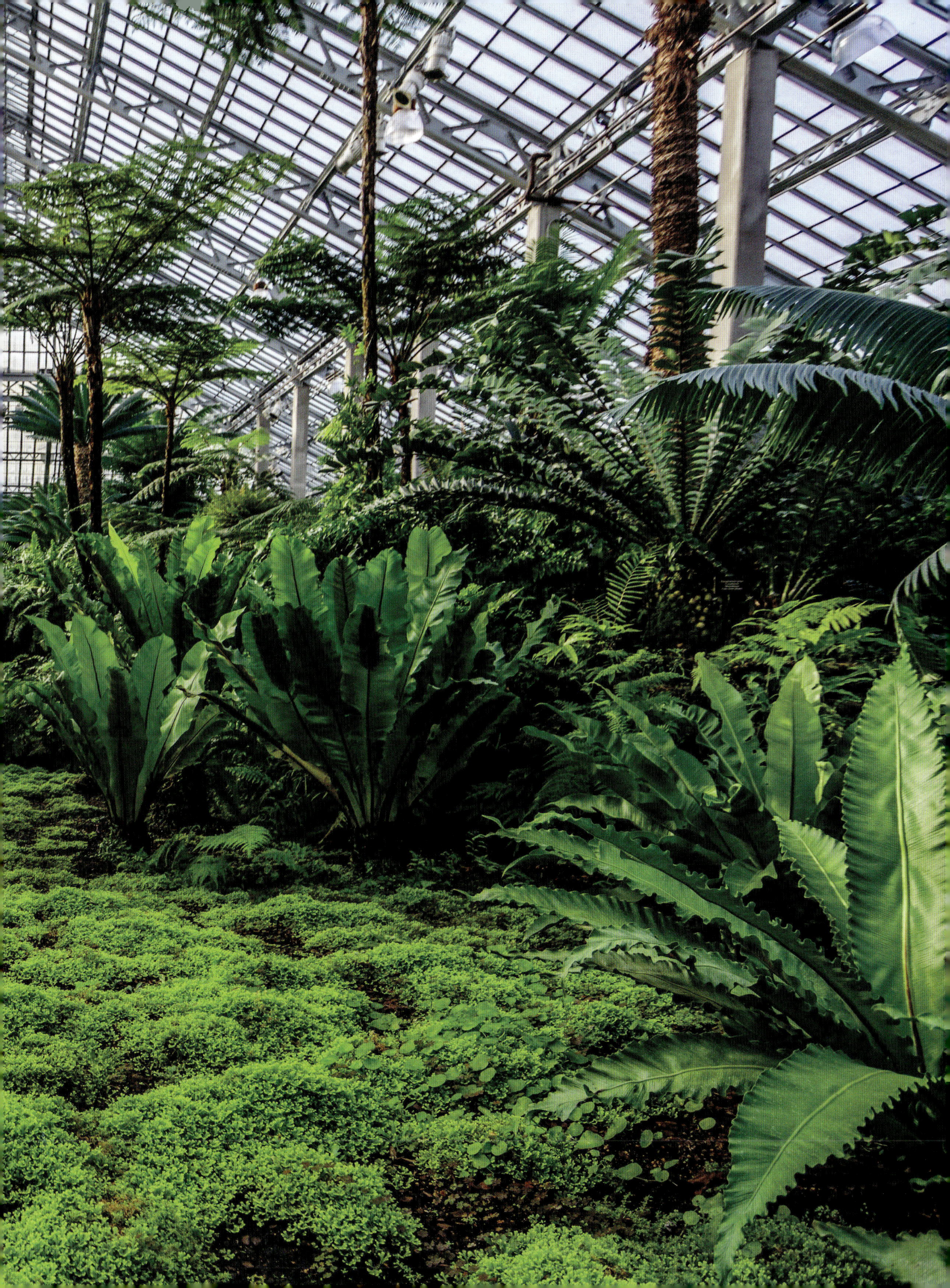

RIGHT:
Chicago Botanic Garden, Illinois, USA
This popular tourist attraction spanning 156ha (385 acres) within the Cook Country Forest Preserve was opened in 1972. It is divided into four zones reflecting local natural habitat: woods, prairie, riparian landscape and lakes and shores. A native plant garden and sensory garden are among the more contemporary attractions here.

BELOW AND OPPOSITE:
Chanticleer, Philadelphia, USA
On the outskirts of Philadelphia, Chanticleer dates from the early 1900s and was built by Adolph and Christine Rosengarten, who had a pharmaceuticals business. Few expenses were spared in its construction, leading the Rosengartens to name their home after the property in Thackeray's novel *The Newcomes*, which was 'mortgaged up to the very castle windows'. Some 14 staff now manage Chanticleer, which is part of the Chanticleer Foundation and open to the public. Productive gardens, ponds, a gravel garden, terraces and a flowery lawn feature.

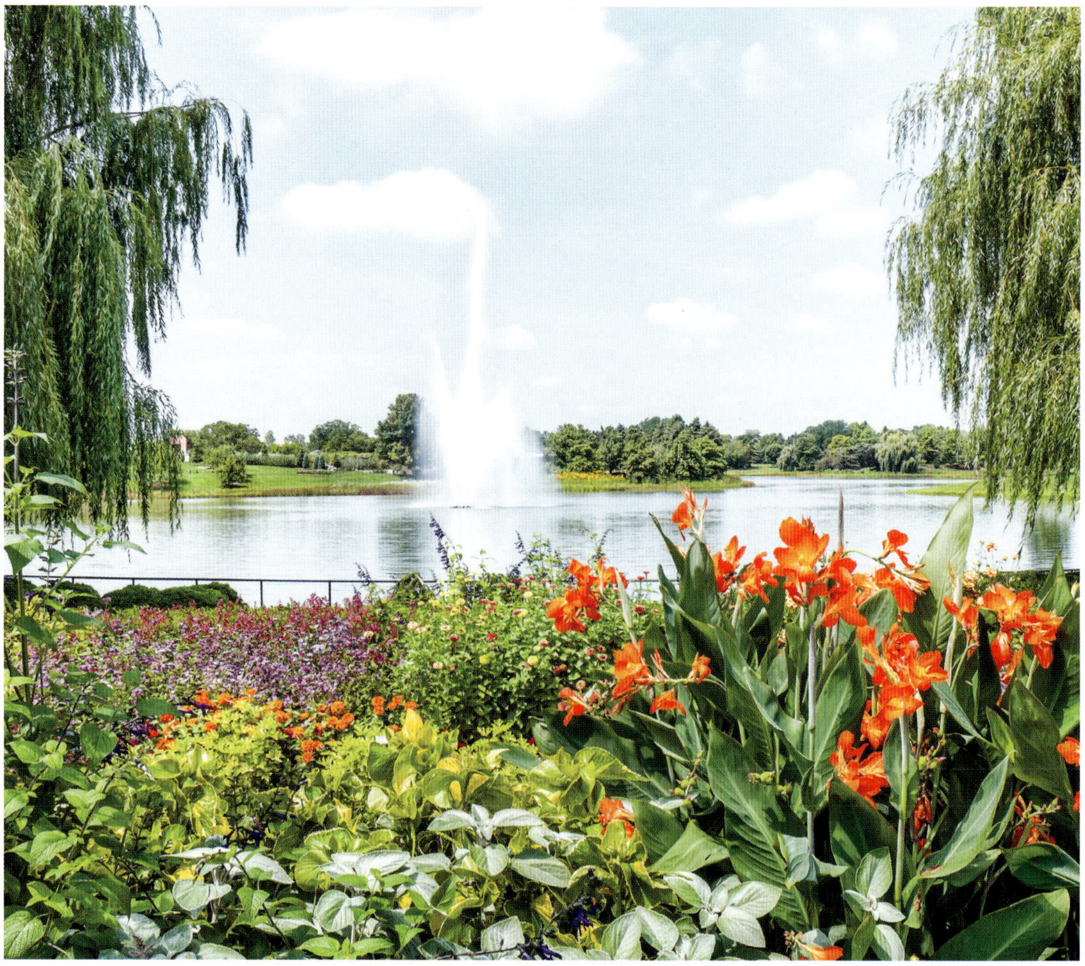

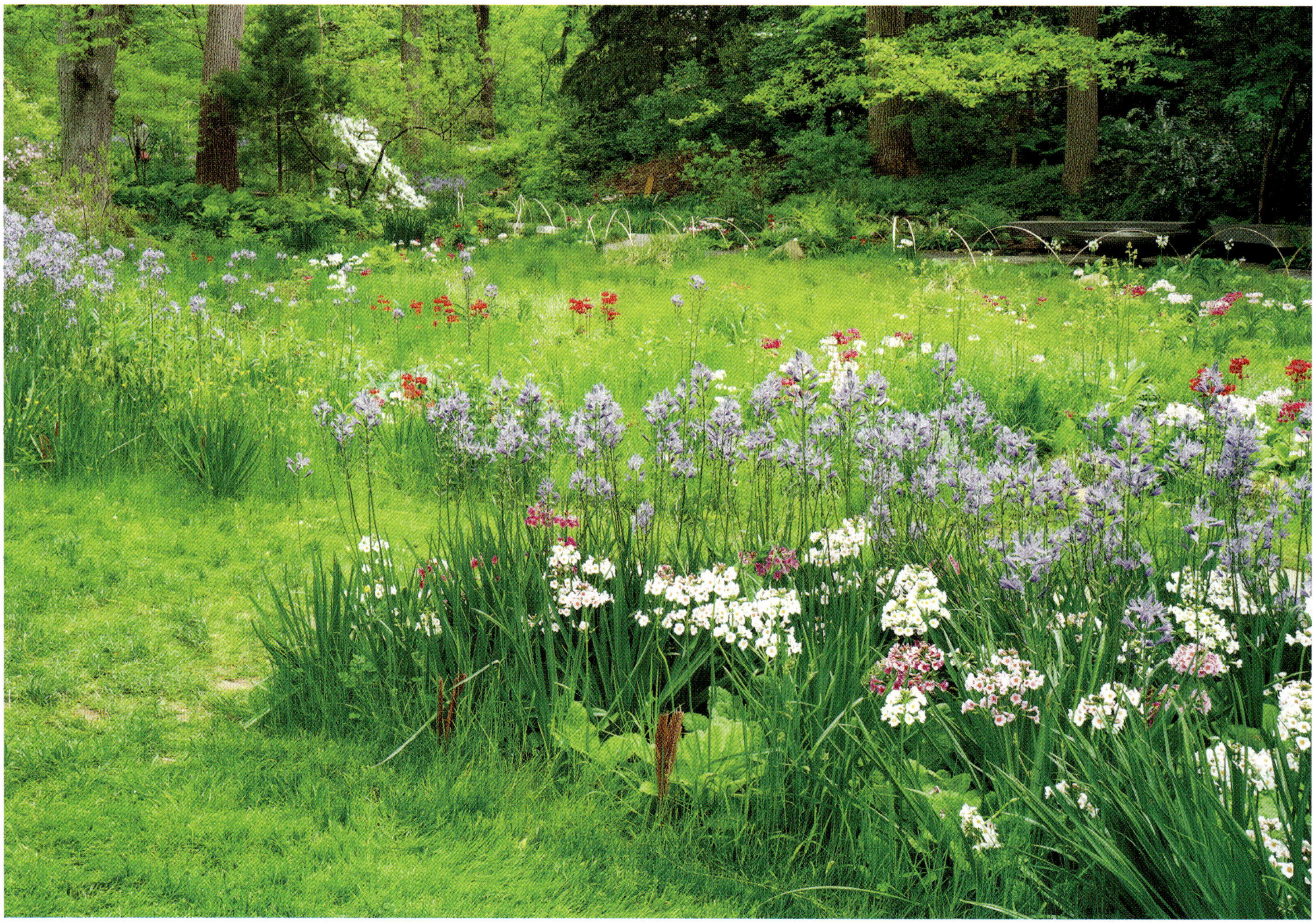

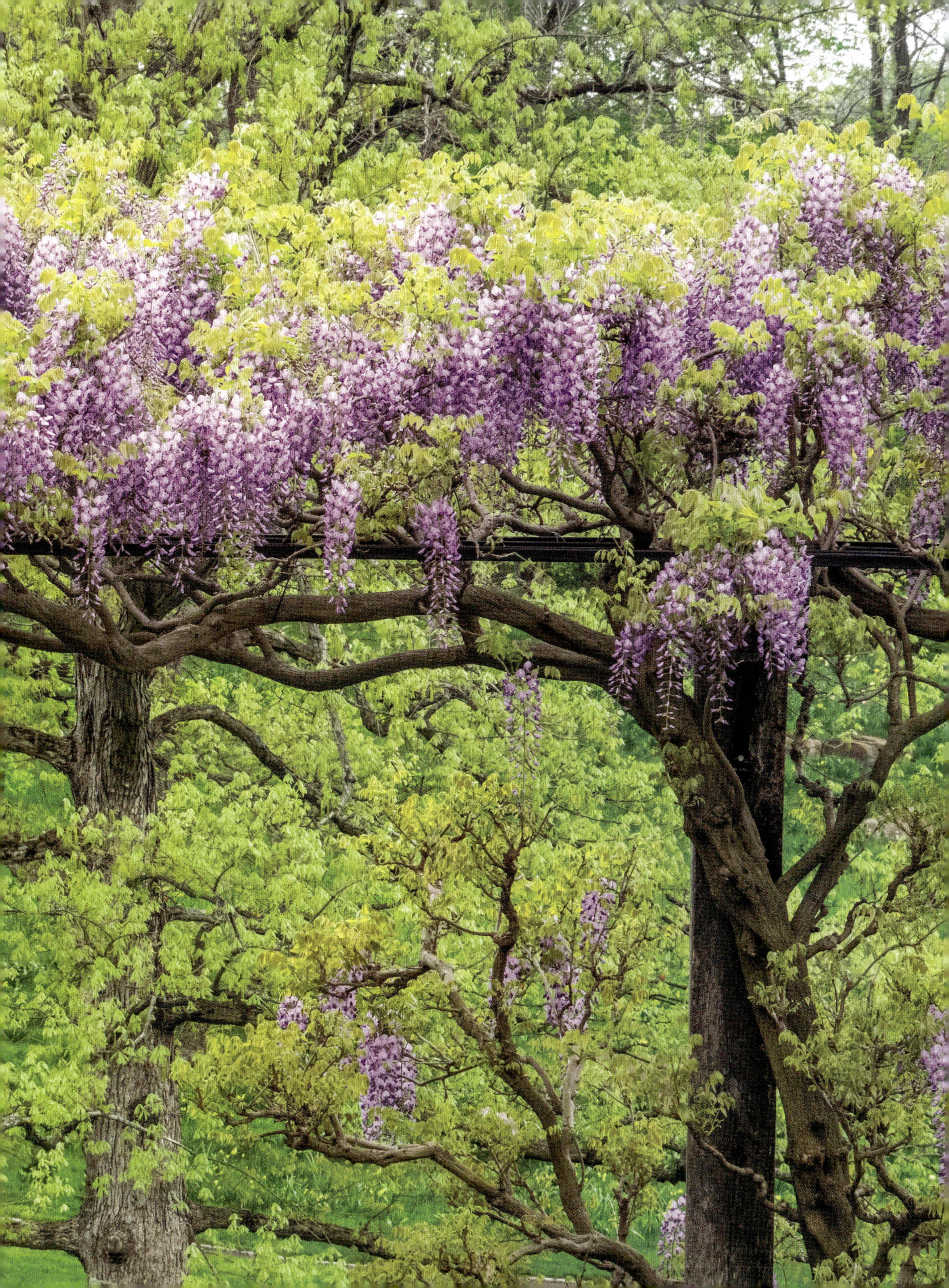

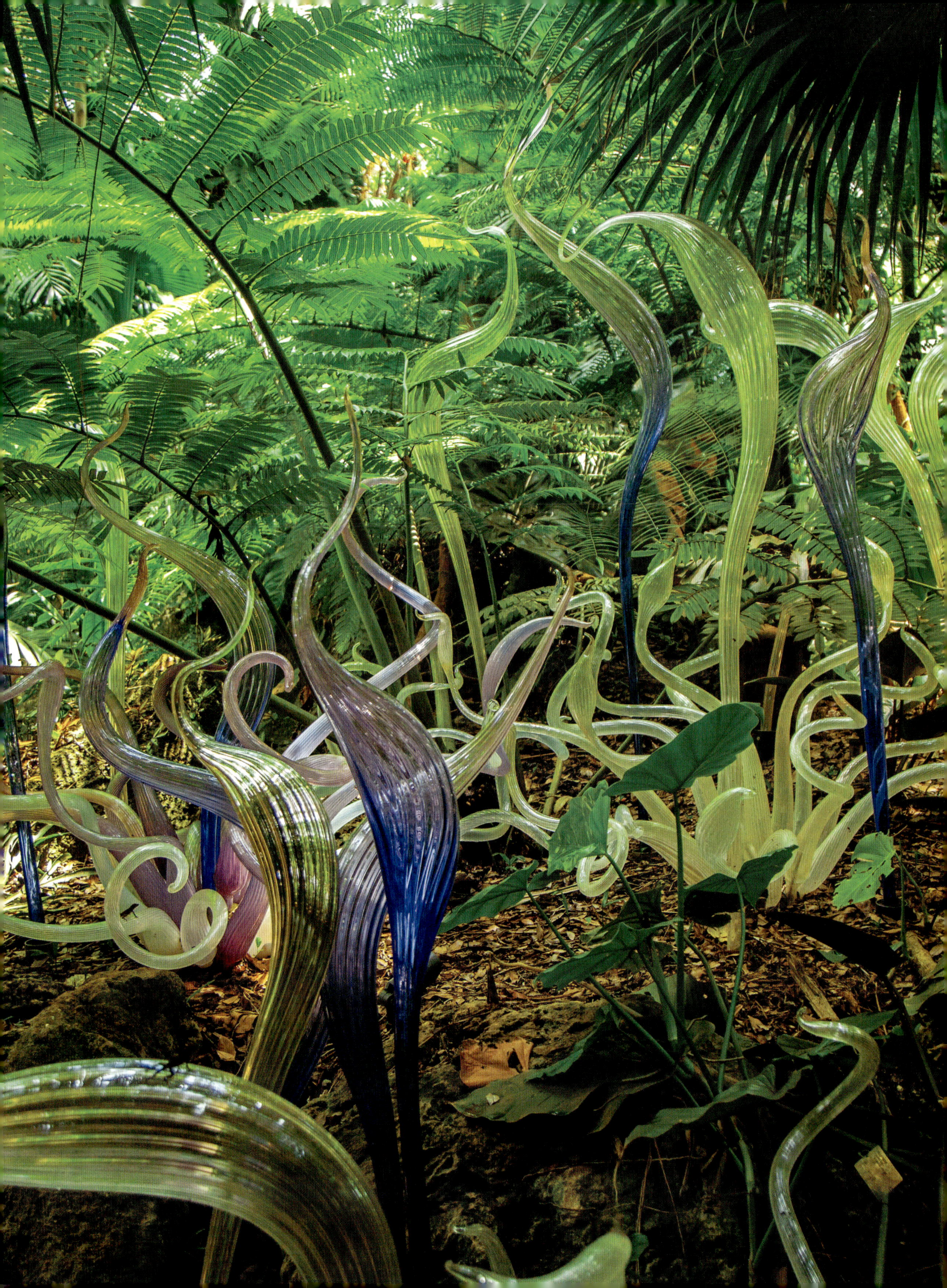

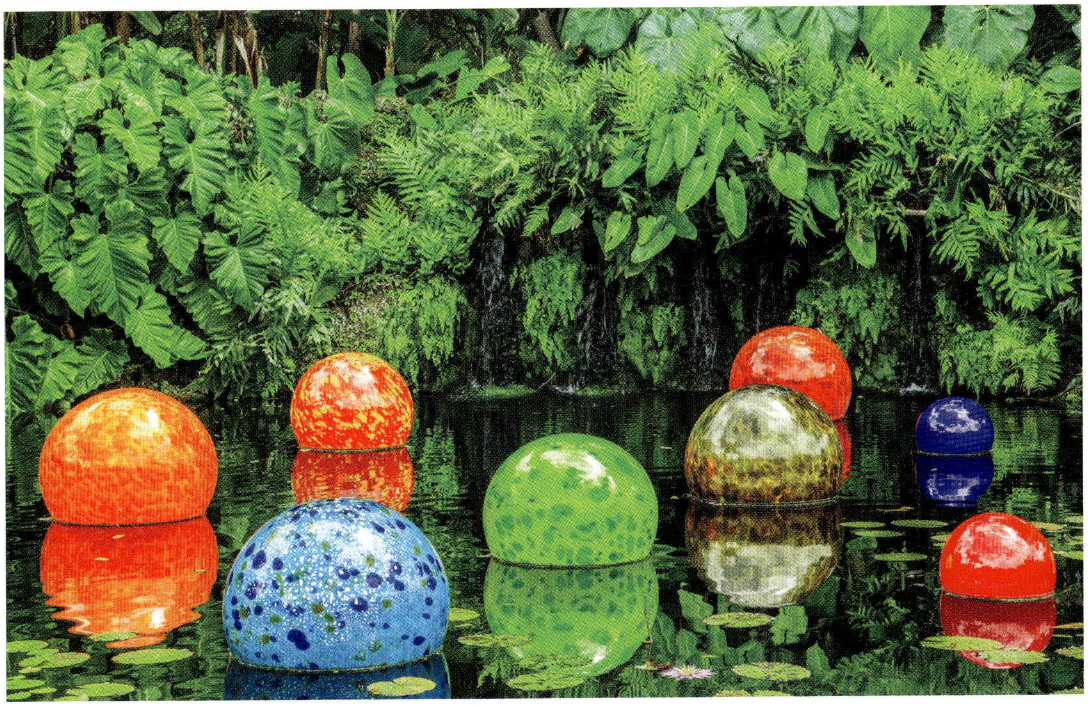

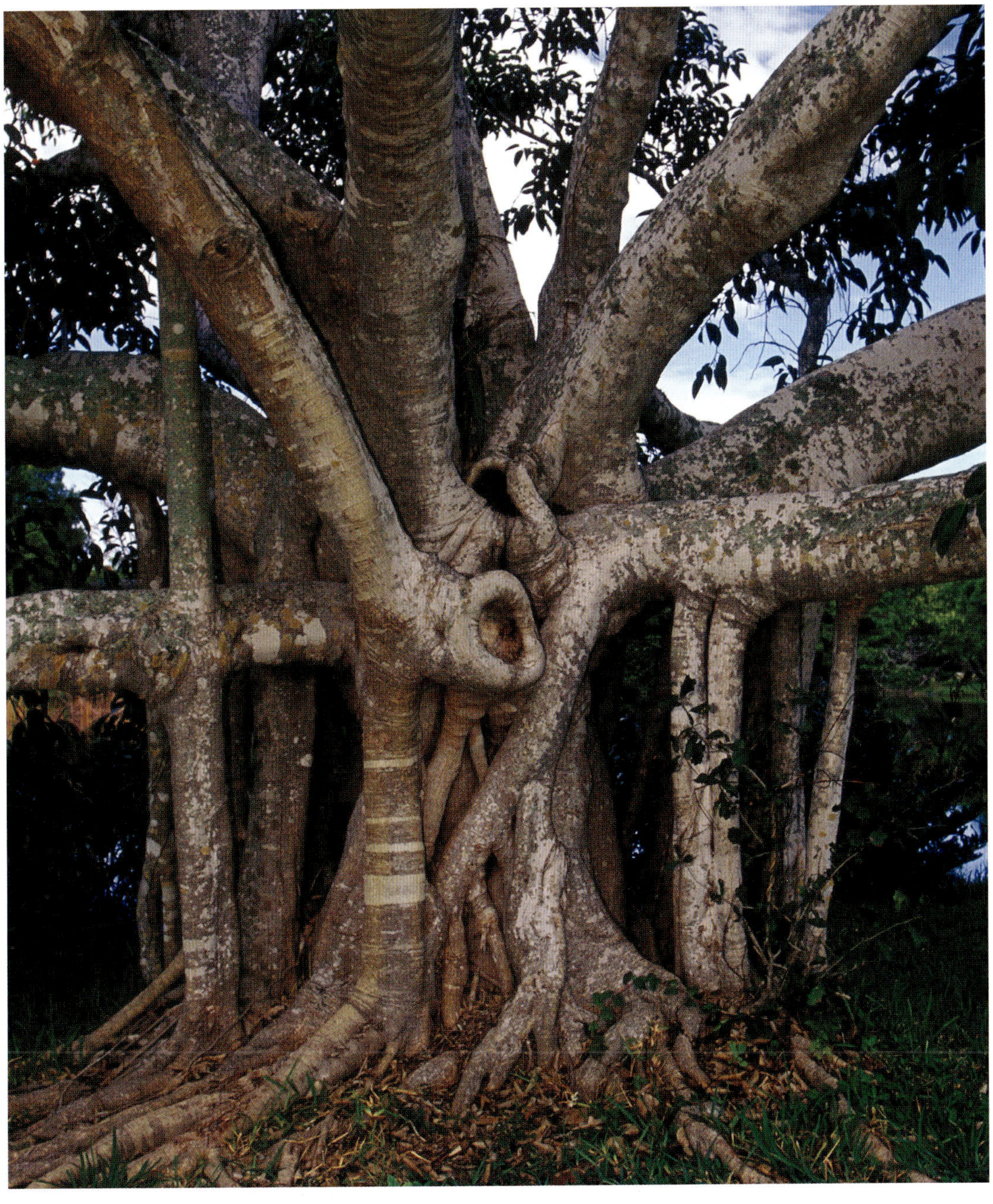

ALL PHOTOGRAPHS:

Fairchild Tropical Botanic Garden, Florida, USA

Just south of Miami, this botanic garden spread over 34ha (84 acres) conducts important research into biodiversity and is also the home of the American Orchid Society. It is named after plant hunter-explorer David Fairchild, who introduced thousands of plants to the United States, not least certain bamboos, mangoes and dates.

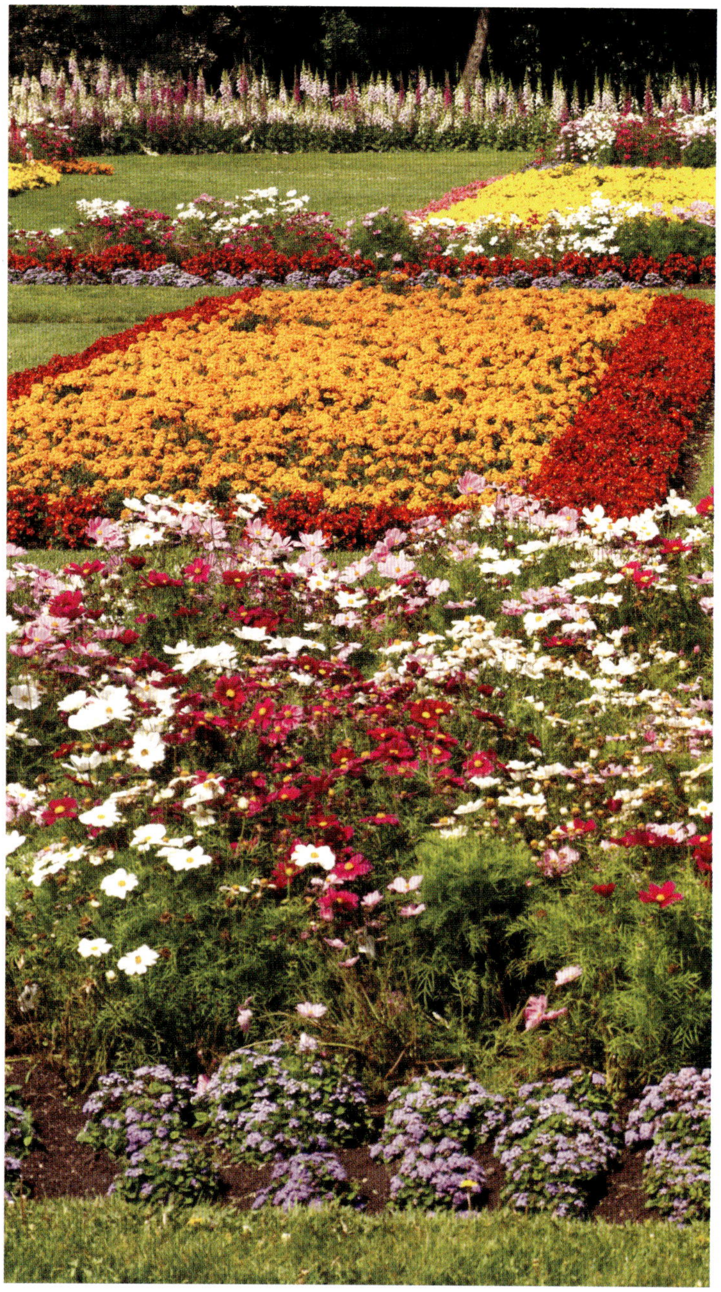

BOTH PHOTOGRAPHS:
Golden Gate Park, California, USA
In San Francisco, this memorable park in the centre of the city is larger but similar in design and function to Central Park in Manhattan. Gardens here comprise meadows, groves and lakes, while the infamous-but-loved Hippie Hill has been a site of counterculture since the 1960s.

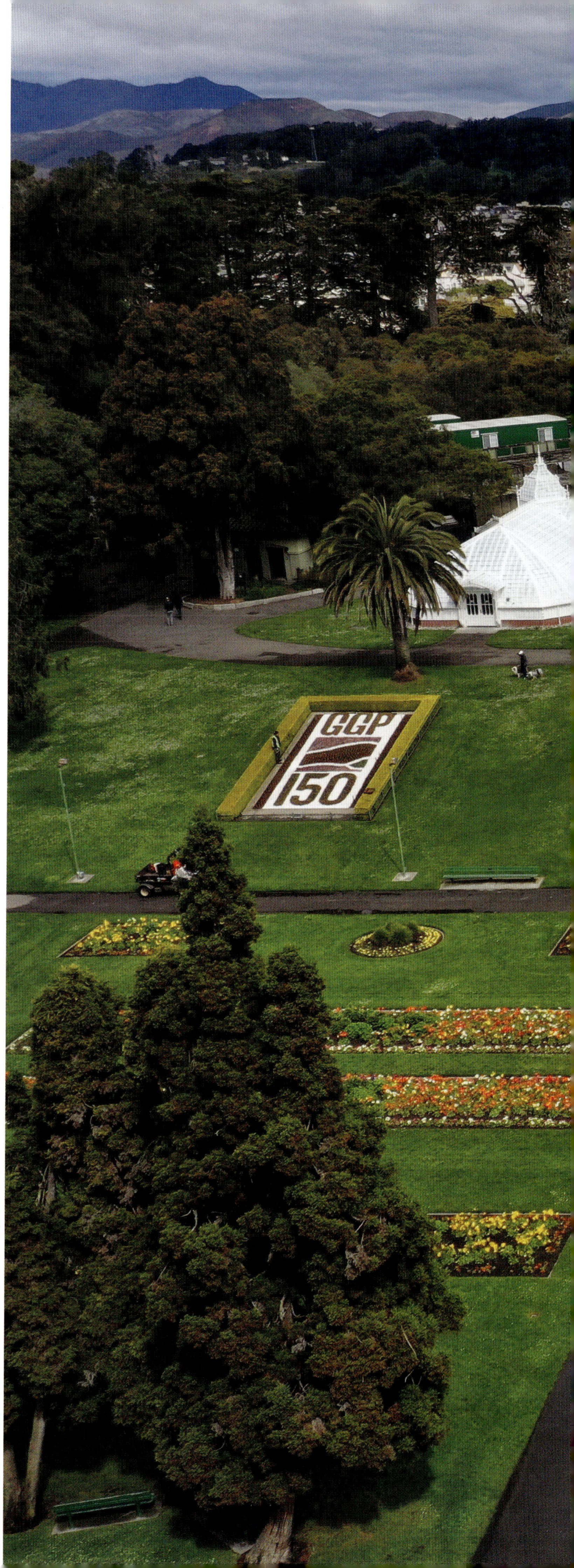

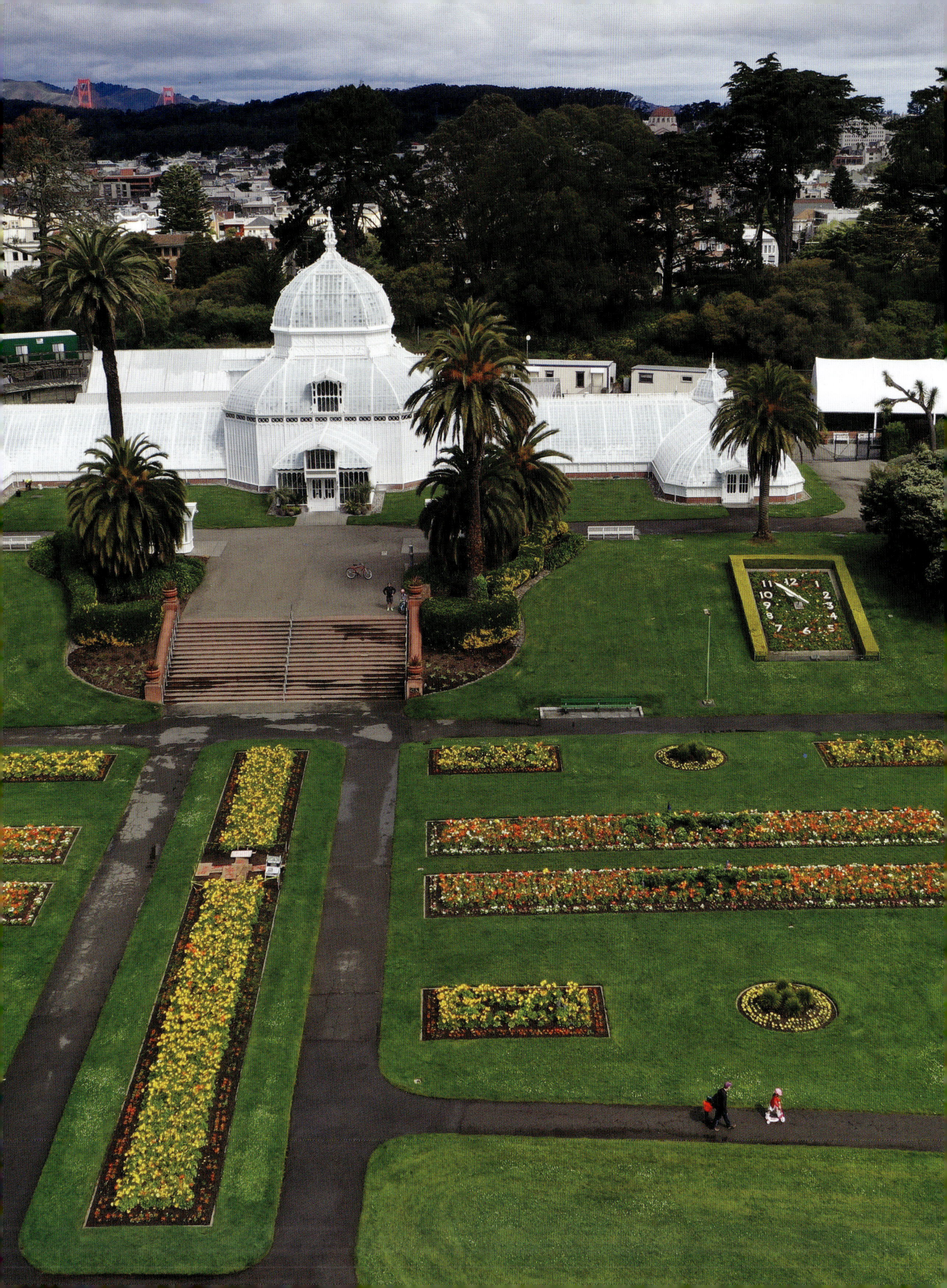

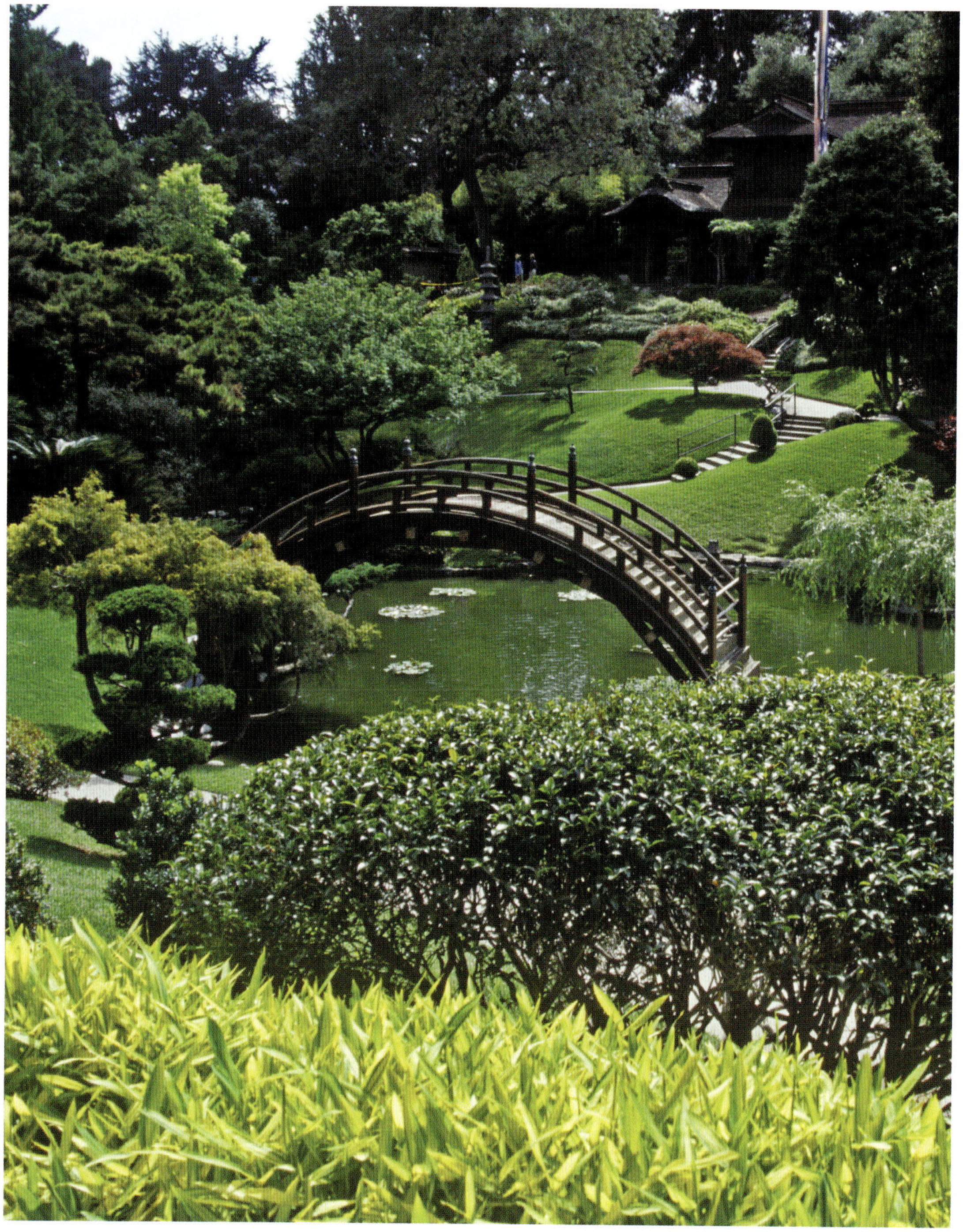

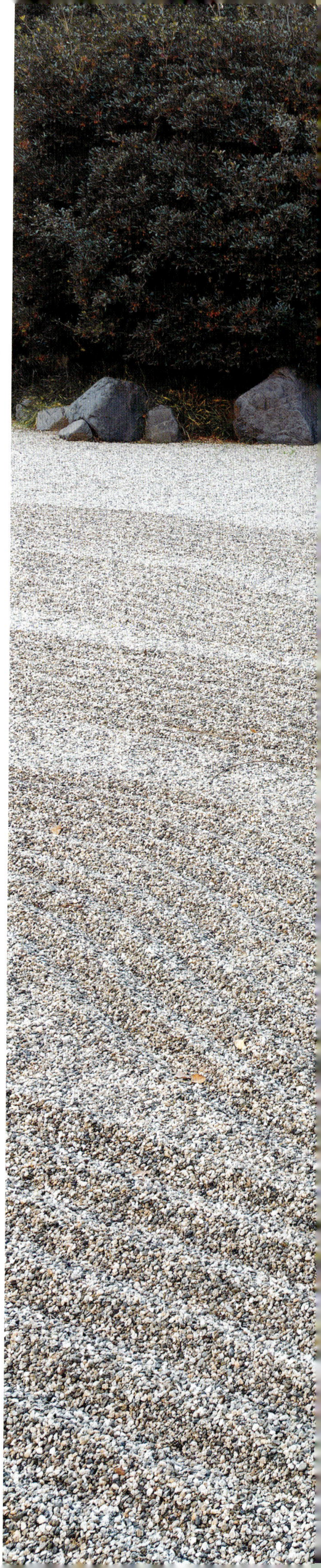

BOTH PHOTOGRAPHS:
Huntington Library and Gardens, California, USA
Dry-climate plants and native species are a hallmark of the California Garden here. It is one of 16 themed gardens, including a Japanese garden, at this popular location in San Marino outside Los Angeles. The Desert Garden holds one of the world's largest collections of cacti and succulents. Research, workshops and lectures are integral to this institution.

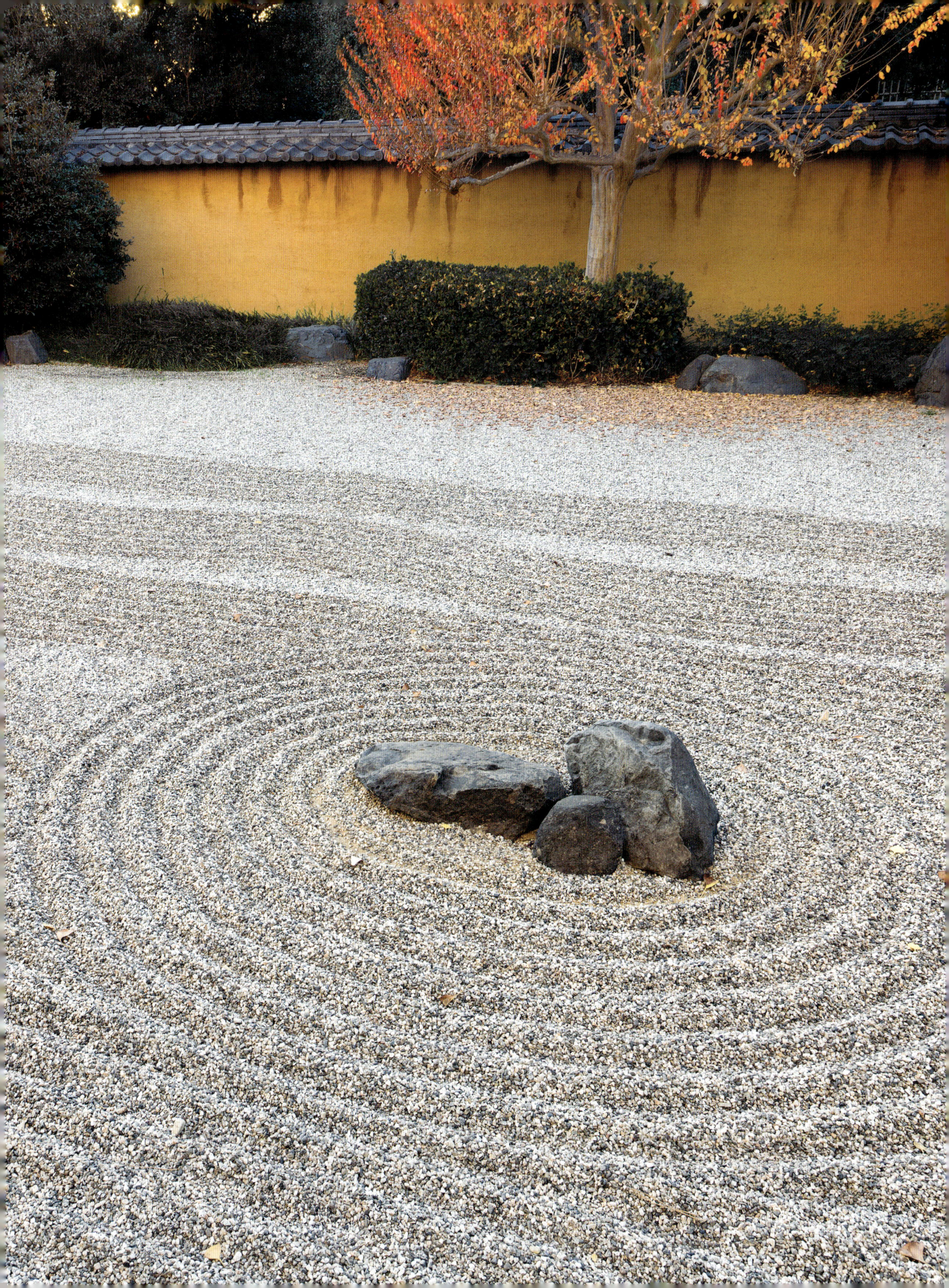

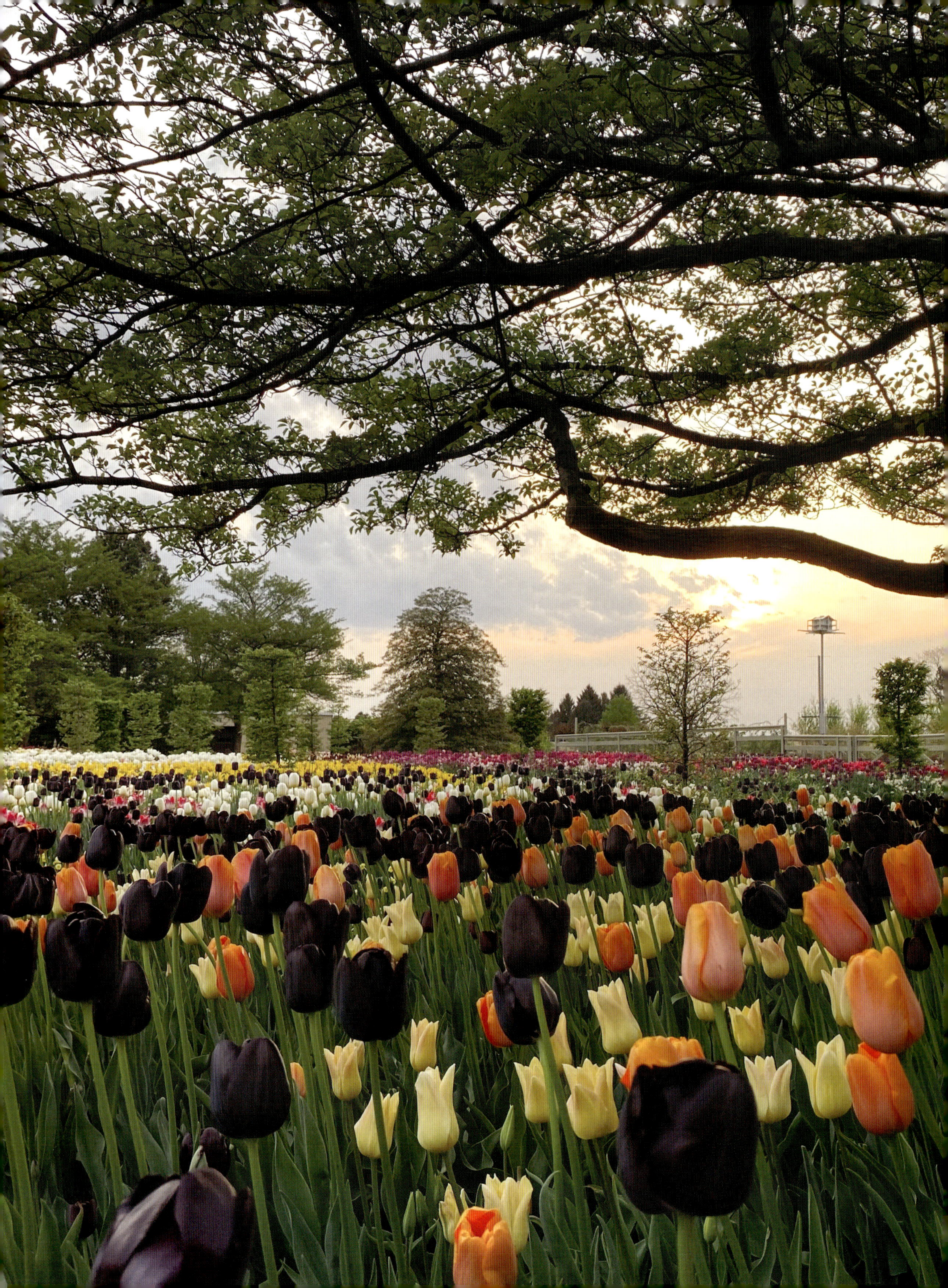

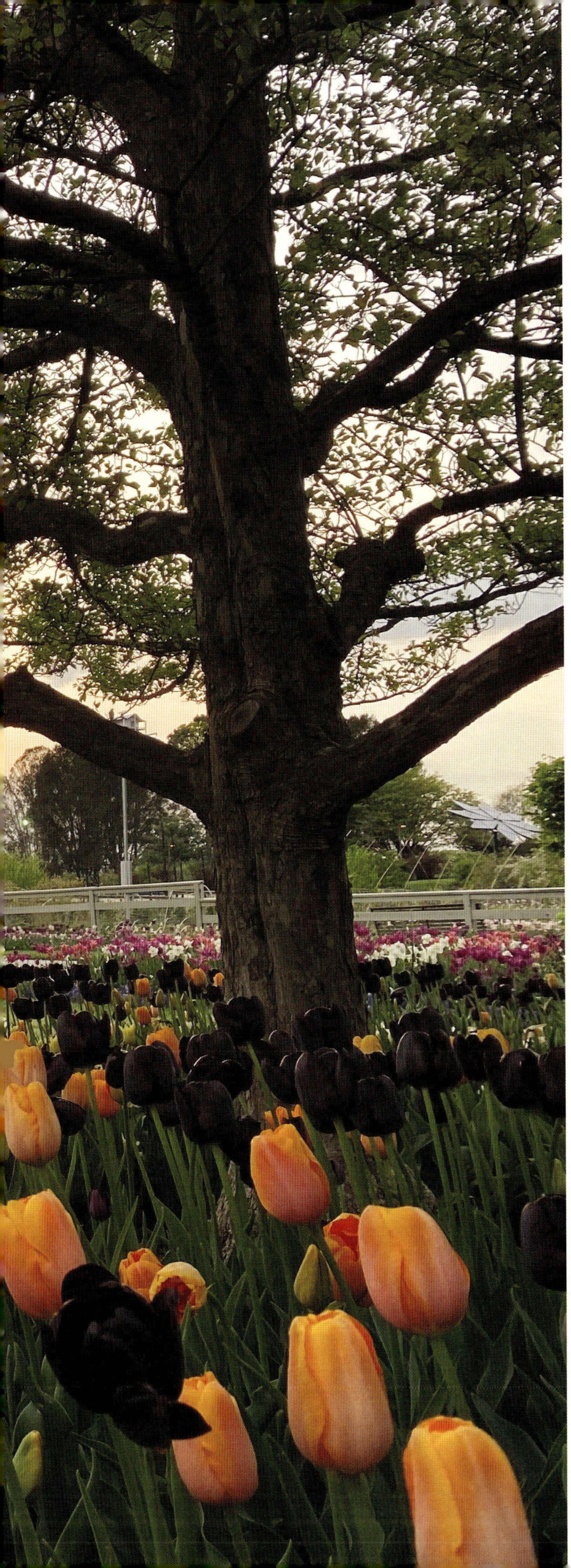

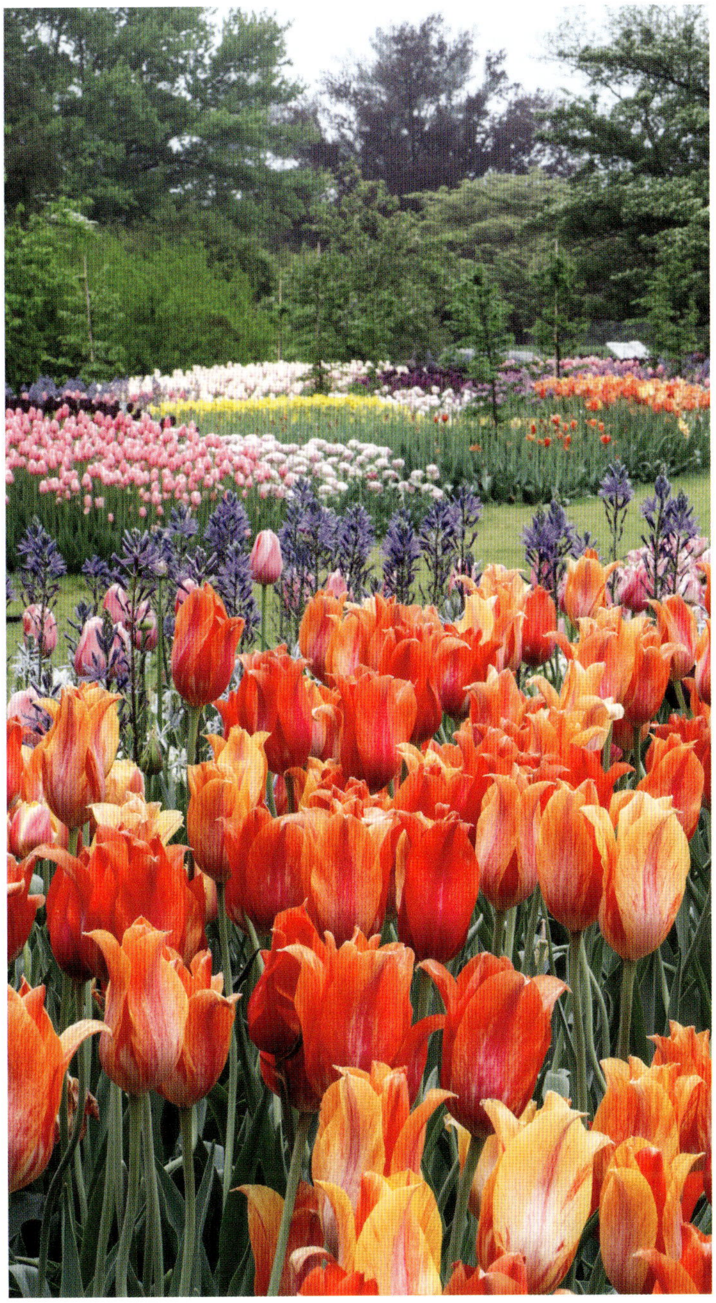

BOTH PHOTOGRAPHS:
Longwood Gardens, Pennsylvania, USA
The extraordinary grounds at Longwood Gardens draw visitors from around the world. This well-regarded botanical garden is one of the finest in the United States and it is an important place of learning and research for horticulturalists and botanists. The Longwood Garden plant collection contains over 9,000 species and varieties and dates to 1798.

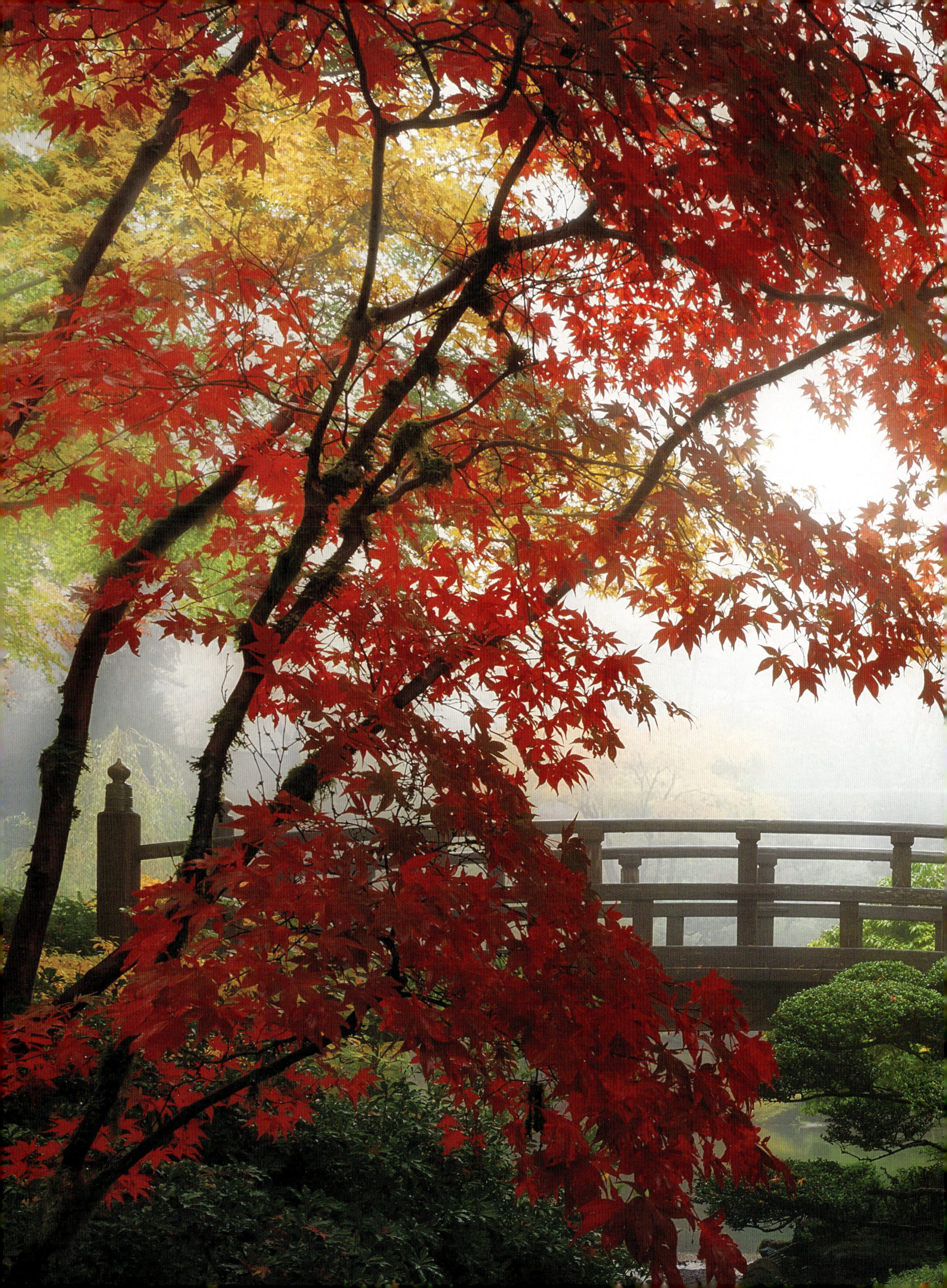

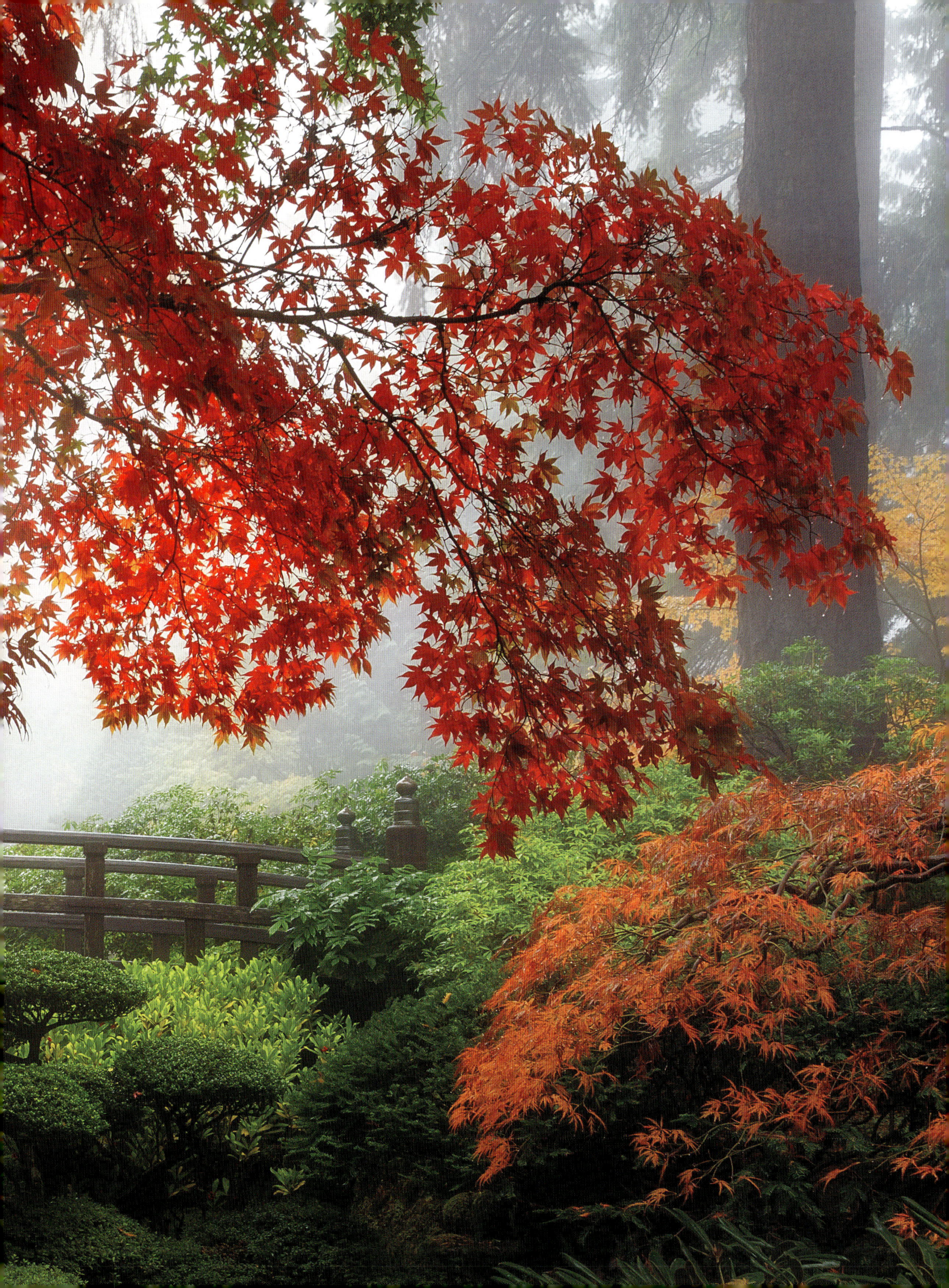

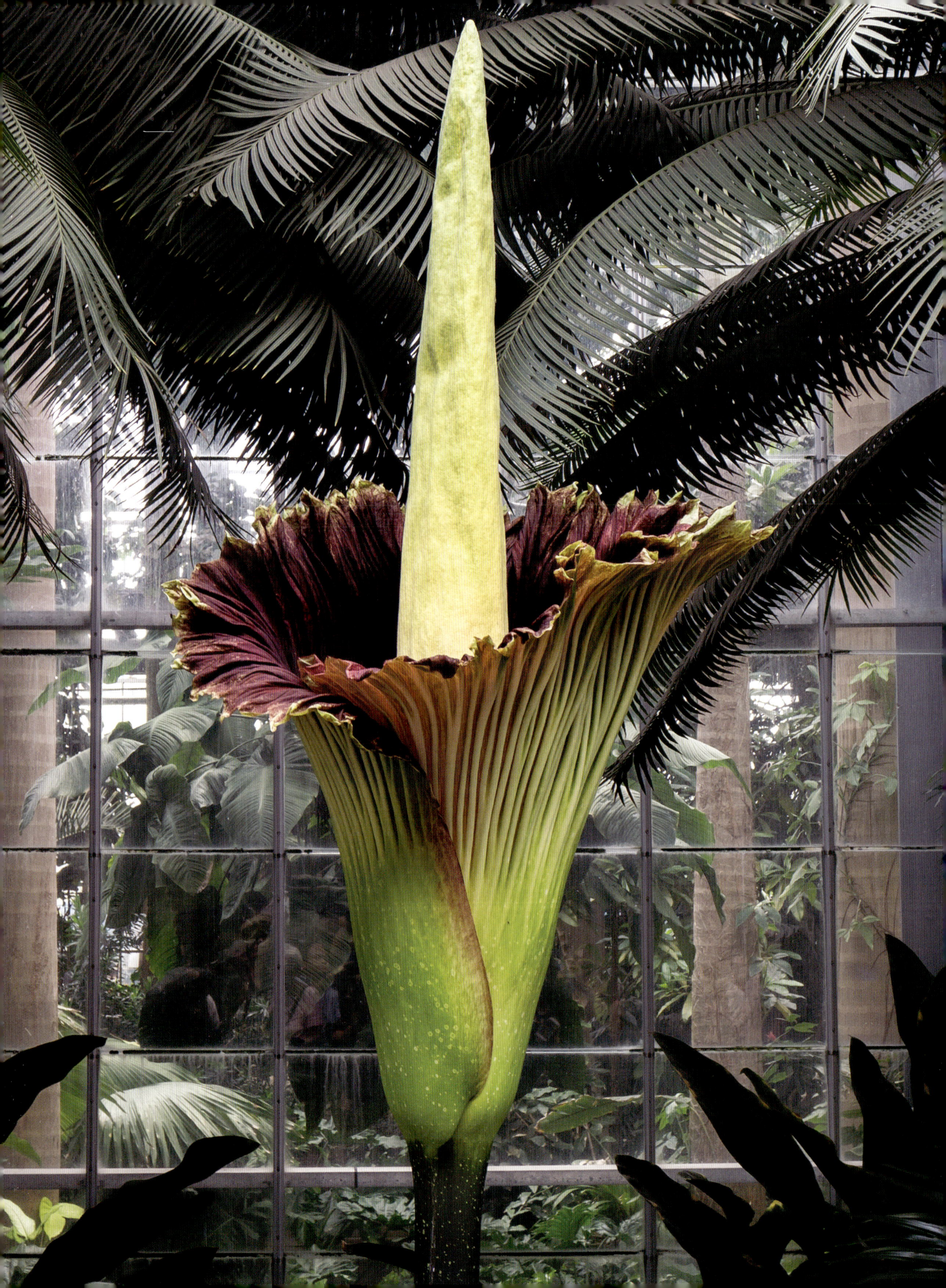

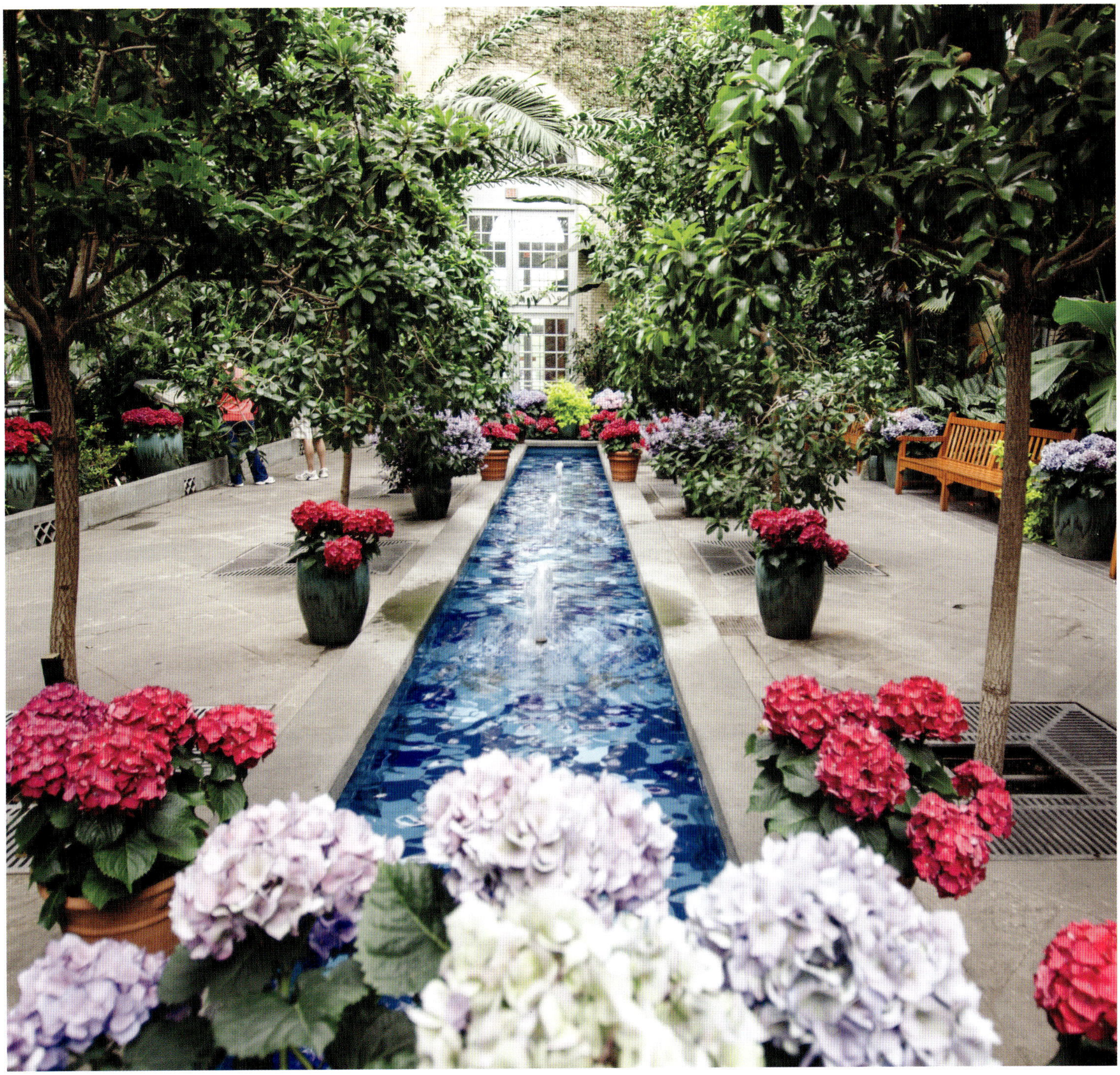

PREVIOUS PAGES:

Portland Japanese Garden, Oregon, USA

With a view of the city of Portland, this considered West Coast garden was borne of the desire to build relations between Oregon and Japan in the 1950s, post World War II – as were many other Japanese gardens around the United States. The garden opened to the public formally in 1967 although the garden continues to evolve, with development taking place as recently as 2017.

OPPOSITE AND ABOVE:

US Botanical Garden, Washington, D.C., USA

This historic garden is housed within the grounds of the United States Capitol. Initiated by George Washington 200 years ago, it can claim to be the oldest continuously operating botanic garden in the United States. Its reported purpose is to promote botanical knowledge, present displays of plants to Congress and the public and foster sustainability and plant conservation.

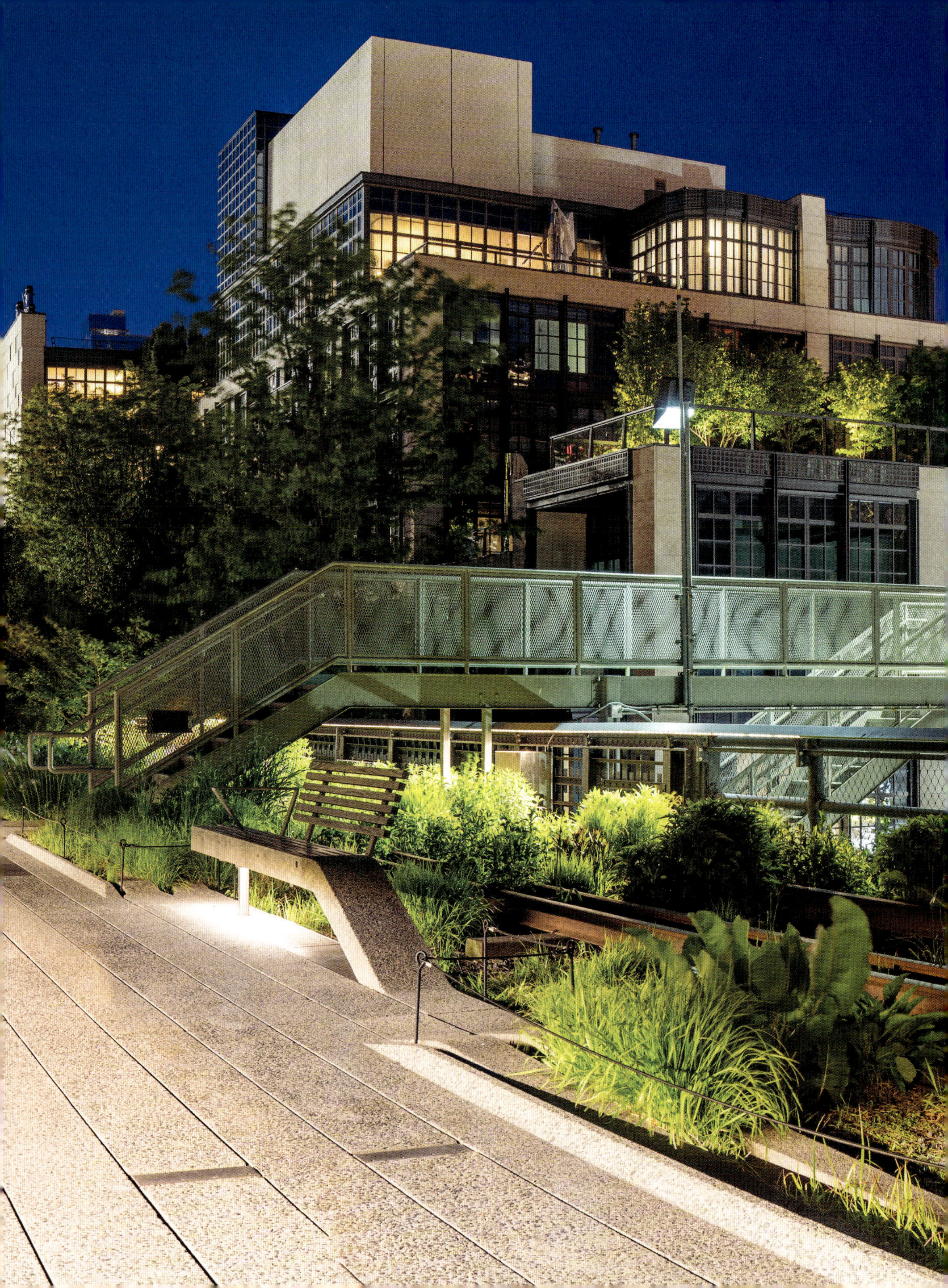

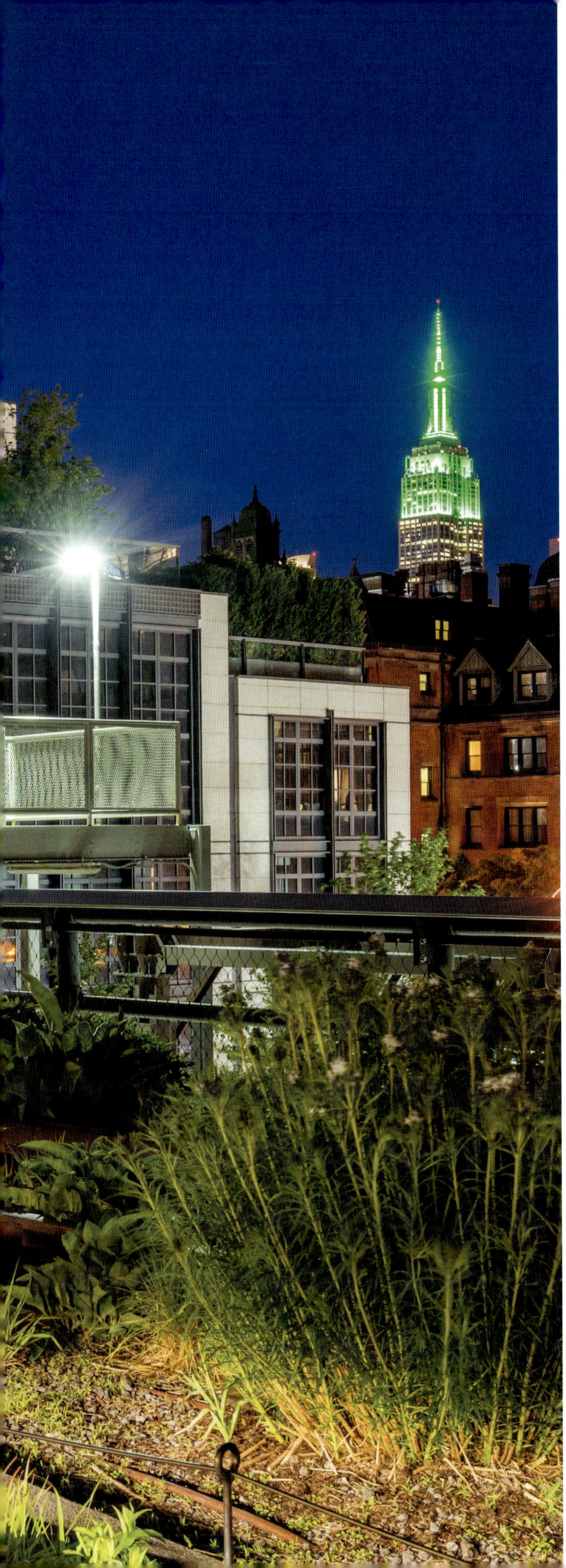

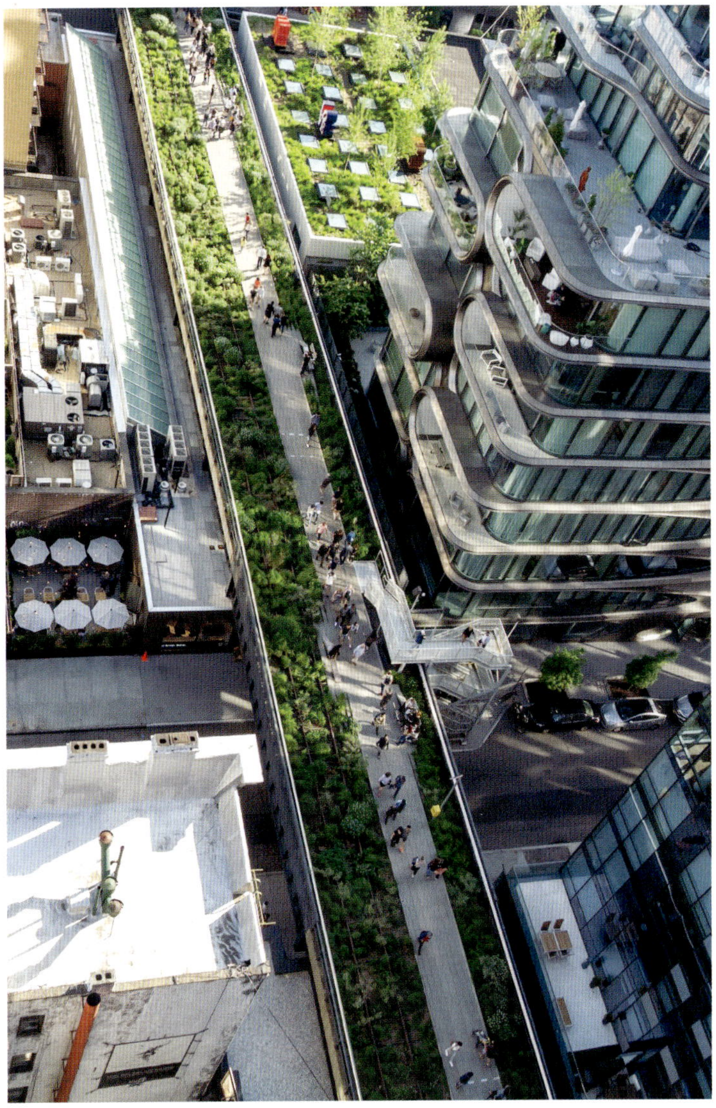

BOTH PHOTOGRAPHS:

The Highline, New York City, USA

From a disused railway line in New York City's Meatpacking District has emerged one of the most compelling gardens in the world. The Highline, designed by master of the New Perennial movement Piet Oudolf, is a sinuous, 2.3km (1.44-mile) long elevated park with planting designed for all seasons of the year. It is maintained and operated by the Friends of the Highline.

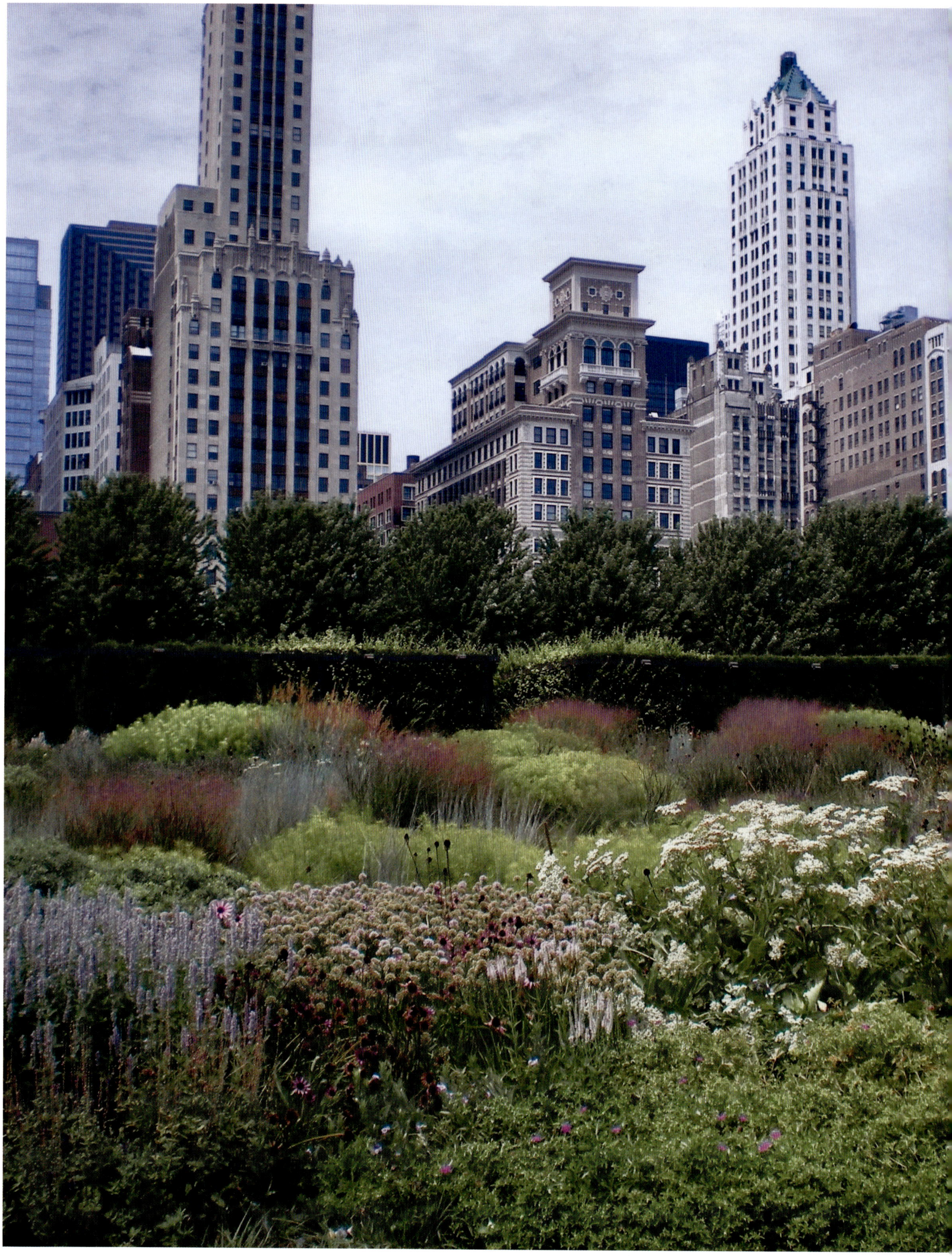

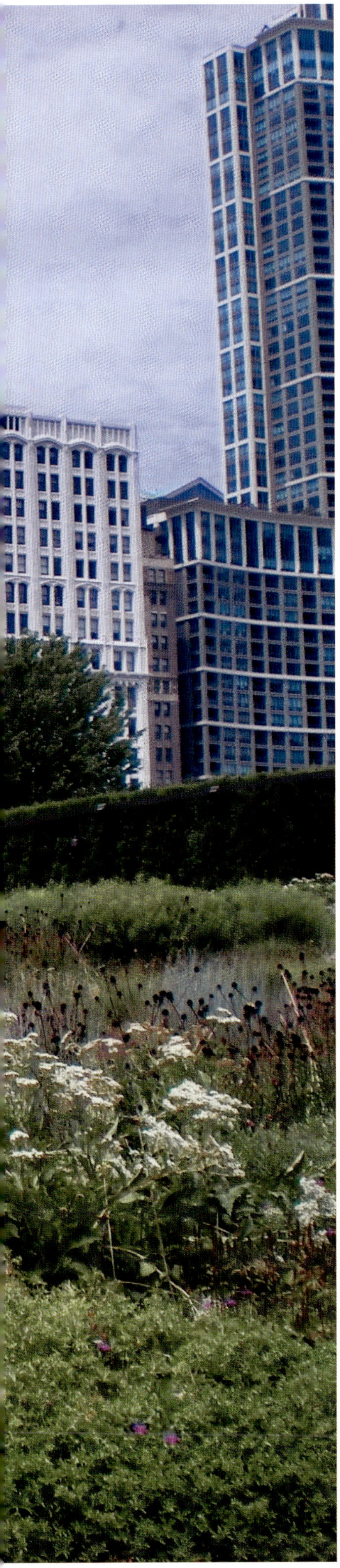

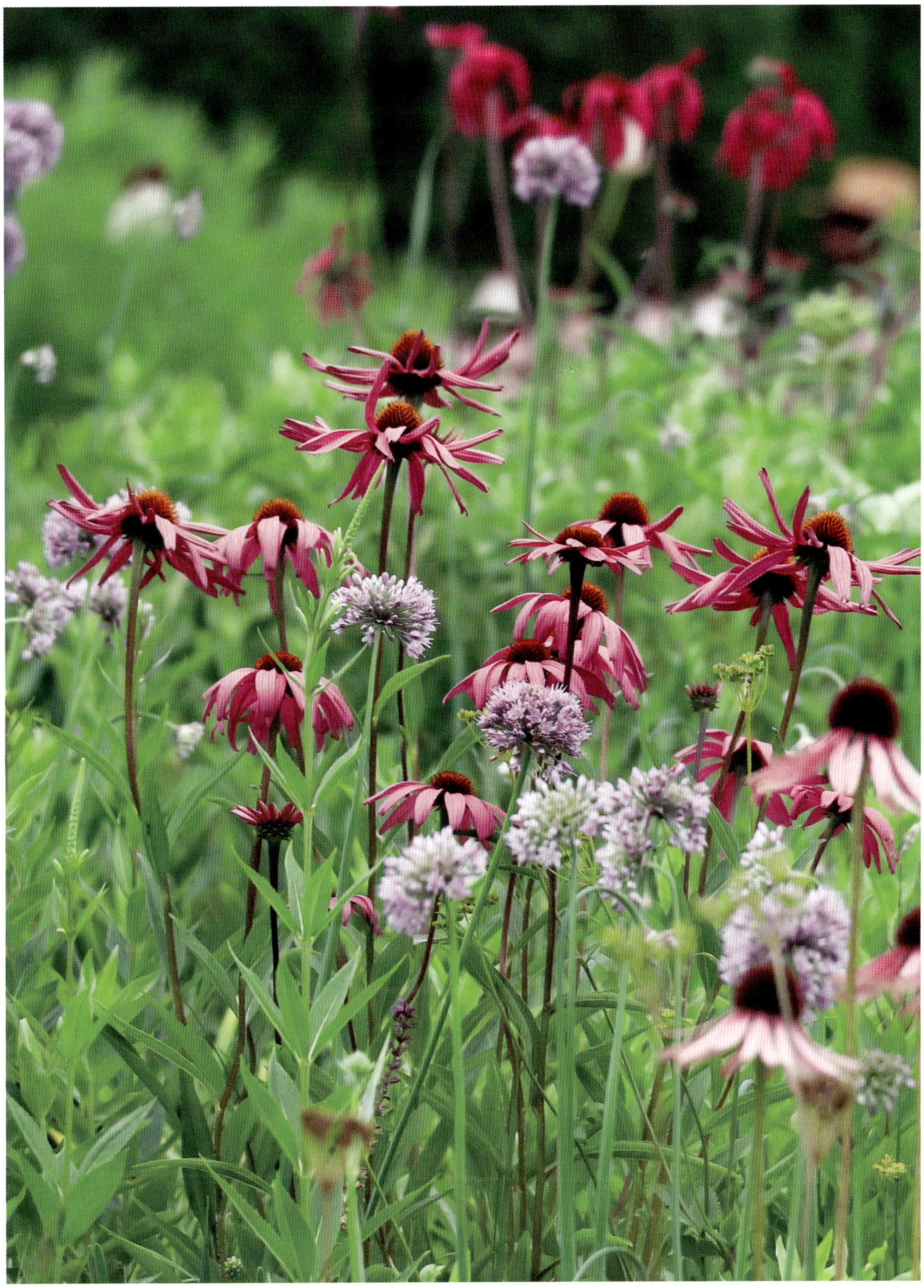

LEFT:
Lurie Gardens Millennium Park, Illinois, USA
The New Perennial planting style, which has come to define a section of horticulture in the first quarter of the 21st century, is triumphant in the Lurie Gardens in Chicago. Designer Piet Oudolf worked with a team of designers to create a 'four-season garden' with emphasis on wildlife, sustainability and enjoyment. A spring bulb display is deftly arranged by eminent Dutch designer Jaqueline van der Kloet.

ABOVE:
Lurie Gardens Millennium Park, Illinois, USA
The gardens are situated on the roof of a parking garage, and have a minimum soil depth of 45cm (18in) in places. Many plant species, such as those in the *Echinacea* genus (pictured), are prairie natives and are a magnate for butterflies, birds and other urban wildlife.

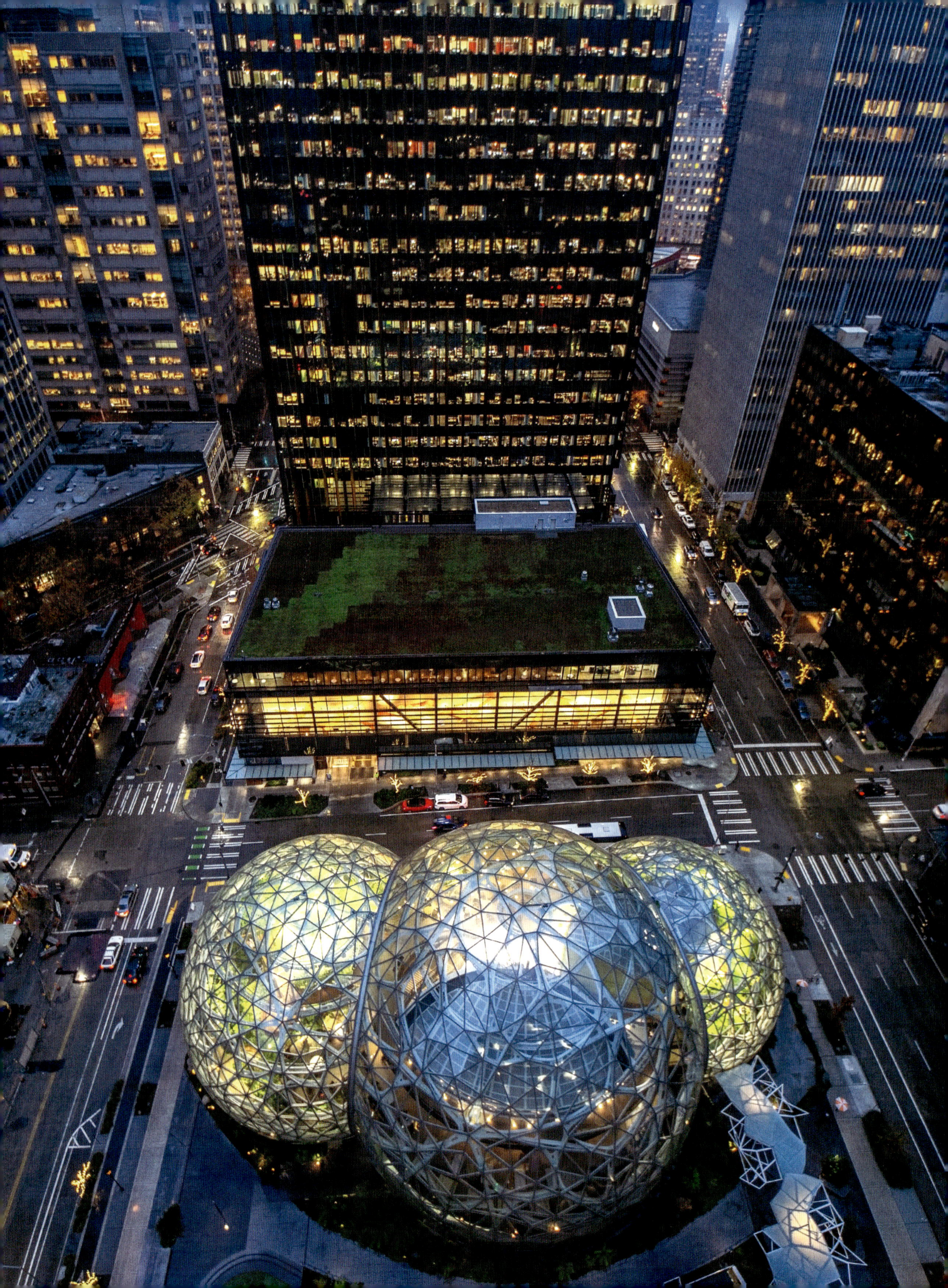

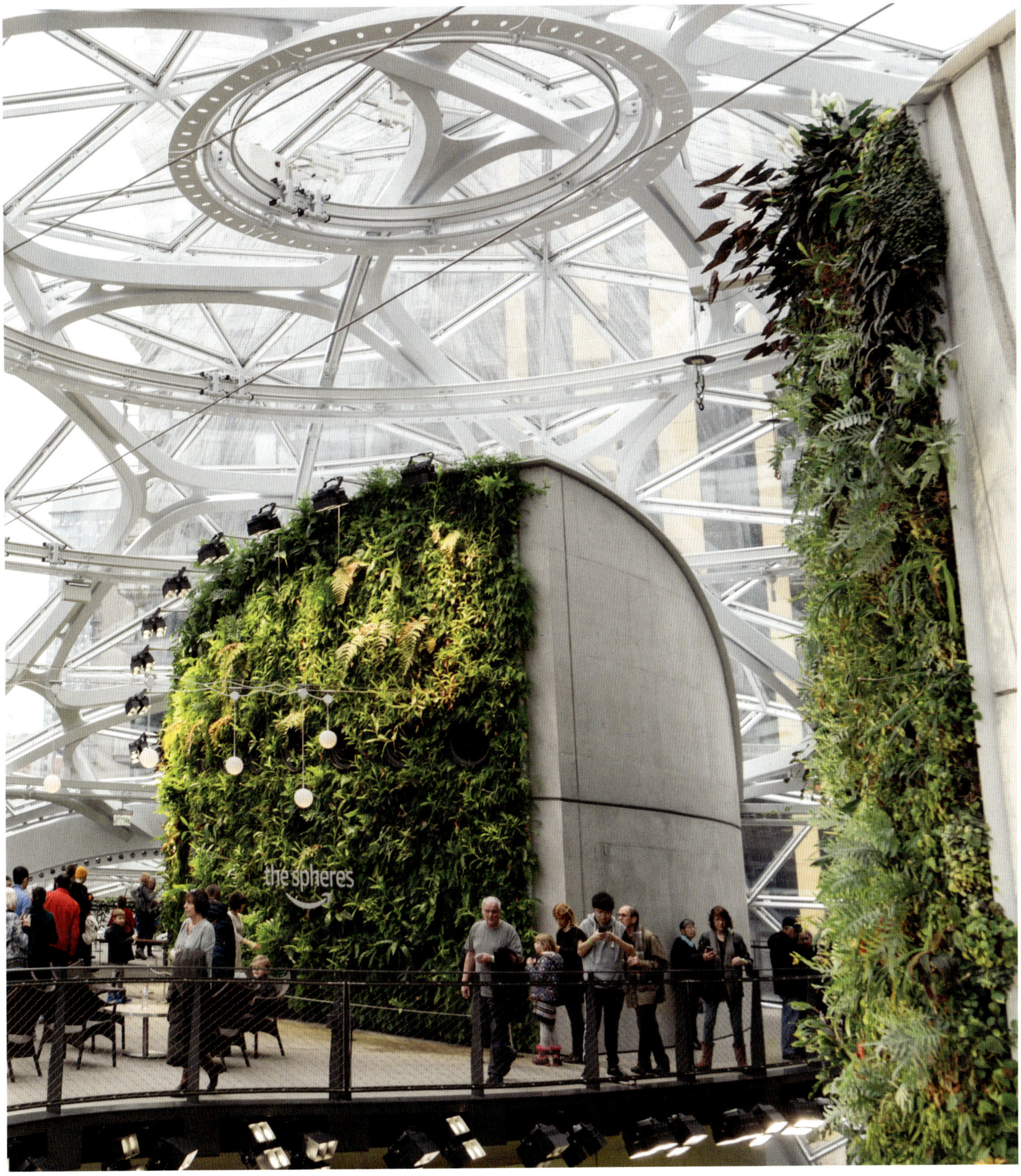

BOTH PHOTOGRAPHS:

Seattle Spheres, Washington, USA

Establishing a direct link to nature is integral to Seattle Spheres, the futuristic-looking office space used by Amazon. Over 40,000 plants grow within the glass-domed building, specifically forming green or living walls. The structure is a reflection of biophilic design, which is gaining traction in buildings around the world, from hospitals and classrooms to office spaces.

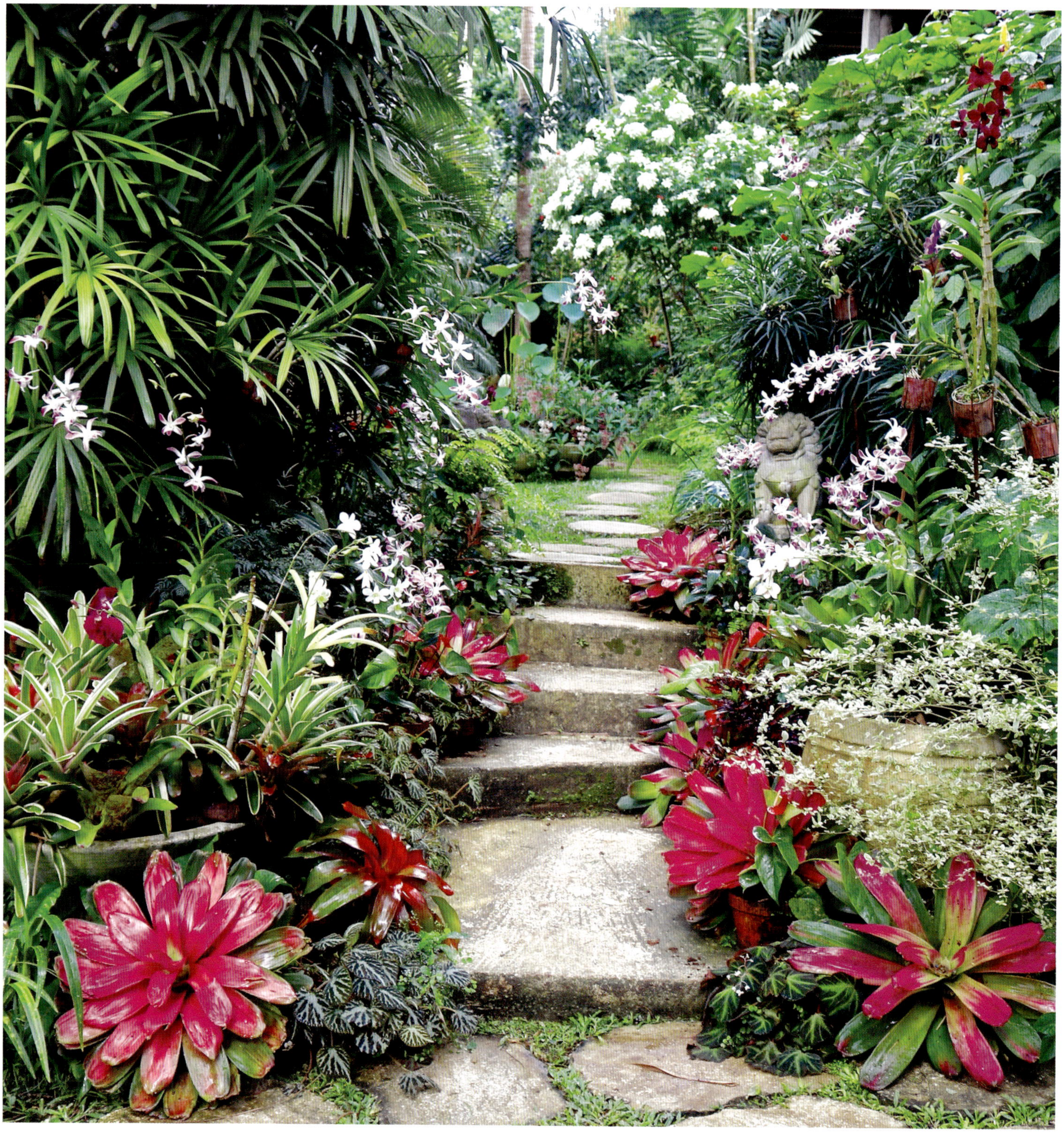

BOTH PHOTOGRAPHS:

Hunte's Botanical Gardens, Barbados

Intended to be a recreation of a Caribbean forest, Hunte's Botanical Gardens, situated on a former sugar plantation in St Joseph, was begun by one Anthony Hunte in the 1950s. Today paths meander through lush tropical planting complete with the vibrant colours and forms associated with the region.

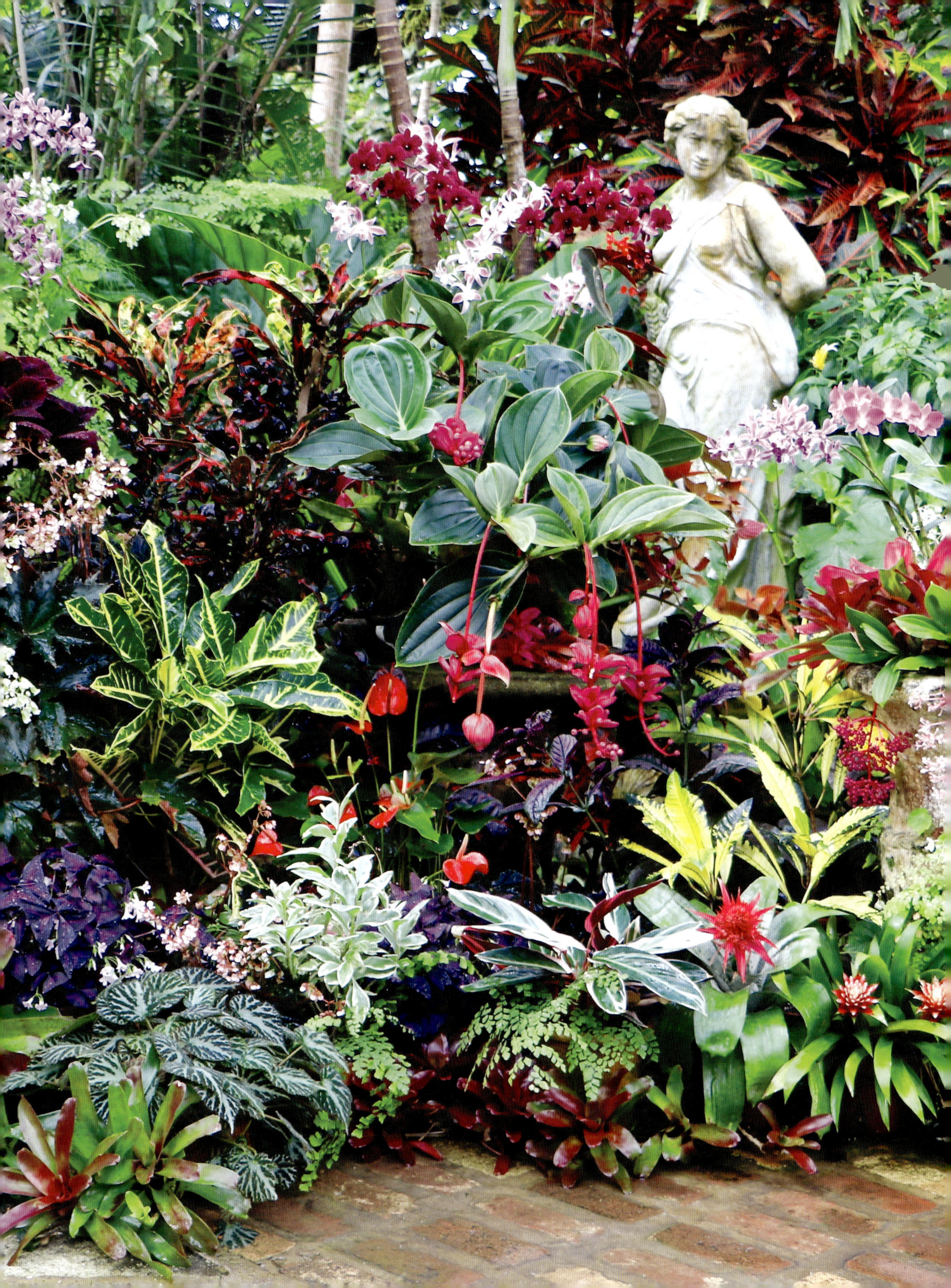

ALL PHOTOGRAPHS:

Vallarta Botanical Gardens, Jalisco, Mexico

Native Mexican plants thrive in this notable botanical garden in Puerto Vallarta on the west coast of Mexico. The intention of this garden is to showcase the great variety of Mexican plant species. Additional attractions include an orchid collection and viewing trails. The gardens are curated by Robert Price, who is also founder of the garden.

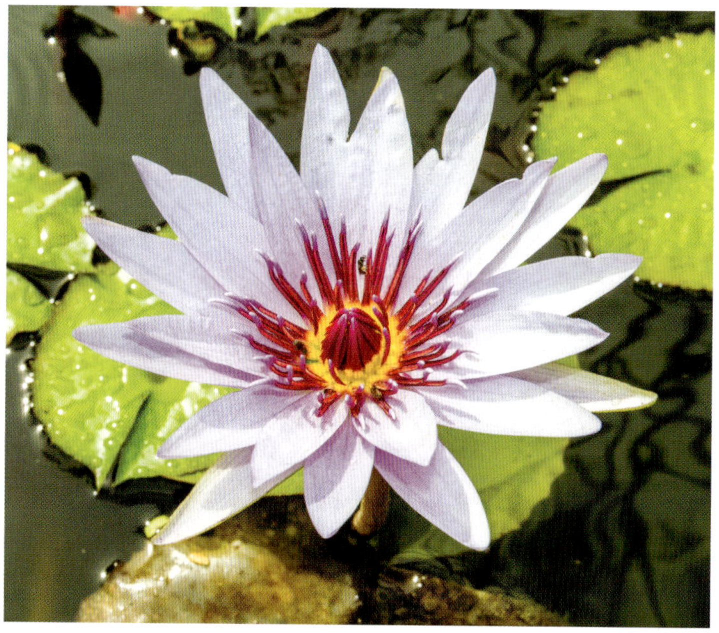

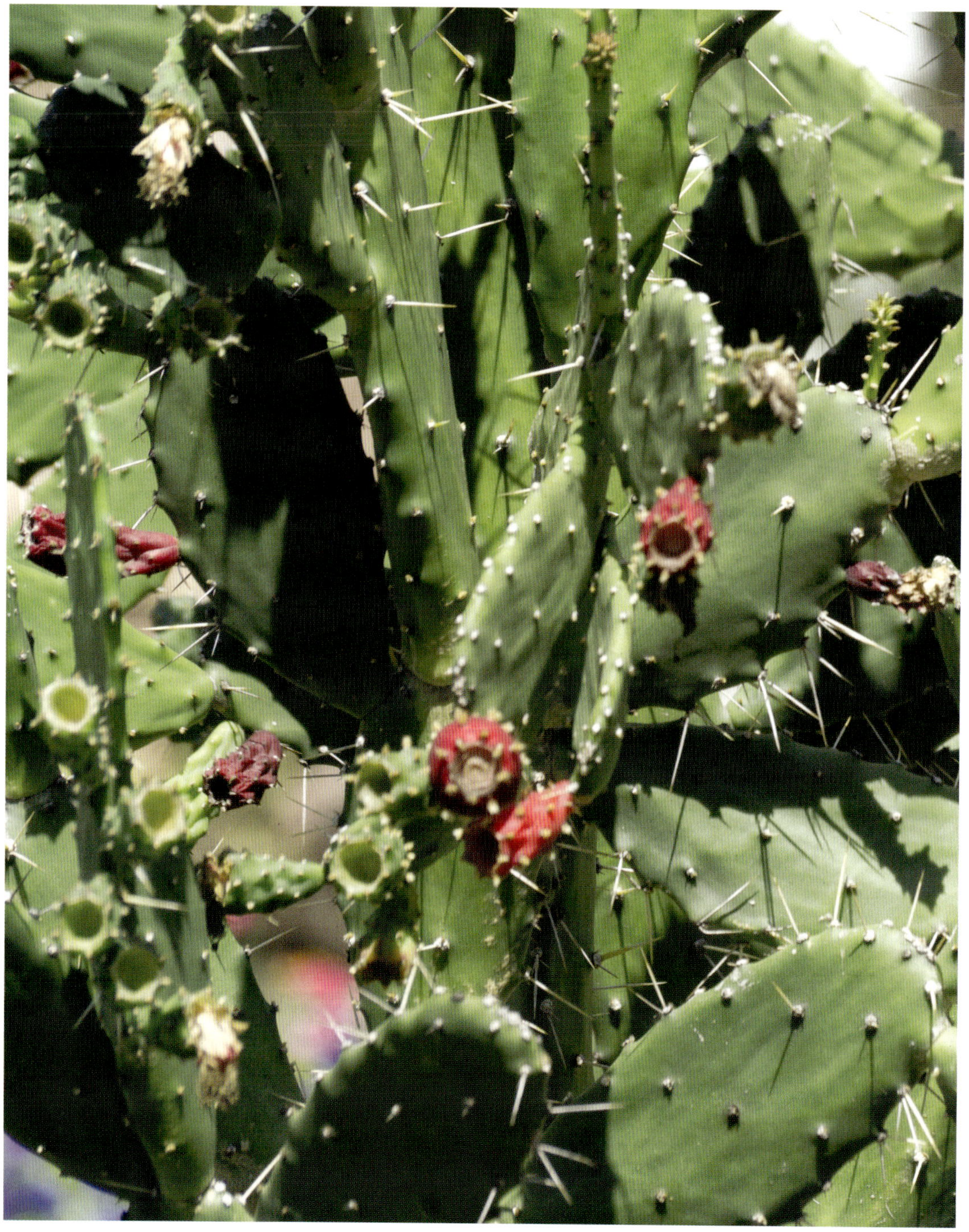

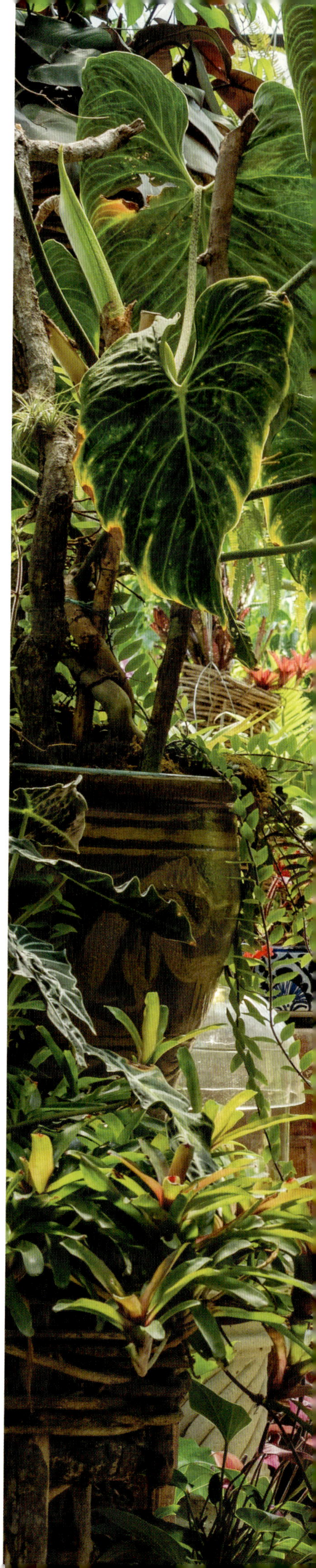

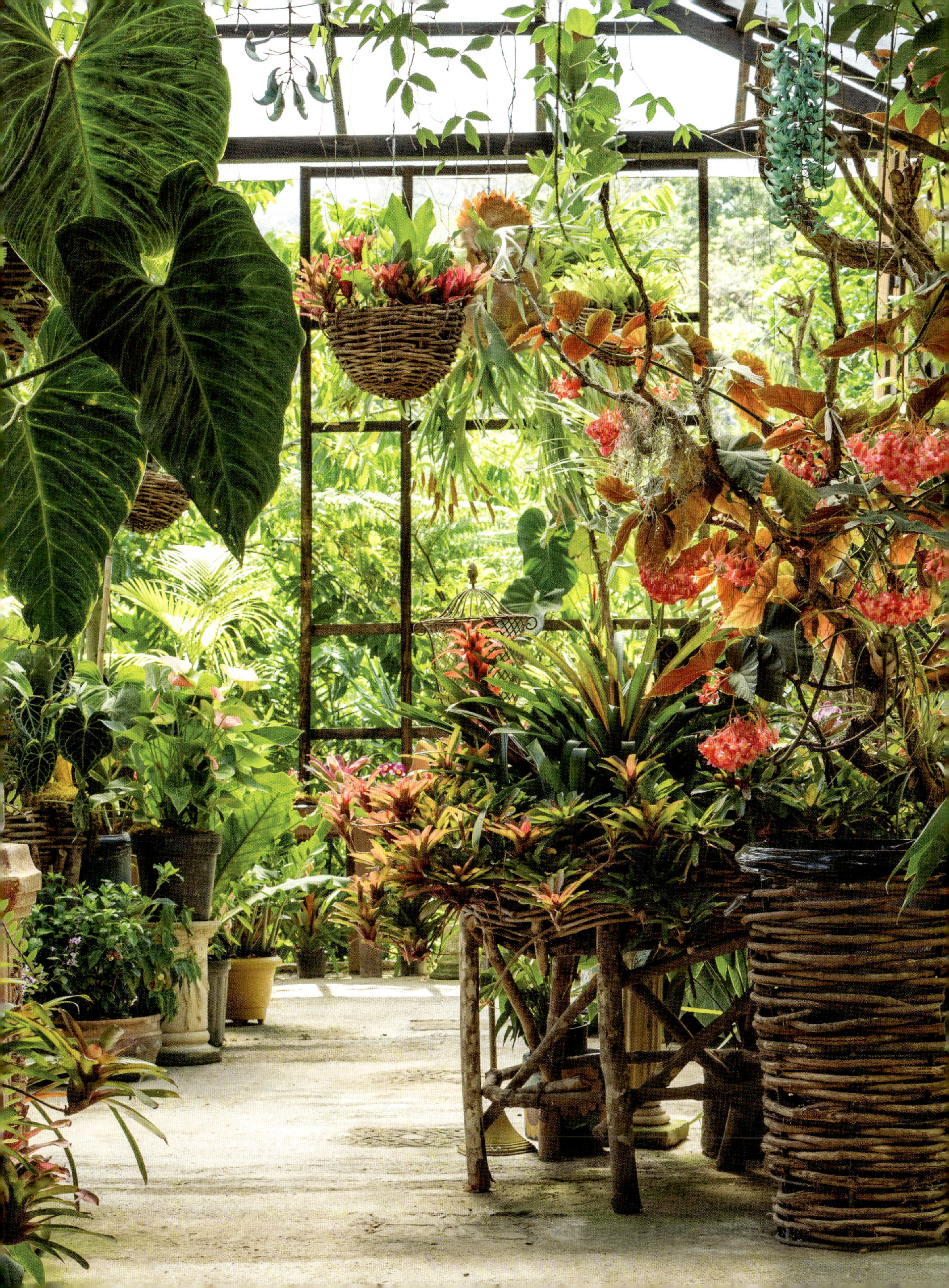

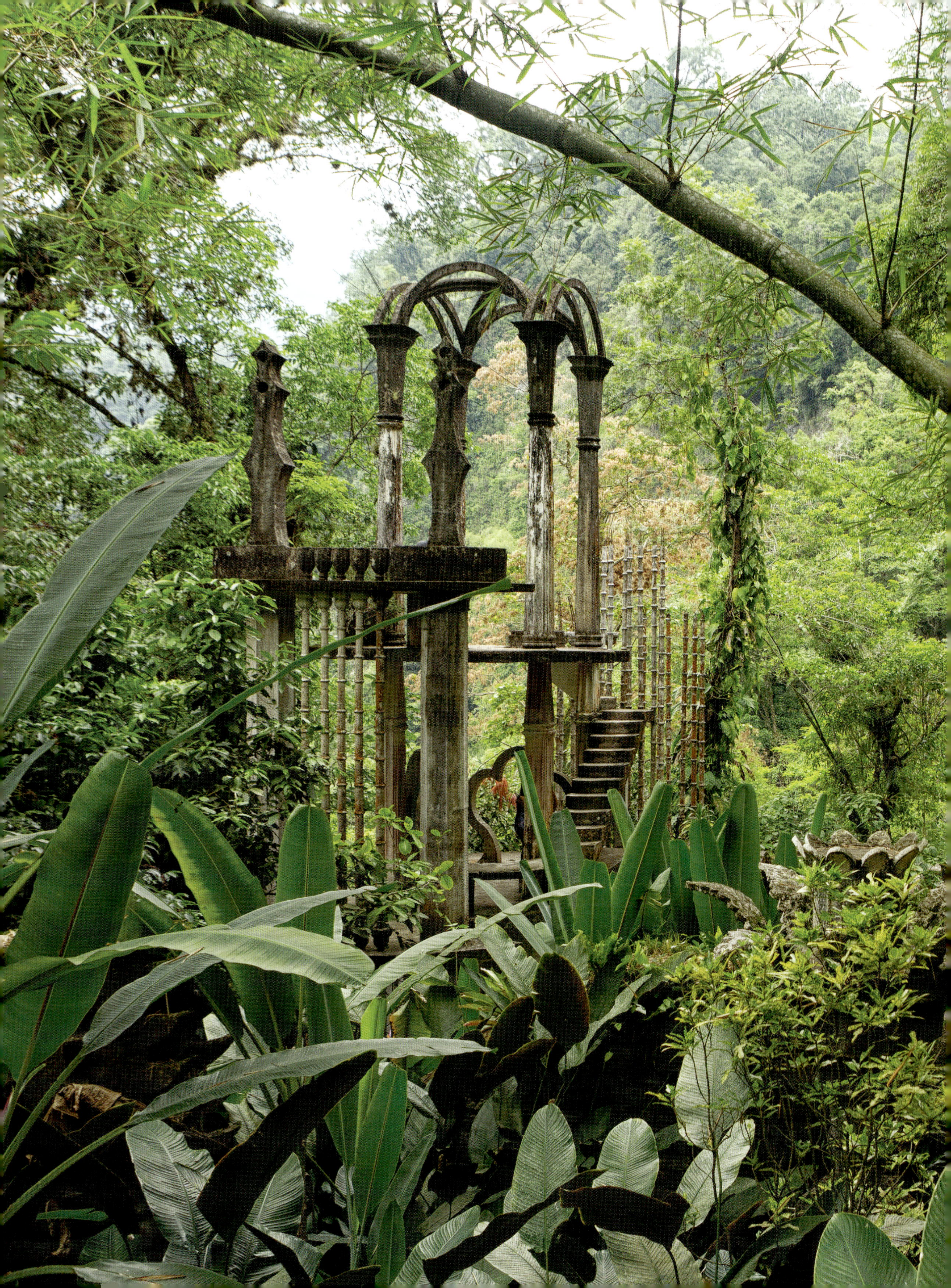

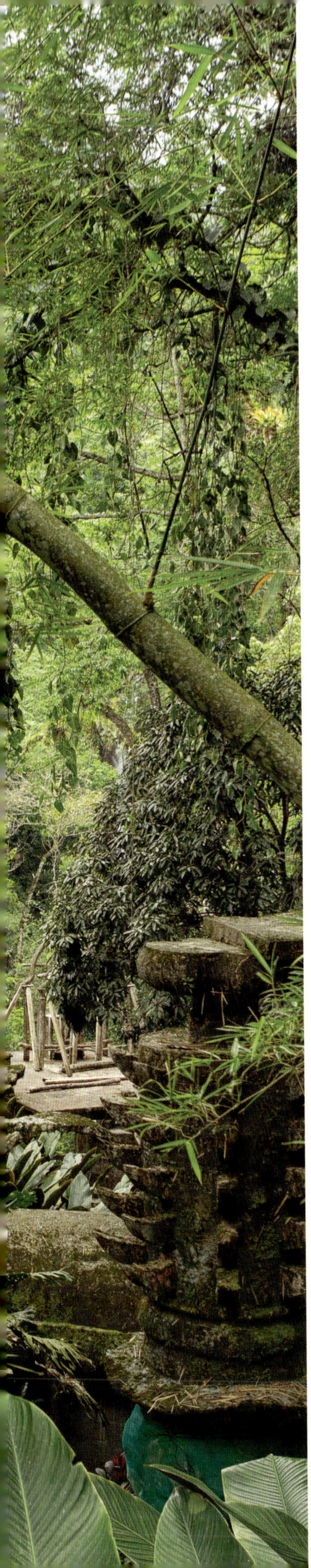

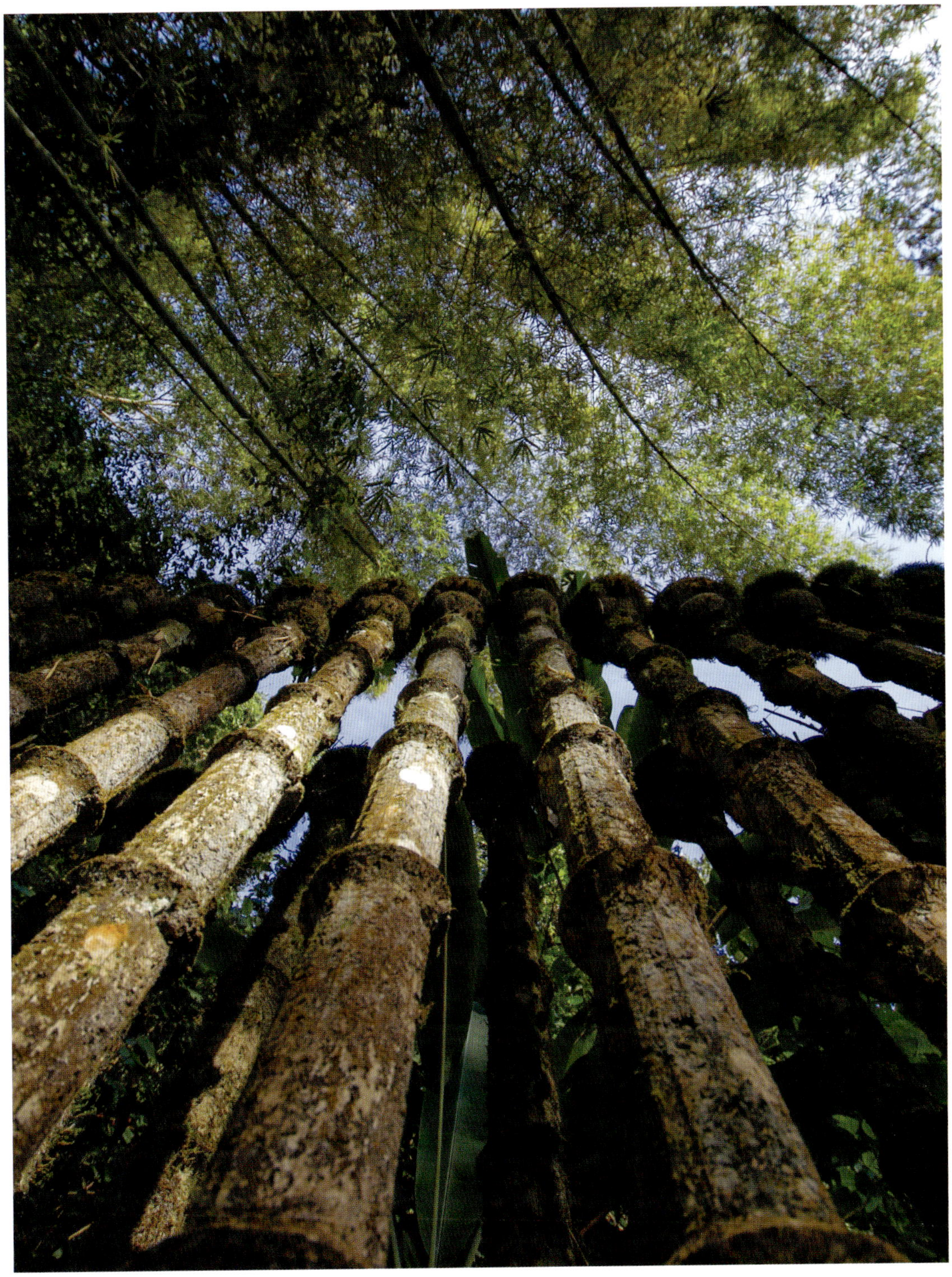

BOTH PHOTOGRAPHS:

Jardín Escultórico Edward James, Las Pozas, San Luis Potosi, Mexico

Edward James was an avid collector of Surrealist art. Having washed up in the small Mexican town of Xilita in the 1940s, he developed one of the most remarkable Surrealist gardens in the world. Arches, columns and Escher-like stairs define this garden which is thick with Mexican vegetation. In a quest to create an everlasting garden, James created numerous sculptures in botanical forms. James died in 1984, whereupon the garden was opened to the public.

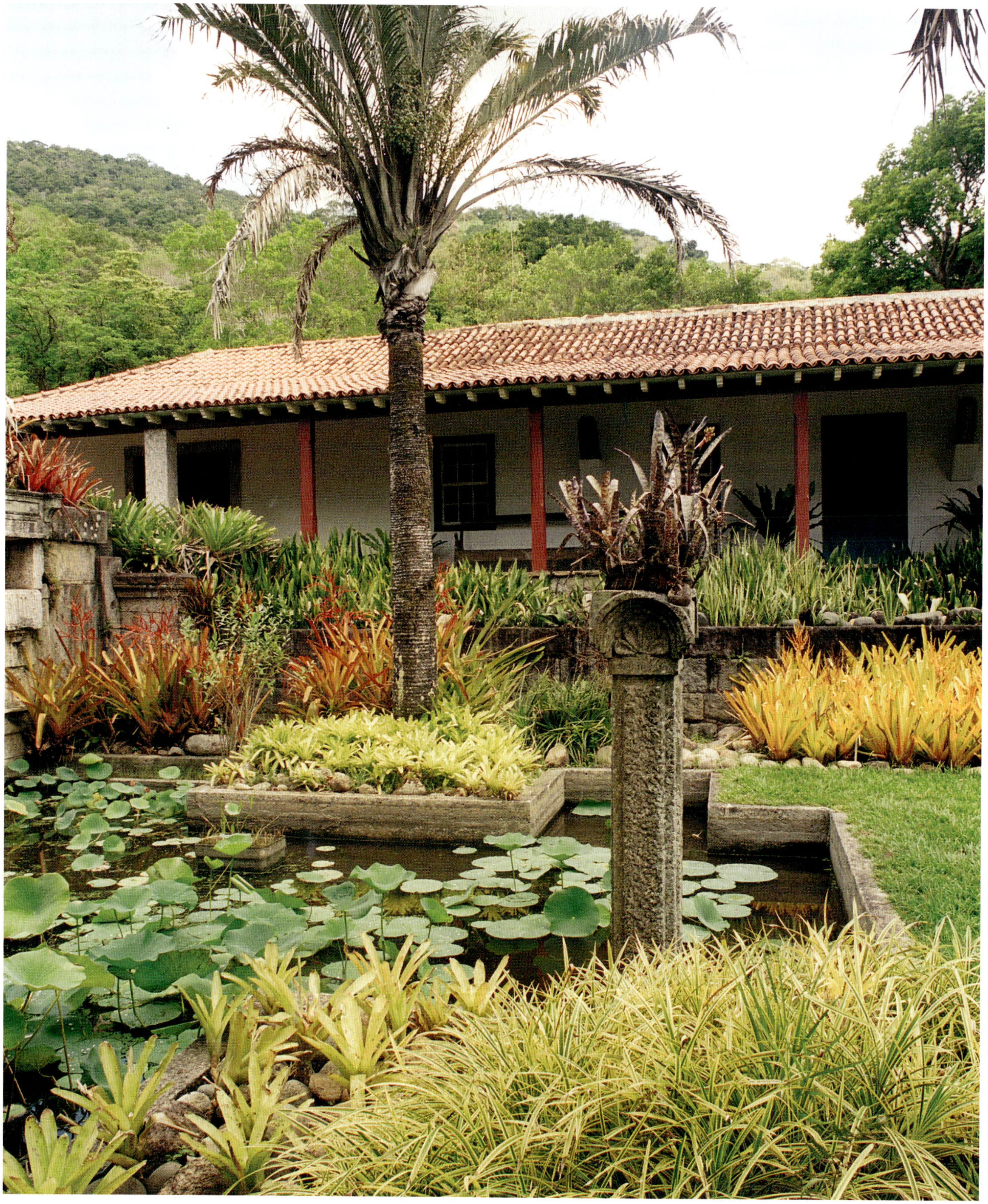

ABOVE:

Sítio Roberto Burle Marx, Rio de Janeiro, Brazil

This UNESCO World Heritage Site on the outskirts of Rio de Janeiro houses a considerable collection of tropical and subtropical plants. The former home of Brazilian landscape architect Roberto Burle Marx, it was built over 40 years to create a "living work of art" drawing on his modernist ideas. Burle Marx was inspired by the Modern Art movement and Portuguese and Brazilian folk traditions.

OPPOSITE:

Jardim Botânico Rio de Janeiro, Brazil

Within sight of the city's famous Christ the Redeemer statue, this botanic garden was founded in 1808 by King John VI of Portugal. It houses a noteworthy collection of tropical plants and highlights the diversity of Brazilian flora. Like other botanical gardens, it began as a place to trial commercial crops, in this case nutmeg, pepper and cinnamon. The garden has an important research facility attached to it.

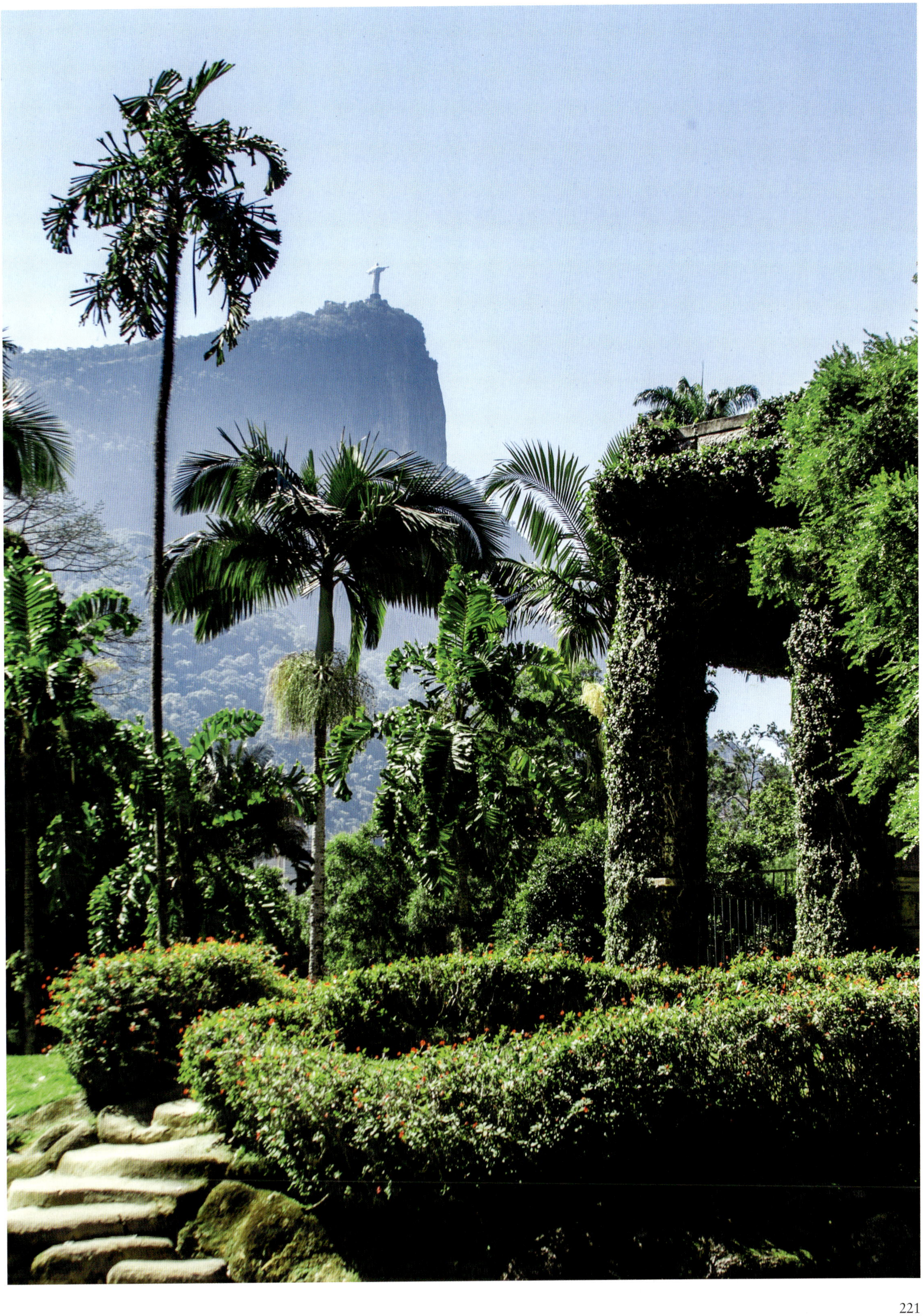

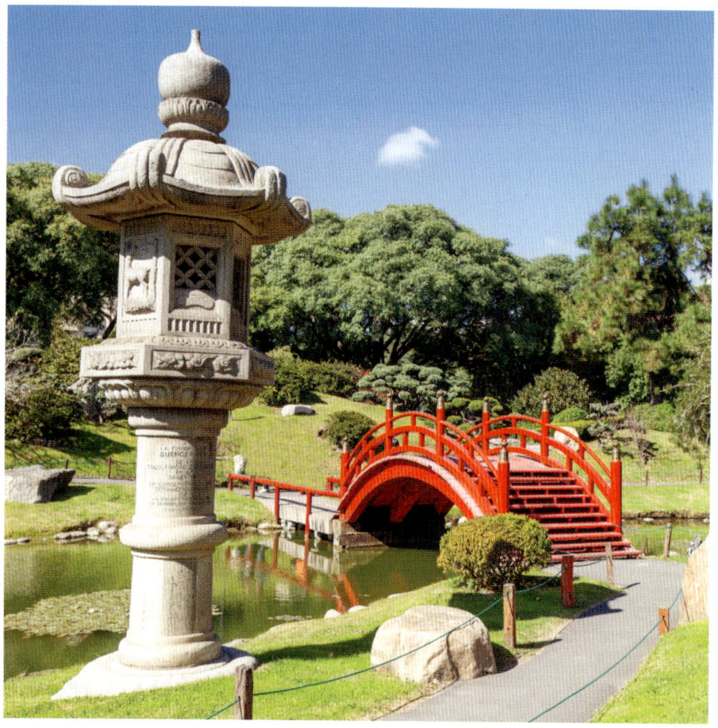

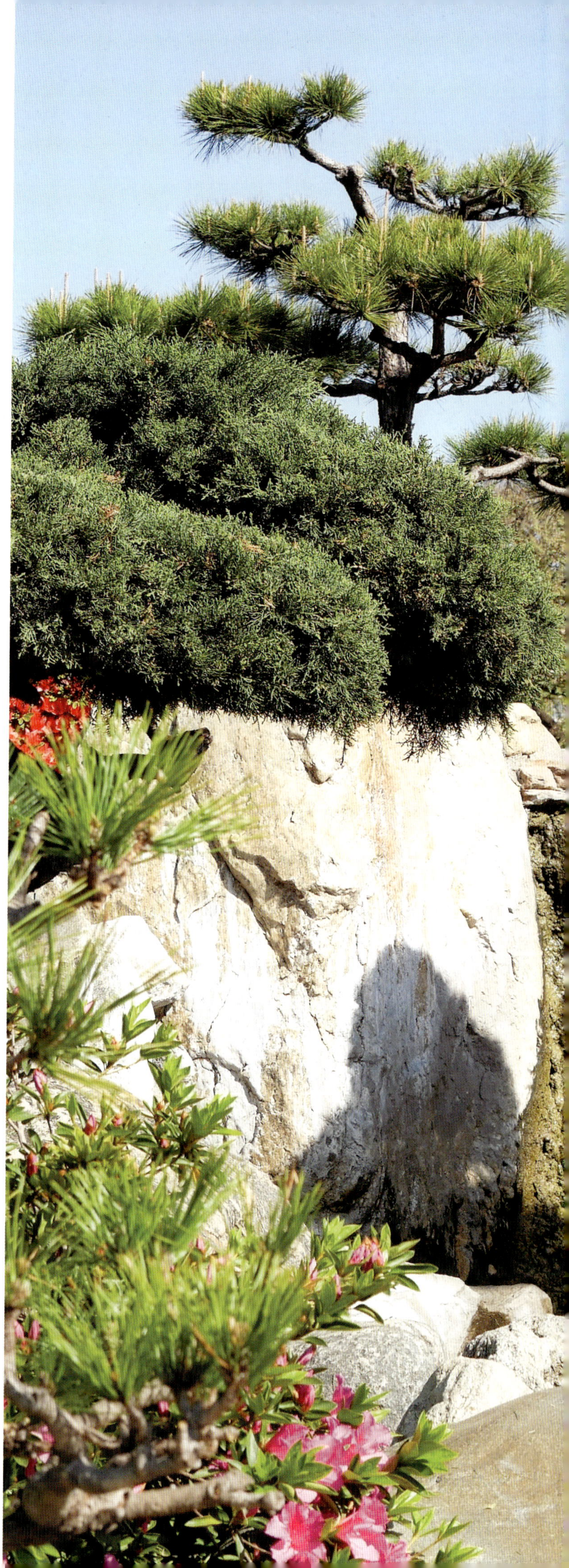

BOTH PHOTOGRAPHS:

Jardín Japonés, Buenos Aires, Argentina

One of the largest Japanese gardens outside Japan in the world, this garden is managed by the Japanese Argentine Cultural Foundation. Construction was completed in 1967, and the public space is valued for cultivating links between the two countries. Features include bonsai, a lake and various Japanese plant species.

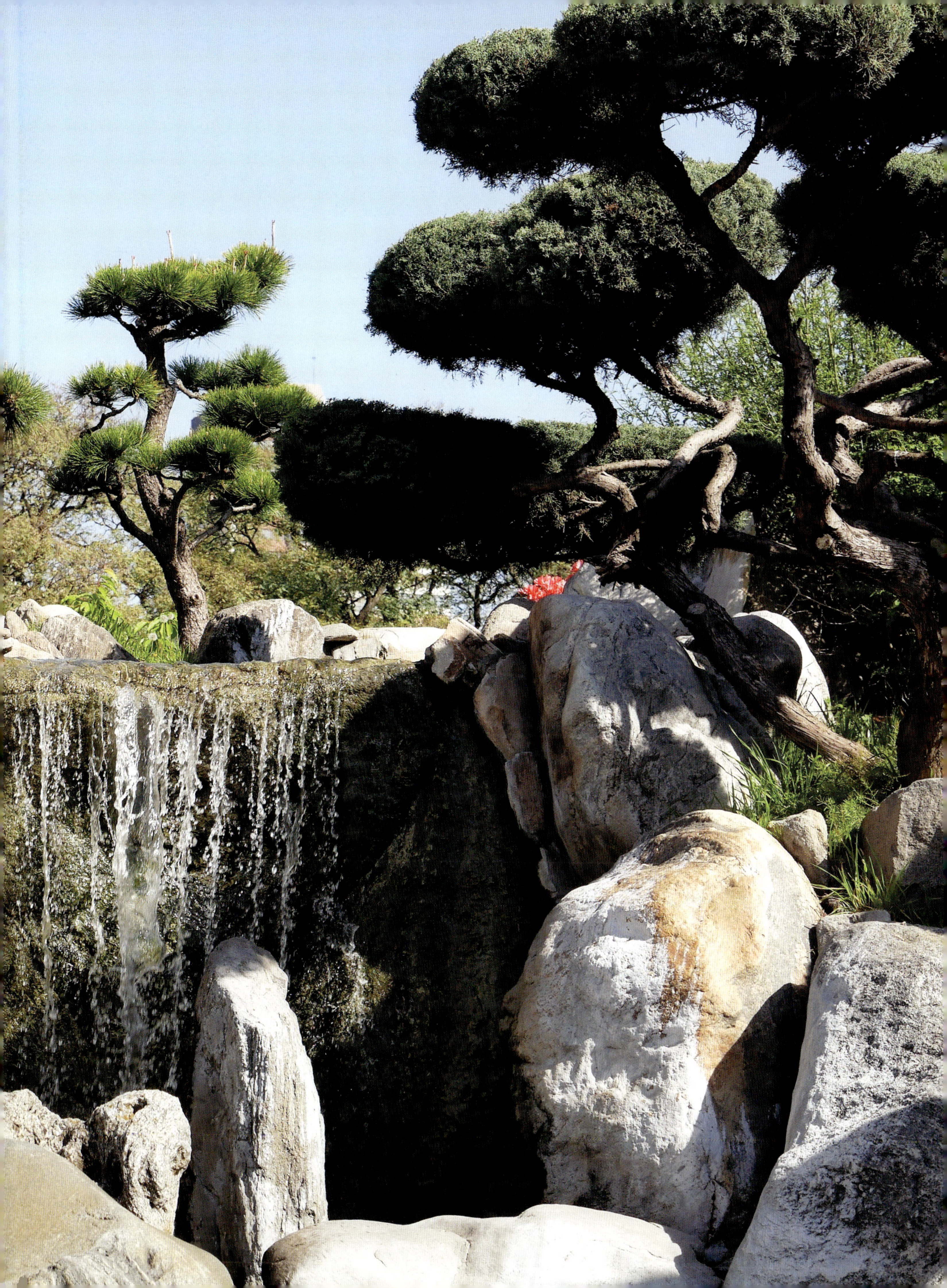

Picture Credits

Alamy: 7 (Leonid Serebrennikov), 10 (Angus Mccomiskey), 11 (Allan Wright), 18 (Jim Monk), 19 top (Madeleine Cardozo), 19 bttom (Christopher Nicholson), 20 (Alex Ramsay), 21 (Martyn Goddard), 28 & 29 (Andrew Kearton), 30 (Susan & Allan Parker), 31 top (Paul Lawrenson), 31 bottom (Arnhel de Serra/National Trust Photo Library), 32/33 (Heinz Wohner/Image Professionals), 34 (Alan Morgan Photography), 37 top (Veronika Lukasova/ZUMA Press), 37 bottom (John Farnham), 42/43 (travelbild), 63 bottom (Visions of America/Purestock), 83 top (Bosiljka Zutich), 87 (Riccardo Sala), 99 (Maurice Savage), 107 top (Derek Harris), 110 (B O'Kane), 113 top (Anders Blomqvist), 130 & 131 (Dinodia Photos), 134 (Hao Wan), 135 (Jochen Schlenker/Robert Harding), 149 (Travelimages), 157 bottom (Ilya Genkin), 166/167 (Micheal Wakely), 176 (Michael Wheatley), 179 top (Philippe Renault/Hemis), 183 top (Greg Vaughn), 183 bottom (Madeleine Jettre), 186 (Lori Epstein), 187 (Tony Quinn), 192/193 (Artur Apresyan), 195 (Danita Delimont), 197 bottom (Robert Fried), 209 (youngchakim), 217 (Greg Vaughn)

Atlanta Botanical Garden: 190 bottom, 191

Blenheim Palace: 26, 27

The Board of Trustees of the Royal Botanic Gardens, Kew: 38

Botanic Gardens and State Herbarium, South Australia: 160, 161

Jason Busch: 158, 159

Château de Villandry: 8

Dreamstime: 18 top left (Steve Luck), 18 bottom left (Sue Cooke), 22 (Stephen Roberts), 35 (Steve Luck), 40/41 (Jackbluee), 48/49 (TravelRider), 56 (Wieslaw Jarek), 57 (Leonid Andronov), 60/61 (Gerald Cummins), 62 (Carabiner), 63 top (Joe Sohm), 64 (Laszlo Konya), 65 (Dudlajzov), 66/67 (Dmitry Rukhlenko), 68 top (Paulgrecaud), 68 bottom (777photography), 74/75 (Leonid Andronov), 76 (Boris Breytman), 78/79 (Minnystock), 80/81 (Roman Plesky), 83 bottom (Selinairina77), 84/85 (Antonello Marangi), 94/95 (Amoklv), 96 top (Dwnld777), 98 (Jeewee), 100/101 (Mikhail Markovskiy), 102 (Marius Dorin Balate), 104/105 (Miroslav Liska), 107 bottom (Artur Nyk), 108 & 109 (Oguz Dikbakan), 113 bottom (Eryk Losik), 116/117 (Arnold Petersen), 118/119 (Siempreverde22), 120 (Suronin), 121 top (Sergey Strelkov), 121 middle (Hossein Lohinejadian), 121 bottom (Murat Tellioglou), 126 (Jayant Bahel), 127 (Naladri Sikder), 132/133 (Shalender Kumar), 142/143 (Tupungato), 144 bottom (Noa80), 145 (Niradj), 152/153 (Nikolai Sorokin), 154 (Lukas Uher), 163 bottom (Mbolina), 164 (Alexander Cimbal), 174 (Hasan Can Balcioglu), 177 (Caroline17), 180/181 (Hasan Can Balcioglu), 194 top (Ellesi), 200 (Joe Sohm), 204/205 (Davidgn), 207 (Mkopka), 216 bottom (Artenz), 221 (Rodrigo De Souza Mendes Junqueira)

Getty Images: 6 (Ian Waldie), 12/13 (David C Tomlinson), 39 (Roger Hutchings), 54/55 (Sylvain Sonnet), 69 (nikitje), 70/71 (Westend61), 111 (Richard I'Anson), 124/125 (Yawar Nazir), 138 (C Dani I Jeske/De Agostini), 139 (John S Lander), 140/141 (Taiwan Nans0410), 144 top & 146/147 (John S Lander), 199 (Justin Sullivan), 220 (Lonely Planet)

Simon Griffiths: 168, 169, 170/171

Hatfield Park & Alex Macey Photography: 23

Heligan Gardens: 44, 45 (James Stephens)

Huntes Gardens: 214, 215

Images courtesy of Longwood Gardens: 202, 203

NSW Department of Planning, Industry & Environment: 156, 157 top

Shutterstock: 14 (Arndale), 15 (Mistervlad), 16 (Jane Bilotska), 17 (Malcolm P Chapman), 24/25 (Chris Noe), 36 (tlorna), 50/51 (Andre Quinou), 52/53 (Mistervlad), 58/59 (Oleg Bakhirov), 72/73 (DR pics), 77 (trabantos), 82 (trabantos), 86 (Marco Rubino), 88 & 89 top (Dorisb.83), 89 bottom (EQRoy), 90 (Sean Pavone), 91 top (A G Baxter), 91 bottom (Luba Shushpanova), 92/93 (trabantos), 96 bottom (tipwam), 97 (Mikhail Markovskiy), 106 (Gardens by Design), 112 (Natalya Sterleva), 114/115 (Dirk M de Boer), 122 (Danita Delimont), 128 (Carlos Neto), 129 (Elena Odareeva), 136/137 (Leonid Andronov), 148 (Maxim Tupikov), 150/151 (Andrei Diomidov), 162 (Greg Brave), 163 top (Pascal Vosicki), 165 (Gary Thomas Photography), 178 (Awana JF), 179 bottom (Simon Eizner), 182 (James Chen), 184/185 (Lee Snider Photo Images), 188/189 & 190 top (Nicholas Lamomtanaro), 194 bottom (Karl Zhong), 196 (Mia2you), 197 top (Neva Fedaeff), 198 (Michael Warwick), 201 (Serge Yatunin), 206 (Erik Cox Photography), 208 (Francois Roux), 210 (Laura Platini), 211 (Molly Shannon), 212 (Marianna Ianovska), 213 (SeaRick1), 216 top (Francisco J Ramos Gallego), 218 (Barna Tanko), 219 (Andrea De la Parra), 222 (Saiko3p) 223 (Tom Payne)

Penny Zino, Flaxmere Garden: 172, 173